T0214145

Lecture Notes in Computer Science   12726

More information about this subseries at http://www.springer.com/series/7410

Kazue Sako · Nils Ole Tippenhauer (Eds.)

Applied Cryptography and Network Security

19th International Conference, ACNS 2021
Kamakura, Japan, June 21–24, 2021
Proceedings, Part I

Editors
Kazue Sako
Waseda University
Tokyo, Japan

Nils Ole Tippenhauer ⓘ
CISPA Helmholtz Center
for Information Security
Saarbrücken, Germany

ISSN 0302-9743   ISSN 1611-3349   (electronic)
Lecture Notes in Computer Science
ISBN 978-3-030-78371-6   ISBN 978-3-030-78372-3   (eBook)
https://doi.org/10.1007/978-3-030-78372-3

LNCS Sublibrary: SL4 – Security and Cryptology

This Springer imprint is published by the registered company Springer Nature Switzerland AG
The registered company address is: Gewerbestrasse 11, 6330 Cham, Switzerland

Preface

We are pleased to present the proceedings of the 19th International Conference on Applied Cryptography and Network Security (ACNS 2021).

ACNS 2021 was planned to be held in Kamakura, Japan. Due to the ongoing COVID-19 crisis, we decided to have a virtual conference again to ensure the safety of all participants. The organization was in the capable hands of Chunhua Su (University of Aizu, Japan) and Kazumasa Omote (University of Tsukuba, Japan) as general co-chairs, and Ryoma Ito (NICT, Japan) as local organizing chair. We are deeply indebted to them for their tireless work to ensure the success of the conference even in such complex conditions.

For the second time, ACNS had two rounds of submission cycles, with deadlines in September 2020 and January 2021, respectively. We received a total of 186 submissions from authors in 43 countries. This year's Program Committee (PC) consisted of 69 members with diverse backgrounds (among them, 27% female experts) and broad research interests. The review process was double-blind and rigorous, and papers were evaluated on the basis of research significance, novelty, and technical quality. 539 reviews were submitted in total, with at least 3 reviews for most papers.

Some papers submitted in the first round received a decision of major revision. The revised version of those papers were further evaluated in the second round and most of them were accepted. After the review process concluded, a total of 37 papers were accepted to be presented at the conference and included in the proceedings, representing an acceptance rate of around 20%.

Among those papers, 27 were co-authored and presented by full-time students. From this subset, we awarded the Best Student Paper Award to Angèle Bossuat (IRISA, France) for the paper "Unlinkable and Invisible γ-Sanitizable Signatures" (co-authored with Xavier Bultel). The reviewers particularly appreciated its clear and convincing motivation and explanation of the intuition behind the approach, and the strong properties achieved by the proposed sanitizable signature scheme. The monetary prize of 1,000 euro was generously sponsored by Springer.

We had a rich program including eight satellite workshops in parallel with the main event, providing a forum to address specific topics at the forefront of cybersecurity research. The papers presented at those workshops were published in separate proceedings.

This year we had three outstanding keynote talks: "Privacy-Preserving Authentication: Concepts, Applications, and New Advances" by Prof. Anja Lehmann (Hasso Plattner Institute, Germany), "Digital Being" presented by Nat Sakimura (OpenID Foundation, Japan), and "Cryptography and the Changing Landscape of Payment Fraud" by Prof. Ross Anderson (University of Cambridge and University of Edinburgh, UK). To them, our heartfelt gratitude for their outstanding presentations.

In this very unusual year, the conference was made possible by the untiring efforts of many individuals and organizations. We are grateful to all the authors for their submissions. We sincerely appreciate the outstanding work of all the PC members and the external reviewers, who selected the papers after reading, commenting, and debating them. Finally, we thank all the people who volunteered their time and energy to put together the conference, speakers and session chairs, and everyone who contributed to the success of the conference.

Last, but certainly not least, we are very grateful to Mitsubishi Electric for sponsoring the conference, and Springer for their help in assembling these proceedings.

June 2021

Kazue Sako
Nils Ole Tippenhauer

Organization

General Co-chairs

Chunhua Su	University of Aizu, Japan
Kazumasa Omote	University of Tsukuba, Japan

Program Co-chairs

Kazue Sako	Waseda University, Japan
Nils Ole Tippenhauer	CISPA, Germany

Publicity Chair

Keita Emura	NICT, Japan

Workshop Chair

Jianying Zhou	Singapore University of Technology and Design, Singapore

Poster Chair

Masaki Shimaoka	University of Tsukuba/SECOM, Japan

Local Organizing Chair

Ryoma Ito	NICT, Japan

Program Committee

Mitsuaki Akiyama	NTT, Japan
Cristina Alcaraz	UMA, Spain
Giuseppe Ateniese	Stevens Institute of Technology, USA
Man Ho Au	The University of Hong Kong, Hong Kong
Lejla Batina	Radboud University, the Netherlands
Alex Biryukov	University of Luxembourg, Luxembourg
Ferdinand Brasser	TU Darmstadt, Germany
Christopher Brzuska	Aalto University, Finland
Alvaro Cardenas	The University of Texas at Dallas, USA
Sudipta Chattopadhyay	SUTD, Singapore
Liqun Chen	University of Surrey, UK
Xiaofeng Chen	Xidian University, China

Reihaneh Safavi-Naini	University of Calgary, Canada
Kazue Sako	Waseda University, Japan
Steve Schneider	University of Surrey, UK
Sooel Son	Korea Advanced Institute of Science and Technology, South Korea
Hung-Min Sun	National Tsing Hua University, Taiwan
Willy Susilo	University of Wollongong, Australia
Pawel Szalachowski	Google, USA
Qiang Tang	University of Sydney, Australia
Vanessa Teague	Thinking Cybersecurity, Australia
Nils Ole Tippenhauer	CISPA Helmholtz Center for Information Security, Germany
A. Selcuk Uluagac	Florida International University, USA
Edgar Weippl	University of Vienna, Austria
Christian Wressnegger	Karlsruhe Institute of Technology, Germany
Kehuan Zhang	The Chinese University of Hong Kong, Hong Kong

Additional Reviewers

Akand, Mamun
Amjad, Ghous
Anada, Hiroaki
Anagnostopoulos, Marios
Banik, Subhadeep
Blazy, Olivier
Booth, Roland
Braeken, An
Briongos, Samira
Bultel, Xavier
Buser, Maxime
Chen, Long
Chen, Xihui
Chen, Yi
Chengjun Lin
Co, Kenneth
Cui, Tingting
Dekker, F. W.
Diao, Wenrui
Diugan, Raluca
Duong, Dung Hoang
Dutta, Sabyasachi
El Hirch, Solane
Eliyan, Lubna
Ersoy, Oguzhan
Feng, Hanwen
Fentham, Daniel
Ferreira Torres, Christof

Florez, Johana
Gan, Qingqing
Gardham, Daniel
Genise, Nicholas
Gerault, David
Ghesmati, Simin
Ghosh, Koustabh
Gontier, Arthur
Grassi, Lorenzo
Guo, Kaiwen
Gálvez, Rafa
Hameed, Muhammad Zaid
Han, Jinguang
Hashimoto, Keitaro
Hirano, Takato
Homoliak, Ivan
Hoshino, Fumitaka
Hou, Zhenduo
Hsu, Chingfang
Hu, Kexin
Huguenin-Dumittan, Loïs
Hülsing, Andreas
Ichikawa, Atsunori
Isobe, Takanori
Isshiki, Toshiyuki
Jangid, Mohit
Jiang, Shaoquan
Jiang, Yuting

Judmayer, Aljosha
Kannwischer, Matthias J.
Kasra, Shabnam
Kim, Joongyum
Laing, Thalia May
Larangeira, Mario
Leurent, Gaëtan
Li, Jiguo
Li, Tianyu
Li, Xinyu
Li, Yanan
Libert, Benoît
Liu, Jia
Lopez, Christian
Lu, Xingye
Lu, Yuan
Ma, Jinhua
Mahawaga Arachchige,
   Pathum Chamikara
Marotzke, Adrian
Mazumdar, Subhra
McMurtry, Eleanor
Mirza, Shujaat
Miteloudi, Konstantina
Moreau, Solène
Niederhagen, Ruben
Ning, Jianting
Nishide, Takashi
Orsini, Emmanuela
Pan, Jiaxin
Pan, Jing
Pang, Bo
Papamartzivanos, Dimitrios
Park, Sunnyeo
Pasquini, Dario
Pereira, Vitor
Pilgun, Aleksandr
Prabel, Lucas
Qiu, Tian
Rabbani, Md Masoom
Ramírez-Cruz, Yunior
Reijsbergen, Daniel
Rivera, Esteban
Roenne, Peter
Sato, Masaya
Schindler, Philipp

Schuldt, Jacob
Schwabe, Peter
Shen, Jun
Shirase, Masaaki
Sideri, Maria
Smith, Zach
Song, Ling
Song, Yongcheng
Song, Zirui
Stifter, Nicholas
Sun, Siwei
Suzuki, Koutarou
Tang, Di
Tengana, Lizzy
Terner, Ben
Tiepelt, Marcel
Tikhomirov, Sergei
Tomita, Toui
Tsohou, Aggeliki
van Bruggen, Christian
van Tetering, Daphne
Vaudenay, Serge
Vitto, Giuseppe
Vliegen, Jo
Wang, Jianfeng
Wang, Qingju
Wang, Yongqi
Weiqiang Wen
Wi, Seongil
Wu, Jiaojiao
Xu, Yanhong
Xue, Haiyang
Yamakawa, Takashi
Yan, Hailun
Yang, Guomin
Yang, Rupeng
Yang, S. J.
Yang, Wenjie
Yin, Qilei
Yoneyama, Kazuki
Yuan, Xingliang
Zeilberger, Hadas
Zhang, Peng
Zhang, Xiaoyu
Zhang, Yuexin
Zhang, Zeyu

Contents – Part I

Embedded System Security

Lattice Cryptography

Contents – Part II

System Security

Cryptography and Its Applications

Cryptographic Protocols

Adaptive-ID Secure Hierarchical ID-Based Authenticated Key Exchange Under Standard Assumptions Without Random Oracles

Ren Ishibashi$^{(\boxtimes)}$ and Kazuki Yoneyama

Ibaraki University, 4-12-1 Nakanarusawacho, Hitachi-shi, Ibaraki 316-8511, Japan
`21NM706R@vc.ibaraki.ac.jp`

Abstract. Hierarchical ID-based authenticated key exchange (HID-AKE) is a cryptographic protocol to establish a common session key between parties with authentication based on their IDs with the hierarchical delegation of key generation functionality. All existing HID-AKE schemes are selective ID secure, and the only known standard model scheme relies on a non-standard assumption such as the q-type assumption. In this paper, we propose a generic construction of HID-AKE that is adaptive ID secure in the HID-eCK model (maximal-exposure-resilient security model) without random oracles. One of the concrete instantiations of our generic construction achieves the first adaptive ID secure HID-AKE scheme under the (standard) k-lin assumption in the standard model. Furthermore, it has the advantage that the computational complexity of pairing and exponentiation operations and the communication complexity do not depend on the depth of the hierarchy. Also, the other concrete instantiation achieves the first HID-AKE scheme based on lattices (i.e., post-quantum).

Keywords: Authenticated key exchange · Hierarchical ID-based authenticated key exchange · HID-eCK model · Adaptive ID security

1 Introduction

Authenticated Key Exchange (AKE) is a cryptographic protocol to share a common session key among multiple parties through unauthenticated networks such as the Internet. In the ordinary PKI-based setting, each party locally keeps its static secret key (SSK) and publishes a static public key (SPK) corresponding to the SSK. Validity of SPKs is guaranteed by a certificate authority. In a key exchange session, each party generates an ephemeral secret key (ESK) and sends an ephemeral public key (EPK) corresponding to the ESK to the other party. A session key is derived from these keys with a key derivation function.

ID-based AKE (ID-AKE) is an ID-based extension of AKE, and the purpose is to remove the management of certificates. Similar to the basic scenario

© Springer Nature Switzerland AG 2021
K. Sako and N. O. Tippenhauer (Eds.): ACNS 2021, LNCS 12726, pp. 3–27, 2021.
https://doi.org/10.1007/978-3-030-78372-3_1

of ID-based encryption (IBE) such as [12–14], a trusted key generation center (KGC) generates a master secret key (MSK), and SSKs of all parties with the MSK according to their IDs. ID-AKE enjoys the same merit as IBE: no need of PKI, and using IDs instead of SPKs. However, at the same time, a problem of scalability is inherited: the workload for a KGC becomes burdensome when running on a large system.

To solve the scalability problem the hierarchical ID-based AKE (HID-AKE) is studied, in which each node can generate SSKs for its children in the hierarchy and delegate the key generation functionality of the KGC to each party. For example, the ID of a party U at level t is represented as $(ID_1, ID_2, \ldots, ID_t)$, and the party can generate the SSK of the party whose the ID $(ID_1, ID_2, \ldots, ID_t, ID_{t+1})$. Thus, it is enough that the KGC just generates MSK and the SSK of the first level party. It is similar to the advantage of hierarchical IBE (HIBE) such as [13] and [15]. Such a hierarchical structure includes hierarchical IDs such as e-mail addresses.

In HID-AKE schemes, we need to take into account forward secrecy and collusion resistance. Forward secrecy means that any adversary cannot obtain information of the session key even if the SSKs are compromised after the completion of the session. Collusion resistance means that disclosure of a party's SSK does not compromise SSKs of higher-level parties. The HID-eCK Security Model [1] guarantees these properties. The HID-eCK model captures maximal-exposure-resilience which means that an adversary is allowed to obtain any non-trivial[1] combination of MSK, SSKs, and ESKs individually. Thus, maximal-exposure-resilience implies forward secrecy and collusion resistance. Exposure of such secret keys may be usually caused in real-world applications. For example, a MSK is exposed when the KGC is corrupted. A SSK is revealed if SSKs are generated in an insecure host machine while it must be generated in a tamper-proof module such as a smart card. Such a failure may be caused to reduce costs for randomness generations in a tamper-proof module. Also, an ESK will be known to the adversary if a weak pseudo-random number generator is implemented. Therefore, it is important to consider such a fail-safe security to apply a cryptographic scheme to practical systems. Fail-safe means that if a cryptographic protocol is implemented in a system in the wrong way by some failure, minimum security properties are still guaranteed. For that reason, it is desirable to satisfy the HID-eCK security.

Currently, there are two HID-AKE schemes that satisfy HID-eCK security, [1] and [2]. However, one [1] is the selective HID-eCK secure scheme in the random oracle (RO) model, and the other [2] is proved in the standard model but it is selective HID-eCK secure under the non-standard assumption (i.e., q-type assumption). The selective ID security means that the adversary must specify target IDs at the beginning of the security experiment. On the other hand,

---

[1] If both SSK and ESK of a party are compromised in the target session, the adversary can obtain the session key trivially. Similarly, if both MSK and ESK are compromised in the target session, the adversary can also compute the session key trivially. We define freshness to consider combinations except this condition.

the adaptive ID security means that the adversary can specify target IDs when the target session is decided in the security experiment. Currently, no adaptive HID-eCK secure scheme under standard assumptions in the standard model is known.

1.1   Contribution

In this paper, we achieve the first adaptive HID-eCK secure HID-AKE scheme without ROs under standard assumptions. Specifically, we introduce a generic construction from an adaptive HID-CCA secure HIB-KEM and an IND-CPA secure KEM. An instantiation of our generic construction with a practical pairing-based HIB-KEM has the following advantages compared with existing schemes.

- Adaptive ID secure under standard assumptions.
- The communication cost and the computational cost of pairing and exponentiation operations are independent of the depth of hierarchy.

The existing scheme in [2] is HID-eCK secure under the non-standard q-type assumption in the standard model. The q-type assumption will change the size of instances depending on the parameter size of the scheme and the security proof. This causes the guaranteed security to be inconsistent even for schemes with the same assumption. On the other hand, standard assumptions, such as the k-lin and the DDH assumptions, are more reliable because the complexity of the assumption does not change according to the scheme and the proof. Our proposed scheme is HID-eCK secure under these standard assumptions in the standard model. In addition, existing schemes [1,2] are selective ID secure HID-AKE schemes, while our proposed scheme is an adaptive ID secure HID-AKE scheme.

Moreover, the computational cost of pairing and exponentiation operations and the communication complexity in the existing scheme in [1] and the computational cost of exponentiation operations in the existing scheme in [2] depend on the depth of hierarchy. Our paring-based instantiation of the generic construction is hierarchy-independent in terms of the computational cost of pairing and exponentiation operations and the communication complexity.

Furthermore, by using HIBE and KEM based on lattices, the first post-quantum HID-AKE scheme can be also constructed. Note that since no adaptive ID secure HIBE from lattices is known, the current instantiation is limited to be selective ID secure. If an adaptive ID secure HIBE from lattices is proposed, we can construct the post-quantum adaptive ID secure HID-AKE scheme.

2   Hierarchical ID-Based eCK Security Model

In this section, we show the definition of the HID-eCK security model [1] for HID-AKE. The HID-eCK model is an extension of the eCK security model of

PKI-based AKE by LaMacchia, Lauter, and Mityagin [8] to HID-AKE. In this paper, we suppose the 2-pass protocol, but it can be easily extended to any n-pass protocol.

Throughout this paper, if X is a set, then by $x \in_R X$ we denote that x is sampled uniformly from X.

2.1   Algorithms

An HID-AKE scheme Π consists of the following algorithms. We denote a party by U_i and its associated identity by $ID_i = (ID_{i.1}, ..., ID_{i.t})$ where $ID_{i.j} \in \{0,1\}^*$. We say that ID_i is a prefix of or equal to the identity ID_i' and denote $ID_i \succ ID_i'$ for $ID_i = (ID_{i.1}, ..., ID_{i.k_1})$ and $ID_i' = (ID_{i.1}, ..., ID_{i.k_1}, ..., ID_{i.k_2})$ for $1 \leq k_1 \leq k_2$. Let ℓ be the maximum depth of the hierarchy in the system. All parties are modeled as a PPT Turing machine.

[Parameters]
A system parameter $params$ is generated for a security parameter κ. All following algorithms implicitly take $params$ as input.

[Key Generation]
The key generation algorithm KeyGen takes a security parameter 1^κ as input, and outputs a master secret key MSK and a master public key MPK, i.e.,

$$\mathsf{KeyGen}(1^\kappa) \to (MSK, MPK).$$

[Key Extraction]
The key extraction algorithm KeyExt takes the master public key MPK, identities $ID_i = (ID_{i.1}, ..., ID_{i.t-1})$ and $ID_i' = (ID_{i.1}, ..., ID_{i.t-1}, ID_{i.t})$, where the identity ID_i is the parent of the identity ID_i', and a static secret key SSK_{ID_i} corresponding to the identity ID_i, and outputs a static secret key $SSK_{ID_i'}$ corresponding to the identity ID_i', i.e.,

$$\mathsf{KeyExt}(MPK, ID_i, ID_i', SSK_{ID_i}) \to SSK_{ID_i'}.$$

In the case of $t = 1$, the key extraction algorithm uses the master secret key MSK instead of a static secret key SSK_{ID_i}, i.e.,

$$\mathsf{KeyExt}(MPK, ID_i, ID_i', MSK) \to SSK_{ID_i'}.$$

[Key Exchange]
Party U_A and party U_B share a session key by performing the following 2-pass protocol. U_A has static secret key SSK_{ID_A} corresponding to $ID_A = (ID_{A.1}, ..., ID_{A.\alpha})$ and U_B has static secret key SSK_{ID_B} corresponding to $ID_B = (ID_{B.1}, ..., ID_{B.\beta})$.

U_A computes ephemeral keys by algorithm EphemeralKey, that takes the master public key MPK, the identity ID_A, the static secret key SSK_{ID_A}, and the identity ID_B, and outputs the ephemeral secret key ESK_{ID_A} and the ephemeral public key EPK_{ID_A}, i.e.,

$$\mathsf{EphemeralKey}(MPK, ID_A, SSK_{ID_A}, ID_B) \rightarrow (ESK_{ID_A}, EPK_{ID_A}).$$

U_A sends EPK_{ID_A} to U_B.

On the other hand, U_B computes ephemeral keys by algorithm EphemeralKey, that takes the master public key MPK, the identity ID_B, the static secret key SSK_{ID_B}, and the identity ID_A, and outputs the ephemeral secret key ESK_{ID_B} and the ephemeral public key EPK_{ID_B}, i.e.,

$$\mathsf{EphemeralKey}(MPK, ID_B, SSK_{ID_B}, ID_A) \rightarrow (ESK_{ID_B}, EPK_{ID_B}).$$

U_B sends EPK_{ID_B} to U_A.

Upon receiving EPK_{ID_B}, U_A computes a session key by algorithm SessionKey, that takes the master public key MPK, the identity ID_A, the static secret key SSK_{ID_A}, the identity ID_B, the ephemeral secret key ESK_{ID_A} and the ephemeral public key EPK_{ID_A}, and the ephemeral public key EPK_{ID_B}, and outputs the session key SK, i.e.,

$$\mathsf{SessionKey}(MPK, ID_A, SSK_{ID_A}, ID_B, ESK_{ID_A}, EPK_{ID_A}, EPK_{ID_B}) \rightarrow SK.$$

Similarly, Upon receiving EPK_{ID_A}, U_B computes a session key by algorithm SessionKey, that takes the master public key MPK, the identity ID_B, the static secret key SSK_{ID_B}, the identity ID_A, the ephemeral secret key ESK_{ID_B} and the ephemeral public key EPK_{ID_B}, and the ephemeral public key EPK_{ID_A}, and outputs the session key SK, i.e.,

$$\mathsf{SessionKey}(MPK, ID_B, SSK_{ID_B}, ID_A, ESK_{ID_B}, EPK_{ID_B}, EPK_{ID_A}) \rightarrow SK.$$

2.2 Session

Let ID_i be an identifier of U_i, and EPK_ID be an ephemeral public key of U_i. An invocation of a protocol is called a session. A session is activated by an incoming message of the form $(\Pi, \mathcal{I}, ID_A, ID_B)$ or $(\Pi, \mathcal{R}, ID_B, ID_A, EPK_{ID_A})$, where Π is a protocol identifier, $\mathcal{I}$ and $\mathcal{R}$ are role identifiers. If U_A is activated with $(\Pi, \mathcal{I}, ID_A, ID_B)$, then U_A is called the session initiator. If U_B is activated with $(\Pi, \mathcal{R}, ID_B, ID_A, EPK_{ID_A})$, then U_B is called the session responder. The initiator U_A sends EPK_{ID_A}, then on receiving an incoming message of the forms $(\Pi, \mathcal{I}, ID_A, ID_B, EPK_{ID_A}, EPK_{ID_B})$ from the responder U_B, U_A outputs the session key SK. The responder U_B sends EPK_{ID_B}, and computes the session key SK.

If U_A is the initiator of a session, the session is identified by $sid = (\Pi, \mathcal{I}, ID_A, ID_B, EPK_{ID_A})$ or $sid = (\Pi, \mathcal{I}, ID_A, ID_B, EPK_{ID_A}, EPK_{ID_B})$. If U_A is the responder of a session, the session is identified by $sid = (\Pi, \mathcal{R}, ID_A, ID_B, EPK_{ID_B}, EPK_{ID_A})$. We say that U_A is the owner of sid if the third coordinate of sid is ID_A. We say that U_A is the peer of sid if the fourth coordinate of session sid is ID_A. We say that a session is completed if a session key is computed in the session. The matching session of $(\Pi, \mathcal{I}, ID_A, ID_B, EPK_{ID_A}, EPK_{ID_B})$ is the session with identifier $(\Pi, \mathcal{R}, ID_B, ID_A, EPK_{ID_A}, EPK_{ID_B})$ and vice versa.

2.3 Adversary

The adversary $\mathcal{A}$, that is modeled as a PPT Turing machine, controls all communications among parties including session activations, by performing the following adversary query.

- Send(*message*): The *message* has one of the following forms: $(\Pi, \mathcal{I}, ID_A, ID_B)$, $(\Pi, \mathcal{R}, ID_B, ID_A, EPK_{ID_A})$, or $(\Pi, \mathcal{I}, ID_A, ID_B, EPK_{ID_A}, EPK_{ID_B})$. Each party performs an internal computation according to the given message and returns the response to $\mathcal{A}$.

A party's secret information is not accessible to the adversary, however, leakage of secret information is captured via the following adversarial queries.

- SessionKeyReveal(*sid*): The adversary obtains the session key for the session *sid* if the session is completed.
- EphemeralKeyReveal(*sid*): The adversary obtains the ephemeral secret key of the owner of the session *sid*.
- StaticKeyReveal(ID_i): The adversary learns the static secret key corresponding to the identity ID_i.
- MasterKeyReveal(): The adversary learns the master secret key of the system.
- EstablishParty(U_i, ID_i): This query allows the adversary to register identity ID_i on behalf of the party U_i and the adversary totally controls that party. If party U_i is established by EstablishParty(U_i, ID_i) query issued by the adversary, then we call U_i dishonest. If not, we call U_i honest.

2.4 Freshness

For the security definition, we need the notion of freshness.

Definition 1 (Freshness). *Let* $sid^* = (\Pi, \mathcal{I}, ID_A, ID_B, EPK_{ID_A}, EPK_{ID_B})$ *or* $(\Pi, \mathcal{R}, ID_B, ID_A, EPK_{ID_A}, EPK_{ID_B})$ *be a completed session between honest party* U_A *with identity* ID_A *and* U_B *with identity* ID_B. *If the matching session exists, then let* $\overline{sid^*}$ *be the matching session of* sid^*. *We say that session* sid^* *is fresh if none of the following conditions hold:*

1. The adversary issues a SessionKeyReveal(sid^*), or SessionKeyReveal($\overline{sid^*}$) query if $\overline{sid^*}$ exists,
2. $\overline{sid^*}$ exists and the adversary makes either of the following queries
    - both StaticKeyReveal(ID) (s.t. $ID \succ ID_A$) and EphemeralKeyReveal (sid^*), or
    - both StaticKeyReveal(ID) (s.t. $ID \succ ID_B$) and EphemeralKeyReveal ($\overline{sid^*}$),

3. $\overline{sid^*}$ does not exist and the adversary makes either of the following queries
   - both StaticKeyReveal(ID) (s.t. $ID \succ ID_A$) and EphemeralKeyReveal (sid^*), or
   - StaticKeyReveal(ID) (s.t. $ID \succ ID_B$),

where

- if the adversary issues MasterKeyReveal() query, we regard that the adversary issues StaticKeyReveal(ID_A) and StaticKeyReveal(ID_B) queries.

2.5 Security Experiment

For the security definition, we consider the following security experiment. Initially, the adversary $\mathcal{A}$ is given a set of honest parties, and makes any sequence of the queries described above. During the experiment, $\mathcal{A}$ makes the following query.

- Test(sid^*): Here, sid^* must be a fresh session. Choose a random bit $b \in_R \{0, 1\}$, and return the session key held by sid^* if $b = 0$, and return a random key if $b = 1$.

The experiment continues until $\mathcal{A}$ makes a guess b'. The adversary wins the game if the test session sid^* is still fresh and if the guess of $\mathcal{A}$ is correct, i.e., $b' = b$. The advantage of the adversary $\mathcal{A}$ in the experiment with the HID-AKE scheme Π is defined as

$$Adv_{\Pi}^{HIDAKE}(\mathcal{A}) = |\Pr[\mathcal{A} \text{ win}] - 1/2|$$

We define the security as follows.

Definition 2 (Security). *We say that an HID-AKE scheme Π is secure in the HID-eCK model, if the following conditions hold:*

1. If two honest parties complete matching sessions, then, except with a negligible probability, they both compute the same session key.
2. For any PPT bounded adversary $\mathcal{A}$, $Adv_{\Pi}^{HIDAKE}(\mathcal{A})$ is negligible in security parameter κ.

Moreover, we say that an HID-AKE scheme Π is adaptive ID secure in the HID-eCK model, if adversary $\mathcal{A}$ can specify a challenge ID when Test(sid^*) query is issued in the security game. Also, we say that an HID-AKE scheme Π is selective ID secure in the HID-eCK model if adversary $\mathcal{A}$ must specify a challenge ID in the beginning of the security game.

3   Building Blocks

3.1   KEM

This section shows the definition of KEM.

Definition 3 (Model for KEM Schemes). *A KEM scheme consists of the following 3-tuple* (wKeyGen, wEnCap, wDeCap):

- $(ek, dk) \leftarrow$ wKeyGen$(1^\kappa; r_g)$: *a key generation algorithm which on inputs* 1^κ *and* $r_g \in \mathcal{RS}_\mathcal{G}$, *where* κ *is the security parameter and* $\mathcal{RS}_\mathcal{G}$ *is a randomness space, outputs a pair of keys* (ek, dk).
- $(K, CT) \leftarrow$ wEnCap$(ek; r_e)$: *an encapsulation algorithm which takes as inputs encapsulation key* ek *and* $r_e \in \mathcal{RS}_\mathcal{E}$, *outputs session key* $K \in \mathcal{KS}$ *and* $CT \in \mathcal{CS}$ *where* $\mathcal{RS}_\mathcal{E}$ *is a randomness space,* $\mathcal{KS}$ *is a session key space, and* $\mathcal{CS}$ *is a ciphertext space.*
- $K \leftarrow$ wDeCap(dk, CT): *a decapsulation algorithm which takes as inputs decapsulation key* dk *and ciphertext* $CT \in \mathcal{CS}$, *and outputs session key* $K \in \mathcal{KS}$.

Definition 4 (IND-CPA Security for KEM). *A KEM scheme is IND-CPA secure for KEM if the following property holds for security parameter* κ; *For any PPT adversary* $\mathcal{A} = (\mathcal{A}_1, \mathcal{A}_2)$, $Adv^{ind-cpa} = |\Pr[r_g \leftarrow \mathcal{RS}_\mathcal{G}; (ek, dk) \leftarrow$ KeyGen$(1^\kappa; r_g); (state) \leftarrow \mathcal{A}_1(ek); b \leftarrow \{0, 1\}; r_e \leftarrow \mathcal{RS}_E; (K_0^*, C_0^*) \leftarrow$ EnCap $(ek; r_e); K_1^* \leftarrow \mathcal{K}; b' \leftarrow \mathcal{A}_2(ek, (K_b^*, C_0^*), state); b' = b] - 1/2| \leq negl$, *where* $\mathcal{K}$ *is the space of session key and state is state information that* $\mathcal{A}$ *wants to preserve from* $\mathcal{A}_1$ *to* $\mathcal{A}_2$.

3.2   Hierarchical ID-Based KEM

This section shows the definition of HIBKEM.

Definition 5 (HIBKEM). *An HIBKEM scheme consists of the following 5-tuple* (MKeyGen, KeyExt, KeyDer, EnCap, DeCap):

- $(MPK, MSK) \leftarrow$ MKeyGen$(1^\kappa; r_g)$: *a master key generation algorithm which on inputs* 1^κ *and* $r_g \in \mathcal{RS}_\mathcal{G}$, *where* κ *is the security parameter and* $\mathcal{RS}_\mathcal{G}$ *is a randomness space, outputs a master public key* MPK *and a master secret key* MSK.
- $dk_i \leftarrow$ KeyExt(MPK, MSK, ID_i): *a key extraction algorithm which on inputs master public key* MPK, *master secret key* MSK, *and* ID_i, *outputs a decapsulation key* dk_i *corresponding to the identity* ID_i.
- $dk_i \leftarrow$ KeyDer$(MPK, dk_{i-1}, ID_i, ID_{i-1})$: *a key delegation algorithm which on inputs master public key* MPK, *decapsulation key* dk_{i-1}, ID_{i-1}, *and* ID_i, *where* ID_{i-1} *is the parent of* ID_i *outputs a decapsulation key* dk_i *corresponding to the identity* ID_i.

- $(K, C) \leftarrow$ EnCap$(MPK, ID; r_e)$: an encapsulation algorithm which on inputs master public key MPK, ID and $r_e \in \mathcal{RS_E}$, outputs session key $K \in \mathcal{KS}$ and ciphertext $C \in \mathcal{CS}$, where $\mathcal{KS}$ is a session key space, $\mathcal{RS_E}$ is a randomness space and $\mathcal{CS}$ is a ciphertext space.
- $K \leftarrow$ DeCap(dk, C): an decapsulation algorithm which on inputs decapsulation key dk and ciphertext $C \in \mathcal{CS}$, outputs session key $K \in \mathcal{KS}$ or $\bot$.

Here, we show the definition of adaptive HID-CCA security for HIBKEM by the following HID-CCA game. The game is played between adversary $\mathcal{A} = (\mathcal{A}_1, \mathcal{A}_2)$ and a challenger.

1. The challenger generates the master public key and the master secret key by $(MPK, MSK) \leftarrow$ MKeyGen$(1^\kappa; r_g)$ and gives MPK to the adversary $\mathcal{A}_1$.
2. The adversary $\mathcal{A}_1$ issues the following queries adaptively.
   (a) Extraction(ID_i): The challenger runs $dk_i =$ KeyExt(MPK, MSK, ID_i) and returns the decapsulation key dk_i corresponding to ID_i.
   (b) Decryption(ID_i, C_i): The challenger runs $K_i \leftarrow$ DeCap(KeyExt$(MPK, MSK, ID_i), C_i$) and returns the session key K_i that is decrypted from the ciphertext C_i.
3. The adversary $\mathcal{A}_1$ outputs the challenge ID $ID^* = (ID_1^*, ..., ID_{\ell^*}^*)$ and state information s, and passes the state information s to the adversary $\mathcal{A}_2$, where the challenge ID is not queried to Extraction for the prefix ID of it in the above phase, i.e., $ID = (ID_1^*, ..., ID_\ell^*)$ (where $\ell \leq \ell^*$) has not been queried.
4. The challenger computes $(C^*, K_0^*) \leftarrow$ EnCap$(MPK, ID^*; r_e^*)$ and randomly chooses $K_1^* \in \mathcal{KS}$. The challenger randomly chooses $b \in \{0, 1\}$ and gives (C^*, K_b^*) to the adversary $\mathcal{A}_2$ as a challenge.
5. The adversary $\mathcal{A}_2$ issues the following queries adaptively.
   (a) Extraction(ID_i): The challenger runs $dk_i =$ KeyExt(MPK, MSK, ID_i) and returns the decapsulation key dk_i corresponding to ID_i, where the prefix ID of the challenge ID ID^* must not be queried.
   (b) Decryption(ID_i, C_i): The challenger runs $K_i \leftarrow$ DeCap(KeyExt$(MPK, MSK, ID_i), C_i$) and returns the session key K_i that is decrypted from the ciphertext C_i, where the pair (ID^*, C^*) must not be queried.
6. adversary $\mathcal{A}_2$ outputs a guess $b' \in \{0, 1\}$.

If $b = b'$, then we say that the adversary wins the game. We also define the adversary's advantage in this game as $Adv_{\mathcal{A}}^{HID-CCA} = |\Pr[b' = b]| - 1/2|$.

Definition 6 (Adaptive HID-CCA Security). *If the advantage of the adversary $\mathcal{A}$ over the challenger in the above HID-CCA game is negligible, then HIBKEM is adaptive HID-CCA secure.*

We define the notion of δ-min-entropy for KEM keys as follows.

Definition 7 (Min-Entropy of KEM Keys [3]). *An HIBKEM scheme is δ-min-entropy HIBKEM if for any ID, MPK, distribution $\mathcal{D}_{KS}$ of variable K defined by $(C, K) \leftarrow$ EnCap$(MPK, ID; r_e)$, distribution $\mathcal{D}_{pub}$ of public information and random $r_e \in \mathcal{RS_E}$, $H_\infty(\mathcal{D}_{KS}|\mathcal{D}_{pub}) \geq \delta$ holds, where H_∞ denotes min-entropy.*

The δ-min-entropy of PKI-based KEM can be defined in the same way.

3.3 Key-Derivation Function

Let KDF : $Salt \times Dom \rightarrow Rng$ be a function with finite domain Dom, finite range Rng, and a space of non-secret random salt $Salt$.

Definition 8 (Key-Derivation Function). *We say that function KDF is a KDF if the following condition holds for a security parameter κ. For any PPT adversary $\mathcal{A}$ and any distribution $\mathcal{D}_{Dom}$ over Dom with $H_\infty(\mathcal{D}_{Dom}) \geq \kappa$, $|\Pr[y \in_R Rng, s \in_R Salt; ; 1 \leftarrow \mathcal{A}(s,y)] - \Pr[x \in_R Dom; s \in_R Salt; y \leftarrow KDF(s,x); 1 \leftarrow \mathcal{A}(s,y)]| \leq negl.$*

3.4 Pseudo-Random Function

We show the definition of Pseudo-Random Function (PRF). Let κ be a security parameter and $\mathbf{F} = \{F_\kappa : Dom_\kappa \times \mathcal{FS}_\kappa \rightarrow Rng_\kappa\}_\kappa$ be a function family with a family of domains $\{Dom_\kappa\}_\kappa$, a family of key spaces $\{\mathcal{FS}_\kappa\}_\kappa$ and a family of ranges $\{Rng_\kappa\}_\kappa$.

Definition 9 (Pseudo-Random Function). *We say that function family $\mathbf{F} = \{F_\kappa\}_\kappa$ is a PRF family if for any PPT distinguisher $\mathcal{D}$, $Adv^{PRF} = |\Pr[1 \leftarrow \mathcal{D}^{F_\kappa(k)}] - \Pr[1 \leftarrow \mathcal{D}^{RF_\kappa(\cdot)}]| \leq negl$, where $RF_\kappa : Dom_\kappa \rightarrow Rng_\kappa$ is a truly random function.*

4 Generic Construction of Hierarchical ID-Based AKE

In this section, we propose a generic construction of HID-AKE (named HID-GC) based on an adaptive HID-CCA secure HIBKEM and an IND-CPA secure KEM. HID-GC satisfies the adaptive HID-eCK security. The protocol of HID-GC is shown in Fig. 1.

4.1 Design Principle

We extend the known generic construction of ID-AKE (ID-GC) by Fujioka et al. [3] to the HID-AKE setting, and use adaptive HID-CCA-secure HIBKEM instead of selective ID-CCA IBKEM in order to achieve adaptive ID security. In the initialization, static secret keys are generated by using the key delegation function (KeyDer of HIBKEM), and each party receives the static secret key corresponding to its ID. In a key exchange session, each party uses the other party's ID to encapsulate the KEM session key by the encapsulation function (EnCap of HIBKEM). In addition, the IND-CPA secure KEM allows us to exchange ek_T and C_T using only the respective ephemeral secret keys, without using the static secret keys of parties. Such a mechanism provides forward secrecy and security against leakage of both static secret keys of the initiator and the responder.

For HID-eCK security, the twisted PRF trick [3] is used as well as ID-GC [3]. The twisted PRF trick computes $F(esk, ssk) \oplus F'(ssk', esk')$ using two PRFs F and F', and uses it instead of directly using ephemeral secret keys, where

(ssk, ssk') are static secret keys and (esk, esk') are ephemeral secret keys. It is especially effective for leakage of ephemeral secret keys. Even if (esk, esk') is exposed, it is impossible to compute $\mathsf{F}(esk, ssk)$ without knowing ssk. Similarly, even if (ssk, ssk') is exposed, it is impossible to compute $\mathsf{F}'(ssk', esk')$ without knowing esk'. In our generic construction of HID-AKE, the output of the twisted PRF trick is used as the randomness of the encapsulation algorithm in HIBKEM. Therefore, the definition of freshness prevents an adversary from obtaining information about the randomness, since both ephemeral secret key and static secret key of the party must not be exposed.

In our security proof of the proposed HID-GC, we use the adaptive HID-CCA secure HIBKEM to prove the security in the adaptive HID-eCK model. Unlike security proofs in the selective ID security model, since the ID space may be a super-polynomial size, parties of the test session cannot be fixed in advance and, thus, we cannot do as in the proof of ID-GC [3]. Moreover, though in the adaptive ID security model of HIBKEM the challenge ciphertext is generated after receiving the target ID from the adversary, in the adaptive ID security model of HID-AKE the adversary can first activate a session with the target IDs to generate ephemeral public keys corresponding to the challenge ciphertext, and then later specifies the test session with the target ID. Due to this difference in the timing, at one glance it is difficult to construct a reduction to the adaptive security of HIBKEM from the adaptive security of HID-AKE. However, since the number of sessions that an adversary can observe in queries is a polynomial size, we can simulate ephemeral public keys of the test session by guessing the order of the test session among activated sessions and generating ephemeral public keys using the target IDs because IDs are specified in the timing of the activation by the adversary. Hence, we can prove the adaptive security.

Note that though HID-GC is not 1-round protocol (i.e., the initiator and the responder can send messages simultaneously) due to the exchange of ek_T and C_T of IND-CPA KEM, if we use KEM with public-key-independent-ciphertext (PKIC-KEM), which is used in the generic construction of 1-round AKE proposed in [16], instead of IND-CPA KEM, HID-GC can be a 1-round protocol without using the twisted PRF trick. An example of PKIC-KEM is the ElGamal KEM.

4.2 Protocol

The protocol of HID-GC consists of HIBKEM (MKeyGen, KeyExt, KeyDer, EnCap, DeCap) and KEM (wKeyGen, wEnCap, wDeCap), as follows.

[Public Parameters]
Let κ be a security parameter, and let $\mathsf{F}, \mathsf{F}' : \{0,1\}^* \times \mathcal{FS} \to \mathcal{RS_E}$, PRF $: \{0,1\}^* \times \mathcal{FS} \to \{0,1\}^\kappa$ be PRFs, where $\mathcal{FS}$ is a key space of PRFs $(|\mathcal{FS}| = \kappa)$, $\mathcal{RS_E}$ is a randomness space of the encapsulation algorithm, and let KDF $: Salt \times \mathcal{KS} \to \mathcal{FS}$ be a KDF with a non-secret random salt $s \in Salt$, where $Salt$ is the salt space and $\mathcal{KS}$ is the session key space of KEM session keys. These are provided as public parameters.

Public Parameter : F, F', PRF, PRF', s

Master Keys : MSK, MPK

U_A(initiator)	U_B(responder)
$dk_A \leftarrow \text{KeyDer}(MPK, dk_{ID_{A-1}}, ID_A, ID_{A-1})$	$dk_B \leftarrow \text{KeyDer}(MPK, dk_{ID_{B-1}}, ID_B, ID_{B-1})$
$r_A \in_R \mathcal{FS}, r'_A \in_R \{0,1\}^k$	$r_B \in_R \mathcal{FS}, r'_B \in_R \{0,1\}^k$
$SSK_A := (dk_A, r_A, r'_A)$	$SSK_B := (dk_B, r_B, r'_B)$

$esk_A \in_R \{0,1\}^k, esk'_A \in_R \mathcal{FS}, esk_{TA} \in_R RS_G$	
$ESK_A := (esk_A, esk'_A, esk_{TA})$	
$s_A \leftarrow F(esk_A, r_A) \oplus F'(r'_A, esk'_A)$	
$(C_B, K_B) \leftarrow \text{EnCap}(ID_B; s_A)$	
$(ek_T, dk_T) \leftarrow \text{wKeyGen}(1^k; esk_{TA})$	

$\xrightarrow{\quad U_A, U_B, C_B, ek_T \quad}$ $esk_B \in_R \{0,1\}^k, esk'_B \in_R \mathcal{FS}, esk_{TB} \in_R RS_E$

$ESK_B := (esk_B, esk'_B, esk_{TB})$

$s_B \leftarrow F(esk_B, r_B) \oplus F'(r'_B, esk'_B)$

$(C_A, K_A) \leftarrow \text{EnCap}(ID_A; s_B)$

$\xleftarrow{\quad U_A, U_B, C_A, C_T \quad}$ $(C_T, K_T) \leftarrow \text{wEnCap}(ek_T; esk_{TB})$

$K_A = DeCap(dk_A, C_A)$	$K_B = DeCap(dk_B, C_B)$
$K_T = wDeCap(dk_T, C_T)$	
$\sigma_1 = KDF(s, K_A)$	$\sigma_1 = KDF(s, K_A)$
$\sigma_2 = KDF(s, K_B)$	$\sigma_2 = KDF(s, K_B)$
$\sigma_3 = KDF(s, K_T)$	$\sigma_3 = KDF(s, K_T)$
$sid := (U_A, U_B, C_B, ek_T, C_A, C_T)$	$sid := (U_A, U_B, C_B, ek_T, C_A, C_T)$

$$SK = PRF(sid, \sigma_1) \oplus PRF(sid, \sigma_2) \oplus PRF(sid, \sigma_3)$$

Fig. 1. Generic Construction HID-GC

[**Master Secret and Public Keys**]
The KGC randomly chooses $r \in \mathcal{RS_G}$ and runs $(MPK, MSK) \leftarrow$ MKeyGen $(1^\kappa, r)$, where $\mathcal{RS_G}$ is a randomness space of the key generation algorithm.
[**Secret Key**]
Party U_P randomly chooses $r_P \in_R \mathcal{FS}$ and $r'_P \in_R \{0,1\}^\kappa$. For party U_P, the KGC or the parent of U_P runs the key extraction algorithm $dk_P \leftarrow$ KeyExt(MPK, MSK, ID_P) or the key delegation algorithm $dk_P \leftarrow$ KeyDer$(MPK, dk_{ID_{P-1}}, ID_P, ID_{P-1})$. Party U_P's static secret key is (dk_P, r_P, r'_P).
[**Key Exchange**]
Let party U_A with $SSK = (dk_A, r_A, r'_A)$ be the initiator, and party U_B with $SSK = (dk_B, r_B, r'_B)$ be the responder.

1. U_A randomly chooses ephemeral secret keys $esk_A \in_R \{0,1\}^\kappa$, $esk'_A \in_R \mathcal{FS}$, and $esk_{TA} \in_R \mathcal{RS_G}$. U_A computes $(ek_T, dk_T) \leftarrow$ wKeyGen$(1^\kappa; esk_{TA})$,

$s_A = \mathsf{F}(esk_A, r_A) \oplus \mathsf{F}'(r'_A, esk'_A)$, $(C_B, K_B) \leftarrow \mathsf{EnCap}(ID_B; s_A)$ and sends (U_A, U_B, C_B, ek_T) to U_B.

2. Upon receiving (U_A, U_B, C_B, ek_T), U_B randomly chooses ephemeral secret key $esk_B \in_R \{0,1\}^\kappa$, $esk'_B \in_R \mathcal{FS}$, and $esk_{TB} \in_R \mathcal{RS}_\mathcal{E}$. U_B computes $s_B = \mathsf{F}(esk_B, r_B) \oplus \mathsf{F}'(r'_B, esk'_B)$, $(C_A, K_A) \leftarrow \mathsf{EnCap}(ID_A; s_B)$, $(C_T, K_T) \leftarrow \mathsf{wEnCap}(ek_T; ek_{TB})$ and sends (U_A, U_B, C_A, C_T) to U_A. U_B computes $K_B \leftarrow \mathsf{DeCap}(dk_B, C_B)$ and shared values as follows.
   - $\sigma_1 = \mathsf{KDF}(s, K_A)$
   - $\sigma_2 = \mathsf{KDF}(s, K_B)$
   - $\sigma_3 = \mathsf{KDF}(s, K_T)$
   U_B sets $sid = (U_A, U_B, C_B, ek_T, C_A, C_T)$ and computes the session key $SK = \mathsf{PRF}(sid, \sigma_1) \oplus \mathsf{PRF}(sid, \sigma_2) \oplus \mathsf{PRF}(sid, \sigma_3)$.

3. Upon receiving (U_A, U_B, C_A, C_T), U_A computes $K_A \leftarrow \mathsf{DeCap}(dk_A, C_A)$, $K_T \leftarrow \mathsf{wDeCap}(dk_T, C_T)$ and shared value as follows.
   - $\sigma_1 = \mathsf{KDF}(s, K_A)$
   - $\sigma_2 = \mathsf{KDF}(s, K_B)$
   - $\sigma_3 = \mathsf{KDF}(s, K_T)$
   U_A sets $sid = (U_A, U_B, C_B, ek_T, C_A, C_T)$ and computes the session key $SK = \mathsf{PRF}(sid, \sigma_1) \oplus \mathsf{PRF}(sid, \sigma_2) \oplus \mathsf{PRF}(sid, \sigma_3)$.

4.3 Security

In this section, we show the security of the proposed HID-GC. The sketch of the proof is given in Sect. 4.1.

Theorem 1. *Assuming that* (MKeyGen, KeyDer, EnCap, DeCap) *is an adaptive HID-CCA secure and δ-min-entropy HIBKEM, and* (wKeyGen, wEnCap, wDeCap) *is an IND-CPA secure and δ-min-entropy KEM,* F, F′, PRF *are PRFs, and* KDF *is a KDF, then HID-GC is adaptive HID-eCK secure.*

Proof. In the experiment of HID-eCK security, we suppose that sid^* is the session identity for the test session, and that at most n sessions are activated. Let κ be the security parameter, and let $\mathcal{A}$ be a PPT (in κ) bounded adversary. We construct a solver $\mathcal{S}$ and a distinguisher $\mathcal{D}$ from $\mathcal{A}$ runs the HID-eCK game.

If Test(sid^*) query is issued for a session by (ID_A, ID_B), then $sid^* = (\Pi, \mathcal{I}, U_A, U_B, (C_B, ek_T), (C_A, C_T))$ or $(\Pi, \mathcal{R}, U_B, U_A, (C_B, ek_T), (C_A, C_T))$ is the session identity of the test session.

Suc denotes the event that $\mathcal{A}$ wins. We consider the following events that cover all cases of the behavior $\mathcal{A}$.

- E_1: test session sid^* has no matching session $\overline{sid^*}$, the owner of sid^* is the initiator and $\mathcal{A}$ queries StaticKeyReveal(ID) s.t. $ID \succ ID_A$.
- E_2: test session sid^* has no matching session $\overline{sid^*}$, the owner of sid^* is the initiator and $\mathcal{A}$ queries EphemeralKeyReveal(sid^*).
- E_3: test session sid^* has no matching session $\overline{sid^*}$, the owner of sid^* is the responder and $\mathcal{A}$ queries StaticKeyReveal(ID) s.t. $ID \succ ID_B$.

-E_4: test session sid^* has no matching session $\overline{sid^*}$, the owner of sid^* is the responder and $\mathcal{A}$ queries EphemeralKeyReveal(sid^*).

-E_5: test session sid^* has matching session $\overline{sid^*}$, and $\mathcal{A}$ queries MasterKeyReveal() or StaticKeyReveal(ID) s.t. $ID \succ ID_A$ and StaticKeyReveal(ID) s.t. ID $\succ ID_B$.

-E_6: test session sid^* has matching session $\overline{sid^*}$, and $\mathcal{A}$ queries EphemeralKeyReveal(sid^*) and EphemeralKeyReveal($\overline{sid^*}$).

-E_7: test session sid^* has matching session $\overline{sid^*}$, and $\mathcal{A}$ queries EphemeralKeyReveal($\overline{sid^*}$) and StaticKeyReveal(ID) s.t. ID $\succ ID_A$.

-E_8: test session sid^* has matching session $\overline{sid^*}$, and $\mathcal{A}$ queries EphemeralKeyReveal(sid^*) and StaticKeyReveal(ID) s.t. ID $\succ ID_B$.

To finish the proof, we investigate events $E_i \wedge Suc(i = 1, \ldots, 8)$ that cover all cases of event Suc. Due to the page limitation, we give the proof of event $E_1 \wedge Suc$, and proofs of other events are given in Appendix A.

Event $E_1 \wedge Suc$. We change the interface of oracle queries and the computation of the session key. These instances are gradually changed over seven hybrid experiments, depending on specific subcases. In the last hybrid experiment, the session key in the test session does not contain information of the bit b. Thus, the adversary clearly only outputs a random guess. We denote these hybrid experiments by $H_0, \ldots, H_6$ and the advantage of the adversary $\mathcal{A}$ when participating in experiment H_i by $\mathbf{Adv}(\mathcal{A}, H_i)$.

Hybrid Experiment H_0: This experiment denotes the real experiment for HID-eCK security and in this experiment the environment for $\mathcal{A}$ is as defined in the protocol. Thus, $\mathbf{Adv}(\mathcal{A}, H_0)$ is the same as the advantage of the real experiment.

Hybrid Experiment H_1: This experiment aborts when sid is matched with multiple sessions.

By the decryption correctness of KEM, the probability of outputting the same ciphertext from different randomness in each session is negligible. Thus, $|Adv(\mathcal{A}, H_1) - Adv(\mathcal{A}, H_0)| \leq negl$.

Hybrid Experiment H_2: This experiment chooses an integer $i^* \in [1, \ell]$ in advance and fixes the session to be the target of the Test query as the i^*-th session. If $\mathcal{A}$ queries a session other than the i^*-th in the Test query, abort the experiment.

The probability that the guess of the test session is correct is $1/\ell$, hence $Adv(\mathcal{A}, H_2) \geq 1/\ell \cdot Adv(\mathcal{A}, H_1)$.

Hybrid Experiment H_3: This experiment changes the way of the computation of initiator's twisted PRF in the test session is changed. Instead of computing $s^* = \mathsf{F}(esk^*, r^*) \oplus \mathsf{F}'(r'^*, esk'^*)$, it is changed as $s^* = \mathsf{F}(esk^*, r^*) \oplus \mathsf{RF}(r'^*)$.

We construct a distinguisher $\mathcal{D}$ that distinguishes if F* is either a pseudo-random function F$'$ or a random function RF from $\mathcal{A}$ in H_2 or H_3. $\mathcal{D}$ performs the following steps.

[Setup]

$\mathcal{D}$ chooses PRF F, F$'$: $\{0,1\}^* \times \mathcal{FS} \to \mathcal{RS}_\mathcal{E}$, PRF : $\{0,1\}^* \times \mathcal{FS} \to \{0,1\}^\kappa$, and a KDF KDF : $Salt \times \mathcal{KS} \to \mathcal{FS}$ with a non-secret random salt $s \in Salt$. These are provided as the public parameters. Also, $\mathcal{D}$ embeds F* into F$'$ of the i^*-th session.

$\mathcal{D}$ sets MPK and MSK according to the protocol.

[Simulation]

$\mathcal{D}$ maintains the list L_{SK} that contains queries and answers of SessionKeyReveal. $\mathcal{D}$ simulates oracle queries by $\mathcal{A}$ as follows.

1. Send$(\Pi, \mathcal{I}, U_P, U_{\bar{P}})$: If the SSK of U_P is not set, $\mathcal{D}$ generates and sets the SSK according to the protocol. If the session is the i^*-th session, $\mathcal{D}$ chooses $ESK^* = (esk^*, esk'^*, esk_T^*)$ according to the protocol and poses r'^* of SSK^* to his oracle F^* (F$'$ or RF) and obtains $x \in \mathcal{RS}_\mathcal{E}$. Also, $\mathcal{D}$ computes $s^* = $ F$(esk^*, r^*) \oplus x$, sets $EPK^* = (C^*, ek_T^*)$, and returns EPK^*. Otherwise, $\mathcal{D}$ computes $EPK = (C_{\bar{P}}, ek_T)$ according to the protocol, returns it, and records $(\Pi, U_P, U_{\bar{P}}, (C_{\bar{P}}, ek_T))$ in L_{SK}.

2. Send$(\Pi, \mathcal{R}, U_{\bar{P}}, U_P, (C_{\bar{P}}, ek_T))$: If the SSK of $U_{\bar{P}}$ is not set, $\mathcal{D}$ generates and sets the SSK according to the protocol. $\mathcal{D}$ computes $EPK = (C_{\bar{P}}, ek_T)$ and SK according to the protocol, and returns EPK, and records $(\Pi, U_P, U_{\bar{P}}, (C_{\bar{P}}, ek_T), (C_P, C_T))$ as the completed session and SK in L_{SK}.

3. Send$(\Pi, \mathcal{I}, U_P, U_{\bar{P}}, (C_{\bar{P}}, ek_T), (C_P, C_T))$: If $(\Pi, U_P, U_{\bar{P}}, (C_{\bar{P}}, ek_T))$ is not recorded in L_{SK}, then $\mathcal{D}$ records this sid as not completed. Also, if the SSK of U_P is not set, $\mathcal{D}$ generates and sets the SSK according to the protocol. Otherwise, $\mathcal{D}$ computes SK according to the protocol and records $(\Pi, U_P, U_{\bar{P}}, (C_{\bar{P}}, ek_T), (C_P, C_T))$ as the completed session and SK in L_{SK}.

4. SessionKeyReveal(sid) :
   (a) If sid is not completed, then $\mathcal{D}$ returns error.
   (b) Otherwise, $\mathcal{D}$ returns SK as recorded in L_{SK}.

5. EphemeralKeyReveal(sid) : $\mathcal{D}$ returns ESK for sid as defined.

6. StaticKeyReveal(ID_i) : If the SSK for ID_i is not set, $\mathcal{D}$ generates and sets the SSK according to the protocol. $\mathcal{D}$ returns the SSK as defined.

7. MasterKeyReveal(): $\mathcal{D}$ returns MSK as defined. Indeed, it is not queried by the freshness definition.

8. EstablishParty(U_i, ID_i) : $\mathcal{D}$ generates and returns SSK for ID_i according to the protocol and marks U_i as dishonest.

9. Test(sid^*) : $\mathcal{D}$ responds to the query as defined, and gives the SSK^* of the owner of sid^* to $\mathcal{A}$.

10. $\mathcal{A}$ outputs a guess $b' \in \{0,1\}$. If $\mathcal{A}$ outputs $b' = 0$, then $\mathcal{D}$ outputs that F* = F$'$, otherwise $\mathcal{D}$ outputs that F* = RF.

[Analysis]

For $\mathcal{A}$, the simulation by $\mathcal{D}$ is the same as the experiment H_2 if F* = F$'$. Otherwise, the simulation by $\mathcal{D}$ is the same as the experiment H_3. Thus, since the advantage of $\mathcal{D}$ is negligible due to the security of the PRF, $|Adv(\mathcal{A}, H_3) - Adv(\mathcal{A}, H_2)| \leq negl$.

Hybrid Experiment H_4: This experiment changes the way of the computation of the initiator's K^* in the i^*-th session. Instead of computing $(C^*, K^*) \leftarrow \mathsf{EnCap}(ID^*; s^*)$ where $s^* = \mathsf{F}(esk^*, r^*) \oplus \mathsf{RF}(r'^*)$, it is changed as choosing $K^* \leftarrow \mathcal{KS}$ randomly.

We construct an adaptive HID-CCA adversary $\mathcal{S}$ from $\mathcal{A}$ in H_3 or H_4. The $\mathcal{S}$ performs the following steps.

[init]

$\mathcal{S}$ receives MPK and $params$ as a public parameter.

[setup]

$\mathcal{S}$ chooses PRF $\mathsf{F}, \mathsf{F}' : \{0,1\}^* \times \mathcal{FS} \rightarrow \mathcal{RS}_{\mathcal{E}}$, PRF $: \{0,1\}^* \times \mathcal{FS} \rightarrow \{0,1\}^\kappa$, and a KDF $KDF : Salt \times \mathcal{KS} \rightarrow \mathcal{FS}$ with a non-secret random salt $s \in Salt$. These are provided as the public parameters.

$\mathcal{S}$ sets as $(params, \mathsf{F}, \mathsf{F}', \mathsf{PRF}, \mathsf{KDF})$ and MPK.

[simulation]

$\mathcal{S}$ maintains the list L_{SK} that contains queries and answers to SessionKeyReveal. $\mathcal{S}$ simulates oracle queries by $\mathcal{A}$ as follows.

1. $\mathsf{Send}(\Pi, \mathcal{I}, U_P, U_{\bar{P}})$: If the SSK of U_P is not set, then $\mathcal{S}$ sets the SSK by the Extraction oracle of the HID-CCA game. If the session is the i^*-th session, $\mathcal{S}$ sets the target ID as $ID^* = ID_{\bar{P}}$. $\mathcal{S}$ receives (C^*, K_b^*) as a challenge from the challenger, computes ek_T according to the protocol, sets it as $EPK^* = (C^*, ek_T)$ and returns EPK^*. Otherwise, $\mathcal{S}$ computes $EPK = (C_{\bar{P}}, ek_T)$ according to the protocol, returns it, and records $(\Pi, U_P, U_{\bar{P}}, (C_{\bar{P}}, ek_T))$ in L_{SK}.

2. $\mathsf{Send}(\Pi, \mathcal{R}, U_{\bar{P}}, U_P, (C_{\bar{P}}, ek_T))$: If the SSK of $U_{\bar{P}}$ is not set, then $\mathcal{S}$ sets the SSK by the Extraction oracle of the HID-CCA game. If $\bar{P} = ID^*$ and $C_{\bar{P}} \neq C^*$, then $\mathcal{S}$ poses $C_{\bar{P}}$ to the Decryption oracle of the HID-CCA game, and obtains $K_{\bar{P}}$, and computes (C_P, C_T) and SK and return EPK, and records $(\Pi, U_P, U_{\bar{P}}, (C_{\bar{P}}, ek_T), (C_P, C_T))$ as a completed session and SK in L_{SK}. Also, if $\bar{P} = ID^*$ and $C_{\bar{P}} = C^*$, then $\mathcal{S}$ sets $K_{\bar{P}} = K_b^*$, computes (C_P, C_T) and SK according to the protocol, and returns EPK. $\mathcal{S}$ records $(\Pi, U_P, U_{\bar{P}}, (C_{\bar{P}}, ek_T), (C_P, C_T))$ as a completed session and SK in L_{SK}. Otherwise, $\mathcal{S}$ computes $EPK = (C_P, C_T)$ and SK according to the protocol, returns EPK, and records $(\Pi, U_P, U_{\bar{P}}, (C_{\bar{P}}, ek_T), (C_P, C_T))$ as a completed session and SK in L_{SK}.

3. $\mathsf{Send}(\Pi, \mathcal{I}, U_P, U_{\bar{P}}, (C_{\bar{P}}, ek_T), (C_P, C_T))$: If the SSK of U_P is not set, then $\mathcal{S}$ sets it by the Extraction oracle. If $(\Pi, U_P, U_{\bar{P}}, (C_{\bar{P}}, ek_T))$ is not recorded in L_{SK}, then $\mathcal{S}$ records this sid as not completed. Also, if the session is the i^*-th session, $\mathcal{S}$ computes SK according to the protocol except $K_{\bar{P}} = K_b^*$, and records $(\Pi, U_P, U_{\bar{P}}, (C_{\bar{P}}, ek_T), (C_P, C_T))$ as a completed session and SK in L_{SK}. Otherwise, $\mathcal{S}$ computes SK and record $(\Pi, U_P, U_{\bar{P}}, (C_{\bar{P}}, ek_T), (C_P, C_T))$ as a completed session and SK in L_{SK}.

4. SessionKeyReveal(sid) :
   (a) If sid is not completed, then $\mathcal{S}$ returns error.
   (b) Otherwise, $\mathcal{S}$ returns SK as recorded in L_{SK}.
5. EphemeralKeyReveal(sid) : $\mathcal{S}$ returns ESK for sid as defined.
6. StaticKeyReveal(ID_i) : If the SSK for ID_i is not set, then $\mathcal{S}$ sets the SSK by the Extraction oracle. $\mathcal{S}$ returns the SSK of ID_i as defined.
7. MasterKeyReveal(): $\mathcal{S}$ aborts. Indeed, it is not queried by the freshness definition.
8. EstablishParty(U_i, ID_i): $\mathcal{S}$ returns SSK for ID_i by the Extraction oracle and marks U_i as dishonest.
9. Test(sid^*) : $\mathcal{S}$ responds to the query as defined and gives the SSK^* of the owner of sid^* to $\mathcal{A}$.
10. If $\mathcal{A}$ outputs b', then $\mathcal{S}$ outputs b'.

[Analysis]
For $\mathcal{A}$, the simulation by $\mathcal{S}$ is same the as the experiment H_3 if the challenge is (C^*, K_0^*). Otherwise, the simulation by $\mathcal{S}$ is same the as the experiment H_4. Thus, since the advantage of $\mathcal{S}$ is negligible due to the security of the adaptive HID-CCA secure HIBKEM, $|Adv(\mathcal{A}, H_4) - Adv(\mathcal{A}, H_3)| \leq negl$.

Hybrid Experiment H_5: This experiment changes the way of the computation of the σ_2^* in the i^*-th session. Instead of computing $\sigma_2^* \leftarrow$ KDF(s, K^*), it is changed as choosing $\sigma_2^* \in \mathcal{FS}$ randomly.

Since K^* is randomly chosen in H_4, it has sufficient min-entropy because HIBKEM is δ-min-entropy KEM. Thus, by the definition of the KDF, $|Adv(\mathcal{A}, H_5) - Adv(\mathcal{A}, H_4)| \leq negl$.

Hybrid Experiment H_6: This experiment changes the way of the computation of SK in the i^*-th session. Instead of computing $SK =$ PRF(sid, σ_1) $\oplus$ PRF(sid, σ_2) $\oplus$ PRF(sid, σ_3), it is changed as $SK =$ PRF(sid, σ_1) $\oplus x \oplus$ PRF(sid, σ_3) where $x \in_R \{0,1\}^\kappa$.

We construct a distinguisher $\mathcal{D}'$ that distinguishes if F^* is either a pseudo-random function PRF or a random function RF from $\mathcal{A}$ in H_5 or H_6. The $\mathcal{D}'$ performs the following steps.
[setup]
   $\mathcal{D}'$ chooses $F, F' : \{0,1\}^* \times \mathcal{FS} \to \mathcal{RS_E}$, PRF $: \{0,1\}^* \times \mathcal{FS} \to \{0,1\}^\kappa$, a KDF KDF $: Salt \times \mathcal{KS} \to \mathcal{FS}$ with a non-secret random salt $s \in Salt$. These are provided as the public parameters. Also, $\mathcal{D}'$ embeds F^* into PRF of the i^*-th session.
   $\mathcal{D}'$ sets MPK and MSK according to the protocol.
[Simulation]
   $\mathcal{D}'$ maintains the list L_{SK} that contains queries and answers to SessionKeyReveal. $\mathcal{D}'$ simulates oracle queries by $\mathcal{A}$ as follows.

1. Send($\Pi, \mathcal{I}, U_P, U_{\bar{P}}$) : If the SSK of U_P is not set, $\mathcal{D}'$ generates and sets the SSK according to the protocol. $\mathcal{D}'$ computes and returns $EPK = (C_{\bar{P}}, ek_T)$ according to the protocol and records $(\Pi, U_P, U_{\bar{P}}, (C_{\bar{P}}, ek_T))$ in L_{SK}.

2. Send($\Pi, \mathcal{R}, U_{\bar{P}}, U_P, (C_{\bar{P}}, ek_T)$) : If the SSK of $U_{\bar{P}}$ is not set, $\mathcal{D}'$ gener-
ates and sets the SSK according to the protocol. $\mathcal{D}'$ computes $EPK = (C_P, C_T)$ and SK according to the protocol, returns EPK, and records $(\Pi, U_P, U_{\bar{P}}, (C_{\bar{P}}, ek_T), (C_P, C_T))$ as the completed session and SK in L_{SK}.
3. Send($\Pi, \mathcal{I}, U_P, U_{\bar{P}}, (C_{\bar{P}}, ek_T), (C_P, C_T)$) : If the SSK of U_P is not set, $\mathcal{D}'$ generates and sets the SSK according to the protocol. If $(\Pi, U_P, U_{\bar{P}}, (C_{\bar{P}}, ek_T))$ is not recorded in L_{SK}, then $\mathcal{D}'$ records this sid as not completed. Also, if the session is the i^*-th session, $\mathcal{D}'$ poses sid to oracle F* (PRF or RF) and obtains $x \in \{0,1\}^\kappa$, and computes $SK^* = \mathsf{PRF}(sid, \sigma_1) \oplus x \oplus \mathsf{PRF}(sid, \sigma_3)$, and records $(\Pi, U_A, U_B, (C_B^*, ek_T^*), (C_A, C_T))$ as the completed session and SK in L_{SK}. Otherwise, $\mathcal{D}'$ computes SK and records $(\Pi, U_P, U_{\bar{P}}, (C_{\bar{P}}, ek_T), (C_P, C_T))$ as the completed session and SK in L_{SK}.
4. SessionKeyReveal(sid) :
    (a) If sid is not completed, then $\mathcal{D}'$ returns error.
    (b) Otherwise, $\mathcal{D}'$ returns SK as recorded in L_{SK}.
5. EphemeralKeyReveal(sid) : $\mathcal{D}'$ returns ESK for sid as defined.
6. StaticKeyReveal(ID_i) : If the SSK for ID_i is not set, $\mathcal{D}$ generates and sets the SSK according to the protocol. $\mathcal{D}'$ returns the SSK as defined.
7. MasterKeyReveal(): $\mathcal{D}'$ returns MSK as defined. Indeed, it is not queried by the freshness definition.
8. EstablishParty(U_i, ID_i) : $\mathcal{D}'$ generates and returns SSK for ID_i according to the protocol and marks U_i as dishonest.
9. Test(sid^*) : $\mathcal{D}'$ responds to the query as defined and gives the SSK^* of the owner of sid^* to $\mathcal{A}$.
10. $\mathcal{A}$ outputs a guess $b' \in \{0,1\}$. If $\mathcal{A}$ outputs $b' = 0$, then $\mathcal{D}'$ outputs that F* = PRF. Otherwise $\mathcal{D}'$ outputs that F* = RF.

[Analysis]
For $\mathcal{A}$, the simulation by $\mathcal{D}'$ is the same as the experiment H_5 if F* = PRF. Otherwise, the simulation by $\mathcal{D}'$ is the same as the experiment H_6. Thus, since the advantage of $\mathcal{D}'$ is negligible due to the security of PRF, $|Adv(\mathcal{A}, H_6) - Adv(\mathcal{A}, H_5)| \leq negl$.

In H_6, the session key in the test session is perfectly randomized. This gives $\mathcal{A}$ no information from the Test query, therefore $Adv(\mathcal{A}, H_6) = 0$ and $\Pr[E_1 \wedge Sec] = negl$.

5   Instantiations

5.1   Pairing-Based Instantiation

Here, we show our pairing-based instantiation under standard assumptions. We can obtain an HID-AKE scheme by instantiating HID-GC using the Langrehr and Pan's HIBKEM scheme $HIBKEM_1 := HIBKEM[MAC_1[\mathcal{U}_{3k,k}], \mathcal{D}_k]$ [4] which is adaptive HID-CPA secure and the ElGamal KEM which is IND-CPA secure. In order to make the HIBKEM scheme from CPA secure to CCA secure, the HID-CPA-secure $(\ell + 1)$-level HIBKEM is used by converting it to HID-CCA secure ℓ-level HIBKEM using the CHK conversion [6]. In the conversion, we use Mohassel's strongly unforgetable digital signature scheme [7] based on hardness of the discrete logarithm problem, and we can omit the generation of the user delegation key (udk) because it is not necessary for the proof of the conversion. The underlying HIBKEM scheme is based on the k-lin assumption derived from the $\mathcal{D}_k$-matrix Diffie-Hellman assumption and the k-lin assumption is the same as the symmetric external Diffie-Hellman assumption (SXDH) (i.e., DDH assumption in G_1 and G_2) in the $k = 1$ case. A comparison of the efficiency with existing schemes is shown in Table 1.

Table 1. Comparison of existing pairing-based schemes and our instantiations

	Model	Resource	Assumption	Computation [pairings, regular-exp]	Communication complexity
[1]	Selective-ID	ROM	GBDH	$[3\ell - 1, \ell + 2]$	$2\ell\kappa$ 256ℓ
[2]	Selective-ID	StdM	$(q+1)-$DBDHE	$[4, \ell + 14]$	13κ 1664
Ours1	Adaptive-ID	StdM	k-lin	$[5k + 1, 8k^2 + 3k + 10]$	$(8k + 13)\kappa$ $1024k + 1664$
Ours2	Adaptive-ID	StdM	SXDH	$[6, 21]$	21κ 2688

GBDH means the gap Bilinear Diffie-Hellman assumption. DBDHE means the Decisional Bilinear Diffie-Hellman Exponent assumption. For concreteness expected communication complexity for a 128-bit implementation is also given. Note that computational costs are estimated without any pre-computation technique and any multi-exponentiation technique.

In existing HID-AKE schemes, the communication and computational complexity of the pairing operation and exponentiation of the scheme in [1] and the computational complexity of exponentiation of the scheme in [2] depend on the depth ℓ, while in our schemes, the communication and computational complexity of the pairing operation and exponentiation are constant and independent of ℓ.[2] Also, the scheme in [1] is in the random oracle model, and the scheme in [2] is in the standard model but under the non-standard assumption, while, our scheme can be proved under the standard assumptions in the standard model.

In our scheme, the size of the static public key and the static secret key are dependent on ℓ. However, both existing HID-AKE schemes [1,2] are selective HID-AKE secure, and our scheme is adaptive HID-eCK.

5.2   Lattice-Based Instantiation

We also achieve the first post-quantum HID-AKE. We propose a concrete instantiation using Agrawal et al.'s HIBE scheme [9], which is INDr-sID-CPA secure under the LWE assumption, and $KEM1$ [11] which is IND-CPA secure KEM scheme under the ring-LWE assumption. In order to make the HIBE scheme

---

[2] However, the number of multiplications depends on ℓ.

from CPA secure to CCA secure, we use the CHK conversion [6]. In the conversion, we use Lyubashevsky and Micciancio's strongly unforgeable one-time signature scheme [10] under the ring-SIS assumption. Also, the HIBE scheme can be transformed into the HIBKEM scheme by using internally generated randomness instead of the plaintext in the HIBE.

Thus, not only in pairing-based but also in lattice-based, we can construct an HID-eCK secure HID-AKE scheme in the standard model. Since the HIBE is selective ID secure, the resultant HID-AKE scheme is selective ID secure.

A   Proof of Other Events

A.1   Event $E_2 \wedge Suc$

The proof in this case is essentially the same as the event $E_1 \wedge Suc$. There is a difference in the experiment H_3. For the computation of s^* in the i^*-th session, in the event $E_1 \wedge Suc$, instead of $s^* = \mathsf{F}(esk^*, r^*) \oplus \mathsf{F}'(r'^*, esk'^*)$, it is changed as $s^* = \mathsf{F}(esk^*, r^*) \oplus \mathsf{RF}(r'^*)$. In the event $E_2 \wedge Suc$, it is changed as $s^* = \mathsf{RF}(esk^*) \oplus \mathsf{F}'(r'^*, esk'^*)$. Since $\mathcal{A}$ cannot obtain r^* of the initiator by the freshness definition in this event, we can construct a distinguisher $\mathcal{D}$ from $\mathcal{A}$ in the similar manner in the proof of the event $E_1 \wedge Suc$.

A.2   Event $E_3 \wedge Suc$

The proof in this case is essentially the same as the event $E_1 \wedge Suc$. There is a difference in the experiment H_3 and H_4. For the computation of the initiator's s^* in the i^*-th session, in H_3 of the event $E_1 \wedge Suc$, instead of $s^* = \mathsf{F}(esk^*, r^*) \oplus \mathsf{F}'(r'^*, esk'^*)$, it is changed as $s^* = \mathsf{F}(esk^*, r^*) \oplus \mathsf{RF}(r'^*)$. In H_3 of the event $E_3 \wedge Suc$, it is changed as $s^* = \mathsf{F}(esk^*, r^*) \oplus \mathsf{RF}(r'^*)$ for the computation of the responder's s^* in the i^*-th session. For the computation of the initiator's K^* in the i^*-th session, in H_4 of the event $E_1 \wedge Suc$, $(C^*, K^*) \leftarrow \mathsf{EnCap}(ID^*; s^*)$, where $s^* = \mathsf{F}(esk^*, r^*) \oplus \mathsf{RF}(r'^*)$, it is changed as choosing $K^* \leftarrow \mathcal{KS}$ randomly. In H_4 of the event $E_3 \wedge Suc$, it is changed as choosing $K^* \leftarrow \mathcal{KS}$ randomly for the computation of the responder's K^* in the i^*-th session. Since $\mathcal{A}$ cannot obtain esk'^* of the responder by the freshness definition in this event, we can construct a distinguisher $\mathcal{D}$ from $\mathcal{A}$ in the similar manner in the proof of the event $E_1 \wedge Suc$.

A.3   Event $E_4 \wedge Suc$

The proof in this case is essentially the same as the event $E_2 \wedge Suc$. There is a difference in the experiment H_3 and H_4. For the computation of the initiator's s^* in the i^*-th session, in H_3 of the event $E_2 \wedge Suc$, instead of $s^* = \mathsf{F}(esk^*, r^*) \oplus \mathsf{F}'(r'^*, esk'^*)$, it is changed as $s^* = \mathsf{RF}(esk^*) \oplus \mathsf{F}'(r'^*, esk'^*)$. In H_3 of the event $E_4 \wedge Suc$, it is changed as $s^* = \mathsf{RF}(esk^*) \oplus \mathsf{F}'(r'^*, esk'^*)$ for the computation of the responder's s^* in the i^*-th session. For the computation of the initiator's K^* in the i^*-th session, in H_4 of the event $E_2 \wedge Suc$, $(C^*, K^*) \leftarrow \mathsf{EnCap}(ID^*; s^*)$, where $s^* = \mathsf{RF}(esk^*) \oplus \mathsf{F}'(r'^*, esk'^*)$, it is changed as choosing $K^* \leftarrow \mathcal{KS}$ randomly. In H_4 of the event $E_4 \wedge Suc$, it is changed as choosing $K^* \leftarrow \mathcal{KS}$ randomly for the computation of the responder's K^* in the i^*-th session. Since $\mathcal{A}$ cannot obtain r^* of the responder by the freshness definition in this event, we can construct a distinguisher $\mathcal{D}$ from $\mathcal{A}$ in the similar manner in the proof of the event $E_2 \wedge Suc$.

A.4   Event $E_5 \wedge Suc$

We change the interface of oracle queries and the computation of the session key. These instances are gradually changed over six hybrid experiments, depending on specific subcases. In the last hybrid experiment, the session key in the test session does not contain information of the bit b. Thus, the adversary clearly only outputs a random guess. We denote these hybrid experiments by $H_0, \ldots, H_5$ and the advantage of the adversary $\mathcal{A}$ when participating in experiment H_i by $\mathbf{Adv}(\mathcal{A}, H_i)$.

Hybrid Experiment H_0: This experiment denotes the real experiment for HID-eCK security and in this experiment the environment for $\mathcal{A}$ is as defined in the protocol. Thus, $\mathbf{Adv}(\mathcal{A}, H_0)$ is the same as the advantage of the real experiment.

Hybrid Experiment H_1: This experiment aborts when sid is matched with multiple sessions.

By the decryption correctness of KEM, the probability of outputting the same ciphertext from different randomness in each session is negligible. Thus, $|Adv(\mathcal{A}, H_1) - Adv(\mathcal{A}, H_0)| \leq negl$.

Hybrid Experiment H_2: This experiment chooses an integer $i^* \in [1, \ell]$ in advance and fixes the session to be the target of the Test query as the i^*-th session. If $\mathcal{A}$ queries a session other than the i^*-th in the Test query, abort the experiment.

The probability that the guess of the test session is correct is $1/\ell$, hence $Adv(\mathcal{A}, H_2) \geq 1/\ell \cdot Adv(\mathcal{A}, H_1)$.

Hybrid Experiment H_3: This experiment changes the way of the computation of the K_T^* in the i^*-th session. Instead of computing $(C_T^*, K_T^*) \leftarrow \mathsf{wEnCap}(ek_T^*, esk_T^*)$, it is changed as $K_T^* \leftarrow \mathcal{KS}$ randomly.

We construct a IND-CPA adversary $\mathcal{S}$ in H_2 or H_3 from $\mathcal{A}$. $\mathcal{S}$ is performs the following steps.
[init]
    $\mathcal{S}$ receives ek_T^* as a challenge.
[setup]
    $\mathcal{S}$ chooses $\mathsf{F}, \mathsf{F}' : \{0,1\}^* \times \mathcal{FS} \to \mathcal{RS}_\mathcal{E}$, $\mathsf{PRF} : \{0,1\}^* \times \mathcal{KS} \to \{0,1\}^\kappa$, and a KDF $\mathsf{KDF} : Salt \times \mathcal{KS} \to \mathcal{FS}$ with a non-secret random salt $s \in Salt$. These are provided as the public parameters.

$\mathcal{S}$ sets params as $(params, \mathsf{F}, \mathsf{F}', \mathsf{PRF}, \mathsf{KDF})$, MPK and MSK.

[simulation]

$\mathcal{S}$ maintains the list L_{SK} that contains queries and answers to SessionKeyReveal. $\mathcal{S}$ simulates oracle queries by $\mathcal{A}$ as follows.

1. Send$(\Pi, \mathcal{I}, U_P, U_{\bar{P}})$: If the SSK of U_P is not set, $\mathcal{S}$ generates and sets the SSK according to the protocol. If the session is the i^*-th session, $\mathcal{S}$ receives (C_T^*, K_{Tb}^*) as a challenge from the challenger and computes $C_{\bar{P}}$ according to the protocol. Also, $\mathcal{S}$ sets $EPK^* = (C_{\bar{P}}, ek_T^*)$ and returns EPK^*. Otherwise, $\mathcal{S}$ computes and returns $EPK = (C_{\bar{P}}, ek_T)$ according to the protocol and records $(\Pi, U_P, U_{\bar{P}}, (C_{\bar{P}}, ek_T))$ in L_{SK}.

2. Send$(\Pi, \mathcal{R}, U_{\bar{P}}, U_P, (C_{\bar{P}}, ek_T))$: If the SSK of $U_{\bar{P}}$ is not set, $\mathcal{S}$ generates and sets the SSK according to the protocol. If the session is the i^*-th session, $\mathcal{S}$ sets $K_T = K_{Tb}^*$, computes C_P and SK according to the protocol, and returns $EPK = (C_P, C_T^*)$. Also, $\mathcal{S}$ records $(\Pi, U_P, U_{\bar{P}}, (C_{\bar{P}}, ek_T), (C_P, C_T^*))$ as the completed session and SK in L_{SK}. Otherwise, $\mathcal{S}$ computes $EPK = (C_P, C_T)$ and SK according to the protocol, returns EPK. Also, $\mathcal{S}$ records $(\Pi, U_P, U_{\bar{P}}, (C_{\bar{P}}, ek_T), (C_P, C_T))$ as the completed session and SK in L_{SK}.

3. Send$(\Pi, \mathcal{I}, U_P, U_{\bar{P}}, (C_{\bar{P}}, ek_T), (C_P, C_T))$: If the SSK of U_P is not set, $\mathcal{S}$ generates and sets the SSK according to the protocol. If $(\Pi, U_P, U_{\bar{P}}, (C_{\bar{P}}, ek_T))$ is not recorded in L_{SK}, then $\mathcal{S}$ records this sid as not completed. Also, if the session is the i^*-th session, $\mathcal{S}$ computes SK according to the protocol, except $K_T = K_T^*$, and records $(\Pi, U_P, U_{\bar{P}}, (C_{\bar{P}}, ek_T), (C_P, C_T))$ as the completed session and SK in L_{SK}. Otherwise, $\mathcal{S}$ computes SK and records $(\Pi, U_P, U_{\bar{P}}, (C_{\bar{P}}, ek_T), (C_P, C_T))$ as the completed session and SK in L_{SK}.

4. SessionKeyReveal(sid) :
   (a) If sid is not completed, then $\mathcal{S}$ returns error.
   (b) Otherwise, $\mathcal{S}$ returns SK as recorded in L_{SK}.

5. EphemeralKeyReveal(sid): $\mathcal{S}$ returns ESK for sid as defined.

6. StaticKeyReveal(ID_i) : If the SSK for ID_i is not set, $\mathcal{S}$ generates and sets the SSK according to the protocol. $\mathcal{S}$ returns the SSK of ID_i as defined.

7. MasterKeyReveal$()$: $\mathcal{S}$ returns MSK as defined.

8. EstablishParty(U_i, ID_i): $\mathcal{S}$ generates and returns SSK for ID_i according to the protocol and marks U_i as dishonest.

9. Test(sid^*) : $\mathcal{S}$ responds to the query as defined and gives the SSK^* of the owner and responder of sid^* to $\mathcal{A}$.

10. If $\mathcal{A}$ outputs b', then $\mathcal{S}$ outputs b'.

[Analysis]

For $\mathcal{A}$, the simulation by $\mathcal{S}$ is the same as the experiment H_2 if the challenge is (C_T^*, K_{T0}^*). Otherwise, the simulation by $\mathcal{S}$ is the same as the experiment H_3. Thus, since the advantage of $\mathcal{S}$ is negligible due to the security of the IND-CPA secure KEM, $|Adv(\mathcal{A}, H_3) - Adv(\mathcal{A}, H_2)| \leq negl$.

Hybrid Experiment H_4: This experiment changes the way of the computation of the σ_3^* in the i^*-th session. Instead of computing $\sigma_3^* \leftarrow \mathsf{KDF}(s, K_T^*)$, it is changed as choosing $\sigma_3^* \in \mathcal{FS}$ randomly.

Since K_T^* is randomly chosen in H_3, it has sufficient min-entropy because KEM is δ-min-entropy KEM. Thus, by the definition of the KDF, $|Adv(\mathcal{A}, H_4) - Adv(\mathcal{A}, H_3)| \leq negl$.

Hybrid Experiment H_5: This experiment changes the way of the computation of SK in the i^*-th session. Instead of computing $SK = \mathsf{PRF}(sid, \sigma_1) \oplus \mathsf{PRF}(sid, \sigma_2) \oplus \mathsf{PRF}(sid, \sigma_3)$, it is changed as $SK = \mathsf{PRF}(sid, \sigma_1) \oplus \mathsf{PRF}(sid, \sigma_2) \oplus x$ where $x \in_R \{0, 1\}^\kappa$.

We construct a distinguisher $\mathcal{D}$ that distinguishes if F^* is either a pseudorandom function PRF and a random function RF from $\mathcal{A}$ in H_4 or H_5. The $\mathcal{D}$ performs the following steps.

[setup]

$\mathcal{D}$ chooses $\mathsf{F}, \mathsf{F}' : \{0,1\}^* \times \mathcal{FS} \to \mathcal{RS_E}$, $\mathsf{PRF} : \{0,1\}^* \times \mathcal{KS} \to \{0,1\}^\kappa$, and a KDF $\mathsf{KDF} : Salt \times \mathcal{KS} \to \mathcal{FS}$ with a non-secret random salt $s \in Salt$. These are provided as the public parameters. Also, $\mathcal{D}$ embeds F^* into PRF of the i^*-th session.

$\mathcal{D}$ sets MPK and MSK according to the protocol.

[simulation]

$\mathcal{D}$ maintains the list L_{SK} that contains queries and answers to SessionKeyReveal. $\mathcal{D}$ simulates oracle queries by $\mathcal{A}$ as follows.

1. Send($\Pi, \mathcal{I}, U_P, U_{\bar{P}}$) : If the SSK of U_P is not set, $\mathcal{D}$ generates and sets the SSK according to the protocol. $\mathcal{D}$ computes and returns $EPK = (C_{\bar{P}}, ek_T)$ according to the protocol, and records $(\Pi, U_P, U_{\bar{P}}, (C_{\bar{P}}, ek_T))$ in L_{SK}.
2. Send($\Pi, \mathcal{R}, U_{\bar{P}}, U_P, (C_{\bar{P}}, ek_T)$) : If the SSK of $U_{\bar{P}}$ is not set, $\mathcal{D}$ generates and sets the SSK according to the protocol. $\mathcal{D}$ computes $EPK = (C_P, C_T)$ and SK according to the protocol, returns EPK, and records $(\Pi, U_P, U_{\bar{P}}, (C_{\bar{P}}, ek_T), (C_P, C_T))$ as the completed session and SK in L_{SK}.
3. Send($\Pi, \mathcal{I}, U_P, U_{\bar{P}}, (C_{\bar{P}}, ek_T), (C_P, C_T)$) : If the SSK of U_P is not set, $\mathcal{D}$ generates and sets the SSK according to the protocol. If $(\Pi, U_P, U_{\bar{P}}, (C_{\bar{P}}, ek_T))$ is not recorded in L_{SK}, then $\mathcal{D}$ records this sid as not completed. Also, if the session is the i^*-th session, $\mathcal{D}$ poses sid to oracle F^* (PRF' or RF) and obtains $x \in \{0,1\}^\kappa$, and computes $SK^* = \mathsf{PRF}(sid, \sigma_1) \oplus \mathsf{PRF}(sid, \sigma_2) \oplus x$. Also $\mathcal{D}$ records $(\Pi, U_A, U_B, (C_B^*, ek_T^*), (C_A, C_T))$ as the completed session and SK in L_{SK}. Otherwise, $\mathcal{D}'$ computes SK, and records $(\Pi, U_P, U_{\bar{P}}, (C_{\bar{P}}, ek_T), (C_P, C_T))$ as the completed session and SK in L_{SK}.
4. SessionKeyReveal(sid) :
   (a) If sid is not completed, then $\mathcal{D}$ returns error.
   (b) Otherwise, $\mathcal{D}$ returns SK as recorded in L_{SK}.
5. EphemeralKeyReveal(sid) : $\mathcal{D}$ returns ESK for sid as defined.
6. StaticKeyReveal(ID_i) : If the SSK for ID_i is not set, $\mathcal{D}$ generates and sets the SSK according to the protocol. $\mathcal{D}$ returns the SSK as defined.
7. MasterKeyReveal(): $\mathcal{D}$ returns MSK as defined.
8. EstablishParty(U_i, ID_i) : $\mathcal{D}$ generates and returns SSK for ID_i according to the protocol and marks U_i as dishonest.

9. Test(sid^*) : $\mathcal{D}$ responds to the query as defined and gives the SSK^* of the owner of sid^* to $\mathcal{A}$.
10. $\mathcal{A}$ outputs a guess $b' \in \{0,1\}$. If $\mathcal{A}$ outputs $b' = 0$, then $\mathcal{D}$ outputs that $\mathsf{F}^* = \mathsf{PRF}$. Otherwise $\mathcal{D}$ outputs that $\mathsf{F}^* = \mathsf{RF}$.

[Analysis]
For $\mathcal{A}$, the simulation by $\mathcal{D}$ is the same as the experiment H_4 if $\mathsf{F}^* = \mathsf{PRF}$. Otherwise, the simulation by $\mathcal{D}$ is the same as the experiment H_5. Thus, since the advantage of $\mathcal{D}$ is negligible due to the security of the PRF, $|Adv(\mathcal{A}, H_5) - Adv(\mathcal{A}, H_4)| \leq negl$.

In H_5, the session key in the test session is perfectly randomized. This gives $\mathcal{A}$ no information from the Test query, therefore $Adv(\mathcal{A}, H_5) = 0$ and $\Pr[E_5 \wedge Sec] = negl$.

A.5 Event $E_6 \wedge Suc$

The proof in this case is essentially the same as the event $E_2 \wedge Suc$. The situation that the ephemeral secret key of $\overline{sid^*}$ is given to $\mathcal{A}$ is the same as sid^* has no matching session because $\mathcal{A}$ can decide arbitrary ephemeral key. Thus, the proof in this event follows that in the event $E_2 \wedge Suc$.

A.6 Event $E_7 \wedge Suc$

The proof in this case is essentially the same as the event $E_1 \wedge Suc$. The situation that the ephemeral secret key of $\overline{sid^*}$ is given to $\mathcal{A}$ is the same as sid^* has no matching session because $\mathcal{A}$ can decide arbitrary ephemeral key. Thus, the proof in this event follows that in the event $E_1 \wedge Suc$.

A.7 Event $E_8 \wedge Suc$

The proof in this case is essentially the same as the event $E_3 \wedge Suc$. The situation that the ephemeral secret key of sid^* is given to $\mathcal{A}$ is the same as sid^* has no matching session because $\mathcal{A}$ can decide arbitrary ephemeral key. Thus, the proof in this event follows that in the event $E_3 \wedge Suc$.

References

1. Fujioka, A., Suzuki, K., Yoneyama, K.: Hierarchical ID-Based authenticated key exchange resilient to ephemeral key leakage. IEICE Trans. Fundam. Electron. Commun. Comput. Sci. **94-A**(6), 1306–1317 (2011)
2. Yoneyama, K.: Practical and exposure-resilient hierarchical ID-Based authenticated key exchange without random oracles. IEICE Trans. Fundam. Electron. Commun. Comput. Sci. **97-A**(6), 1335–1344 (2014)
3. Fujioka, A., Suzuki, K., Xagawa, K., Yoneyama, K.: Strongly secure authenticated key exchange from factoring, codes, and lattices. Des. Codes Cryptogr. **76**(3), 469–504 (2015)

4. Langrehr, R., Pan, J.: Tightly secure hierarchical identity-based encryption. PKC **1**, 436–465 (2019)
5. Blazy, O., Kiltz, E., Pan, J.: (Hierarchical) identity-based encryption from affine message authentication. In: Garay, J.A., Gennaro, R. (eds.) CRYPTO 2014. LNCS, vol. 8616, pp. 408–425. Springer, Heidelberg (2014). https://doi.org/10.1007/978-3-662-44371-2_23
6. Boneh, D., Canetti, R., Halevi, S., Katz, J.: Chosen-ciphertext security from identity-based encryption. SIAM J. Comput. **36**(5), 1301–1328 (2007)
7. Mohassel, P.: One-time signatures and chameleon hash functions. In: Biryukov, A., Gong, G., Stinson, D.R. (eds.) SAC 2010. LNCS, vol. 6544, pp. 302–319. Springer, Heidelberg (2011). https://doi.org/10.1007/978-3-642-19574-7_21
8. LaMacchia, B., Lauter, K., Mityagin, A.: Stronger security of authenticated key exchange. In: Susilo, W., Liu, J.K., Mu, Y. (eds.) ProvSec 2007. LNCS, vol. 4784, pp. 1–16. Springer, Heidelberg (2007). https://doi.org/10.1007/978-3-540-75670-5_1
9. Agrawal, S., Boneh, D., Boyen, X.: Efficient lattice (H)IBE in the standard model. In: Gilbert, H. (ed.) EUROCRYPT 2010. LNCS, vol. 6110, pp. 553–572. Springer, Heidelberg (2010). https://doi.org/10.1007/978-3-642-13190-5_28
10. Lyubashevsky, V., Micciancio, D.: Asymptotically efficient lattice-based digital signatures. J. Cryptol **31**(3), 774–797 (2018)
11. Peikert, C.: Lattice cryptography for the internet. In: Mosca, M. (ed.) PQCrypto 2014. LNCS, vol. 8772, pp. 197–219. Springer, Cham (2014). https://doi.org/10.1007/978-3-319-11659-4_12
12. Boneh, D., Franklin, M.: Identity-based encryption from the Weil pairing. In: Kilian, J. (ed.) CRYPTO 2001. LNCS, vol. 2139, pp. 213–229. Springer, Heidelberg (2001). https://doi.org/10.1007/3-540-44647-8_13
13. Boneh, D., Boyen, X.: Efficient selective-ID secure identity-based encryption without random oracles. In: Cachin, C., Camenisch, J.L. (eds.) EUROCRYPT 2004. LNCS, vol. 3027, pp. 223–238. Springer, Heidelberg (2004). https://doi.org/10.1007/978-3-540-24676-3_14
14. Waters, B.: Efficient identity-based encryption without random oracles. In: Cramer, R. (ed.) EUROCRYPT 2005. LNCS, vol. 3494, pp. 114–127. Springer, Heidelberg (2005). https://doi.org/10.1007/11426639_7
15. Gentry, C., Silverberg, A.: Hierarchical ID-based cryptography. In: Zheng, Y. (ed.) ASIACRYPT 2002. LNCS, vol. 2501, pp. 548–566. Springer, Heidelberg (2002). https://doi.org/10.1007/3-540-36178-2_34
16. Yoneyama, K.: One-round authenticated key exchange without implementation tricks. J. Inf. Process. **24**(1), 9–19 (2016)

Analysis of Client-Side Security for Long-Term Time-Stamping Services

Long Meng[✉] and Liqun Chen

Department of Computer Science, The University of Surrey, Guildford, UK
{lm00810,liqun.chen}@surrey.ac.uk

Abstract. Time-stamping services produce time-stamp tokens as evidences to prove that digital data existed at given points in time. Time-stamp tokens contain verifiable cryptographic bindings between data and time, which are produced using cryptographic algorithms. In the ANSI, ISO/IEC and IETF standards for time-stamping services, cryptographic algorithms are addressed in two aspects: (i) Client-side hash functions used to hash data into digests for nondisclosure. (ii) Server-side algorithms used to bind the time and digests of data. These algorithms are associated with limited lifespans due to their operational life cycles and increasing computational powers of attackers. After the algorithms are compromised, time-stamp tokens using the algorithms are no longer trusted. The ANSI and ISO/IEC standards provide renewal mechanisms for time-stamp tokens. However, the renewal mechanisms for client-side hash functions are specified ambiguously, that may lead to the failure of implementations. Besides, in existing papers, the security analyses of long-term time-stamping schemes only cover the server-side renewal, and the client-side renewal is missing. In this paper, we analyse the necessity of client-side renewal, and propose a comprehensive long-term time-stamping scheme that addresses both client-side renewal and server-side renewal mechanisms. After that, we formally analyse and evaluate the client-side security of our proposed scheme.

1 Introduction

Digital data is ubiquitous in our modern world. To prove the existence time of digital data, a time-stamping service produces verifiable cryptographic bindings between digital data and time to form time-stamp tokens. Such cryptographic bindings could be digital signatures, hash values, message authentication codes etc. Most of the bindings are generated through cryptographic algorithms. Therefore, time-stamp tokens are valid only when the underlying cryptographic algorithms remain secure.

For time-stamping services specified in the ANSI [1], IETF [2] and ISO/IEC [3–6] standards, the cryptographic algorithms used to generate time-stamp tokens could be categorized into two sides: (i) Client-side hash functions used to hash data into digests for nondisclosure; (ii) Server-side algorithms used to bind digests of a data item and a given point in time. These algorithms are

© Springer Nature Switzerland AG 2021
K. Sako and N. O. Tippenhauer (Eds.): ACNS 2021, LNCS 12726, pp. 28–49, 2021.
https://doi.org/10.1007/978-3-030-78372-3_2

time-restricted due to their limited operational life cycles and the increasing computational power of attackers [7]. For instance, the upcoming quantum computers are considered to break some broadly-used signature algorithms [8] and to increase the speed of attacking hash functions [9]. Once the algorithms are compromised, the corresponding time-stamp tokens are no longer valid.

However, for many types of digital data, the validity of time-stamp tokens need to be maintained for a long time. For example, the identity information of citizens should be kept permanently; the health records of people follow their lifetimes; mp3 files produced by musicians may last for decades etc. In these cases, the validity periods of time-stamp tokens need to be longer than any individual cryptographic algorithm's lifetime. For the purpose of this paper, *if a time-stamping service (or scheme) is able to prove the existence of data at given points in time through valid and secure time-stamp tokens in a long period of time, which is not bounded with the lifetimes of underlying cryptographic algorithms, we say it is a Long-Term Time-Stamping (LTTS) service (or scheme).* Clearly, for a long-term time-stamping service, time-stamp tokens should be constantly renewed.

The ANSI [1] and ISO/IEC [3–6] standards provide time-stamp renewal mechanisms for both client-side and server-side algorithms. For server-side renewal, the standards clearly say that a requester sends a time-stamp request with inputting a new server-side algorithm identifier, hash value(s) of a data item, and a previous time-stamp token on this data item to a Time-Stamping Authority (TSA), the TSA then produces a new time-stamp token on the input content using the indicated algorithm.

However, the client-side renewal mechanisms in both standards are specified ambiguously. In the ISO/IEC standard, the renewal of client-side hash functions is not mentioned as a motivation for time-stamp renewal, and how to implement the client-side renewal is not explicitly specified. In the ANSI standard, a list of reasons for time-stamp renewal includes that a requester needs to replace the hash value using a stronger hash function, but when a requester "needs" to replace the hash value is not specified in detail. These ambiguities may cause the failure of client-side renewal implementations and therefore the failure of long-term time-stamping services.

In the existing papers [10] and [11], long-term time-stamping schemes based on signatures and hash functions have been formally analysed respectively (the details will be introduced in Sect. 2). Nevertheless, the analyses are only related to renewal mechanisms of server-side algorithms, the client-side renewal is not covered. Specifically, in the security model of [10], the client-side renewal is not discussed, and client-side hash functions are treated as random oracles. This security notion does not truly model the case of practical implementations. In [11], the client-side hash functions are not considered.

The motivation of this work is based on the following observation. The security of client-side is as significant as server-side, since the time-stamp tokens are generated on the hash values of data items. If the client-side hash functions are broken and the client-side renewal mechanism is not performed effectively, the time-stamp tokens are no longer valid regardless whether the server-side is secure or not. Even if a client-side renewal mechanism is clearly specified, a formal security analysis of the mechanism is necessary and it does not exist in the literature.

In this paper, we provide following contributions:

- We firstly analyse several possible failures of client-side renewal implementations by complying with the ANSI and ISO/IEC standards, and discuss the importance of a well-specified client-side renewal mechanism.
- We then propose a comprehensive long-term time-stamping scheme that addresses both client-side and server-side renewal mechanisms.
- After that, we formally analyse the client-side security of our proposed long-term time-stamping scheme, and provide a quantified evaluation to the client-side security level.

2 Related Works

In 1990 [12], Haber and Stornetta introduced the first concept of digital time-stamping with two techniques: linear linking and random witness. In this paper, they also proposed a solution for time-stamp renewal, in which a time-stamp token could be renewed by time-stamping the token with a new implementation before the old implementation is compromised.

In 1993 [13], Bayer, Haber and Stornetta proposed another time-stamping technique: publish linked trees into a widely visible medium (e.g., newspapers). Besides, they spotted that the renewal idea in the 1990 paper [12] is insufficient to time-stamp a digital certificate alone (without the original data being certified). They proposed a corrected renewal solution: time-stamping a (data, signature) pair or a (data, time-stamp) pair to extend the signature or time-stamp's lifetime.

In further years, the ideas of [12,13] have been polished and recorded into various standards: The NIST standard specified several signature-based time-stamping applications for proving time evidences of digital signatures [14]; the IETF standard [2] (an update is [15]) specified signature-based time-stamping protocols; the ISO/IEC and ANSI standards cover various time-stamping mechanisms and renewal mechanisms. Notice that the time-stamping services in both the NIST and IETF are not specified in long-term, the ANSI and ISO/IEC standards contain the specifications for long-term time-stamping services.

Apart from the standards, the ideas of [13] have been extended into several long-term integrity schemes [16–22], but the security analyses of such schemes were not given until 2016, Geihs et al. formalized this idea separately into a signature-based long-term integrity scheme [10], and a hash-based long-term time-stamping scheme [11] in 2017. These two schemes are related to the security of two types of server-side algorithms: signature schemes and hash functions, and their renewal mechanisms, but the renewal mechanisms for client-side hash functions are not addressed. In [10], the client-side hash functions are ideally modelled as random oracles, and the renewal of client-side hash functions is not discussed; in [11], the client-side hash functions are not considered in the scheme, time-stamp tokens carry out on actual data items.

Similarly, in Geihs' PhD thesis [23] (includes [10,11]), the signature-based time-stamping scheme is slightly different with [10]: time-stamp tokens are created on a data item and signature pair, and the consideration of client-side hash functions is removed. For all these analyses [10,11,23], the client-side security is guaranteed with ideal assumptions.

Nevertheless, the papers [10,11,23] provide substantial frameworks for analysing the security of long-term time-stamping schemes. For example, they presented a new computational framework based on [24], and a global time model based on [25] for modelling the computational power of long-lived adversaries; they created "long-term unforgeability" model for the integrity of signature-based time-stamping [10]; they constructed "long-term extraction" model for the integrity of hash-based time-stamping [11], which is an integration of "extraction-based" time-stamping proposed in [26] and "preimage awareness" hash functions defined in [27].

In addition, the security of hash functions in time-stamping has been explored [28–31], and only in [29] Buldas et al. analysed the security of client-side hash functions. They proposed a new notion named "unpredictability preservation" and argued that this property, rather than collision resistance or second preimage resistance (the definitions are in Sect. 3.1), is necessary and sufficient for client-side hash functions in secure time-stamping. However, their conclusions are not in the case of long-term time-stamping since the time-stamping renewal is not considered in their works.

In this paper, we create a "long-term integrity" model for our long-term time-stamping scheme including both client-side and server-side renewal (will be introduced in Sect. 6.3). In this model, we follow the computational framework of long-lived adversaries, and refer to the analysis results of server-side security in [10,11,23]. In our analysis, we mainly focus on analysing the security at the client-side.

3   Review the ANSI and ISO/IEC Time-Stamping Services

The ISO/IEC 18014 standard specifies time-stamping services in four parts: the framework in Part 1 [3], mechanisms producing independent tokens in Part 2[4], mechanisms producing linked tokens in Part 3 [5], and traceability of time sources in Part 4 [6]. The ANSI X9.95 standard [1] specifies both independent and linked tokens, which are similar to the mechanisms specified by the ISO/IEC in [3–5].

In this section, we review some common specifications from the first three parts of the ISO/IEC 18014 [3–5] and the ANSI X9.95 [1] standards, which includes the definition of hash functions, two types of time-stamp tokens and time-stamp transactions between entities.

3.1   Hash Functions

A secure hash function [32] maps a string of bits of variable (but usually upper bounded) length to a fixed-length string of bits, satisfying the following three properties:

- *Preimage Resistance*: it is computationally infeasible to find, for a given output, an input which maps to this output.
- *Second Preimage Resistance*: it is computationally infeasible to find a second input which maps to the same output.
- *Collision Resistance*: it is computationally infeasible to find any two distinct inputs which map to the same output.

Note that the hash functions discussed in this paper are compression functions. That means, the collision resistance of a hash function implies preimage resistance [33,34]. In other words, if a hash function is collision resistant, then it is also preimage resistant; if a hash function is not preimage resistant, then it is not collision resistant.

3.2   Types of Time-Stamp Tokens

There are two types of time-stamp tokens that can be generated by a time-stamping service:

1. *Independent tokens*: An independent time-stamp token can be verified without involving other time-stamp tokens. The protection mechanism used to generate this type of tokens can be digital signatures, message authentication codes (MAC), archives or transient keys [1]. For instance, for signature-based time-stamping, a Time-Stamping Authority (TSA) digitally signs a data item and a time value that results a cryptographic binding between the data and time. The data, time and the corresponding signature together form a time-stamp token.
2. *Linked tokens*: A linked time-stamp token is associated with other time-stamp tokens produced by the same methods. The protection mechanism used to generate this type of tokens can be hash functions and a public repository, therefore a time-stamping service generating this type of tokens is referred to "hash-based time-stamping" or "repository-based time-stamping". In specific, a TSA hashes a data item and a time value together and aggregates the hash output with other data items produced at the same time, (e.g., uses a Merkle Tree [35]). The aggregation result can be linked to other data produced at previous times, (e.g., uses linear chain linking [12]). Eventually, the aggregation or linking result is published at a widely visible media (e.g., newspapers). The data, time record, published information, and group values that are contributed to determine the published result, together form a time-stamp token.

3.3   Time-Stamp Transactions

There are two time-stamp transactions that are performed between a requester and one or more TSAs, or between a requester and a verifier, respectively:

1. Time-stamp request transaction: A requester sends a *time-stamp request* to a TSA and the TSA returns a *time-stamp response* to the requester.

2. Time-stamp verification transaction: A requester sends a *verification request* to a verifier and the verifier returns a *verification response* to the requester.

The data formats of a time-stamp request and response are shown in Fig. 1. A *time-stamp request* contains a "messageImprint" field, which is comprised of a hash value of a data item and its hash function identifier, an "extensions" field and other information.

More specifically, the "extensions" field contains three types of additional information: ExtHash, ExtMethod and ExtRenewal, which work as follows:

1. ExtHash: In this field, a requester could submit multiple "messageImprint" fields, in which each hash value could be computed from a different hash function so that it prevents the failure of any single hash function.
2. ExtMethod: In this field, a requester could indicate a specific protection mechanism (e.g., a digital signature scheme) to bind the data item and time.
3. ExtRenewal: In this field, a requester could submit an existing time-stamp token on the data item in the purpose of extending the validity period of the time-stamp token.

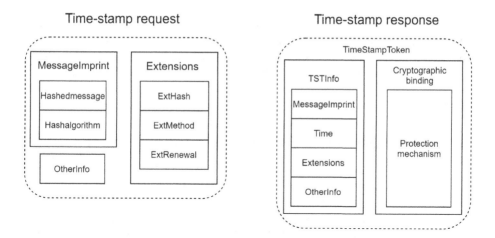

Fig. 1. Data formats of time-stamp request and time-stamp response

After the TSA receives the request, it adds the current time to the request content to form a "TSTInfo" structure, and produces a cryptographic binding on the TSTInfo by using the indicated protection mechanism or a default one if it is not indicated. The TSTInfo and the cryptographic binding together form a time-stamp token, then the TSA returns a *time-stamp response* with the time-stamp token to the requester.

In order to validate the time-stamp token, the requester could send a *verification request* that contains the time-stamp token to a verifier at time t_v. For a single time-stamp token that has not been renewed, the verifier checks the following:

- The token is syntactically well-formed.
- Every hash value of the data item is correctly computed through the corresponding hash function.
- At least one of the hash functions that is used to generate digests of the data item is collision resistant at t_v.
- The protection mechanism of the time-stamp token is not broken at t_v.
- The cryptographic binding is correctly computed on the data and time.

If all above conditions are held, the time-stamp token is valid at time t_v, so the verifier returns a *verification response* with a "true" result to the requester. Otherwise, the verifier returns a "false" result to the requester.

For a renewed time-stamp token, the verifier checks the validity of each nested time-stamp token at the time it was generated or renewed, and validity of the latest time-stamp token at t_v following the above checking steps. The verifier returns a *verification response* with a "true" result to the requester if all verifications are successful, or a "false" otherwise.

4   Discussions on Client-Side Renewal

In Sect. 3, we have reviewed some common specifications in the ANSI and ISO/IEC time-stamping services. In this section, we observe that the client-side renewal mechanisms in both standards are not explained thoroughly, which may cause some ambiguities for implementations. To make our discussions clear, we analyse several possible scenarios that the client-side hash functions are not renewed correctly by following the standards and their consequences.

4.1   The Ambiguities in the ANSI and ISO/IEC Standards

As specified in Sect. 3.3, a time-stamp token consists of hash value(s) of a data item, a time value and a cryptographic binding. The cryptographic algorithms used in the token include client-side hash functions and server-side algorithms. However, the lifetimes of these cryptographic algorithms are restricted due to the operational life cycles or advanced computational architectures. Once the algorithms are compromised, the time-stamp token becomes invalid and the existence of the data item could not be proved after that. Thus, time-stamp tokens should be constantly renewed to extend their validity periods.

In both the ANSI and ISO/IEC standards, the server-side renewal could be achieved by using the "ExtMethod" and "ExtRenewal" fields as following: when the server-side algorithm in the time-stamp token is close to the end of its lifecycle, or there is strong evidence that it will be compromised in the near future, the requester associates the time-stamp token in the "ExtRenewal" field, and indicates a new server-side algorithm in the "ExtMethod" field. The TSA then maintains these contents in the "TSTInfo" structure, and generates a new time-stamp token on TSTInfo using the indicated algorithm.

For client-side hash functions, as Sect. 3.3 shows, the ISO/IEC and ANSI standards both introduce the "ExtHash" field that allows multiple hash values of a data item to be submitted in the time-stamp request, but how to renew the client-side hash functions are not introduced clearly. For example, as the quote from the ISO/IEC 18014-1 [3], Section 5.7, Time-stamp renewal:

"Time-stamped data may be time-stamped again at a later time. This process is called time-stamp renewal and may optionally be implemented by the TSA. This may be necessary for example for the following reasons:

- *The mechanism used to bind the time value to the data is near the end of its operational life cycle (e.g., when using a digital signature and the public key certificate is about to expire).*
- *The cryptographic function used to bind the time value to the data is still trusted; however, there is strong evidence that it will become vulnerable in the near future (e.g., when a hash function is close to begin broken by new attacks or available computing power).*
- *The issuing TSA is about to terminate operations as a service provider."*

We can see that the "mechanism used to bind the time value and data" and "cryptographic function used to bind the time value to the data" do not include the client-side hash functions, which means that the client-side hash functions are not defined as a motivation for time-stamp renewal. Apart from this, there are no other specifications in the ISO/IEC standard about how to renew client-side hash functions.

In the ANSI standard [1], the client-side renewal is briefly addressed in the definition of the "renewal" term, as the quote from the ANSI X9.95 [1], Section 3.29, Renewal:

- *"A renewal is the extension of the validity of an existing time stamp token. Legitimate reasons to renew a TST include: (i) the public key certificate used to verify the TSA digital signature is nearing its expiration date, or (ii) a requestor needs to replace the hash value using a stronger hash algorithm."*

We can see that "a requestor could replace the hash value using a stronger hash algorithm" is a statement that allows requesters to replace the client-side hash value, but when to replace the hash value, how many hash values should be replaced are not specified. The ambiguities in both standards may mislead the implementers to ignore or improperly operate client-side renewal.

4.2 Possible Failed Implementations of Client-Side Renewal

Based on the observations in Sect. 4.1, we further analyse some possible scenarios for implementations that do not effectively renew client-side hash functions. Note that the following three cases are arguably compatible with both the ISO/IEC and ANSI time-stamping standards.

- Case 1: A requester only submits one hash value of a data item without renewal.
- Case 2: A requester submits multiple hash values of a data item without renewal.

– Case 3: A requester replaces hash values using stronger hash functions after all current hash functions are not collision resistant.

Case 1: Let D denote a data item, and the hash value of D is h_0, which is computed through a client-side hash function H_0, i.e., $h_0 = H_0(D)$. The requester sends the pair (h_0, H_0) to a TSA, the TSA generates a time-stamp token TST_0 at time t_0. When the server-side algorithm in TST_0 is nearly compromised, the requester sends (h_0, H_0, TST_0) to a TSA, the TSA produces a new time-stamp token TST_1 on the input at time t_1. Repeat the server-side renewal in a long-term period, the requester eventually has $TST_0, ..., TST_n$ $(n \in \mathcal{N})$.

Assume the collision resistance of H_0 is broken at time t_{b0}. After t_{b0}, the verification condition "at least one client-side hash function is not broken at t_v" is failed. Thus, time-stamp tokens generated after t_{b0} are verified as "false", the time-stamping service could prove the existence time of data item D at most between t_0 and t_{b0}. After t_{b0}, any server-side renewal does not extend the validity of time-stamp tokens any more.

Case 2: Let D denote a data item, and the hash values of D are $h_0, ..., h_m$, which are computed through client-side hash functions $H_0, ..., H_m$ separately, i.e., $h_0 = H_0(D), ..., h_m = H_m(D)$. The requester sends $(h_0, H_0), ..., (h_m, H_m)$ to a TSA, the TSA generates a time-stamp token TST_0 at time t_0. After that, the server-side renewal is implemented correctly in a long-term period, the requester obtains $TST_0, ..., TST_n$ $(n \in \mathcal{N})$ at the end.

Assume the collision resistance of $H_0, ..., H_m$ are all broken at time t_{bm}. After t_{bm}, the verification condition "at least one client-side hash function is not broken at t_v" is failed. The time-stamp tokens produced after t_{bm} are verified as "false", the time-stamping service could prove the existence time of D at most between t_0 and t_{bm}, not any longer.

Case 3: With the same notation as in Case 2, if the requester replaces one or more hash values in $h_0, ..., h_m$ using stronger hash functions at time $t_1 > t_{bm}$, for the same reason as Case 1 and Case 2, the new time-stamp token generated at t_1 is valid, but the time-stamp tokens generated before t_1 are verified as "false". The time-stamping service only proves the existence of D at t_1 or after, and certainly can not prove its existence at time t_0.

Summary: If a requester does not renew client-side hash functions correctly, the time-stamping service is only able to prove the existence of data items with limited time periods, when at least one of the client-side hash functions in the set is collision resistant. Multiple hash values only extend the lifetime of a single hash function, but the overall lifetime of them is still limited. In other words, a time-stamping service without correct client-side renewal does not satisfy the definition of "long-term" in Sect. 1. In order to achieve a long-term time-stamping service, the client-side renewal is necessary and should be specified clearly.

5   Proposed Long-Term Time-Stamping Scheme

In this section, we propose a comprehensive long-term time-stamping scheme that describes how the client-side hash functions and server-side algorithms are used and renewed. Notice that the server-side protection mechanism is not described as a particular one, which could be any of the mechanisms for an independent token or a linked token, as specified in either the ISO/IEC 18014-2 [4], ISO/IEC 18014-3 [5] or the ANSI X9.95 [1].

Table 1. Notation

$n \in \mathcal{N}$	Total number of time-stamp renewal processes
$i \in \{0, \, n\}$	Index number of time-stamp renewal
D	The data item to be time-stamped
$H_0^*, \, ..., \, H_n^*$	Client-side hash functions' identifiers, each of them could be a set of identifiers
$h_0^*, \, ..., \, h_n^*$	Hash values computed through hash function $H_0^*, \, ..., \, H_n^*$ respectively, each of them could be a set of hash values
$t_0, \, ..., \, t_n$	Time points of requesting time-stamp renewal
$TST_0, \, ..., \, TST_n$	Time-stamp tokens generated at time $t_0, \, ..., \, t_n$ respectively
$C_0, \, ..., \, C_n$	Cryptographic binding in time-stamp token $TST_0, \, ..., \, TST_n$ respectively

Our proposed scheme has three functionalities: time-stamp generation, time-stamp renewal and time-stamp verification. Figure 2 shows the time-stamp generation and renewal together, the notation is listed in Table 1. *For simplicity, we assume that each hash value also contains its hash identifier, e.g., we denote $(h_0^*, \, H_0^*)$ pair as h_0^*. For every pair $(h_0, \, H_0)$ in $(h_0^*, \, H_0^*)$ satisfying $h_0 = H_0(D)$,*

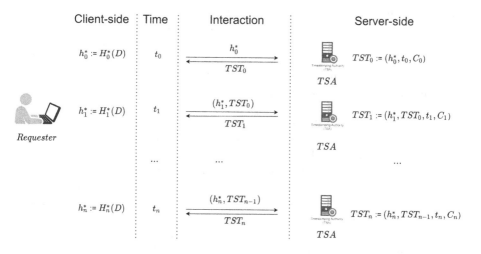

Fig. 2. The proposed long-term time-stamping scheme

we denote them as $h_0^* = H_0^*(D)$. Note that some message formats that are not relevant to security analysis are omitted.

5.1 Time-Stamp Generation

As the top row in Fig. 2, at time t_0 $(i = 0)$: a requester computes one or more hash values of D and sends them to a TSA. i.e., $h_0^* = H_0^*(D)$. The TSA generates a cryptographic binding C_0 on (h_0^*, t_0), and returns the time-stamp token $TST_0 :=$ (h_0^*, t_0, C_0) to the requester.

5.2 Time-Stamp Renewal

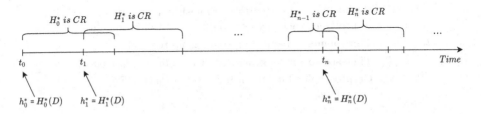

Fig. 3. Timeline of client-side renewal (CR represents "Collision Resistant")

As the second to the last row in Fig. 2, at time t_i $(i \in \{1, n\})$: the requester sends (h_i^*, TST_{i-1}) to a TSA. The TSA produces a new time-stamp token $TST_i := (h_i^*, TST_{i-1}, t_i, C_i)$ to the requester. h_i and C_i are determined with different renewal mechanisms as follows:

1. **Server-side renewal:** When the server-side algorithm is about to be compromised or reach the end of its life cycle, the requester remains the previous hash value(s) of D, i.e., $h_i^* = h_{i-1}^*$, then indicates a stronger server-side algorithm in the time-stamp request. The TSA generates a new cryptographic binding C_i with the indicated server-side algorithm.
2. **Client-side renewal:** When the collision resistance of all client-side hash functions in the latest time-stamp token are about to be broken, and at least one of them is still collision resistant, the requester computes one or more new hash values of D using stronger hash functions, i.e., $h_i^* = H_i^*(D)$, then replaces some of the old hash values with the new ones, or directly adds the new ones into the time-stamp request. The TSA generates a new cryptographic binding C_i using the server-side algorithm used in C_{i-1}. As the timeline shows in Fig. 3, each renewal should happen between the current set of hash functions are all compromised.
3. **Both-side renewal:** A combination of the above two cases: when the security of server-side algorithm and collision resistance of client-side hash functions are all threatened as above scenarios, the requester computes one or more new hash values of D with stronger hash functions, i.e., $h_i^* = H_i^*(D)$, replaces the

old hash values with new ones, or adds the new ones into the request, and then indicates a stronger server-side algorithm in the request. The TSA generates a new cryptographic binding C_i with the indicated server-side algorithm.

*Note that the message format of C_i depends on the server-side protection mechanisms and their details are not discussed in this paper. We stress that the scheme is applicable for any type of server-side protection mechanism.

5.3 Time-Stamp Verification

At the verification time t_v, the verifier receives a time-stamp token TST_i ($i \in \{0, n\}$) and checks the following conditions:

- The time-stamp token is syntactically well-formed.
- The hash values of D through H_0^*, ..., H_i^* match the corresponding hash values in time-stamp tokens, i.e., $h_0^* = H_0^*(D)$, $h_1^* = H_1^*(D)$, ..., $h_i^* = H_i^*(D)$.
- At least one hash function in H_0^* and in H_1^* is collision resistant when H_0^* is renewed, ..., at least one hash function in H_{i-1}^* and in H_i^* is collision resistant when H_{i-1}^* is renewed, at least one hash function in H_i^* is collision resistant at time t_v.
- The server-side algorithm used in C_0 and C_1 are secure at the time the one for C_0 is renewed, ..., the server-side algorithm used in C_{i-1} and C_i are secure at the time the one for C_{i-1} is renewed, the server-side algorithm for C_i is secure at t_v.
- Cryptographic binding C_0, ..., C_i are correctly computed on the corresponding input content.

If all above conditions are satisfied, we say the time-stamp token TST_i is valid at time t_v, and the verifier returns "true" to the requester if the verifications are successful. Otherwise, return a "false" to the requester. The valid time-stamp token TST_i indicates that the data item D existed at the time t_0.

6 Security Notions

In this section, we formalize the syntax of a long-term time-stamping scheme, the security assumptions that are required for analysis, and the security properties that a long-term time-stamping scheme should satisfy.

6.1 Syntax of a Long-Term Time-Stamping Scheme

As defined as follows, a comprehensive long-term time-stamping scheme consists of three algorithms, which are respectively associated with time-stamp generation, time-stamp renewal and time-stamp verification.

Definition 1 *(Long-term time-stamping (LTTS) scheme). A LTTS scheme is a tuple of the following algorithms (TSGen, TSRen, TSVer):*

- $TSGen(h_0^*) \rightarrow TST_0$: the algorithm $TSGen$ takes as input a set of hash values h_0^*, outputs a time-stamp token TST_0.
- $TSRen(h_i^*, \ TST_{i-1}) \rightarrow TST_i$: the algorithm $TSRen$ takes as input a set of hash values h_i^* and a previous time-stamp token TST_{i-1}, outputs a new time-stamp token TST_i.
- $TSVer(D, \ TST_i, \ VD, \ t_v) \rightarrow b$: the algorithm $TSVer$ takes as input a data item D, a time-stamp token TST_i, the necessary verification data VD (e.g., revocation lists of cryptographic algorithms that can be updated over time), and the verification time t_v, outputs $b = 1$ if the time-stamp token is valid, otherwise outputs $b = 0$.

6.2 Security Assumptions

In the following models and proofs, we assume that

1. The verifier correctly performs the verification algorithm.
2. TSAs correctly perform the $TSGen$ and $TSRen$ algorithms.
3. The verification data VD is trusted and cannot be tampered.
4. Each cryptographic algorithm is associated with a validity period and provides correct outputs within their validity periods.

6.3 Security Models and Definitions

A long-term time-stamping (LTTS) scheme should achieve three security properties: correctness, nondisclosure, and long-term integrity. The formal definitions of these properties are given as follows:

Correctness. This property means that assuming every entity is honest, a long-term time-stamping scheme is able to prove existence of data items in a long period of time that is not bounded with the lifetimes of underlying cryptographic algorithms. The formal definition of correctness is given below.

Definition 2 *(Correctness). Let* $LTTS = (TSGen, \ TSRen, \ TSVer)$ *be a long-term time-stamping scheme,* D *be a data item to be time-stamped,* TST_n *($n \in \mathcal{N}$) is a time-stamp token produced as follows.*

At time t_0*, a requester computes a set of hash values of* D*, i.e.,* $h_0^* = H_0^*(D)$*, then the algorithm* $TSGen$ *takes input* h_0^* *(includes identifiers* H_0^**) and outputs a time-stamp token* TST_0*. Then for* $i = 1, \ ..., \ n$*, at time* t_i*, the algorithm* $TSRen$ *takes as input a set of hash values* $h_i^* = H_i^*(D)$ *and a time-stamp token* TST_{i-1} *at a point in time when the server-side algorithm and client-side hash functions in* TST_{i-1} *are still secure, and outputs a time-stamp token* TST_i*. In the end, at a point in time* $t_v > t_n$*, the algorithm* $TSVer$ *takes as input the data item* D*, the time-stamp token* TST_n*, the verification data* VD *and verification time* t_v*. Assume at* t_v*, at least one client-side hash function in* H_n^* *is still collision resistant, and the server-side algorithm in* TST_n *is still secure.*

For a long-term time-stamping scheme to be correct, it must satisfy that if a time-stamp token TST_n *is generated for any data item* D *following the above process, the verification algorithm outputs* $TSVer(D, \ TST_n, \ VD, \ t_v) = 1$*.*

Nondisclosure. This property means that the data item to be time-stamped is not exposed to any party except for the requester and verifier. Similar to the definition of a long-term time-stamping scheme, if the nondisclosure could be achieved with limited duration that is bounded by the lifetimes of corresponding cryptographic algorithms, we say it is *short-term nondisclosure*, otherwise it is *long-term nondisclosure*. The formal definition of nondisclosure in a long-term time-stamping scheme is as follows.

Definition 3 *(Nondisclosure). A long-term time-stamping service provides nondisclosure for data items to be time-stamped if it is computationally infeasible for any party except the requester and verifier to reveal the data items.*

Long-Term Integrity. The security notion of long-term integrity is based on the concept of "compromising" a time-stamping scheme. In specific, we say an attacker is able to compromise a time-stamping scheme, if it is able to claim that a data object exists at a point in time that actually it does not exist, or to tamper valid time-stamp tokens without being detected. Thus, we say a time-stamping scheme has "long-term integrity" if an attacker is unable to compromise the time-stamping scheme in a long period of time that is not bounded with the lifetimes of underlying cryptographic algorithms.

The long-term integrity model is defined as a game running between a long-lived adversary $\mathcal{A}$, a simulator $\mathcal{B}$ and a set of TSAs. As same in [10,11,23], $\mathcal{A}$ is modelled as a set of computing machines that have abilities to develop computational power and computing architectures with time increasing, but also being restricted within each time period. $\mathcal{B}$ has computational resources comparable to $\mathcal{A}$. Besides, $\mathcal{A}$ is able to advance time by calling a global clock oracle $Clock(t)$, and communicate with TSAs through available queries in different time periods. Based on timely manner, the long-term integrity model could be divided into two stages:

Stage 1 $(t = t_0)$:

1. Set time and power: $\mathcal{A}$ is able to set current time as t_0 by querying the oracle $Clock(t)$, i.e., $t_{cur} = t_0$, and use computing machine $\mathcal{M}_0$ and computational power $\mathcal{P}_0$.
2. Request time-stamps: The adversary $\mathcal{A}$ is able to select a secure TSA, then send one or more hash values of a data object x to the TSA. The TSA returns a time-stamp token TST_0 to $\mathcal{A}$. i.e., $h_0^* := H_0^*(x)$, $TST_0 \leftarrow h_0^*$. H_0^* and the server-side algorithm used in TST_0 are secure against $(\mathcal{M}_0, \mathcal{P}_0)$.

Stage 2 $(t = t_i, \ i \in \{1, \ n\})$:

1. Set time and power: $\mathcal{A}$ is able to set current time as t_i by querying the oracle $Clock(t)$, i.e., $t_{cur} = t_i$, and use computing machine $\mathcal{M}_i$ and computational power $\mathcal{P}_i$.
2. Request time-stamp renewal: The adversary $\mathcal{A}$ is able to select a secure TSA, then send one or more hash values of a data object x with a previous time-stamp token TST_{i-1} to the TSA. The TSA returns a new time-stamp token

TST_i to $\mathcal{A}$. i.e., $h_i^* = H_i^*(x)$, $TST_i \leftarrow (h_i^*, TST_{i-1})$. H_i^*, H_{i-1}^* and the server-side algorithm used in TST_i are secure against $(\mathcal{M}_i, \mathcal{P}_i)$.

3. Compromise TSAs: The adversary $\mathcal{A}$ is able to select an expired TSA, and obtain the relevant secret information kept by the TSA (e.g., the private key for signature-based time-stamping).

The winning conditions of the long-lived adversary $\mathcal{A}$ and the simulator $\mathcal{B}$ are defined as:

- $\mathcal{A}$: At any point in time t_v, $\mathcal{A}$ outputs a pair (x', TST), $\mathcal{A}$ wins the game if the pair (x', TST) is not queried from the TSAs, and $TSVer(x', VD, t_v, TST) = 1$.
- $\mathcal{B}$: At any point in time t_v, $\mathcal{B}$ breaks any set of the client-side hash functions, or any of the server-side algorithms within their validity periods.

We denote the probability that $\mathcal{A}$ wins the game as $\mathcal{A}_{LTTS}^{LTI}$. Until time t_v, the sum probability that $\mathcal{B}$ breaks at least one client-side hash function within its validity period is denoted as $\mathcal{B}_{t_v}^{CS}$, and the sum probability that $\mathcal{B}$ breaks at least one server-side algorithm within its validity period is denoted as $\mathcal{B}_{t_v}^{SS}$. Furthermore, we define the $\mathcal{B}_{t_v}^{Cryp}$ as the sum probability of the failure of cryptographic algorithms within their validity periods:

$$\mathcal{B}_{t_v}^{Cryp} = \mathcal{B}_{t_v}^{CS} + \mathcal{B}_{t_v}^{SS}.$$

Definition 4 (Long-term Integrity). *Let $LTTS = (TSGen, TSRen, TSVer)$ be a long-term time-stamping scheme, let $\mathcal{A}$ and $\mathcal{B}$ be a long-lived adversary and a simulator respectively as specified in the game above. we say a LTTS has long-term integrity if there exists a constant c for $\mathcal{B}$ such that for any point in time t_v,*

$$\mathcal{A}_{LTTS}^{LTI} \leq c \cdot \mathcal{B}_{t_v}^{Cryp}.$$

7   Security Analysis

In terms of the security models and definitions in Sect. 6.3, we now prove our proposed long-term time-stamping scheme holding each security property.

7.1   Proof of Correctness

Theorem 1. *The proposed long-term time-stamping scheme is correct.*

Proof. In our proposed $LTTS = (TSGen, TSRen, TSVer)$, we assume that a data item D has been through the $TSGen$ and $TSRen$ algorithms separately at time t_0 and time t_i for $i \in \{1, n\}$ as the process described in Definition 2, and finally outputs a time-stamp token TST_n ($n \in \mathcal{N}$). At time $t_v > t_n$, the verification algorithms takes input D, TST_n, VD and t_v, the verification result could be analysed for each condition specified in Sect. 5.3 as follows:

First, the time-stamp token TST_n is generated through $TSGen$ and $TSRen$ legitimately, so every enclosed time-stamp token TST_0, ..., TST_n is syntactically correct.

Second, every set of hash values h_i^* of the data item D are computed through the corresponding set of hash functions H_i^*, and every cryptographic binding is generated by the $TSGen$ and $TSRen$ algorithms, it is clear that the hash values of D through H_0^*, ..., H_i^* match the corresponding hash values in time-stamp tokens, and all cryptographic bindings are correctly computed on the corresponding input contents.

Third, since the algorithm $TSRen$ is implemented every time before client-side hash functions in the latest time-stamp tokens are all broken, and also before the server-side algorithm in the latest cryptographic binding is compromised, the validity or client-side hash functions and server-side algorithms are all guaranteed at their renewal times. With the assumption that at t_v, at least one client-side hash function in TST_n is still collision resistant, and the server-side algorithm in TST_n is still secure, all verification steps are satisfied. Therefore, the verification algorithm outputs $TSVer(D, TST_n, VD, t_v) = 1$ and the theorem follows.   □

7.2   Proof of Nondisclosure

Theorem 2. *The proposed long-term time-stamping scheme is able to provide nondisclosure for data items when all client-side hash functions are preimage resistant.*

Proof. Assume a requester obtains a time-stamp token, which contains a set of hash values of a data item D. These hash values are computed using a set of client-side hash functions, $H_0^* = (H_0, ..., H_m)$, i.e., $h_0 = H_0(D)$, ..., $h_m = H_m(D)$. Assume that the preimage resistance of H_0, ..., H_m are compromised at t_{p0}, ..., t_{pm} respectively, and that the hash function H_f is one of H_0, ..., H_m, the preimage resistance of H_f is broken at t_{pf}, with $\{t_{p0}, ..., t_{pm}\}_{min} = t_{pf}$ ($\{...\}_{min}$ denotes the earliest time in the set). Then at time $t_0 < t < t_{pf}$, if an attacker is able to find a preimage for any of h_0, ..., h_m with non-negligible possibilities, the preimage resistance of at least one of H_0, ..., H_m is broken within its validity period, which contradicts our assumption. After time t_{pf}, the attacker is able to attack at least the hash function H_f that determine preimages of h_f to D with non-negligible possibilities. Thus, the proposed time-stamping scheme provides short-term nondisclosure in the duration (t_0, t_{pf}). Therefore, the theorem follows.   □

7.3   Proof of Long-Term Integrity

Based on the assumptions discussed in Sect. 6.2, TSAs and the verifier are trusted parties and always perform operations correctly. The integrity of data objects only relies on the security of client-side hash functions and server-side algorithms.

In this paper, we do not limit out discussion with a specific server-side protection mechanism. A time-stamp token could be any type as introduced in Sect. 3.2.

For the security of server-side mechanisms, the existing security analyses from [10] and [11] have proved the security of a signature-based long-term time-stamping scheme as well as a hash-based one. As introduced in Sect. 2, these two schemes satisfy the long-term integrity property under the condition that client-side security is guaranteed. Thus, their results can be fitted in our analysis. We assume that server-side security is satisfied in our proposed scheme, and focus on the analysis of client-side security. In other words, as defined in Sect. 6.3, the probability of the adversary breaking the scheme through server-side is reduced to $\mathcal{B}_{t_v}^{SS}$.

Theorem 3. *If the security of server-side is guaranteed, the proposed time-stamping scheme has long-term integrity.*

Proof. That the server-side security is guaranteed means that all the time-stamp tokens $TSTs$ must be created by the corresponding trusted TSAs. The adversary $\mathcal{A}$ can only join the long-term integrity game as defined in Sect. 6.3 to obtain these tokens. These token are not tampered after their generations.

If $\mathcal{A}$ wins the game, it must output a time-stamp token $TST = (TST_0, ..., TST_n)$ on a data item x', which is distinct to the original x value that was used to request any of $TST_0, TST_1, ..., TST_n$ but somehow to manage letting $TSVer(x', VD, t_v, TST) = 1$. Based on Sect. 5.3, this equation guarantees that at time t_i for $i \in \{1, n\}$, the two corresponding sets of client-side hash functions used by $\mathcal{A}$, denoted by $H_{i-1}^* = (H_{(i-1)1}, H_{(i-1)2}, ..., H_{(i-1)m_{i-1}})$ and $H_i^* = (H_{i1}, H_{i2}, ..., H_{im_i})$, must both contain at least one collision resistant hash function. Besides, each set of hash values $H_i^*(x)$ is a part of token TST_i. Now let us check the following reasoning:

At time t_0, $\mathcal{A}$ submits a set of hash values $H_0^*(x)$ of a data item x to a TSA, the TSA returns a time-stamp token TST_0 on $H_0^*(x)$. Assume that the set of hash functions $H_0^* = (H_{01}, H_{02}, ..., H_{0m_0})$, H_{0j} for $j \in \{1, m_0\}$ is collision resistant at t_0.

At time t_1, $\mathcal{A}$ decides to renew the token TST_0 by using another set of client-side hash functions $H_1^* = (H_{11}, H_{12}, ..., H_{1m_1})$. Since at least one of the hash functions in H_0^*, which is still collision resistant at this time, we assume H_{0j} is still collision resistant at t_1, although it may have become weak, and the corresponding hash value $H_{0j}(x)$ is a part of TST_0. Then $\mathcal{A}$ can submit $(H_1^*(x), TST_0)$ for requesting a time-stamp renewal and obtains TST_1 (Case 1) or $\mathcal{A}$ may submit $(H_1^*(x'), TST_0)$ for requesting a time-stamp renewal and obtains TST_1 (Case 2). If Case 2 happens, there must have $H_{0j}(x) = H_{0j}(x')$ with a pair of collisions (x, x'). $\mathcal{B}$ can then obtain this pair. This result is contradict to the assumption that H_{0j} is collision resistant at t_1. If Case 1 happens, let us carry on with our reasoning. The TSA returns a renewed time-stamp token TST_1. We now assume that $H_{1j} \in H_1^*$ for $j \in \{1, m_1\}$ is collision resistant at time t_1.

At time t_2, H_{0j} and all other client-side hash functions used at t_0 may have been broken, but we assume that H_{1j} is still collision resistant, and the hash value $H_{1j}(x)$ is a part of TST_1. Now repeating the previous situation, $\mathcal{A}$ can submit $(H_2^*(x), TST_1)$ for requesting another time-stamp renewal and obtains TST_2 (Case 1) or $\mathcal{A}$ may submit $(H_2^*(x'), TST_1)$ for requesting another time-stamp renewal and obtains TST_2 (Case 2). Again, Case 2 allows $\mathcal{B}$ to obtain a pair of collisions satisfying $H_{1j}(x) = H_{1j}(x')$ and it contradicts the assumption, and Case 1 leads us to continue our reasoning.

Carrying on our argument as before, only Case 1 for each time-stamp renewal is considered. We assume that $H_{(n-1)j}$ for $j \in \{1, m_{(n-1)}\}$ is collision resistant at both t_{n-1} and t_n, and the hash value $H_{(n-1)j}(x)$ is a part of TST_{n-1}. If $\mathcal{A}$ finally submits $(H_n^*(x'), TST_{n-1})$ and successfully obtains TST_n, then $\mathcal{B}$ obtains a pair of collisions (x, x') satisfying $H_{(n-1)j}(x) = H_{(n-1)j}(x')$.

In summary, based on the above reasoning, as long as $\mathcal{A}$ wins the game, $\mathcal{B}$ can break at least one client-side hash function within its validity period. Therefore, the winning probability of $\mathcal{A}$ through client-side is reduced to the same level of the probability that $\mathcal{B}$ breaks at least one client-side hash function within its validity period. With adding the probability of the failure of server-side algorithms $\mathcal{B}_{t_v}^{SS}$, there exists a constant c such that:

$$\mathcal{A}_{LTTS}^{LTI} \leq c \cdot (\mathcal{B}_{t_v}^{CS} + \mathcal{B}_{t_v}^{SS}).$$

Thus, we have proved Theorem 3.   □

8 Evaluations of Client-Side Security Level

In this section, we determine the client-side security level $\mathcal{L}_{CS}$ in practical, which represents the probability of a long-lived adversary as defined in Sect. 6.3 breaks the client-side security of the proposed scheme. In terms of the ISO/IEC and ANSI standards, multiple hash values are allowed in every time-stamp request, and the system is available to set up policies for the number of client-side hash functions in every time-stamp request, and the interval of time-stamp renewal. Therefore, there are two parameters that affect the client-side security level:

1. l^{set}: the security level of a set of client-side hash functions in a time-stamp request, which means the probability that a long-lived adversary as defined in Sect. 6.3 breaks all collision resistant hash functions in the set within their validity periods.
2. n: the number of sets of client-side hash functions in time-stamp tokens, which means the number of client-side renewal process.

Assume the security level of each set of client hash functions are l_1^{set}, ..., l_n^{set} respectively. The winning probability of the adversary is the aggregated probability of the failure of every set of client-side hash functions:

$$\mathcal{L}_{CS} = \sum_{i=1}^{n} l_i^{set}.$$

We can see that the more sets of client-side hash functions are used in the scheme, the higher probability that the adversary breaks the client-side security of the proposed scheme. The stronger of each set of client-side hash functions, the lower probability that the adversary breaks the client-side security of the proposed scheme.

Furthermore, the security level of a set of client-side hash functions l^{set} is decided by another two parameters:

1. l: the security level of a specific client-side hash function in the set, which means the probability of a long-lived adversary as defined in Sect. 6.3 breaks the collision resistance of the specific hash function within its validity period.
2. m: the number of client-side hash functions required in a set.

Assume the security level of each hash function in a set is l_1, ..., l_m respectively. Then the probability of the failure of a whole set of hash functions, is equal to the probability that every hash function in the set fails:

$$l^{set} = \prod_{i=1}^{m} l_m.$$

Based on the bounded computational resources in each time period, a long-lived adversary has not enough resources to break the collision resistance of whole set of hash functions. That means, the computational resources of the adversary is not enough to break at least one of the hash functions in the set. If the adversary owns computational power to break some of the hash functions, then the security level of these hash functions are equal to 1, the l^{set} is only determined by the security level of the other hash functions.

Summary: The evaluation results show that with more times the client-side renewal happens, the probability of the adversary breaks the scheme increases; for multiple hash values submitted in each time-stamp request, the more collision resistant hash functions are required in each time-stamp request, the lower probability of the adversary breaks the scheme.

9   Conclusions

In this paper, we have discussed the importance of client-side renewal: it is not enough for a requester to only use the same set of multiple hash values in an initial time-stamping request as well as a time-stamp renewal request, new hash values computed through stronger hash functions should be used before the failure of current set of hash functions. This argument is straightforward but is not explicitly addressed in the ISO/IEC and ANSI standards. Then we propose a long-term time-stamping scheme with specifications of both client-side and server-side mechanisms. We have proved that our scheme achieves correctness, short-term nondisclosure and long-term integrity properties. Finally, we have provided a quantified evaluation for the client-side security level of our proposed scheme.

We argue that the short-term nondisclosure of our scheme could be accepted, since the integrity could naturally be required for much longer time than nondisclosure. For instance, intellectual-property data is usually protected in secret for a certain period before it is released but its integrity should be maintained in perpetuity.

As the future work, we will implement the proposed scheme in a timestamping service environment to measure the timing overhead and to determine the network channel affectation. Besides, our research could be carried on covering other renewable applications that require long-term integrity. The renewal mechanisms in time-stamping services may have other application scenarios and such applications and their security analyses should be explored.

Acknowledgements. This work is supported by the European Union's Horizon 2020 research and innovation program under grant agreement No. 779391 (FutureTPM) and grant agreement No. 952697 (ASSURED).

References

1. American National Standard Institute (ANSI). ANSI X9.95-2016 - Trusted Timestamp Management and Security (2016)
2. Adams, C., Cain, P., Pinkas, D., Zuccherato, R.: RFC 3161: Internet X. 509 Public Key Infrastructure Time-Stamp Protocol (TSP) (2001)
3. ISO/IEC 18014–1:2008. Information technology - Security techniques - Timestamping services - part 1: Framework. Standard (2008)
4. ISO/IEC 18014–2:2009. Information technology - Security techniques - Timestamping services - part 2: Mechanisms producing independent tokens. Standard (2009)
5. ISO/IEC 18014–3:2009. Information technology - Security techniques - Timestamping services - part 3: Mechanisms producing linked tokens. Standard (2009)
6. ISO/IEC 18014–4:2015. Information technology - Security techniques - Timestamping services - part 4: Traceability of time sources. Standard (2015)
7. Lenstra, A.K.: Key length. Contribution to the handbook of information security (2004)
8. Shor, P.W.: Polynomial-time algorithms for prime factorization and discrete logarithms on a quantum computer. SIAM Rev. **41**(2), 303–332 (1999)
9. Grover, A.K.: A fast quantum mechanical algorithm for database search. In: Proceedings, 28th Annual ACM Symposium on the Theory of Computing, pp. 212–219 (1996)
10. Geihs, M., Demirel, D., Buchmann, J.: A security analysis of techniques for longterm integrity protection. In: 2016 14th Annual Conference on Privacy, Security and Trust (PST), pp. 449–456. IEEE (2016)
11. Buldas, A., Geihs, M., Buchmann, J.: Long-term secure time-stamping using preimage-aware hash functions. In: Okamoto, T., Yu, Y., Au, M.H., Li, Y. (eds.) ProvSec 2017. LNCS, vol. 10592, pp. 251–260. Springer, Cham (2017). https://doi.org/10.1007/978-3-319-68637-0_15
12. Haber, S., Stornetta, W.S.: How to time-stamp a digital document. In: Menezes, A.J., Vanstone, S.A. (eds.) CRYPTO 1990. LNCS, vol. 537, pp. 437–455. Springer, Heidelberg (1991). https://doi.org/10.1007/3-540-38424-3_32

13. Bayer, D., Haber, S., Stornetta, W.S.: Improving the efficiency and reliability of digital time-stamping. In: Capocelli, R., Vaccaro, U. (eds.) Sequences II, pp. 329–334. Springer, New York (1993). https://doi.org/10.1007/978-1-4613-9323-8_24
14. National Institute of Standards and Technology (NIST). Recommendation for Digital Signature Timeliness. Standard (2009)
15. Pope, N., Santesson, S.: RFC 5816: Esscertidv2 update for RFC 3161 (2010)
16. Pinkas, D., Pope, N., Ross, J.: CMS Advanced Electronic Signatures (CAdES). IETF Request for Comments, 5126 (2008)
17. Centner, M.: XML Advanced Electronic Signatures (XAdES) (2003)
18. Haber, S., Kamat, P.: A content integrity service for long-term digital archives. In: Archiving Conference, volume 2006, pp. 159–164. Society for Imaging Science and Technology (2006)
19. Gondrom, T., Brandner, R., Pordesch, U.: Evidence Record Syntax (ERS). Request For Comments-RFC, 4998 (2007)
20. Blazic, A.J., Saljic, S., Gondrom, T. Extensible Markup Language Evidence Record Syntax (XMLERS). Technical Report, IETF RFC 6283 (2011). http://www.ietf.org/rfc/rfc6283.txt
21. Lekkas, D., Gritzalis, D.: Cumulative notarization for long-term preservation of digital signatures. Comput. Secur. **23**(5), 413–424 (2004)
22. Vigil, M., Cabarcas, D., Buchmann, J., Huang, J.: Assessing trust in the long-term protection of documents. In: 2013 IEEE Symposium on Computers and Communications (ISCC), pp. 000185–000191. IEEE (2013)
23. Geihs, M.: Long-Term Protection of Integrity and Confidentiality-Security Foundations and System Constructions. Ph.D. thesis, Technische Universität (2018)
24. Canetti, R., Cheung, L., Kaynar, D.K., Lynch, N.A., Pereira, O.: Modeling computational security in long-lived systems, version 2. IACR Cryptology ePrint Archive, p. 492 (2008)
25. Schwenk, J.: Modelling time for authenticated key exchange protocols. In: Kutyłowski, M., Vaidya, J. (eds.) ESORICS 2014. LNCS, vol. 8713, pp. 277–294. Springer, Cham (2014). https://doi.org/10.1007/978-3-319-11212-1_16
26. Buldas, A., Laur, S.: Knowledge-binding commitments with applications in time-stamping. In: Okamoto, T., Wang, X. (eds.) PKC 2007. LNCS, vol. 4450, pp. 150–165. Springer, Heidelberg (2007). https://doi.org/10.1007/978-3-540-71677-8_11
27. Dodis, Y., Ristenpart, T., Shrimpton, T.: Salvaging Merkle-Damgård for practical applications. In: Joux, A. (ed.) EUROCRYPT 2009. LNCS, vol. 5479, pp. 371–388. Springer, Heidelberg (2009). https://doi.org/10.1007/978-3-642-01001-9_22
28. Buldas, A., Saarepera, M.: On provably secure time-stamping schemes. In: Lee, P.J. (ed.) ASIACRYPT 2004. LNCS, vol. 3329, pp. 500–514. Springer, Heidelberg (2004). https://doi.org/10.1007/978-3-540-30539-2_35
29. Buldas, A., Laur, S.: Do broken hash functions affect the security of time-stamping schemes? In: Zhou, J., Yung, M., Bao, F. (eds.) ACNS 2006. LNCS, vol. 3989, pp. 50–65. Springer, Heidelberg (2006). https://doi.org/10.1007/11767480_4
30. Buldas, A., Jürgenson, A.: Does secure time-stamping imply collision-free hash functions? In: Susilo, W., Liu, J.K., Mu, Y. (eds.) ProvSec 2007. LNCS, vol. 4784, pp. 138–150. Springer, Heidelberg (2007). https://doi.org/10.1007/978-3-540-75670-5_9
31. Buldas, A., Niitsoo, M.: Can we construct unbounded time-stamping schemes from collision-free hash functions? In: Baek, J., Bao, F., Chen, K., Lai, X. (eds.) ProvSec 2008. LNCS, vol. 5324, pp. 254–267. Springer, Heidelberg (2008). https://doi.org/10.1007/978-3-540-88733-1_18

32. ISO/IEC 10118 (all parts). Information technology - Security techniques - Hash functions. Standard
33. Katz, J., Lindell, Y.: Introduction to Modern Cryptography. CRC Press, Boca Raton (2014)
34. Vanstone, S.A., Menezes, A.J., van Oorschot, P.C.: Handbook of Applied Cryptography. CRC Press, Boca Raton (1996)
35. Merkle, R.C.: A certified digital signature. In: Brassard, G. (ed.) CRYPTO 1989. LNCS, vol. 435, pp. 218–238. Springer, New York (1990). https://doi.org/10.1007/0-387-34805-0_21

Towards Efficient and Strong Backward Private Searchable Encryption with Secure Enclaves

Viet Vo[1,2], Shangqi Lai[1], Xingliang Yuan[1(✉)], Surya Nepal[2], and Joseph K. Liu[1]

[1] Department of Software Systems and Cybersecurity, Monash University, Melbourne, Australia
{Viet.Vo,Shangqi.Lai,Xingliang.Yuan,Joseph.Liu}@monash.edu
[2] Data61, CSIRO, Sydney, Australia
Surya.Nepal@data61.csiro.au

Abstract. Dynamic searchable symmetric encryption (DSSE) can enable a cloud server to search and update over the encrypted data. Recently, forward and backward privacy in DSSE receive wide attention due to the rise in a number of emerging attacks exploiting the leakage in data update operations. Forward privacy ensures newly added data is not related to queries issued in the past, whilst backward privacy ensures previously deleted data is not revealed in the queries. Unfortunately, achieving strong forward and backward privacy, i.e., only revealing insertion timestamps of search results, requires the adoption of oblivious data structures, which incur heavy computation and communication overhead at both the client and server-side. In this paper, we resort to secure enclaves, aka Intel SGX, to tackle the above problem. Specifically, we propose Maiden, the first strong backward-private DSSE scheme without relying on ORAM. Our key idea is to keep track of the states of updates and the deletion information inside the secure enclave to prevent the leakage from the server. To speed up, we further leverage a compressed data structure to maintain a sketch of addition operations in the enclave to facilitate the fast generation of search tokens of non-deleted data. We conduct formal security analysis and perform comprehensive evaluations on both synthetic and real-world datasets. Our results confirm that Maiden outperforms the prior work.

1 Introduction

With the advent of cloud computing, outsourcing data to cloud storage becomes an increasingly common way to keep big data economically and reliably. Yet it exposes sensitive data to the server which cannot always be trusted. Although this issue can be mitigated by encrypting the data before uploading it, this solution also prevents the data from being searched. To solve the above problem, the notion of searchable symmetric encryption (SSE) was introduced [48] to enable search over the encrypted data. In past years, SSE schemes [11,17,32,48]

© Springer Nature Switzerland AG 2021
K. Sako and N. O. Tippenhauer (Eds.): ACNS 2021, LNCS 12726, pp. 50–75, 2021.
https://doi.org/10.1007/978-3-030-78372-3_3

were proposed to handle secure search over static datasets. In order to support dynamic operations, dynamic SSE (DSSE) [10,30] is proposed to support secure updates (addition and deletion) on the encrypted data while preserving the search functionality. However, recent studies show that the update operation incurs more information leakage, which ca n be exploited by several attacks [9,57] to break the security of SSE.

Most recent work on DSSE schemes focuses on the forward and backward privacy of DSSE introduced by Stefanov et al. [49] and formalised by Bost et al. [4,5]. In general, forward privacy guarantees the updates cannot be associated with prior queries. Since it can mitigate adaptive file injection attacks [57], several studies have been presented to construct a forward-private DSSE scheme [4,5,21]. On the other hand, backward privacy ensures that the queries do not link to deleted documents. As defined in [5], the strongest backward-private (Type-I) schemes should only reveal the documents that currently match the queries, i.e., the deleted document is hidden from the server. Although the above notion is desirable, recent work [5,24] demonstrates that Type-I backward privacy is difficult to achieve in an efficient way as it has to hide the access pattern on updated data. Complex cryptographic primitives, e.g., ORAM, are required to achieve the goal, but this introduces formidable computation and communication costs, which bring stupendous obstacle in deploying those Type-I DSSE schemes in practice.

A practical solution for designing a Type-I backward-private DSSE scheme is to resort to the trusted execution environment (TEE), i.e., Intel SGX. Due to its advantages on performance and functionality, SGX has been applied to accelerate the oblivious data structure [36]. Intuitively, a basic approach is to port the existing strong backward-private DSSE scheme Orion [24] as an SGX-based application. However, as we demonstrated later in Sect. 6, this approach simply migrates the heavy ORAM operations from client-server to enclave-server, and they are still the performance bottleneck. Recently, Amjad et al. [1] proposed another SGX-based DSSE scheme with Type-I backward privacy (i.e., Fort). They show that it is not necessary to use ORAM to keep the entire index, while only the states of updates need to be stored in ORAM to hide the access pattern on addition and deletion. Also, the search in Fort can be ORAM-free with the help of SGX. Unfortunately, Fort [1] only has a theoretical construction, and our analysis and empirical evaluation demonstrate that it is still not scalable when handling large datasets.

Contributions: Our contributions in this work can be summarised as follows:

- We thoroughly analyse a basic scheme named Orion*, i.e., direct migration of the latest strong backward-private DSSE scheme Orion [24] to TEE, and the latest art of TEE-based scheme Fort [1]. We identify their limitations both theoretically and empirically. As the implementation of Fort and Orion* is not available, we implement them from scratch for evaluations and comparisons.
- We propose Maiden, the first Type-I backward-private DSSE scheme without relying on ORAM. Maiden is designed to keep the states of updates, the deletion information, and a sketch of insertions inside TEE, so as to eliminate the leakage in updates and allow minimally necessary leakage during the

search. We formalise the security model of the scheme and perform security analysis accordingly.

- We conduct comprehensive evaluations on our proposed scheme Maiden, Fort, and Orion*. Our experiment shows that the addition throughput of Maiden is 13–36× higher than Orion*. Maiden takes a negligible time to perform document deletion. The search latency in Maiden is 70–90× faster than Fort and Orion* when using a large synthesis dataset. With a real-world dataset, Maiden is 575× and 291× faster than those schemes, respectively.

Organisation: We discuss related works in Sect. 2. Section 3 presents preliminaries of our work. Section 4 analyses the limitations of baseline approaches that aim to build strong backward-private DSSE scheme via TEE. In this section, we also highlight our design and introduce the detail protocols of Maiden. Section 5 analyses the security of the proposed scheme. In Sect. 6, we evaluate Maiden and compare it with the baseline schemes. Section 7 discusses SGX side-channels and how existing countermeasures can be applied to our design. Section 8 concludes the paper.

2   Related Work

Searchable Encryption. The notion of searchable symmetric encryption (SSE) is firstly introduced by Song et al. [48]. Later, Curtmola et al. [17] and Kamara et al. [30] formalised the security model of static and dynamic SSE (DSSE), respectively. Since SSE was formalised, extensive studies have been made to improve the security [4–6,49], functionality [10,11] and performance [10,11,19, 24,50] of SSE. Recently, the community focuses on designing DSSE schemes with forward and backward privacy to resolve the security issues [9,57] of it.

Forward and Backward Privacy in DSSE. Stefanov et al. [49] introduced the notion of forward and backward privacy, and Bost [4] provided the security model of forward-privacy DSSE. The follow-up work [6] further studied the backward-privacy model and categorised the backward-privacy DSSE schemes into three types based on the security level they achieved. A line of work for efficient DSSE constructions with backward privacy [6,19,24,50] has been present. This includes Type-I schemes (the highest security level) Moneta [6] and Orion [24], Type-II schemes Fides [6], Mitra [24], SD_a and SD_d [19], and Type-III schemes Janus, $Diana_{del}$ [6], Horus [24], Janus++ [50] and QOS [19]. To achieve better (Type-I and Type-II) security, all the above schemes employ ORAMs and multi-rounds of interaction, which noticeably increases the protocol complexity. In this work, we will study how to achieve a stronger security level of backward privacy with low computation and interaction costs by introducing trusted execution to DSSE schemes.

DSSE with Trusted Execution. Amjad et al. [1] are the first to study hardware-assisted DSSE schemes with backward privacy. They proposed three schemes supporting Type-I (Fort), II (Bunker-B) and III (Bunker-A) DSSE to enable single-keyword query with the help of Intel SGX. However, the practical

Table 1. Comparison with previous SGX-supported Type-I *backward-private* schemes. N denotes the total number of keyword/document pairs. a_w presents the total number of entries of addition updates performed on w. n_w is the number of (current, non-deleted) documents containing w. Let d_w denote the number of deletions performed on w. D and W denote the total number of documents, and the total number of keywords, respectively. Orion* presents the scheme of porting the *Client* in Orion [24] to TEE.

Type-I Scheme	Communication Enclave-Server			Enclave Computation			Enclave Storage
	Add	Del	Search	Add	Del	Search	
Orion*	$\mathcal{O}(log^2 N)$	$\mathcal{O}(log^2 N)$	$\mathcal{O}(n_w log^2 N)$	$\mathcal{O}(log^2 N)$	$\mathcal{O}(log^2 N)$	$\mathcal{O}(n_w log^2 N)$	$\mathcal{O}(1)$
Fort [1]	$\mathcal{O}(1)$	$\mathcal{O}(1)$	$\mathcal{O}(n_w)$	$\mathcal{O}(log^2 N)$	$\mathcal{O}(1)$	$\mathcal{O}(n_w)+\mathcal{O}(\Sigma_{\forall w} d_w)$	$\Sigma_{\forall w} d_w$
Maiden	$\mathcal{O}(1)$	$\mathcal{O}(1)$	$\mathcal{O}(n_w)$	$\mathcal{O}(1)$	$\mathcal{O}(1)$	$\mathcal{O}(n_w)$	$\mathcal{O}(WlogD)$ $+\mathcal{O}(a_w W)$ $+\mathcal{O}(N)$

performance of these schemes has not been investigated. Lastly, Vo et al. [53] proposed Type-II backward-private SGX-SE1 and SGX-SE2 schemes. These two schemes store database states within the enclave to reduce the communication between the client and enclave as well as the enclave and server. In addition, they maintain the deletion information within the enclave to save communication costs during queries. This also reduces the query delay since it does not require to re-encrypt accessed database entries after queries like in Bunker-B. As a result, the above schemes outperform Bunker-B in both search latency and update computation/communication. Although these schemes are efficient and highly-scalable to large databases, they cannot achieve Type-I backward privacy.

Table 1 compares the two existing Type-I DSSE schemes and our newly proposed scheme Maiden. While Fort [1] and Maiden are designed for TEE, Orion* directly migrates the latest cryptographic-based Type-I DSSE Orion [24] into SGX. Maiden highly reduces the communication and computation overhead during Update and Search. Although it consumes more storage than the other two schemes, our evaluation results show that this will not affect the efficiency of Maiden.

Encrypted Search Systems with Trusted Execution. Another active research line aims to design search systems [3,14,23,28,36,59] over encrypted data based on hardware-assisted trusted execution environment (TEE). Those systems can support efficient query over encrypted document [3,23,28], SQL queries on database tables [14,20,36,52] and complicated analytic tasks [59]. Note that those works target different problems and applications.

3 Preliminaries

3.1 Trusted Execution Environment

Trusted Execution Environment (TEE) like Intel SGX provides a secure and isolated execution environment for applications and their data when running on

TEE-enabled platforms. The trusted execution part of the application, named enclave, is located and executed in a dedicated memory portion of physical RAM with strong protection mechanism enforced by TEE. Other processes running on the same CPU, including OS and hypervisor, cannot access the isolated memory or tamper with the execution. TEE is equipped with the remote attestation mechanism, which allows an enclave to prove to a remote client that it is running untampered code. Also, it establishes a secure channel between the enclave and client to communicate. The TEE threat model we considered in this work is discussed in Sect. 3.3.

3.2 Dynamic Searchable Symmetric Encryption

We briefly overview the definition of DSSE given by the literature [4,6,49]. In Sect. 3.3, we will provide the security model of DSSE in this work. We consider a document $\mathsf{doc} = (id, \mathbf{w})$ consists of an identifier id and a list of keywords $\mathbf{w}$. DB is an inverted index built from a set of documents. A set of documents containing a keyword w can be retrieved from DB via $\mathsf{DB}(w) = \{id_i | w \in \mathbf{w}_i\}$. Let N denote the total number of keyword/document pairs, D is the total number of documents, and W is the total number of keywords in DB. Also, we set a_w to be the number of updates regarding w, n_w to be the total number of documents matching w ($|\mathsf{DB}(w)|$) and d_w to be the number of deletions regarding w.

A dynamic SE scheme $\Sigma = (\mathsf{Setup}, \mathsf{Search}, \mathsf{Update})$ consists of three protocols between a client and a server as follows:

$\mathsf{Setup}(1^\lambda, \mathsf{DB})$: The protocol inputs a security parameter λ and outputs a secret key K, a state ST for the client, and an empty encrypted database EDB that will be stored at the server.

$\mathsf{Search}(K, w, ST; \mathsf{EDB})$: The protocol allows to query w based on the state ST, the secret key K and the state ST from the client, and the encrypted database EDB from the server. After that, it outputs the search result Res containing documents matching w.

$\mathsf{Update}(K, (\mathsf{op}, \mathsf{in}), ST; \mathsf{EDB})$: The protocol takes K, ST, an input in associated with an operation op from the client, and EDB, where $\mathsf{op} \in \{add, del\}$, and in consists of a document identifier id and a set of keywords in that document. If $\mathsf{op} = del$, in only contains the deleted id. The protocol inserts or removes in from EDB upon op.

3.3 Security Model

Our Assumptions with TEE. We assume that the TEE like SGX *Enclave* can protect the code and data inside the enclave. Meanwhile, the communication between the *Client* and the *Enclave* is secured by the secure channel established during attestation. There exist some SGX side-channel attacks such as cache and page-fault side-channel attacks [8,25,46,55] and transient execution attacks (i.e., SgxPectre [12] and Foreshadow [51]). Like many other hardware-supported works [1,36,53,59], we consider side-channel attacks and transient execution attacks against SGX are out of our scope. We are aware that the security in future SGX versions will be improved by both hardware and software-based countermeasures. We also consider Denial-of-service (DoS) and power analysis attacks [37] are also out of our focus, i.e., the enclave is always available whenever the client invoked or queried. Finally, we assume that all the used crypto and other supporting libraries of SGX are trusted with their correctness, and the SGX enclave executes correctly with memory-safe implementation to avoid memory-corruption attacks [15,44]. Note that we later discuss how to deploy our proposed scheme in practical enclave that are vulnerable SGX-related attacks in Sect. 7.

The Security of DSSE. We follow the same notion of DSSE security defined [4, 6]. In particular, the security of a DSSE scheme Σ is parameterised by a leakage profile $\mathcal{L} = (\mathcal{L}^{Stp}, \mathcal{L}^{Updt}, \mathcal{L}^{Srch})$, where $\mathcal{L}^{Stp}$ depicts the leakage during setup, $\mathcal{L}^{Updt}$ depicts the leakage during updates, and $\mathcal{L}^{Srch}$ depicts the leakage during queries. A secure DSSE scheme will not reveal information about DB beyond the leakage $\mathcal{L}$. This can be formalised by standard real/ideal game paradigm:

Definition 1. *Consider the probabilistic experiments $\mathbf{Real}_A(\lambda)$ and $\mathbf{Ideal}_{A,S}(\lambda)$, where $\mathbf{Real}_A(\lambda)$ runs a real instantiation of a DSSE scheme Σ, and $\mathbf{Ideal}_{A,S}(\lambda)$ uses a stateful simulator S to simulate Σ via the leakage function $\mathcal{L}$. A probabilistic polynomial time (PPT) adversary A can adaptively submit queries to the above instantiations and get query results. Σ is $\mathcal{L}$-adaptively secure iff $\mathbf{Real}_A(\lambda)$ and $\mathbf{Ideal}_{A,S}(\lambda)$ are indistinguishable for any PPT adversary.*

Forward and Backward Privacy. In order to control the information disclosure during updates, the DSSE scheme presented in this work aims to achieve forward and backward privacy [6]. The *forward privacy* ensures that each update leaks no information about the keyword that was queried in the past and currently is in the document to be updated. The *backward privacy* guarantees that when a keyword-document pair (w, id) is added and then deleted, subsequent searches on w do not reveal id. There are three types of *backward privacy*, which varies the information leakage to the server, from Type-I to Type III [6]. Following the verbatim from [4,6], we let TimeDB(w) be the insertion pattern on the non-deleted documents *currently* matching w and the timestamps of inserting them to the database. Formally,

$$\mathsf{TimeDB}(w) = \{(u, id) : (u, add, (w, id)) \in Q$$
$$\text{and } \forall u', (u', del, (w, id)) \notin Q\}$$

where u is a timestamp indicating when (w, id) is added into the database, while u' is a timestamp indicating when (w, id) is removed from the database.

Type-I *backward privacy* is the most secure [6], and it only reveals the insertion pattern of what time the current (non-deleted) documents matching to w was added (i.e., TimeDB(w)). Note that, the timestamps of the current matching documents equivalent to the timestamps when they were inserted [6]. There have been many non-SGX supported SSE schemes supporting this advance security notion (e.g., Type-I *backward privacy* with Moneta and Orion [6], Type-II with

Fides and Mitra [6], Type-III with Janus [6], Horus [24], and Janus++ [50]). However, there is only one SGX-supported Type-I *backward-private* schemes, which is Fort [1]. Nonetheless, the enclave's computation in the Search operation and the *search latency* in Fort have not been thoroughly investigated as stated in the author's work [1].

Threat Model. We follow existing works [1,23] to consider a semi-honest adversary at the server-side. Although the adversary will not deviate from the protocol, he/she is capable of accessing the entire software stack (including hypervisor and OS) except the program running in the enclave. In addition, the adversary can inspect the untrusted memory and track the access pattern (the address and the time of access). The goal of the attacker is to learn extra information about the historical updates on EDB and client's query keywords from the leakage both revealed by hardware and the leakage function defined in Sect. 5.

4   Our Proposed Type-I Backward-Private Scheme

In this section, we firstly review the existing attempts on designing a TEE-based Type-I backward-private scheme and indicate why they still fall short under the TEE setting. Then, we highlight our design intuition and present the detailed construction of our scheme.

4.1   Baseline Approaches

A basic attempt to build a Type-I *backward-private* scheme is to utilise ORAM. In particular, the latest construction (Orion [24]) leverages two oblivious map OMAPs to store the database index and states. These two OMAPs ensure the update and query operations are oblivious, and thus Orion can achieve Type-I backward privacy. Since the existing work demonstrates how to use TEE (Intel SGX) to accelerate the oblivious data structure [36], one can directly employ SGX to fulfil the *Client*'s role in non-TEE supported schemes. And then, the *Server* in those schemes can be executed in untrusted memory area outside the *Enclave*. However, this solution still maintains the high communication overhead between the *Enclave* and the *Server* during Update *addition/deletion* and Search due to the use of multiple oblivious maps at the *Server* (see Table 1 for porting the *Client* of Orion [24] to the *Enclave*).

The second approach (Fort) [1] proposed by Amjad et al. reduces that communication overhead between the *Enclave* and the *Server* via two solutions. First, it asks the *Server* to only maintain one oblivious map OMAP. The map stores the pair $(F(w, id), label)$ during Update, where *label* is the token used to insert (w, id) pair into the index map M_I. Secondly, the *Enclave* in Fort stores a $Stash_{del} = \Sigma_{\forall w} d_w$ that maintains the deleted *labels* d_w of every keyword w. The *Client* in Fort holds keyword state $st_w = (version, count)$ where *version* increases after every Search, and *count* gets updated for every Update op $\in \{add, del\}$ on w. During Update, the *Enclave* generates an update token $(label, value)$, where $label := F_{K_1}(w||version||count)$ and $value := Enc(K_2, id||op)$, to insert into M_I.

Whenever the *label* is inserted into M_I, the newly generated pair $(F(w, id), label)$ is obliviously added to the OMAP. If the op of Update is *deletion*, the *Enclave* obliviously retrieves the corresponding *label* from the OMAP and then appends it to $Stash_{del}$. The *Enclave* will execute dummy operations on OMAP to hide whether the Update is for *addition* or *deletion*. The Search operation of Fort is Type-I *backward-private* because the *Enclave* only sends (reveals) n_w currently matching *labels* to the *Server* after locally discarding deleted *labels* found in $Stash_{del}$. The complexity of Fort can be found in Table 1.

Amjad et al. [1] acknowledged that the cost of identifying and discarding the deleted *labels* of the query keyword w in $Stash_{del}$ of Fort could slow down the *search latency*. However, that cost was not investigated thoroughly in their work [1]; only a theoretical scheme was proposed. Therefore, we had re-implemented the *Enclave*'s computation of Fort and found that the scanning could take up to 8.02×10^6 *ms* just to scan 10^4 tokens when $Stash_{del} = 10^7$. That insufficient cost is added to the *search latency* upon Search operation of Fort.

Remarks on Fort's Optimisation. Amjad et al. [1] note that Fort can be optimised by replacing the usage of $Stash_{del}$ in the *Enclave* by an OMAP to be stored in the untrusted *Server*. In this way, the *Enclave* does not need to perform the linear scanning of identifying and discarding deleted labels of the query keywords. Instead, the *Enclave* obliviously retrieves them from the OMAP during Search. However, this access will downgrade the security of the scheme. The reason is that it additionally leaks the number of deletions of the query keyword during Search, i.e., the number of ORAM accesses can be exposed.

4.2 Design Intuition

As analysed, Fort relies on TEE (a hardware *Enclave*) to protect the supporting information for Search, which is the deletion information in $Stash_{del}$. The deleted labels in $Stash_{del}$ need to be retrieved via ORAM accesses to the *Server* during Update *deletion* before Search happens. But, this causes the intensive linear scaning operation during Search if the $Stash_{del}$ or the number of generated undeleted/deleted tokens of query keywords is large.

Similar to Fort, we also rely on TEE to protect the supporting information for Search. But, we let the *Enclave* store a normal state map M_c of all (w, id) pairs received during Update *addition*. Based on our assumption, the *Enclave* can protect code and data inside the *Enclave*, migrating M_c to the *Enclave* does not affect the security of our protocol while it fully eliminates ORAM operations for Type-I DSSE schemes. By doing so, our design neither does require the *Server* to store any OMAP data structure in Setup, nor access to that in Update *deletion*. Instead, we simply track the deleted *id* within the *Enclave*. In addition, Maiden also employs a sketch addition BF, i.e., a Bloom filter, to compress all (w, id) pairs added during Update *addition*. With the latest states of tracked keywords, BF, and deleted *id* list, the *Enclave* is able to generate the query tokens for currently matching documents. This helps the scheme to achieve Type-I backward-privacy (i.e., leaking only TimeDB(w)), without exposing historical

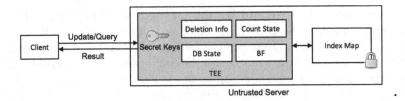

Fig. 1. High-level illustration of Maiden

Setup(1^λ)	*Enclave:*
Client: 1: Initialise $k_\Sigma, k_{BF} \xleftarrow{\$} \{0,1\}^\lambda$, and integers l, h 2: Attest and establish a secure channel to *Enclave* 3: Send (k_Σ, k_{BF}, l, h) to *Enclave*;	4: Initialise $R_k \xleftarrow{\$} \{0,1\}^\lambda$; 5: Init maps ST, M_c, and a list d 6: Initialise $BF \leftarrow 0^l$ and $\{H'_j\}_{j\in[h]}$; *Server:* 7: Initialise an index map M_I;

Fig. 2. Setup protocol in Maiden where the *Client* is *storage-free*

deletion information to the *Server*. Yet, storing M_c in the *Enclave* may cause the paging overhead in SGX *Enclave Page Cache* (EPC). Nonetheless, we observe that the access with the EPC paging is still one to two orders of magnitude faster than the linear scan in Fort and the ORAM accesses from the *Enclave* to the *Server* in a basic scheme that ports Orion to TEE (see Sect. 6).

4.3 The Detailed Protocol

Figure 1 presents the design overview of Maiden. The design contains three participants: the trusted *Client*, the TEE denoted as the *Enclave* within the *Server* and the untrusted *Server*. Maiden equips with a lightweight *Client*, which does not maintain any data structure locally. On the other hand, the untrusted *Server* only maintains a normal *index map* M_I to store the mapping between *label* and *value*. The *Enclave* keeps the deletion information. To accelerate the query process, the *Enclave* also has three state maps: The first one is the database state map ST which stores the update counter for each keyword. It indicates the number of updates regarding the keyword. We migrate it from the *Client* to the *Enclave* to reduce the workload for generating query/update tokens. The second one is a count state map M_c maintaining the mapping between (w, id) and the corresponding count. The third one is a compressed state map BF stored as a Bloom filter. This indicates whether a given keyword is in a given document, which can be used to facilitate the query process.

To communicate with the *Server*, the *Client* leverages the remote attestation mechanism to establish a secure channel with the *Enclave*. Then, the *Client* can remotely access the database via Setup, Update (add/del documents), and Search operations. The *Enclave* receives the above operations and manipulates

---

Update(op, in)

Client:

1: **if** op = *add* **then**// in=(doc,id)
2:   send (op, in) to *Enclave*;
3: **else** // op = *del*
4:   Send (op, in = (doc', id));
5: **end if**

Enclave:

6: **if** op = *add* **then**
7:   Parse doc to $D = \{(w, id)\}$;
8   $T \leftarrow \{\emptyset\}$
9:   **for** $(w, id) \in D$ **do**
10:     $k_w \leftarrow F(k_\Sigma, w)$;
11:     $c \leftarrow ST[w]$; $c \leftarrow c + 1$

12:     $k_{id} \leftarrow H_1(k_w, c)$;
13:     $(u, v) \leftarrow (H_2(k_w, c), \mathsf{Enc}(k_{id}, id))$
14:     add (u, v) to T;
15:     $M_c[F(k_w, id)] \leftarrow c$;
16:     $BF[H'_j(k_{BF}, w \parallel id)] \leftarrow 1$ for $j \in [1, h]$;
17:     $ST[w] \leftarrow c$;
18:   **end for**
19:   send T to *Server*; // in batch
20: **else:** // op = *del*, in = (doc', id)
21:   add id to d;
22:   Set dummy entries (u', v') in T
23: **end if**

Server:

24:   $M_I[u] \leftarrow v$ for (u, v) in T;

Fig. 3. Update protocol in Maiden

Search(w)

Enclave:

1: Receive w from *Client*;
2: $k_w \leftarrow F(k_\Sigma, w)$;
3: $st_{(w,c)} \leftarrow \{\emptyset\}, Q \leftarrow [\emptyset]$;
4: **for** id in d **do**
5:   **if** $BF[H'_j(k_{BF}, w \parallel id)]_{j \in [h]} = 1$ **then**
6:     $c \leftarrow M_c[F(k_w, id)]$;
7:     $st_{(w,c)} \leftarrow \{c\} \cup st_{(w,c)}$;
8:   **end if**
9: **end for**

10: $st_{(w,c)} \leftarrow \{0, \ldots, ST[w]\} \setminus st_{(w,c)}$
11: **for** c in $st_{(w,c)}$ **do**
12:   $(u, k_{id}) \leftarrow (H_2(k_w, c), H_1(k_w, c))$;
13:   $Q \leftarrow \{(u, k_{id})\} \cup Q$;
14: **end for**
15: send Q to *Server*; //in batch

Server:

16: $id\_List \leftarrow \{\emptyset\}$;
17: **for** (u, k_{id}) in Q **do**
18:   $id \leftarrow \mathsf{Dec}(k_{id}, M_I[u])$;
19:   $id\_List \leftarrow \{id\} \cup id\_List$
20: send id_List to *Enclave*;

Fig. 4. Search protocol in Maiden

---

the encrypted database stored on the untrusted *Server* on behalf of the *Client*. The detailed procedures of Maiden are provided in Fig. 2, 3 and 4.

Setup. During Setup, the *Client* attests the *Enclave* and then establishes a secure channel for later communication. The *Enclave* maintains the latest keyword state ST, list d of deleted ids, a Bloom filter BF, and importantly a state map M_c that tracks the state c of (w, id). It also receives necessary keys (K_Σ, K_{BF}) provisioned by the *Client*. The *Server* maintains an encrypted map M_I to facilitate the index search.

Update. The *Client* directly provides a tuple (op = *add*, in = {doc, id}) to the *Enclave* via the secure channel. Then, the *Enclave* generates update tokens $T = \{(u, v)\}$ for $\forall(w, id) \in$ doc to update the index map M_I, where $(u_i, v_i) \leftarrow (H_2(k_w, c), \mathsf{Enc}(k_{id}, id))$ with k_{id} generated from $ST[w]$. After that, the *Enclave* tracks the latest state c of $F(k_w, id)$ in the map M_c. This state tracking later enables retrieving the states of deleted doc with id containing w in Search. In addition, the *Enclave* updates the membership of $(w||id)$ to BF. If the Update is *deletion*, given a tuple of (doc', id) sent by the *Client*, the *Enclave* adds id to the list d. It also adds dummy token entries (u', v') generated from doc' to M_I to hide the *deletion* op.

Search. The *Client* sends a query keyword w to the *Enclave* for receiving documents matching the keyword. The *Enclave* first performs the membership testing for $(w, id_i), id_i \in d$. With the help of the internal map M_c, the *Enclave* can retrieve the state of (w, id_i) if id_i was deleted. Then, the *Enclave* can generate the query tokens $\{(u, k_{id})\}$, where $(u, k_{id} \leftarrow (H_2(k_w, c), H_1(k_w, c))$, for undeleted states based on the latest state $ST[w]$ after eliminating deleted ones. Upon receiving the query tokens, the *Server* returns the currently matching document id_List to the *Enclave*.

The Efficiency of Maiden. The asymptotic search complexity of Maiden is $\mathcal{O}(n_w)$. The scheme relies on the interval map M_c to compute n_w query tokens. It does not need to communicate to the *Server* to find the states of deleted documents. As a trade-off, the scheme maintains a storage of $(\mathcal{O}(W \log D) + \mathcal{O}(a_w W) + \mathcal{O}(N))$, where the significant factor $\mathcal{O}(N)$ presents the size of M_c. The access pattern on M_c during Search is protected by the *Enclave*. Our experiments show that Maiden is still more than two orders of magnitude faster than the *linear scanning* cost in Fort even when Maiden suffers large memory overhead.

Remarks: Maiden employs a BF for keeping track of *addition*, which facilitates the search token generation in Search. A false positive can be introduced when non-member (w, id) pairs map to set bit positions in the BF vector. This turns out w presumably presented in the deleted document id by the wrong testing. We note that this false match does not affect the correctness of search. The state $ST[w]$ only tracks the matching states for truly existing (w, id) pairs (see line 17 in Fig. 3), and no valid state can be found in M_c if w does not exist in the document id (see line 6 in Fig. 4). Therefore, an invalid state cannot be used to generate query tokens (see line 10 in Fig. 4).

Like many other SSE works [1,5,19,24,50,53] that focus on the search document index, Search protocol in Maiden only retrieves the document identifiers ids of currently matching documents docs containing the query keyword. We note that encrypted data blocks of the documents can be independently outsourced to an oblivious data structure stored in the *Server*. The idea of using this data structure is to hide document update patterns for the document access. Once the *Enclave* obtains the currently matching ids, it can perform oblivious access to the *Server* to retrieve these data blocks and return them to the *Client* via the established secure channel.

5   Security Analysis

Maiden contains the leakage of Update and Search operations. We formulate the leakage and define $\mathbf{Real}_A(\lambda)$ and a $\mathbf{Ideal}_{A,S}(\lambda)$ game for an adaptive adversary $\mathcal{A}$ and a polynomial time simulator S with the security parameter λ as follows.

Let $\mathcal{L}$ be a stateful leakage function $\mathcal{L} = (\mathcal{L}^{Stp}, \mathcal{L}^{Updt}, \mathcal{L}^{Srch}, \mathcal{L}^{hw})$, where the first three functions are inherited from DSSE *Server* (see Sect. 3.3). They define the information exposed to the *Server* in Setup, Update and Search, respectively. Besides, $\mathcal{L}^{hw}$ defines the inherent leakage of the used SGX *Enclave* communicating with the *Server*. In Setup, Maiden only leaks the data structure of M_I (i.e., the encrypted index). We note that the state map M_c is protected by SGX *Enclave* and it is not exposed to the *Server*. In Update(op $= \{add, del\}$, in), Maiden leaks the data access pattern T_{M_I} of encrypted entries to be inserted in M_I. Hence, $\mathcal{L}^{Updt}(\text{op}, \text{in}) = \{T_{M_I}\}$. In Search($w$), Maiden leaks the access pattern on M_I when the *Enclave* queries n_w, named $\text{ap}_{M_I}(w)$. Then, formally $\mathcal{L}^{Srch}(w) = \{\text{ap}_{M_I}(w)\}$. We define $\mathcal{L}^{hw}(M_I)$ as the hardware leakage during Update and Search. That includes memory addresses, the time log, and the size of the manipulated memory area. We write $\mathcal{L}^{hw.Updt}(\text{op}, \text{in}) \leftarrow (M_I)^{Updt}$, which outputs the trace τ of $\{(v, s, t)\}$ on M_I, where v is the encrypted data inserted into M_I, s is the memory size of v, and t is the accessing timestamp of op. We note $\mathcal{L}^{hw.Srch}(w) \leftarrow (M_I)^{Srch}(w)$, which also leaks the trace τ of entries matching w in M_I. We let EDB_k be the state of EDB after updated by the k-th operation $(\text{op}, \text{in})_k$.

Definition 2. *Consider* Maiden *scheme that consists of three protocols* Setup, Update, *and* Search. *Consider the probabilistic experiments* $\textbf{Real}_{\mathcal{A}}(\lambda)$ *and* $\textbf{Ideal}_{\mathcal{A},\mathcal{S}}(\lambda)$, *whereas* $\mathcal{A}$ *is a stateful adversary, and* $\mathcal{S}$ *is a stateful simulator that gets the leakage function* $\mathcal{L}$.

$\textbf{Real}_{\mathcal{A}}(\lambda)$: The challenger runs Setup(1^λ). Then, $\mathcal{A}$ chooses a database DB = $\{\text{doc}_i\}_{i \in Z}$ and makes a polynomial number of Updates (addition/deletion) with (op, in), where Z is a natural number of documents, and (op $= add$, in $= \{\text{doc}_i, id_i\}$) or (op $= del$, in $= \{\text{doc}', id_i\}$). Accordingly, the challenger runs those updates with Update(op, in) and eventually returns the tuple $(M_I)^{Updt}$ to $\mathcal{A}$. After that, $\mathcal{A}$ adaptively chooses the keyword w (*resp.*, (op, in)) to search (*resp.*, update). In response, the challenger runs Search(w) (*resp.*, Update(op,in)) and returns the transcript of each operation. The challenger also returns $(M_I)^{Srch}$ to $\mathcal{A}$. Finally, $\mathcal{A}$ outputs a bit b.

$\textbf{Ideal}_{\mathcal{A},\mathcal{S}}(\lambda)$: The challenger runs $\mathcal{S}(\mathcal{L}^{Stp}(1^\lambda))$. $\mathcal{A}$ chooses a DB = $\{\text{doc}_i\}_{i \in Z}$, and makes a polynomial number of Updates (addition/deletion) with (op, in) to the $\mathcal{S}$, where Z is a natural number of documents, and (op $= add$, in $= \{\text{doc}_i, id_i\}$) or (op $= del$, in $= \{\text{doc}', id_i\}$) By using $\mathcal{L}^{Updt}$ and $\mathcal{L}^{hw.Updt}$, $\mathcal{S}$ creates a tuple of (M_I) and send them to the *Server*. Then, $\mathcal{A}$ adaptively chooses the keyword w (*resp.*, (op, in)) to search (*resp.*, update). The challenger returns the transcript simulated by $\mathcal{S}(\mathcal{L}^{Srch}(w), \mathcal{L}^{hw.Srch}(w))$ (*resp.*, $\mathcal{S}(\mathcal{L}^{Updt}(\text{op}, \text{in}), \mathcal{L}^{hw.Updt}(\text{op}, \text{in}))$). Finally, $\mathcal{A}$ returns a bit b.

We say Maiden is $\mathcal{L}$-secure against adaptive chosen-keyword attacks if for all probabilistic polynomial-time algorithms $\mathcal{A}$, there exist a PPT simulator $\mathcal{S}$ such that

$$|Pr[\textbf{Real}_{\mathcal{A}}(\lambda) = 1] - Pr[\textbf{Ideal}_{\mathcal{A},\mathcal{S}}(\lambda) = 1]| \leq negl(\lambda)$$

Theorem 1. *Assuming the map M_c is secure and protected by SGX Enclave, and the communication between the Client and the Enclave is secure,* Maiden *is an adaptively-secure SSE scheme with $(\mathcal{L}^{Updt}(\text{op}, \text{in}) = \text{op}, \mathcal{L}^{hw.Updt}(\text{op}, \text{in}) = (M_I)^{Updt})$, and $(\mathcal{L}^{Srch}(w) = \text{TimeDB}(w), \mathcal{L}^{hw.Srch}(w) = (M_I)^{Srch})$.*

Proof. We now prove Theorem 1 by describing a PPT simulator $\mathcal{S}$ for which a PPT adversary $\mathcal{A}$ can distinguish $\mathbf{Real}_{\mathcal{A}}(\lambda)$ and $\mathbf{Ideal}_{\mathcal{A},\mathcal{S}}(\lambda)$ with negligible probability. We now describe $\mathcal{S}$ as follows:

- $\mathcal{S}.Init(1^{\lambda})$. It generates a random key $\tilde{K} = (\tilde{k}_{\Sigma}, \tilde{k}_{BF})$ to simulate the key components that the enclave contains (see Fig. 2). $\mathcal{S}$ also creates an empty M_I. It then sets $\text{EDB}_0 \leftarrow M_I$ and sends it to the *Server*, and set $st_{\mathcal{S}}$ to null.
- $\mathcal{S}.Update(st_{\mathcal{S}}, \mathcal{L}^{Updt}(\text{op}, \text{in})_k, \mathcal{L}^{hw.Updt}(\text{op}, \text{in})_k, \text{EDB}_{k-1})$. Recall that $\mathcal{L}^{Updt}(\text{op}, \text{in})_k = \{T_{M_I}\}_k$, and $\mathcal{L}^{hw.Updt}(\text{op}, \text{in})_k = \tau_k$. $\mathcal{A}$ selects a doc with id and send a tuple of $(\text{op} = add, in = \{\text{doc}, id\})$ or $(\text{op} = del, \text{in} = \{\text{doc}', id\})$ to $\mathcal{S}$, where doc' is a dummy doc. Upon receiving doc, $\mathcal{S}$ computes new entries and sends them to the *Server* for the insertion to M_I. We note that $\mathcal{S}$ computes these new entries by simulating the output of the secure hardware (i.e., TEE). To do so, the simulator first takes encrypted data in $\{T_{M_I}\}_k$ and decrypts them using $\tilde{k}_{\Sigma}$. Based on the timestamps and data sizes revealed in τ_k, $\mathcal{S}$ tries to locally updates $st_{\mathcal{S}}$, and generates new tokens for (w, id) pairs in doc. It then sends these new tokens to the *Server*.
- $\mathcal{S}.Search(st_{\mathcal{S}}, \mathcal{L}^{Srch}(w)_k, \mathcal{L}^{hw.Srch}(w)_k, \text{EDB}_{k-1})$. $\mathcal{A}$ choose a keyword w and sends it to $\mathcal{S}$. Recall that $\mathcal{L}^{Srch}(w)_k = \text{TimeDB}(w)$. Then, with $\mathcal{L}^{hw.Srch}(w)$ and $st_{\mathcal{S}}$, $\mathcal{S}$ simulates the outputs of the secure hardware and sends them to the *Server*. Finally, let R_w be the set of document identifiers corresponding to the queried keyword, as derived from $\text{TimeDB}(w)$. $\mathcal{S}$ sends R_w to $\mathcal{A}$.

Consider the $\mathbf{Ideal}_{\mathcal{A},\mathcal{S}}(\lambda)$ game with the described simulator $\mathcal{S}$, the produced transcript is indistinguishable from the one produced during $\mathbf{Real}_{\mathcal{A}}(\lambda)$ as the map M_I get entries inserted in the same document addition manner, the state protected by secure TEE, and the document identifiers of the query keyword are also the same.

We note that $\mathcal{A}$ knows the timestamps when encrypted entries are inserted into the index map M_I in both *addition/deletion* Updates, but $\mathcal{A}$ cannot distinguish the Update is *addition* or *deletion*. The reason is the map M_I always get entries inserted during the doc *addition/deletion* under $\mathcal{A}$'s view. During Search, Maiden only reveals n_w during the query on M_I. The rest information of d_w and M_c are within the *Enclave*. Therefore, $\mathcal{A}$ cannot match the accessed positions in Search to any previous document Update on particular w. This ensures that Maiden only reveals $\text{TimeDB}(w)$.

6 Experiment and Evaluation

SGX-Supported Schemes for Evaluation. We develop Maiden and two baseline schemes Orion* and Fort for comparison by using Intel SGX SDK and C++[1].

---

[1] Source code: https://github.com/MonashCybersecurityLab/SGXSSE.

Table 2. Statistics of the datasets used in the evaluation.

Name	# of keywords	# of docs	# of keyword-doc pairs
DS1	500	10,000	119,286
DS2	1,000	1,000,000	8,281,451
Enron	23,355	85,000	8,895,865

The prototype of Maiden contains three components of *Client*, the *Enclave*, and the *Server*. They follow the scheme's protocols as presented in Sect. 4.3. We leverage standard *ecalls/ocalls* interfaces provided by SGX SDK to implement the communication between these components. In all experiments, we set a batch size to 1×10^4 when the *Enclave* sends query tokens to the *Server* during Search via the *ocall* interface. Note that, we use the same Bloom filter's configuration for all the following used datasets, with the false positive rate 10^{-4} and it can store up to 1.5×10^7 pairs.

For baseline schemes, we first choose Orion [24] since it is publicly known as the most optimal non-TEE supported Type-I *backward-private* scheme with $\mathcal{O}(n_w log^2 N)$ search latency. We migrate the *Client* of Orion to the *Enclave*, and name this ported version as Orion*. The *Enclave* in Orion* stores the map $LastInd[w]$ that maintains the most recently inserted file identifier matching w, and the map $UpdtCnt[w]$ tracking the total number of currently matched documents of w. The *Server* in Orion* maintains two oblivious maps (OMAPs) to facilitate the Update and Search operations, as presented in the original scheme. They are OMAP_{upd} and OMAP_{src}, respectively. We carefully port the implementation of Orion to the *Enclave* and also construct the OMAP_{upd} and OMAP_{src} in the *Server* by using oblivious data structures initiated by AVL trees [24], as introduced in the original Orion scheme. We refer readers to the original work [24] for the detailed protocols of the scheme.

In addition, we also implement the *Enclave* component of Fort during Search for comparison since the implementation of Fort is not publicly available. In details, for a given sampled $Stash_{del}$ cached in the *Enclave*, we ask the *Enclave* to generate deleted/undeleted query tokens for a query keyword w. Then, the *Enclave* linearly scans $Stash_{del}$ to identify and discard a portion of the deleted tokens existing in the $Stash_{del}$. We only measure the scanning time and consider it as the *search latency* for Fort.

For both three schemes, we leverage built-in cryptographic primitives in `sgx_tcrypto` library to implement required cryptographic operations. The prototypes of these schemes are deployed into an Intel SGX-equipped station with Intel core i7 2.6 GHz and 32 GB RAM.

Experimental Datasets: We use two synthesis datasets (a small DS1: 70 MB, and a large DS2: 4 GB), and a portion of public Enron email dataset[2] (895 MB). The synthesis datasets are generated from the American English keyword

[2] Enron email dataset: https://www.cs.cmu.edu/~./enron/.

Table 3. Avg. (μs) for adding/deleting a (w, id) pair when adding/deleting a portion of DS1 and DS2.

Scheme	Add 100% docs		Del 25% docs		Del 50% docs		Del 75% docs	
	DS1	DS2	DS1	DS2	DS1	DS2	DS1	DS2
Maiden	19	43	1.24	1.4	2.09	2.4	3.01	3.3
Orion*	361	601	575	5,059	820	8,564.1	1,021.3	11,495.1

Table 4. Number of *ocalls* for data communication between *Enclave* and *Server* in adding/deleting a portion of documents

Scheme	Add 100% docs		Del 25% docs		Del 50% docs		Del 75% docs	
	DS1	DS2	DS1	DS2	DS1	DS2	DS1	DS2
Maiden	12	829	1*	1*	1*	1*	1*	1*
Orion*	8.9×10^4	6.2×10^6	7.86×10^5	1.34×10^7	9.2×10^5	1.7×10^7	3.2×10^6	3.6×10^7

*: Maiden performs 1 *ocall* per doc in non-batch setting to add dummy entries to M_I

frequency data and sampled by using the Zipf's law distribution. With DS1, the keyword's state map M_c of Maiden can fit in the limited memory protected by SGX *Enclave* (i.e., 98 MB), while the map causes *paging overhead* when DS2 is used. The *paging overhead* is essential to enable *Enclave Page Cache* (EPC) perform page swaps of Intel SGX [16]. Table 2 summarises these used datasets.

6.1 The Performance on the Synthesis Datasets

Insertion and Deletion. We first evaluate the time for insertion and deletion an (w, id) pair under different schemes when using datasets DS1 and DS2. As shown in Table 3, Orion* takes 361 and 601 μs to insert a pair to DS1 and DS2, respectively. That latency is about $(13$–$36)\times$ significantly higher than Maiden. The reason is because the *Enclave* in Orion* needs to update/traverse the AVL tree structures of both OMAP$_{upd}$ and OMAP$_{src}$ stored in the *Server*. Table 4 confirms that the communication (i.e., *ocalls*) in Orion* during *addition* is about $(4.6 \times 10^3$–$1.4 \times 10^5)\times$ more than Maiden. It is clearly that Maiden is more efficient because it only updates the local state map M_c within the *Enclave*. With Maiden, the number of *ocalls* contacting to the *Server* is negligible (12 *ocalls* with DS1, 829 *ocalls* with DS2). This communication is purely made when the *Enclave* inserts encrypted entries to the index map M_I.

Similar with the *addition*, Orion* operates on both OMAP$_{upd}$ and OMAP$_{src}$ to retrieve/update new state for every (w, id) pairs with the recently inserted document identifiers. Therefore, the time to delete a document with Orion* scales to the number of keywords in that document. Averagely, Orion* takes $6,325$ ms to delete a document containing 8–14 keywords. Table 4 reports the latency when deleting a portion of documents in DS1 and DS2. In contrast, Maiden takes a negligible time cost to delete a document. The main reason behind it is because Maiden only tracks the identifiers of those deleted documents within the *Enclave*.

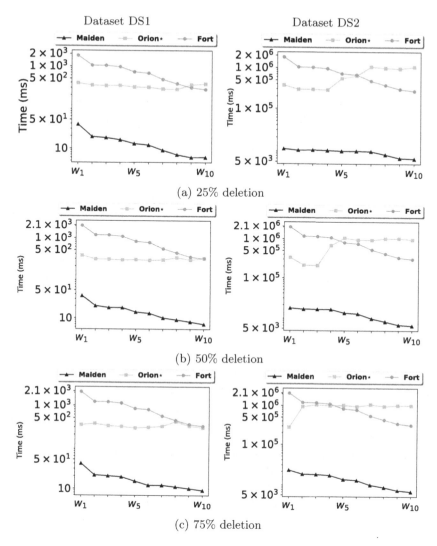

Fig. 5. The query delay of querying the i-th most frequent keyword in the DS1 and DS2 datasets after deleting a portion of documents

It only takes 1 *ocall* per a deleted document to insert dummy entries into the index map M_I to hide the operation.

Query Delay. Next, we monitor the search latency between Fort, Orion⋆, and Maiden when using datasets DS1 and DS2. We choose to query the top-10 keywords in the datasets after deleting a portion of documents. With DS1, we insert 1×10^4 documents, then delete 25%, 50%, and 75% of the documents, respectively. Similarly, with DS2, we insert 1×10^6 documents, and also delete these portions of the documents. Figure 5 reports the search latency under different schemes. The result shows that Fort has the downward trend when querying less-frequent keywords. The reason is because those keywords have fewer number of undeleted/deleted tokens to be scanned against the map $Stash_{del}$ stored in the Enclave. Averagely, scanning a token (w, id) of the most frequent keyword in DS1 takes 18 μs when $Stash_{del} = 1 \times 10^5$. In the larger dataset DS2, this cost is averagely 284.2 μs to scan just an (w, id) pair for the most frequent keyword when $Stash_{del} = 6.3 \times 10^6$. The more documents deleted, the longer time Fort takes to scan the tokens of query keywords. Querying the most frequent keyword in DS2 after deleting 75% documents takes more than 2×10^6 ms. With Orion*, the scheme takes 1.4×10^3 ms less than Fort to query the most frequent keyword w (with the frequency of 1×10^4) in the small dataset DS1 after deleting 25% documents. The reason is because Orion* only computes the tokens of currently documents matching the query keyword w. However, the latency to query documents matching a keyword in the larger dataset DS2 is non-trivial. It takes about 9.2×10^5 ms to query a keyword in the top-10 frequent keywords in DS2 after deleting 75% documents. The reason for it is because the Enclave in Orion* needs to retrieve matching nodes from a large AVL tree (with 2^{23} AVL nodes in DS2) of $OMAP_{src}$, where the tree's nodes are stored in the random positions of the underlying ORAM structure stored in the Server. In addition, the oblivious accesses in Orion* also include the cost of mapping visited AVL nodes to new ORAM positions, and encrypting/writing them back to the Server.

Figure 5 shows that Maiden completely outperforms Fort and Orion* in both DS1 and DS2. With the small dataset DS1, querying the most frequency keyword with Maiden is 10× and 47× faster than Orion* and Fort, respectively, after deleting 25% documents in DS1. With the large dataset DS2, the difference is about 35× and 174× faster than Orion* and Fort, respectively. When deleting 75% documents in DS2, Maiden is more efficient than Orion* and Fort about 12× and 95× when querying the most frequent keyword. Even when querying the 10-th frequent keyword, that difference varies from 45–175×. Note that, the main difference in the search of Maiden compared to others is how it generates the query tokens of currently matching documents for query keywords. Unlike Fort, Maiden does not require intensive computation (i.e. linear scanning undeleted/deleted tokens of query keywords against the large $Stash_{del}$), neither does Maiden perform oblivious accesses to the Server to identify the state of currently matching identifiers like Orion*. We note that membership testing with Bloom filter in Search of Maiden is $\mathcal{O}(1)$. With tracked deleted identifiers in the list d, the Enclave in Maiden can directly retrieve the deleted state of deleted documents matching the query keyword. The difference between DS1 and DS2 is that the size of the state map M_c in Maiden triggers paging overhead in SGX Enclave. We monitor that M_c in DS1 takes 2.27 MB, while the latter exceeds 157 MB. The paging cost is added to the search latency of Maiden when the EPC swaps pages to access the states of deleted (w, id) from the map. Nonetheless, with paging access, we observe that Maiden is averagely 75× and 90× faster than Orion* and Fort when querying the top-10 frequent keywords in DS2 after

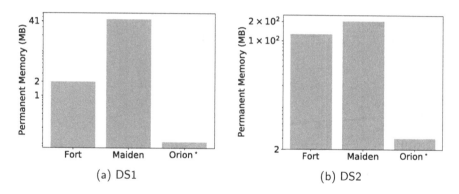

Fig. 6. The permanent memory in the *Enclave* in the datasets DS1 $(1 \times 10^4$ documents) and DS2 $(1 \times 10^6$ documents) and deleted 25% portion of them

deleting 25% documents of the dataset. With 75% documents deleted in DS2, the difference is in the range 70–72× faster than Orion* and Fort.

Memory Storage. Finally, we present the memory storage in the *Enclave* of the three schemes. As shown in Fig. 6, Maiden takes the largest memory, about 41 MB, among others when using dataset DS1. The main reason is because the storage of M_c (i.e., 2.27 MB) and the configured Bloom filter 38 MB (i.e., $P_e = 10^{-4}$) . When using DS2, the memory storage is about 200 MB due to the large state map M_c (i.e., 157 MB). We note that, deleting more documents, i.e., 75% documents in DS1 and DS2 does not affect significantly the memory consumption in the *Enclave* of Maiden. The reason is because only the identifiers of these deleted documents are appended in the list d of the scheme. Note that, the size of d is only about 30 KB and 3 MB when deleting 75% documents in DS1 and DS2, respectively. With Orion*, the memory consumption in the *Enclave* is negligible because the scheme only maintains the number of current documents and the most recently inserted document identifiers matching every keyword in the maps $UpdtCnt[w]$ and $LastInd[w]$, respectively. With Fort, the scheme maintains $Stash_{del} = \Sigma_{\forall w} d_w$ in the *Enclave*. Hence, with the DS2, deleting 25% documents requires about 121 MB to store 6.4×10^6 deleted tokens.

6.2 The Performance on the Enron Email Dataset

Query Latency. We use a portion of real world Enron email dataset to demonstrate the efficient of Maiden when the paging overhead in SGX Enclave occurs. We insert 85,000 email documents and test the average query delay with a small deletion portion 25%. With this deletion portion, there is no paging overhead in Fort. Figure 7 a reports the query delay when querying the top-10 frequent keyword in Enron dataset. The result shows that Maiden is averagely 291× and 575× faster than Orion* and Fort, respectively. We obtain that Maiden is more efficient than Fort and Orion* during Search with the used Enron dataset. The reason is because Enron actually has more keywords in the same deletion portion

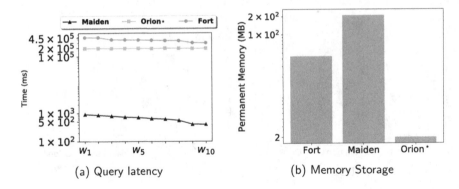

Fig. 7. Query latency and memory storage between schemes in the Enron dataset

compared to the used dataset DS2 (see Table 2). With DS2, the rate of cache hit in Fort is 1.56×10^{-1}, an order of magnitude higher than that rate (i.e., 1.52×10^{-2}) when Enron dataset is used. We note that reducing the false positive rate P_e of the Bloom filter used in Maiden does not change much its search performance. Changing $P_e = 10^{-6}$ from $P_e = 10^{-4}$, it only incurs averagely an additional 120 ms latency to search the top-10 frequent keywords.

Memory Storage. Clearly, Maiden needs the largest SGX Enclave memory to store the state map M_c of the all (w, id) pairs in the dataset ($\sim$170 MB). Fort consumes a minimal storage $Stash_{del} = 44$ MB to store 2.3×10^6 deleted tokens. The limitation of Maiden is the memory bottleneck in the SGX Enclave. In the future work, we will improve the memory efficient of the scheme. In the meantime, we expect the new version Intel SGXv2 to increase the size of the *enclave page cache* more greatly and support dynamic page allocation [35].

7   SGX-Related Attacks and Defence Discussion

With Intel SGX's security guarantee, CPU is the only trustworthy component where enclave's code and data are handled in plain-text format, all other components including operating system (OS), memory, hypervisor, memory bus, etc. are treated as untrusted. Whenever the code/data are moved out of the CPU, i.e., into untrusted DRAM memory space, they are encrypted and integrity protected. However, there have been many side-channel attacks showing that it is not impossible to infer/steal the secrets protected by the SGX enclaves. Those attacks leverage the side information revealed by cache [8,25,43], page table [46,54,55], transient execution [12,51] and others [2,33,37]. In this section, we discuss significant SGX-related attacks and existing defences, and consider how they can be applied to our proposed scheme.

7.1   Cache Side-Channel Attacks and Defence

While enclave's code and data are encrypted and authenticated by the CPU, they are still stored unencrypted in CPU's caches and registers to facilitate the execution. Therefore, by monitoring the cache channels, an adversary can learn fine-grained data leakage of the enclave. These cache-based attacks have been investigated at L1/L2 caches (on the same shared CPU core with hyper-threading) and L3 cache (cross-CPU core attacks). With shared L1/L2 cache channels, an adversarial process and a victim enclave process interleaved on the same physical CPU core, sharing both L1 cache that stores code and data, and L2 cache that unifies code and data at fine granularity level. Therefore, the adversary can infer the memory content of the victim enclave via the cache data access pattern. This is also known as time-sliced cache attacks [8,25,40]. With L3 cache channel, i.e., the last level cache (LLC) shared between CPU-cores, Schwartz et al. [43] developed an unprivileged program injected in a malicious enclave to conceal the secret key of a co-located victim enclave running on the same host machine. The simplest way to prevent the adversarial hyperthread from accessing to the shared L1/L2 cache channels of the victim enclave's process is by disabling hyper-threading [34]. However, this solution is not highly recommended since it obstructs other applications' performance and restricts CPUID instruction access from the victim enclave. Alternatively, preferred solutions to mitigate these cache channel attacks are transaction memory randomisation [7,27] and oblivious execution approaches [38,41,42] to obfuscate the cache data access pattern, and/or using Varys-protected run-time environment [39].

Transaction Memory Randomisation: Dr. SGX [7] applies a hardening randomisation technique to all data locations in enclave's memory at cache-line granularity. By randomising every eight data blocks at once, it makes the cache tracing of enclave's data is harder. Cloak [27] is also another mitigation solution using memory transaction technique. It uses Intel Transactional Synchronization Extension (TSX) to construct atomic memory operations that obliviously hide the memory access of enclave's data. The idea is that the enclave is requested to touch all cache lines before it accesses to the real data. Therefore, an adversary, monitoring the cache channel, learns nothing about the enclave's data access. We note that Dr. SGX is built as a compiler tool and Cloak simply just requires annotating enclave's data. Therefore, they can be applied directly to current SGX-supported (backward-private) SE schemes, (i.e., Maiden, Fort [1], Orion*, and SGX-SE1 and SGX-SE2 [53]), without changing the schemes' design. As a trade-off, they require an increasing overhead of averagely $4.8\times$ for Dr. SGX, and $2.48\times$ for Cloak, respectively. The penalty overhead is added to the complexity of enclave's computation in Update and Search operations for all the schemes (see Table 1).

Oblivious Memory Execution: Oblivious execution is also another approach to hide all enclave's code and data access. For example, Raccoon [41] provides annotation guides to hide the data access regarding different data sizes in the enclave. For small-size secrets, the data access is hidden by using Path ORAM. Otherwise, Raccoon uses Advanced Vector Extensions (AVX) intrinsic operations provided by Intel to stream over large data structures. In addition, Raccoon also obfuscates control flows by using oblivious operation primitives extended from CMOV x86 instructions. Applying Racoon to current backward-private SE schemes' operations will add about 16× penalty overhead. We also note that this solution can be plugged directly to the current implementation of the schemes, without changing the design. Alternatively, ZeroTrace [42] also proposes efficient oblivious memory primitives by using Circuit-ORAM. It runs on top of a software memory controller. Therefore, applying ZeroTrace to the implementation of the backward-private schemes requires a minor modification of using the memory controller interface for all enclave's accesses, without changing the (backward-private) SE schemes' implementation design. Other oblivious primitives of memory assignments and comparisons, and oblivious array access [38] can be directly adapted to the schemes' implementation. Again, using oblivious data structures like ORAM will reduce the efficiency, and designing an TEE-based SSE schemes that can address memory access side-channels without using ORAM is still an open question.

Side-Channel Protected Runtime Environment: To mitigate the cache-channel attacks, Varys [39] provides a trusted core reservation technique that ensures the CPU-core only shares its caches to Varys's benign threads, preventing adversarial threads from using the same caches. In particular, for single-thread application like Maiden, Fort [1], Orion*, and SGX-SE1 and SGX-SE2 [53], we realise that Varys would simply pair that application thread with a service thread to reserve the complete core, and schedule it for runtime monitoring. Varys was reportedly to incur 15% penalty overhead in previous case studies [39]. Therefore, we assume that it would not impact much on the performance of these SE schemes. In addition, Varys is built as a Low Level Virtual Machine (LLVM)-based compiler; therefore, it also does not affect the schemes' code structure.

7.2   Page-Table Side-Channel Attacks and Defence

Apart from exploiting CPU caches, enclave's code and data are stored in Enclave Page Cache (EPC), which is the a subset of a contiguous Processor Reserved Memory (PRM) of DRAM. Every 4 KB enclave page of code and data is allocated from the EPC (including paging). With SGX design, the page table is managed by the (untrusted) OS. Therefore, it reveals the page-level access patterns of the victim enclave. The malicious OS can trigger page faults from requested pages during the enclave execution to learn the enclave's control flow and memory access. That page fault channel is sufficiently informative to extract the rich text information [55], or secret key bits [46] of victim enclaves. While increasing high page fault rate, these attacks consequently trigger asynchronous enclave exit (AEX) to report the accessing address of the faulting page to the (malicious) OS (i.e., even up to 11000 exits per second [54]). Therefore, a common system-level solution to thwart page-table side-channel attacks is to monitor and detect AEXs due to interrupts of page faults, like T-SGX [45] and Déjá Vu [13]. This solution allows the enclave to stop its execution if the detection occurs. Using this detection solution is a separated configuration and it also does not affect the designs of the SE schemes. Alternatively, Varys [39], an LLVM-based compiler, also introduces a monitoring mechanism for enclave exits so that the application thread running in the enclave can be terminated, without revealing further faulty pages' addresses to the OS. Other studies [22,47] also provide a self-verification mechanism to the enclave when page faults occur with an extra 1.2–2.4× overhead. We note that these compiler-based tools do not cause any impact on the SE scheme's code structure and implementation.

7.3 Transient Execution Attacks and Defence

Recent works also exploit the CPU execution design to steal enclave's secrets. The execution of a program in Intel CPUs (i.e., Intel's Skylake microarchitecture) is facilitated by two parts including a *frontend* component and an *Execution Engine*. While the *frontend* performs speculative execution predicting branch instruction to speed up the program's execution, the *Execution Engine* can execute instructions in out-of-order fashion so that multiple instructions can be executed in parallel. It has been shown that both these two parts can be exploited. For instance, Chen et al. [12] demonstrated SgxPectre attack that poisons the branch prediction of a victim enclave so that malicious injected secret-leaking instructions can be executed when the victim enclave runs. Unlike SgxPectre attack, Foreshadow [51] exploits the out-of-order execution to access even pages where the victim enclave's memory lies in. It exploits OS's system calls to trigger page faults and then uses Meltdown-like technique to access enclave's data before the page fault is handled. After that, it uses caching side-channel attack (i.e., Flush+Reload [56]) to read enclave's secrets from CPU's cache. We note that these attacks cannot solely mitigated by software solutions. It would include updates to OS, hypervisors, and CPU microcode. We refer interested readers to [18,26] for additional details about these hardware countermeasures.

7.4 Other Attacks and Defence

Apart from side-channel and transient execution attacks, recent studies found that SGX Enclave is also vulnerable to memory-corruption attacks [2,33]. These attacks often assume that the adversary has knowledge of vulnerabilities in the enclave's legacy code (i.e., stack overflow, data type confusion, format string vulnerability, etc.). Therefore, the untrusted code outside the enclave could pass parameters or invokes specific functions in the enclave, which subsequently perform sensitive computations. Since SGX instructions of *ecalls* (i.e., **EEN-TER**) and *ocalls* (i.e., **EEXIT**) do not clear CPU registers, thereby they allow the execution of (vulnerable) trusted code in the enclave to pass sensitive results/access to untrusted code (i.e., gaining access to CPU registers [2], or exfiltrating confidential code and data from enclave memory [33]). Mitigation solutions could be either 1) restricting the enclave's permission from accessing pages containing malicious code injection [58], 2) providing memory-safe access for variables/objects in SGX [31], 3) designing memory randomisation scheme for SGX enclave [44], or 4) static host-to-enclave code analysis tool [15]. We note that memory-corruption attacks are out of our focus since we consider that SE schemes used in our experiment and evaluation are memory-safe implementation.

Finally, adversaries can rely on power management software [37] to induce memory errors and cause overflows in the SGX runtime. Particularly, they can change protected values in the EPC region and direct in-enclave pointers to untrusted memory via this attack. Unlike prior attacks, this attack does not require any knowledge on code/memory. Fortunately, the issue has been fixed by recent microcode and BIOS updates offered by Intel [29].

8   Conclusion

In this paper, we design an efficient and strong backward-private DSSE scheme using TEE. Our scheme is the first to achieve Type-I backward privacy without relying on ORAM. We carefully investigate the limitations of prior theoretical TEE-supported scheme. Our proposed design reduces the overhead computation of the SGX enclave and also reduces the communication between the enclave and server. We implement prior works and our scheme and conduct a detailed evaluation on the performance under different schemes. The results show that our design is more efficient in the update operation and query latency. We also discuss SGX-related attacks and the deployment of our scheme in practical enclaves.

Acknowledgements. The authors would like to thank the anonymous reviewers for their valuable comments. The work was supported in part by the Australian Research Council Discovery Project grants DP180102199 and DP200103308, a Data61-Monash Collaborative Research Project (D61 Challenge: E01), and an Oceania Cyber Security Centre industry co-funded project.

References

1. Amjad, G., Kamara, S., Moataz, T.: Forward and backward private searchable encryption with SGX. In: EuroSec 2019 (2019)
2. Biondo, A., Conti, M., Davi, L., Frassetto, T., Sadeghi, A.R.: The guard's dilemma: efficient code-reuse attacks against intel SGX. In: USENIX Security 2018 (2018)
3. Borges, G., Domingos, H., Ferreira, B., Leitão, J., Oliveira, T., Portela, B.: BISEN: efficient boolean searchable symmetric encryption with verifiability and minimal leakage. In: IEEE SRDS 2019 (2019)
4. Bost, R.: Σοφος - forward secure searchable encryption. In: ACM CCS 2016 (2016)
5. Bost, R., Fouque, P.A.: Thwarting leakage abuse attacks against searchable encryption - a formal approach and applications to database padding. Cryptology ePrint Archive, Report 2017/1060 (2017). https://eprint.iacr.org/2017/1060
6. Bost, R., Minaud, B., Ohrimenko, O.: Forward and backward private searchable encryption from constrained cryptographic primitives. In: ACM CCS 2017 (2017)
7. Brasser, F., Capkun, S., Dmitrienko, A., Frassetto, T., Kostiainen, K., Sadeghi, A.R.: DR.SGX: automated and adjustable side-channel protection for SGX using data location randomization. In: ACSAC 2019 (2019)
8. Brasser, F., Müller, U., Dmitrienko, A., Kostiainen, K., Capkun, S., Sadeghi, A.R.: Software grand exposure: SGX cache attacks are practical. In: WOOT 2017 (2017)
9. Cash, D., Grubbs, P., Perry, J., Ristenpart, T.: Leakage-abuse attacks against searchable encryption. In: ACM CCS 2015 (2015)

10. Cash, D., Jaeger, J., Jarecki, S., Jutla, C.: Dynamic searchable encryption in very large databases: data structures and implementation. In: NDSS 2014 (2014)
11. Cash, D., Jarecki, S., Jutla, C., Krawczyk, H., Roşu, M.C., Steiner, M.: Highly-scalable searchable symmetric encryption with support for boolean queries. In: CRYPTO 2013 (2013)
12. Chen, G., Chen, S., Xiao, Y., Zhang, Y., Lin, Z., Lai, T.H.: Sgxpectre: stealing intel secrets from SGX enclaves via speculative execution. In: Euro S&P 2019 (2019)
13. Chen, S., Zhang, X., Reiter, M.K., Zhang, Y.: Detecting privileged side-channel attacks in shielded execution with déjà vu. In: ASIA CCS 2017 (2017)
14. Christian, P., Kapil, V., Manuel, C.: EnclaveDB: a secure database using SGX. In: IEEE S&P 2018 (2018)
15. Cloosters, T., Rodler, M., Davi, L.: TeeRex: discovery and exploitation of memory corruption vulnerabilities in SGX enclaves. In: USENIX Security 2020, pp. 841–858 (2020)
16. Costan, V., Devadas, S.: Intel SGX explained. In: IACR Cryptol. ePrint Arch. (2016)
17. Curtmola, R., Garay, J., Kamara, S., Ostrovsky, R.: Searchable symmetric encryption: improved definitions and efficient constructions. In: ACM CCS 2006 (2016)
18. Cutress, I.: Analyzing core i9-9900K performance with spectre and melt-down hardware mitigations. Intel Corp (2018). https://www.anandtech.com/show/13659/analyzing-core-i9-9900k-performance-with-spectre-and-meltdown-hardware-mitigations
19. Demertzis, I., Chamani, J.G., Papadopoulos, D., Papamanthou, C.: Dynamic searchable encryption with small client storage. In: NDSS 2020 (2020)
20. Eskandarian, S., Zaharia, M.: Oblidb: oblivious query processing for secure databases. In: Proceedings of the VLDB Endow. (2019)
21. Etemad, M., Küpçü, A., Papamanthou, C., Evans, D.: Efficient dynamic searchable encryption with forward privacy. In: PET 2018 (2018)
22. Fu, Y., Bauman, E., Quinonez, R., Lin, Z.: SGX-LAPD: thwarting controlled side channel attacks via enclave verifiable page faults. In: RAID (2017)
23. Fuhry, B., Bahmani, R., Brasser, F., Hahn, F., Kerschbaum, F., Sadeghi, A.: HardIDX: practical and Secure Index with SGX. In: DBSec 2017 (2017)
24. Ghareh Chamani, J., Papadopoulos, D., Papamanthou, C., Jalili, R.: New constructions for forward and backward private symmetric searchable encryption. In: ACM CCS 2018, pp. 1038–1055 (2018)
25. Götzfried, J., Eckert, M., Schinzel, S., Müller, T.: Cache attacks on intel SGX. In: EuroSec 2017 (2017)
26. Gruss, D., Lipp, M., Schwarz, M., Fellner, R., Maurice, C., Mangard, S.: KASLR is dead: long live KASLR. In: Bodden, E., Payer, M., Athanasopoulos, E. (eds.) ESSoS 2017. LNCS, vol. 10379, pp. 161–176. Springer, Cham (2017). https://doi.org/10.1007/978-3-319-62105-0_11
27. Gruss, D., Lettner, J., Schuster, F., Ohrimenko, O., Haller, I., Costa, M.: Strong and efficient cache side-channel protection using hardware transactional memory. In: USENIX Security 2017, pp. 217–233 (2017)
28. Hoang, T., Ozmen, M.O., Jang, Y., Yavuz, A.A.: Hardware-supported ORAM in effect: practical oblivious search and update on very large dataset. In: PET 2019 (2019)
29. Intel: Intel processors voltage settings modification advisory (2020). https://www.intel.com/content/www/us/en/security-center/advisory/intel-sa-00289.html
30. Kamara, S., Papamanthou, C., Roeder, T.: Dynamic searchable symmetric encryption. In: ACM CCS 2012, pp. 965–976 (2012)

31. Kuvaiskii, D., et al.: SGXBOUNDS: memory safety for shielded execution. In: EuroSys 2017, pp. 205–221 (2017)
32. Lai, S., et al.: Result pattern hiding searchable encryption for conjunctive queries. In: ACM CCS 2018, pp. 745–762 (2018)
33. Lee, J., et al.: Hacking in darkness: return-oriented programming against secure enclaves. In: USENIX Security 2017, pp. 523–539 (2017)
34. Marshall, A., Howard, M., Bugher, G., Harden, B.: Security best practices for developing windows azure applications. Microsoft Corp **42**, 12–15 (2010)
35. McKeen, F., et al.: Intel® software guard extensions (intel® SGX) support for dynamic memory management inside an enclave. In: HASP 2016 (2016)
36. Mishra, P., Poddar, R., Chen, J., Chiesa, A., Popa, R.A.: Oblix: an efficient oblivious search index. In: IEEE S&P 2018 (2018)
37. Murdock, K., et al.: Plundervolt: software-based fault injection attacks against intel SGX. In: IEEE S&P 2020 (2020)
38. Ohrimenko, O., et al.: Oblivious multi-party machine learning on trusted processors. In: USENIX Security 2016 (2016)
39. Oleksenko, O., et al.: Varys: Protecting SGX enclaves from practical side-channel attacks. In: USENIX ATC 2018 (2018)
40. Osvik, D.A., Shamir, A., Tromer, E.: Cache attacks and countermeasures: the case of AES. In: Topics in Cryptology - CT-RSA 2006 (2006)
41. Rane, A., Lin, C., Tiwari, M.: Raccoon: closing digital side-channels through obfuscated execution. In: USENIX Security 2015 (2015)
42. Sasy, S., Gorbunov, S., Fletcher, C.W.: Zerotrace: oblivious memory primitives from intel SGX. In: NDSS 2018 (2018)
43. Schwarz, M., Weiser, S., Gruss, D., Maurice, C., Mangard, S.: Malware guard extension: using SGX to conceal cache attacks. In: Polychronakis, M., Meier, M. (eds.) DIMVA 2017. LNCS, vol. 10327, pp. 3–24. Springer, Cham (2017). https://doi.org/10.1007/978-3-319-60876-1_1
44. Seo, J., et al.: SGX-shield: enabling address space layout randomization for SGX programs. In: NDSS (2017)
45. Shih, M.W., Lee, S., Kim, T., Peinado, M.: T-SGX: eradicating controlled-channel attacks against enclave programs. In: NDSS (2017)
46. Shinde, S., Chua, Z.L., Narayanan, V., Saxena, P.: Preventing page faults from telling your secrets. In: ACM AsiaCCS 2016 (2016)
47. Sinha, R., Rajamani, S., Seshia, S.A.: A compiler and verifier for page access oblivious computation. In: ESEC/FSE 2017 (2017)
48. Song, D., Wagner, D., Perrig, A.: Practical techniques for searches on encrypted data. In: IEEE S&P 2000, pp. 44–55 (2000)
49. Stefanov, E., Papamanthou, C., Shi, E.: Practical dynamic searchable symmetric encryption with small leakage. In: NDSS 2014 (2014)
50. Sun, S.F., et al.: Practical backward-secure searchable encryption from symmetric puncturable encryption. In: ACM CCS 2018 (2018)
51. Van Bulck, J., et al.: Foreshadow: extracting the keys to the intel SGX kingdom with transient out-of-order execution. In: USENIX Security 2018 (2018)
52. Vinayagamurthy, D., Gribov, A., Gorbunov, S.: Stealthdb: A scalable encrypted database with full SQL query support. In: PET 2019 (2019)
53. Vo, V., Lai, S., Yuan, X., Sun, S.F., Nepal, S., Liu, J.K.: Accelerating forward and backward private searchable encryption using trusted execution. In: ACNS 2020 (2020)
54. Wang, W., et al.: Leaky cauldron on the dark land: understanding memory side-channel hazards in SGX. In: CCS 2017 (2017)

55. Xu, Y., Cui, W., Peinado, M.: Controlled-channel attacks: deterministic side channels for untrusted operating systems. In: IEEE S&P 2015 (2015)
56. Yarom, Y., Falkner, K.: FLUSH+RELOAD: a high resolution, low noise, L3 cache side-channel attack. In: USENIX Security 2014 (2014)
57. Zhang, Y., Katz, J., Papamanthou, C.: All your queries are belong to us: The power of file-injection attacks on searchable encryption. In: USENIX Security 2016 (2016)
58. Zhao, W., Lu, K., Qi, Y., Qi, S.: Mptee: bringing flexible and efficient memory protection to intel SGX. In: EuroSys 2020 (2020)
59. Zheng, W., Dave, A., Beekman, J.G., Popa, R.A., Gonzalez, J.E., Stoica, I.: Opaque: an oblivious and encrypted distributed analytics platform. In: USENIX NSDI 2017 (2017)

Secure and Fair Protocols

CECMLP: New Cipher-Based Evaluating Collaborative Multi-layer Perceptron Scheme in Federated Learning

Yuqi Chen[1,2], Xiaoyu Zhang[1,2(✉)], Yi Xie[1], Meixia Miao[3], and Xu Ma[4]

[1] State Key Laboratory of Integrated Service Networks (ISN), Xidian University, Xi'an 710071, China
xiaoyuzhang@xidian.edu.cn
yuqichen,xieyi@stu.xidian.edu.cn
[2] State Key Laboratory of Cryptology, P. O. Box 5159, Beijing 100878, China
[3] School of Cyberspace Security, Xi'an University of Posts and Telecommunications, Xi'an 710121, China
[4] School of Cyber Science and Engineering, Qufu Normal University, Qufu 273165, China
xma@qfnu.edu.cn

Abstract. Due to the large volume of available datasets and powerful computing infrastructures, federated learning has been widely explored in many scenarios, e.g. medical screening, and image processing. It refers to all participants to jointly learn shared models under the orchestration of the server without exposing their datasets. In federated learning, since the data qualities of the participants are extremely diverse, reliability is used to measure the data qualities of the participants. To make the learning task liberally and non-discriminative, participants' reliability privacy related to their data quality should be well preserved. However, the existing work assumed that the reliability of participants is transparent for the server provider, resulting in a severe challenge in practical applications. To thwart this challenge, we propose a novel federated learning scheme, which prevents each participant's training set privacy and reliability privacy from being revealed to the public. Moreover, to further reduce the impact of unreliable participants and improve training efficiency, we design a cipher-based reliability weighted method to differentiate and intensify different contributions of the (un)reliable participants for joint model training. Security analysis shows that our proposed scheme can achieve the desired security requirements. Moreover, extensive performance evaluations demonstrate that our design achieves higher accuracy and is more robust against unreliable participants than conventional federated learning.

Keywords: Federated learning · Privacy preservation · Cipher-based weighted method

K. Sako and N. O. Tippenhauer (Eds.): ACNS 2021, LNCS 12726, pp. 79–99, 2021.
https://doi.org/10.1007/978-3-030-78372-3_4

1   Introduction

In recent years, a large amount of data has been generated and released for driving neoteric scientific discoveries. Hence, effective, rational and responsible utilization of these massive data has become a huge challenge. Fortunately, thanks to the powerful computing infrastructures, collaborative machine learning has provided a novel technique for dealing with these large amounts of data. The term "collaborative learning" refers to a new learning mode in which participants at various performance levels work together toward a common classifier training by leveraging their own datasets. Then, the well-trained classifier will make an accurate prediction on the new input sample, powering its widespread use in an extremely wide variety of applications such as image processing [13,14,17,18], smart medical [2,3,26], and game playing [22,31]. However, these user-related data are often crowdsourced from sensors deployed on wearable or mobile devices, comprising of personal sensitive information, *e.g.*, location, medical history anamnesis, personally identifiable information, and private images, etc. Therefore, it will lead to critical privacy concerns if we directly share and use these data in collaborative deep learning without any protection measures.

Federated learning, introduced by Mcmahan et al. [8] in 2016, provides a promising solution to the privacy leakage problems in collaborative learning. It refers to a learning setting where many participants collaboratively train a shared classifier under the orchestration of a parameter server while keeping the training data decentralized and privately. Concretely, in federated learning, all participants duplicate a global classifier and update it by iteratively minimizing the loss function over local datasets over many epochs, and then they only submit the model parameters or the calculated gradients in non-plaintext form to the server. Henceforth, a longstanding goal pursued by cryptography and machine learning research communities is how to efficiently and effectively complete the above learning process without revealing sensitive information concerning to the participants. [6,7,20,21,23,24,33].

To this end, extensive privacy-preserving techniques, including secure multi-party computation (SMC) [12], differential privacy (DP) [9], and homomorphic encryption (HC) [25], have been fully utilized into federated learning algorithms. Very recently, to protect the whole gradients as well as reduce the communication overheads, Shokri et al. [29] proposed a privacy-preserving deep learning scheme, which allowed participants to share a small portion of gradients with a parameter server. However, it had been proved by Aono et al. [6] that sharing a portion of gradients also results in privacy leakage. Besides, Aono et al. [6] designed a privacy-preserving deep learning scheme via additively homomorphic encryption technique. Compared with the scheme in [29], Geyer et al. [10] proposed a differentially private federated learning approach that can maintain client-level differential privacy at the cost of a minor model performance loss. So far, these approaches are only suitable for the scenario where all the participants contribute the same data quality to the joint model training. Nevertheless, in real-world federated learning, the training data generated and collected from a variety of participants differ in quality and reliability. The reason is that different terminal devices have diverse abilities to generate raw data, and it may occur some extraordinary errors during data collection, storage, processing, and aggregation. Zhao et al. [35] firstly took the unreliable participant *i.e.,* participants with low quality data, into account in collaborative learning. In order to make the learning procedure fair and non-discriminative, reliability privacy of participants related to their data quality can be regarded as one of privacy concerns that need to be protected. Besides, functional mechanism [34] is applied to perturb the loss function of model training to avoid potential privacy leakage from sharing gradients.

Although the method proposed in [35] is capable for preserving each participant's training data with taking the existence of the unreliable participants into account, there still exist some key defects: 1) while the data quality privacy of each participant cannot be inferred by other participants, it is transparent for the parameter server, especially for the malicious server. The parameter server may reveal the data quality privact of the participant with low data quality. This may cause unfairness and discrimination to participants with low data quality in the learning process. 2) In the case discussed earlier, the method of calculating reliability score used in [35] to improve training efficiency is invalid since that data quality of each participant is also non-transparent for the cloud server. 3) Based on DP technique, privacy-preserving collaborative deep learning with unreliable participants introduces a certain model accuracy loss, which may result in significant performance degradation in some specific domains.

1.1   Our Contributions

Our main contributions can be summarized as below.

- We propose a participants' reliability privacy-preserving federated learning scheme with unreliable participants based on homomorphic encryption technique. Except for the training dataset and its corresponding gradients, the data quality, *i.e.,* reliability privacy of each participant can also be preserved, decoupling the learning process being unfair and discriminative.
- We design a novel cipher-based gradients weighted method which makes participants dedicate discrepant contributions to the joint model training, relying on their private data quality without revealing them. In this way, our design has an advantage over conventional federated learning in performance.
- We conduct extensive experimental study on our design by using three benchmark datasets and the results confirm that our proposed scheme is effective and efficient.

1.2   Related Work

Privacy-preserving machine learning attracts more attentions from both the cryptography and machine learning communities. Previous works have concentrated on preserving the training data privacy and model privacy by leveraging cryptographic techniques such as garbled circuit, secure multi-party computation and homomorphic encryption. With the ever-growing volume of data generated, machine learning based on cloud computing has been widely explored for its available infrastructure and feasibility in massive data learning. In [11], Gilad-Bachrach et al. proposed CryptoNets, which allows to conduct model training and prediction on encrypted data, but it requires considerable computation resources. Mohassel et al. [20] presented SecureML based on secure two-party computation, implementing a general system for privacy-preserving machine learning with a two-server model. Based on SIMD, Liu et al. [19] proposed MiniONN, which converts any existing neural networks to an oblivious neural network for prediction task. Riazi et al. [28] presented a hybrid secure computation framework for machine learning applications, named Chameleon. Besides, this method introduces a trusted third-party. Then, Juevekar et al. [15] improved the scheme in [28] by exploring effective use of packed ciphertexts.

Differential privacy also can be utilized to perturb the model parameters [27], the objective function [35], or the calculated gradients [29] in collaborative deep learning in order to hide the original training data privacy. Aggregation of independently trained neural networks using DP is presented in [27]. Unfortunately, directly averaging neural-network parameters does not necessarily contribute to a better shared model. In [29], participants only contributed a small portion of gradients to the joint model training, targeting at reduce communication overhead. The differential privacy is achieved by adding noises to truncated weights. However, the total privacy budget is increasing with the numbers of parameters. Zhao et al. [35] proposed a privacy-preserving collaborative deep learning, which firstly takes the data quality privacy into consideration. While the data quality privacy of each participant cannot be inferred by other participants, it is still transparent for the parameter server. Besides, all the above solutions inevitable result in utility loss by leveraging DP technique.

1.3   Organization

The rest of this paper is organized as follows. Section 2 presents some preliminary knowledge and tools used in this paper, followed by a description of the system model and security requirements in Sect. 3. In Sect. 4, we give a concrete construction for the CECMLP scheme. Security analysis and extensive performance evaluations are elaborated in Sect. 5 and Sect. 6, respectively. Finally, Sect. 7 concludes this paper and discusses future work.

2   Preliminaries

In this section, some preliminaries about privacy-preserving collaborative deep learning [29], homomorphic cryptosystem [25], and cipher-based multi-layer perceptron (CMLP) are presented. The key notations defined in this paper are shown in Table 1.

Table 1. Key notations

Notations	Description
W_{shared}	Parameters of the shared model
W_{new}	New parameters of the shared model computed in the **Eval** Phase
W_i	Local model parameters of the participant i
w_i	Local model parameters in integer form of the participant i
G_i	Local model gradients of the participant i
D_e	Evaluating dataset
N	Number of the participants
E	Size of the evaluating dataset
d	Preserved precision of floating-point numbers

2.1   Privacy-Preserving Collaborative Deep Learning

Privacy-preserving collaborative deep learning enables several data owners to train a common model collaboratively with their local datasets keeping privately. In general, the system model of privacy-preserving collaborative deep learning consists of a parameter server and multiple participants. In this setting, the parameter server keeps a public shared model and the participants own the corresponding duplicate model as well as their local private datasets. The following procedures are repeatedly conducted to train the shared model with the contribution from the participants' private datasets.

Privacy-Preserving Collaborative Deep Learning

1. The participants download the parameters W_{shared} from the parameter server and update the local parameters $W_i(1 \leq i \leq N)$ with W_{shared}, where N represent the number of the participants.
2. The participants train the local model on their local datasets by conducting stochastic gradient descent (SGD) algorithm, *i.e.*, $W_i = W_i + G_i(1 \leq i \leq N)$, where the gradients $G_i(1 \leq i \leq N)$ are the vectors of increments of local parameters in the training epoch.
3. The participants upload the local parameters $W_i(1 \leq i \leq N)$ to the parameter server. On receiving the local parameters from the participants, the parameter server updates the global shared model. For averaging method, the global model is updated by adding the average of all parameters, *i.e.*, $W_{shared} = \frac{1}{N}\sum_{i=1}^{N} W_i = W_{shared} + \frac{1}{N}\sum_{i=1}^{N} G_i$.

2.2   Homomorphic Encryption

Homomorphic encryption is a cryptosystem that allows meaningful operations on ciphertext. When decrypting the result of this computation, the plaintext matches the result of operations as if they had been performed on plaintext. Paillier cryptosystem [25] is an additively homomorphic encryption scheme, while does not support homomorphic multiplication. We extend Paillier and design a novel homomorphic encryption algorithm, which support encrypting floating-point number and performing homomorphic operations needed in our work. The homomorphic encryption algorithm is formalized as $HE = (\mathbf{KeyGen}, \mathbf{Enc},$ $\mathbf{Dec}, \mathbf{Add}, \mathbf{Mul}, \mathbf{Max}, \mathbf{Equal})$.

- $(pk, sk) \leftarrow \mathbf{KeyGen}(1^\lambda)$: $\mathbf{KeyGen}$ algorithm returns a key pair (pk, sk) which is also a Paillier key pair and $pk = (n, g)$, where n is the modulus and $g \in \mathbb{Z}_{n^2}^*$.
- $c \leftarrow \mathbf{Enc}_{pk}(M)$: To encrypt a floating-point number, the floating-point number is encoded into an integer firstly. Then, by encrypting the integer with Paillier public key pk, the algorithm outputs the ciphertext c.
- $M \leftarrow \mathbf{Dec}_{sk}(c)$: $\mathbf{Dec}$ decrypts the ciphertext c to obtain an integer plaintext. Then, the integer plaintext is decoded into a floating-point number.
- $c' \leftarrow \mathbf{Add}(c_1, c_2)$: $\mathbf{Add}$ enables homomorphic addition of two ciphertext c_1 and c_2.
- $c' \leftarrow \mathbf{Prod}(c_1, m_2)$: On inputting the ciphertext c_1 and the plaintext m_2, homomorphic production result c is returned, s.t. $\mathbf{Dec}_{sk}(c') = m_2\mathbf{Dec}_{sk}(c_1)$.
- $c' \leftarrow \mathbf{Mul}(c_1, c_2)$: $\mathbf{Mul}$ is a homomorphic multiplication protocol which enables one to obtain the homomorphic multiplication result with the help of private key owner without revealing the result.
- $c' \leftarrow \mathbf{Max}(c_1, c_2)$: $\mathbf{Max}$ is a protocol which enables one to obtain the ciphertext which has a larger corresponding plaintext.
- $c' \leftarrow \mathbf{Equal}(c_1, c_2)$: $\mathbf{Equal}$ is a protocol which enables one to obtain the ciphertext of the result c' by comparing c_1 and c_2, where $c' = \mathbf{Enc}_{pk}(1)$ if $\mathbf{Dec}_{sk}(c_1) = \mathbf{Dec}_{sk}(c_2)$, $c' = \mathbf{Enc}_{pk}(0)$ otherwise.

2.3   Cipher-Based Multi-Layer Perceptron

CMLP is a model transformed from a multi-layer perceptron (MLP) by encrypting the parameters of the MLP. Holding a CMLP, one can exploit the CMLP to make a prediction on an encrypted input data and obtain an encrypted confidence vector.

A multi-layer perceptron generally consists of several fully connected layers, which are composed of several neurons. Let x and y be the input and output of one neural layer respectively. Each neuron takes outputs of $|X|$ neurons in the previous layer as its input, where $|X|$ is the number of neurons of the previous layer. Then, the output of ith neuron in the layer can be formalized as Eq. (1), where y_i represents the output value of ith neuron, w_{ij} represents the weight of the connection between jth neuron in the previous layer and ith neuron, x_j represents the output of jth neuron in the previous layer, b_i represents bias of the neuron, and f is the activation function. The purpose of using activation function is to introduce non-linear to the model. In this work, we apply rectified linear unit (ReLU) $f(x) = \text{ReLU}(x) = \max(0, x)$ as the activation function of MLP model.

$$y_i = f(\sum_{j=0}^{|X|} w_{ij}x_j + b_i) \qquad (1)$$

CMLP has the same structure as the original model. The input, output, and parameters are encrypted exploiting HE represented in Sect. 2.2. For each layer, the activation of neuron is shown as Eq. (2), where $\bar{y}_i = \mathbf{Enc}_{pk}(y_i)$ is encrypted activation, $\bar{w}_{ij} = \mathbf{Enc}_{pk}(w_{ij})$ is encrypted parameter, $\bar{x}_j = \mathbf{Enc}_{pk}(x_j)$ is encrypted input, $\bar{b}_i = \mathbf{Enc}_{pk}(b_i))$ is encrypted bias, $\oplus$ is homomorphic addition $\mathbf{Add}$, and $\otimes$ is homomorphic multiplication $\mathbf{Mul}$, $\bar{f}$ is homomorphic activation function. In this work, we design a homomorphic ReLU function $\bar{f}(\bar{x}) = \mathbf{Max}(\mathbf{Enc}_{pk}(0), \bar{x})$, which is implement by the $\mathbf{Max}$ presented in 2.2.

$$\bar{y}_i = \bar{f}(\sum_{j=0}^{|X|} \bar{w}_{ij} \otimes \bar{x}_j \oplus \bar{b}_i) \qquad (2)$$

Based on the above homomorphic encryption algorithm HE, the definition of CMLP is formalized as $CMLP = (\mathbf{Pred}, \mathbf{Eval})$.

- $\mathbf{Enc}_{pk}(\hat{y}) \leftarrow \mathbf{Pred}(\mathbf{Enc}_{pk}(W), \mathbf{Enc}_{pk}(x))$: On inputting the encrypted model parameter $\mathbf{Enc}_{pk}(W)$ and the encrypted input data $\mathbf{Enc}_{pk}(x)$, $\mathbf{Pred}$ computes the encrypted confidence vector $\mathbf{Enc}_{pk}(\hat{y})$.
- $N_c \leftarrow \mathbf{Eval}(\mathbf{Enc}_{pk}(W), \mathbf{Enc}_{pk}(D))$: Given the encrypted model parameter $\mathbf{Enc}_{pk}(W)$, on inputting the encrypted dataset D, $\mathbf{Eval}$ returns the encrypted correct number N_c of parameter W.

3   System Model and Security Requirements

The system model and security requirements of our proposed cipher-based evaluating collaborative multi-layer perceptron (CECMLP) training scheme are introduced in this section.

3.1   System Model

As shown in Fig. 1, the system model of the proposed CECMLP consists of three entities, including the parameter server, the participants, and the evaluator.

- **Parameter server.** The main task of the parameter server is to send the shared model parameters to all the participants and update the shared model parameters on receiving aggregated parameters sent from the evaluator. Note that the parameter server send the shared model parameters in plaintext form in Fig. 1. Optionally, some security protocol (*e.g.*, SSL) can be used to prevent eavesdropping by the adversary when the parameter server sending the shared model parameters.

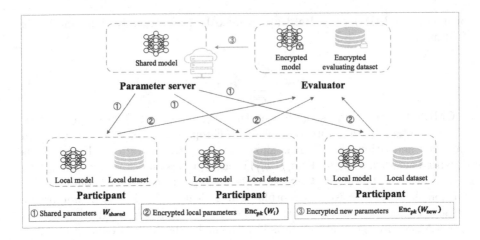

Fig. 1. System model of CECMLP

- **Participants.** The participants have local datasets which are used to train the shared model collaboratively. Each iteration mainly consists of two phases: 1) The participants update the local model parameters with the shared model parameters received from the parameter server and train local model over their own datasets. 2) After training, the participants encrypt the local model parameters with the public key of the parameter server and send it to the evaluator. We remark that the difference in data quality among the participants is taken into consideration in this work.
- **Evaluator.** The evaluator holds a small evaluating dataset collected and encrypted by the parameter server. In order to ensure the accuracy of evaluation, the distribution of the evaluating dataset should be independent and identically distributed with the real data. When collecting the encrypted parameters from the participants, the evaluator validates the encrypted parameters exploiting the encrypted evaluating set and obtains the encrypted reliability scores for the parameters. New model parameters are obtained by aggregating the participants' parameters with the reliability score as weight. When the new model parameters are computed, the evaluator sends them to the parameter server.

3.2   Definition of CECMLP

Definition 1. *The cipher-based evaluating collaborative multi-layer perceptron CECMLP =* (**Setup, Download, Training, Evaluate, Update**) *consists of the following five phases.*

- **Setup.** The parameter server initializes the shared model and generates its key pair and encrypts the evaluating set with its public key. Then, it sends the encrypted evaluating set to the evaluator.

- **Download**. The participants download the current shared model parameters from the parameter server and update their local models.
- **Training**. The participants train the local models over their local datasets. After training, the participants encrypt the local parameters with the public key of the parameter server and send them to the evaluator.
- **Evaluate**. When received the encrypted parameters of the participants, the evaluator computes the reliability scores of the participants via exploiting HE and $CMLP$. Then, the evaluator computes the new parameters and sends it to the parameter server.
- **Update**. When received the new parameters, the parameter server updates the current shared model parameters.

3.3   Security Requirements

In our proposed CECMLP scheme, all three entities are honest-but-curious, which means that they will perform obeying the protocol honestly, but they are curious about the private information of other participants and they can exploit the imformation they hold to speculate on participants' privacy information. We assume that either of them are non-colluding. The security requirements we target at achieving are presented below.

- **Dataset privacy.** The private dataset owned by the participants are not directly shared with others in collaborative learning procedure.
- **Gradient privacy.** Utilizing the gradients that calculated via training on the local dataset, membership inference attack and inversion attack can be performed. Therefore, the model parameters of the participants should be encrypted before being uploaded to the evaluator to prevent gradient leakage.
- **Participants' reliability privacy.** The reliability of the participants represent the quality of their local datasets. In CECMLP, the accuracy of the uploaded parameters represents the reliability of this parameters. reliability of the participants contain data distribution, data quality and other private information about the local datasets. Therefore, the reliability of the participants should be treated as their private information.

4   The Proposed Construction

In this section, we illustrate our proposed cipher-based evaluating collaborative multi-layer perceptron (CECMLP) scheme.

4.1   High Description

In this paper, we focus on reducing the influence of the unreliable participants in federated learning while protecting participants' reliability privacy. An obvious method to make good use of the participants with diverse abilities is that the global model considers the reliability of the participants as the weights for adopting the parameters uploaded by them. However, it is unpractical to predict the data quality of the participants since the participants would not directly share their private data set with others. Therefore, the reliability of participants are unknown to all entities. To this end, we propose CECMLP.

The main idea is that the reliability of the participants are evaluated before computing the new parameters. Concretely, to avoid revealing the participants' reliability privacy to the public, the calculated local model parameters are encrypted before being collected. Then, based on HE technique and the proposed CMLP, an evaluator is introduced to evaluate the reliability of the participants. In this way, the evaluator is capable of assessing the reliability of all the participants without decryption. Moreover, the evaluator utilizes cipher-based reliability weighted method to aggregate and compute the new model parameters, and then sends them to the parameter server for the shared model renewal. Therefore, the proposed CECMLP can guarantee the reliability privacy of the participants, and it is robust against the unreliable participants.

4.2 Construction of CECMLP

- **Setup.** The parameter server generates (pk, sk) as its key pair by running **KeyGen** algorithm on inputting the security parameter λ. Then, the parameter server: 1) initializes the parameters of the shared model randomly, 2) encrypts every examples in the evaluating dataset D_e using private key sk and sends $\mathbf{Enc}_{pk}(D_e)$ to the evaluator. Encrypting an example (x, y) represents encrypting the data x and its label y, *i.e.*, $(\mathbf{Enc}_{pk}(x), \mathbf{Enc}_{pk}(y))$.
- **Download.** The participants download the current shared model parameters W_{shared} via SSL protocol. When receiving the shared model, the participants update the local models with the received parameters W_{shared}.
- **Training.** The participants update the local model parameters by training over their local datasets. After training, the local model parameters $W_i = W_{shared} + G_i (1 \leq i \leq N)$ are obtained. Then, the participants encrypt the local model parameters $W_i (1 \leq i \leq N)$ with pk and send $\mathbf{Enc}_{pk}(W_i)(1 \leq i \leq N)$ to the evaluator. Floating-point vector W_i is encoded into integer vector, such that $w_i = \lfloor 10^d W_i \rfloor$, where d is an integer. For simplicity, we assume that floating-point number only has d decimal. Then, we have $w_i = 10^d W_i$. When w_i has been computed, $\widehat{\mathbf{Enc}}$ is run to encrypt w_i and the ciphertext $\mathbf{Enc}_{pk}(W_i)$ is obtained, where $\widehat{\mathbf{Enc}}$ represents Paillier encryption. Therefore, we have $\mathbf{Enc}_{pk}(W_i) = \widehat{\mathbf{Enc}}_{pk}(10^d w_i)$. Similarly, when decrypting $\mathbf{Enc}_{pk}(W_i)$, integer plaintext w_i is computed firstly by exploiting $\widehat{\mathbf{Dec}}$, which represents Paillier decryption, then the floating-point plaintext W_i can be obtained by calculating $W_i = \frac{w_i}{10^d}$.

- **Evaluate.** When receiving the ciphertexts from all the participants, the evaluator evaluates $\mathbf{Enc}_{pk}(W_i)(1 \leq i \leq N)$ on the encrypted evaluating dataset $\mathbf{Enc}_{pk}(D_e)$ and obtains the reliability scores of the participants. Then, the evaluator computes the new shared model parameters based on the parameters and the reliability scores of all the participants. To aggregate the new shared model parameters, the evaluator processes the following steps:

Algorithm 1. Mul protocol

Sign subprotocol

Input: S_0 holds $c = \mathbf{Enc}_{pk}(M)$. S_1 holds sk.
Output: S_0 obtains the encrypted sign $\widehat{\mathbf{Enc}}_{pk}(s)$
$\quad S_0$:
1: Randomly choose r, such that $1 \le r \le \frac{n}{2 \cdot 10^d}$.
2: Compute $c' = \mathbf{Enc}_{pk}(rM)$ and send c' to S_1.
$\quad S_1$:
3: Decrypt c' to get rM. If $rM > 0$, let $s = 1$. If $rM == 0$, let $s = 0$. If $rM < 0$, let $s = -1 = n - 1 \mod n$.
4: Compute and send $\widehat{\mathbf{Enc}}_{pk}(s)$ to S_0.

SecMul subprotocol

Input: S_0 holds $c_1 = \widehat{\mathbf{Enc}}_{pk}(m_1)$, $c_2 = \widehat{\mathbf{Enc}}_{pk}(m_2)$. S_1 holds sk.
Output: S_0 obtains $c = \widehat{\mathbf{Enc}}_{pk}(m_1 m_2)$
$\quad S_0$:
1: Randomly choose r_1, r_2, such that $1 \le r_1, r_2 \le n - 1$.
2: Compute $c'_1 = \widehat{\mathbf{Enc}}_{pk}(m_1 + r_1)$ and $c'_2 = \widehat{\mathbf{Enc}}_{pk}(m_2 + r_2)$. Then, send c'_1, c'_2 to S_1.
$\quad S_1$:
3: Decrypt c'_1 and c'_2 to get $m_1 + r_1$ and $m_2 + r_2$.
4: Compute $t = (m_1 + r_1)(m_2 + r_2) \mod n$. Then, encrypt t with pk and send $\widehat{\mathbf{Enc}}_{pk}(t)$ to S_0.
$\quad S_0$:
5: Compute $\widehat{\mathbf{Enc}}_{pk}(-m_1 r_2)$, $\widehat{\mathbf{Enc}}_{pk}(-m_2 r_1)$, and $\widehat{\mathbf{Enc}}_{pk}(-r_1 r_2)$.
6: Utilize homomorphic addition to compute $c = \widehat{\mathbf{Enc}}_{pk}(t - m_1 r_2 - m_2 r_1 - r_1 r_2) = \widehat{\mathbf{Enc}}_{pk}(m_1 m_2)$.

Mul protocol

Input: S_0 holds $c_1 = \mathbf{Enc}_{pk}(M_1)$, $c_2 = \mathbf{Enc}_{pk}(M_2)$. S_1 holds sk.
Output: S_0 obtains $c = \mathbf{Enc}_{pk}(M_1 M_2)$
$\quad S_0$:
1: Run **SecMul** on c_1 and c_2 with S_1 to get $c' = \widehat{\mathbf{Enc}}_{pk}(t)$, where $t = 10^d M_1 10^d M_2$.
2: Run **Sign** on c' with S_1 to get $\widehat{\mathbf{Enc}}_{pk}(s)$.
3: Run **SecMul** on c' and $\widehat{\mathbf{Enc}}_{pk}(s)$ with S_1 to obtain $\widehat{\mathbf{Enc}}_{pk}(st)$
4: Randomly choose R, such that $1 \le R \le \frac{n}{10^d} - 2$.
5: Compute $c'_{masked} = \widehat{\mathbf{Enc}}_{pk}(st + 10^d R)$ and send c'_{masked} to S_1.
$\quad S_1$:
6: Receive c'_{masked} and decrypt it to get $st + 10^d R$.
7: Compute $\frac{st + 10^d R}{10^d} = \frac{st}{10^d} + R$.
8: Send $\widehat{\mathbf{Enc}}_{pk}(\frac{st}{10^d} + R)$ to S_0.
$\quad S_0$:
9: Run **Add** on $\widehat{\mathbf{Enc}}_{pk}(\frac{st}{10^d} + R)$ and $\widehat{\mathbf{Enc}}_{pk}(-R)$ to obtain $\widehat{\mathbf{Enc}}_{pk}(\frac{st}{10^d})$.
10: Run **SecMul** on $\widehat{\mathbf{Enc}}_{pk}(s)$ and $\widehat{\mathbf{Enc}}_{pk}(\frac{st}{10^d})$ to obtain $c = \widehat{\mathbf{Enc}}_{pk}(\frac{s^2 t}{10^d}) = \widehat{\mathbf{Enc}}_{pk}(10^d M_1 M_2) = \mathbf{Enc}_{pk}(M_1 M_2)$.

Algorithm 2. Max protocol

Input: S_0 holds $c_1 = \mathbf{Enc}_{pk}(M_1)$, $c_2 = \mathbf{Enc}_{pk}(M_2)$. S_1 holds sk.
Output: S_0 obtains $c' = \arg\max_i \mathbf{Dec}_{sk}(c_i)$

S_0:
1: Compute $c_{dif} = \mathbf{Add}(c_1, c_2)$.
2: Compute $\bar{c}_{dif} = \mathbf{Prod}(c_{dif}, r)$, where r is a random integer.
3: Send $\bar{c}_{dif}$ to S_1.
   S_1:
4: Decrypt $\bar{c}_{dif}$. If $\mathbf{Dec}_{sk} \geq 0$ send $s = 1$ to S_0, else send $s = -1$ to S_0.
   S_0: If $s = 1$, $c' = c_1$, else $c' = c_2$

- The evaluator exploits **Eval** to obtain ciphertext of correct number $N_{c,i}(1 \leq i \leq N)$, which are the ciphertexts of the numbers that the CMLP with parameters $\mathbf{Enc}_{pk}(W_i)(1 \leq i \leq N)$ correctly predict on $\mathbf{Enc}_{pk}(D_e)$. For each encrypted example $(\mathbf{Enc}_{pk}(x), \mathbf{Enc}_{pk}(y))$, the evaluator computes the ciphertext of confidence vector $\mathbf{Enc}_{pk}(\hat{y})$. The computations of each layer in CMLP is processed as Eq. 2, where the **Mul** and **Max** is represented in Algorithm 1 and Algorithm 2. On obtaining the ciphertext of confidence vector, the evaluator utilizes **Max** protocol to find the prediction of CMLP $p = \arg\max_j \hat{y}_j (1 \leq i \leq C)$, where C is the number of classification classes. To compare the prediction of CMLP p with the encrypted label $\mathbf{Enc}_{pk}(y)$, in the same token, the evaluator computes $c_p = \mathbf{Prod}(\mathbf{Add}(\mathbf{Enc}_{pk}(p), -\mathbf{Enc}_{pk}(y)), r)$ and sends c_p to the parameter server, the parameter server decrypts c_p and sends comparison result to the evaluator. If $\mathbf{Dec}_{sk}(c_p) = 0$, the parameter server sends $\widehat{\mathbf{Enc}}_{pk}(1)$, otherwise the parameter server sends $\widehat{\mathbf{Enc}}_{pk}(0)$ otherwise. By computing the summation of comparison results for all the encrypted examples in evaluating set, $N_{c,i}(1 \leq i \leq N)$ can be obtained.
- The ciphertexts of correct numbers $N_{c,i}(1 \leq i \leq N)$ are not used directly as reliability score. To compute reliability score $s_i(1 \leq i \leq N)$ based on $N_{c,i}(1 \leq i \leq N)$, the evaluator finds the homomorphic maximum $N_{c,max}$ and minimum $N_{c,min}$ in $N_{c,i}(1 \leq i \leq N)$, where $max = \arg\max_i \mathbf{Dec}_{sk}(N_{c,i})$ and $min = \arg\min_i \mathbf{Dec}_{sk}(N_{c,i})$. Then, the evaluator computes homomorphic difference D between $N_{c,max}$ and $N_{c,min}$ utilizing **Add**. After that, for each participant i, the reliability score s_i is computed as $s_i = \mathbf{Add}(\mathbf{Add}(N_{c,i}, -N_{c,min}), D)$.
- When the encrypted reliability scores of all the participants have been calculated, the evaluator aggregates all the encrypted parameters with reliability scores as weights to obtain the ciphertext of new parameters $\mathbf{Enc}_{pk}(W_{new}) = \sum_{i=1}^{N} \mathbf{Mul}(s_i, \mathbf{Enc}_{pk}(W_i))$ and sends it to the parameter server. The homomorphic sum of all reliability scores of the participants $s_{sum} = \sum_{i=1}^{N} s_i$ is also sent to the parameter server.
- **Update.** On receiving $\mathbf{Enc}_{pk}(W_{new})$ and s_{sum}, the parameter server decrypts the ciphertexts to obtain W_{new} and $\mathbf{Dec}_{sk}(s_{sum})$. Then, the parameter server

computes the current shared model parameters as $W_{shared} = \frac{W_{new}}{\mathbf{Dec}_{sk}(s_{sum})} = \sum_{i=1}^{N} \frac{s_i}{\sum_{j=1}^{N} s_j} W_i$.

Algorithm 3. Compute the reliability scores of the participants

---

Input: Set of the encrypted parameters of the participants $\{\mathbf{Enc}_{pk}(W_i)|1 \leq i \leq N\}$, the encrypted evaluating dataset $\mathbf{Enc}_{pk}(D_e)$
Output: The reliability scores of the participants
1: **for** each $1 \leq i \leq N$ **do**
2:    Compute $N_{c,i} = \mathbf{Eval}(\mathbf{Enc}_{pk}(W_i), \mathbf{Enc}_{pk}(D_e))$
3: **end for**
4: Find the homomorphic max $N_{c,max}$ in $\{N_{c,i} | 1 \leq i \leq N\}$ utilizing **Max**.
5: Find the homomorphic min $N_{c,min}$ in $\{N_{c,i} | 1 \leq i \leq N\}$ utilizing **Max**.
6: Compute the homomorphic difference c_{dif} between $N_{c,max}$ and $N_{c,min}$ utilizing **Add**.
7: **for** each $1 \leq i \leq N$ **do**
8:    Compute $s_i = N_{c,i} - N_{c,min} + c_{dif}$ utilizing **Add**.
9: **end for**
10: **return** $\{s_i|1 \leq i \leq N\}$

Note that the proposed CECMLP also work for other machine learning models, *i.e.*, CNN and SVM, which can implemented with addition, multiplication, and maximum. To this end, in this paper, we only focus on the implementation of MLP which is a special case of CNN model and will not discussion about implementation of other models anymore.

5   Security Analysis

The security analysis of our proposed CECMLP is presented in this section.

Theorem 1. *In CECMLP, dataset privacy and gradient privacy of the participant is guaranteed, if all the participants, the parameter server and the evaluator are non-colluding.*

Proof. The privacy of the gradients is presented firstly. In CECMLP, the participants only upload the encrypted parameters to the evaluator. While for any participant i, gradients can be computed by calculating the difference between the parameter of the participant i and shared model parameter before training, *i.e.*, $G_i = W_i - W_{shared}$. For an adversarial participant adv, only the parameters of shared model W_{shared} is visible to the adversary. The adversary can calculate the difference G of parameters between two adjacent **Training** phases, where $G = \sum_{i=1}^{N} \frac{s_i}{\sum_{j=1}^{N} s_j} G_i$. Since that the adversary only knows G_{adv}, it is hard for it to infer any other participant's gradients.

For the parameter server, it is similar to the condition of adversarial participant. The parameter server can only obtain parameters of the shared model W_{shared} in every iteration. Although the evaluator evaluates the encrypted parameter collaboratively with the parameter server, the evaluator masks the ciphertext with a blinding factor in the process to avoid revealing private information to the parameter server. Because we assume that the evaluator and the parameter server are non-colluding. Considering a malicious parameter server who eavesdrops the communication channel between the participant and the evaluator, SSL protocol can be utilized to guarantee the communication security against eavesdropping from the parameter server.

For the evaluator, it only obtains the encrypted parameters of the participant. Guaranteed by the Paillier cryptosystem, malicious evaluator cannot obtain the plaintext of parameters of the participant without the private key of the parameter server. In **Evaluate** phase, the evaluator utilizes **Eval** to compute an encrypted reliability score of each participant and uses the encrypted parameters as well as the reliability score to aggregate the encrypted new parameters. All calculations are performed on ciphertexts via homomorphic operations and protocols. Therefore, the evaluator cannot obtain any information about parameters of the participant without colluding with the parameter server, let alone inferring gradients of the participant. As mentioned before, the gradient vector of the participant i can be obtain by calculating the difference between the participant's parameter vector and the shared model parameter vector, $i.e.$, $G_i = W_i - W_{shared}$. Participants encrypt the local parameters with the parameter server's public key pk_s before uploading them to the evaluator. Without sk_s, the evaluator cannot obtain the plaintext of the model parameters. So far, we have proved that dataset privacy and gradient privacy of the participant information is guaranteed in CECMLP.   □

Theorem 2. *In CECMLP, the participant's reliability privacy is guaranteed, if all the participants, the evaluator and the parameter server are non-colluding.*

Proof. In CECMLP, model accuracy represents the reliability of parameters in **Evaluate** phase. The evaluator calculates reliability score s_i by counting the number of samples that classified correctly. As shown in Sect. 4.2, The evaluator utilizes CMLP to make a prediction to an encrypted example. Then, the evaluator compares the prediction and the encrypted label and obtains an encrypted compare result. By calculating the sum of the encrypted compare results of evaluating dataset via **Add**, $\text{Enc}_{pk}(s_i)$ is obtained. Since that the evaluator does not have the private key, the evaluator cannot obtain the plaintext of reliability score. Though the parameter server can obtain the new parameter $W_{new} = \sum_{i=1}^{N} s_i W_i$, it still knows nothing about W_i and s_i. Therefore, the parameter server does not have the ability to compute the value of s_i of any participant. Similarly, for the participant i, it knows nothing except for W_{shared} and W_i. Therefore, the participant i cannot calculate reliability score of any participant. In a conclusion, reliability privacy of the participants is protected against being revealed to all entities.   □

6   Experiments

In this section, we evaluate the proposed CECMLP on a Windows 10 PC with an Intel Core i5-4590 CPU @3.30 GHz and a 8G RAM.

6.1   Datasets and Model Architectures

– **Datasets.** We use two real-world datasets to evaluate the proposed scheme, namely MNIST [4] and SVHN [5]. Concretely, MNIST dataset consists of 60000 training examples and 10000 testing examples. Each example contains a 28×28 image with a handwritten digit on its center and a label in 0–9. SVHN can be seen as similar to MNIST. It consists of 73257 digits for training, 26032 digits for testing, each examples contains a 32×32 RGB image and a label in 1–10.
– **Model architectures.** We use MLP with two hidden layers for the classification tasks. For different dataset, the number of the neurons in each layer is shown in Table 2. The activation function of each hidden layer is ReLU. We train those model exploiting stochastic gradient descent (SGD) learning algorithm with mini-batch size, learning rate, and momentum set as 64, 0.001, and 0.5.

Table 2. Neuron numbers in each layer of MLP

	MNIST	SVHN
Input layer	28 * 28	32 * 32 * 3
First hidden layer	1000	255
Second hidden layer	500	255
Output layer	10	10

6.2   Efficiency Analysis

To show the efficiency of CECMLP, we represent the theoretical analysis of all phases and experiment results of predicting encrypted example with CMLP on MNIST. We implement CMLP exploiting C++ programming language and Crypto++ library [1]. We set the security parameter with 128, and set the floating-point number correct to 8 decimal places, *i.e.*, set $d = 8$. Since MLP is not sensitive to the precision of data and parameters, setting $d = 8$ would not result in obvious deviation of prediction result.

Table 3 shows the theoretical analysis of the computation and the communication cost in all phases for all entities, where $|D_e|$ and N represent the size of the evaluating dataset and the number of the participants. For the computation cost, **KeyGen, Enc, Dec, Pred, Equal, Max, Add,** and **Mul** represent the computation complexities of the corresponding operation respectively. While, for the communication cost, those symbols represent the communication complexities of the corresponding operation. For brevity, we use some shorthands to replace some notation in Table 3. We use $\mathcal{P}$, $\mathcal{E}$, and $\mathcal{PS}$ to represent *Participants*, *Evaluator*, and *Parameter Server*. **Cp** and **Cm** are used to represent *Computation Cost* and *Communication Cost*. For homomorphic algorithms, we use **KG, E, D, A, M**, and **PEM** to represent **KeyGen, Enc, Dec, Add, Mul**, and **Pred + Equal + Max** respectively. The five phases, **Setup, Download, Training, Evaluate**, and **Update** are represented by $\mathbf{P_S}$, $\mathbf{P_D}$, $\mathbf{P_T}$, $\mathbf{P_E}$, and $\mathbf{P_U}$ respectively. Table 4 shows the computation experiment results of **Enc, Dec, Add, Mul, Max**, and **Pred**. Note that performing **Pred** once makes prediction on one sample. While, it is reasonable to considering the evaluator as a powerful party, *e.g.*, having multiple computation cores, so that the evaluator has the ability to make prediction on one data batch with **Pred** simultaneously.

Table 3. Computation and communication cost for CECMLP

Phases		$\mathbf{P_S}$	$\mathbf{P_D}$	$\mathbf{P_T}$	$\mathbf{P_E}$	$\mathbf{P_U}$
$\mathcal{P}$	**Cp**	–	–	$O(1)\mathbf{E}$	–	–
	Cm	$O(1)$	$O(1)$	$O(1)$	–	–
$\mathcal{E}$	**Cp**	–	–	–	$O(N|D_e|)(\mathbf{PEM} + \mathbf{A}) + O(N)\mathbf{M}$	–
	Cm	$O(|D_e|)$	–	$O(N)$	$O(N|D_e|)(\mathbf{PEM}) + O(N)\mathbf{M}$	–
$\mathcal{PS}$	**Cp**	$\mathbf{KG} + O(|D_e|)\mathbf{E}$	–	–	$O(N|D_e|)(\mathbf{PEM}) + O(N)\mathbf{M}$	$O(1)\mathbf{D}$
	Cm	$O(|D_e| + N)$	$O(N)$	–	$O(N|D_e|)(\mathbf{PEM}) + O(N)\mathbf{M}$	$O(1)$

Table 4. Experiment result of homomorphic operations.

Algorithms	Enc	Dec	Add	Mul	Max	Pred
Time cost (usec)	17	14	0.17	336	23	422047571

6.3 Evaluation of CECMLP

Our proposed CECMLP is evaluated by comparing with conventional federated learning (FL), SecProbe [35], centralized learning (CL). The FL scheme is the standard federated learning system which does not take the participants' reliability into consideration and update the shared model parameters by averaging the participants' updates. The SecProbe scheme utilizes functional mechanism and exponential mechanism to prevent the reliability privacy of the participants. In theoretically, the performance of SecProbe is worse than FL. In CL scheme, the server centralizes the datasets of the participants and directly train shared model over centralized dataset. Obviously, the CL can achieve the best performance but give no privacy guarantee to the datasets of the participants. The performance of CL scheme can be seen as the upper bound of any other schemes.

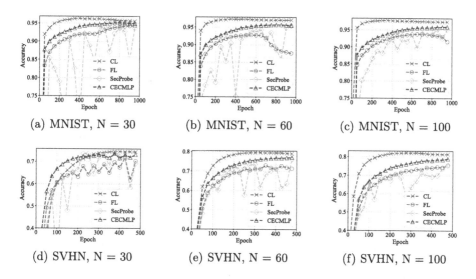

(a) MNIST, N = 30   (b) MNIST, N = 60   (c) MNIST, N = 100

(d) SVHN, N = 30   (e) SVHN, N = 60   (f) SVHN, N = 100

Fig. 2. Convergences of three schemes with different participant number

– **Training convergence.** We vary the number of the participants N in CECMLP, FL, SecProbe, and CL. Each participant holds a local dataset which contains 600 examples. 30% of the participants are unreliable participants. Figure 2 shows the convergences of all schemes on two datasets. The x-axis denotes the number of training epochs, and y-axis denotes the accuracy of the schemes. Table 5 shows the best accuracy of all schemes on MNIST. It is obvious that CL achieves the highest accuracy, and CECMLP achieves the second highest accuracy. The reason why CECMLP achieves higher accuracy than FL does may be that CECMLP aggregates the participants' parameters with referring the reliability of them, which enables the reliable participants to influence the shared model more. SecProbe exploits the functional mechanism which reduces its performance than FL. As a result, CECMLP achieves a better performance than SecProbe.

Table 5. Accuracy of different schemes on MNIST

	CL	CECMLP	SecProbe [35]	FL
MNIST	97.37%	95.74%	95.58%	95.28%

– **Influence of size of evaluating dataset.** We evaluate the influence of size of evaluating dataset E. In this experiment, E in CECMLP is set to 100, 500, and 1000. As shown in Fig. 3, with larger E, CECMLP achieves higher accuracy.

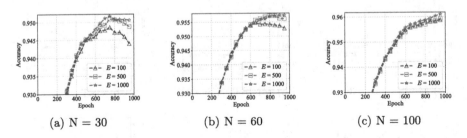

| (a) N = 30 | (b) N = 60 | (c) N = 100 |

Fig. 3. Convergences of CECMLP on MNIST with different evaluating dataset size

– **Robustness against the unreliable participants.** In this experiment, we vary the rate of the unreliable participants R and evaluate the robustness of CECMLP, FL, SecProbe, and CL against the unreliable participants. Figure 4 shows the best accuracy of all learning schemes with 30%, 50%, 70% unreliable participants respectively. As R raises, the accuracy of all schemes decreases for affected by the unreliable participants. As shown in Table 6, it is observed that CECMLP is the robustest scheme except for CL. The reason may be that CECMLP aggregates parameters refers to the participants' reliability and reduces the influence of the unreliable participants.

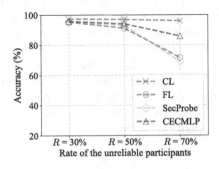

Fig. 4. Convergences of different scheme on MNIST with different unreliable rate

Table 6. Accuracy of different schemes on MNIST with different R

	CL	CECMLP	SecProbe [35]	FL
$R = 0.3$	97.37%	95.74%	95.58%	95.28%
$R = 0.7$	95.92%	85.80%	69.00%	71.56%
Decrease rate	1.54%	9.94%	26.58%	23.72%

7 Conclusion

In this paper, we propose a novel federated learning towards reliability privacy protection of participants. Except for the training dataset and its corresponding gradients, the reliability privacy of the participants can also be preserved, decoupling the learning process being unfair and discriminative. The reliability of the participants are evaluated by the cipher-based gradients weighted method. In this way, the proposed method has an advantage over conventional federated learning in performance and prevents the reliability privacy of the participants simultaneously. Experimental evaluations demonstrate the practical performance of our scheme as well as the robustness against the unreliable participants.

Acknowledgement. This work is supported by National Natural Science Foundation of China (No. 61902315).

References

1. Crypto++ Homepage. https://www.cryptopp.com/
2. Choi, E., Bahadori, M.T., Song, L., Stewart, W.F., Sun, J.: GRAM: graph-based attention model for healthcare representation learning. In: Proceedings of the 23rd ACM SIGKDD International Conference on Knowledge Discovery and Data Mining (KDD), Halifax, pp. 787–795. ACM (2017). https://doi.org/10.1145/3097983.3098126
3. Choi, E., Bahadori, M.T., Schuetz, A., Stewart, W.F., Sun, J.: Doctor AI: predicting clinical events via recurrent neural networks. In: Proceedings of the 1st Machine Learning in Health Care (MLHC), Los Angeles, pp. 301–318 (2016). JMLR.org
4. LeCun, Y., Bottou, L., Bengio, Y., Haffner, P.: Gradient-based learning applied to document recognition. Proc. IEEE **86**(11), 2278–2324 (1998)
5. Netzer, Y., Wang, T., Coates, A., Bissacco, A., Wu, B., Ng, A.Y.: Reading digits in natural images with unsupervised feature learning. In: Proceedings of NIPS Workshop on Deep Learning and Unsupervised Feature Learning (2011)
6. Phong, L.T., Aono, Y., Hayashi, T., Wang, L., Moriai, S.: Privacy-preserving deep learning via additively homomorphic encryption. IEEE Trans. Inf. Forensics Secur. **13**(5), 1333–1345 (2018)
7. Bonawitz, K., et al.: Practical secure aggregation for privacy-preserving machine learning. In: Proceedings of the 2017 ACM SIGSAC Conference on Computer and Communications Security (CCS), pp. 1175–1191. ACM, New York (2017). https://doi.org/10.1145/3133956.3133982

8. McMahan, B., Moore, E., Ramage, D., Hampson, S., Arcas, B.A.y.: Communication-efficient learning of deep networks from decentralized data. In: Proceedings of the 20th International Conference on Artificial Intelligence and Statistics (AISTATS), Cambridge, MA, pp. 1273–1282. PMLR (2017)

9. Dwork, C.: Differential privacy: a survey of results. In: Agrawal, M., Du, D., Duan, Z., Li, A. (eds.) TAMC 2008. LNCS, vol. 4978, pp. 1–19. Springer, Heidelberg (2008). https://doi.org/10.1007/978-3-540-79228-4_1

10. Geyer, R.C., Klein, T., Nabi, M.: Differentially private federated learning: a client level perspective. arXiv preprint (2018). arXiv:1712.07557

11. Gilad-Bachrach, R., Dowlin, N., Laine, K.E., Naehrig, M., Wernsing, J.: CryptoNets: applying neural networks to encrypted data with high throughput and accuracy. In: Proceedings of the 33rd International Conference on Machine Learning (ICML), Cambridge, MA, pp. 201–210. PLMR (2016)

12. Goldreich, O.: Secure multi-party computation. Manuscript, Preliminary version (1998)

13. He, K., Zhang, X., Ren, S., Sun, J.: Deep residual learning for image recognition. In: Proceedings of the 29th IEEE Conference on Computer Vision and Pattern Recognition (CVPR), Piscataway, NJ, pp. 770–778. IEEE (2016). https://doi.org/10.1109/CVPR.2016.90

14. Huang, G., Liu, Z., Maaten, L., Weinberger, K.Q.: Densely connected convolutional networks. In: Proceedings of the 30th IEEE Conference on Computer Vision and Pattern Recognition (CVPR), Piscataway, NJ, pp. 2261–2269. IEEE(2017). https://doi.org/10.1109/CVPR.2017.243

15. Juvekar, C., Vaikuntanathan, V., Chandrakasan, A.: GAZELLE: a low latency framework for secure neural network inference. In: Proceedings of the 27th USENIX Security Symposium (USENIX), Berkeley, pp. 1651–1669. USENIX (2018)

16. Hitaj, B., Ateniese, G., Perez-Cruz, F.: Deep models under the GAN: information leakage from collaborative deep learning. In: Proceedings of the 2017 ACM SIGSAC Conference on Computer and Communications Security (CCS), pp. 603–618. ACM, New York (2017). https://doi.org/10.1145/3133956.3134012

17. Simonyan, K., Zisserman, A.: Very deep convolutional networks for large-scale image recognition. In: Proceedings of International Conference on Learning Representations (ICLR), pp. 1–14. ICLR (2015)

18. Krizhevsky, A., Sutskever, I., Hinton, G.E.: ImageNet classification with deep convolutional neural networks. Commun. ACM **60**(6), 84–90 (2017)

19. Liu, J., Juuti, M., Lu, Y., Asokan, N.: Oblivious neural network predictions via MiniONN transformations. In: Proceedings of the 2017 ACM SIGSAC Conference on Computer and Communications Security (CCS), pp. 619–631. ACM, New York (2017). https://doi.org/10.1145/3133956.3134056

20. Mohassel, P., Zhang, Y.: SecureML: A system for scalable privacy-preserving machine learning. In: Proceedings of the 2017 IEEE Symposium on Security and Privacy (SP), Piscataway, NJ, pp. 19–38. IEEE (2017). https://doi.org/10.1109/SP.2017.12

21. Mohassel, P., Rindal, P.: ABY3: A mixed protocol framework for machine learning. In: Proceedings of the 2018 ACM SIGSAC Conference on Computer and Communications Security (CCS), pp. 35–52. ACM, New York (2018). https://doi.org/10.1145/3243734.3243760

22. Moravčík, M., et al.: DeepStack: expert-level artificial intelligence in heads-up no-limit poker. Science **356**(6337), 508–513 (2017)

23. Ma, X., et al.: Secure multiparty learning from the aggregation of locally trained models. J. Netw. Comput. Appl. **167**, 102754102754 (2020)

24. Li, J., Kuang, X., Lin, S., Ma, X., Tang, Y.: Privacy preservation for machine learning training and classification based on homomorphic encryption schemes. Inf. Sci. **526**, 166–179 (2020)
25. Paillier, P.: Public-key cryptosystems based on composite degree residuosity classes. In: Stern, J. (ed.) EUROCRYPT 1999. LNCS, vol. 1592, pp. 223–238. Springer, Heidelberg (1999). https://doi.org/10.1007/3-540-48910-X_16
26. Paparrizos, J., White, R.W., Horvitz, E.: Screening for pancreatic adenocarcinoma using signals from web search logs: feasibility study and results. J. Oncol. Pract. **12**(8), 737–744 (2016)
27. Pathak, M., Rane, S., Raj, B.: Multiparty differential privacy via aggregation of locally trained classifiers. In: Proceedings of Advances in Neural Information Processing Systems 23 (NIPS), pp. 1876–1884. Curran Associates, New York (2010)
28. Riazi, M.S., Weinert, C., Tkachenko, O., Songhori, E.M., Schneider, T., Koushanfar, F.: Chameleon: a hybrid secure computation framework for machine learning applications. In: Proceedings of the 2018 on Asia Conference on Computer and Communications Security (ASIACCS), pp. 707–721. ACM, New York (2018). https://doi.org/10.1145/3196494.3196522
29. Shokri, R., Shmatikov, V.: Privacy-preserving deep learning. In: Proceedings of the 22nd ACM SIGSAC Conference on Computer and Communications Security (CCS), pp. 1310–1321. ACM, New York (2015). https://doi.org/10.1145/2810103.2813687
30. Shokri, R., Stronati, M., Song, C., Shmatikov, V.: Membership inference attacks against machine learning models. In: Proceedings of the 2017 IEEE Symposium on Security and Privacy (SP), Piscataway, NJ, pp. 3–18. IEEE (2017). https://doi.org/10.1109/SP.2017.41
31. Silver, D., et al.: Mastering the game of go with deep neural networks and tree search. Nature **529**(7587), 484–489 (2016)
32. Yang, Z., Chang, E.C., Liang, Z.: Adversarial neural network inversion via auxiliary knowledge alignment. arXiv preprint (2019). arXiv:1902.08552
33. Zhang, X., Chen, X., Liu, J.K., Xiang, Y.: DeepPAR and DeepDPA: privacy-preserving and asynchronous deep learning for industrial IoT. IEEE Trans. Industr. Inf. **16**(3), 2081–2090 (2020)
34. Zhang, J., Zhang, Z., Xiao, X., Yang, Y., Winslett, M.: Functional mechanism: regression analysis under differential privacy. In: Proceedings of the VLDB Endowment, vol. 5, no. 11, pp. 1364–1375. ACM, New York (2012). https://doi.org/10.14778/2350229.2350253
35. Zhao, L., Wang, Q., Zou, Q., Zhang, Q., Chen, Y.: Privacy-preserving collaborative deep learning with unreliable participants. IEEE Trans. Inf. Forensics Secur. **15**, 1486–1500 (2020)

Blind Polynomial Evaluation and Data Trading

Yi Liu[1,3] [iD], Qi Wang[1,2(✉)] [iD], and Siu-Ming Yiu[3]

[1] Guangdong Provincial Key Laboratory of Brain-inspired Intelligent Computation,
Department of Computer Science and Engineering, Southern University of Science
and Technology, Shenzhen 518055, China
`liuy7@mail.sustech.edu.cn, wangqi@sustech.edu.cn`
[2] National Center for Applied Mathematics (Shenzhen), Southern University
of Science and Technology, Shenzhen 518055, China
[3] Department of Computer Science, The University of Hong Kong, Pokfulam,
Hong Kong SAR, China
`smyiu@cs.hku.hk`

Abstract. Data trading is an emerging business, in which data sellers
provide buyers with, for example, their private datasets and get paid from
buyers. In many scenarios, sellers prefer to sell pieces of data, such as statistical results derived from the dataset, rather than the entire dataset.
Meanwhile, buyers wish to hide the results they retrieve. Since it is not
preferable to rely on a trusted third party (TTP), we are wondering, in
the absence of TTP, whether there exists a *practical* mechanism satisfying the following requirements: the seller Sarah receives the payment if
and only if she *obliviously* returns the buyer Bob the *correct* evaluation
result of a function delegated by Bob on her dataset, and Bob can only
derive the result for which he pays. Despite a lot of attention data trading has received, a *desirable* mechanism for this scenario is still missing.
This is due to the fact that general solutions are inefficient when the
size of datasets is considerable or the evaluated function is complicated,
and that existing efficient cryptographic techniques cannot fully capture
the features of our scenario or can only address very limited computing
tasks.

In this paper, we propose the *first desirable* mechanism that is practical and supports a wide variety of computing tasks—evaluation of arbitrary functions that can be represented as polynomials. We introduce a
new cryptographic notion called *blind polynomial evaluation* and instantiate it with an explicit protocol. We further combine this notion with the
blockchain paradigm to provide a *practical* framework that can satisfy
the requirements mentioned above.

Keywords: Blind polynomial evaluation · Blockchain · ElGamal
encryption · Encryption switching protocol · Paillier encryption

© Springer Nature Switzerland AG 2021
K. Sako and N. O. Tippenhauer (Eds.): ACNS 2021, LNCS 12726, pp. 100–129, 2021.
https://doi.org/10.1007/978-3-030-78372-3_5

1   Introduction

Nowadays, data trading is an emerging business, which may involve different kinds of data, such as financial data, commercial data, and personal data. As the public gradually realizes the value of data, data trading has attracted more and more attention. Traditional data trading trivially seeks help from a central platform as a trusted third party (TTP). In most trading strategies, sellers send the entire dataset directly to buyers, which is fairly exchanged under the coordination of the central platform.

Unfortunately, in these solutions, central platforms are heavily relied on and have to be assumed to act honestly. Once the central platform is corrupted, the interests of parties will be significantly hurt. Furthermore, in many data trading scenarios, sellers may prefer to sell only certain calculation results on the dataset rather than exposing the entire dataset *at one time*. At the same time, buyers in a blind fashion wish to hide from sellers the results they retrieve. Therefore, it would be preferable to design a practical mechanism for selling only function evaluation results and capturing requirements like correctness, privacy, consistency, and fairness, but without the existence of TTP.

An illustration of such a scenario is shown above. More precisely, without the help of TTP, the seller Sarah possessing dataset x receives the payment *if and only if* she *obliviously* helps the buyer Bob possessing a function f get the result $f(x)$ *correctly*. Meanwhile, Bob can *only* derive the result for which he pays from the data trading. Besides, we should ensure the *consistency* of datasets in two transactions, *i.e.*, for each transaction (with the same buyer or with different buyers), Sarah should use the same dataset x. In addition, for the reason that datasets during data trading tend to remain unchanged and consistent, we prefer a pre-processing procedure that amortizes the processing cost of datasets rather than a one-time solution. Here we call a solution *one-time* if every execution of such a solution involves a new entire processing procedure of the dataset.

However, even if data trading is more and more important, desirable solutions meeting the above requirements are still unknown. Although general solutions, such as Yao's garbled circuits [30] using universal circuit [27,31] and fully homomorphic encryption [14] (see more discussion in Sect. 2.2 and Sect. 2.3) can theoretically be used as a component for this scenario, they are infeasible for *practical use* when the sizes of datasets are considerable and the evaluated functions are complicated. Furthermore, existing efficient frameworks cannot *fully* capture the features of our scenario and practical cryptographic tools can only cover *limited* computing tasks. Thus, despite the existence of theoretical solutions, the following question remains open:

How to construct a practical mechanism for the requirements of data trading mentioned above, with the capability of supporting a wide variety of computing tasks?

We answer this question in the present paper.

1.1 Our Results

In this paper, we focus on arbitrary functions that can be represented as polynomials and propose the *first* practical solution that fulfills all aforementioned requirements. We remark that the evaluation of polynomials is powerful and can be utilized in many applications. To further motivate our results, we illustrate some potential applications from three aspects: (i) Polynomial evaluation supports many statistical numerical calculations, including mean, variance, determinant, inner product, Minkowski distance, etc. (ii) Since many functions can be approximated by *Taylor polynomials*, our work supports approximate evaluations of these functions. (iii) Datasets can be specially designed to support many operations through polynomial evaluation. Here we provide a toy example. Suppose that a seller holds a dataset containing the gender and salary of employees at a company. In cells for gender, female employees are specifically represented by zero and male by one. If a buyer intends to calculate the total salary of employees of a particular gender, he requires selecting and summing the salary items of employees of that gender. We denote the gender and salary as b_i and s_i, respectively, for the term of the index i. Then calculating the total salary of female employees is equivalent to evaluating the polynomial $\sum_i (s_i - b_i s_i)$ on the dataset and that of male employees equals $\sum_i b_i s_i$.

To capture the features of the scenario for polynomial evaluations on private datasets, we introduce a new cryptographic notion called *blind polynomial evaluation*. This notion can be viewed as a subset of two-party computation (2PC) problems [29] and is of independent interest. We further combine our blind polynomial evaluation protocol with the blockchain paradigm to provide a practical solution that achieves fairness of exchange for the scenario of data trading.

Here we briefly introduce the underlying insights. We borrow the idea from [6] of using two compatible homomorphic encryption schemes and introducing a switching mechanism between them to support complicated computing tasks. But we note that the scenario we consider is anyhow different from that of [6] (for a comparison, see Sect. 2.4). Through this mechanism, buyers can evaluate their polynomials on sellers' encrypted datasets via additively and multiplicatively homomorphic properties simultaneously. This idea is simple, but it is a *highly nontrivial* approach for two main reasons: two schemes should be *compatible*, and switching should be guaranteed to perform *correctly*. For our scenario, we need to ensure that two encryption schemes are switched *secretly* and *correctly* when one party holds the complete private keys and intends to behave dishonestly. In addition, we also consider the fact that almost all multiplicatively homomorphic encryption schemes do not support encryption of zero, but it is indeed required in some scenarios. We customize a new multiplicatively homomorphic encryption scheme to resolve this situation. Furthermore, we introduce how to achieve fair exchange of the final result over blockchain.

We summarize the main contributions of this work in the following.

1. Considering the scenario of data trading, we introduce a new cryptographic notion, namely, blind polynomial evaluation. We propose a generic construction of this notion with communication cost $\mathcal{O}(k)$, where k is the number of terms of polynomials.
2. We propose a *small-constant-round* protocol to instantiate the generic construction to support polynomial evaluation over $\mathbb{Z}_n^*$, where n is a strong RSA modulus having two distinct prime factors of the same length, under standard computational hardness assumptions. Furthermore, we extend our instantiation from polynomial evaluation over $\mathbb{Z}_n^*$ to that over $\mathbb{Z}_n$.
3. We integrate our blind polynomial evaluation protocol with the blockchain paradigm to support fair exchange in the data trading scenario.
4. We analyze our protocol in terms of both round complexity and a *proof-of-concept* implementation to provide evidence that the protocol is practical.

The rest of the present paper is organized as follows. In Sect. 2, we introduce some related work, with an emphasis on both relevance and difference compared to our work. We then introduce the notion of blind polynomial evaluation together with a generic construction and corresponding definitions in Sect. 3. The protocol to instantiate the generic construction over $\mathbb{Z}_n^*$ is presented in Sect. 4, and is further extended from $\mathbb{Z}_n^*$ to $\mathbb{Z}_n$ in Sect. 5. In Sect. 6, we show how to combine our blind polynomial evaluation protocol with the blockchain paradigm to achieve fair exchange for data trading. Finally, analysis of the practicality of our protocol is given in Sect. 7. All proofs of security can be found in the full version of this paper [18].

2   Related Work

In this section, we recall some classical definitions and results that are related to our work.

2.1   Oblivious Polynomial Evaluation

Naor and Pinkas [22] proposed a cryptographic notion named *oblivious polynomial evaluation* (OPE), and then an extended version called *oblivious multivariate polynomial evaluation* [26] was proposed. These notions are for the scenario that a receiver holding a value x (resp. vector $\boldsymbol{x}$) intends to compute $p(x)$ (resp. $p(\boldsymbol{x})$) with the help of a sender possessing a private univariate (resp. multivariate) polynomial p. By the protocol, the receiver gets only $p(x)$ (resp. $p(\boldsymbol{x})$), and the sender can infer no information about x (resp. $\boldsymbol{x}$) from the interaction.

We note that the scenario of data trading we now consider is different from OPE. On the one hand, the receiver of the evaluation result is the polynomial provider in our setting, while the data provider in OPE. This difference leads to very different security definitions. On the other hand, most OPE protocols are designed for one-time use. Such solutions are not preferable and could lead to data inconsistencies among transactions as we have mentioned in Sect. 1.

2.2 Universal Circuit and Garbled Circuit

For a fixed universal circuit U_n such that $U_n(x, C) = C(x)$ for any circuits having at most n gates, it is easy to see that universal circuits combined with the garbled circuit technique can theoretically be used for the data trading scenario we consider. However, overhead is prohibitive for the following four main reasons.

- For polynomial evaluation, complicated polynomials lead to boolean circuits with considerable sizes. Meanwhile, representations of boolean circuits using universal circuits involve a significant expansion of the circuit size—$\mathcal{O}(n \log n)$ with significant constant terms as well as the low-order terms.
- To ensure data consistency, a costly consistency check of the entire dataset may need to be encoded in the circuit.
- To be secure against malicious parties, expensive techniques (*e.g.*, cut-and-choose approach) should be involved.
- The solution will be a one-time use solution.

In contrast, our solution is efficient and overcomes all of these issues.

2.3 Homomorphic Encryption

Homomorphic encryption is an encryption scheme that allows computations to be performed on encrypted data, such that the decryption of the final result equals the result directly computed from the plaintexts. As a classic example, ElGamal [13] cryptosystem is multiplicatively homomorphic. For additively homomorphic encryption schemes, one of the well-known schemes is Paillier cryptosystem [23], which supports additions of encrypted values and multiplications between encrypted values and constants. Although these cryptosystems (named *partially homomorphic encryption* (PHE)) are practically used in many applications, they support very limited computing tasks (such as only addition or multiplication) and are limited in many other applications. In 2009, Gentry proposed the first *fully homomorphic encryption* (FHE) [14], from which it is possible to perform arbitrary computations. Following Gentry's seminal work, some FHE schemes are proposed afterward. The noted barrier of FHE is that current FHE schemes are still inefficient and prohibitive, especially for datasets of considerable size and complicated functions. For example, polynomial evaluation via FHE is prohibitive when the degree of polynomials is not a *very small constant* and the polynomial cannot be written in a batch-friendly form. In contrast, our protocol is efficient and will not be subject to these limitations.

2.4   Encryption Switching Protocol

The notion of encryption switching protocol was formalized by Couteau, Peters, and Pointcheval [6] in 2016 (see [3] for a more general construction). The encryption switching protocol applies to the scenario that two parties *secretly share* two private keys for a multiplicatively homomorphic encryption scheme and an additively homomorphic encryption scheme, respectively. Both of them can individually encrypt a message, but neither of them can decrypt a ciphertext unless they cooperate to perform threshold decryption. This leads to a framework for two parties to cooperatively switch a ciphertext from one cryptosystem to the other and follow a deterministic computation path on the ciphertexts together until a computation result is reached. The encryption switching protocol also shows efficiency in practice [5]. Although we utilize this encryption switching idea in our work, we are considering a *different* scenario: one party holds the two complete private keys while the other holds only the corresponding public keys. In this scenario, given an encrypted value, the party holding the two private keys can decrypt this ciphertext and learn the corresponding plaintext herself, which leads to entirely different definitions and solutions from [3,6].

2.5   Fairness Based on Blockchain

The blockchain paradigm is the underlying data structure, along with the emergence of Bitcoin [21]. It is deployed in a peer-to-peer (P2P) network, where all nodes follow a consensus mechanism. Ethereum [28] is the first platform that introduced blockchain-based smart contracts. After the deployment of a smart contract, nodes in the network execute the instructions specified by this smart contract and users. If the majority of nodes honestly follow the consensus mechanism, a blockchain can be deemed as a (semi-)honest third party with a *public* execution transcript.

It is known that general protocols in the absence of a third party cannot guarantee fairness when one of the parties is corrupted for 2PC problems [4]. Because of the emergence of the blockchain and smart contracts, some researchers recently integrated them into protocols as a third party to achieve fairness. A few of blockchain-based protocols, such as [1,2,16], ensure fairness of 2PC via a mechanism called *claim-or-refund*, in which a malicious party who aborts ahead of specified time will be forced to pay a monetary penalty.

For data trading, a few results based on the blockchain are also proposed to ensure data consistency through the claim-or-refund mechanism, such as [8,10,11]. These results mainly focus on data delivery, in which data sellers intend to sell an entire dataset or file. A few other results are proposed for collecting data from specified data generators, such as [15,19,20]. As a comparison, in our scenario, only two parties are involved, and the result evaluated on the function delegated by the buyer is delivered instead of the entire dataset.

3   Definitions and Generic Construction

According to earlier discussion in Sect. 1, we need a practical mechanism to capture the requirements of correctness, privacy, consistency and fairness for the data trading scenario. In this section, we model such a data trading scenario as a cryptographic notion called *blind polynomial evaluation*, aiming to resolve concerns of the first three requirements during data trading. The concern of fairness will be postponed to Sect. 6.

3.1   Blind Polynomial Evaluation

We consider the scenario that a seller Sarah initially uploads her entire dataset $\boldsymbol{x}$ in an encrypted form (denoted by $\boldsymbol{c_x}$) to a public place (*e.g.*, cloud) and publishes a hash value of $\boldsymbol{c_x}$ for consistency check. Then she can start trading data with potential buyers who have downloaded $\boldsymbol{c_x}$. We note that for Business-to-Customer (B2C) scenarios, the seller Sarah can indeed play the role of the storage server, and here we use *public place* to generalize the description that may also involve Customer-to-Customer (C2C) scenarios. It is typically cheap for individual sellers to use cloud storage service, and in this way sellers even do not need to store $\boldsymbol{c_x}$ locally. Since Sarah only needs to encrypt her dataset once, this approach avoids one-time use cost. We also note that once Sarah wants to update a portion of the dataset, she can only update this portion and the hash value. Moreover, since buyers can download the encrypted dataset without interaction with Sarah before a data trading, this approach, in some sense, largely saves Sarah's communication cost. Furthermore, the hash value of $\boldsymbol{c_x}$ ensures data consistency of transactions. Once the encrypted dataset is uploaded, Bob, as a potential buyer, can download $\boldsymbol{c_x}$ and check the hash value of $\boldsymbol{c_x}$.

Sarah, as a sender, in a blind fashion helps Bob, as a receiver, evaluates on the dataset $\boldsymbol{x}$ a function that belongs to the set $\mathcal{P}$, which contains all ℓ-variate polynomials with $k+1$ terms in the sparse representation of

$$P(\boldsymbol{x}) = \sum_{i=0}^{k} b_i \prod_{j=1}^{\ell} x_j^{d_{ij}},$$

where $\boldsymbol{x} \in (\mathbb{Z}_n^*)^\ell$, κ is the security parameter, $\ell, k \in \mathcal{O}(\kappa^c)$ for large enough constant $c > 0$, all $b_i, d_{ij} \in \mathcal{O}(2^\kappa)$, and $d_{0j} = 0$ for $j = 1\ldots\ell$. We denote the terms of $P(\boldsymbol{x})$ by $P_i(\boldsymbol{x}) = b_i \prod_{j=1}^{\ell} x_j^{d_{ij}}$ for $i = 1, \ldots, k$ and $P_0(\boldsymbol{x}) = b_0$, such that $P(\boldsymbol{x}) = \sum_{i=0}^{k} P_i(\boldsymbol{x})$. Note that polynomials with the number of variates less than ℓ and number of terms less than $k+1$ can also be written in this form by simply setting certain b_i and d_{ij} to be 0. We call such a procedure *blind polynomial evaluation* and define its functionality of this notion as follows.

Definition 1. *The two-round functionality of the blind polynomial evaluation protocol between a receiver and a sender is presented below.*

1. (a) *The receiver inputs an encrypted vector* $\boldsymbol{c_x}$ *corresponding to a plaintext vector* $\boldsymbol{x}$ *and public information* pi. *The sender inputs a trapdoor* td *and public information* pi$'$.
   (b) *If* pi $=$ pi$'$, td *is correct for* $\boldsymbol{c_x}$ *and* pi, *both parties receive* continue *and proceed to the next round. Otherwise, both parties receive* $\perp$ *with abortion.*
2. (a) *The receiver inputs the description of a polynomial* $P \in \mathcal{P}$.
   (b) *If* $P \in \mathcal{P}$, *the receiver receives the evaluation result* $P(\boldsymbol{x})$ *and the sender receives* nothing. *Otherwise, both parties receive* $\perp$ *with abortion.*

We note that pi (resp. pi$'$) includes public parameters such as public keys for c_x. From this definition, the receiver only receives the result $P(\boldsymbol{x})$ at the end without leaking any more information to the sender. Here, we allow buyer to set the polynomial $P(\boldsymbol{x}) = x_i$ to retrieve the i-th entry of $\boldsymbol{x}$. Our goal is for the seller to avoid revealing the entire dataset at one time, and it is acceptable that buyer retrieves the entire dataset via numerous transactions. If the scenario is to avoid leaking information of single entries, the dataset could simply be processed by differential privacy [9] techniques at the beginning.

As stated in Sect. 1.1, to support polynomial evaluation on encrypted datasets, and meanwhile, to make it *practical*, we utilize in our construction two *compatible* homomorphic encryption schemes $\Pi_\times$ and Π_+, where $\Pi_\times$ is multiplicatively homomorphic, and Π_+ is additively homomorphic. Here we call two schemes $\Pi_\times$ and Π_+ *compatible* if the plaintext space of Π_+ is a ring $\mathbb{R}$ and that of $\Pi_\times$ is a monoid $\mathbb{M}$ with $\mathbb{R} \cap \mathbb{M} = \mathbb{R}^*$, where $\mathbb{R}^*$ is the set of invertible elements of $\mathbb{R}$ [3]. The main idea of our construction is that Sarah first encrypts via $\Pi_\times$ all entries of the dataset, which then allows Bob to multiply encrypted values of the encrypted dataset directly. After multiplications, Sarah, in a *blind* manner, helps Bob switch all encrypted multiplication results to ciphertexts of Π_+, which again allows Bob to add encrypted values of these ciphertexts. Finally, we let Sarah once again in a *blind* fashion provide Bob with the final decrypted result.

To avoid duplicate definitions, in the rest of this section we denote the multiplicatively homomorphic encryption scheme as $\Pi_\times = (\mathsf{KGen}, \mathsf{Enc}, \mathsf{Dec}, \mathsf{Mul})$ with a key pair $(\mathsf{pk}_\times, \mathsf{sk}_\times)$, message space $\mathcal{M}_\times$, and ciphertext space $\mathcal{C}_\times$, and the additively homomorphic encryption scheme as $\Pi_+ = (\mathsf{KGen}, \mathsf{Enc}, \mathsf{Dec}, \mathsf{Add}, \mathsf{Mul})$ with a key pair $(\mathsf{pk}_+, \mathsf{sk}_+)$, message space $\mathcal{M}_+$, and ciphertext space $\mathcal{C}_+$. Here we require Π_+ to support efficient multiplication of an encrypted value and a constant. Since most additively homomorphic encryption schemes have this property, this requirement can be easily satisfied. We assume that $\Pi_\times$ and Π_+ are *compatible* and both IND-CPA (Indistinguishability under Chosen Plaintext Attack) secure. We write $r \leftarrow_\$ S$ for sampling r uniformly from a set S.

3.2 Definitions of Building Blocks

To formalize our idea, we introduce the following building blocks. We first recall the definition of twin-ciphertext pair.

Definition 2 (Twin-Ciphertext Pair [6]). *For two encryption schemes* $\Pi_\times$ *and* Π_+, *we call a pair of ciphertexts* $(c_\times, c_+) \in (\mathcal{C}_\times, \mathcal{C}_+)$ *a twin-ciphertext pair* *if $c_\times$ is an encryption of a message $m_\times$ under $\Pi_\times$, c_+ is an encryption of a message m_+ under Π_+, $m_\times, m_+ \in \mathcal{M}_\times \cap \mathcal{M}_+$ and $m_\times = m_+$.*

Then in Table 1, we present some languages for relations and their corresponding zero-knowledge ideal functionality. The functionality $\mathcal{F}_{zk}^{TwinCtx}$ is for proving that a ciphertext pair is a twin-ciphertext pair, $\mathcal{F}_{zk}^{EncValue}$ is for proof of encrypted value for Π_+, and $\mathcal{F}_{zk}^{sk_+}$ is for proof of private key sk_+ of the scheme Π_+. Each ideal functionality receives the statement from both the prover and verifier, and a witness from the prover. It outputs accept to the verifier if the statement from both parties are the same and true, and reject otherwise.

Table 1. Languages for relations and their zero-knowledge ideal functionalities.

Language for relation	Functionality
$L_{TwinCtx} = \{(c_\times \in \mathcal{C}_\times, c_+ \in \mathcal{C}_+, pk_\times, pk_+) \mid \exists (m_\times, m_+, r_+, sk_\times), s.t.$ $sk_\times$ is the private key of $pk_\times \wedge m_\times = \Pi_\times.Dec_{pk_\times}(c_\times, sk_\times)$ $\wedge\, c_+ = \Pi_+.Enc_{pk_+}(m_+; r_+) \wedge m_\times = m_+\}$	$\mathcal{F}_{zk}^{TwinCtx}$
$L_{EncValue} = \{(c_+ \in \mathcal{C}_+, m_+ \in \mathcal{M}_+, pk_+) \mid \exists (r_+), s.t.$ $c_+ = \Pi_+.Enc_{pk_+}(m_+; r_+)\}$	$\mathcal{F}_{zk}^{EncValue}$
$L_{sk_+} = \{(pk_+) \mid \exists (sk_+), s.t. sk_+$ is the private key of $pk_+\}$	$\mathcal{F}_{zk}^{sk_+}$

3.3   Construction

We here present our generic construction of blind polynomial evaluation between the sender, *i.e.*, seller Sarah, and the receiver, *i.e.*, buyer Bob, in the $(\mathcal{F}_{zk}^{TwinCtx}, \mathcal{F}_{zk}^{EncValue}, \mathcal{F}_{zk}^{sk_+})$-hybrid model in Fig. 1.

Now we define the security of this construction. For the receiver's security, we should guarantee that: (i) A malicious sender cannot deviate from the protocol without being detected (with protocol abortion); (ii) The view of the sender can be simulated, *i.e.*, the sender *learns nothing*. The ideal functionalities indeed guarantee the first requirement in the hybrid model, that is, the sender must return the correct switched ciphertexts and the decryption result. We now define the receiver's security in the hybrid model against malicious senders as follows.

Definition 3 (Receiver's Security). *For all adversaries $\mathcal{A}$ running in probabilistic polynomial-time (PPT) with input pi, $sk_\times$, sk_+, and auxiliary input z playing the sender's role in the $(\mathcal{F}_{zk}^{TwinCtx}, \mathcal{F}_{zk}^{EncValue}, \mathcal{F}_{zk}^{sk_+})$-hybrid model, there exists a PPT simulator $\mathcal{S}$ given pi, $sk_\times$, sk_+ and z in the ideal model of blind polynomial evaluation, such that the output of $\mathcal{S}$ is (perfectly) indistinguishable from the view of $\mathcal{A}$.*

Inputs: The receiver Bob takes as input the description of a polynomial $P \in \mathcal{P}$, an encrypted vector c_x of $\Pi_\times$ corresponding to a vector x. The sender Sarah takes as input the keys $\mathsf{sk}_\times$ and sk_+ (*i.e.*, the trapdoor td) for $\Pi_\times$ and Π_+, respectively. Both parties also take as input the public information pi containing $\mathsf{pk}_\times$, pk_+.

1. Sarah checks if keys $\mathsf{sk}_\times$ and sk_+ are correct, and aborts if they are incorrect. Bob, as the verifier, calls $\mathcal{F}_{\mathsf{zk}}^{\mathsf{sk}_+}$ with the prover Sarah for pk_+. If $\mathcal{F}_{\mathsf{zk}}^{\mathsf{sk}_+}$ outputs **accept**, Bob continues. Otherwise, Bob halts and outputs $\bot$.
2. Bob computes on c_x according to the term P_i to derive $c_{\times,P_i(x)}$ for $i = 1, \ldots, k$. If a coefficient $b_i = 0$, Bob picks a random ciphertext of $\Pi_\times$ as $c_{\times,P_i(x)}$.
3. Bob interacts with Sarah for all $c_{\times,P_i(x)}$'s, $i = 1, \ldots, k$, following the *encryption switching procedure* below to switch the underlying encryption scheme of these ciphertexts. At the end, Bob retrieves switched ciphertexts $c_{+,P_i(x)}$'s, $i = 1, \ldots, k$.
   (a) Bob picks $s \leftarrow_\$ \mathcal{M}_\times$ and computes $c_s \leftarrow \Pi_\times.\mathsf{Enc}_{\mathsf{pk}_\times}(s)$. Then Bob computes $c'_{\times,P_i(x)} \leftarrow \Pi_\times.\mathsf{Mul}_{\mathsf{pk}_\times}(c_{\times,P_i(x)}, c_s)$ to randomize $c_{\times,P_i(x)}$, and sends $c'_{\times,P_i(x)}$ to Sarah.
   (b) If $c'_{\times,P_i(x)} \in \mathcal{C}_\times$, Sarah decrypts $c'_{\times,P_i(x)}$, re-encrypts the decrypted value via Π_+ with pk_+ to derive $c'_{+,P_i(x)}$, and sends it to Bob. Otherwise, Sarah halts and outputs $\bot$.
   (c) Bob, as the verifier, calls $\mathcal{F}_{\mathsf{zk}}^{\mathsf{TwinCtx}}$ with the prover Sarah for $(c'_{\times,P_i(x)}, c'_{+,P_i(x)})$. If $\mathcal{F}_{\mathsf{zk}}^{\mathsf{TwinCtx}}$ outputs **accept**, Bob continues. Otherwise, Bob halts and outputs $\bot$.
   (d) Bob computes $c_{+,P_i(x)} \leftarrow \Pi_+.\mathsf{Mul}_{\mathsf{pk}_+}(c'_{+,P_i(x)}, s^{-1})$, where s^{-1} is the multiplicative inverse of s (such an inverse exists as $\Pi_\times$ and Π_+ are compatible).
4. Bob computes $c_{+,P_0(x)} \leftarrow \Pi_+.\mathsf{Enc}_{\mathsf{pk}_+}(b_0)$ and sums encrypted values of $c_{+,P_i(x)}$ for $i = 0, \ldots, k$ (except $b_i = 0$) to obtain $c_{+,P(x)}$, which is the encrypted $P(x)$.
5. Bob retrieves the final result $m = P(x)$ via the following *result retrieval procedure*.
   (a) Bob picks $s \leftarrow_\$ \mathcal{M}_+$ and encrypts it via $c_s \leftarrow \Pi_+.\mathsf{Enc}_{\mathsf{pk}_+}(s)$. Then Bob computes $c'_{+,P(x)} \leftarrow \Pi_+.\mathsf{Add}_{\mathsf{pk}_+}(c_{+,P(x)}, c_s)$ and sends it to Sarah.
   (b) If $c'_{+,P(x)} \in \mathcal{C}_+$, Sarah decrypts it and sends the decrypted value m' to Bob.
   (c) Bob, as the verifier, calls $\mathcal{F}_{\mathsf{zk}}^{\mathsf{EncValue}}$ with the prover Sarah for $c'_{+,P(x)}$ and m'. If $\mathcal{F}_{\mathsf{zk}}^{\mathsf{EncValue}}$ outputs **accept**, Bob continues. Otherwise, Bob halts and outputs $\bot$.
   (d) Bob outputs the decrypted result $m \leftarrow m' - s$.

Fig. 1. Generic construction with $\mathcal{F}_{\mathsf{zk}}^{\mathsf{TwinCtx}}$, $\mathcal{F}_{\mathsf{zk}}^{\mathsf{EncValue}}$, and $\mathcal{F}_{\mathsf{zk}}^{\mathsf{sk}_+}$.

For the sender's security, it is necessary to ensure that after the evaluation of a polynomial P, the receiver cannot obtain more information than he should, *i.e.*, Bob only retrieves $P(x)$. In the hybrid model, a malicious Bob can only cause abortion or send different ciphertexts to Sarah instead of the ciphertexts according to an honest evaluation for $P(x)$. If Bob sends values in incorrect forms, he will be rejected and the protocol aborts. Since Bob obtains nothing, this behavior does not offend our security goal. If he sends ciphertexts that are different from an honest evaluation, but in the correct form, he indeed evaluates a different polynomial P' from P. We notice that if $\Pi_\times$ and Π_+ are both IND-CPA secure, Bob gains no advantage after he receives ciphertexts from Sarah (see more in Sect. 6.1). Hence, it is reasonable to let malicious Bob pick a polynomial P after seeing c_x and before the execution of the protocol, and then Bob behaves semi-honestly during the protocol. Hence, we define the adversary that plays the role of the receiver as $\mathcal{A} = (\mathcal{A}_0, \mathcal{A}_1)$: $\mathcal{A}_0$ takes as input c_x and pi, and outputs the description of a polynomial $P \in \mathcal{P}$; $\mathcal{A}_1$ takes as input the description of P, c_x and pi, and acts as a semi-honest adversary to evaluate P on the encrypted dataset c_x with the sender. We abuse the notion representation slightly and use P to represent the description of the polynomial P if the context is clear.

Definition 4 (Sender's Security). *For every* PPT *adversary* $\mathcal{A} = (\mathcal{A}_0, \mathcal{A}_1)$ *in the* $(\mathcal{F}_{zk}^{\mathsf{TwinCtx}}, \mathcal{F}_{zk}^{\mathsf{EncValue}}, \mathcal{F}_{zk}^{\mathsf{sk+}})$*-hybrid model with input* c_x, pi *and auxiliary input* z *playing receiver's role, once the description of a polynomial is output via* $P \leftarrow \mathcal{A}_0(c_x, \mathrm{pi}, z)$, *there exists a* PPT *simulator* $\mathcal{S}$ *taking* c_x, pi *and* P *as input in the ideal model, such that the view simulated by* $\mathcal{S}$ *and the view of the semi-honest* $\mathcal{A}_1$ *in the hybrid model taking* c_x, pi, *and* P *as input are computationally indistinguishable.*

For the above generic construction, we have the theorem as follows.

Theorem 1. *If* $\Pi_\times$ *and* Π_+ *are both* IND-CPA, *the generic construction in the* $(\mathcal{F}_{zk}^{\mathsf{TwinCtx}}, \mathcal{F}_{zk}^{\mathsf{EncValue}}, \mathcal{F}_{zk}^{\mathsf{sk+}})$*-hybrid model guarantees both receiver's and sender's security.*

Therefore, to guarantee both receiver's and sender's security, we should ensure that both $\Pi_\times$ and Π_+ are IND-CPA secure, and functionalities $\mathcal{F}_{zk}^{\mathsf{TwinCtx}}$, $\mathcal{F}_{zk}^{\mathsf{EncValue}}$, and $\mathcal{F}_{zk}^{\mathsf{sk+}}$ are securely realized in the presence of *malicious* adversaries.

4   Instantiation of Blind Polynomial Evaluation over $\mathbb{Z}_n^*$

To instantiate the generic construction of blind polynomial evaluation, we utilize a variant of ElGamal encryption scheme from [6] with the plaintext space of $\mathbb{Z}_n^*$ and the Paillier encryption scheme from [23] with the plaintext space of $\mathbb{Z}_n$, where n is a strong RSA modulus having two distinct prime factors of the same length. It is easy to see that these two schemes are compatible. Given these two schemes, we then provide protocols that securely realize $\mathcal{F}_{zk}^{\mathsf{TwinCtx}}$, $\mathcal{F}_{zk}^{\mathsf{EncValue}}$, and $\mathcal{F}_{zk}^{\mathsf{sk+}}$ in the presence of malicious adversaries, which immediately leads to a secure blind polynomial evaluation protocol based on the generic construction.

For the following description, let κ and t be the security parameters, and negl be a negligible function. Algorithms implicitly take as input 1^κ. Our instantiation in this paper relies on the following computational hardness assumptions.

- The Decisional Diffie-Hellman (DDH) assumption in a cyclic group $\mathbb{G} = \langle g \rangle$ of order $q \in \Theta(2^\kappa)$ is that for all PPT adversaries $\mathcal{A}$, we have

$$\Pr\left[\mathcal{A}(\mathbb{G}, q, g, g^x, g^y, z_b) = b : \begin{array}{l} x, y \leftarrow_{\$} \mathbb{Z}_q; z_0 = g^{xy}; \\ z_1 \leftarrow_{\$} \mathbb{G}; b \leftarrow_{\$} \{0, 1\} \end{array}\right] \leq 1/2 + \mathsf{negl}(\kappa) \ .$$

– The Decisional Composite Residuosity (DCR) assumption in $\mathbb{Z}_{n^2}^*$, where $n \in \Theta(2^\kappa)$ is a strong RSA modulus, is that for all PPT adversaries $\mathcal{A}$, we have

$$\Pr\left[\mathcal{A}(n, z_b) = b : \begin{array}{l} r \leftarrow_\$ \mathbb{Z}_n^*; z_0 = r^n \bmod n^2; \\ z_1 \leftarrow_\$ \mathbb{Z}_{n^2}^*; b \leftarrow_\$ \{0,1\} \end{array}\right] \le 1/2 + \mathsf{negl}(\kappa) .$$

– The Quadratic Residuosity (QR) assumption in $\mathbb{Z}_n^*$, where $n \in \Theta(2^\kappa)$ is a strong RSA modulus, is that for all PPT adversaries $\mathcal{A}$, we have

$$\Pr\left[\mathcal{A}(n, z_b) = b : \begin{array}{l} r \leftarrow_\$ \mathbb{Z}_n^*; z_0 \leftarrow r^2 \bmod n; \\ z_1 \leftarrow_\$ \mathbb{J}_n; b \leftarrow_\$ \{0,1\} \end{array}\right] \le 1/2 + \mathsf{negl}(\kappa) ,$$

where $\mathbb{J}_n$ is the set of all elements of $\mathbb{Z}_n^*$ whose *Jacobi symbols* are $+1$.

4.1 ElGamal Encryption over $\mathbb{Z}_n^*$

We slightly modify a variant of ElGamal encryption scheme $\mathbb{Z}_n^*$-EG over $\mathbb{Z}_n^*$ introduced in [6] and use it as the multiplicatively homomorphic encryption scheme $\Pi_\times$. The description of $\mathbb{Z}_n^*$-EG is given below.

Key Generation. The key generation algorithm KGen takes as input the security parameter 1^κ and generates a strong RSA modulus $n = pq$ where $p, q \in \Theta(2^\kappa)$ are distinct randomly-chosen safe primes having the same length. Then the algorithm follows the procedure below:

1. Compute $g_0 \leftarrow_\$ \mathbb{Z}_n^*$, $g \leftarrow -g_0^2$ to obtain a generator of $\mathbb{J}_n$ of order $\lambda = \mathsf{lcm}(p-1, q-1)$. Here $\mathbb{J}_n$ is the set of all elements of $\mathbb{Z}_n^*$ whose *Jacobi symbols* are $+1$.
2. Compute $v = [p^{-1} \bmod q] \cdot p \bmod n$, such that $v \equiv 0 \bmod p$ and $v \equiv 1 \bmod q$, and $\chi \leftarrow (1-v) \cdot g^{t_p} + v \cdot g^{t_q} \bmod n$ for an even $t_p \leftarrow_\$ \mathbb{Z}_\lambda$ and an odd $t_q \leftarrow_\$ \mathbb{Z}_\lambda$. Compute θ, such that $g^{2\theta} = \chi^2$, based on the Chinese Remainder Theorem.
3. Pick $s \leftarrow_\$ \mathbb{Z}_\lambda$, and set $h \leftarrow g^s$. Note that such (s, h) are components of the private key and the public key in the generic ElGamal encryption scheme.
4. Output the public key $\mathsf{pk}_\times \leftarrow (n, g, \chi, h)$ and the private key $\mathsf{sk}_\times \leftarrow (s, \theta, p, q)$. Note that we can derive λ, v, t_p, t_q from $\mathsf{sk}_\times$.

Encryption. The encryption algorithm Enc takes as input a message $m \in \mathbb{Z}_n^*$ and a public key $\mathsf{pk}_\times$, and encodes m in $\mathbb{J}_n$ via $(m_1, m_2) \leftarrow (g^a, \chi^{-a} m) \in \mathbb{J}_n^2$ for $a \leftarrow_\$ \{1, \ldots, \lfloor n/2 \rfloor\}$ that satisfies $J_n(m) = (-1)^a$. Here J_n is an algorithm to compute the Jacobi symbol of a given value. Then the algorithm computes $c_J \leftarrow \mathbb{J}_n\text{-EG.Enc}(m_2) = (c_0 = g^r, c_1 = m_2 h^r)$ for $r \leftarrow_\$ \{1, \ldots, \lfloor n/2 \rfloor\}$. Finally, the algorithm returns the ciphertext $c \leftarrow (c_J = (c_0, c_1), m_1)$.

Decryption. The decryption algorithm Dec takes as input a ciphertext $c = (c_J = (c_0, c_1), m_1)$ and a key pair $(\mathsf{pk}_\times, \mathsf{sk}_\times)$, checks whether $J_n(c_1) = 1$ and outputs $\bot$ if it is not. If the check passes, the algorithm recovers m_2 via $m_2 \leftarrow \mathbb{J}_n\text{-EG.Dec}(c_J) = c_1/c_0^s \bmod n$ and computes $m_0 \leftarrow (1-v) \cdot m_1^{t_p} + v \cdot m_1^{t_q} \bmod n$. Finally, the algorithm returns the message $m \leftarrow m_0 m_2 \bmod n$.

Multiplication. The multiplication algorithm Mul takes as input two ciphertexts $c = (c_0, c_1, m_1)$ and $c' = (c_0', c_1', m_1')$, and outputs $c'' = (c_0 \cdot c_0', c_1 \cdot c_1', m_1 \cdot m_1') = (c_0'', c_1'', m_1'')$. Assume that m is the plaintext of c and m' is the plaintext of c'. We can easily verify that c'' is the ciphertext of $m \cdot m'$.

For simplicity, we may omit the parameters $\mathsf{pk}_\times$ and $\mathsf{sk}_\times$ from input parameters of the above algorithms in the setting of no confusion. We may also use $\mathbb{Z}_n^*$-EG.Enc$(m; r, a)$ to explicitly indicate the random coins (r, a) for encryption. The correctness of $\mathbb{J}_n$-EG is the same as the generic ElGamal encryption scheme: $c_1/c_0^s = (m_2 h^r)/g^{rs} = (m_2 g^{rs})/g^{rs} = m_2$ in $\mathbb{J}_n$. For an isomorphism f from $\mathbb{Z}_n^*$ to $\mathbb{Z}_p^* \times \mathbb{Z}_q^*$: $f(x) = ([x \bmod p], [x \bmod q])$, it is easily verified that

$$m_0 = (1 - v) \cdot m_1^{t_p} + v \cdot m_1^{t_q} \bmod n \leftrightarrow (m_1^{t_p}, m_1^{t_q}) = (g^{at_p}, g^{at_q})$$
$$= (g^{t_p}, g^{t_q})^a \leftrightarrow \left((1 - v) \cdot g^{t_p} + v \cdot g^{t_q} \bmod n\right)^a \bmod n = \chi^a \bmod n$$

and $m_0 m_2 = \chi^a \chi^{-a} m \bmod n = m$.

In [6], the authors proved the above $\mathbb{Z}_n^*$-EG is IND-CPA secure under the DDH assumption in $\mathbb{J}_n$ and the QR assumption in $\mathbb{Z}_n^*$.

4.2   Paillier Encryption over $\mathbb{Z}_n$

We use as the additively homomorphic encryption scheme the Paillier encryption scheme [23] $\mathbb{Z}_n$-P, $i.e.$, $\Pi_+ = \mathbb{Z}_n$-P. Its description is as follows.

Key Generation. The algorithm KGen takes as input a security parameter 1^κ, and generates a strong RSA modulus $n = pq$, where $p, q \in \Theta(2^\kappa)$ are randomly-chosen safe primes having the same length. Then the algorithm outputs a key pair ($\mathsf{pk}_+ = n$, $\mathsf{sk}_+ = (p, q)$). From sk_+, we can compute $\lambda \leftarrow \mathrm{lcm}(p - 1, q - 1)$ and $d \leftarrow [\lambda^{-1} \bmod n] \cdot \lambda \bmod n\lambda$. Note that the public key $\mathsf{pk}_+ = n$ is equal to n of the public key $\mathsf{pk}_\times$ of $\mathbb{Z}_n^*$-EG.

Encryption. The algorithm Enc takes as input a message $m \in \mathbb{Z}_n$ and the public key pk_+, and outputs the ciphertext $c \leftarrow (1 + n)^m r^n \bmod n^2$, where $r \leftarrow_\$ \mathbb{Z}_n^*$.

Decryption. The algorithm Dec takes as input a ciphertext c, the key pair $(\mathsf{pk}_+, \mathsf{sk}_+)$, and returns the plaintext $m = ([c^d \bmod n^2] - 1)/n$.

Addition. The algorithm Add takes as input two ciphertexts c and c', and outputs $c'' = c \cdot c' \bmod n^2$. Assume that m is the plaintext of c and m' is the plaintext of c'. We can easily check that c'' is the ciphertext of $m + m'$.

Multiplication. The scalar multiplication algorithm Mul takes as input a ciphertext c and a constant s, and outputs $c' = c^s \bmod n^2$. Note that computing a constant power of a ciphertext is equivalent to multiplying its encrypted value by this constant.

Randomness Extraction. The algorithm ExtractR takes as input a ciphertext c and a key pair $(\mathsf{pk}_+, \mathsf{sk}_+)$. It first computes $m \leftarrow \mathbb{Z}_n$-P.Dec$_{\mathsf{pk}_+}(c, \mathsf{sk}_+)$ and $c_0 \leftarrow c \cdot (1 + n)^{-m}$. Since p and q have the same length, we have $\gcd(\lambda, n) = 1$. Hence, the algorithm can find a value x, such that $n \cdot x \bmod \lambda = 1$. Finally, the algorithm outputs the random coin $r \leftarrow c_0^x \bmod n$.

Since $c^d \equiv (1+n)^{md} r^{nd} \equiv (1+n)^{m[\lambda^{-1} \bmod n] \cdot \lambda} r^{n[\lambda^{-1} \bmod n] \cdot \lambda} \equiv (1+n)^m \equiv 1 + mn \bmod n^2$, we can easily extract the message via $m \leftarrow ([c^d \bmod n^2] - 1)/n$. We remark that $\mathbb{Z}_n$-P is IND-CPA secure under the DCR assumption [23]. For simplicity, we may omit the parameters pk_+ and sk_+ from input parameters of the above algorithms when the setting is clear. We may also use $\mathbb{Z}_n$-P.Enc$(m; r)$ to explicitly indicate the random coins r for encryption.

4.3   Instantiation of Functionalities

We introduce how to securely realize $\mathcal{F}_{\mathsf{zk}}^{\mathsf{TwinCtx}}$, $\mathcal{F}_{\mathsf{zk}}^{\mathsf{EncValue}}$, and $\mathcal{F}_{\mathsf{zk}}^{\mathsf{sk}_+}$ based on $\mathbb{Z}_n^*$-EG and $\mathbb{Z}_n$-P. We provide protocols that are *public-coin honest-verifier zero-knowledge proof of knowledge*. There are several approaches to compile such protocols to protocols against malicious verifiers with *low overhead*, such as the Fiat-Shamir heuristic [12]. Note that we could simply use proof of factoring techniques, such as [24] to securely realize $\mathcal{F}_{\mathsf{zk}}^{\mathsf{sk}_+}$ for $\mathbb{Z}_n$-P.

We use ideas of [7] to realize $\mathcal{F}_{\mathsf{zk}}^{\mathsf{EncValue}}$ in Fig. 2. Here the prover Sarah can use $\mathbb{Z}_n$-P.ExtractR to extract the random coins r_+ of the ciphertext c_+.

Inputs: Both the prover P and the verifier V take as input $c_+ \in \mathbb{Z}_{n^2}^*$, $m_+ \in \mathbb{Z}_n$, $\mathsf{pk}_+ = n$. P also takes as input the witness $r_+ \in \mathbb{Z}_n^*$.

1. P picks $s \leftarrow_\$ \mathbb{Z}_n^*$ and sends $a \leftarrow \mathbb{Z}_n$-P.Enc$_{\mathsf{pk}_+}(0; s) = s^n \bmod n^2$ to V.
2. V returns $e \leftarrow_\$ \{0,1\}^t$ to P if $a \in \mathbb{Z}_{n^2}^*$. Otherwise, V outputs reject.
3. P computes and sends to V the value $z \leftarrow s r_+^e \bmod n$.
4. V computes $c' = c_+ (1+n)^{-m_+} \bmod n^2$. V outputs **accept** if $z^n \equiv a c'^e \bmod n^2$ and c', a, and z are all relatively prime to n. Otherwise, V outputs **reject**.

Fig. 2. Protocol EncValue associated with $\mathbb{Z}_n$-P.

Proposition 1. *The protocol* EncValue *associated with* $\mathbb{Z}_n$-P *is public-coin honest-verifier zero-knowledge proof of knowledge.*

Before we provide the protocol for $\mathcal{F}_{\mathsf{zk}}^{\mathsf{TwinCtx}}$, we introduce a zero-knowledge ideal functionality $\mathcal{F}_{\mathsf{zk}}^{\mathsf{EncOne}}$ associated with the language that a given ciphertext $c_\times$ encrypts 1 as follows:

$$L_{\mathsf{EncOne}} = \{(c_\times = ((c_0, c_1), m_1) \in (\mathbb{Z}_n^*)^3, \mathsf{pk}_\times = (n, g, \chi, h)) \mid \exists (s, \theta), s.t.$$
$$h = g^s \bmod n \wedge \chi^2 \equiv g^{2\theta} \bmod n \wedge c_1 = m_1^{-\theta} c_0^s \bmod n\}.$$

If the plaintext of $c_\times = ((c_0 = g^r, c_1 = m_2 h^r), m_1 = g^a)$ is 1, which is encoded by $(m_1, m_2) = (g^a, \chi^{-a}) \in \mathbb{J}_n^2$ for an even a, we should have $c_1 = \chi^{-a} h^r = g^{-\theta a} g^{sr} = m_1^{-\theta} c_0^s$. Hence, the protocol that could be used to realize $\mathcal{F}_{\mathsf{zk}}^{\mathsf{EncOne}}$ is given in Fig. 3 and the proposition for its security is in the following.

Inputs: Both the prover P and the verifier V take as input $\mathsf{pk}_\times = (n, g, \chi, h))$ and $(c_\times = ((c_0, c_1), m_1) \in (\mathbb{Z}_n^*)^3$. P also takes as input the witness (s, θ).

1. P randomly picks $u, v \leftarrow_\$ \mathbb{Z}_n$, computes $d_1 \leftarrow g^{2u} \bmod n$, $d_2 \leftarrow g^v \bmod n$, $d_3 \leftarrow m_1^{-u} c_0^v \bmod n$, and sends d_1, d_2, and d_3 to V.
2. V randomly picks $e \leftarrow_\$ \{0,1\}^t$ and sends it to P if $d_1, d_2, d_3 \in (\mathbb{Z}_n^*)^3$. Otherwise, V outputs **reject**.
3. P computes $z_1 \leftarrow u + e\theta \bmod \lambda$, $z_2 \leftarrow v + es \bmod \lambda$, and sends it to V.
4. V checks $g^{2z_1} \equiv d_1(\chi^e)^2 \bmod n$, $g^{z_2} \equiv d_2 h^e \bmod n$, and $m_1^{-z_1} c_0^{z_2} \equiv d_3 c_1^e \bmod n$. V outputs **accept** if all equations hold, and **reject** otherwise.

Fig. 3. Protocol EncOne associated with $\mathbb{Z}_n^*$-EG.

Proposition 2. *The protocol* EncOne *associated with* $\mathbb{Z}_n^*$-EG *is complete, sound, and honest-verifier zero-knowledge.*

For $\mathcal{F}_{\mathsf{zk}}^{\mathsf{TwinCtx}}$, the prover Sarah proves to the verifier Bob that a given ciphertext pair is a twin-ciphertext pair. We separate the protocol realizing $\mathcal{F}_{\mathsf{zk}}^{\mathsf{TwinCtx}}$ into two phases: offline and online phases, to obtain a more practical protocol[1].

For the offline phase (Fig. 4), the prover Sarah possessing $\mathsf{sk}_\times$ first generates a random ciphertext pair (c_0, c_0'), such that $c_0 = \mathbb{Z}_n^*\text{-EG.Enc}(m_0) = (c_{0J} = (c_{00}, c_{01}), m_{01})$ and $c_0' = \mathbb{Z}_n\text{-P.Enc}(m_0'; r_0')$, where $m_0 = m_0'$. Then P sends it to the verifier Bob and convinces Bob that it is indeed a twin-ciphertext pair without revealing information about the plaintexts and the corresponding random coins. The generated (c_0, c_0') will then be used in the online phase of TwinCtx.

In the online phase (Fig. 5), Sarah proves a given ciphertext $(c_\times, c_+)$ is a twin-ciphertext pair using (c_0, c_0'), as required in $\mathcal{F}_{\mathsf{zk}}^{\mathsf{TwinCtx}}$.

Intuitively, since m' is a random message and both $\mathbb{Z}_n$-P and $\mathbb{Z}_n^*$-EG are IND-CPA secure, m and the random coins of $(c_\times, c_+)$ will be preserved if (c_0, c_0') is correctly generated in the offline phase. We have the following proposition.

Proposition 3. *The* TwinCtx *protocol associated with* $\mathbb{Z}_n^*$-EG *and* $\mathbb{Z}_n$-P *is public-coin honest-verifier zero-knowledge proof of knowledge.*

Here each execution of TwinCtx generates and consumes a (random) twin-ciphertext pair, which is not desirable. We now introduce how to improve the efficiency of the TwinCtx protocol using the idea in [6,17]. We first recall the notion *multi-exponentiation with encrypted bases* (MEB). The zero-knowledge functionality $\mathcal{F}_{\mathsf{zk}}^{\mathsf{MEB}}$ is for the relation associated with the language below:

$$L_{\mathsf{MEB}} = \{(n, \{\omega_i\}_{i=1}^k \in \{0,1\}^{\kappa \cdot k}, C, \{c_i\}_{i=1}^k \in (\mathbb{Z}_{n^2})^{k+1} \mid \exists (r, \{m_i, r_i\}_{i=1}^k), s.t.$$

$$\forall i \in \{1, \ldots, k\} c_i = \mathbb{Z}_n\text{-P.Enc}(m_i; r_i) \wedge C = \mathbb{Z}_n\text{-P.Enc}(\prod_{i=1}^k m_i^{\omega_i}; r)\}.$$

---

[1] Such an approach is similar to that of [6]. However, their security goal indeed cannot be achieved since the random coins of the ElGamal encryption cannot be extracted and the group order is hidden. We overcome the security faults for our scenario.

Inputs: Both the prover P and the verifier V take as input $c_0 = (c_{0J} = (c_{00}, c_{01}), m_{01}) \in (\mathbb{Z}_n^*)^3$, $c_0' \in \mathbb{Z}_{n^2}^*$, $\mathsf{pk}_+ = n$, $\mathsf{pk}_\times = (n, g, \chi, h)$. P also takes as input $(s, \theta) \in \mathsf{sk}_\times$, $m_0 = m_0' \in \mathbb{Z}_n$ and $r_0' \in \mathbb{Z}_n^*$, such that $c_0' = \mathbb{Z}_n\text{-P.Enc}_{\mathsf{pk}}(m_0'; r_0')$.

1. P generates t random ciphertext pairs (c_i, c_i'), such that $c_i = \mathbb{Z}_n^*\text{-EG.Enc}(m_i; r_i, a_i) = (c_{iJ} = (c_{i0}, c_{i1}), m_{i1})$, $c_i' = \mathbb{Z}_n\text{-P.Enc}(m_i'; r_i')$, and $m_i = m_i'$, for $i = 1, \ldots, t$. Then P sends them to V.
2. V picks $e = e_1 \cdots e_t \leftarrow \{0,1\}^t$ and returns e to P if $c_i \in (\mathbb{Z}_n^*)^3$ and $c_i' \in \mathbb{Z}_{n^2}^*$. Otherwise, V outputs reject.
3. For $i = 1, \ldots, t$,
   - if $e_i = 0$, P sends to V the values m_i, r_i, a_i and r_i';
   - if $e_i = 1$, P computes $R_i \leftarrow m_0/m_i \bmod n$, and encodes it as $(R_{i1}, R_{i2}) \leftarrow (g^{a_{R_i}}, \chi^{-a_{R_i}} R_i) \in \mathbb{J}_n^2$ for $a_{R_i} \leftarrow_\$ \{1, \ldots, \lfloor n/2 \rfloor\}$, such that $J_n(R_i) = (-1)^{a_{R_i}}$. Then P computes $\rho_i' \leftarrow r_i'^{R_i} \cdot r_0^{-1} \bmod n$. Finally, P sends R_i, a_{R_i} to V.
4. For $i = 1, \ldots, t$,
   - if $e_i = 0$, V checks the validity of (c_i, c_i') via $c_i = \mathbb{Z}_n^*\text{-EG.Enc}(m_i; r_i, a_i)$ and $c_i' = \mathbb{Z}_n\text{-P.Enc}(m_i; r_i')$;
   - if $e_i = 1$, V reconstructs $(R_{i1}, R_{i2}) \leftarrow (g^{a_{R_i}}, \chi^{-a_{R_i}} R_i) \in \mathbb{J}_n^2$, computes $D_i \leftarrow ((c_{i0} \cdot (c_{00})^{-1}, c_{i1} \cdot R_{i2} \cdot (c_{01})^{-1}), m_{i1} \cdot R_{i1} \cdot (m_{01})^{-1}) \in \mathbb{J}_n^3$ and $D_i' \leftarrow c_i'^{R_i} \cdot (c_0')^{-1} \bmod n^2$. Then, P proves to V that $D_i = \mathbb{Z}_n^*\text{-EG.Enc}(1)$ and $D_i' = \mathbb{Z}_n\text{-P.Enc}(0; \rho_i')$ hold using $\mathcal{F}_{\mathsf{zk}}^{\mathsf{EncOne}}$ and $\mathcal{F}_{\mathsf{zk}}^{\mathsf{EncValue}}$.

If all verifications are accepted, V outputs **accept**, and **reject** otherwise.

Fig. 4. Protocol TwinCtx for $\mathbb{Z}_n^*$-EG and $\mathbb{Z}_n$-P—offline Phase.

Inputs: Both the prover P and the verifier V take as input $c_\times = (c_J = (c_{\times 0}, c_{\times 1}), m_{\times 1}) \in (\mathbb{Z}_n^*)^3$, $c_+ \in \mathbb{Z}_{n^2}^*$, $\mathsf{pk}_+ = n$, and $\mathsf{pk}_\times = (n, g, \chi, h)$. They have input a *twin-ciphertext pair* (c_0, c_0'), where $c_0 = ((c_{00}, c_{01}), m_{01})$ and c_0' from the offline phase. P also takes as input $(s, \theta) \in \mathsf{sk}_\times$, $m \in \mathbb{Z}_n$ and $r_+ \in \mathbb{Z}_n^*$, such that $c_+ = \mathbb{Z}_n\text{-P.Enc}_{\mathsf{pk}}(m; r_+)$, and (m_0', r_0') from the offline phase.

1. P computes $R \leftarrow m/m_0'$, and encodes R as $(R_1, R_2) \leftarrow (g^{a_R}, \chi^{-a_R} R) \in \mathbb{J}_n^2$ for $a_R \leftarrow_\$ \{1, \ldots, \lfloor n/2 \rfloor\}$, such that $J_n(R) = (-1)^{a_R}$. P computes $\rho_+ \leftarrow r_0'^R \cdot r_+^{-1} \bmod n$, and sends R, a_R to V.
2. V reconstructs $(R_1, R_2) \leftarrow (g^{a_R}, \chi^{-a_R} R) \in \mathbb{J}_n^2$, computes $D_\times \leftarrow ((c_{00} \cdot (c_{\times 0})^{-1}, c_{01} \cdot R_2 \cdot (c_{\times 1})^{-1}), m_{01} \cdot R_1 \cdot (m_{\times 1})^{-1}) \in \mathbb{J}_n^2$ and $D_+ \leftarrow c_0'^R \cdot (c_+)^{-1} \bmod n^2$. P proves to V that $D_\times = \mathbb{Z}_n^*\text{-EG.Enc}_{\mathsf{pk}_\times}(1)$ and $D_+ = \mathbb{Z}_n\text{-P.Enc}_{\mathsf{pk}_+}(0; \rho_+)$ hold using $\mathcal{F}_{\mathsf{zk}}^{\mathsf{EncOne}}$ and $\mathcal{F}_{\mathsf{zk}}^{\mathsf{EncValue}}$. If they hold, V outputs **accept**, and **reject** otherwise.

Fig. 5. Protocol TwinCtx for $\mathbb{Z}_n^*$-EG and $\mathbb{Z}_n$-P—online Phase.

A protocol to realize $\mathcal{F}_{zk}^{MEB}$ was proposed in [6], and then it was improved and its security was formally proved in [17]. We can use the 5-round protocol in [17] to batch the executions of the online phase of TwinCtx. In this setting, the prover P wants to prove to the verifier V that all pairs of $(c_i, c_i')_{i=1,\ldots,k}$ where $c_i = \mathbb{Z}_n^*\text{-EG.Enc}(m_i; r_i, a_i)$ and $c_i' = \mathbb{Z}_n\text{-P.Enc}(m_i'; r_i')$ are all twin-ciphertext pairs, i.e., $m_i = m_i'$ given only one random twin-ciphertext pair generated in the offline phase of TwinCtx. Here the common reference string (CRS) contains the description of a pseudo-random generator (PRG). The procedure for batching the executions of the online phase of TwinCtx is as follows.

1. V sends $\omega \leftarrow_\$ \{0,1\}^\kappa$ to P.
2. Both parties use ω as a seed for PRG to generate $(\omega_i)_{i=1,\ldots,k}$. Then both parties take ω_ith power for each entry of c_i and add them together to obtain C, such that $C = \mathbb{Z}_n^*\text{-EG.Enc}(\prod_{i=1}^k m_i^{\omega_i}; \sum_{i=1}^k \omega_i r_i, \sum_{i=1}^k \omega_i a_i)$. P picks $\rho \leftarrow_\$ \mathbb{Z}_n^*$ and sends $C' \leftarrow \mathbb{Z}_n\text{-P.Enc}(\prod_{i=1}^k m_i'^{\omega_i}; \rho)$ to V.
3. P and V uses $\mathcal{F}_{zk}^{MEB}$ on $((\omega_i)_{i=1,\ldots,k}, C', (c_i')_{i=1,\ldots,k})$.
4. If $\mathcal{F}_{zk}^{MEB}$ returns accept, P and V perform the online phase of TwinCtx for (C, C'), and V outputs what TwinCtx outputs. Otherwise, V returns reject.

MEB proves that C' is indeed the ciphertext of $\prod_{i=1}^k m_i'^{\omega_i}$. If $\prod_{i=1}^k m_i^{\omega_i} = \prod_{i=1}^k m_i'^{\omega_i}$ for random $(\omega_i)_{i=1,\ldots,k}$, we have $m_i = m_i'$ for $i = 1, \ldots, k$ with an overwhelming probability. Here we note that the messages from P in Step 2 and Step 3 can be combined, and the two protocols, MEB [17] and TwinCtx, can be performed in parallel. We can further pack the procedure, such that the online phase and the offline phase of TwinCtx are executed simultaneously. More precisely, the online phase uses the generated random twin-ciphertext pair, and meanwhile the offline phase proves that this generated ciphertext pair is indeed a twin-ciphertext pair. Such an approach can reduce the number of rounds of the encryption switching procedure (Step 3 of the generic construction) to 6.

5   Extension from $\mathbb{Z}_n^*$ to $\mathbb{Z}_n$

The $\mathbb{Z}_n^*$-EG scheme encrypts values in $\mathbb{Z}_n^*$. However, in some scenarios, it would be nice if one can encrypt the element 0. We illustrate a method to extend the protocol from $\mathbb{Z}_n^*$ to $\mathbb{Z}_n$ in this section. We recall the definition of computational equality as follows for our further discussion.

Definition 5 (Computational Equality [6]). *For two finite sets S_1 and S_2 with cardinalities $|S_1|, |S_2| \in \Theta(\kappa^c)$ for large enough constant $c > 0$, we call them computationally equal if for every PPT adversary $\mathcal{A}$, we have*

$$\Pr[m \in S_1 \oplus S_2 : m \leftarrow \mathcal{A}(S_1, S_2)] \leq \mathsf{negl}(\kappa) ,$$

where $S_1 \oplus S_2$ denotes the symmetric difference of S_1 and S_2.

We claim that $\mathbb{Z}_n$ and $\mathbb{Z}_n^* \cup \{0\}$ is computationally equal, since if we can find a value $m \in \mathbb{Z}_n \oplus (\mathbb{Z}_n^* \cup \{0\})$, we can factor the RSA modulus n, which contradicts the assumption that it is computationally hard to factor n. Hence, we only need to include 0 in the $\mathbb{Z}_n^*$-EG plaintext space to extend from $\mathbb{Z}_n^*$ to $\mathbb{Z}_n$.

The ciphertext of the new encryption scheme $\mathbb{Z}_n$-EG is a tuple $C = (c, u)$, where u is called *zero indicator*. A messages m is encrypted as follows.

- If $m \neq 0$, we compute $c \leftarrow \mathbb{Z}_n^*\text{-EG.Enc}(m)$, $u \leftarrow \mathbb{Z}_n^*\text{-EG.Enc}(1)$.
- If $m = 0$, we compute $c \leftarrow \mathbb{Z}_n^*\text{-EG.Enc}(r)$ for $r \leftarrow_\$ \mathbb{Z}_n^*$, and $u \leftarrow \mathbb{Z}_n^*\text{-EG.Enc}(\bar{g})$, where $\bar{g} \in \mathbb{J}_n$ is a predefined fixed value for $\mathbb{Z}_n$-EG.

Multiplication of two encrypted values with tuples (c_1, u_1) and (c_2, u_2) is by doing element-wise multiplications of these tuples. If the multiplication involves an encrypted zero, the zero indicator encrypts a *non-one* value and the first entry c encrypts a *random* value. Otherwise, the zero indicator encrypts 1, and c encrypts the multiplication result. To decrypt a tuple (c, u), the decryption algorithm decrypts the zero indicator via $z \leftarrow \mathbb{Z}_n^*\text{-EG.Dec}_{\mathsf{pk}_\times}(u, \mathsf{sk}_\times)$. If $z \neq 1$, the algorithm outputs $m \leftarrow 0$. Otherwise, the algorithm outputs $m \leftarrow \mathbb{Z}_n^*\text{-EG.Dec}_{\mathsf{pk}_\times}(c, \mathsf{sk}_\times)$. Because $\mathbb{Z}_n$-EG is based on $\mathbb{Z}_n^*$-EG, it is obvious that $\mathbb{Z}_n$-EG is also IND-CPA secure. Otherwise, we can construct a distinguisher to break the IND-CPA security of $\mathbb{Z}_n^*$-EG. For the zero indicator, we can further encrypt values $\bar{g} \in \mathbb{J}_n$ without encoding and thus obtain *shorter* ciphertexts.

The extension from $\mathbb{Z}_n^*$ to $\mathbb{Z}_n$ affects the encryption switching procedure in the generic construction (Step 3), and we now illustrate how to modify this procedure in Fig. 6. Our goal is to switch a $\mathbb{Z}_n$-EG ciphertext (c, u) to a $\mathbb{Z}_n$-P ciphertext. Let the maximum degree of the polynomial P be $d_{\max}$. For u inside (c, u), we know that u encrypts one value of $\{1, \bar{g}, \ldots, \bar{g}^{d_{\max}}\}$. We thus can construct a Lagrange polynomial L of (at most) degree $d_{\max}$, which maps 1 to 1 and values in $\{\bar{g}, \ldots, \bar{g}^{d_{\max}}\}$ to 0. If we evaluate L on the encrypted value of u, we derive encrypted 1 for ciphertexts of non-zero values and encrypted 0 for ciphertexts of zero according to the zero indicator. Then this encrypted evaluation result multiplied by the encrypted value of c leads to the switched ciphertext.

The procedure in Fig. 6 utilizes the zero-knowledge functionality $\mathcal{F}_{\mathsf{zk}}^{\mathsf{EncMul}}$ for the multiplication of encrypted values relation associated with the language:

$$L_{\mathsf{EncMul}} = \{(c_a, c_b, c_c \in (\mathbb{Z}_{n^2}^*)^3, \mathsf{pk}_+ = n) \mid \exists (a, b, c, r_a, r_b, r_c), s.t.$$
$$ab \equiv c \bmod n \wedge \forall x \in \{a, b, c\}, \mathbb{Z}_n\text{-P.Enc}_{\mathsf{pk}_+}(x; r_x) = c_x\}.$$

The protocol that realizes $\mathcal{F}_{\mathsf{zk}}^{\mathsf{EncMul}}$ can be found in [7]. Note that since α and β are random, $c'_{a+\alpha}$ and $c'_{b+\beta}$ do not leak any information about a, b, Sarah learns no information about C, c_+ and v during the protocol.

Similar to the $\mathbb{Z}_n^*$ case, we can pack the encryption switching procedure for the $\mathbb{Z}_n$ case. More precisely, Bob can switch for both c and terms of Lagrange polynomial L on u simultaneously via batching TwinCtx. After obtaining the switched ciphertexts (c_+ and v), Bob starts Step 3 of the encryption switching procedure from $\mathbb{Z}_n$-EG to $\mathbb{Z}_n$-P in parallel. Hence, we derive a 6-round procedure. We present an illustration of this procedure for switching one ciphertext in Fig. 7, and a very similar approach can be used to switch multiple ciphertexts.

Inputs: The receiver Bob takes as input $\mathsf{pk}_\times$, pk_+, and $\mathsf{sk}_\times$. The sender Sarah takes as input $C = (c, u)$, $\mathsf{pk}_\times$, pk_+.

1. Bob switches the encryption scheme of c from $\mathbb{Z}_n^*$-EG to $\mathbb{Z}_n$-P according to Step 3 of the generic construction, and obtains c_+. Bob executes Step 2 – 4 of the generic construction to evaluate the Lagrange polynomial L mentioned above on the encrypted value of u, and obtains a $\mathbb{Z}_n$-P ciphertext v. Denote the plaintext of c_+ by a and the plaintext of v by b, i.e., $b \in \{0, 1\}$.

2. Bob picks $\alpha, \beta \leftarrow_\$ \mathbb{Z}_n$ and computes ciphertexts $c_\alpha \leftarrow \mathbb{Z}_n\text{-P.Enc}_{\mathsf{pk}_+}(\alpha)$, $c_\beta \leftarrow \mathbb{Z}_n\text{-P.Enc}_{\mathsf{pk}_+}(\beta)$, $c_{a+\alpha} \leftarrow \mathbb{Z}_n\text{-P.Add}_{\mathsf{pk}_+}(c_+, c_\alpha)$, $c_{b+\beta} \leftarrow \mathbb{Z}_n\text{-P.Add}_{\mathsf{pk}_+}(v, c_\beta)$. Then Bob sends $c_{a+\alpha}$ and $c_{b+\beta}$ to Sarah. Meanwhile, Bob locally computes $c_{a\beta} \leftarrow \mathbb{Z}_n\text{-P.Mul}_{\mathsf{pk}_+}(c_+, \beta)$, $c_{b\alpha} \leftarrow \mathbb{Z}_n\text{-P.Mul}_{\mathsf{pk}_+}(v, \alpha)$, and $c_{\alpha\beta} \leftarrow \mathbb{Z}_n\text{-P.Enc}_{\mathsf{pk}_+}(\alpha\beta)$.

3. Sarah extracts $a' \leftarrow \mathbb{Z}_n\text{-P.Dec}_{\mathsf{pk}_+}(c_{a+\alpha}, \mathsf{sk}_+)$ and $b' \leftarrow \mathbb{Z}_n\text{-P.Dec}_{\mathsf{pk}_+}(c_{b+\beta}, \mathsf{sk}_+)$, and the corresponding random coins via $\mathbb{Z}_n\text{-P.ExtractR}$. Then Sarah computes $c_c' \leftarrow \mathbb{Z}_n\text{-P.Enc}_{\mathsf{pk}_+}(a' \cdot b')$, and sends c_c' to Bob. Sarah, as the prover, calls $\mathcal{F}_{\mathsf{zk}}^{\mathsf{EncMul}}$ with Bob, as the verifier, for the multiplication relation of $c_{a+\alpha}$, $c_{b+\beta}$, and c_c'.

4. If the output of $\mathcal{F}_{\mathsf{zk}}^{\mathsf{EncMul}}$ is accept, Bob outputs $c_c \leftarrow c_c' \cdot c_{a\beta}^{-1} \cdot c_{b\beta}^{-1} \cdot c_{\alpha\beta}^{-1} \bmod n^2$, which is the switched ciphertext of C. Otherwise, Bob outputs $\bot$ and halts.

Fig. 6. Encryption switching procedure from $\mathbb{Z}_n$-EG to $\mathbb{Z}_n$-P with $\mathcal{F}_{\mathsf{zk}}^{\mathsf{EncMul}}$.

6   Fair Exchange on Blockchain

In this section, we introduce how to achieve fairness via blockchain, such that the buyer Bob receives the evaluation result if and only if the seller Sarah gets paid from Bob. We first briefly introduce the underlying ideas.

We stress that Sarah has a negligible advantage to provide an incorrect result without being rejected if the blind polynomial evaluation protocol guarantees receivers' security. Meanwhile, Bob obtains no more information than the result $P(x)$ and cannot have any information about $P(x)$ before Step 5 of the generic construction. Therefore, we can compile the protocol EncValue associated with $\mathbb{Z}_n$-P via Fiat-Shamir heuristic to make it non-interactive, and deploy the proof verification process on smart contracts to achieve fair exchange. More precisely, Bob programs a smart contract, uploads parameters for EncValue, and freezes his payment on the contract. This smart contract receives Sarah's decrypted result, together with the proof, and verifies the proof. If the verification returns accept, Sarah will retrieve the payment automatically. Bob can remove the blind factor to obtain the final result. We call this approach *active* verification.

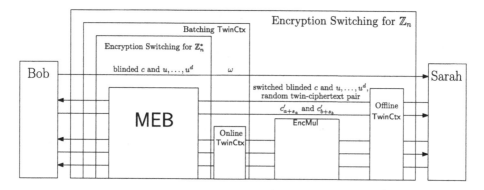

Fig. 7. Packing encryption switching procedure for the $\mathbb{Z}_n$ case.

It is indeed possible to further reduce the cost. It is reasonable to assume that Sarah behaves mostly honestly, since Sarah may trade data many times with different buyers, and it will influence Sarah's credit if she is detected to behave dishonestly. We could require Sarah to pay a deposit on the smart contract when she submits her proof. The smart contract now does not verify this proof. Alternatively, Bob verifies the proof off-chain, *i.e.*, Bob retrieves the proof from the smart contract and verifies it locally. If the proof is accepted, Sarah can retrieve the payment and her deposit after a specified period called *complaint period*. Hence, we save the cost of on-chain verification. Otherwise, Bob starts the verification procedure on the smart contract during the complaint period. If the smart contract indeed rejects the proof, it transfers the payment together with Sarah's deposit to Bob to penalize dishonest Sarah. Hence, if the latency of the complaint period is acceptable, this *passive* verification approach is cheaper. In what follows, we give a formal description and analysis for the ideas above.

6.1   Procedure Obliviousness

Before introducing the fair exchange protocol, we explicitly define for blind polynomial evaluation a security property called *procedure obliviousness*. Informally, the blind polynomial evaluation protocol achieves *procedure obliviousness* if the receiver of the protocol learns nothing beyond the public information c_x and pi before the *result retrieval procedure* of the generic construction. This property is to ensure that buyers must learn nothing if he aborts before the seller can claim the payment. The definition is given as follows.

Definition 6 (Procedure Obliviousness). *For every* PPT *adversary $\mathcal{A}$ with input c_x, pi and auxiliary input z playing receiver's role until the beginning of the fifth step in the generic construction, there exists a* PPT *simulator $\mathcal{S}$ taking c_x, pi, z as input in the ideal model, such that the view simulated by $\mathcal{S}$ is computationally indistinguishable from the view of $\mathcal{A}$.*

Our generic construction in Sect. 3 indeed achieves procedure obliviousness.

Theorem 2. *The generic construction in the hybrid model with the ideal functionalities* $\mathcal{F}_{zk}^{TwinCtx}$, $\mathcal{F}_{zk}^{EncValue}$, *and* $\mathcal{F}_{zk}^{sk+}$ *achieves procedure obliviousness.*

6.2 Security Requirements

Given that the blind polynomial evaluation protocol is procedure obliviousness, we proceed to introduce the fair exchange protocol for the result retrieval procedure of the generic construction over blockchain. Note that in this procedure, the seller Sarah will receive the blinded ciphertext $c'_{+,P(x)}$ from the buyer Bob. Now to achieve a fair exchange of the decryption result and the payment, we move the transfer of the decryption result for $c'_{+,P(x)}$ and the verification of EncValue protocol to blockchain. After the fair exchange, Bob can simply remove the blind factor to obtain the final result to finish the data trading procedure.

We first define the security requirements for the fair exchange of the data trading scenario between a data buyer and a data seller via *termination, buyer fairness*, and *seller fairness* in the following.

Termination. If at least one party is honest, the protocol will terminate, and all coins for the contract will be unlocked.

Buyer Fairness. An honest buyer is guaranteed that only if the seller provides the *correct* decryption result of the ciphertext c given by the buyer, the buyer will pay the seller p coins.

Seller Fairness. An honest seller is ensured that only if the buyer pays p coins to the seller, the buyer can learn the decryption result.

6.3 Protocol

We remark that our goal in this section is to integrate the transfer of the decryption result and the verification of EncValue protocol into the blockchain paradigm to achieve the security requirements defined in Sect. 6.2.

We first introduce how to compile the EncValue protocol for a Paillier ciphertext c, i.e., $c'_{+,P(x)}$ in the generic construction, via the Fiat-Shamir heuristic to make it non-interactive and secure against malicious verifiers. Given a cryptographic hash function $H: \{0,1\}^* \mapsto \{0,1\}^t$, the prover first picks $s \leftarrow_s \mathbb{Z}_n^*$ and computes the value a as in EncValue. Then the prover computes $e \leftarrow H(n, c, m, a)$ to generate the challenge e. Finally, the prover computes z as in EncValue and sends (m, e, z) to verifiers. To verify the proof, verifiers compute $a \leftarrow z^n c'^{-e} \mod n^2$ and output accept if and only if $e \leftarrow H(n, c, m, a)$. Note that the size of the non-interactive proof is short to be deployed on blockchain, e.g., 0.28125 KB for $\|n\| = 2048$ and $t = 256$. The idea for the fair exchange of the evaluation result is to use a blockchain-enabled smart contract as a judge for the verification of this non-interactive proof when disputes happen.

The description of our fair exchange protocol basically follows the symbols and framework used in [10] (and also in [11]). As the same as [10], we abstract the communication by the synchronous communication model. This model assumes that the protocol is executed in rounds and all parties are aware of the current round. At the beginning of each round, parties receive all messages sent to them in the previous round. Meanwhile, all messages are sent within one round and received within the next round, *i.e.*, the communication is instantaneous.

We model the hash function (*e.g.*, keccak 256) used in the Fiat-Shamir heuristic via the global random oracle $\mathcal{H}$ and use the global ledger $\mathcal{L}$ (see [10] for more information) to model a blockchain (*e.g.*, Ethereum). Here we focus on the *passive verification* approach as described in Sect. 6. The ideal functionality $\mathcal{G}_{\mathsf{FairExchange}}^{\mathcal{L},\mathcal{H}}$ is to model the blockchain-enabled smart contract $\mathcal{G}_{\mathsf{FairExchange}}$ with access to $\mathcal{L}$ and $\mathcal{H}$. Note that $\mathcal{G}_{\mathsf{FairExchange}}^{\mathcal{L},\mathcal{H}}$, acting as a judge smart contract over the blockchain, interacts with $\mathcal{L}$, $\mathcal{H}$, the buyer Bob, and the seller Sarah. The description of $\mathcal{G}_{\mathsf{FairExchange}}^{\mathcal{L},\mathcal{H}}$ is given in Fig. 8, and the description of the four-phase protocol for fair exchange between an honest buyer Bob and an honest seller Sarah is given in Fig. 9. In practice, because of the transparency of blockchain, both parties can check the code of the smart contract and start the protocol only if the smart contract correctly realizes the functionality of $\mathcal{G}_{\mathsf{FairExchange}}^{\mathcal{L},\mathcal{H}}$.

In the initiation phase, $\mathcal{G}_{\mathsf{FairExchange}}^{\mathcal{L},\mathcal{H}}$ receives from the buyer Bob the public key $\mathsf{pk}_+ = n$ for the Paillier encryption, the Paillier ciphertext c, as well as the price p for the evaluation result. Then $\mathcal{G}_{\mathsf{FairExchange}}^{\mathcal{L},\mathcal{H}}$ locks p coins from Bob via $\mathcal{L}$ for the payment. The buyer Bob also sends n and c to the seller Sarah.

If the message from Bob and $\mathcal{G}_{\mathsf{FairExchange}}^{\mathcal{L},\mathcal{H}}$ are consistent, Bob submits the decryption result and corresponding non-interactive zero-knowledge proof derived from EncValue to $\mathcal{G}_{\mathsf{FairExchange}}^{\mathcal{L},\mathcal{H}}$ in the submission phase. Additionally, $\mathcal{G}_{\mathsf{FairExchange}}^{\mathcal{L},\mathcal{H}}$ locks p coins from Bob via $\mathcal{L}$, which would be used to penalize dishonest Bob.

In the complaint phase, upon receiving the acknowledgment of Sarah's submitted message from $\mathcal{G}_{\mathsf{FairExchange}}^{\mathcal{L},\mathcal{H}}$, Bob could locally run the verification of the non-interactive zero-knowledge proof. If the proof is incorrect, Bob needs to send the message to complain the dispute during the complaint phase *in time*. Once $\mathcal{G}_{\mathsf{FairExchange}}^{\mathcal{L},\mathcal{H}}$ receives the complaint during the complaint phase, $\mathcal{G}_{\mathsf{FairExchange}}^{\mathcal{L},\mathcal{H}}$ verifies the non-interactive zero-knowledge proof and resolves the dispute. If the verification is indeed incorrect, $\mathcal{G}_{\mathsf{FairExchange}}^{\mathcal{L},\mathcal{H}}$ unlocks $2p$ coins to Bob (p coins sent back to honest Bob and p coins for penalizing dishonest Sarah sending incorrect proof). Otherwise, $\mathcal{G}_{\mathsf{FairExchange}}^{\mathcal{L},\mathcal{H}}$ unlocks these $2p$ coins to Sarah. If the verification of the proof is accepted, Bob sends $(finalize, id)$ to finalize the fair exchange.

If no *complain* message or *finalize* message from Bob is sent to $\mathcal{G}_{\mathsf{FairExchange}}^{\mathcal{L},\mathcal{H}}$ during the complaint phase, Sarah sends $(finalize, id)$ to $\mathcal{G}_{\mathsf{FairExchange}}^{\mathcal{L},\mathcal{H}}$ in the payout phase. Then $\mathcal{G}_{\mathsf{FairExchange}}^{\mathcal{L},\mathcal{H}}$ unlocks the $2p$ coins to Sarah.

We note that smart contract for *active verification* approach mentioned in Sect. 6 is similar to $\mathcal{G}_{\mathsf{FairExchange}}^{\mathcal{L},\mathcal{H}}$. The smart contract for active verification merges the submission, complaint, and payout phases together, *i.e.*, the smart contract verifies the proof once it receives the *submit* message. If the proof is correct, coins are sent to the seller. Otherwise, coins are sent back to the buyer.

The ideal functionality $\mathcal{G}_{\mathsf{FairExchange}}^{\mathcal{L},\mathcal{H}}$ locally stores addresses $addr_{\mathrm{Bob}}$ and $addr_{\mathrm{Sarah}}$ for both Bob and Sarah, respectively. It also maintains price p, state s, and the corresponding parameters for EncValue: n, c, m, e, and z.

───────────────────────**Initiation**───────────────────────

Upon receiving $(initiate, id, n, c, p)$ from the buyer Bob, store n, c, and p, and send $(freeze, id, \mathrm{Bob}, p)$ to $\mathcal{L}$. If $\mathcal{L}$ responds with $(frozen, id, \mathrm{Bob}, p)$, set $s = initialized$ and send $(initialized, id, n, c, p)$ to all parties.

───────────────────────**Submission**───────────────────────

Upon receiving $(submit, id, m, e, z)$ from the seller Sarah when $s = initialized$, send $(freeze, id, \mathrm{Sarah}, p)$ to $\mathcal{L}$. If $\mathcal{L}$ responds with $(frozen, id, \mathrm{Sarah}, p)$, set $s = submitted$, store m, e, and z, and send $(submitted, id, m, e, z)$ to all parties. Otherwise, if no such a message from Sarah was received, send $(unfreeze, id, \mathrm{Bob}, p)$ to $\mathcal{L}$ and abort.

───────────────────────**Complaint**───────────────────────

Upon receiving $(complain, id)$ from the buyer Bob when $s = submitted$, compute $c' \leftarrow c \cdot (1 + n)^{-m} \bmod n^2$, $a \leftarrow z^n \cdot c'^{-e} \bmod n^2$, set $s = finalized$, and verify whether the equation $e = \mathcal{H}(n, c, m, a)$ holds.

- If the equation holds, send $(unfreeze, id, \mathrm{Sarah}, 2p)$ to $\mathcal{L}$, $(sold, id)$ to all parties, and terminate.
- If the equation does not hold, send $(unfreeze, id, \mathrm{Bob}, 2p)$ to $\mathcal{L}$, $(not\ sold, id)$ to all parties, and terminate.

If the message from Bob is $(finalize, id)$ when $s = submitted$, set $s = finalized$, send $(unfreeze, id, \mathrm{Sarah}, 2p)$ to $\mathcal{L}$, output $(sold, id)$, and terminate. Otherwise, if no such messages from Bob were received, proceed to the *payout* phase.

───────────────────────**Payout**───────────────────────

Upon receiving $(finalize, id)$ from Sarah when $s = submitted$, set $s = finalized$, send $(unfreeze, id, \mathrm{Sarah}, 2p)$ to $\mathcal{L}$, output $(sold, id)$, and terminate.

Fig. 8. Ideal functionality $\mathcal{G}_{\mathsf{FairExchange}}^{\mathcal{L},\mathcal{H}}$ for fair exchange smart contract.

6.4   Security Analysis

We now analyze the security requirements mentioned in Sect. 6.2 for the fair exchange protocol.

Termination. The protocol always terminates, and all coins for the contract will be unlocked in one of the following cases when at least one parties act honestly.

No Abort. This case occurs when both parties act honestly, *i.e.*, Bob sends a *complain* message or *finalize* message to $\mathcal{G}_{\mathsf{FairExchange}}^{\mathcal{L},\mathcal{H}}$ in the complaint phase. According to the description of $\mathcal{G}_{\mathsf{FairExchange}}^{\mathcal{L},\mathcal{H}}$, all coins will be unlocked at the end of the protocol.

The description of the fair exchange protocol consists of the behavior of the honest buyer Bob and seller Sarah.

────────────────────────────**Initiation**────────────────────────────

Buyer Bob: Upon receiving input (buy, id, n, c, p), Bob sends (buy, id, n, c) to Sarah and $(initiate, id, n, c, p)$ to $\mathcal{G}_{\mathsf{FairExchange}}^{\mathcal{L},\mathcal{H}}$. Then he proceeds to the *submission* phase.
Seller Sarah: Upon receiving input $(sell, id, n, c, m, r, p)$, Sarah proceeds to the *submission* phase.

────────────────────────────**Submission**────────────────────────────

Seller Sarah: Upon receiving (buy, id, n, c) from Bob, Sarah checks if she receives $(initialized, id, n, c, p)$ from $\mathcal{G}_{\mathsf{FairExchange}}^{\mathcal{L},\mathcal{H}}$. If it is, Sarah computes $c' \leftarrow c \cdot (1+n)^{-m} \bmod n^2$, picks $s \leftarrow_\$ \mathbb{Z}_n^*$, and computes $a = s^n \bmod n^2$, $e \leftarrow \mathcal{H}(n, c, m, a)$, and $z \leftarrow s \cdot r^e$. Then Sarah sends $(submit, id, m, e, z)$ to $\mathcal{G}_{\mathsf{FairExchange}}^{\mathcal{L},\mathcal{H}}$.
If either message $(initialized, id, n, c, p)$ from $\mathcal{G}_{\mathsf{FairExchange}}^{\mathcal{L},\mathcal{H}}$ or (buy, id, n, c) from Bob was not received, Sarah instead terminates the protocol.
Buyer Bob: Upon receiving $(submitted, id, m, e, z)$ from $\mathcal{G}_{\mathsf{FairExchange}}^{\mathcal{L},\mathcal{H}}$, Bob proceeds to the *complaint* phase. If no message $(submitted, id, m, e, z)$ from $\mathcal{G}_{\mathsf{FairExchange}}^{\mathcal{L},\mathcal{H}}$ was received, Bob terminates the protocol.

────────────────────────────**Complaint**────────────────────────────

Buyer Bob: Bob computes $c' \leftarrow c \cdot (1+n)^{-m} \bmod n^2$, $a \leftarrow z^n \cdot c'^{-e} \bmod n^2$. Bob then verifies whether $e = \mathcal{H}(n, c, m, a)$ holds. If it holds, Bob terminates the protocol by sending $(finalize, id)$ to $\mathcal{G}_{\mathsf{FairExchange}}^{\mathcal{L},\mathcal{H}}$ and outputs $(bought, id, m)$. Otherwise, Bob sends $(complain, id)$ to $\mathcal{G}_{\mathsf{FairExchange}}^{\mathcal{L},\mathcal{H}}$ and outputs $(not\ sold, id)$.
Seller Sarah: Upon receiving $(sold, id)$ or $(not\ sold, id)$ from $\mathcal{G}_{\mathsf{FairExchange}}^{\mathcal{L},\mathcal{H}}$, Sarah outputs this message and terminates the protocol. Otherwise, if no such a message from $\mathcal{G}_{\mathsf{FairExchange}}^{\mathcal{L},\mathcal{H}}$ was received, Sarah proceeds to the *payout* phase.

────────────────────────────**Payout**────────────────────────────

Seller Sarah: Sarah sends $(finalize, id)$ to $\mathcal{G}_{\mathsf{FairExchange}}^{\mathcal{L},\mathcal{H}}$ and outputs $(sold, id)$.

Fig. 9. Protocol associated with $\mathcal{G}_{\mathsf{FairExchange}}^{\mathcal{L},\mathcal{H}}$ between honest buyer Bob and seller Sarah.

Buyer Bob Aborts. After the initiation phase, Bob's abortion cannot stop the execution of $\mathcal{G}_{\mathsf{FairExchange}}^{\mathcal{L},\mathcal{H}}$ when an honest Sarah involves. In case that Bob does not send $(finalize, id)$ in the complaint phase, Sarah could send $(finalize, id)$ to $\mathcal{G}_{\mathsf{FairExchange}}^{\mathcal{L},\mathcal{H}}$ in the payout phase and coins will be sent to Sarah. Therefore, all coins will be unlocked at the end of the protocol.

Seller Sarah Aborts. This case occurs when Sarah does not submit decryption result and the corresponding non-interactive zero-knowledge proof in the submission phase. Here $\mathcal{G}_{\mathsf{FairExchange}}^{\mathcal{L},\mathcal{H}}$ will ask $\mathcal{L}$ to unlock all p coins back to Bob and terminate the protocol.

Buyer Fairness. The non-interactive zero-knowledge proof derived from Enc-Value guarantees the correctness of the decryption result for the ciphertext c. Note that a computationally bounded seller cannot provide a correct proof due to the security of EncValue compiled by the Fiat-Shamir heuristic under the random oracle model except a negligible probability.

Suppose that the decryption result m is incorrect, $i.e.$, the proof is incorrect. In that case, an honest buyer can complain to $\mathcal{G}_{\mathsf{FairExchange}}^{\mathcal{L},\mathcal{H}}$ on time to prevent the payment and retrieve coins back. Since the verification of the proof on $\mathcal{G}_{\mathsf{FairExchange}}^{\mathcal{L},\mathcal{H}}$ is the same as the verification executed by the honest buyer, coins will be back to the buyer. Thus, the seller here cannot retrieve the payment, and the protocol achieves buyer fairness.

Seller Fairness. For seller fairness, we should ensure that once the buyer learns the decryption result of c, the honest seller should be paid. From the protocol, the buyer Bob learns the decryption result of c only if the honest seller Sarah submits it. For a submission of an honest seller, the buyer can choose to send $complain$ or $finalize$ to $\mathcal{G}_{\mathsf{FairExchange}}^{\mathcal{L},\mathcal{H}}$, or does nothing.

Suppose the buyer sends a $complain$ message to $\mathcal{G}_{\mathsf{FairExchange}}^{\mathcal{L},\mathcal{H}}$. In that case, the correct proof will still be accepted by $\mathcal{G}_{\mathsf{FairExchange}}^{\mathcal{L},\mathcal{H}}$. Then the honest seller will receive the payment, together with her p coins frozen in the submission phase. For the $finalize$ message, $2p$ coins will be sent to the seller directly. If the buyer does nothing, the honest seller can send the message $finalize$ to $\mathcal{G}_{\mathsf{FairExchange}}^{\mathcal{L},\mathcal{H}}$ to retrieve the payment together with her own p coins frozen in the submission phase. Therefore, the protocol achieves seller fairness.

6.5   Possible Attacks and Countermeasures

We note that a malicious seller in practice may try to submit incorrect proof and hope that the buyer does not verify the proof or send $complain$ on time. For this case, our solution is to penalize the malicious seller when her submitted proof is incorrect. In the submission phase, the seller is required to deposit p coins on $\mathcal{G}_{\mathsf{FairExchange}}^{\mathcal{L},\mathcal{H}}$ when she submits the decryption result and the proof. Hence, if the proof is incorrect, the buyer can complain to $\mathcal{G}_{\mathsf{FairExchange}}^{\mathcal{L},\mathcal{H}}$ and retrieve these p coins to penalize the seller.

A malicious buyer may be able to perform a $Denial\ of\ Service\ (DoS)$ attack. In a normal interaction of the data trading, the buyer Bob will perform computation on the encrypted dataset, run the $encryption\ switching\ procedure$ with the seller Sarah, and execute the fair exchange protocol to retrieve the final decryption result. However, malicious Bob may perform a DoS attack by performing the encryption switching procedure with Sarah using garbage ciphertexts. These garbage ciphertexts are generated randomly rather than through computation on encrypted data. Then malicious Bob will always abort before the $result\ retrieval$ $procedure$, $i.e.$, the fair exchange protocol. We note that the seller needs to conduct more computation than Bob during the TwinCtx protocol. Hence, if Bob launches this attack, though malicious Bob learns nothing from the protocol, it is unfair for Sarah to perform much more useless computation than Bob (since Bob here only generates garbage ciphertexts and acts as a verifier in TwinCtx).

This DoS attack cannot be avoided, but we still have countermeasures. A black-list approach may be a possible solution, but alternatively, we provide another solution here. The solution is to let the buyer deploy the smart contract and freeze some coins on the contract before the data trading. These frozen coins can only be retrieved back at the end of the fair exchange, after a specified period, or directly treated as the payment. If the malicious buyer performs the DoS attack, he needs to pay the fee for the smart contract's deployment and freeze some coins on the smart contract at first, and thus we make it expensive to carry out such a DoS attack.

For the fair exchange protocol, if Sarah does not submit the decryption result and the corresponding proof, Bob is allowed to retrieve his coins frozen for the payment back. However, in practice, updates of blockchain follow a consensus mechanism, which allows malicious buyers to launch an attack based on this scenario of getting the payment back. In practice, it takes some time for the seller's submission to be confirmed on blockchain because of the consensus mechanism. At this point, after seeing the seller's submission, the malicious buyer can quickly submit a request to the smart contract to retrieve the frozen payment pretending that the seller has not submitted the decryption result. In this way, the malicious buyer's request may be confirmed by blockchain before the seller's submission. Thus, the malicious buyer gets the answer submitted by the seller while getting back the frozen payment. Our solution to this attack is to set a time limit for the withdrawal of frozen payments in smart contracts. Within this period, the seller can submit the decryption result and proof, and the buyer is allowed to retrieve the frozen payment only after this period. Therefore, if the seller can submit the decryption result in time, malicious buyers' request to retrieve the frozen payment will not be accepted, so the attack cannot succeed.

7 Analysis

7.1 Round Complexity

We count the number of rounds of our two instantiations (both using the batch technique for TwinCtx) for protocols that are honest-verifier zero-knowledge (HVZK) or compiled by Fiat-Shamir heuristic. Since the offline phase of TwinCtx involves a cut-and-choose procedure, we do *not recommend* compiling this procedure via the Fiat-Shamir heuristic, and it is regarded as a *three-round* protocol even for the Fiat-Shamir heuristic. The total number of rounds of the protocol is equal to the number of rounds of the encryption switching procedure plus the number of rounds of the decryption procedure. For both the cases of $\mathbb{Z}_n^*$ and $\mathbb{Z}_n$, our instantiations only need 5 rounds under the Fiat-Shamir heuristic and 10 rounds under HVZK, which is very cheap for practical use.

7.2 Experimental Performance

We provide a *proof-of-concept* implementation to evaluate the performance of our blind polynomial evaluation protocol. The protocol is implemented in C++

using the `NTL library` [25] for the underlying modular arithmetic on a single core of MacBook Air (2018) with a 1.6 GHz Intel©Core i5 CPU, 8 GB of RAM, running macOS 10.15.4.

Table 2 provides the experimental performance of basic operations and ciphertext sizes in our instantiations. We give the total running time of per 10000 addition and multiplication operations, respectively. For the instantiation over $\mathbb{Z}_n$, we use zero indicators encrypting values of $\mathbb{J}_n$, as mentioned in Sect. 5.

Table 2. Experimental performance of basic operations and size of ciphertexts.

Ptx space	$\|n\|$	$10k \times$ Mul	$10k \times$ Add	ElGamal ctx	Paillier ctx
$\mathbb{Z}_n^*$	1024	0.2173 s	0.1996 s	0.375 KB	0.25 KB
$\mathbb{Z}_n$	1024	0.3834 s	0.1971 s	0.625 KB	0.25 KB
$\mathbb{Z}_n^*$	2048	0.6271 s	0.6199 s	0.750 KB	0.50 KB
$\mathbb{Z}_n$	2048	1.0387 s	0.6143 s	1.250 KB	0.50 KB

Table 3 presents the experimental performance of batching executions of TwinCtx and corresponding communication cost for security parameter $t = 32$. We measure the running time for both the verifier and the prover when a random twin-ciphertext has been generated. The parameter k denotes the number of ciphertext pairs that are proved to be twin-ciphertext pairs. As the bottleneck of the protocol, its performance is efficient and practical.

Table 3. Performance of batching the executions of TwinCtx for $t = 32$.

$\|n\|$	k	Verifier	Prover	Communication cost
1024	128	0.6421 s	4.6771 s	172.50 KB
1024	256	1.1878 s	9.2474 s	316.81 KB
1024	512	2.3242 s	18.5823 s	605.44 KB
2048	128	4.2374 s	28.7013 s	344.44 KB
2048	256	8.1683 s	58.3467 s	632.75 KB
2048	512	16.1003 s	117.2097 s	1209.38 KB

7.3 Cost on Blockchain

We give a *proof-of-concept* implementation for the blockchain part illustrated in Sect. 6 by deploying it on a private network of Ethereum. We measure the computation cost via *gas consumption* of the smart contract execution, which only depends on the instructions executed by the Ethereum Virtual Machine.

Table 4 presents the gas consumption and total transaction fee for both active and passive verification, with different security parameters κ.[2] Although our proof-of-concept implementation is not fully optimized, the gas consumption and fees are acceptable, especially for the passive verification approach.[3]

Table 4. Gas consumption of functions and total transaction fee for $t = 256$.

Mode	$\|n\|$	initiate	submit	complain	getPaid	Total Fee
Active	1024	620167	2807188	None	None	$5.41
Active	2048	1061626	13408995	None	None	$22.84
Passive	1024	635495	586386	2636802	30271	$1.98
Passive	2048	1076542	950408	13190574	30271	$3.25

Acknowledgments. We thank the reviewers for their detailed and helpful comments. Y. Liu and Q. Wang were partially supported by the National Science Foundation of China under Grant No. 61672015 and Guangdong Provincial Key Laboratory (Grant No. 2020B121201001). Y. Liu and S.-M. Yiu were also partially supported by ITF, Hong Kong (ITS/173/18FP).

References

1. Andrychowicz, M., Dziembowski, S., Malinowski, D., Mazurek, L.: Secure multi-party computations on bitcoin. In: 2014 IEEE Symposium on Security and Privacy, SP 2014, Berkeley, CA, USA, 18–21 May 2014, pp. 443–458. IEEE Computer Society (2014)
2. Bentov, I., Kumaresan, R.: How to use Bitcoin to design fair protocols. In: Garay, J.A., Gennaro, R. (eds.) CRYPTO 2014, Part II. LNCS, vol. 8617, pp. 421–439. Springer, Heidelberg (2014). https://doi.org/10.1007/978-3-662-44381-1_24
3. Castagnos, G., Imbert, L., Laguillaumie, F.: Encryption switching protocols revisited: switching modulo p. In: Katz, J., Shacham, H. (eds.) CRYPTO 2017, Part I. LNCS, vol. 10401, pp. 255–287. Springer, Cham (2017). https://doi.org/10.1007/978-3-319-63688-7_9

---

[2] Assume that the gas price is 10 `Gwei` (a common price, albeit lower fees is possible). The total transaction fees (of US dollar) are calculated according to the *average price* of gas and coin on April 12th, 2020 (see more in https://etherscan.io/chart/gasprice). For the total fee, we take into account the total gas consumption of all functions for active verification and all functions except `complain` for passive verification.

[3] Note that since our implementation involves big integers and Ethereum today can only support integers represented by 256 bits, we have to use an external library. However, library instructions from therein will be pulled into the calling contract in the compilation. Hence, once a new version of Ethereum has better support of external library call, the cost of our protocol can further be *dramatically reduced*.

4. Cleve, R.: Limits on the security of coin flips when half the processors are faulty (extended abstract). In: Hartmanis, J. (ed.) Proceedings of the 18th Annual ACM Symposium on Theory of Computing, Berkeley, California, USA, 28–30 May 1986, pp. 364–369. ACM (1986)

5. Couteau, G., Peters, T., Pointcheval, D.: Secure distributed computation on private inputs. In: Garcia-Alfaro, J., Kranakis, E., Bonfante, G. (eds.) FPS 2015. LNCS, vol. 9482, pp. 14–26. Springer, Cham (2016). https://doi.org/10.1007/978-3-319-30303-1_2

6. Couteau, G., Peters, T., Pointcheval, D.: Encryption switching protocols. In: Robshaw, M., Katz, J. (eds.) CRYPTO 2016, Part I. LNCS, vol. 9814, pp. 308–338. Springer, Heidelberg (2016). https://doi.org/10.1007/978-3-662-53018-4_12

7. Damgård, I., Jurik, M., Nielsen, J.B.: A generalization of Paillier's public-key system with applications to electronic voting. Int. J. Inf. Sec. 9(6), 371–385 (2010)

8. Delgado-Segura, S., Pérez-Solà, C., Navarro-Arribas, G., Herrera-Joancomartí, J.: A fair protocol for data trading based on bitcoin transactions. Future Gener. Comput. Syst. 107, 832–840 (2017)

9. Dwork, C.: Differential privacy. In: Bugliesi, M., Preneel, B., Sassone, V., Wegener, I. (eds.) ICALP 2006, Part II. LNCS, vol. 4052, pp. 1–12. Springer, Heidelberg (2006). https://doi.org/10.1007/11787006_1

10. Dziembowski, S., Eckey, L., Faust, S.: FairSwap: how to fairly exchange digital goods. In: Lie, D., Mannan, M., Backes, M., Wang, X. (eds.) Proceedings of the 2018 ACM SIGSAC Conference on Computer and Communications Security, CCS 2018, Toronto, ON, Canada, 15–19 October 2018, pp. 967–984. ACM (2018)

11. Eckey, L., Faust, S., Schlosser, B.: OptiSwap: fast optimistic fair exchange. In: Sun, H., Shieh, S., Gu, G., Ateniese, G. (eds.) ASIA CCS 2020: The 15th ACM Asia Conference on Computer and Communications Security, Taipei, Taiwan, 5–9 October 2020, pp. 543–557. ACM (2020)

12. Fiat, A., Shamir, A.: How to prove yourself: practical solutions to identification and signature problems. In: Odlyzko, A.M. (ed.) CRYPTO 1986. LNCS, vol. 263, pp. 186–194. Springer, Heidelberg (1987). https://doi.org/10.1007/3-540-47721-7_12

13. ElGamal, T.: A public key cryptosystem and a signature scheme based on discrete logarithms. In: Blakley, G.R., Chaum, D. (eds.) CRYPTO 1984. LNCS, vol. 196, pp. 10–18. Springer, Heidelberg (1985). https://doi.org/10.1007/3-540-39568-7_2

14. Gentry, C.: Fully homomorphic encryption using ideal lattices. In: Mitzenmacher, M. (ed.) Proceedings of the 41st Annual ACM Symposium on Theory of Computing, STOC 2009, Bethesda, MD, USA, May 31 – June 2 2009, pp. 169–178. ACM (2009)

15. Koutsos, V., Papadopoulos, D., Chatzopoulos, D., Tarkoma, S., Hui, P.: Agora: a privacy-aware data marketplace. In: 40th IEEE International Conference on Distributed Computing Systems, ICDCS 2020, Singapore, November 29 - December 1, 2020, pp. 1211–1212. IEEE (2020)

16. Kumaresan, R., Vaikuntanathan, V., Vasudevan, P.N.: Improvements to secure computation with penalties. In: Weippl, E.R., Katzenbeisser, S., Kruegel, C., Myers, A.C., Halevi, S. (eds.) Proceedings of the 2016 ACM SIGSAC Conference on Computer and Communications Security, Vienna, Austria, 24–28 October 2016, pp. 406–417. ACM (2016)

17. Liu, Y., Wang, Q., Yiu, S.-M.: An improvement of multi-exponentiation with encrypted bases argument: smaller and faster. In: Wu, Y., Yung, M. (eds.) Inscrypt 2020. LNCS, vol. 12612, pp. 397–414. Springer, Cham (2021). https://doi.org/10.1007/978-3-030-71852-7_27

18. Liu, Y., Wang, Q., Yiu, S.: Blind polynomial evaluation and data trading. IACR Cryptol. ePrint Arch. **2021**, 413 (2021). https://eprint.iacr.org/2021/413
19. Lu, Y., Tang, Q., Wang, G.: ZebraLancer: private and anonymous crowdsourcing system atop open blockchain. In: 38th IEEE International Conference on Distributed Computing Systems, ICDCS 2018, Vienna, Austria, 2–6 July 2018, pp. 853–865. IEEE Computer Society (2018)
20. Lu, Y., Tang, Q., Wang, G.: Dragoon: private decentralized hits made practical. In: 40th IEEE International Conference on Distributed Computing Systems, ICDCS 2020, Singapore, November 29 – December 1 2020, pp. 910–920. IEEE (2020)
21. Nakamoto, S., et al.: Bitcoin: a peer-to-peer electronic cash system (2008)
22. Naor, M., Pinkas, B.: Oblivious polynomial evaluation. SIAM J. Comput. **35**(5), 1254–1281 (2006)
23. Paillier, P.: Public-key cryptosystems based on composite degree residuosity classes. In: Stern, J. (ed.) EUROCRYPT 1999. LNCS, vol. 1592, pp. 223–238. Springer, Heidelberg (1999). https://doi.org/10.1007/3-540-48910-X_16
24. Poupard, G., Stern, J.: Short proofs of knowledge for factoring. In: Imai, H., Zheng, Y. (eds.) PKC 2000. LNCS, vol. 1751, pp. 147–166. Springer, Heidelberg (2000). https://doi.org/10.1007/978-3-540-46588-1_11
25. Shoup, V.: NTL: a library for doing number theory. http://www.shoup.net/ntl
26. Tassa, T., Jarrous, A., Ben-Ya'akov, Y.: Oblivious evaluation of multivariate polynomials. J. Math. Cryptol. **7**(1), 1–29 (2013)
27. Valiant, L.G.: Universal circuits (preliminary report). In: Chandra, A.K., Wotschke, D., Friedman, E.P., Harrison, M.A. (eds.) Proceedings of the 8th Annual ACM Symposium on Theory of Computing, Hershey, Pennsylvania, USA, 3–5 May 1976, pp. 196–203. ACM (1976)
28. Wood, G., et al.: Ethereum: a secure decentralised generalised transaction ledger. Ethereum Project Yellow Paper **151**(2014), 1–32 (2014)
29. Yao, A.C.: Protocols for secure computations (extended abstract). In: 23rd Annual Symposium on Foundations of Computer Science, Chicago, Illinois, USA, 3–5 November 1982, pp. 160–164. IEEE Computer Society (1982)
30. Yao, A.C.: How to generate and exchange secrets (extended abstract). In: 27th Annual Symposium on Foundations of Computer Science, Toronto, Canada, 27–29 October 1986, pp. 162–167. IEEE Computer Society (1986)
31. Zhao, S., Yu, Yu., Zhang, J., Liu, H.: Valiant's universal circuits revisited: an overall improvement and a lower bound. In: Galbraith, S.D., Moriai, S. (eds.) ASIACRYPT 2019, Part I. LNCS, vol. 11921, pp. 401–425. Springer, Cham (2019). https://doi.org/10.1007/978-3-030-34578-5_15

Coin-Based Multi-party Fair Exchange

Handan Kılınç Alper[1]([⊠]) and Alptekin Küpçü[2]

[1] Web3.0 Foundation, Zug, Switzerland
handan@web3.foundation
[2] Koç University, Istanbul, Turkey
akupcu@ku.edu.tr

Abstract. Multi-party fair exchange (MFE) considers scenarios where fairness means that either all exchanges as agreed upon between multiple parties take place, or no item changes hands. The two-party case was widely studied starting with the seminal work of Asokan et al. in ACM CCS 1998. The state-of-the-art MFE protocol was shown by Kılınç and Küpçü in CT-RSA 2015. Unfortunately, it only works on items that can be efficiently verifiably encrypted, which, in particular, means that it cannot efficiently handle exchange of large files in a peer-to-peer file sharing scenario. In this work, first, we extend the optimistic two-party fair computation definition of Cachin and Camenisch in CRYPTO 2000 for the MFE setting, and prove security of our protocol with ideal-real simulation. Secondly, we extend the CT-RSA 2015 solution of Kılınç and Küpçü in a way that our protocol enables parties to exchange any item, be it a large file. While doing so, we employ electronic payments, where if a party does not obtain the desired item at the end of the protocol, the payment of the item's owner will be obtained instead. Third, we achieve asymptotic optimality with $O(1)$ rounds and $O(n^2)$ messages, where n is the number of participating parties. Finally, we also provide experimental results from our prototype code.

Keywords: Multi-party fair exchange · Optimistic model · Electronic payments · Threshold cryptography

1 Introduction

Exchange protocols are suitable for scenarios where people want to exchange their electronic goods such as signing electronic contracts [31,45], online shopping, file sharing [23], or certified e-mail delivery [1]. These exchanges can be in numerous exchange topologies that define who want whose goods. The most well-known one is the complete topology where parties want to receive all other parties' goods (e.g., electronic contract signing, where each party needs the signatures of all other parties). Another popular topology is the ring topology, where a group of parties in some order wants to the receive previous party's good. Ring topology is particularly suitable for online shopping: a customer wants to buy online an item from a seller: the seller sends the item to the customer, the customer sends approval for the payment to her bank, the customer's bank sends

K. Sako and N. O. Tippenhauer (Eds.): ACNS 2021, LNCS 12726, pp. 130–160, 2021.
https://doi.org/10.1007/978-3-030-78372-3_6

the actual payment to the seller's bank, and finally the seller's bank puts the money to the seller's account. In all these scenarios, fairness is an ultimate security requirement: either all parties in the exchange protocol receive the electronic goods that they want, or no one receives anything useful.

Unfortunately, it is a known fact that fairness cannot be achieved without honest majority [29,49]. In the two party setting, to minimize the requirement of a trusted third party (TTP), Asokan et al. [4,5] introduced the notion of *optimistic fair exchange*, where the TTP participates in the exchange protocol if and only if a dispute between the participants occurs. While previous definitions were game-based, in CRYPTO 2000, Cachin and Camenisch [16] provided an ideal world definition for fair and secure multi party computation, which we adapt for the multi-party fair exchange (MFE) setting. Thus, our first contribution is this adaptation and security proof in the ideal-real model.

Verifiable encryption [17,19] under the TTP's key is the main cryptographic primitive in an optimistic fair exchange protocol, because if any party cheats (e.g., does not send his item), other parties ask the TTP to decrypt the verifiable encryption and receive the item. One may consider verifiable encryption as an encryption together with a zero knowledge proof that the encrypted value is correct. Since the encryption is verifiable, meaning that it is the encryption of the correct item, the parties receive the missing item at the end when the TTP decrypts it. For example, if parties exchange signatures, then it is efficiently possible to show that the encryption includes a signature of the contract with the signing key of the party. Our second contribution lies in the following question: What if the item is a large file with a known hash value? Although there has been significant progress on the efficiency of zero-knowledge proofs in the recent years, verifiably encrypting such files is still not practical, thereby eliminating the previous MFE solutions for practical use in this scenario. In this paper, we find a solution for this multi-party large-file exchange problem that works for any exchange topology. To achieve fairness efficiently, we consider a different fairness definition: if a party receives a wrong item, then (s)he can get the coin of the party who provided the wrong item. Note that, some existing two-party protocols (e.g., [12,40,43]) also apply this type of fairness definitions, and recently Dziembowski et al. [27] used this type of fairness for file-exchange in two party scenario using smart contracts. One may consider scenarios such as peer-to-peer file sharing, where the hash of the file to be exchanged is known beforehand (e.g., via a trusted Tracker [23]). Our solution is inspired by the solution of Kılınç and Küpçü [37] that is practical in the multi-party setting, but only for items that can be efficiently verifiably encrypted. Our contribution is as follows:

- Our coin-based multi-party fair exchange (CMFE) protocol is the *first* practical multi-party exchange protocol that enables multiple parties to exchange verifiable items that cannot be efficiently put in a verifiable encryption. For example, files may be verifiable via their hashes, but still there is no efficient way of putting a large file into a public-key verifiable encryption. Our CMFE protocol enables very efficient exchange of any size of items, by relaxing the fairness definition and employing electronic payments.

- Our CMFE has an easy setup phase, which is employed only *once* for exchanging *multiple* sets of items, thus improving efficiency even further for *repeated exchanges* among the same set of participants. The topology can change between repetitions, without the need to redo the setup.
- We construct CMFE with generic cryptographic primitives, and instantiate it with practical solutions in the random oracle model and show its concrete efficiency. For 10 parties, after a setup phase that takes at most 1.35 s and 527 KB, each exchange costs less than 87 ms and 105 KB overhead over unfairly exchanging the files.
- CMFE has asymptotically optimal performance with round complexity of $O(1)$ and message complexity of $O(n^2)$ for n parties (for optimality, see the combinatorial proofs in [34,45,50]).
- We prove the fairness of CMFE via ideal-real world simulation considering it as a multi-party computation protocol.
- As an independent contribution, we define and use a verifiable deniable (k,n)-threshold encryption scheme and show in the Appendix A that ElGamal threshold scheme leads to an efficient instantiation.

2   Related Work

Two-party fair exchange (2FE) is a well studied problem [5–7,10,26,40,48], while multi-party fair exchange (MFE) does not have the same popularity. Most of the MFE protocols were constructed for the ring topology, where each party expects an item only from the previous one. The one by Ba et al. [9] is not an optimistic protocol and needs a trusted initiator besides the TTP. In addition, it has the passive conspiracy problem [30], where a malicious party conspires with an honest party. Gonzales-Deleito and Markowitch [32] removed the trust on a party but their resolution protocol requires some parties being online, which is not a reliable assumption. Liu and Hu [44] remove the passive conspiracy problem of Bao et al. [9], but they still rely on the existence of online parties. In all these ring-topology MFE protocols, no formal fairness proof exists. Instead, case-by-case analyses are done to show that fairness is satisfied.

In addition, there is a **fundamental difference between the fairness notion** in these protocols and that of ours. According to their definition, there will be no honest party that does not receive his desired item from the previous party but sends his item to the next party. It implies that some parties may receive their desired items while some other parties do not receive or send anything. For instance, consider a ring topology with parties P_0, P_1, P_2, P_3 and P_4, and assume that P_1 and P_3 are malicious and colluding. In this case, the following scenario can happen using the fairness notion in these protocols: P_0 receives an item from P_4 and P_0 sends an item to P_1, and similarly P_4 receives an item from P_3 and P_4 sends an item to P_0. However, P_2 did not send or receive any item. This was previously considered fair. Whereas, according to our definition, we need that either all parties receive their desired item or receive monetary compensation from the party who did not send his item, or no party receives anything useful. We think that our way of defining fairness where the whole exchange topology must be fairly completed is more suitable for multi-party fair exchange (e.g., the online shopping scenario in the ring topology in Sect. 1 should be fair according to our fairness understanding). Otherwise, MFE protocols could have been simply achieved via multiple executions of two-party fair exchange protocols.

Asokan et al. [4] protocol is the first optimistic MFE protocol that works for any topology. Parties are restricted to "exchangeable items" where the TTP can replace or revoke the items. In case the revocation or replacement is not possible, the TTP signs an affidavit to be used external dispute handling system such as a court. In exchange protocols where affidavit signature of the TTP is not useful, this protocol shrinks the set of possible items to be exchanged. The resolution protocol also requires the parties to be online all the time as in [9,32], since the TTP may ask to re-execute the exchange. In addition, the protocol needs broadcast to send the items, rendering the protocol inefficient.

Kılınç and Küpçü [37] constructed the first optimistic MFE protocol with optimal round and message complexity in all topologies and has the first formal fairness proof via ideal-real world simulation. Unfortunately, for practicality, they also restrict the items to be those that can be efficiently verifiably encrypted. As an important technical difference, since the file cannot be efficiently verifiably encrypted, we employ symmetric-key encryption of the item, and then encrypt this key under a shared public key, as well as the public key of the TTP. This dual encryption is necessary to enable optimistic exchange and resolution with the TTP both. Then, differently from [37], verifiable escrows (verifiable encryption under the TTP's public key) of both the payments and the decryption keys are necessary in our solution. We also employ digital signatures to tie messages in the exchange to each other. Moreover, we need to introduce additional resolution protocols that deal with payments. Finally, the introduction of the symmetric-key encryption complicates our security proof, requiring a whole new approach. Overall, while we do employ ideas from [37], the technical contribution is non-trivial. As a minor drawback, the TTP in CMFE is more powerful: it can spend the payments put down by the honest parties. Reducing the trust put on the TTP is left as future work. See Table 1 for the overall comparison of our protocol and existing multi-party fair exchange protocols.

Blockchain-Based Fair Exchange: In recent years, blockchain started to replace the TTP in fair exchange protocols [3,11,13,14,27,36,38,39] by giving monetary compensation instead of the item to resolve fairness issues. However, except FairSwap [27], which is a two-party fair exchange protocol, none of those provide fair exchange efficiently for the exchange of very large files. FairSwap [27] uses an efficient proving system based on Merkle trees to let the smart contract detect the exchange of wrong items without knowing the whole item. Instantaneous Decentralized Poker (IDP) [14] provides an optimistic multi-party fair exchange with smart contracts that consists of a combination of multi-party computation that outputs the encrypted exchange items and fair exchange of keys. The fairness of this combination has been proven by Gordon et al. [33].

Table 1. Comparison with existing MFE protocols with n parties. TTP-party independence exists if the TTP does not have to contact a prespecified party to resolve the fairness problem with another party. TTP privacy exists if the TTP does not learn any information about the identity of the parties and exchanged items. TTP partial privacy exists if TTP does not obtain whole item.

	Topology	Num. messages	Large item exchange	TTP-party independence	TTP privacy
Bao et al. [9]	Ring	$O(n)$	Impractical	No	None
González-Deleito and Markowitch [32]	Ring	$O(n^2)$	Impractical	No	None
Liu and Hu [44]	Ring	$O(n)$	Impractical	No	None
Asokan et al. [4]	All	$O(n^3)$	Impractical	No	None
Kılınç and Küpçü (MFE) [37]	All	$O(n^2)$	Impractical	Yes	Private
Ours (CMFE)	**All**	$\mathbf{O(n^2)}$	**Practical**	**Yes**	**Partial**

Table 2. Fair exchange and secure computation protocols that use coin-based fairness definition. '-' shows that the notion is not applicable.

	Type	Topology	Large item exchange	Trusted entity
Küpçü and Lysyanskaya [40]	2FE	–	Practical	TTP
[3,11,13,14,36,38,39]	Fair MPC	All	–	Blockchain
FairSwap [27]	2FE	–	Practical	Blockchain
Ours (CMFE)	**MFE**	**All**	**Practical**	**TTP**

However, IDP does not handle whether the items of the parties are correct or not while providing fairness unless checking the correctness of them is encoded in the MPC functionality. As we discussed previously, encrypting, for example, a 1 GB file and showing that it is the encryption of the file with the expected hash value decreases the efficiency significantly because the circuit size of such a proving system is huge. In a nutshell, there does not exist any MFE protocol on smart contracts that enables exchanging very large items efficiently. We also consider it as a future work. Overall, there exists no efficient and optimistic MFE protocol to exchange very large files (see Table 2) even with the coin-based fairness notion as we employ in this paper.

3   Definitions and Preliminaries

The fairness model of our coin-based MFE protocol is built on the ideal/real world simulation as in the security model of secure multi-party computation (MPC) protocols, because an MFE protocol is an MPC protocol (see [37]).

Optimistic Fair Secure MPC: We extend the two-party fair and secure computation definition by Cachin and Camenisch in CRYPTO 2000 [16] to the multi-party case in the spirit of the standard secure computation definition. Besides extending it to multi-party case, we slightly modify the ideal world definition to fit the nature of fair exchange where the parties first provide some kind of promise (e.g., verifiable encryption) before executing the item exchange.

Ideal World: It consists of honest party(s) $\mathcal{P}_h$, an adversary $\mathcal{A}$ that corrupts the parties in set $\mathcal{P}_c$, the TTP, and the ideal functionality U^ϕ_{fs}. Here, ϕ is the function that parties want to compute with their inputs and promise is a some promise function, whose security is as defined below.

Definition 1 (Security of Promise). *The function* promise $: \mathcal{W} \to \mathcal{X}$ *is a secure promise function if for all PPT adversary $\mathcal{A}$ there exists another adversary $\mathcal{B}$ such that for all $w \leftarrow_D \mathcal{W}$ chosen according to a distribution D and for all polynomial functions H and* Leak, *there exists a negligible function such that*

$$\Pr[\mathcal{A}(1^\ell, \mathsf{promise}(w), H(w)) = \mathsf{Leak}(w)] - \Pr[\mathcal{B}(1^\ell, H(w)) = \mathsf{Leak}(w)] < \mathsf{negl}(\ell).$$

Here, $H(w)$ models the public information related to w (e.g., H is a hash function the exchange item with known hash scenario). Informally, knowing $\mathsf{promise}(w)$ does not improve our current knowledge about w. We now define the ideal protocol for secure and fair MFE.

U^ϕ_{fs} for security and fairness

- (*Promise*) U^ϕ_{fs} receives inputs $\{w_i, \mathsf{promise}(w_i)\}_{P_i \in \mathcal{P}_h}$ from the honest parties and relays $\{\mathsf{promise}(w_i)\}_{P_i \in \mathcal{P}_h}$ to $\mathcal{A}$. If $\mathcal{A}$ sends the message ABORT, then U^ϕ_{fs} sends $\perp$ to all of the parties and halts. Otherwise, U^ϕ_{fs} receives the inputs $\{w_i, \mathsf{promise}(w_i)\}_{P_i \in \mathcal{P}_c}$ from $\mathcal{A}$. If w_i's are valid, U^ϕ_{fs} sends $\{\mathsf{promise}(w_i)\}_{P_i \in \mathcal{P}_c}$ to the honest parties. Otherwise, U^ϕ_{fs} sends $\perp$ to all of the parties and halts.
- (*Computation*) If the protocol is not halted, U^ϕ_{fs} computes $\phi(w_1, ..., w_n) = (\phi_1(w_1, ..., w_n), \phi_2(w_1, ..., w_n), ..., \phi_n(w_1, ..., w_n))$. Let $\phi_i = \phi_i(w_1, ..., w_n)$ be the ith output. Then, he sends $\{\phi_i\}_{P_i \in \mathcal{P}_c}$ to $\mathcal{A}$ and expects back a response from the TTP.
- (*Fair Exchange*) The TTP sends $\{b_i \in \{\mathcal{Y}_i \cup \perp \cup \text{CONTINUE}\}\}_{P_i \in \mathcal{P}_h}$ to U^ϕ_{fs}. An honest TTP always responds as $\{b_i = \text{CONTINUE}\}_{P_i \in \mathcal{P}_h}$. For each $P_i \in \mathcal{P}_h$, U^ϕ_{fs} does the following: If $b_i = \text{CONTINUE}$, sends ϕ_i to P_i. Else, sends b_i to P_i.

Observe that an honest TTP always sends CONTINUE for each honest party. In this case, U^ϕ_{fs} guarantees that either the adversary obtains $\{\mathsf{promise}(w_i)\}_{P_i \in \mathcal{P}_c}$ and honest parties obtain nothing, or each party P_i obtains ϕ_i. Therefore, as long as the function promise is secure according to Definition 1, fairness is guaranteed with U^ϕ_{fs}. Even though we never consider malicious TTP in CMFE (because otherwise fairness is not possible [29,49]), for the sake of generality, U^ϕ_{fs} covers the case where the TTP is controlled by the adversary: $b_i = \bot$ represents the TTP not responding to an honest party P_i, breaking fairness, and any other $b_i \in \mathcal{Y}_i$ denotes that the TTP resolves with the party P_i such that P_i learns an incorrect output, where $\mathcal{Y}_i$ is the domain of ϕ_i. In U_{fs}^ϕ, promise(w_i) represents the information that parties provide each other before exchanging real items in exchange protocols. We note that U_{fs}^ϕ also covers MFE protocols without promise. These protocols can consider promise(w_i) as a null function.

The outputs of honest parties and of $\mathcal{A}$ in an ideal execution between the honest party(s) and $\mathcal{A}$ controlling the corrupted parties where U_{fs}^ϕ computes ϕ is denoted $IDEAL_{\phi,\text{TTP},\mathcal{A}(aux),\mathcal{P}_c}^{fs}(\{w_i\}_{1\leq i\leq n}, \ell)$, where $\{w_i\}_{1\leq i\leq n}$ are the private inputs of P_i, aux is an auxiliary input, and ℓ is the security parameter.

Real World: No ideal functionality U_{fs}^ϕ exists in the real protocol π to compute the functionality ϕ. A PPT $\mathcal{A}$ controls the set $\mathcal{P}_c$ of parties. The TTP participates in the protocol when a dispute arises. $REAL_{\pi,\text{TTP},\mathcal{A}(aux),\mathcal{P}_c}^{fs}(w_1, w_2, ...w_n, \ell)$ denotes the outputs of honest party(s) P_h and $\mathcal{A}$ in π that may employ the TTP where $\{w_i\}_{1\leq i\leq n}, aux$, and ℓ are as above.

Definition 2 (Fair and Secure Multi-Party Exchange). *Let π be a PPT protocol and let ϕ be a PPT MFE functionality. If $\exists$ a PPT simulator $\mathcal{S}$ for every non-uniform PPT adversary $\mathcal{A}$ attacking π and for all $w_1, w_2, ..., w_n$ s.t.*

$$\{IDEAL_{\phi,\mathcal{S}(aux),\mathcal{P}_c}^{fs}(\{w_i\},\ell)\}_{\ell\in\mathbb{N}} \equiv_c \{REAL_{\pi,\text{TTP},\mathcal{A}(aux),\mathcal{P}_c}^{fs}(\{w_i\},\ell)\}_{\ell\in\mathbb{N}}$$

then, we say that π securely realizes U_{fs}^ϕ. If the promise function of U_{fs}^ϕ is secure according to Definition 1 and π realizes U_{fs}^ϕ, then we call that π is fair.

We denote an exchange topology by $\Upsilon = (\Upsilon_S, \Upsilon_R)$ where $\Upsilon_R, \Upsilon_S \in \{0,1\}^{n\times n}$ where $\Upsilon_R[i,i] = \Upsilon_S[i,i] = 0$. If $\Upsilon_S[i,j] = 1$, it indicates P_i has to send his item $f_{i\to j}$ to P_j. Similarly, $\Upsilon_R[i,j] = 1$, it indicates the P_i needs to receive the item $f_{j\to i}$ of P_j. Each item $f_{i\to j}$ where $\Upsilon_S[i,j] = 1$ has a public description $H_{i\to j}$ which lets a receiver party P_j verify whether the received item is correct with a item validation function H.

Definition 3 (Coin-based MFE (CMFE) Functionality). *The functionality ϕ of a CMFE with parties $\mathcal{P} = \{P_1, P_2, ..., P_n\}$ defined on topology $\Upsilon \in \{0,1\}^{n\times n}$, item validation function H, the list of item definitions H_{ij} for all $\Upsilon_S[i:j] = 1$ is the function: $\phi(z_1, z_2, ..., z_n) = (\phi_1(z_1, z_2, ..., z_n), \phi_2(z_1, z_2, ..., z_n), ..., \phi_n(z_1, z_2, ..., z_n))$ where $z_i = \{(coin_{i\to j}, f_{i\to j})\}_{\forall j:\Upsilon_S[i,j]=1}$. The output is $\phi_i = \{\rho_j : \forall j \text{ s.t. } \Upsilon_R[j,i] = 1\}$, where $\rho_j = f_{j\to i}$ if $H_{j\to i} = H(f_{j\to i})$, or $\rho_j = coin_{j\to i}$ otherwise.*

Here, $f_{i\to j}$ is the item that a party P_i wants to exchange, and $coin_{i\to j}$ is a collateral (e.g. an electronic payment [21,22]) that is issued to any P_j who wants the items of P_i when P_i does not give his items. In exchange protocols, validity of an item can be verified by a publicly known item description (e.g., the item description is the hash of the item and validation function is the hash function). For example, in BitTorrent [23], hashes of files are already obtained in the torrent file before the exchange begins; hence they are known by each party.

Adversarial Model: The TTP resolves the disputes *atomically*, dealing with one party at a time until that resolution protocol is finished. The communication channel is defined similar to previous work [8, 40–42], such that there are loosely-synchronized clocks (e.g., we employ large timeouts on the order of potentially hours or days since they only affect dispute resolution, not the execution of the protocol), and while the communication channel is under the adversary's control, it is assumed that the adversary cannot prevent the honest parties from reaching the TTP before the specified time interval ends. Essentially, we are in a bounded-delay model [35], where the delay the adversary can enforce on the communication between the honest parties and the TTP is bounded by some α, which is assumed to be less than the timeouts stated in the protocols. Note that there is no bound on the delay on the messages between the parties; only those between a party and the TTP has a bounded delay. Thus, message passing between parties and local aborts can be done in an asynchronous manner, but communication with the TTP must be done via loosely synchronized clocks with bounded adversarial delay [35]. Secure channels are used for exchanging the decryption shares and endorsement of a coin. A secure and server-authenticated channel (e.g., TLS) is employed when contacting the TTP. The adversary may control up to $n-1$ out of n parties in the exchange, and is PPT.

Definition 4 ((k, n)-Threshold Encryption [52]). *It consists of the following PPT algorithms where the number of parties is n and the threshold is k:*

- ThGen$(1^\ell, k, n) \rightarrow (\text{pk}, v, \{x_i\}_{1 \leq i \leq n})$: *It takes a security parameter ℓ in unary and parameters k, n as input and outputs a public key pk, a verification key v, and a secret key x_i for each party P_i.*
- ThEnc$(\text{pk}, m) \rightarrow E$: *It takes the public key pk and a message m as input and outputs the ciphertext E.*
- ThDShare$(x_i, \text{pk}, E) \rightarrow d_i$: *It takes a private key x_i, the public key pk, and a ciphertext E as input and outputs the decryption share d_i.*
- ThDSProve$(x_i, \text{pk}, d_i, E) \rightarrow \text{DSproof}_i$: *It takes as input a private key x_i, a ciphertext E, the public key pk, a decryption share d_i, and outputs a proof DSproof_i that the decryption share is valid.*
- ThDSVerify$(v, \text{pk}, E, d_i, \text{DSproof}_i) \rightarrow \text{valid/invalid}$: *It takes the verification key v, the public key pk, a ciphertext E, and a decryption share d_i with its proof DSproof_i as input and outputs either valid or invalid based on the verification of the proof.*
- ThDec$(DS, \text{pk}, E) \rightarrow m$: *It takes a set of decryption shares DS where $|DS| \geq k$, pk, and a ciphertext E as input and outputs a plaintext m.*

We use the zero-knowledge functionality $U^{\text{ZK-}\mathcal{R}}$ below with two parties P_i as a prover and P_j as a verifier for the security of ThDSProve and ThDSVerify where the prover is the party who proves that the d_i is correctly constructed for the encryption E and the verifier is the party who wants to verify that d_i is a correct decryption share for E.

$U^{\mathsf{ZK}\text{-}\mathcal{R}}$ **with a relation** $\mathcal{R}$

- $U^{\mathsf{ZK}\text{-}\mathcal{R}}$ receives $(\mathsf{prove}, id||P_i||P_j, w, \delta)$ from party P_i.
- If $(w, \delta) \in \mathcal{R}$, then $U^{\mathsf{ZK}\text{-}\mathcal{R}}$ outputs $(\mathsf{proof}, id||P_i||P_j, \delta)$ to P_j. Otherwise, $U^{\mathsf{ZK}\text{-}\mathcal{R}}$ outputs $(\mathsf{disproof}, id||P_i||P_j, \delta)$ to P_j.

Definition 5 (Deniable (k, n)-Threshold Encryption). *It consists of all algorithms in Definition 4 and also the PPT algorithm below. Assume that we have $E = \mathsf{ThEnc}(\mathsf{pk}, m)$ where its corresponding valid decryption shares are $DS = \{d_{i_1}, d_{i_2}, ..., d_{i_t}\}$ where $\{i_1, i_2, ..., i_t\} \subseteq \{1, 2, ..., n\}$ and $t = |DS| < k$.*

- $\mathsf{ThDeny}(E, DS, \mathcal{I}, m', \mathsf{pk}) \to DS'$: *It takes as input a ciphertext E, decryption shares DS, an index set $\mathcal{I}$ such that $|\mathcal{I}| = k - |DS|$ and $\{i_1, i_2, ..., i_t\} \notin \mathcal{I}$, a fake plaintext m', and the public key pk. It outputs a set of fake decryption shares DS' for the indices in $\mathcal{I}$ such that $\mathsf{ThDec}(DS' \cup DS, \mathsf{pk}, E) \to m'$.*

Definition 6 ((Labeled) Public Key Encryption). *A (labeled) public key encryption scheme with security parameter ℓ and message space $\mathcal{M}$ consists of the following PPT algorithms: Key generation algorithm: $\mathsf{PkGen}(1^\ell) \to (\mathsf{sk}, \mathsf{pk})$. Encryption algorithm: $\mathsf{PkEnc}(\mathsf{pk}, m; lbl) \to E$ where $m \in \mathcal{M}$ is a message and lbl is label which can be empty and E is the ciphertext. lbl is public and integrated to E such that it cannot be modified. Decryption algorithm: $\mathsf{PkDec}(\mathsf{sk}, E) \to m$.*

Deniable encryption is employed in our security proof, to enable simulation to succeed while initially encrypting random junk. Encryption labels are employed to tie different messages together, as well as indicate exchange parameters to the TTP. Below, we give the definition of verifiable escrow, which is the same cryptographic primitive as verifiable encryption [17, 19]. We use the name *escrow* to indicate that the key of the encryption scheme belongs to the TTP.

Definition 7 (Verifiable Escrow [17, 19]). *Let $\psi = [\mathcal{R}, W, \Delta]$ be a description of a binary relation $\mathcal{R}$ on $W \times \Delta$, and $\mathcal{M}$ be a message space. A verifiable escrow scheme is a (labelled) public key encryption scheme with the following two additional potentially interactive PPT algorithms: $\mathsf{ProveEnc}$ run by a prover who encrypts the message and $\mathsf{VerifyEnc}$ run by a verifier who receives the ciphertext.*

- $\mathsf{ProveEnc}(\mathsf{pk}_T, w, \delta; lbl) \to (\mathsf{VS}, \mathsf{VSproof})$: *It takes as input pk, a witness $w \in W$, and a statement $\delta \in \Delta$, and outputs the ciphertext $\mathsf{VS} = \mathsf{PkEnc}(\mathsf{pk}_T, w; lbl)$ and a proof $\mathsf{VSproof}$ that $(w, \delta) \in \mathcal{R}$.*
- $\mathsf{VerifyEnc}(\mathsf{pk}_T, \delta, \mathsf{VS}, \mathsf{VSproof}) \to 1/0$: *It takes as input $\mathsf{pk}_T, \delta, \mathsf{VS}$ and the proof $\mathsf{VSproof}$, and outputs 1 if $(w, \delta) \in \mathcal{R}$, or 0 if $(w, \delta) \notin \mathcal{R}$.*

We give below the security of $\mathsf{ProveEnc}$ and $\mathsf{VerifyEnc}$ with the functionality $U^{\mathsf{VS}\text{-}\mathcal{R}}$ for two parties P_i as a prover and P_j as a verifier which satisfies the security properties of these algorithms: completeness, soundness, and zero knowledge

[17,19]. The ideal verifiable *escrow* functionality $U^{\mathsf{VS}\text{-}\mathcal{R}}$ checks that pk_T is the public key of the TTP.

$U^{\mathsf{VS}\text{-}\mathcal{R}}$ with a relation $\mathcal{R}$ and TTP's public key pk_T

- $U^{\mathsf{VS}\text{-}\mathcal{R}}$ receives $(\mathsf{VSprove}, id||P_i||P_j, item, \delta, \mathsf{pk}', lbl)$ from party P_i.
- If $(item, \delta) \notin \mathcal{R}$ or $\mathsf{pk}' \neq \mathsf{pk}_T$, then $U^{\mathsf{VS}\text{-}\mathcal{R}}$ sends $(\mathsf{VSdisproof}, id||P_i||P_j, item, \delta, \mathsf{pk}', label, \perp)$ to the party P_j. Otherwise, $U^{\mathsf{VS}\text{-}\mathcal{R}}$ computes the ciphertext $\mathsf{PkEnc}(\mathsf{pk}_T, item; lbl) \rightarrow E$ and sends $(\mathsf{VSproof}, id||P_i||P_j, \delta, \mathsf{pk}_T, lbl, E)$ to P_j.

Remark that $U^{\mathsf{VS}\text{-}\mathcal{R}}$ covers the security condition that the label *lbl* cannot be modified and attached to the ciphertext.

In Sect. 7, we show how to efficiently initialize these functionalities and primitives using previous work and present concrete performance numbers.

Endorsed E-cash: Endorsed e-cash [18] consists of two pieces: unendorsed coin '*coin*^{u}' and endorsement '*e*'. *coin*^{u} cannot be used as a coin without *e*. In addition, no one except the owner of *coin*^{u} can construct a valid *e* for *coin*^{u}. The endorsement can be efficiently verifiably escrowed and can be verified to endorse the matching unendorsed coin. Note that in our protocol, we can employ any electronic payment scheme, as long as it can be efficiently verifiably escrowed (e.g., electronic checks [22]). For the formal security definitions, we refer the reader to [18], since those are not necessary for understanding our paper. In our protocol, honest parties' endorsements' are never given to any other party.

Symmetric Encryption Scheme with the message space $\mathcal{M}$ consists of the key generation algorithm $\mathsf{SymGen}(1^\ell) \rightarrow K$, encryption algorithm $\mathsf{SymEnc}(K, m) \rightarrow E$ and the decryption algorithm $\mathsf{SymDec}(K, E) \rightarrow m$ where $m \in \mathcal{M}$ and ℓ is the security parameter.

Signature Scheme consists of the key generation algorithm $\mathsf{SgGen}(1^\ell) \rightarrow (sg, vk)$, the signing algorithm $\mathsf{SgSign}(sg_i, m) \rightarrow S$ and the verification algorithm $\mathsf{SgVerify}(vk, S, m) \rightarrow 0/1$ where $m \in \{0,1\}^*$ where ℓ is the security parameter.

Notation Parties and their names in the protocol are represented by P_i, where $i \in \{1, ..., n\}$. $\mathcal{P}_h$ denotes the set of honest parties, and the set of $\mathcal{P}_c$ denotes the corrupted parties controlled by the adversary $\mathcal{A}$. $E_k(m)$ is used to denote a ciphertext with a plaintext m and a key is k. VS is used to show verifiable escrow. We denote by f and *coin* the item and the coin used during the exchange. In general, $X_{i \rightarrow j}$ represents that P_i has generated X for P_j where $X \in \{\mathsf{VS}, E, f, coin\}$. We let d_i^k denote a decryption share of the encryption E_i generated by a party P_k (i.e., $\mathsf{ThDShare}(x_k, \mathsf{pk}, E_i) \rightarrow d_i^k$). Usually, we denote simulated values separately e.g., the encryption of a random message is shown with $\tilde{E}_i$ and its corresponding valid decryption shares are shown with $\tilde{d}_i$. We use the ideal functionalities, $U^{\mathsf{ZK}\text{-}\mathcal{R}_{ds}}, U^{\mathsf{VS}\text{-}\mathcal{R}_{vs\text{-}ds}}$ and $U^{\mathsf{VS}\text{-}\mathcal{R}_{coin}}$ where the relations are, respectively:

$$\mathcal{R}_{ds} = \{((x_i, r), (\mathsf{pk}, d_i, v)|\mathsf{ThDShare}^r(x_i, \mathsf{pk}, E) \rightarrow d_i\}, \tag{1}$$

where ThDShare^r runs ThDShare with random coins r, and

$$\mathcal{R}_{vs\text{-}ds} = \{(((\{d_i, \mathsf{DSproof}_i\}), (\mathsf{pk}, \mathsf{pk}_T, \{E_i\}, v))| \\ \forall i, \mathsf{ThDSVerify}(v, \mathsf{pk}, E_i, d_i, \mathsf{DSproof}_i) \rightarrow valid\} \tag{2}$$

showing that E_i is the encryption of valid decryption shares and their proofs. For electronic payments,

$$\mathcal{R}_{coin} = \{(e, coin^u)|e \text{ is the endorsement of unendorsed coin } coin^u\} \tag{3}$$

which denotes that a valid e-coin payment is escrowed.

4   Overview of Our Techniques

2FE vs. MFE: The classical MFE for any topology, where all parties obtain their desired items or none of them obtain anything, is especially more difficult than 2FE because the protocol should guarantee that *all* parties get items at the same time [37], *even when some parties do not need to exchange items with each other* according to the exchange topology (e.g., P_3 and P_1 on the left-hand side in Fig. 1, or P_4 and P_2 on the right-hand side of Fig. 1). For example, we should avoid cases in the ring topology in Fig. 1 such that P_4 obtains her item before P_2 obtains his item or a certificate that lets him get the item from the TTP. We prevent this type of unfair case by dividing the protocol into phases and let the participants obtain their items at the very end of the protocol. However, the issue in such phase-based protocols is synchronization: i.e., to move to the next phase if and only if other parties move as well.

Fig. 1. Graph representation of the ring topology (left) and a random topology (right). f_i is the item of party P_i. The direction of the arrow shows the party who wants to receive it.

Broadcast vs. Threshold Cryptography: One of the ways for this synchronization could be broadcasting at the end of every phase to inform others with the current view. However, broadcasting increases the message complexity to $O(n^3)$, which is far from the optimal message complexity of $O(n^2)$ that we aim for. Instead of broadcasting, we use the idea by Kılınç and Küpçü [37] connecting the parties with threshold cryptography. Thanks to the threshold cryptography, if a party cannot complete any intermediate phase successfully, others do not obtain any item (from any other party) at the last phase of the protocol. This nice property removes the need for informing other parties regarding whether the phase is completed or not, and thus decreasing the message complexity.

Resolutions with the TTP is another issue that requires special attention in an MFE protocol in any topology. One of the main requirements to achieve fairness is that the TTP should never help a party to obtain an item until making sure that others can also obtain their items. In a 2FE protocol, this issue could be solved much easily. For example, the TTP could ask the party who comes to resolve to give his own item in exchange of helping him to obtain the other party's item. This way, when the other party comes, the TTP can give the item that the other party wants. However, this solution cannot work in an MFE protocol unless the TTP contacts the other parties to give their items, which is not ideal. The protocol should not assume that the TTP knows how and when to contact the parties; instead, we can only assume that the TTP is a server machine that is available, and the parties should initiate contact, only when they need to. Another requirement from the TTP specific to coin-based fairness is that the TTP should never provide a coin to a party who comes for resolution, until it makes sure that others can obtain either a coin or their desired item and also the party who comes for the resolution *cannot* obtain the desired item.

Overview of CMFE: CMFE has three phases. In the first phase (Setup), parties generate a public-key for the threshold encryption using their private shares and then exchange coins that can be activated only by the TTP.

In the second phase (-EIE- Phase), they encrypt their item with a symmetric key and send this encryption to the parties who want their item. Also, each party sends the encryption of the symmetric key under the threshold encryption scheme to everyone. Thus, everyone needs each other because each party must obtain the decryption shares from all other parties, even if they do not expect their item, to be able to decrypt the encrypted item. A signature is used to bind these values together to be used for resolutions. If a party does not receive the ciphertexts or valid signatures, she aborts *locally*.

In the final phase (-DSE- Phase), they fairly exchange the decryption shares for each item so that the symmetric keys are reconstructed. Even if there is one party who locally aborts in the EIE phase, no party obtains any item or payment because this party never sends the decryption shares of hers during the DSE phase, and her shares are essential to decrypt all encrypted items. The DSE phase consists of two steps. In the first step, they send a verifiable escrow of the decryption shares. If a party does not receive it, it executes a resolution protocol with the TTP just to complain and comes back to the TTP later. Besides, this party does not continue to the next step. In the second step, all parties who have received the verifiable escrow send each other the decryption shares. If a party does not receive them, this party contacts the TTP and gives the verifiable escrow so that the TTP decrypts and learns some decryption shares. However, the TTP does not release them to anyone until it collects all missing decryption shares of the parties who complained. Remark that since the party who complained did not send the decryption shares, the rest of the parties, including the malicious parties who did not send the verifiable escrow, have to contact and give the verifiable escrow to the TTP if they want to obtain the item or the payment. Otherwise, no one is able to get any item or payment. We note that all parties need each other after the EIE-phase because the only way to obtain any item is to receive the decryption shares from all parties. This is intentional for achieving the fairness goal: either all parties obtain their desired item/payment or none of them obtains anything. If the TTP succeeds in collecting the missing decryption shares for all victims, it gives all of them to the parties who comes after a deadline. After decrypting the encrypted item, either with the help of the TTP or at the end of the DSE phase, if a party does not obtain the right item, then she does a resolution with the TTP by proving efficiently (without sending the large encrypted item) that the decrypted item is not the one she expected and obtains the payment of the cheating party.

5   Coin-Based MFE Protocol (CMFE)

CMFE consists of n parties and a TTP. TTP acts in CMFE if and only if a party does not follow the protocol and a dispute arises. Each party has an item f_i to be exchanged according to the topology Υ. For simplicity of presentation, we describe our protocol by assuming that each party P_i will share only one item f_i instead of different items being shared with different receivers. The TTP has a secret/public key pair $(\mathsf{sk}_T, \mathsf{pk}_T)$ generated by $\mathsf{PkGen}(1^\ell)$ where ℓ is the security parameter. The public values $\mathsf{pk}_T, \Upsilon, H$ and hashes $H_{f_1}, \ldots, H_{f_n}$ of the items as the item descriptions and timeouts t_1, t_2 are known by every party. The details follow (see also Fig. 2).

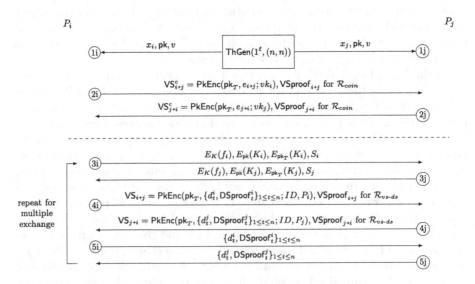

Fig. 2. Our CMFE Protocol in the complete topology.

Setup Phase (① and ② in Fig. 2): Each party P_i runs ThGen of a threshold encryption scheme with the threshold n and obtains its secret share x_i, the public key pk, and the verification key v of a deniable (n, n)-threshold encryption. Then, each P_i generates a signature signing-verification key-pair (sg_i, vk_i) by running SgGen(1^ℓ). Then, each party P_i generates a verifiable escrow of the endorsement $e_{i \to j}$ of an unendorsed coin $coin_{i \to j}^u$ with pk_T for each P_j, and sends the encryption $\mathsf{VS}_{i \to j}^c = \mathsf{PkEnc}(\mathsf{pk}_T, e_{i \to j}; vk_i)$ proving that the payment is valid $((e_{i \to j}, coin_{i \to j}^u) \in \mathcal{R}_{coin})$ (see Relation (3)) where $coin_i^u$ is sent in clear.

The label of $\mathsf{VS}_{i \to j}^c$ is vk_i because it is necessary to link a later escrow (explained below) with this one, so that the TTP can understand that both were sent by the same party. Upon receipt, each party verifies the values. This ensures that the coin will be valid once endorsed with the endorsement in the escrow[1]. Remark that labels are non-malleable so that a malicious party cannot modify them; e.g., cannot replace vk_i with another vk_i' labelled to the verifiable escrow to fool the TTP with the signatures which are not generated by P_i.

The parties execute the Setup Phase only once. They can continue exchanging multiple sets of items with the same set of parties by repeating only the following phases. If a party P_i receives the coin of a party P_j during a dispute, to continue with the next item exchange, P_j needs to send a new $\mathsf{VS}_{j \to i}^c$ to only P_i, without the need to repeat the Setup Phase completely (note that electronic payment schemes have methods to either prevent or penalize double spenders, and hence we do not need to worry about some coin being used multiple times in our protocol). In some sense, think of every participant putting down some money; if theirs are spent, they need to renew it to continue.

Encrypted Item Exchange (EIE) Phase (③ in Fig. 2): The aim of this phase is to transmit the encrypted item to the parties expecting it according to Υ. First, parties agree on two time parameters t_1 and t_2 where $t_1 > \alpha$ and $t_2 - t_1 > \alpha$ (hence allowing parties to reach the TTP even with adversarial delay; see the adversarial model in Sect. 3), the topology Υ, and unique identification id of the protocol (e.g., a counter).[2] t_1 and t_2 are two deadlines to execute some of the resolutions with the TTP. If the protocol executed honestly without the help of the TTP, parties never take into account t_1 and t_2 in any step of the CMFE. We denote the whole identifier of the protocol by $ID = \{id, t_1, t_2, \Upsilon, v, \mathsf{pk}\}$.

Each party P_i encrypts their item f_i (e.g., a file) using a symmetric encryption scheme with a key K_i generated by SymGen(1^ℓ) and obtains $E_K(f_i) = \mathsf{SymEnc}(K_i, f_i)$. Then, P_i encrypts K_i with the public key pk of the threshold-encryption scheme: $E_{\mathsf{pk}}(K_i) = \mathsf{ThEnc}(\mathsf{pk}, K_i)$. In addition, she encrypts K_i with pk_T and obtains $E_{\mathsf{pk}_T}(K_i) = \mathsf{PkEnc}(\mathsf{pk}_T, K_i)$ which is useful during the resolutions. She generates the signature $S_i = \mathsf{SgSign}(sg_i, E_{\mathsf{pk}_T}(K_i)\|H_{f_i}\|H(E_K(f_i))\|ID)$. S_i enables the TTP to understand that VS_i^c and $E_{\mathsf{pk}_T}(K_i)$ are encrypted by the same party (remember,

---

[1] For example, the verifiable escrow can be Camenisch-Shoup verifiable escrow [19], which can be efficiently used to verifiably encrypt endorsed E-cash coins [18].

[2] Time parameters and topology can also be agreed in the Setup Phase if they will remain constant.

VS_i^c contains the signature verification key in its public non-malleable label) and to learn the hash of the item and hash of its encryption. P_i sends $E_K(f_i), E_{pk_T}(K_i), E_{pk}(K_i), S_i$ to each party P_j where $\Upsilon_S[i,j] = 1$ in *a secure channel*. We note that we need only in this step a secure channel to hide the encrypted item from other parties who does not want the item and preserve privacy against the TTP. A party does not continue to the next phase till she receives all expected encryptions and signatures. After receiving all encryptions and valid signatures, each party P_i sends ciphertexts of keys, signatures and hashes $\{E_{pk}(K_j), E_{pk_T}(K_j), S_j, H_{f_j}, H(E_K(f_j))\}_{\forall j: \Upsilon_S[j,i]=1}$ to each party P_t where $t \neq j, \Upsilon_S[j,t] = 0$. P_i sends these to all parties who do not have them because she needs help from all parties to decrypt $E_{pk}(K_j)$ ((n,n)-threshold encryption). When a party receives these, he verifies signatures to check if they belong to the exchange with ID. No party continues to the next phase without completing the EIE phase: receiving all messages that they are supposed to receive and verifying signatures. If anything goes wrong, parties can locally abort and no party receives anything, so fairness preserved.

Decryption Share Exchange (DSE) Phase (④ and ⑤ in Fig. 2): This is almost the same as the MFE protocol [37] except labeling. This phase guarantees a fair exchange of symmetric keys. P_i first finds out the decryption shares that she needs to generate based on Υ. For this, she generates a decryption share and a proof with its secret share x_i for **all parties** depending on the items that they expect to receive (see FindDS below). For example, if P_u wants the item of P_v (i.e., $\Upsilon_R[u,v] = 1$), then P_i generates a decryption share of the encryption $E_{pk}(K_v)$ with x_i for each party $P_j \neq P_i$ as follows:

FindDS$(\Upsilon_R, DS_j, j, x_i)$ where $DS_j = \emptyset$ initially

---

for all t where $\Upsilon_R[j,t] = 1$

$d_t^i \leftarrow$ ThDShare$(x_i, pk, E_{pk}(K_t))$ and DSproof$_t^i \leftarrow$ ThDSProve$(x_i, pk, d_t^i, E_{pk}(K_t))$

add $(d_t^i, \text{DSproof}_t^i)$ to DS_j

After populating DS_j, P_i generates verifiable escrow. For this, she runs ProveEnc$(pk_T, DS_j, \delta; lbl)$ with $\delta = (pk, pk_T, \{E_{pk}(K_t)\}_{\forall t: \Upsilon_R[j,t]=1}, v)$ and $lbl = \{ID\|P_i\}$ and gets $VS_{i \to j} = $ PkEnc$(pk_T, DS_j; lbl)$ and its proof $VSproof_{i \to j}$. $VSproof_{i \to j}$ proves that $(DS_j, \delta) \in \mathcal{R}_{vs\text{-}ds}$ (see Relation (2)). In simple terms, $VS_{i \to j}$ includes the encryption of the decryption shares generated by P_i that is used to decrypt the encrypted items that P_j needs to receive. After receiving them, P_j verifies $VS_{i \to j}$ with VerifyEnc$(pk_T, \delta, VS_{i \to j}, VSproof_{i \to j})$ and the label.

Remark: The name P_i in the label is used to show the owner of VS. The party names can be random and distinct in each exchange, as long as the parties know each others' names, and so it does not violate the privacy of the parties. ID is to show the protocol parameters to the TTP. Putting in wrong labels is not helpful to the adversary to break fairness as it can be seen in the resolution protocols.

After sending the verifiable escrows, P_i waits for verifiable escrows from each P_j. If anything is wrong with some $VS_{j \to i}$ (e.g., verification fails or the label is not as expected), or P_i does not receive a verifiable escrow from a party, she goes to the TTP for **Resolve 1** before t_1 and does not continue with the next.

If P_i receives all verifiable escrows, P_i continues with the step ⑤. P_i sends DS_j to each party P_j. Then, she waits for the correct DS_i from each P_j. If there exists $\{d_t^j, \mathsf{DSproof}_t^j\} \in DS_i$ such that $\mathsf{ThVerify}(v, \mathsf{pk}, d_t^j, \mathsf{DSproof}_t^j) \to$ invalid) or if she does not receive some of them from P_j, she performs **Resolve 2** with the TTP, before t_2 and after t_1 (executing Resolve 2 necessitates running **Resolve 3** as well, at the latest at time t_2, where the parties may receive the decryption shares that they are missing; see the resolution protocols for details). Otherwise, P_i continues with the next step without waiting.

After receiving all the necessary values, P_i decrypts each $E_{\mathsf{pk}}(K_t)$ by running $\mathsf{ThDec}(\{d_t^j\}_{j=1}^n, \mathsf{pk}, E_{\mathsf{pk}}(K_t))$ and obtains the key to decrypt $E_K(f_t)$ for all t, $\Upsilon_R[i,t] = 1$. Next, P_i decrypts $E_K(f_t)$ to obtain some f_t'. It is possible, since the item was not verifiably encrypted, that K_t or f_t' are wrong and the decrypted file f_t' has a different hash (i.e. $H(f_t') \neq H_{f_t}$). In this case, P_i runs **Resolve 4**.

Resolve 1: This resolution is the same as Resolve 1 in [37]. We give a more generic version for any topology. The goal of Resolve 1 is to *record* the corrupted parties that did *not* send their verifiable escrow in ④. The parties do *not* learn any decryption shares here; instead they just complain about other parties. Resolve 1 needs to be done **before t_1** (Lines 2–4 in Algorithm 1). The complainant party P_i gives ID, P_j to the TTP where P_j is the party that did not send his proper $\mathsf{VS}_{j\to i}$ to P_i (complainee). The TTP creates a new complaintList for the protocol with ID if it is the first resolution for the protocol with ID. If there exists a list for ID, it checks if it is marked as DONE to make sure not to execute a resolution for an exchange that has been already done. The complaintList consists of tuples containing information about a dispute between two parties because of missing or wrong VS. The first part of the tuple is the complainant, the second part is the complainee, and the third part is the names of the expected shares from the complainee according to Υ (Line 10 in Algorithm 1). The name of an expected share d_t^j is denoted by $share_t^j$. The TTP also creates a list called solvedList, which is empty in Resolve 1 (Line 8 in Algorithm 1). In the next resolution protocols, the TTP adds any valid decryption shares obtained to solvedList. See Algorithm 1.

Algorithm 1. Resolve 1

1: P_i sends ID, P_j where P_j is the party that did not send his proper $\mathsf{VS}_{j\to i}$ to P_i.
2: **if** currenttime $> t_1$ **then**
3:     **send** msg "Abort Resolve 1"
4: **else**
5:     complaintList = GetComplaintList(ID)
6:     **if** complaintList == NULL **then**
7:         complaintList = EmptyList(pk, v, t_1, t_2, id, Υ) // initialize empty list
8:         solvedList = EmptyList(pk, v, t_1, t_2, id, Υ) // will be used in Resolve 2
9:     **else if** complaintList $\neq$ DONE **then**
10:         complaintList.add($P_i, P_j, \{share_t^j\}_{\forall t, \Upsilon_R[i,t]=1}$)
11:     **else**
12:         **send** message "The protocol is aborted"
13:     **end if**
14:     **send** message "Come after t_1 for **Resolve 2**"
15: **end if**

Remark that cheating on ID in Resolve 1 causes to have a completely different complaintList which has no relation with the real one created by the correct ID given by an honest party. So, it is not helpful for a malicious party who wants an honest party's item, because an honest party never comes with a wrong ID.

Resolve 2: It is the resolution protocol where the parties contact with the TTP to provide some verifiable escrows to help the TTP to solve the problems recorded in Resolve 1. However, the TTP does *not* send any decryption shares in Resolve 2. He just stores the decryption shares obtained from the verifiable escrows given by the parties who come for Resolve 2 in solvedList.

The party P_i, who comes for Resolve 2 **between t_1 and t_2**, gives all the verifiable escrows that he has already received from the other parties and his own verifiable escrow to the TTP in case of some owner of verifiable escrows complained in Resolve 1. So, the TTP decrypts and verifies all verifiable escrows that any party needs according to complaintList (Line 8–9 in Algorithm 2). After the decryption, the TTP adds the decryption shares and proofs to solvedList to distribute them in Resolve 3 if all the complains are solved (Line 10 in Algorithm 2). Then, the TTP checks if any party in complaintList requires these decryption shares. If there are some parties in complaintList who need them, the TTP removes the corresponding name of the decryption shares, which are in the third part of each tuple, marking that decryption share as received (Line 13–17 in Algorithm 2). If the third part of any tuple is empty after removal, the TTP removes that tuple from complaintList (Line 19 in Algorithm 2) because it obtained all the decryption shares for which a party in Resolve 1 complained.

If the complaintList is not empty during Resolve 2, P_i comes after t_2 for **Resolve 3** (Line 25 in Algorithm 2). Otherwise, P_i performs Resolve 3 and obtains all the decryption shares together with their proofs that he requests immediately. Hence, in our model, the latest time an honest party would have Resolve 3 performed is $t_2 + \alpha$ (including adversarial delay).

Resolve 3: Resolve 3 is the only resolution protocol that the TTP may give the missing decryption shares to the parties. If the complaintList still has parties, even after t_2, then the TTP answers each party saying that the protocol is **aborted** (Line 12 in Algorithm 3) because the TTP could not obtain all the missing decryption shares. It also marks complaintList with ID as DONE so that no party executes Resolve1-2-3 with ID anymore. If the TTP aborts, it means nobody is able to learn any item. The reason behind this is the following: Remark that the parties who executed Resolve 1 do not send the decryption shares in the last step of CMFE (step ⑤). Thus, their decryption shares are not known by any other party. It implies that it is not possible for the rest of parties, including the ones who did not send the verifiable escrow in step ④, to decrypt any encryption of the key ($E^{K_{pk}}$), and so it is not possible for them to decrypt the encryption of the item (E^{f_K}). If the complaintList is *empty*, then the TTP decrypts any verifiable escrow with a correct label that is provided to him (Line 6 in Algorithm 3). If the complainants from Resolve 1 come, he gives the stored decryption shares and proofs according to the topology Υ (Line 8 in Algorithm 3).

Algorithm 2. Resolve 2

```
1:  P_i gives ID and V, the set of all verifiable escrows and their proof that P_i generated and received.
2:  if t_1 < currenttime < t_2 then
3:      complaintList = GetComplaintList(ID)
4:      if complaintList == DONE or complaintList == NULL then
5:          send message "The protocol is aborted" and halt
6:      end if
7:      for all VS_{j→i} in V do
8:          if (*, P_j, *) ∈ complaintList AND VerifyEnc(pk_T, δ, VS_{j→i}, VSproof_{j→i}) → valid then
9:              shares = PkDec(sk_T, VS_{j→i}) = {d_t^j, DSproof_t^j}_{∀t, Υ_R[i,t]=1}
10:             P_j.solvedList.Append(shares)
11:             for all (P_u, P_j, *) ∈ complaintList  // all parties that complained about P_j in Resolve 1
                do
12:                 lst = complaintList[(P_u, P_j)]  // returns {share_k^j}_{∀k. Υ_R[u,k]=1}
13:                 for all share_k^j ∈ lst do
14:                     if (d_k^j, DSproof_k^j) ∈ shares then
15:                         remove share_k^j from lst
16:                     end if
17:                 end for
18:                 if lst = ∅ then
19:                     remove (P_u, P_j, ∅) from complaintList
20:                 end if
21:             end for
22:         end if
23:     end for
24: end if
25: if complaintList is empty then
26:     send message "Perform Resolve 3"
27: else
28:     send message "Come after t_2 for Resolve 3"
29: end if
```

Resolve 4: The MFE protocol [37] does not have Resolve 4. Note that if the parties reach this point, all complaints were already resolved in the Resolve 1-2-3. The party P_i who does not obtain the valid item comes for Resolve 4 to obtain the coin of the party P_j who gave the invalid item. P_i gives ID, P_j and $E_{pk_T}(K_j), VS_{j→i}^c, S_j, H_{f_j}, H(E_K(f_j))$ to the TTP. The TTP decrypts $E_{pk_T}(K_j)$ and sends K_j to P_i (Line 7 - 8 in Algorithm 4) if the complaintList is empty and if P_i should receive f_j according to Υ (Line 6 in Algorithm 4). If K_j is a correct key, then P_j obtains the item by decrypting $E_{pk_T}(K_j)$ with K_j. If K_j is a wrong key, meaning that it decrypts $E_K(f_j)$ to some f_j' with $H(f_j') \neq H_{f_j}$, then P_i proves that K_j is not correct using the subprotocol [12,27] below (Line 9 in Algorithm 4), and obtains the endorsement e_j in VS_j^c from the TTP (Line 11 in Algorithm 4), thereby obtaining the payment of P_j. Here, the TTP obtains the correct hashes by verifying the signature S_j of hashes with the verification key of P_j in the label of $VS_{j→i}^c$ (Line 2 in Algorithm 4). If An honest party would have performed Resolve 4 the latest at time $t_2 + 2\alpha$ (another delay after Resolve 3)

Prove Incorrect Key: The trivial solution to prove that the decryption of $E_K(f_j)$ with a key K_j is not equal to H_{f_j} is to send of $E_K(f_j)$ and S_j. In this case, the TTP first checks whether $H(E_K(f_j))$ matches with the hash in the signature S_i. Then, it decrypts $E_K(f_j)$ with the K_j that is obtained by decrypting $E_{pk_T}(K_j)$ and checks whether the hash of the decryption is equal

---

Algorithm 3. Resolve 3

1: P_i gives ID and $\mathcal{M}$, which is the set of malicious parties that did not behave well in step ④ or ⑤, and $\mathcal{VS}$ is a set of verifiable escrows that belongs to parties in $\mathcal{M}$ who performed step ④ properly.
2: complaintList = GetComplaintList(ID)
3: if complaintList is empty then
4:   for all P_j in $\mathcal{M}$ do
5:     if $\mathsf{VS}_{j \to i} \in \mathcal{VS}$ and $ID \in$ label of $\mathsf{VS}_{j \to i}$ then
6:       send PkDec(sk_T, VS_j)
7:     else
8:       send $\{d_t^j, \mathsf{DSproof}_t^j\}_{\forall t, \varUpsilon_S[t,i]=1} \subseteq$ solvedList
9:     end if
10:   end for
11: else if $currenttime > t_2$ then
12:   send message "Protocol is aborted"
13: else
14:   send message "Try after t_2"
15: end if

Algorithm 4. Resolve 4

1: P_i sends $v, \mathsf{pk}, t_1, t_2, id, \varUpsilon, P_j$ and $E_{\mathsf{pk}_T}(K_j), \mathsf{VS}_j^c, S_j, H_{f_j}, H(E_K(f_j))$ to the TTP where P_j is the party whose item with hash H_{f_j} could not be obtained. The TTP does the following:
2: if $currenttime < t_2$ or SgVerify($vk_j, E_{\mathsf{pk}_T}(K_j)||H_{f_j}||H(E_K(f_j)), S_j$) is invalid then
3:   send msg "Abort Resolve 4"
4: end if
5: complaintList = GetComplaintList ($\mathsf{pk}, v, id, t_1, t_2, \varUpsilon$)
6: if complaintList is empty and $\varUpsilon_R[i,j] = 1$ then
7:   $K_j = $ PkDec($\mathsf{sk}_T, E_{\mathsf{pk}_T}(K_j)$)
8:   send K_j
9:   execute "Prove Incorrect" with P_i and obtain output // only if requested by P_i
10:   if output is true then
11:     send PkDec(sk_T, VS_j^c) // P_i obtains coin of P_j instead of f_j
12:   else
13:     send msg "Abort Resolve 4"
14:   end if
15: else
16:   send msg "Abort Resolve 4"
17: end if

---

to H_{f_j}. If it is not equal, the sub protocol 'Prove Incorrect Key' outputs true. However, this solution requires heavy communication between the party and the TTP since the item so its encryption is potentially large. Besides, in the case that the key in $E_{\mathsf{pk}_T}(K)$ is correct, the TTP learns all file and privacy against the TTP is violated. Therefore, we prefer the communication efficient proving techniques based on Merkle tree [47] by Belenkiy et al. [12] or by Dziembowski et al. [27]. In this case, the hashes should be Merkle roots, and the TTP challenges parts of the file. We note that in both techniques, the TTP receives some parts of the file but not necessarily the complete file. Providing better privacy against the TTP during resolutions is left as future work.

Multiple Exchanges with Single Setup: As long as the coins are not used, multiple sets of items can be exchanged with a single setup. Even when coins are used, it is indeed enough for those parties to renew their coins rather than executing a full setup. Thus, step ① need not be renewed but step ② may need to be (selectively) renewed.

6   Fairness Proof of CMFE

Theorem 1. *Assuming that the verifiable deniable (n,n)-threshold encryption scheme is IND-CPA secure, the public key encryption scheme used for VS's and E_{pk_T}'s (the encryption scheme used to encrypt with the TTP's public key) is IND-CCA secure, the payment scheme is unforgeable, the symmetric encryption scheme is semantically secure, the signature scheme is existentially-unforgeable under adaptive chosen-message attack, and the hash function is chosen from a (target) collision resistant family (for the "proving key is not correct" protocol), the CMFE protocol with the topology Υ in $U^{\mathsf{VS}\text{-}\mathcal{R}_{coin}}, U^{\mathsf{VS}\text{-}\mathcal{R}_{vs\text{-}ds}}$, and $U^{\mathsf{ZK}\text{-}\mathcal{R}_{ds}}$ hybrid models [20] realizes U_{fs}^{ϕ} where* promise = SymEnc *where ϕ is as in Definition 3 with $z_i = (\{coin_{i \to j}\}_{\forall j, \Upsilon_S[i,j]=1}, (f_i, K_i))$. (f_i, K_i) is valid if $H(f_i) = H_{f_i}$.*

Before starting the proof, we want to make it clear that promise = SymEnc in Theorem 1 is a secure promise function according to Definition 1.

Proof. We do our proof in the $U^{\mathsf{VS}\text{-}\mathcal{R}_{coin}}$, $U^{\mathsf{VS}\text{-}\mathcal{R}_{vs\text{-}ds}}$, and $U^{\mathsf{ZK}\text{-}\mathcal{R}_{ds}}$ hybrid model [20]. The simulator $\mathcal{S}$ simulates the honest parties in $\mathcal{P}_h$ in the real world, and the corrupted parties in $\mathcal{P}_c$ in the ideal world. $\mathcal{S}$ also simulates the TTP in the real world if any resolution protocol occurs, since the TTP is an honest party. First, $\mathcal{S}$ generates $(\mathsf{sk}_T, \mathsf{pk}_T)$ as the TTP does and publishes pk_T.

Setup Phase: $\mathcal{S}$ behaves as ThGen and generates all secret keys, the public key pk, and the verification key v. $\mathcal{S}$ distributes each secret key x_j to each corrupted party P_j together with pk, v. After the key distribution, $\mathcal{S}$ behaves as $U^{\mathsf{VS}\text{-}\mathcal{R}_{coin}}$. It sends $(\mathsf{VSproof}, sid\|P_i\|P_j, coin_{i \to j}^u, \mathsf{pk}, label, \tilde{\mathsf{VS}}_{i \to j}^c)$ on behalf of each $P_i \in \mathcal{P}_h$ where $\tilde{\mathsf{VS}}_{i \to j}^c$ includes fake endorsements. Then, it waits for $(\mathsf{VSprove}, sid\|P_i\|P_j, e_{i,j}, coin_{i \to j}^u, \mathsf{pk}, v_i)$ from $P_i \in \mathcal{P}_c$. $\mathcal{S}$ does not proceed to the next phase until it receives all the necessary values properly.

EIE Phase: $\mathcal{S}$ receives from U_{fs}^{ϕ} the promises of honest parties, which are $\{E_K(f_i)\}_{P_i \in \mathcal{P}_h}$. At this point, it has the encryption of honest parties' items. In the real world, it needs to send the encryption of the key of these ciphertexts under the keys pk and pk_T, but it does not know the actual symmetric keys employed. For this, it picks some random keys $\{\tilde{K}_i\}_{P_i \in \mathcal{P}_h}$ and encrypts them under pk and pk_T. We denote these fake key encryptions by $\{E_{\mathsf{pk}}(\tilde{K}_i), E_{\mathsf{pk}_T}(\tilde{K}_i)\}_{P_i \in \mathcal{P}_h}$. It generates the signatures $\{S_i\}_{P_i \in \mathcal{P}_h}$ as in the EIE Phase, and sends them to the corrupted parties. It also saves the signatures that it sends as (i, S_i) to the list *SignList*. At the same time, it waits for the ciphertexts and signatures from the corrupted parties, and it does not execute the next step before successfully completing this one. Whenever it receives ciphertexts from the corrupted parties, $\mathcal{S}$ learns a symmetric key K_j and an item f_j' of malicious parties as follows: Assume that a corrupted party P_j gave $E_{\mathsf{pk}}(K_j)$ to an honest party P_i. $\mathcal{S}$ decrypts $E_{\mathsf{pk}}(K_j)$ ($\mathcal{S}$ knows the secret shares of the corrupted parties from the setup phase) and obtains K_j. Then, it decrypts $E_K(f_j)$ with K_j and obtains f_j'. If $H(f_j') \neq H_{f_j}$, it decrypts $E_{\mathsf{pk}_T}(K_j)$ with sk_T and obtains a key. If this does not equal to K_j, it decrypts $E_K(f_j)$ with this key. If again the hash of the item is not equal to H_{f_j}, it means that the corrupted party did not encrypt the correct item. If S obtains the correct f_j, it stores it as an item of the corrupted party P_j given to P_i. Otherwise, it stores a (or one of the) random item f_j obtained from $E_{\mathsf{pk}}(K_j)$ as an item of P_j given to P_i.

DSE Phase: S does the same computations as in the step ④ on behalf of the honest parties. Then, S as $U^{\mathsf{VS}-\mathcal{R}_{vs-ds}}$ waits for $(\mathsf{VSprove}, sid||P_i||P_j, w, \delta, \mathsf{pk}_T, \{d_t^i, \mathsf{DSproof}_t^i\}_{\forall t, \Upsilon_R[j,t]}, lbl)$ from each corrupted party P_i for a party P_j where $(w, \delta) = (\{d_t^i, \mathsf{DSproof}_t^i\}_{\forall t, \Upsilon_R[j,t]}, (\mathsf{pk}, \mathsf{pk}_T, \{E_{\mathsf{pk}}(K_t)\}_{\forall t, \Upsilon_R[j,t]}, v))$ as in Relation 2. Whenever S receives this message with valid a witness and statement from a corrupted party P_i for an honest party P_j, it stores $\{d_t^i, \mathsf{DSproof}_t^i\}_{\forall t, \Upsilon_R[j,t]=1}$. It also sends to each corrupted party P_i the message $(\mathsf{VSproof}, id||P_j||P_i, \delta, \mathsf{pk}_T, lbl, \tilde{VS}_{j\to i})$ on behalf of each honest party P_i. $\tilde{VS}_{j\to i})$ is a random encryption. At this point, one of the following situations must have happened: (1) S stores all the decryption shares of the corrupted parties and (2) S has some missing decryption shares of the corrupted parties.

Case (1): By time t_1, if S received all $\{d_j^i, \mathsf{DSproof}_j^i\}_{P_i \in \mathcal{P}_c}$ to be given to some honest parties, it means that all parties may obtain the items or coins because S in the real world is now able to learn all decryption shares (or coins) from the corrupted parties via Resolve 1, 2, 3, 4 (i.e., if verifiable escrows of all corrupted parties were received by some honest party, even if corrupted parties do not execute the next step, honest ones are able to obtain the decryption shares of the corrupted parties via resolutions. Also, any honest party P who did not receive any verifiable escrow in the DSE phase from corrupted parties can learn all the decryption shares too, because the honest parties who have the verifiable escrows from the corrupted parties execute Resolve 2 since P will not send their decryption shares in the next phase). Since it is guaranteed that everyone gets the item or the coin, S sends all $\{coin_j, f_j, K_j\}_{P_j \in \mathcal{P}_c}$ for each honest party P_i where $\Upsilon_S[j,i] = 1$ to U together with the promises $\{E_K(f_j)\}_{P_j \in \mathcal{P}_c}$ as ideal adversary and $\{b_i = \mathrm{CONTINUE}\}_{P_i \in \mathcal{P}_h}$ as TTP to U_{fs}^ϕ. Afterwards, U_{fs}^ϕ checks the correctness of each item f_j using their public hash values. If some of them is not the correct item, U_{fs}^ϕ sends corresponding coins to the parties in the ideal world instead of item (f_j, K_j). Besides, U_{fs}^ϕ sends $\{f_i, K_i\}_{P_i \in \mathcal{P}_h}$ to S. It is sure that U_{fs}^ϕ outputs $\{f_i, K_i\}_{P_i \in \mathcal{P}_h}$ to S because those come from the honest parties in the ideal world; so neither can be a coin.

S should send his decryption shares to the corrupted parties in the real world. However, S sent the encryption of random keys $\{\tilde{K}_j\}_{P_j \in \mathcal{P}_h}$ in the EIE phase. So, it cannot send the correct decryption shares of random ciphertexts $\{E_{\mathsf{pk}}(\tilde{K}_j)\}_{j \in \mathcal{P}_h}$. Instead, for each $E_{\mathsf{pk}}(\tilde{K}_j)$ where $P_j \in \mathcal{P}_h$, S runs ThDeny algorithm to obtain decryption shares that make decryption of $E_{\mathsf{pk}}(\tilde{K}_j)$ be K_j that learned from U_{fs}^ϕ. Assume that the correct decryption shares of $E_{\mathsf{pk}}(\tilde{K}_j)$ is $\{d_j^i = \mathsf{ThDShare}(x_i, \mathsf{pk}, E_{\mathsf{pk}}(\tilde{K}_j))\}_{P_i \in \mathcal{P}}$ and the index set of honest parties is $\mathcal{I}$ such that for all $i \in \mathcal{I}$, $P_i \in \mathcal{I}$. For all $E_{\mathsf{pk}}(\tilde{K}_j)$ where $P_j \in \mathcal{P}_h$, S obtains fake $\{d_j^i\}_{P_i \in \mathcal{P}_h}$

by running $\mathsf{ThDeny}(E_{\mathsf{pk}}(\tilde{K}_j), \{\tilde{d}_j^t\}_{P_t \in \mathcal{P}_c}, \mathcal{I}, K_j, \mathsf{pk})$ (See Definition 5) and uses $\{d_j^i\}_{i \in \mathcal{P}_h}$ when simulating the step ④ for each $E_{\mathsf{pk}}(\tilde{K}_j)$. For each encryption $\mathsf{VS}_{j \to i}$ where $P_j \in \mathcal{P}_c$, S also runs $\mathsf{ThDeny}(E_{\mathsf{pk}}(K_j), \{\tilde{d}_j^t\}_{P_t \in \mathcal{P}_c}, \mathcal{I}, K_j, \mathsf{pk})$ and obtains valid decryption shares $\{d_j^i\}_{i \in \mathcal{P}_h}$ for $E_{\mathsf{pk}}(K_j)$. S acts as $U^{\mathsf{ZK}\text{-}\mathcal{R}_{ds}}$ and sends as $\mathsf{DSproof}_i$, $(\mathsf{proof}, id||P_i||P_j, (\mathsf{pk}, E_{\mathsf{pk}}(\tilde{K}_i)(\text{or } E_{\mathsf{pk}}(K_j)), \{d_t^i\}_{\forall t, \Upsilon_R[j,t]}, v))$ to each $P_j \in \mathcal{P}_c$ on behalf of $P_i \in \mathcal{P}_h$. If all corrupted parties send their valid decryption shares, then the simulation ends by the simulator outputting the items and keys (if correct item is obtained in the real protocol) or coins of the malicious parties (if item is incorrect, then S uses the coins obtained during setup) on behalf of the real honest parties and whatever the adversary outputs on behalf of the ideal corrupted parties.

Case (2): S behaves as the TTP and adds the corrupted parties who did not send their verifiable escrows to the complaintList, because in reality the honest party(s) would have complained about them before t_1 in Resolve 1. In addition, if a corrupted party performs Resolve 1, S behaves like the TTP and adds the complainant and his complainee to the complaintList. Moreover, S does not send any of P_i's decryption shares to others if it does not receive a valid verifiable escrow from at least one corrupted party, as in the real protocol. If some of the corrupted parties come for Resolve 2, S behaves exactly as the TTP and clears the parties from the complaintList according to the given verifiable escrows. Each time it clears the complaintList, it learns the decryption shares of the complainee. It performs Resolve 2 as honest parties. In the end, if complaintList is empty, it means that S learned all the decryption shares of the corrupted parties. If so, it sends $\{f_j, K_j, E_K(f_j)\}_{P_j \in \mathcal{P}_c}$ for each honest party P_i where $\Upsilon_S[j,i] = 1$ as an ideal adversary and also $\{b_i = \text{CONTINUE}\}_{P_i \in \mathcal{P}_h}$ as TTP to U_{fs}^ϕ. U_{fs}^ϕ sends $\{f_i, K_i\}_{P_i \in \mathcal{P}_h}$ to S. S learns the decryption shares as described in case (1). S outputs the received items on behalf of real honest parties. If complaintList is not empty at time t_2, S sends message ABORT to U_{fs}^ϕ and will return an abort message to all Resolve 3 attempts. S outputs $\perp$ on behalf of real honest parties. In all cases, S simulates the resolutions. It simulates Resolve 2 by replacing the line 9 in Algorithm 2 and Resolve 3 by replacing the lines between 5–6 in Algorithm 3 with the following where $proof = (\mathsf{proof}, id||P_j||P_i, (\mathsf{pk}, \tilde{\mathsf{VS}}_j, \{d_t^j\}_{P_t \in \mathcal{P}}, v))$:

Resolve 2:
if $(*, (P_j, h_j), *) \in$ complaintList and
$\mathsf{VerifyEnc}(\mathsf{pk}_T, \delta, \mathsf{VS}_{j \to i}, \mathsf{VSproof}_{j \to i})$ valid
    if $P_j \in \mathcal{P}_h$
    $shares = \{d_t^j\}_{P_t \in \mathcal{P}}, proof$
    else: $shares = \mathsf{PkDec}(\mathsf{sk}_T, \mathsf{VS}_j)$

Resolve 3:
if $\mathsf{VS}_j \in V$ and has correct label
    if $P_j \in \mathcal{P}_h$
    send $shares = \{d_t^j\}_{P_t \in \mathcal{P}}, proof$
    else:
    send $\mathsf{PkDec}(\mathsf{sk}_T, \mathsf{VS}_j)$

The reason of this change in the simulations of Resolve 2 and 3 is that S sent random verifiable escrows in the DSE phase. So, as a TTP, it cannot send directly the decryption of random escrow to the party who comes for Resolve 2. It also simulates Resolve 4 as follows:

Resolve 4:

We replace lines 2–4 of Algorithm 4 with the ones below instead of actually verifying the signatures using SgVerify. So, the signatures of the honest parties that are not generated by the simulator are never accepted.

if $currenttime < t_2$ **or** ($P_j \in \mathcal{P}_h$ **and** $(j, S_j) \notin SignList$): **send** msg "Abort"
else: as in 2–4 in Algorithm 4

We replace line 7 of Algorithm 4 with below to give the correct key K_j of honest parties since $\mathcal{S}$ sent a random encryption as an encryption of the key in EIE.

if $P_j \in \mathcal{P}_h$: $K = K_j$ //the key send from $U_{f_s}^\phi$ **else:** $K = \mathsf{PkDec}(E_j^{K_{\mathsf{pk}_T}}, \mathsf{sk}_T)$

We replace line 11 of Algorithm 4 with below so that the honest parties' fake endorsements are never exposed.

if $P_j \in \mathcal{P}_h$: **send** msg "Abort Resolve 4" **else:** as in line 11 in Algorithm 4

Finally, the simulator outputs whatever the adversary $\mathcal{A}$ outputs on behalf of ideal corrupted parties. This finishes our description of the simulator. We now show the simulator's actions remain indistinguishable from the adversary's view.

Lemma 1. *The view of $\mathcal{A}$ in his interaction with the simulator $\mathcal{S}$ is indistinguishable from the view in his interaction with real honest parties and the TTP.*

We prove this lemma via a sequence of hybrid games. The initial game corresponds to the real protocol, whereas the final game corresponds to the simulator $\mathcal{S}$ described above. In each game, we change one (or more) step of CMFE with the steps which are different in the simulation above.

G 1 : The adversary $\mathcal{A}$ who corrupts the parties in $\mathcal{P}_c$ in CMFE wants to break the fairness. We simulate the honest parties $\mathcal{P}_h$ and TTP in the real protocol.

G 2 : It is the same as the previous game except that we simulate Resolve 2 and 3 as in the simulator and only line 7 of Resolve 4 as the simulator above. So, everything is the same as Game 1 except, instead of decrypting verifiable escrows and encryptions of honest parties, it returns the (already known) decryption shares and keys of the honest parties. Remark that at this point, $\{d_i^j\}$'s and K_j's are correct, since we did not start putting fake decryption shares yet. Because of the correctness of the verifiable encryption scheme, this game is indistinguishable from the previous game.

G 3 : It is the same as the previous game except that we simulate lines 2–4 of Resolve 4 as described in the simulation. The only difference between G 2 and G 3 is in the case that the TTP receives a valid signature that is not generated by an honest party. One can easily prove that this case happens with negligible probability due to the unforgeability of the signature scheme.

G 4 : It is the same as the previous game except that we simulate line 11 of Resolve 4 as described in the simulation. The only difference between G 4 and G 3 is in the case that the TTP outputs true by running the sub protocol "Prove Key is not Correct" even though the key is correct. We can easily prove that this case happens with negligible probability via the security of this sub protocol. Therefore, this game is indistinguishable from the previous game. Note that this reduction shows that a malicious party cannot get both the file and coin of an honest party at the same time.

G 5 : It is the same as the previous game except that the honest provers send encryption of random decryption shares in step ④. Intuitively, they are indistinguishable by the IND-CCA security of the verifiable escrow.

The reduction from G 4 to G 5 is the following:

We define hybrid game $H_{5,i}$ where first i parties behave as in G 4 and the rest of the simulated parties behaves as in G 5. For the sake of clarity of the hybrid argument, assume without loss of generality that $\mathcal{P}_h = \{P_j\}_{1 \leq j \leq m}$. $H_{5,0}$ is equivalent to G 5 and $H_{5,m}$ is equivalent to G 4. We use the hybrid argument to show the indistinguishability of $H_{5,0}$ and $H_{5,m}$. If the adversary manages to distinguish $H_{5,0}$ and $H_{5,m}$ with non-negligible advantage, it must distinguish $H_{5,i}$ and $H_{5,i+1}$ for some i. If so, we can construct an adversary $\mathcal{B}$ which breaks the IND-CCA security of the verifiable escrow scheme, as follows:

The IND-CCA challenger sends a pk_T, and $\mathcal{B}$ publishes it as the public key of the TTP. Then, $\mathcal{B}$ guesses i in range $[0, m-1]$, and does the following: For $P_j \in \{P_1, ..., P_i\}$, $\mathcal{B}$ asks the challenger to encrypt $\{d_t^j, \mathsf{DSproof}_t^j\}_{\forall t, \Upsilon_R[k,t]=1}$ and gets the encryption part of $\mathsf{VS}_{j \to k}$. For $P_j \in \{P_{i+2}, ..., P_m\}$, $\mathcal{B}$ asks challenger to encrypt $\{r_k\}_{1 \leq t \leq n}$ for some random r_k from the same distribution of decryption shares and obtain encryption part of $\mathsf{VS}_{j \to k}$.

As the challenge query, $\mathcal{B}$ sends $m_0 = \{d_t^{i+1}, \mathsf{DSproof}_t^{i+1}\}_{\forall t, \Upsilon_R[k,t]=1}$ for a $P_k \in \mathcal{P}$ and sets m_1 randomly and obtains back $\mathsf{VS}_{i+1 \to k}$. It then picks $b' \in \{0, 1\}$. If $b' = 0$, it asks challenger to encrypt $\{d_t^{i+1}, \mathsf{DSproof}_t^{i+1}\}_{\forall t, \Upsilon_R[u,t]=1}$ and obtain encryption part of $\mathsf{VS}_{i+1 \to u}$ for all $P_u \in \mathcal{P} \backslash \{P_k\}$. If $b' = 1$, it asks challenger to encrypt $\{r_u\}_{P_u \in \mathcal{P} \backslash \{P_k\}}$ and obtain encryption part of $\mathsf{VS}_{i+1 \to u}$ for all $P_u \in \mathcal{P} \backslash \{P_k\}$. It then continues interacting with the adversary as prescribed. Observe that if m_0 is encrypted by the IND-CCA challenger and $b' = 0$, then this corresponds to hybrid $H_{5,i+1}$, and if m_1 and $b' = 1$ is encrypted, then this is hybrid $H_{5,i}$.

If corrupted parties do not send the decryption shares in step ④, then $\mathcal{B}$ calls decryption oracle to decrypt the corresponding encryption in VS values to learn the missing decryption shares and continues simulation. Note that we do not need to query the decryption oracle for $\mathsf{VS}_{i+1 \to k}$ during resolutions, since we changed the simulation of Resolve 2 and Resolve 3 since G 3 (i.e., TTP does not decrypt the verifiable escrows of the honest parties).

If the guess of i and b' was correct and the adversary distinguishes between G 4 and G 5 with $\mathsf{adv}(\ell)$ advantage, then $\mathcal{B}$ can guess whether m_0 or m_1 was encrypted with the same advantage. Hence the IND-CCA security of the verifiable escrow is broken with at least $\mathsf{adv}(\ell)/2m$ advantage. Since $\mathsf{adv}(\ell)/2m$ must be negligible if we use a secure verifiable escrow scheme, $\mathsf{adv}(\ell)$ must be negligible as well, meaning that this behaviour of our simulator remains indistinguishable to the adversary.

G 6 : It is the same as the previous game except that we encrypt random keys $\tilde{K}$ and fake endorsements with pk_T to obtain $E_{\mathsf{pk}_T}(\tilde{K})$ and $\tilde{\mathsf{VS}}^c$ for honest parties. They are indistinguishable because of the IND-CCA-security of the encryption scheme (a very similar reduction as in G 5) and $\tilde{\mathsf{VS}}^c, E_{\mathsf{pk}_T}(\tilde{K})$ of honest parties are never decrypted in the resolution protocols in G 4.

G 7 : It is the same as the previous game except that we simulate the honest provers by encrypting random keys with pk in step ③ and using decryption shares outputted by ThDeny algorithm. More specifically, each honest prover P_i encrypts a random item $\tilde{K}_i$ and sends the encryption $E_{\mathsf{pk}}(\tilde{K}_i) = \mathsf{ThEnc}(\mathsf{pk}, \tilde{K}_i)$ to all other parties. Normally, the valid decryption shares of the honest parties and the corrupted parties for $E_{\mathsf{pk}}(\tilde{K}_i)$ are $\{\tilde{d}_i^j = \mathsf{ThDShare}(x_j, \mathsf{pk}, E_{\mathsf{pk}}(\tilde{K}_i))\}_{P_j \in \mathcal{P}}$. Instead of the valid ones, at step ⑤ each honest party P_j uses fake decryption shares as a decryption shares of $\{E_{\mathsf{pk}}(\tilde{K}_i)\}_{P_i \in \mathcal{P}_h}$. The fake decryption shares $\{d_i^j\}_{P_j \in \mathcal{P}_h}$ for each $E_{\mathsf{pk}}(\tilde{K}_i)$ are the output of $\mathsf{ThDeny}(E_{\mathsf{pk}}(\tilde{K}_i), \{\tilde{d}_i^j\}_{P_j \in \mathcal{P}_c}, \mathcal{I}, K_i, \mathsf{pk})$. Intuitively, G 6 and G 7 are indistinguishable because of the IND-CPA security of the deniable threshold encryption scheme. The reduction is as follows:

We define hybrid game $H_{7,i}$, where the first i honest parties behave as in G 6 and the rest of the simulated parties behave as in G 7. For the sake of clarity, assume without loss of generality that $\mathcal{P}_h = \{P_i\}_{1 \leq i \leq m}$. $H_{7,0}$ is equivalent to G 7 and $H_{7,m}$ is equivalent to G 6. We use the hybrid argument to show the indistinguishability of $H_{7,0}$ and $H_{7,m}$. Against the adversary, $\mathcal{B}$ plays the honest parties $\{P_i\}_{1 \leq i \leq m}$. Against the IND-CPA challenger, $\mathcal{B}$ plays the honest parties $\{P_i\}_{m+1 \leq i \leq n}$. If the adversary distinguishes $H_{7,0}$ and $H_{7,m}$ with non-negligible advantage, it must distinguish $H_{7,i}$ and $H_{7,i+1}$ for some i. If so, we can construct an adversary $\mathcal{B}$ which breaks the IND-CPA security of the threshold encryption scheme, as follows:

$\mathcal{B}$ picks i in range $[1, m]$. Then, $\mathcal{B}$ obtains secret keys $\{x_{m+1}, x_{m+2}, ..., x_n\}$, the public key pk, and the verification key v from the IND-CPA challenger. As the challenge query, $\mathcal{B}$ sends the actual item K_{i+1} and a random item $\tilde{K}_{i+1}$ and receives $E_{\mathsf{pk}}(K_{i+1}^*)$, which either encryption of K_{i+1} or $\tilde{K}_{i+1}$.

Then, $\mathcal{B}$ simulates each party $P_j \in \{P_1, ..., P_i\}$ as encrypting the correct item K_j, each party $P_j \in \{P_{i+2}, P_{i+3}, ..., P_m\}$ as encrypting a random item $\tilde{K}_j$, and P_{i+1} using $E_{\mathsf{pk}}(K_{i+1}^*)$ as the key encryption of P_{i+1}. During the simulation of $U^{\mathsf{VS}\text{-}\mathcal{R}_{vs\text{-}ds}}$, it learns the decryption shares of the corrupted parties from the adversary. $\mathcal{B}$ does not know the secret keys $x_1, x_2, ..., x_m$ but it can generate the decryption shares of the honest parties as follows:

- For the decryption shares for the encrypted keys of the corrupted parties and decryption shares of the encrypted items of $\{P_j\}_{1 \leq j \leq i}$: $\{d_j^t\}_{P_t \in \mathcal{P}_h} = \mathsf{ThDeny}(E_{\mathsf{pk}}(K_j), \{d_j^t\}_{P_t \in \mathcal{P}_c}, \mathcal{I}, K_j, \mathsf{pk})$
- For the decryption shares of the encrypted items of $\{P_j\}_{i+2 \leq j \leq m}$: $\{d_j^t\}_{P_t \in \mathcal{P}_h} = \mathsf{ThDeny}(E_{\mathsf{pk}}(\tilde{K}_j), \{\tilde{d}_j^t\}_{P_t \in \mathcal{P}_c}, \mathcal{I}, K_j, \mathsf{pk})$
- For the decryption shares of the challenge ciphertext $E_{\mathsf{pk}}(K_{i+1}^*)$ of P_{i+1}: $\{d_{i+1}^t\}_{P_t \in \mathcal{P}_h} = \mathsf{ThDeny}(E_{\mathsf{pk}}(K_{i+1}^*), \{d_{i+1}^t\}_{P_t \in \mathcal{P}_c}, \mathcal{I}, K_{i+1}, \mathsf{pk})$

It simulates the proofs of all decryption shares via $U^{\mathsf{ZK}\text{-}\mathcal{R}_{ds}}$. Observe that if $E_{\mathsf{pk}}(K_{i+1}^*)$ is not the encryption of K_{i+1} then $\mathcal{B}$ simulates $H_{7,i+1}$. Otherwise, it simulates $H_{7,i}$. Therefore, if the guess of i was correct and the adversary distinguishes between G 7 and G 6 with $\mathsf{adv}(\ell)$ advantage, then $\mathcal{B}$ can guess whether the actual item K_{i+1} or a random item was encrypted with the same advantage. Hence the IND-CPA security of the threshold encryption scheme is broken with at least $\mathsf{adv}(\ell)/m$ advantage. Since $\mathsf{adv}(\ell)/m$ must be negligible if we use a secure verifiable deniable threshold encryption scheme, $\mathsf{adv}(\ell)$ must be negligible as well, meaning that this behavior of our simulator remains indistinguishable to the adversary.

G 7 is the same as our simulation of CMFE. Since G 7 and G 1 are indistinguishable, our simulation is indistinguishable as well.

Lemma 2. *The distributions of the outputs of honest and corrupted players in ideal and real worlds are indistinguishable according to Definition 2.*

Proof. We showed in the previous lemma that the simulator's actions, on behalf of the honest parties in the real world, are indistinguishable from the CMFE protocol. We also need to show the joint output of honest and corrupted parties are indistinguishable in the real and ideal worlds.

$\mathcal{S}$ receives promises $\{E_K(f_j)\}_{P_j \in \mathcal{P}_h}$ from U_{fs}^{ϕ} and starts the simulation. $\mathcal{S}$ sends the message $\{coin_i, (f_i, K_i)\}_{P_i \in \mathcal{P}_h}$ and promises $\{E_K(f_i)\}_{P_i \in \mathcal{P}_h}$ as an ideal adversary and $\{b_i = \text{CONTINUE}\}_{P_i \in \mathcal{P}_h}$ as TTP to U_{fs}^{ϕ} whenever it is guaranteed that the honest parties would get their desired items (coin or item). At these cases (Case 1 and Case 2), each $P_j \in \mathcal{P}_h$ where $\Upsilon_S[j, i] = 1$ outputs K_i and f_i if $H(f_i) = H_{f_i}$, and $coin_i$ otherwise, in the ideal world. Similarly, at these cases, the simulated honest parties also obtain K_i and f_i if $H(f_i) = H_{f_i}$, and $coin_i$ otherwise, in the real world as discussed in the simulation. $\mathcal{S}$ sends ABORT message to U_{fs}^{ϕ} after the end of the EIE phase when complaintList is not empty at time t_2. After the end of the EIE phase, if $\mathcal{S}$ sends ABORT message, it means that the adversary in the real world only has the promises of the honest parties, which do not leak any information according to Definition 1. Indeed, $\mathcal{S}$ outputs in the ideal world on behalf of corrupted parties whatever $\mathcal{A}$ outputs in the real world; hence adversarial parties' outputs in both worlds will always be indistinguishable.

The outputs of parties in the ideal world are identically distributed to the outputs of parties in the real protocol. It completes the proof of Theorem 1. □

Security of Multiple Exchanges with Single Setup: Once the setup is performed, all remaining actions of $\mathcal{S}$ can be repeated for each set of item exchanges. Observe that the $\mathcal{S}$ never uses the secret keys, which means that the interaction with the adversary cannot leak any useful information about the secret keys. Moreover, the honest parties' coins are never given to the adversary. Therefore, we can simulate multiple exchanges with a single setup phase.

7 Performance Analysis

While we did not implement the full protocol, we provide performance numbers based on the performance of the underlying primitives taken from Cashlib [15] and Charm [2] libraries. The yardstick of the values were obtained from a DELL Latitude E7240 laptop with a 2.10 GHz i7 processor and 8 GB of RAM running Ubuntu 16.04 LTS. The security parameter for the public-key operations is 1024 bits. KB represents kilobytes, MB is megabytes, and ms is milliseconds. We do not include the network latency in our measurements, leaving it out of scope. We note that CMFE works in optimal complexity in terms of the number of rounds. Moreover, observe that the timeouts regarding resolution protocols do not affect the execution time of the protocol. Given these numbers, our protocol is ready for deployment in practice.

For the underlying primitives, we employ El Gamal [28] public key encryption, Cramer-Shoup [24] based verifiable escrows, Endorsed E-cash [18] for coins, Camenish-Shoup [19] based verifiable escrows for coin endorsements, and RSA [51] signatures. Zero knowledge proofs of knowledge are taken from ZKPDL [46] implementation of efficient Sigma proofs [25] in the random oracle model.

Per participant, the communication complexity is $O(n^2)$ and the computational complexity is $O(n)$.

Optimizations: Observe that, a party's coin is decrypted by the TTP only if during Resolve 4, some party manages to prove that this party sent a wrong key/file. Therefore, if a party is honest, her coin will *never* be obtained by another party. So, an honest party can prepare only one coin and VS^c, and can send the same coin to all other parties.[3] Moreover, if parties may wish to change the topology during CMFE repetitions after a single setup, then they need to initially perform a complete topology type of one-time setup, where every pair of parties exchange unendorsed coins and verifiably encrypted endorsements. But, if a topology will be fixed for all the subsequent exchanges, the setup can be more efficient. Consider the ring topology: Since the only other party who can obtain a party's coin in Resolve 4 is the succeeding party in the ring, it is enough that each party sends her unendorsed coin and verifiably encrypted endorsement only to the succeeding party in the ring. This makes the per-participant cost of the Setup Phase for the ring topology independent of the number of participants. Below, we provide performance numbers with these optimizations.

Communication Overhead: Table 3 shows that the total bit overhead of CMFE is about 527 KB in the complete topology and 70 KB in the ring topology for 10 participants. Since the Setup Phase of CMFE is executed once among the same set of participants, if we do not consider this phase (for repeated exchanges), the bit complexity for 10 parties is around 105 KB for the complete topology and 20 KB for the ring topology.

Computation Overhead: We analyze the time complexity of CMFE in Table 4. The total computation is around 1.3 s in the complete topology and 0.4 s in the ring topology for 10 parties. The setup is costly due to the electronic coin requirement (and hence would be much faster with non-anonymous electronic

---

[3] Of course, a malicious party can also do so, but remember that offline e-cash schemes have penalties for double spenders, which is outside our scope.

checks). If we do not consider the Setup Phase, then the computation time decreases to 87 ms in the complete topology and 59 ms in the ring topology.

The main benefit of CMFE comes from not only repeated exchanges, but also the fact that CMFE is the *first* multi-party fair exchange protocol that enables efficient fair exchange of items that cannot be efficiently verifiably encrypted.

Table 3. The size of messages in CMFE for each participant. The values in parenthesis show the size of the messages in CMFE without the Setup Phase. The unit of values is KB. # is the number of parties.

#	Complete T. (KB)	Ring T. (KB)
2	49.8 (2.94)	49.8 (2.94)
4	155.9 (15.38)	54.87 (7.20)
6	270.9 (36.62)	59.93 (11.46)
8	394.6 (66.61)	64.98 (15.72)
10	527.1 (105.34)	70.04 (19.98)

Table 4. Required time for each party for the computations in CMFE. The values in parenthesis show the time of computation in CMFE without the Setup Phase. The unit of the values is millisecond. # is the number of parties.

#	Complete T. (ms)	Ring T. (ms)
2	387.5 (12.08)	387.5 (12.08)
4	623.1 (25.70)	400.1 (23.95)
6	861.8 (42.63)	412.4 (35.82)
8	1104.6 (63.52)	424.9 (47.68)
10	1350.3 (87.34)	437.3 (59.55)

Future Work: We leave reducing the trust on and increasing the privacy against, or incentivizing the TTP as future work. The realistic valuation of the exchange items is another open problem outside of the cryptographic scope.

Acknowledgements. We acknowledge the support of the Turkish Academy of Sciences and TÜBİTAK (the Scientific and Technological Research Council of Turkey) project 119E088.

A   Deniable (n, n)- El Gamal Threshold Encryption

In this section, we use a group $\mathbb{G}$ with a generator g of a prime order p with respect to a security parameter ℓ. All operations are group operations. We use multiplicative group notation.

Deniable (n, n)-threshold El-Gamal encryption consists of the probabilistic polynomial time (PPT) protocols below:

- ThGen(ℓ, n, n): It is an interactive protocol. Each party P_i picks $x_i \in \mathbb{Z}_p$ as a secret share. Then, he sends $h_i = g^{x_i}$ as a verification key by proving the relation $\mathcal{R}_{dl} = \{(x_i, (\mathbb{G}, p, g))|h_i = g^{x_i}\}$ denoting knowledge of the discrete logarithm. At the end, all parties agree on the public key $h = \prod g^{x_i}$ and the verification key $v = \{g^{x_1}, g^{x_2}, ..., g^{x_n}\}$.
- ThEnc$(h, m) \rightarrow (a, b)$ where $(a, b) = (g^r, mh^r)$ for random $r \in \mathbb{Z}_p$.
- ThDShare$(x_i, h, E) \rightarrow d_i$ where $d_i = a^{x_i}$ and a is the first part of E.

- ThDSProve$(x_i, E, h, d_i) \rightarrow p_i$ where $p_i = (c, D)$ such that $c = H(W_1, W_2)$, $W_1 = g^r$, $W_2 = a^r$ and $D = r - x_i c \mod p$. Remark that p_i is the proof of the relation $\mathcal{R}_{dleq} = \{(x_i, (\mathbb{G}, p, g, h_i, a, d_i | x_i = \log_g h_i = \log_a d_i\}$.
- ThDSVerify(v, h, E, d_i, p_i) outputs valid if $c = H(g^D h_i^c, a^D d_i^c)$. Otherwise it outputs invalid.
- ThDec$(\{d_i\}_{1 \leq i \leq n}, E) \rightarrow m$ where $m = \frac{b}{\prod d_i} = \frac{mh^r}{g^r \Sigma x_i} = \frac{mh^r}{h^r}$
- ThDeny$(E, DS', \mathcal{I}, m_1, h) \rightarrow DS''$. Assume that $DS' \subset DS$ where DS is the decryption shares of $E = ThEnc(h, m_0)$ with $|DS'| < n$ and $\mathcal{I}$ is the index set of missing decryption shares. ThDeny first picks randomly an index $i \in \mathcal{I}$ and then randomly picks d_j for all $j \in \mathcal{I} \setminus i$. Then, finds a decryption share d_i as follows: $d_i = \frac{b}{m_1 \prod_{j \in \mathcal{I} \setminus i} d_j}$ and then outputs $DS'' = \{d_t\}_{t \in \mathcal{I}}$.

References

1. Abadi, M., Glew, N.: Certified email with a light on-line trusted third party: design and implementation. In: World Wide Web, pp. 387–395. ACM (2002)
2. Akinyele, J.A., et al.: Charm: a framework for rapidly prototyping cryptosystems. J. Cryptographic Eng. **3**(2), 111–128 (2013)
3. Andrychowicz, M., Dziembowski, S., Malinowski, D., Mazurek, L.: Secure multi-party computations on bitcoin. In: SP, pp. 443–458. IEEE (2014)
4. Asokan, N., Schunter, M., Waidner, M.: Optimistic protocols for multi-party fair exchange. Technical report, IBM Research RZ2892 (1996)
5. Asokan, N., Shoup, V., Waidner, M.: Optimistic fair exchange of digital signatures. IEEE J. Sel. Areas Commun. **18**, 591–610 (2000)
6. Ateniese, G.: Efficient verifiable encryption (and fair exchange) of digital signatures. In: ACM CCS, pp. 138–146. ACM (1999)
7. Ateniese, G., Nita-Rotaru, C.: Stateless-recipient certified e-mail system based on verifiable encryption. In: Preneel, B. (ed.) CT-RSA 2002. LNCS, vol. 2271, pp. 182–199. Springer, Heidelberg (2002). https://doi.org/10.1007/3-540-45760-7_13
8. Avoine, G., Vaudenay, S.: Optimistic fair exchange based on publicly verifiable secret sharing. In: Wang, H., Pieprzyk, J., Varadharajan, V. (eds.) ACISP 2004. LNCS, vol. 3108, pp. 74–85. Springer, Heidelberg (2004). https://doi.org/10.1007/978-3-540-27800-9_7
9. Bao, F., Deng, R., Nguyen, K.Q., Varadharajan, V.: Multi-party fair exchange with an off-line trusted neutral party. In: DEXA, pp. 858–862. IEEE (1999)
10. Bao, F., Deng, R.H., Mao, W.: Efficient and practical fair exchange protocols with off-line TTP. In: IEEE Symposium on Security and Privacy, pp. 77–85 (1998)
11. Baum, C., David, B., Dowsley, R.: Insured MPC: efficient secure computation with financial penalties. In: Bonneau, J., Heninger, N. (eds.) FC 2020. LNCS, vol. 12059, pp. 404–420. Springer, Cham (2020). https://doi.org/10.1007/978-3-030-51280-4_22
12. Belenkiy, M., et al.: Making P2P accountable without losing privacy. In: WPES (2007)
13. Bentov, I., Kumaresan, R.: How to use bitcoin to design fair protocols. In: Garay, J.A., Gennaro, R. (eds.) CRYPTO 2014. LNCS, vol. 8617, pp. 421–439. Springer, Heidelberg (2014). https://doi.org/10.1007/978-3-662-44381-1_24

14. Bentov, I., Kumaresan, R., Miller, A.: Instantaneous decentralized poker. In: Takagi, T., Peyrin, T. (eds.) ASIACRYPT 2017. LNCS, vol. 10625, pp. 410–440. Springer, Cham (2017). https://doi.org/10.1007/978-3-319-70697-9_15

15. Brownie cashlib cryptographic library. http://github.com/brownie/cashlib

16. Cachin, C., Camenisch, J.: Optimistic fair secure computation. In: Bellare, M. (ed.) CRYPTO 2000. LNCS, vol. 1880, pp. 93–111. Springer, Heidelberg (2000). https://doi.org/10.1007/3-540-44598-6_6

17. Camenisch, J., Damgård, I.: Verifiable encryption, group encryption, and their applications to separable group signatures and signature sharing schemes. In: Okamoto, T. (ed.) ASIACRYPT 2000. LNCS, vol. 1976, pp. 331–345. Springer, Heidelberg (2000). https://doi.org/10.1007/3-540-44448-3_25

18. Camenisch, J., Lysyanskaya, A., Meyerovich, M.: Endorsed e-cash. In: Security and Privacy, pp. 101–115. IEEE (2007)

19. Camenisch, J., Shoup, V.: Practical verifiable encryption and decryption of discrete logarithms. In: Boneh, D. (ed.) CRYPTO 2003. LNCS, vol. 2729, pp. 126–144. Springer, Heidelberg (2003). https://doi.org/10.1007/978-3-540-45146-4_8

20. Canetti, R.: Security and composition of multiparty cryptographic protocols. J. Cryptol. **13**, 143–202 (2000). https://doi.org/10.1007/s001459910006

21. Chaum, D.: Blind signatures for untraceable payments. In: Chaum, D., Rivest, R.L., Sherman, A.T. (eds.) Advances in Cryptology, pp. 199–203. Springer, Boston, MA (1983). https://doi.org/10.1007/978-1-4757-0602-4_18

22. Chaum, D., den Boer, B., van Heyst, E., Mjølsnes, S., Steenbeek, A.: Efficient offline electronic checks. In: Quisquater, J.-J., Vandewalle, J. (eds.) EUROCRYPT 1989. LNCS, vol. 434, pp. 294–301. Springer, Heidelberg (1990). https://doi.org/10.1007/3-540-46885-4_31

23. Cohen, B.: Incentives build robustness in BitTorrent. WEPS **6**, 68–72 (2003)

24. Cramer, R., Shoup, V.: Universal hash proofs and a paradigm for adaptive chosen ciphertext secure public-key encryption. In: Knudsen, L.R. (ed.) EUROCRYPT 2002. LNCS, vol. 2332, pp. 45–64. Springer, Heidelberg (2002). https://doi.org/10.1007/3-540-46035-7_4

25. Damgård, I.: On Σ-protocols. University of Aarhus, Department for Computer Science, Lecture Notes (2002)

26. Dodis, Y., Lee, P.J., Yum, D.H.: Optimistic fair exchange in a multi-user setting. In: Okamoto, T., Wang, X. (eds.) PKC 2007. LNCS, vol. 4450, pp. 118–133. Springer, Heidelberg (2007). https://doi.org/10.1007/978-3-540-71677-8_9

27. Dziembowski, S., Eckey, L., Faust, S.: FairSwap: how to fairly exchange digital goods. In: ACM SIGSAC, pp. 967–984 (2018)

28. ElGamal, T.: A public key cryptosystem and a signature scheme based on discrete logarithms. IEEE Trans. Inf. Theory **31**(4), 469–472 (1985)

29. Even, S., Yacobi, Y.: Relations among public key signature systems. Technical report, Technical Report 175, Technion, Haifa, Israel (1980)

30. Franklin, M., Tsudik, G.: Secure group barter: multi-party fair exchange with semi-trusted neutral parties. In: Hirchfeld, R. (ed.) FC 1998. LNCS, vol. 1465, pp. 90–102. Springer, Heidelberg (1998). https://doi.org/10.1007/BFb0055475

31. Garay, J.A., MacKenzie, P.: Abuse-free multi-party contract signing. In: Jayanti, P. (ed.) DISC 1999. LNCS, vol. 1693, pp. 151–166. Springer, Heidelberg (1999). https://doi.org/10.1007/3-540-48169-9_11

32. González-Deleito, N., Markowitch, O.: An optimistic multi-party fair exchange protocol with reduced trust requirements. In: Kim, K. (ed.) ICISC 2001. LNCS, vol. 2288, pp. 258–267. Springer, Heidelberg (2002). https://doi.org/10.1007/3-540-45861-1_20

33. Gordon, D., Ishai, Y., Moran, T., Ostrovsky, R., Sahai, A.: On complete primitives for fairness. In: Micciancio, D. (ed.) TCC 2010. LNCS, vol. 5978, pp. 91–108. Springer, Heidelberg (2010). https://doi.org/10.1007/978-3-642-11799-2_7

34. Guerraoui, R., Wang, J.: Optimal fair computation. In: Gavoille, C., Ilcinkas, D. (eds.) DISC 2016. LNCS, vol. 9888, pp. 143–157. Springer, Heidelberg (2016). https://doi.org/10.1007/978-3-662-53426-7_11

35. Katz, J., Maurer, U., Tackmann, B., Zikas, V.: Universally composable synchronous computation. In: Sahai, A. (ed.) TCC 2013. LNCS, vol. 7785, pp. 477–498. Springer, Heidelberg (2013). https://doi.org/10.1007/978-3-642-36594-2_27

36. Kiayias, A., Zhou, H.-S., Zikas, V.: Fair and robust multi-party computation using a global transaction ledger. In: Fischlin, M., Coron, J.-S. (eds.) EUROCRYPT 2016. LNCS, vol. 9666, pp. 705–734. Springer, Heidelberg (2016). https://doi.org/10.1007/978-3-662-49896-5_25

37. Kılınç, H., Küpçü, A.: Optimally efficient multi-party fair exchange and fair secure multi-party computation. In: Nyberg, K. (ed.) CT-RSA 2015. LNCS, vol. 9048, pp. 330–349. Springer, Cham (2015). https://doi.org/10.1007/978-3-319-16715-2_18

38. Kumaresan, R., Bentov, I.: Amortizing secure computation with penalties. In: ACM SIGSAC, pp. 418–429 (2016)

39. Kumaresan, R., Vaikuntanathan, V., Vasudevan, P.N.: Improvements to secure computation with penalties. In: ACM SIGSAC, pp. 406–417 (2016)

40. Küpçü, A., Lysyanskaya, A.: Usable optimistic fair exchange. Computer Networks, pp. 50–63 (2012)

41. Küpçü, A.: Distributing trusted third parties. ACM SIGACT News Distrib. Comput. Column **44**, 92–112 (2013)

42. Küpçü, A., Lysyanskaya, A.: Optimistic fair exchange with multiple arbiters. In: Gritzalis, D., Preneel, B., Theoharidou, M. (eds.) ESORICS 2010. LNCS, vol. 6345, pp. 488–507. Springer, Heidelberg (2010). https://doi.org/10.1007/978-3-642-15497-3_30

43. Lindell, A.Y.: Legally-enforceable fairness in secure two-party computation. In: Malkin, T. (ed.) CT-RSA 2008. LNCS, vol. 4964, pp. 121–137. Springer, Heidelberg (2008). https://doi.org/10.1007/978-3-540-79263-5_8

44. Liu, Y., Hu, H.: An improved protocol for optimistic multi-party fair exchange. In: EMEIT, vol. 9, pp. 4864–4867. IEEE (2011)

45. Mauw, S., Radomirovic, S., Dashti, M.T.: Minimal message complexity of asynchronous multi-party contract signing. In: CSF, pp. 13–25. IEEE (2009)

46. Meiklejohn, S., Erway, C.C., Küpçü, A., Hinkle, T., Lysyanskaya, A.: ZKPDL: a language-based system for efficient zero-knowledge proofs and electronic cash. In: USENIX Security Symposium (2010)

47. Merkle, R.C.: A digital signature based on a conventional encryption function. In: Pomerance, C. (ed.) CRYPTO 1987. LNCS, vol. 293, pp. 369–378. Springer, Heidelberg (1988). https://doi.org/10.1007/3-540-48184-2_32

48. Micali, S.: Simple and fast optimistic protocols for fair electronic exchange. In: PODC, pp. 12–19. ACM (2003)

49. Pagnia, H., Gärtner, F.C.: On the impossibility of fair exchange without a trusted third party. Technical report, TUD-BS-1999-02 (1999)

50. Radomirovic, S.: A construction of short sequences containing all permutations of a set as subsequences. Electron. J. Comb. **19**(4), 31 (2012)

51. Rivest, R., Shamir, A., Adleman, L.: A method for obtaining digital signatures and public-key cryptosystems. ACM Commun. **21**, 120–126 (1978)

52. Shoup, V., Gennaro, R.: Securing threshold cryptosystems against chosen ciphertext attack. J. Cryptol. **15**, 75–96 (2002)

Cryptocurrency and Smart Contracts

P2DEX: Privacy-Preserving Decentralized Cryptocurrency Exchange

Carsten Baum[1], Bernardo David[2], and Tore Kasper Frederiksen[3(✉)]

[1] Aarhus University, Aarhus, Denmark
cbaum@cs.au.dk
[2] IT University of Copenhagen, Copenhagen, Denmark
bernardo@bmdavid.com
[3] Alexandra Institute, Aarhus, Denmark
tore.frederiksen@alexandra.dk

Abstract. Cryptocurrency exchange services are either trusted central entities that have been routinely hacked (losing over 8 billion USD), or decentralized services that make all orders public before they are settled. The latter allows market participants to "front run" each other, an illegal operation in most jurisdictions. We extend the "Insured MPC" approach of Baum *et al.* (FC 2020) to construct an efficient universally composable privacy preserving decentralized exchange where a set of servers run private cross-chain exchange order matching in an outsourced manner, while being financially incentivised to behave honestly. Our protocol allows for exchanging assets over multiple public ledgers, given that users have access to a ledger that supports standard public smart contracts. If parties behave honestly, the on-chain complexity of our construction is as low as that of performing the transactions necessary for a centralized exchange. In case malicious behavior is detected, users are automatically refunded by malicious servers at low cost. Thus, an actively corrupted majority can only mount a denial-of-service attack that makes exchanges fail, in which case the servers are publicly identified and punished, while honest clients do not to lose their funds. For the first time in this line of research, we report experimental results on the MPC building block, showing the approach is efficient enough to be used in practice.

Keywords: Multiparty computation · Secure asset exchange · Front-running · Blockchain

1 Introduction

Decentralized cryptocurrencies based on permissionless ledgers such as Bitcoin [43] allow for users to perform financial transactions without relying

---

This work was supported by the Concordium Foundation, by Protocol Labs grant S²LEDGE and by the Independent Research Fund Denmark with grants number 9040-00399B (TrA²C) and number 9131-00075B (PUMA).

K. Sako and N. O. Tippenhauer (Eds.): ACNS 2021, LNCS 12726, pp. 163–194, 2021.
https://doi.org/10.1007/978-3-030-78372-3_7

on central authorities. However, exchanging coins among different decentralized cryptocurrency platforms still mainly rely on centralized exchange services which must hold tokens during the exchange process, making them vulnerable to theft. Centralized exchange hacks have resulted in over 8 Billions dollars' worth of tokens being stolen [44], out of which over 250 Million dollars' worth of tokens were stolen in 2019 alone. The main alternative is to use decentralized exchange services (*e.g.* [13]) that do not hold tokens during the exchange process but are vulnerable to front-running attacks, since they make all orders public before they are finalized. This allows for illegal market manipulation, for example by leveraging the discrepancy between the most extreme buying and selling prices to buy tokens at the smallest offered price and immediately selling them at the highest accepted price.

Given the astounding volume of financial losses from centralized exchange hacks, constructing alternatives that are not vulnerable to token theft is clearly of great importance. However, ensuring that exchange orders remain private and avoiding front-running has also been identified as a chief concern [10,28], since this vulnerability reduces user trust and rules out regulatory compliance. In essence, a solution is needed for reconciling order privacy, market fairness and token security. In this work, we address the question:

Can we securely & efficiently exchange cryptocurrency tokens while preserving order privacy, avoiding front-running and ensuring users never lose tokens?

1.1 Our Contributions

We introduce universally composable privacy preserving decentralized exchanges immune to token theft and front-running, as well as optimizations to make our approach feasible in practice. Our main contributions are summarized as follows:

- **Privacy:** A provably secure privacy preserving decentralized exchange protocol, which is immune to both front-running and secret key theft.
- **Security:** An Universally Composable [18] analysis of our protocol, showing our approach is secure in real world settings.
- **Efficiency:** The first experimental results showing that Multiparty Computation on blockchains can be practical (*i.e.* faster than block finalization).
- **Usability:** An architecture that allows for deployment of a decentralized-exchange-as-a-service where users only need to do very lightweight computation and complete a *single* blockchain transfer in connection with a *single* round of efficient communication with the servers.

As the main building blocks of our work, we use publicly verifiable secure multiparty computation (MPC) [5] and threshold signatures with identifiable abort [21,33,34]. MPC allows for users to compute on private data without revealing this data to each other, which is a central concern in our solution. Moreover, using tools for public verifiability [4], it is possible to prove to any third party that a given computation output has been obtained without revealing inputs, which is paramount for proving validity in decentralized permissionless systems. We use standard (public) smart contracts to implement a financial punishment system that incentivizes servers executing our protocol to behave honestly and ensures that users are reimbursed in case servers cheat.

If parties do not cheat, our protocol *requires no on-chain communication* except for the transactions needed to perform the exchanges and uses MPC only for privately matching orders (to avoid front-running). We prove security against an actively dishonest majority and argue how clients can be refunded in case of malicious behaviour by up to $n-1$ servers. We analyse our solution in the Universal Composability (UC) framework [18], which guarantees security even in complex situations where multiple protocols are executed concurrently with each other (*i.e.* real world scenarios as the Internet or decentralized cryptocurrency systems). To that end, we introduce a treatment of decentralized exchanges in the UC framework, allowing us to prove that our protocol is secure even in these realistic scenarios.

1.2   Our Techniques

The Protocol in a Nutshell: Clients $C_1, \ldots, C_m$ wish to exchange tokens between ledgers $\mathcal{L}_a$ and $\mathcal{L}_b$ using servers $\mathcal{P}_1, \ldots, \mathcal{P}_n$ that facilitate the privacy-preserving exchange. Any number of ledgers can be involved, as long as all parties can use a standard smart contract (*e.g.* Ethereum) on a ledger $\mathcal{L}_{\mathsf{Ex}}$. Moreover, all ledger pairs $\mathcal{L}_a, \mathcal{L}_b$ must use cryptocurrency systems that allow for publicly proving that a double spend happened, *e.g.* Bitcoin UTXOs [43] (which can be emulated by attaching unique IDs to coins in account-based systems like Ethereum). Our protocol works as follows:

- **Smart Contract Setup:** The servers send a collateral deposit to a smart contract on ledger $\mathcal{L}_{\mathsf{Ex}}$ that guarantees that the servers do not cheat.
- **Off-chain communication:** After setup, *only off-chain protocol messages are exchanged* between the servers unless cheating happens, in which case cheating servers can be identified by publicly verifiable proofs [4] and punished.
- **Main Protocol Flow:** Performing exchanges between client C_i who wants to exchange tokens from ledger $\mathcal{L}_a$ held at their address $\mathsf{Addr}_i^{\mathsf{src}}$ with tokens from C_j who holds tokens in ledger $\mathcal{L}_b$ at address $\mathsf{Addr}_j^{\mathsf{src}}$ (or any other tuple of users/ledgers/addresses):
  1. *Burner address setup:* The servers set up threshold signature addresses $\mathsf{Addr}_i^{\mathsf{ex}}$ and $\mathsf{Addr}_j^{\mathsf{ex}}$ on each ledger $\mathcal{L}_a$ and $\mathcal{L}_b$.
  2. *Private order placement:* Clients transfer their tokens to server threshold addresses on each ledger (*i.e.* clients C_i and C_j transfer their tokens from addresses $\mathsf{Addr}_i^{\mathsf{src}}$ and $\mathsf{Addr}_j^{\mathsf{src}}$ on ledgers $\mathcal{L}_a$ and $\mathcal{L}_b$ to addresses $\mathsf{Addr}_i^{\mathsf{ex}}$ and $\mathsf{Addr}_j^{\mathsf{ex}}$, respectively) and send to the servers the addresses $\mathsf{Addr}_j^{\mathsf{trg}}$ and $\mathsf{Addr}_i^{\mathsf{trg}}$ on $\mathcal{L}_a$ and $\mathcal{L}_b$ where they will receive exchanged tokens if their orders match, respectively. They also send *secret shared* order information, describing the prices they charge for their tokens in a way that the servers do not learn the prices.

3. *Confirmation:* If the servers have correctly received the secret orders and deposits from all the clients on each ledger, they proceed. Otherwise, they generate and send to the smart contract refund transactions transferring tokens from $\mathtt{Addr}_i^{\mathsf{ex}}$ and $\mathtt{Addr}_j^{\mathsf{ex}}$ back to client addresses $\mathtt{Addr}_i^{\mathsf{src}}$ and $\mathtt{Addr}_j^{\mathsf{src}}$, respectively. $\mathcal{C}_i$ and $\mathcal{C}_j$ retrieve these transactions and post them to $\mathcal{L}_a$ and $\mathcal{L}_b$, respectively.

4. *Private Matching:* The servers execute a publicly verifiable MPC protocol (*e.g.* [5]) to run *any* order matching algorithm on secret-shared orders so that they can publicly prove that either a given set of orders have been matched or that a server has cheated, never learning non-matched orders.

5. *Pay out:* Servers publish signed transactions for the final exchange operations to addresses $\mathtt{Addr}_j^{\mathsf{trg}}$ and $\mathtt{Addr}_i^{\mathsf{trg}}$ on $\mathcal{L}_a$ and $\mathcal{L}_b$ for matched order pairs to pay out the exchange to the clients.

- **Cheating Recovery:** The main cheating scenario is that a server sent an invalid message or failed to send a message. In that case, an honest server complains to the smart contract on $\mathcal{L}_{\mathsf{Ex}}$ and all servers have to send valid protocol messages to complete the protocol to the smart contract. If a server $\mathcal{P}_i$ does not send a valid message, it is identified as a cheater.

  Any server $\mathcal{P}_i$ identified as a cheater loses its deposit to the smart contract, which is used to reimburse the clients and the honest servers for their work.

Security Guarantees: Our main protocol achieves *security against an actively dishonest majority of servers* without requiring the clients to put up expensive collateral deposits, which is the case in previous approaches (*e.g.* [5]) where all parties must provide such deposits. Moreover, we describe a modification where even in a catastrophic failure where *all* servers become corrupted, even though the client's orders may leak, *all clients are guaranteed to be refunded* by the smart contract.

Efficiency: Unless cheating happens, *all communication is off-chain* and the only information stored on-chain on any ledger are the transactions necessary to perform the exchange itself (improving on [5]). If cheating happens, the smart contract must identify and punish the cheater, but *this cost is covered by the cheater's deposit.* Moreover, *MPC is only used to match orders* in the Private Matching phase, while other operations are executed via efficient off-chain protocols. Finally, we do the first full implementation of the MPC component in a secure computation with financial incentives setting, showing that *MPC on blockchains is efficient in practice* (in particular for our matching application).

Alternative Approaches: Our protocol can be modified in the following ways:

- **Preventing Denial-of-Service attacks by Clients:** In our outlined protocol, either all clients transfer their money after registration or they all get reimbursed. Then, a client who registers but does not transfer funds could participate in a Denial-of-Service attack. We explain in Sect. 4.3 how to modify our protocol to avoid this.

- **Incentivizing Servers:** Clients may pay fees to servers so that it is profitable to execute a server. This can be achieved in a simple manner as part of the pay out step. Concretely the servers will also post transactions to their respective addresses, from the burner addresses used by the clients during the exchange, instead of only posting a transaction paying out the exchange to the recipient.
- **Guaranteed Success with Honest Majority of Servers:** Assuming an honest majority of servers, we can obtain a much more efficient protocol by replacing the MPC protocol [5] used for the Private Matching with a much cheaper honest majority MPC protocol. Moreover, in this case we can achieve guaranteed output delivery, meaning that the *privacy preserving exchange always works* regardless of the minority of malicious servers.
- **Resilience under full corruption:** Even though we consider a dishonest majority where at least one server is honest, our technique can be modified for the setting where all servers may be corrupted. If users are allowed to register their orders (and destination addresses) on the smart contract, they can prove that all servers have misbehaved and get reimbursed with tokens from the exchange smart contract ledger, similarly to the approach of [31].

1.3   Related Work

MPC with Financial Incentives: A feature required by the MPC scheme in our applications is that if a cheating party obtains the output, then all the honest parties should do so as well (so all parties learn matching orders). Protocols which guarantee this are also called *fair* but known to be impossible to achieve with dishonest majorities [26]. Recently, [2,11] initiated a line of research that aims at incentivizing fairness in MPC by imposing cryptocurrency based financial penalties on misbehaving parties. Several works [5,9,12,40,41] improved the performance with respect to on-chain storage and the size of the collateral deposits from each party, while others obtained stronger notions of fairness [25,37]. None of these works implemented the MPC component of this approach.

In our work, we rely on such techniques to ensure that servers cannot profit from forcing exchange operations to fail. However, even the state-of-the-art [5] of these works only considers the single blockchain setting (not allowing for exchanges) and suffers from indefeasibly high overheads in both off-chain/on-chain complexity that would make exchange operations infeasible. We address these issues with an MPC protocol that operates on multiple blockchains, but building a decentralized exchange service where we only use MPC for matching orders; then later generating matched order transactions via an efficient threshold signature. We propose concrete improvements on the off-chain/on-chain overhead of [5] with the first concrete implementation of techniques from [4,6]. Furthermore, we achieve optimal communication (no more than in centralized exchanges) in the optimistic setting, where no party behaves maliciously. For the first time in this line of work [2,5,9,11,12,40,41], *we fully implement the MPC component* of such a solution showing it is efficient in practice, whereas previous works only focused on on-chain efficiency (which is still optimal in our protocol).

Privacy Preserving Smart Contracts: Another related line of work [14, 16, 39] has focused on constructing privacy preserving smart contracts that can be checked for correct execution without revealing private inputs on-chain. However, these are intrinsically unfit for our application because they require a trusted party to learn all private inputs in order to generate zero-knowledge proofs showing that a given computation output was obtained. This would allow a corrupted trusted party (or insecure SGX enclave [15]) to perform front running (or even steal funds), *i.e.* the same issues of centralized exchanges.

Distributed Markets and Exchanges: The use of MPC in traditional stock market exchanges has been considered in [23, 24, 42] but these works focus on matching stock market orders and do not address the issue of ensuring that exchange transactions are performed correctly, which we do. Many commercial decentralized exchange services (*e.g.* [13]) exist, but they are not private and suffer from front-running as discussed before. A front-running resistant approach is suggested in [10] but it relies on insecure trusted hardware [15] and has no privacy.

Fair Two-Party Data Exchange: Dziembowski *et al.* [31] showed how to use financial incentives and a proof of cheating to enforce honest behaviour when two parties are exchanging pre-images of a hash function using a distributed ledger. Despite showing security in UC, their approach would not directly be efficient for cross-chain token exchange, nor generalize to exchange order matching.

2   Preliminaries

Let τ be the computational and κ the statistical security parameter. We use n to denote the number of servers and m for the clients. Let $y \xleftarrow{\$} F(x)$ denote running the randomized algorithm F with input x and implicit randomness, and obtaining the output y. $y \leftarrow F(x)$ is used for a deterministic algorithm. For a finite set $\mathcal{X}$, let $x \xleftarrow{\$} \mathcal{X}$ denote x chosen uniformly at random from $\mathcal{X}$. For $k \in \mathbb{N}$ we write $[k]$ for $\{1, \ldots, k\}$. We say a function $f(x)$ is negligible in x (or negl(x) to denote an arbitrary such function) if $f(x)$ is positive and for every positive polynomial $p(x) \in \text{poly}(x)$ there exists a $x' \in \mathbb{N}$ such that $\forall x \geq x' : f(x) < 1/p(x)$. Two ensembles $X = \{X_{\tau,z}\}_{\tau \in \mathbb{N}, z \in \{0,1\}^*}$ and $Y = \{Y_{\tau,z}\}_{\tau \in \mathbb{N}, z \in \{0,1\}^*}$ of binary random variables are said to be *computationally indistinguishable*, denoted by $X \approx_c Y$, if for all z it holds that $|\Pr[\mathcal{D}(X_{\tau,z}) = 1] - \Pr[\mathcal{D}(Y_{\tau,z}) = 1]| \in \text{negl}(\tau)$ for every probabilistic poly-time algorithm (distinguisher) $\mathcal{D}$ in τ.

2.1   (Global) Universal Composability and Verifiability

In this work, the (Global) Universal Composability or (G)UC framework [18, 20] is used to analyze security. Due to space constraints, we refer interested readers to the aforementioned works for more details. We generally use $\mathcal{F}$ to denote an ideal functionality and Π for a protocol.

Several functionalities in this work allow *public verifiability*. To model this, we follow the approach of Badertscher *et al.* [3] and allow the set of verifiers $\mathcal{V}$ to be dynamic by adding register and de-register instructions as well as instructions that allow $\mathcal{S}$ to obtain the list of registered verifiers. All functionalities with public verifiability include the following interfaces, which can also be used by other functionalities to register as a verifier of a publicly verifiable functionality, and which are omitted henceforth for simplicity:

Register: Upon receiving (REGISTER, sid) from some verifier $\mathcal{V}_i$, set $\mathcal{V} = \mathcal{V} \cup \mathcal{V}_i$ and return (REGISTERED, sid, $\mathcal{V}_i$) to $\mathcal{V}_i$.

Deregister: Upon receiving (DEREGISTER, sid) from some verifier $\mathcal{V}_i$, set $\mathcal{V} = \mathcal{V} \setminus \mathcal{V}_i$ and return (DEREGISTERED, sid, $\mathcal{V}_i$) to $\mathcal{V}_i$.

Is Registered: Upon receiving (IS-REGISTERED, sid) from $\mathcal{V}_i$, return. (IS-REGISTERED, sid, b) to $\mathcal{V}_i$, where $b = 1$ if $\mathcal{V}_i \in \mathcal{V}$ and $b = 0$ otherwise.

Get Registered: Upon receiving (GET-REGISTERED, sid) from the ideal adversary $\mathcal{S}$, the functionality returns (GET-REGISTERED, sid, $\mathcal{V}$) to $\mathcal{S}$.

2.2 The Global Clock

As some parts of our work are inherently synchronous, we model the different "rounds" of it using a UC clock functionality $\mathcal{F}_{\mathsf{Clock}}$ as in [3,36,37]. This functionality is assumed to be a global functionality, which means that other ideal functionalities will be granted access to it. And while in the real protocol execution all parties send messages to and receive them from $\mathcal{F}_{\mathsf{Clock}}$, in the simulated case only the ideal functionality, other global functionalities as well as the dishonest parties will do so. Hybrid functionalities in the simulation might also be given access, but this is not necessary in our setting. For simplicity, we do not introduce a session management in $\mathcal{F}_{\mathsf{Clock}}$ as it is not necessary to state our result. Throughout this work, we will write "update $\mathcal{F}_{\mathsf{Clock}}$" as a short-hand for "send (UPDATE, sid) to $\mathcal{F}_{\mathsf{Clock}}$" (Fig. 1).

Functionality $\mathcal{F}_{\mathsf{Clock}}$

$\mathcal{F}_{\mathsf{Clock}}$ is parameterized by a variable ν, sets $\mathcal{P}, \mathcal{F}$ of parties and functionalities respectively. It keeps a Boolean variable $d_{\mathcal{J}}$ for each $\mathcal{J} \in \mathcal{P} \cup \mathcal{F}$, a counter ν as well as an additional variable u. All $d_{\mathcal{J}}$, ν and u are initialized as 0.

Clock Update: Upon receiving a message (UPDATE) from $\mathcal{J} \in \mathcal{P} \cup \mathcal{F}$:
1. Set $d_{\mathcal{J}} = 1$.
2. If $d_F = 1$ for all $F \in \mathcal{F}$ and $d_p = 1$ for all honest $p \in \mathcal{P}$, then set u $\leftarrow$ 1 if it is 0.

Clock Read: Upon receiving a message (READ) from any entity:
1. If u = 1 then first send (TICK, sid) to $\mathcal{S}$. Next set $\nu \leftarrow \nu + 1$, reset $d_{\mathcal{J}}$ to 0 for all $\mathcal{J} \in \mathcal{P} \cup \mathcal{F}$ and reset u to 0.
2. Answer the entity with (READ, ν).

Fig. 1. Functionality $\mathcal{F}_{\mathsf{Clock}}$ for a global clock.

2.3   Client-Input MPC with Publicly Verifiable Output

We focus on MPC with security against a static, rushing and malicious adversary $\mathcal{A}$ corrupting up to $n - 1$ of the n servers where m clients provide the actual inputs and where all clients might be malicious. This specific setting of MPC is called *out-sourced MPC* and can efficiently be realized in a black box manner on top of a "standard" MPC scheme where the servers are providing the output [35]. We let the MPC functionality compute the result **y** and share its output in a verifiable way such that any potential verifier can either check that the output is correct or identify a cheater, and hence allow for incentivized fairness. In Fig. 2 we formally define functionality $\mathcal{F}_{\mathsf{Ident}}$ adapted from [5] that captures this style of MPC. We remark that differently from [5], we use a publicly verifiable version [4] of the original protocol of [5] with optimizations from [6] where no homomorphic commitments are needed and, in case no cheating is detected, no interaction with the smart contract is needed apart from the initial deposits from servers executing $\mathcal{F}_{\mathsf{Ident}}$ and the final output. Intuitively it specified an out-sourced MPC functionality where clients $\mathcal{C}_1, \ldots, \mathcal{C}_m$ supply private input that is computed on in MPC by the servers $\mathcal{P}_1, \ldots, \mathcal{P}_n$ and where the output of the computation is verifiably shared between the servers in such a manner that the shares can verified by an external verifier $\mathcal{V}$ after the completion of the protocol to identify any potential malicious behaviour. As $\mathcal{F}_{\mathsf{SC}}$ will need to interact with $\mathcal{F}_{\mathsf{Ident}}$ to verify outputs, we consider $\mathcal{F}_{\mathsf{Ident}}$ as a global functionality. This does, however, not change anything concerning it's implementation or security proof, as $\mathcal{F}_{\mathsf{Ident}}$ does not keep a common state across multiple sessions and ignores requests from other sessions.

2.4   (Threshold) Signatures

In our work we rely on signatures and identifiable threshold signatures to represent transactions on ledgers. Therefore we will assume the existence of two UC functionalities: $\mathcal{F}_{\mathsf{Sig}}$ which is a standard functionality in UC [19] (with key generation, signature generation and signature verification), as well as our own formalization of general UC identifiable threshold signatures $\mathcal{F}_{\mathsf{TSig}}$ (which can be seen as a generalization of signatures such as [21,22]). In comparison to normal signatures, $\mathcal{F}_{\mathsf{TSig}}$ has a two-step process of signature generation, where the parties first generate shares ρ of the overall signature σ which later on are aggregated in a share combination phase. This share combination also exposes parties that generated some shares wrongly. Additionally, $\mathcal{F}_{\mathsf{TSig}}$ also creates the signing key in a distributed way. We treat both $\mathcal{F}_{\mathsf{Sig}}$ and $\mathcal{F}_{\mathsf{TSig}}$ as global UC functionalities, which means that both local and other global UC functionalities can verify signatures on them. This is meaningful as we assume that ledgers are global functionalities too, hence validating their transactions should be consistent among any different session. Due to space constraints, the formalizations of both $\mathcal{F}_{\mathsf{Sig}}, \mathcal{F}_{\mathsf{TSig}}$ only appear in the full version [7].

Functionality $\mathcal{F}_{\mathsf{Ident}}$

For each session, $\mathcal{F}_{\mathsf{Ident}}$ interacts with servers $\mathcal{P} = \{\mathcal{P}_1, \ldots, \mathcal{P}_n\}$, clients $\mathcal{C} = \{\mathcal{C}_1, \ldots, \mathcal{C}_m\}$ and also provides an interface to register external verifiers $\mathcal{V}$. It is parameterized by a circuit C with inputs $x^{(1)}, \ldots, x^{(m)}$ and output $\mathbf{y} \in \mathbb{F}^g$. $\mathcal{S}$ provides a set $I_{\mathcal{P}} \subset [n]$ of corrupt parties and $I_{\mathcal{C}} \subseteq [m]$ of corrupt clients. $\mathcal{F}_{\mathsf{Ident}}$ only interacts with $\mathcal{P}, \mathcal{C}, \mathcal{V}$ and $\mathcal{S}$ of the respective session sid.

Throughout **Init**, **Input**, **Evaluate** and **Share**, $\mathcal{S}$ can at any point send (ABORT, sid) to $\mathcal{F}_{\mathsf{Ident}}$, upon which it sends (ABORT, sid, $\perp$) to all parties and terminates. Throughout **Reveal**, $\mathcal{S}$ at any point is allowed to send (ABORT, sid, J) to $\mathcal{F}_{\mathsf{Ident}}$. If $J \subseteq I_{\mathcal{P}}$ then $\mathcal{F}_{\mathsf{Ident}}$ will send (ABORT, sid, J) to all honest parties and terminate.

Init: Upon first input (INIT, sid) by all parties in $\mathcal{P}$ set $\mathbf{rev}, \mathbf{ver}, \mathbf{ref} \leftarrow \emptyset$.

Input: Upon first input (INPUT, $sid, j, x^{(j)}$) by $\mathcal{C}_j$ and input (INPUT, $sid, j, \cdot$) by all servers the functionality stores the value $(j, x^{(j)})$ internally.

Evaluate: Upon first input (COMPUTE, sid) by all parties in $\mathcal{P}$ and if the inputs $(j, x^{(j)})_{j \in [m]}$ for all clients have been stored internally, compute $\mathbf{y} \leftarrow C(x^{(1)}, \ldots, x^{(m)})$ and store $\mathbf{y}$ locally.

Share: Upon first input (SHARE, sid) by $\mathcal{P}_i \in \mathcal{P}$ and if **Evaluate** was finished:
1. For each $i \in I_{\mathcal{P}}$ let $\mathcal{S}$ provide $\mathbf{s}^{(i)} \in \mathbb{F}^g$.

2. For each $\mathcal{P}_i \in \overline{I_{\mathcal{P}}}$ sample $\mathbf{s}^{(i)} \xleftarrow{\$} \mathbb{F}^g$ subject to the constraint that $\mathbf{y} = \sum_{i \in [n]} \mathbf{s}^{(i)}$.

Optimistic Reveal: Upon input (OPTIMIST-OPEN, sid, i) by each honest $\mathcal{P}_i$ and if **Share** is completed, then send (OUTPUT, $sid, \mathbf{y}$) to $\mathcal{S}$. If $\mathcal{S}$ sends (CONTINUE, sid) then send (OUTPUT, $sid, \mathbf{y}$) to each honest $\mathcal{P}_i$, otherwise send (OUTPUT, $sid, \perp$).

Reveal: On input (REVEAL, sid, i) by $\mathcal{P}_i$, if $i \notin \mathbf{rev}$ send (REVEAL, $sid, i, \mathbf{s}^{(i)}$) to $\mathcal{S}$.
- If $\mathcal{S}$ sends (REVEAL-OK, sid, i) then set $\mathbf{rev} \leftarrow \mathbf{rev} \cup \{i\}$, send (REVEAL, $sid, i, \mathbf{s}^{(i)}$) to all parties in $\mathcal{P}$.
- If $\mathcal{S}$ sends (REVEAL-NOT-OK, sid, i, J) with $J \subseteq I_{\mathcal{P}}, J \neq \emptyset$ then send (REVEAL-FAIL, sid, i) to all parties in $\mathcal{P}$ and set $\mathbf{ref} \leftarrow \mathbf{ref} \cup J$.

Test Reveal: Upon input (TEST-REVEAL, sid) from a party in $\mathcal{P} \cup \mathcal{V}$ return (REVEAL-FAIL, $sid, \mathbf{ref}$) if $\mathbf{ref} \neq \emptyset$. Otherwise return (REVEAL-FAIL, $sid, [n] \setminus \mathbf{rev}$).

Allow Verify: Upon input (START-VERIFY, sid, i) from party $\mathcal{P}_i \in \mathcal{P}$ set $\mathbf{ver} \leftarrow \mathbf{ver} \cup \{i\}$. If $\mathbf{ver} = [n]$ then deactivate all interfaces except **Test Reveal** and **Verify**.

Verify: Upon input (VERIFY, $sid, \mathbf{z}^{(1)}, \ldots, \mathbf{z}^{(n)}$) by $\mathcal{V}_i \in \mathcal{V}$ with $\mathbf{z}^{(j)} \in \mathbb{F}^g$:
- If $\mathbf{ver} \neq [n]$ then return (VERIFY-FAIL, $sid, [n] \setminus \mathbf{ver}$).
- Else, if $\mathbf{ver} = [n]$ and $\mathbf{rev} \neq [n]$ then send to $\mathcal{V}_i$ what **Test Reveal** sends.
- Else set $\mathbf{ws} \leftarrow \{j \in [n] \mid \mathbf{z}^{(j)} \neq \mathbf{s}^{(j)}\}$ and return (OPEN-FAIL, $sid, \mathbf{ws}$).

Fig. 2. Functionality $\mathcal{F}_{\mathsf{Ident}}$ for MPC with publicly verifiable output.

Functionality $\mathcal{F}_{BB}$

$\mathcal{F}_{BB}$ contains a list $\mathcal{M} \in \{0,1\}^*$ of messages $m \in \{0,1\}^*$ which is initially empty.

Post: Upon receiving $(\text{POST}, m, \text{vk}, \sigma)$ from some entity contact $\mathcal{F}_{Sig}$ or $\mathcal{F}_{TSig}$ belonging to vk. If σ verifies for m and vk then send $(\text{POST}, m, \text{vk}, \sigma)$ to $\mathcal{S}$ and append (m, vk) to $\mathcal{M}$.

Read: Upon receiving (READ) from some entity, return $\mathcal{M}$.

Fig. 3. The bulletin board functionality $\mathcal{F}_{BB}$ that abstractly describes the source and target public ledgers of transactions.

2.5 Bulletin Boards and Smart Contracts

Our approach does not require dealing with the specifics of blockchain consensus, since we hold tokens in addresses controlled by threshold signatures in such a way that transactions can only be issued when all servers cooperate. Since at least one server is assumed to be honest, we do not have to confirm whether a transaction is registered. Even when we address the case of total server corruption, our approach only requires identifying an attempt of double spending a client's deposit regardless of which transaction of the double spends gets finalized on the ledger. Hence, in this work we do neither fully formalize distributed ledgers as was done in previous work [3], nor do we use other existing simplified formulations such as [37]. Instead, for the sake of simplicity, we use a public bulletin board functionality $\mathcal{F}_{BB}$ (see Fig. 3) to represent ledgers. What this functionality affords, is basically to allow storage of authenticated messages as well as make them available for all users. In Appendix A we also define the functionality $\mathcal{F}_{SC}$ which describes our needs of the smart contract functionality run by the ledger.

2.6 Representing Cryptocurrency Transactions

In order to focus on the novel aspects of our protocol, we represent cryptocurrency transactions under a simplified version of the Bitcoin UTXO model [43]. For the sake of simplicity we only consider operations of the "Pay to Public Key" (P2PK) type, even though any other types of transaction can be supported as long as it is possible to publicly prove that a double spend happened and to generate transactions in a distributed manner. In particular, even a privacy preserving cryptocurrency that publicly reveals double spends could be integrated to our approach by constructing a specific purpose multiparty computation protocol for generating transactions in that cryptocurrency. *Representing Addresses:* An address $\text{Addr} = \text{vk}$ is simply a signature verification key, where vk and subsequent signatures σ are generated by the signature scheme used in the cryptocurrency (represented by $\mathcal{F}_{Sig}$ and $\mathcal{F}_{TSig}$).

Representing Transactions: We represent a transaction in our simplified UTXO model by the tuple $\mathsf{tx} = (\mathsf{id}, \mathsf{In}, \mathsf{Out}, \mathsf{Sig})$, where $\mathsf{id} \in \{0,1\}^\tau$ is a unique transaction identification, $\mathsf{In} = \{(\mathsf{id}_1, \mathsf{in}_1), \ldots, (\mathsf{id}_m, \mathsf{in}_m)\}$ is a set of pairs of previous transaction id's $\mathsf{id} \in \{0,1\}^\tau$ and their values $\mathsf{in} \in \mathbb{N}$, $\mathsf{Out} = \{(\mathsf{out}_1, \mathsf{Addr}_1), \ldots, (\mathsf{out}_n, \mathsf{Addr}_n)\}$ is a set of pairs of values $\mathsf{out} \in \mathbb{N}$ and signature verification keys Addr and $\mathsf{Sig} = \{\sigma_1, \ldots, \sigma_m\}$ is a set of signatures σ.

Transaction Validity: A transaction $\mathsf{tx} = (\mathsf{id}, \mathsf{In}, \mathsf{Out}, \mathsf{Sig})$ is considered valid if, for all $(\mathsf{id}_i, \mathsf{in}_i) \in \mathsf{In}$ and $(\mathsf{out}_j, \mathsf{Addr}_j) \in \mathsf{Out}$, the following conditions hold:

- There exists a valid transaction $\mathsf{tx}_i = (\mathsf{id}_i, \mathsf{In}_i, \mathsf{Out}_i, \mathsf{Sig}_i)$ in the public ledger (in our case represented by $\mathcal{F}_{\mathsf{BB}}$ and $\mathcal{F}_{\mathsf{SC}}$) such that $(\mathsf{in}_i, \mathsf{Addr}_i) \in \mathsf{Out}_i$.
- There exists $\sigma_i \in \mathsf{Sig}$ such that σ_i is a valid signature of $\mathsf{id}|\mathsf{In}|\mathsf{Out}$ under Addr_i according to the cryptocurrency's signature scheme ($\mathcal{F}_{\mathsf{Sig}}$ or $\mathcal{F}_{\mathsf{TSig}}$).
- It holds that $\sum_{i=1}^m \mathsf{in}_i = \sum_{j=1}^n \mathsf{out}_j$.

Generating Transactions: A party controlling the corresponding signing keys for valid UTXO addresses $\mathsf{Addr}_1, \ldots, \mathsf{Addr}_m$ containing values $\mathsf{in}_1, \ldots, \mathsf{in}_m$ can generate a transaction that transfers the funds in these addresses to output addresses $\mathsf{Addr}_{out,1}, \ldots, \mathsf{Addr}_{out,n}$ by proceeding as follows:

1. Choose a unique $\mathsf{id} \in \{0,1\}^\tau$.
2. Choose values $\mathsf{out}_1, \ldots, \mathsf{out}_n$ such that $\sum_{i=1}^m \mathsf{in}_i = \sum_{j=1}^n \mathsf{out}_j$.
3. Generate $\mathsf{In}, \mathsf{Out}$ as described above and sign $\mathsf{id}|\mathsf{In}|\mathsf{Out}$ with the instances of $\mathcal{F}_{\mathsf{Sig}}$ or $\mathcal{F}_{\mathsf{TSig}}$ corresponding to $\mathsf{Addr}_1, \ldots, \mathsf{Addr}_m$, obtaining $\mathsf{Sig} = \{\sigma_1, \ldots, \sigma_m\}$.
4. Output $\mathsf{tx} = (\mathsf{id}, \mathsf{In}, \mathsf{Out}, \mathsf{Sig})$.

3 Modeling Fair Decentralized Exchanges in UC

In this section we formalize a decentralized exchange on a high level. We assume that there are m clients $\mathcal{C}_1, \ldots, \mathcal{C}_m$. These clients can exchange between ℓ ledgers $\mathcal{L}_1, \ldots, \mathcal{L}_\ell$. Each $\mathcal{C}_j$ controls an amount of tokens $\mathsf{am}_j^{\mathsf{src}}$ in an address $\mathsf{vk}_j^{\mathsf{src}}$ which is on ledger $\mathcal{L}_j^{\mathsf{src}}$. The goal of $\mathcal{C}_j$ is to acquire $\mathsf{am}_j^{\mathsf{trg}}$ tokens on ledger $\mathcal{L}_j^{\mathsf{trg}}$ which should be transferred to address $\mathsf{vk}_j^{\mathsf{trg}}$.

In order to compute transactions there exist two deterministic poly-time algorithms compSwap and makeTX. On a high level, compSwap takes the exchange order of each client between two specific ledgers, $\mathcal{L}_a$ and $\mathcal{L}_b$, as input and returns the order matches. Whereas makeTX takes as input the order matches computed by compSwap for *each* possible pair of ledgers along with some metadata and returns a list of all, unsigned, transactions to be carried out to complete the exchange over all ledgers. More concretely, a bit δ_j indicates for each client $\mathcal{C}_j$ whether said client wants to buy $\mathsf{am}_j^{\mathsf{src}}$ tokens on $\mathcal{L}_a$ using *at most* $\mathsf{am}_j^{\mathsf{trg}}$ tokens from $\mathcal{L}_b$, or if they want to sell $\mathsf{am}_j^{\mathsf{src}}$ tokens from $\mathcal{L}_a$ for *at least* $\mathsf{am}_j^{\mathsf{trg}}$ tokens on $\mathcal{L}_b$. compSwap then returns a list of transfer orders. More concretely, a list of tuples where each tuple contains two quantities, am_j and $am_{j'}$ and the identifiers of two clients; client $\mathcal{C}_j$ who should have am_j of its tokens transferred on $\mathcal{L}_a$ to the other client $\mathcal{C}_{j'}$ and client $\mathcal{C}_{j'}$ should transfer $am_{j'}$ of its tokens on $\mathcal{L}_b$ to $\mathcal{C}_j$. As our protocol will use individual burner addresses for each $\mathcal{C}_j$ controlled by the servers, we assume for the computation that the asset was transferred by $\mathcal{C}_j$ to an address vk_j^{ex} using a transaction with id id_j.

compSwap computes swaps between two ledgers. It takes as input $m' \leq m$ tuples of the form $(\mathcal{C}_j, \delta_j, am_j^{src}, am_j^{trg})$ where $\mathcal{C}_j, am_j^{src}, am_j^{trg} \in \mathbb{N}$ where $\delta_j = 0$ if $\mathcal{C}_j$ wants to swap from the first to the second and $\delta_j = 1$ if it wants to swap from the second to the first ledger. It outputs a list of tuples $(\mathcal{C}_j, am_j, \mathcal{C}_{j'}, am_{j'})$, where $am_j, am_{j'} \in \mathbb{N}$, which is viewed as a vector $\mathbf{y}^{a,b} \in \mathbb{N}^g$ for some g.

makeTX takes the $\ell \cdot (\ell - 1)$ outputs of compSwap for each pair of ledgers $\mathcal{L}_a, \mathcal{L}_b$ with $1 \leq a < b \leq \ell$ as well as a tuple $(\mathcal{C}_j, \mathcal{L}_j^{src}, \mathcal{L}_j^{trg}, id_j, vk_j^{ex}, vk_j^{src}, vk_j^{trg}, am_j^{src})$ for each $\mathcal{C}_j$ as input. It then outputs ℓ transaction orders (id_a, In_a, Out_a) (still missing the signatures however), one for each $\mathcal{L}_a$, such that

1. $In_a = \{(id_j, am_j^{src})\}$ for some $\mathcal{C}_j$ where $\mathcal{L}_j^{src} = \mathcal{L}_a$ and $\mathcal{C}_j$ transferred the amount am_j^{src} to vk_j^{ex} in a transaction with id id_j.
2. $Out_a = \{(out_a^i, Addr_a^i)\}$ where each $Addr_a^i$ is either vk_j^{src} for $\mathcal{C}_j$ with $\mathcal{L}_j^{src} = \mathcal{L}_a$ or $vk_{j'}^{trg}$ for $\mathcal{C}_{j'}$ with $\mathcal{L}_{j'}^{trg} = \mathcal{L}_a$.
3. $\sum_j in_a^j = \sum out_a^i$ and id_a is computed as a hash of In_a, Out_a.

Algorithms compSwap and makeTX only model the generation of UTXO-style transaction descriptions that can later be turned into valid transactions by creating a signature Sig_a for each $\mathcal{L}_a$. The exchange *security* requirements are then modeled in the functionality (*e.g.* requiring that e.g. each $\mathcal{C}_j$ either gets its asset back or also an asset on the other ledger according to some matching rule of transactions). The exchange functionality $\mathcal{F}_{EX}$ as well as the protocol Π_{Ex} will later use the algorithms compSwap, makeTX to generate the transactions. Looking ahead we note that compSwap will be computed using outsourced MPC through $\mathcal{F}_{Ident}^{a,b}$, keeping the input am_j^{src}, am_j^{trg} from each client hidden from every server whereas makeTX will be computed openly. We furthermore note that since there is always an honest party that can influence the choice of algorithms so that the chosen algorithms are fair.

Functionality $\mathcal{F}_{\mathsf{EX}}$ (Part 1)

$\mathcal{F}_{\mathsf{EX}}$ interacts with the set of servers $\mathcal{P} = \{\mathcal{P}_1, \ldots, \mathcal{P}_n\}$, a set of m clients $\mathcal{C} = \{\mathcal{C}_1, \ldots, \mathcal{C}_m\}$ as well as the global functionality $\mathcal{F}_{\mathsf{Clock}}$ to which it is registered. $\mathcal{F}_{\mathsf{EX}}$ is parameterized by the compensation amount q and the security deposit $d = mq$. $\mathcal{S}$ specifies an adversary controlling a set of corrupted servers $I \subset [n]$ and clients $J \subseteq \mathcal{C}$. Let $\mathcal{L}_1, \ldots, \mathcal{L}_\ell$ be the available ledgers.

Init: Upon input (INPUT, sid, coins(d)) by each honest $\mathcal{P}_i$:

1. Send (KEYGEN, sid) to $\mathcal{F}_{\mathsf{TSig}}$. If $\mathcal{F}_{\mathsf{TSig}}$ returns a key vk then save it internally and continue, if it instead aborts then return coins(d) to each honest $\mathcal{P}_i$ and stop.

2. Update $\mathcal{F}_{\mathsf{Clock}}$ and wait for a message from $\mathcal{S}$. If $\mathcal{S}$ sends coins($|I| \cdot d$) send (KEY, sid, vk) to each honest $\mathcal{P}_i$, otherwise reimburse all honest $\mathcal{P}_i$ with coins(d).

Enroll Client: Upon input (ENROLL, sid, $\mathcal{L}_j^{\mathsf{src}}$, $\mathsf{vk}_j^{\mathsf{src}}$, $\mathsf{am}_j^{\mathsf{src}}$, $\mathcal{L}_j^{\mathsf{trg}}$, $\mathsf{vk}_j^{\mathsf{trg}}$) from a client $\mathcal{C}_j \in \mathcal{C} \setminus J$ or $\mathcal{S}$ if $\mathcal{C}_j \in J$ and if **Init** finished:

1. If $\mathcal{C}_j$ was enrolled already then return.

2. Send (ENROLL, sid, $\mathcal{L}_j^{\mathsf{src}}$, $\mathsf{vk}_j^{\mathsf{src}}$, $\mathsf{am}_j^{\mathsf{src}}$, $\mathcal{L}_j^{\mathsf{trg}}$, $\mathsf{vk}_j^{\mathsf{trg}}$) to $\mathcal{S}$. If $\mathcal{S}$ sends (OK, sid) then send (KEYGEN, sid) to $\mathcal{F}_{\mathsf{TSig}}$ to generate $\mathsf{vk}_j^{\mathsf{ex}}$ as well as (SIGN, sid, m) (obtaining ρ) and (COMBINE, sid, m, ρ, vk) to obtain σ.

3. If $\mathcal{F}_{\mathsf{TSig}}$ aborts then send (ABORT, sid) to $\mathcal{C}_j$. If it did not abort then send (PROCEED?, sid, σ, $\mathsf{vk}_j^{\mathsf{ex}}$) to the caller. If the caller was an honest $\mathcal{C}_j$ then wait for input (VALUE, sid, $\mathsf{am}_j^{\mathsf{trg}}$, id_j) where id_j is a transaction id of an honestly generated transaction on $\mathcal{L}_j^{\mathsf{src}}$ from $\mathsf{vk}_j^{\mathsf{src}}$ to $\mathsf{vk}_j^{\mathsf{ex}}$ with amount $\mathsf{am}_j^{\mathsf{src}}$. Send (INPUTPROVIDED, sid, $\mathcal{C}_j$) to $\mathcal{S}$.

Exchange: Upon input (EXCHANGE, sid) by all honest $\mathcal{P}_i$ and if **Init** finished:

1. Send (CLIENTS?, sid) to $\mathcal{S}$ and wait for $\mathsf{am}_j^{\mathsf{src}}$, id_j for each $\mathcal{C}_j \in J$ or alternatively for a message that $\mathcal{C}_j$ did not transfer to $\mathsf{vk}_j^{\mathsf{ex}}$.

2. Send (CONFIRM, sid, $\{\mathsf{am}_i^{\mathsf{src}}, \mathsf{id}_i\}_{i \in [m]}$) to all servers in $\mathcal{P}$. If no honest server $\mathcal{P}_i$ for $i \notin I$ answers with (CONFIRMED, sid, $\{\mathsf{am}_i^{\mathsf{src}}, \mathsf{id}_i\}_{i \in [m]}$) (meaning a client did not make a transaction) enter **Abort without Output**.

3. Send (SIGN, sid, $\mathcal{C}_j | \mathsf{id}_j$, vk) (receiving ρ_j) and (COMBINE, sid, $\mathcal{C}_j | \mathsf{id}_j$, ρ_j, vk) to $\mathcal{F}_{\mathsf{TSig}}$ for each $\mathcal{C}_j \in \mathcal{C}$. If any of them aborts then enter **Abort without Output**.

4. For each $a, b \in [\ell]$, $1 \le a < b \le \ell$ let $\mathcal{C}^{a,b}$ be the clients swapping between $\mathcal{L}_a$ and $\mathcal{L}_b$. For $\mathcal{C}_j \in \mathcal{C}^{a,b}$ define the $m' \le m$ values $h_j = (\mathcal{C}_j, \delta_j, \mathsf{am}_j^{\mathsf{src}}, \mathsf{am}_j^{\mathsf{trg}})$ where δ_j is 0 if $\mathcal{L}_j^{\mathsf{src}} = \mathcal{L}_a$ and 1 otherwise. Compute $\mathbf{y}^{a,b} \leftarrow \mathsf{compSwap}(h_1, \ldots, h_{m'})$. If $\mathcal{S}$ sends (ABORT, sid) enter **Abort without Output**.

Fig. 4. Functionality $\mathcal{F}_{\mathsf{EX}}$ for secure decentralized exchange.

Functionality $\mathcal{F}_{\mathsf{EX}}$ (Part 2)

Open: Upon input (OPEN, sid) by each honest $\mathcal{P}_i$ and if **Exchange** finished:

1. Send (SIGN, $sid, open, \mathsf{vk}$) to $\mathcal{F}_{\mathsf{TSig}}$ and obtain ρ. Then send (COMBINE, $sid, open, \rho, \mathsf{vk}$) to $\mathcal{F}_{\mathsf{TSig}}$. If $\mathcal{F}_{\mathsf{TSig}}$ aborted then enter **Abort without Output**, otherwise send (OUTPUTS, $sid, \{\mathbf{y}^{a,b}\}$) to $\mathcal{S}$.

2. Locally compute for each $\mathcal{L}_a$ the values $t_a = (\mathsf{id}_a, \mathsf{In}_a, \mathsf{Out}_a)$ using makeTX. Let the length of In_a be r and denote the burner addresses as $\mathsf{vk}_c^{\mathsf{ex}}$ for $c \in [r]$.

3. For each $\mathcal{L}_a$ and $c \in [r]$ send (SIGN, $sid, t_a, \mathsf{vk}_c^{\mathsf{ex}}$) to $\mathcal{F}_{\mathsf{TSig}}$ to obtain ρ_a^c. Then send (COMBINE, $sid, t_a, \rho_a^c, \mathsf{vk}_c^{\mathsf{ex}}$) to $\mathcal{F}_{\mathsf{TSig}}$. If $\mathcal{F}_{\mathsf{TSig}}$ aborted enter **Abort with Output**.

4. Send (SIGN, $sid, done, \mathsf{vk}$) to $\mathcal{F}_{\mathsf{TSig}}$ to obtain ρ. Then send (COMBINE, $sid, done, \rho, \mathsf{vk}$) to $\mathcal{F}_{\mathsf{TSig}}$. If $\mathcal{F}_{\mathsf{TSig}}$ aborted then enter **Abort with Output**.

5. Update $\mathcal{F}_{\mathsf{Clock}}$. Then send (SUCCESS, sid, tx_a) to each $\mathcal{C}_j$ with $\mathcal{L}_a \in \{\mathsf{vk}_j^{\mathsf{src}}, \mathsf{vk}_j^{\mathsf{trg}}\}$, send $\mathsf{coins}(d)$ back to each honest $\mathcal{P}_i$ and $\mathsf{coins}(|I| \cdot d)$ to $\mathcal{S}$.

Abort with Output:

1. Update $\mathcal{F}_{\mathsf{Clock}}$ twice and send (ABORT?, sid) to $\mathcal{S}$. If $\mathcal{S}$ responds with (ABORT, sid, I_1) where $\emptyset \neq I_1 \subseteq I$ then update $\mathcal{F}_{\mathsf{Clock}}$. Afterwards send $\mathsf{coins}(d)$ to each honest $\mathcal{P}_i$, $\mathsf{coins}((|I| - |I_1|)d)$ to $\mathcal{S}$ and $\mathsf{coins}(|I'|d/m)$ to each client $\mathcal{C}_j$.

2. If $\mathcal{S}$ did not abort then update $\mathcal{F}_{\mathsf{Clock}}$. Afterwards for each $\mathcal{L}_a$ and $c \in [r]$ send (SIGN, $sid, t_a, \mathsf{vk}_c^{\mathsf{ex}}$) to $\mathcal{F}_{\mathsf{TSig}}$ to obtain ρ_a^c (with the same notation as **Open**). Then send (COMBINE, $sid, t_a, \rho_a^c, \mathsf{vk}_c^{\mathsf{ex}}$) to $\mathcal{F}_{\mathsf{TSig}}$. If $\mathcal{F}_{\mathsf{TSig}}$ aborted overall with the set of parties $I_2 \subset I$ cheating update $\mathcal{F}_{\mathsf{Clock}}$. Afterwards send $\mathsf{coins}(d)$ to each honest $\mathcal{P}_i$, $\mathsf{coins}((|I| - |I_2|)d)$ to $\mathcal{S}$, $\mathsf{coins}(|I'|d/m)$ to each client $\mathcal{C}_j$ and return.

3. Otherwise update $\mathcal{F}_{\mathsf{Clock}}$, compute tx_a for each $\mathcal{L}_a$, send (SUCCESS, sid, tx_a) to each $\mathcal{C}_j$ with $\mathcal{L}_a \in \{\mathsf{vk}_j^{\mathsf{src}}, \mathsf{vk}_j^{\mathsf{trg}}\}$, $\mathsf{coins}(d)$ to each honest $\mathcal{P}_i$ and $\mathsf{coins}(|I| \cdot d)$ to $\mathcal{S}$.

Abort without Output:

1. Update $\mathcal{F}_{\mathsf{Clock}}$ twice.

2. Send (ABORTC?, sid) to $\mathcal{S}$ which responds with (ABORTC, $sid, J_1, \{\mathsf{id}_j\}_{j \in J \setminus J_1}$) where $J_1 \subseteq J$. Then send (ABORT?, sid) to $\mathcal{S}$. If $\mathcal{S}$ responds with (ABORT, sid, I_1) where $\emptyset \neq I_1 \subseteq I$ update $\mathcal{F}_{\mathsf{Clock}}$, send $\mathsf{coins}(d)$ to each honest $\mathcal{P}_i$, send $\mathsf{coins}((|I| - |I_1|)d)$ to $\mathcal{S}$ and $\mathsf{coins}(|I'|d/(m - |J_1|))$ to each $\mathcal{C}_j \in \mathcal{C} \setminus J_1$.

3. If $\mathcal{S}$ did not abort then update $\mathcal{F}_{\mathsf{Clock}}$. Afterwards for each $\mathcal{C}_j$ compute $t_j = (\mathsf{id}_j, \mathsf{In}_j, \mathsf{Out}_j)$ by setting $\mathsf{In}_j = (\mathsf{id}_j, \mathsf{am}_j^{\mathsf{src}})$ and $\mathsf{Out}_j = (\mathsf{am}_j^{\mathsf{src}}, \mathsf{vk}_j^{\mathsf{src}})$ and determining id_j as the hash of $\mathsf{In}_j, \mathsf{Out}_j$.

4. For each $\mathcal{C}_j$ send (SIGN, $sid, t_j, \mathsf{vk}_j^{\mathsf{ex}}$) to $\mathcal{F}_{\mathsf{TSig}}$ and obtain ρ_j. Then send (COMBINE, $sid, t_j, \rho_j, \mathsf{vk}_j^{\mathsf{ex}}$) to $\mathcal{F}_{\mathsf{TSig}}$. If $\mathcal{F}_{\mathsf{TSig}}$ aborted overall with the set of parties $I_2 \subset I$ cheating then update $\mathcal{F}_{\mathsf{Clock}}$. Afterwards send $\mathsf{coins}(d)$ to each honest $\mathcal{P}_i$, $\mathsf{coins}((|I| - |I_2|)d)$ to $\mathcal{S}$ and $\mathsf{coins}(|I_2|d/m)$ to each client $\mathcal{C}_j$.

5. If $\mathcal{F}_{\mathsf{TSig}}$ did not abort update $\mathcal{F}_{\mathsf{Clock}}$. Compute tx_j for each $\mathcal{C}_j$ and send (REIMBURSE, sid, tx_j) to $\mathcal{C}_j$, $\mathsf{coins}(d)$ to each honest $\mathcal{P}_i$ and $\mathsf{coins}(|I| \cdot d)$ to $\mathcal{S}$.

Fig. 5. Functionality $\mathcal{F}_{\mathsf{EX}}$ for secure decentralized exchange.

3.1 The Fair Exchange Functionality

Functionality[1] $\mathcal{F}_{\mathsf{EX}}$ as depicted in Fig. 4 and 5 generates the transactions for clients via burner addresses. As our protocol later uses the global clock, $\mathcal{F}_{\mathsf{EX}}$ also accesses $\mathcal{F}_{\mathsf{Clock}}$. The transactions that $\mathcal{F}_{\mathsf{EX}}$ will generate must be verifiable on other ledgers and its signatures therefore come from a global threshold signing functionality $\mathcal{F}_{\mathsf{TSig}}$. $\mathcal{F}_{\mathsf{EX}}$ accesses $\mathcal{F}_{\mathsf{TSig}}$ in order to generate these, giving the adversary $\mathcal{S}$ extra influence in the process. Notice that $\mathcal{F}_{\mathsf{EX}}$ implements a fair secure swap given that compSwap and makeTX implement swapping algorithms. $\mathcal{S}$ only learns the swap data $\mathbf{y}^{a,b}$ after all transactions were determined but does not learn the input orders like a centralized exchange does. $\mathcal{S}$ can only cause an abort before the output is released by causing signature generation to fail. In this case, all clients get reimbursed with either their original assets or with a deposit (here coins) from $\mathcal{S}$. If the functionality progressed far enough that $\mathcal{S}$ learned the output, then it can only abort by losing its coins. Otherwise, the swap output transactions will always be given to the clients.

4 Realizing the Exchange Functionality

We now describe a protocol Π_{Ex} that GUC-realizes $\mathcal{F}_{\mathsf{EX}}$, making sketch from Sect. 1.2 more precise. As the smart contract which is used, abstractly described in $\mathcal{F}_{\mathsf{SC}}$ (see Appendix A), is rather complex, we outline the interplay between Π_{Ex} and $\mathcal{F}_{\mathsf{SC}}$ beforehand. Due to space limitations, the smart contract description and its formalization $\mathcal{F}_{\mathsf{SC}}$ as well as the full protocol Π_{Ex} can be found in Appendix A.

4.1 Overview of the Protocol

Π_{Ex} runs between n servers $\mathcal{P}$ and m clients $\mathcal{C}$. The clients can exchange between ℓ ledgers $\mathcal{L}$. Each $\mathcal{C}_j$ controls an amount of tokens $\mathsf{am}_j^{\mathsf{src}}$ on an address with public key $\mathsf{vk}_j^{\mathsf{src}}$ on ledger $\mathcal{L}_j^{\mathsf{src}}$. The goal of $\mathcal{C}_j$ is to acquire $\mathsf{am}_j^{\mathsf{trg}}$ tokens on $\mathcal{L}_j^{\mathsf{trg}}$ to an address with public key $\mathsf{vk}_j^{\mathsf{trg}}$.

Smart Contract Setup. Initially, no servers or clients are registered anywhere. The servers $\mathcal{P}$ run a pre-processing step where they use $\mathcal{F}_{\mathsf{TSig}}$ to (internally) sample a common key sk for threshold-signing along with a public key vk for threshold-signature verification. Each $\mathcal{P}_i$ also sends its individual verification key $\widehat{\mathsf{vk}}_i$ to all other servers. Finally the servers set up $\ell \cdot (\ell - 1)$ instances $\mathcal{F}_{\mathsf{Ident}}^{a,b}$ to accept inputs by clients who want to transfer between $\mathcal{L}_a$ and $\mathcal{L}_b$.

To initiate the protocol each server sends $\mathsf{vk}, \widehat{\mathsf{vk}}_1, \ldots, \widehat{\mathsf{vk}}_n, \mathsf{coins}(d)$ to $\mathcal{F}_{\mathsf{SC}}$. $\mathcal{F}_{\mathsf{SC}}$ will wait for a certain period and then check if all servers put in enough

---

[1] Throughout this work, we treat $\mathcal{F}_{\mathsf{EX}}$ as an ordinary UC functionality and not a global functionality (which would intuitively make more sense). This is due to subtle issues that would arise in the proof if $\mathcal{F}_{\mathsf{EX}}$ was global, namely the simulator would not be able to equivocate the necessary outputs.

deposit[2] and signed messages consistently. If so, then the coins are locked and $\mathcal{F}_{SC}$ transitions to a state ready, otherwise the servers are reimbursed and $\mathcal{F}_{SC}$ goes back to its initial state init.

1. Burner Address Setup. If a client $\mathcal{C}_j$ wants to exchange an asset from $\mathcal{L}_j^{src}$ to $\mathcal{L}_j^{trg}$ it checks if $\mathcal{F}_{SC}$ is in state ready. If so then $\mathcal{C}_j$ sends a registration message to all $\mathcal{P}$, who generate a burner address/public key vk_j^{ex} on $\mathcal{L}_j^{src}$ using $\mathcal{F}_{TSig}$. The servers sign the client's data and vk_j^{ex} using sk and send the signature to $\mathcal{C}_j$.

2. Private Order Placement. If the signature is correct, then $\mathcal{C}_j$ transfers am_j^{src} from vk_j^{src} to vk_j^{ex} and inputs its transfer information into the correct $\mathcal{F}_{Ident}^{a,b}$.

3. Confirmation. Servers wait until all transfers to burner addresses were made and inputs were provided to $\mathcal{F}_{Ident}^{a,b}$ by all clients. They then sign information about the transactions to the burner addresses using sk. If either of this fails, then at least one $\mathcal{P}_i$ signs an "abort" message using sk_i and sends it to $\mathcal{F}_{SC}$.

4. Private Matching. Afterwards the servers run compSwap on all $\mathcal{F}_{Ident}^{a,b}$ to match transactions. If **Share** of each $\mathcal{F}_{Ident}$ is completed, all servers sign a message "ok" using sk that every server obtains. If this fails then each $\mathcal{P}_i$ signs an "abort" message and sends it to $\mathcal{F}_{SC}$. If signing succeeded but a server sent "abort", then all $\mathcal{P}_i$ respond by sending the signed "ok" to $\mathcal{F}_{SC}$. If signing "ok" was successful then all $\mathcal{P}_i$ use **Optimistic Reveal** of $\mathcal{F}_{Ident}^{a,b}$, i.e. the swaps.

5. Pay Out. The servers will compute the resulting transactions $tx_a = (id_a, In_a, Out_a, Sig_a)$ using makeTX and by making signatures using $\mathcal{F}_{TSig}$ under all burner addresses of each $\mathcal{L}_a$. These tx_a are then sent to clients $\mathcal{C}_j$ that are touched by the transfer. In case of an error a server sends "abort" to $\mathcal{F}_{SC}$. Once all transactions were signed, the servers sign a message *done* using sk and send this message to $\mathcal{F}_{SC}$. Upon receiving *done* signed by sk $\mathcal{F}_{SC}$ reimburses all $\mathcal{P}_i$.

Cheating Recovery. If any server sends an "abort" to $\mathcal{F}_{SC}$, then $\mathcal{F}_{SC}$ waits if any other server publishes an "ok" or "done" signed by sk. If "done" is published after an "abort" then $\mathcal{F}_{SC}$ reimburses all $\mathcal{P}_i$.

  If "ok" is published then each $\mathcal{P}_i$ runs **Reveal** and **Allow Verify** for each $\mathcal{F}_{Ident}^{a,b}$ and then posts all sk-signed client registrations, transaction ids as well as $\mathcal{F}_{Ident}$-shares $s_i^{a,b}$. This allows each server to compute $y^{a,b} = \sum_i s_i^{a,b}$ and hence id_a, In_a, Out_a for each $\mathcal{L}_a$ using makeTX. For each such transaction the server then computes its shares of Sig_a which it also posts. All this information allows $\mathcal{F}_{SC}$ to check if all servers revealed correct shares and signature shares or not. In case of cheating $\mathcal{F}_{SC}$ sends the cheaters' deposit to all registered clients and reimburses all honest servers. If posted data was correct, $\mathcal{F}_{SC}$ instead reimburses

---

[2] To ensure that all clients can be reimbursed in case of a malicious server, the deposit from each server must have value equal or greater to the total value of input given by clients during an exchange. However, in practice only a small percentage of this would be sufficient to incentivize honest behaviour and the requirement could even be considered equivalent to the *reserve requirement* of banks.

all servers. Each client C_j identifies from $\mathcal{F}_{SC}$ the parts necessary to compute its swap transactions locally and then posts these to finalize the swap.

If no "ok" or "done" is published then each server posts all client registrations signed by sk to $\mathcal{F}_{SC}$ as well as the transactions that each client C_j made to vk_j^{ex} from vk_j^{src}. After a certain delay passed the servers create reimbursing transactions tx_j for each C_j. For this, each server $\mathcal{P}_i$ generates its share of the signature using $\mathcal{F}_{TSig}$ and sends this share to $\mathcal{F}_{SC}$, signed under $\widehat{sk}_i$.

$\mathcal{F}_{SC}$ parses all signed client registrations and transactions, locally generates id_j, In_j, Out_j for each C_j and checks that each $\mathcal{P}_i$ generated its signature share correctly. If any share is missing or if $\mathcal{P}_i$ did not provide a valid share, then the deposit of all cheaters is shared among all clients. Finally, each honest server is reimbursed. If all reimbursement transactions can be made, then each C_j reads its transactions from $\mathcal{F}_{SC}$ and posts them on $\mathcal{F}_{BB}$ while $\mathcal{F}_{SC}$ reimburses all servers.

Protocol Π_{Ex} (Part 1)

We have n servers $\mathcal{P}$ and m clients $\mathcal{C}$. The clients exchange between ℓ ledgers $\mathcal{L}$ known to $\mathcal{P}$. Each C_j starts with an amount of asset am_j^{src} signed by vk_j^{src} on ledger $\mathcal{L}_j^{src}$. The goal of C_j is to acquire am_j^{trg} on $\mathcal{L}_j^{trg}$ by a transfer to vk_j^{trg}.
The protocol runs in the presence of $\mathcal{F}_{Clock}, \mathcal{F}_{SC}$ and multiple instances of $\mathcal{F}_{Sig}, \mathcal{F}_{TSig}$.

Initialize:
1. All $\mathcal{P}$ set up $\ell \cdot (\ell - 1)$ instances $\mathcal{F}_{Ident}^{a,b}$ where $1 \leq a < b \leq \ell$ to accept inputs by clients who want to transfer between $\mathcal{L}_a$ and $\mathcal{L}_b$ and run **Init** on each $\mathcal{F}_{Ident}^{a,b}$.

2. The servers $\mathcal{P}$ use $\mathcal{F}_{TSig}$ to sample a common key vk. Furthermore each $\mathcal{P}_i$ uses $\mathcal{F}_{Sig}$ to generate an individual public verification key $\widehat{vk}_i$, which it shares with all $\mathcal{P}$.

3. Let $t = (vk, \{\widehat{vk}_i\}_{i\in[n]}, \{\mathcal{L}_j\}_{j\in[\ell]}, \{\mathcal{F}_{Ident}^{a,b}\}_{a,b\in[\ell]}^{a<b})$. If $\mathcal{F}_{SC}$ is in state init then each $\mathcal{P}_i$ first computes a signature $\sigma_{\widehat{vk}_i}(t)$ on t using $\mathcal{F}_{Sig}$ for the key $\widehat{vk}_i$ and then sends $(POST, sid, t, \widehat{vk}_i, \sigma_{\widehat{vk}_i}(t))$ to $\mathcal{F}_{SC}$. Afterwards, each $\mathcal{P}_i$ sends $(LOCK\text{-}IN, sid, coins(d))$ to $\mathcal{F}_{SC}$ updates $\mathcal{F}_{Clock}$.

Enroll Client: Upon message $(ENROLL, sid, am_j^{src}, \mathcal{L}_j^{src}, vk_j^{src}, \mathcal{L}_j^{trg}, vk_j^{trg})$ by C_j:
1. If **state** = **ready** then all $\mathcal{P}_i$ use $\mathcal{F}_{TSig}$ to generate a fresh key vk_j^{ex} on $\mathcal{L}_j^{src}$. Let $t_j = (C_j, \mathcal{L}_j^{src}, am_j^{src}, vk_j^{src}, vk_j^{ex}, \mathcal{L}_j^{trg}, vk_j^{trg})$. Then the servers use $\mathcal{F}_{TSig}$ to generate a signature $\sigma_{vk}(t_j)$ for the key vk. All $\mathcal{P}_i$ send $(OK, sid, t_j, \sigma_{vk}(t_j))$ to C_j.

2. Upon receiving $(OK, sid, t_j, \sigma_{vk}(t_j))$ C_j checks if $\sigma_{vk}(t_j)$ is valid using vk from $\mathcal{F}_{SC}$. Then it creates a transaction $\overline{tx}_j = (\overline{id}_j, \overline{In}_j, \overline{Out}_j, \overline{Sig}_j)$ where $\overline{id}_j$ is fresh for $\mathcal{L}_j^{src}$, $\overline{In}_j = (id_j, am_j^{src})$, $\overline{Out}_j = (am_j^{src}, vk_j^{ex})$ and $\overline{Sig}_j = \sigma_{vk_j^{src}}(id|In|Out)$ where id is the id of an unspent transaction for vk_j^{src} and the signature is produced by $\mathcal{F}_{Sig}$ for the key vk_j^{src}. Finally, C_j sends $\overline{tx}_j$ to $\mathcal{F}_{BB}$ corresponding to $\mathcal{L}_j^{src}$.

3. Let $\mathcal{L}_a = \mathcal{L}_j^{src}$ and $\mathcal{L}_b = \mathcal{L}_j^{trg}$. Each C_j sends $(INPUT, sid, j, (C_j, 0, am_j^{src}, am_j^{trg}))$ to $\mathcal{F}_{Ident}^{a,b}$ if $a < b$, otherwise it sends $(INPUT, sid, j, (C_j, 1, am_j^{src}, am_j^{trg}))$ to $\mathcal{F}_{Ident}^{b,a}$.

Fig. 6. The protocol Π_{Ex}.

4.2 The Protocol

We discuss the practical deployment considerations of the protocol in Sect. 5 and describe the full protocol in Figs. 6, 7 and 8 and now prove our main theorem:

Theorem 1. *The protocol Π_{Ex} GUC-implements the functionality $\mathcal{F}_{\mathsf{EX}}$ in the $\mathcal{F}_{\mathsf{SC}}, \mathcal{F}_{\mathsf{Ident}}, \mathcal{F}_{\mathsf{Clock}}, \mathcal{F}_{\mathsf{Sig}}, \mathcal{F}_{\mathsf{TSig}}, \mathcal{F}_{\mathsf{BB}}$-hybrid model against any PPT-adversary corrupting at most $n - 1$ of the n servers statically.*

Proof. In order to prove the claim we construct a PPT simulator $\mathcal{S}$ which will, in the ideal setting, interact with $\mathcal{A}$, $\mathcal{F}_{\mathsf{EX}}$ and all the hybrid and global functionalities in such a way that $\mathcal{F}_{\mathsf{EX}} \circ \mathcal{S} \approx \Pi_{\mathsf{Ex}} \circ \mathcal{A}$ for any PPT environment $\mathcal{Z}$, i.e. that the interaction created by $\mathcal{S}$ is indistinguishable from a protocol transcript in a composed setting. Additionally, the global functionalities will be present in both cases and $\mathcal{Z}$ will be able to perform queries to these.

$\mathcal{S}$, on a high level, runs as follows:

- Upon learning the sets I, J of corrupted servers and clients $\mathcal{S}$ simulates honest servers $\mathcal{P}_i$ and honest clients $\mathcal{C}_j$ in a simulated instance of Π_{Ex}.
- $\mathcal{S}$ follows the protocol Π_{Ex} but with dummy inputs for $\mathcal{P}_i$ and $\mathcal{C}_j$. $\mathcal{S}$ will observe $\mathcal{A}$'s behaviour during the protocol execution and from it extract inputs that it sends to $\mathcal{F}_{\mathsf{EX}}$ on behalf of the dishonest servers and clients.
- During **Initialize** $\mathcal{S}$ will forward all messages sent by $\mathcal{A}$ to $\mathcal{F}_{\mathsf{TSig}}$ for generating the key vk. It generates keys $\widehat{\mathsf{vk}}_i$ for all the simulated servers and sends these to $\mathcal{A}$. It then for each party sends a signature on t as in the protocol, where different values are signed by different honest parties if $\mathcal{A}$ sent different keys to different honest servers. $\mathcal{S}$ will additionally provide messages $\mathsf{coins}(d)$ by each simulated honest party to $\mathcal{F}_{\mathsf{SC}}$. If $\mathcal{F}_{\mathsf{EX}}$ activates the clock and time progresses then it sends $\mathsf{coins}(|I| \cdot d)$ to $\mathcal{F}_{\mathsf{EX}}$, otherwise it aborts.
- During **Enroll Client** $\mathcal{S}$ will simulate sign-up of honest clients based on the output of $\mathcal{F}_{\mathsf{EX}}$ by sending the respective message to $\mathcal{A}$. It forwards all interactions of $\mathcal{A}$ to $\mathcal{F}_{\mathsf{TSig}}$ concerning the burner address. Ultimately it creates "fake" inputs for each honest $\mathcal{C}_j$ to the respective $\mathcal{F}_{\mathsf{Ident}}$ instance. For all the dishonest clients $\mathcal{S}$ observes $\mathcal{F}_{\mathsf{SC}}$ as well as the instances of $\mathcal{F}_{\mathsf{BB}}$. Upon receiving an enrollment message to all simulated honest servers it sends the respective message to $\mathcal{F}_{\mathsf{EX}}$. Their inputs will be extracted from the respective instances of $\mathcal{F}_{\mathsf{Ident}}$ which can be observed by $\mathcal{S}$. Alternatively send a message to $\mathcal{F}_{\mathsf{EX}}$ if a dishonest client neither provided any input nor made a transfer.
- During **Exchange** $\mathcal{S}$ follows what the honest servers would do in the protocol and forwards messages to $\mathcal{F}_{\mathsf{TSig}}$ accordingly. It aborts if the computation on any $\mathcal{F}_{\mathsf{Ident}}$ fails or if the sharing fails. Finally, it sends the respective message to $\mathcal{F}_{\mathsf{EX}}$.
- During **Open** either start the abort if $\mathcal{F}_{\mathsf{EX}}$ does so or obtain the outputs $\mathbf{y}^{a,b}$ from $\mathcal{F}_{\mathsf{EX}}$. In case that $\mathcal{S}$ obtains the output then make the output from $\mathcal{F}_{\mathsf{Ident}}$ to $\mathcal{A}$ appear to be the correct corresponding output and run their

Protocol Π_{Ex} (Part 2)

Exchange: Upon (EXCHANGE, sid) by all servers:

1. Each $\mathcal{P}_i$ checks that each $\mathcal{C}_j$ provided input to its respective $\mathcal{F}_{\text{Ident}}^{a,b}$ and that $\overline{\text{tx}}_j$ has been approved (with the right amount of asset) on the respective $\mathcal{F}_{\text{BB}}$-instance. If this is the case then all $\mathcal{P}$ use $\mathcal{F}_{\text{TSig}}$ to generate a signature $\sigma_{\text{vk}}(u_j)$ with $u_j = (\mathcal{C}_j, \overline{\text{id}}_j)$ for the transaction id $\overline{\text{id}}_j$ of $\overline{\text{tx}}_j$. If the transaction is not present or the signing with $\mathcal{F}_{\text{TSig}}$ fails then $\mathcal{P}_i$ uses $\mathcal{F}_{\text{Sig}}$ to generate the signature $\sigma_{\widehat{\text{vk}}_i}(u_j)$ and sends (POST, sid, $abort$, $\widehat{\text{vk}}_i$, $\sigma_{\widehat{\text{vk}}_i}(u_j)$) to $\mathcal{F}_{\text{SC}}$. It then updates $\mathcal{F}_{\text{Clock}}$, sends (ABORT, sid) to all $\mathcal{P}$ and enters **Abort**.

2. $\mathcal{P}_i$ runs **Evaluate** and **Share** on each $\mathcal{F}_{\text{Ident}}^{a,b}$ where the circuit evaluated runs compSwap for the registered number of parties. If $\mathcal{P}_i$ obtained an abort from any $\mathcal{F}_{\text{Ident}}^{a,b}$ then it sends (POST, sid, $abort$, $\widehat{\text{vk}}_i$, $\sigma_{\widehat{\text{vk}}_i}(u_j)$) to $\mathcal{F}_{\text{SC}}$, updates $\mathcal{F}_{\text{Clock}}$, sends (ABORT, sid) to all $\mathcal{P}$ and enters **Abort**.

3. If all of this succeeds, then all $\mathcal{P}_i$ compute $\sigma_{\text{vk}}(ok)$ using $\mathcal{F}_{\text{TSig}}$ and send it to all servers. If $\mathcal{P}_i$ did not obtain the signature then it sends (POST, sid, $abort$, $\widehat{\text{vk}}_i$, $\sigma_{\widehat{\text{vk}}_i}(u_j)$) to $\mathcal{F}_{\text{SC}}$, updates $\mathcal{F}_{\text{Clock}}$, sends (ABORT, sid) to all $\mathcal{P}$ and enters **Abort**.

4. If no abort message was obtained then each $\mathcal{P}_i$ updates $\mathcal{F}_{\text{Clock}}$. Then it checks state of $\mathcal{F}_{\text{SC}}$. If state $=$ abort then it runs **Abort**, else it runs **Open**.

Open:

1. Each $\mathcal{P}_i$ runs **Optimistic Reveal** for each $\mathcal{F}_{\text{Ident}}^{a,b}$. If a server $\mathcal{P}_i$ obtained an abort from any $\mathcal{F}_{\text{Ident}}^{a,b}$ then it sends (POST, sid, $abort$, $\widehat{\text{vk}}_i$, $\sigma_{\widehat{\text{vk}}_i}(u_j)$) to $\mathcal{F}_{\text{SC}}$, updates $\mathcal{F}_{\text{Clock}}$, sends (ABORT, sid) to all $\mathcal{P}$ and enters **Abort**.

2. If no abort was received then each $\mathcal{P}_i$ obtained $\mathbf{y}^{a,b} \in \mathbb{F}^g$ for each $\mathcal{F}_{\text{Ident}}^{a,b}$. For each $\mathcal{L}_a$ $\mathcal{P}_i$ then computes $\text{tx}_a = (\text{id}_a, \text{In}_a, \text{Out}_a, \text{Sig}_a)$ as follows:
   (a) Compute $(\text{id}_a, \text{In}_a, \text{Out}_a)$ using makeTX from all $\mathbf{y}^{a,b}$ as well as all client registrations and $\overline{\text{id}}_j$.
   (b) Compute $\text{Sig}_a = \sigma_{\text{vk}_c^{\text{ex}}}(\text{id}_a|\text{In}_a|\text{Out}_a)$ using $\mathcal{F}_{\text{TSig}}$ for each vk_c^{ex} where $c \in [r]$ and r is the number of burner addresses in In_a.
   Finally, all servers will compute $\sigma_{\text{vk}}(done)$ using $\mathcal{F}_{\text{TSig}}$. If a server $\mathcal{P}_i$ obtained an abort from any $\mathcal{F}_{\text{TSig}}$ then it sends (POST, sid, $abort$, $\widehat{\text{vk}}_i$, $\sigma_{\widehat{\text{vk}}_i}(u_j)$) to $\mathcal{F}_{\text{SC}}$, updates $\mathcal{F}_{\text{Clock}}$, sends (ABORT, sid) to all $\mathcal{P}$ and enters **Abort**.

3. If no $\mathcal{F}_{\text{TSig}}$ aborted then send tx_a to each $\mathcal{C}_j$ with $\mathcal{L}_a \in \{\text{vk}_j^{\text{src}}, \text{vk}_j^{\text{trg}}\}$.

4. All $\mathcal{P}_i$ send (POST, sid, $done$, $\sigma_{\text{vk}}(done)$, vk) to $\mathcal{F}_{\text{SC}}$.

Abort: If $\mathcal{P}_i$ sends or receives (ABORT, sid) at any point:

1. If $\mathcal{P}_i$ received (ABORT, sid) from another server then update $\mathcal{F}_{\text{Clock}}$.

2. If $\mathcal{F}_{\text{SC}}$ is in state abort and $\mathcal{P}_i$ has the message $\sigma_{\text{vk}}(done)$ then it sends (POST, sid, $done$, $\sigma_{\text{vk}}(done)$, vk) to $\mathcal{F}_{\text{SC}}$. Else if $\mathcal{P}_i$ has the message $\sigma_{\text{vk}}(ok)$ then it sends (POST, sid, ok, $\sigma_{\text{vk}}(ok)$, vk) to $\mathcal{F}_{\text{SC}}$. Afterwards it updates $\mathcal{F}_{\text{Clock}}$.

3. If it obtains coins(d) from $\mathcal{F}_{\text{SC}}$ then it outputs coins(d) and terminates.

4. If $\mathcal{F}_{\text{SC}}$ is in state reimburse1 then run **Abort without Output**. If $\mathcal{F}_{\text{SC}}$ is in state ok1 then run **Abort with Output**.

Fig. 7. The protocol Π_{Ex}.

Protocol Π_{Ex} (Part 3)

Abort with Output:

1. For each registered C_j the servers send $(\text{POST}, sid, t_j, \sigma_{vk}(t_j), vk)$ and $(\text{POST}, sid, u_j, \sigma_{vk}(u_j), vk)$ to $\mathcal{F}_{SC}$ where $t_j = (C_j, \mathcal{L}_j^{src}, am_j^{src}, vk_j^{src}, vk_j^{ex}, \mathcal{L}_j^{trg}, vk_j^{trg})$ and $u_j = (C_j, \overline{id}_j)$.

2. Each $\mathcal{P}_i$ runs **Reveal** and **Allow Verify** for each $\mathcal{F}_{Ident}^{a,b}$, followed by sending $(\text{POST}, sid, s_i^{a,b}, \sigma_{\widehat{vk}_i}(s_i^{a,b}), \widehat{vk}_i)$ to $\mathcal{F}_{SC}$ and updates $\mathcal{F}_{Clock}$. If $\mathcal{P}_i$ or C_j obtains $\text{coins}(d)$ from $\mathcal{F}_{SC}$ then it outputs $\text{coins}(d)$ and terminates.

3. Otherwise $\mathcal{P}_i$ recovers all $y^{a,b}$ from $\mathcal{F}_{SC}$ and does the following for each $\mathcal{L}_a$:
   (a) Determine id_a, In_a, Out_a using $\texttt{makeTX}$ from all $y^{a,b}$ as well as all t_j, u_j.
   (b) Compute $\rho_i^{a,c}$ by sending $(\text{SIGN}, sid, id_a|In_a|Out_a)$ to $\mathcal{F}_{TSig}$ for each vk_c^{ex} where $c \in [r]$ and r is the length of In_a. Set $v_j = (\rho_i^{a,1}, \ldots, \rho_i^{a,r})$.

4. $\mathcal{P}_i$ sends $(\text{POST}, sid, v_j, \sigma_{\widehat{vk}_i}(v_j), \widehat{vk}_i)$ for $a \in [\ell]$ to $\mathcal{F}_{SC}$ and updates $\mathcal{F}_{Clock}$.

5. If $\mathcal{P}_i$ obtains $\text{coins}(d)$ from $\mathcal{F}_{SC}$ then it outputs $\text{coins}(d)$ and terminates.

6. Each C_j checks if $\mathcal{F}_{SC}$ contains data for a transaction tx_a if $\mathcal{L}_a \in \{vk_j^{src}, vk_j^{trg}\}$. If so then C_j reconstructs tx_a. Otherwise it outputs the coins obtained from $\mathcal{F}_{SC}$.

Abort without Output:

1. For each registered client C_j the servers send $(\text{POST}, sid, t_j, \sigma_{vk}(t_j), vk)$ to $\mathcal{F}_{SC}$ where $t_j = (C_j, \mathcal{L}_j^{src}, am_j^{src}, vk_j^{src}, vk_j^{ex}, \mathcal{L}_j^{trg}, vk_j^{trg})$. Furthermore, each client C_j sends $(\text{POST}, sid, \overline{id}_j|\overline{In}_j|\overline{Out}_j, \sigma_{vk_j^{src}}(\overline{id}_j|\overline{In}_j|\overline{Out}_j), vk_j^{src})$ to $\mathcal{F}_{SC}$ where $\overline{id}_j|\overline{In}_j|\overline{Out}_j$ are from the transaction $\overline{tx}_j$ that C_j made to vk_j^{ex} and where $\sigma_{vk_j^{src}}(\overline{id}_j|\overline{In}_j|\overline{Out}_j)$ is from the signatures $\overline{Sig}_j$ that are part of $\overline{tx}_j$. Then each $\mathcal{P}_i$ updates $\mathcal{F}_{Clock}$.

2. Next, each $\mathcal{P}_i$ for each C_j computes the transaction tx_j as follows:
   (a) Set $In_j = (id_j, am_j^{src})$ and $Out_j = (am_j^{src}, vk_j^{src})$.
   (b) Determine id_j as the hash of In_j, Out_j. Set $t_j = (id_j, In_j, Out_j)$.
   (c) Compute ρ_j^i by sending $(\text{SIGN}, sid, t_j, vk_j^{ex})$ to $\mathcal{F}_{TSig}$.

3. Each $\mathcal{P}_i$ sends $(\text{POST}, sid, \rho_j^i, \sigma_{\widehat{vk}_i}(\rho_j^i), \widehat{vk}_i)$ to $\mathcal{F}_{SC}$ and updates $\mathcal{F}_{Clock}$.

4. If $\mathcal{P}_i$ obtains $\text{coins}(d)$ from $\mathcal{F}_{SC}$ then it outputs $\text{coins}(d)$ and terminates.

5. Each C_j checks if $\mathcal{F}_{SC}$ contains data for a transaction tx_j. If so then C_j reconstructs tx_j. Otherwise it outputs the coins coins it obtained from $\mathcal{F}_{SC}$.

Fig. 8. The protocol Π_{Ex}.

output phases[3]. Then forward all interactions towards $\mathcal{F}_{TSig}$ of $\mathcal{A}$. If a "done" message gets signed then let each honest server send it to $\mathcal{F}_{SC}$. Upon obtaining $\text{coins}(|I| \cdot d)$ back from $\mathcal{F}_{Ex}$ let $\mathcal{F}_{SC}$ forward these to $\mathcal{A}$.

- If $\mathcal{F}_{EX}$ runs **Abort without Outputs** $\mathcal{S}$ simulates the behavior of the honest servers by sending the signed messages that they learned during **Enroll Client** to $\mathcal{F}_{SC}$. Furthermore it fetches the transaction tx from $\mathcal{F}_{BB}$ that the

---

[3] This is possible, even if $\mathcal{F}_{Ident}$ is global, as $\mathcal{S}$ can alter all messages between $\mathcal{A}$ and global functionalities. This will not be noticeable for $\mathcal{Z}$ as $\mathcal{F}_{Ident}$ only outputs information for a specific sid to TMs acting in that session.

honest client made to send money to the burner address and puts it on $\mathcal{F}_{SC}$ as an honest client does in the protocol. If $\mathcal{A}$ does not send certain messages to $\mathcal{F}_{SC}$ then identify the respective sets J_1, I_1 and send them to $\mathcal{F}_{EX}$. If $\mathcal{F}_{EX}$ sends any $\mathsf{coins}(d)$ back to $\mathcal{S}$ then let $\mathcal{F}_{SC}$ distribute these accordingly.

– Simulate **Abort with Output** like **Output without Abort** is simulated.

It is easy to see that the messages which an adversary reads during the simulated protocol are consistent with the values that are returned both to the honest parties and servers and with the outputs of the ideal functionality. The state of $\mathcal{F}_{Clock}$ during each protocol step is identical with that during the simulated protocol instance. Moreover, whenever the simulated protocol aborts then this also leads to an abort of $\mathcal{F}_{EX}$ and when honest servers let $\mathcal{F}_{EX}$ abort then this is reflected in $\mathcal{F}_{SC}$. Honest clients never abort in the simulation as they cannot abort in Π_{Ex} either. Finally, the coins that $\mathcal{A}$ puts into $\mathcal{F}_{SC}$ and obtains from $\mathcal{F}_{SC}$ are identical with those that $\mathcal{S}$ inputs into $\mathcal{F}_{EX}$ or obtains from it. □

4.3   Preventing Denial of Service Attacks by Clients

In Π_{Ex} as sketched above, any client that registers but does not transfer funds causes an abort of the exchange. This can be avoided with an extension of Π_{Ex} that we outline below. We did not include this extension in the formalization of Π_{Ex} in order to keep the protocol description as small as possible.

To avoid the attack, all $\mathcal{P}_i$ in Step 3 of the protocol (**Confirmation**) sign information on which clients will be included and which will be excluded in the exchange, using $\mathcal{F}_{TSig}$. For each excluded $\mathcal{C}_j$, the servers send the signed message of exclusion to $\mathcal{C}_j$. If $\mathcal{C}_j$'s transaction tx_j to vk_j^{ex} on $\mathcal{L}_j^{src}$ was confirmed after this signature was generated, then $\mathcal{C}_j$ sends this signature together with tx_j and its registration information to $\mathcal{F}_{SC}$ as proof that it should be reimbursed[4]. Upon having obtained this, $\mathcal{F}_{SC}$ requires all $\mathcal{P}_i$ to create a signature on a reimbursement transaction to $\mathcal{C}_j$. If a server $\mathcal{P}_i$ does not send it's signature share, then $\mathcal{C}_j$ will be reimbursed from the collateral of $\mathcal{P}_i$ on the exchange ledger.

Observe that tx_j might not be a valid transaction on $\mathcal{L}_j^{src}$, but the reimbursement transaction will only be valid if tx_j was valid (as it spends tx_j), hence a malicious $\mathcal{C}_j$ cannot obtain funds of an honest party. Also, if a dishonest $\mathcal{P}_i$ refuses to sign an honest $\mathcal{C}_j$'s reimbursement transaction, then $\mathcal{C}_j$ will be reimbursed on the exchange ledger with funds of $\mathcal{P}_i$.

5   Implementation

To demonstrate feasibility of our approach, we describe a simple algorithm for order matching, i.e. $\mathsf{compSwap}$, along with an efficient MPC-based privacy preserving implementation of this, based on the ring-variant of the SPDZ protocol [30], called SPDZ_{2^k} [29].

---

[4] All this information was signed by $\mathcal{F}_{TSig}$ and must therefore be valid.

We implemented a *limited* order-matching function, $C_{compSwap}$ realizing the algorithm compSwap, which we describe in full detail in the full version. We note that $C_{compSwap}$ is a simplified version of standard limit-order price-focused matching algorithms, in the sense that it assumes all orders are for a constant amount of tokens from ledger $\mathcal{L}_a$ and only matches according to price. That is, the algorithm sorts the buy and sell orders according to their maximum and minimum limits respectively. Then the largest acceptable buy price is then matched with the smallest acceptable sell price, assuming the buy price is larger than the sell price. The clearing price will then be the average of the two prices. The price describes how many tokens of $\mathcal{L}_b$ must be swapped to get a constant amount of the tokens on $\mathcal{L}_a$. Orders which are not matched are simply discarded, without disclosing their price limits. We chose to implement this simple matching algorithm as it provides a minimally useful example of what is required by compSwap by performing oblivious sorting and selecting, which are they key aspects we can expect from any reasonable choice of algorithm.

Complexity of Matching. It is easy to see that comparison is the key primitive used in our order matching. In most arithmetic MPC schemes this primitive can be realized using $O(\log(k))$ multiplication gates and rounds of communication where k is the max bit-length of the numbers being computed on [29]. Besides being used for deciding whether a buy and sell order should be matched, comparison is also the key component in most oblivious sorting algorithms. In

Table 1. Complexity of the matching protocol implementation in SPDZ$_{2^k}$.

Orders (m)	k = 32, #mult	k = 26 #rounds	k = 64, #mult	k = 57 #rounds
4	2269	151	4075	158
8	7417	262	13351	275
16	22833	410	41151	431
32	66465	595	119871	626
64	184449	817	332799	862
128	492097	1077	888127	1169

particular, Batcher's Odd-Even Merge-sort [38, Sec. 5.4.3], which our implementation uses, has comparison depth $O(\log^2(m))$ and uses a total of $O(m\log^2(m))$ comparisons. For this reason the overall round complexity of our concrete order-matching algorithm, $C_{compSwap}$, ends up at $O(\log(k)\cdot\log^2(m))$ with multiplication gate complexity of $O(k\cdot m\log^2(m))$. The communication complexity associated with a multiplication gate is $O(k+\kappa)$ bits for SPDZ$_{2^k}$ [29]. Hence we get at most $O((k+\kappa)\cdot m)$ bit in bandwidth usage per round. The total amount used for each of the different choices of m and k by our implementation, including overhead by the framework, is expressed in Table 1.

Implementation of Matching. We implemented and ran $C_{compSwap}$ using the Fresco framework [1], which is an open-source MPC framework in Java for secure computation in the dishonest majority setting. We chose Fresco as it offers a simple API allowing quick construction of MPC applications. Furthermore, since it is Java-based, it also allows for easy cross-platform deployment and integration with other software. Additionally, Fresco is a commonly used framework for prototyping MPC applications [27,29] and supports a bring-your-own-backend approach, allowing easy switching of the underlying MPC scheme without having to modify the program to be executed. Most importantly however, Fresco is actively maintained, has high test coverage and offers an extensive API of operations, making it a great choice for prototyping MPC protocols, with a focus on potential real-world deployment, despite it not being the fastest option available.

We note that we could have optimized our implementation by using newer and more efficient approaches to MPC, such as approaches mixing both the binary and arithmetic setting [32]. However, the goal of our implementation has been to show feasibility and an upper bound on the time it would require to execute our protocol using a fully tested, documented and maintained framework. Thus we leave such possible optimizations as future work.

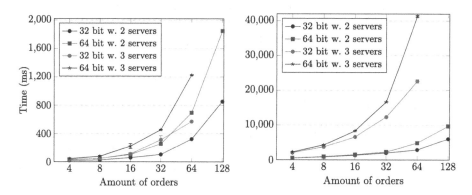

Fig. 9. Online phase of LAN execution of oblivious matching using SPDZ_{2^k} on AWS m5.xlarge.

Benchmarking Matching. We benchmarked the online execution of the matching protocol in several different settings using Amazon's Web Services EC2. We show these benchmarks in Fig. 9 based on the average of 30 iterations (executed after 30 "warm-up" iterations) and note that memory usage never gets above 536 MB regardless of test. For all tests we used m5.xlarge instances running Ubuntu 18.04 LTS. This means that each instance has 4 virtual CPUs and 16 GiB of RAM along with a LAN connections of up to a 10 Gbps with less than 0.1 ms latency, when running instances in the same data-center. For the WAN setting we also used m5.xlarge instances, but data centers in different countries. For the setting with 2 servers, one was located in Ireland and another in the U.K., with a latency of around 10 ms. For the setting with 3 servers, we kept the servers in Ireland and the U.K., but added a third server in Germany, with a latency of up to 25 ms between the Germany and Ireland servers.

When working over 32-bit integers ($k = 32$), the statistical security parameter is $\kappa = 26$, whereas when working over the 64-bit integers ($k = 64$) we have $\kappa = 57$. This is due to the underlying implementation of SPDZ_{2^k} in Fresco, and was originally made for efficiency choices [29].

From Fig. 9 we notice a steep increase in execution time when expanding the amount of orders and when moving from 2 to 3 servers. This is especially true in the WAN setting. This is to be expected due to the underlying SPDZ$_{2^k}$ protocol having round complexity in the multiplicative depth of the circuit being computed and where each round involves every party sending two ring elements to *all* other parties. Thus the overall execution time of the protocol becomes highly depended on the underlying network, in particular its latency, when increasing the amount of servers. This is also the case when increasing the amount of orders as the round complexity is bounded by $O(\log(k) \cdot \log^2(m))$ and multiplication gate complexity is bounded by $O(k \cdot m \log^2(m))$.

We imagine our protocol being run by a small set of servers, either run by a single or a few public organizations, whose servers will be in physically distinct locations, running distinct systems and administered by different people. For this reason we only benchmark for 2–3 servers, but note that if high scalability is desired one can simply change the underlying MPC scheme to a constant round scheme such as BMR [8] as done in "Insured MPC" [5].

We note that Fig. 9 only shows the online execution time. However, each multiplication gate used for such an execution requires to be preprocessed in advance in SPDZ$_{2^k}$. This preprocessing is independent of the input of the function to be computed and can thus be done before the clients even submit their exchange orders. The most efficient SPDZ$_{2^k}$ triple generation protocol with benchmarks is due to Damgård *et al.* [29], offering a throughput of 26,455 triples/second for $k = 32$ and 9,496 triples/second for $k = 64$ in the 2 server setting on LAN. Thus this can be done completed in about 1.5 min for $m = 128$ and $k = 64$.

Table 2. Complexity of the (threshold) signatures required by Π_{Ex} for its different phases. Time estimates are based on [34, Table 1].

	$\mathcal{F}_{\mathsf{TSig}}$ KEYGEN	$\mathcal{F}_{\mathsf{TSig}}$ SIGN	$\mathcal{F}_{\mathsf{Sig}}$ SIGN pr server	$\mathcal{F}_{\mathsf{Sig}}/\mathcal{F}_{\mathsf{TSig}}$ VERIFY pr server	Wall-clock time (sec.) for $m = 128$			
					2 servers		3 servers	
					LAN	WAN	LAN	WAN
Initialize	1	0	1	0	1	1	1	1
Enroll	m	m	m	0	125	125	246	246
Exchange	0	$m+1$	0	0	63	63	124	124
Open	0	$<m+1$	0	0	63	63	124	124
Abort w. out.	0	$<m$	0	0	62	62	123	123
Abort wo. out.	0	m	0	0	62	62	123	123

Signatures. We outline the computational need and timing estimates of $\mathcal{F}_{\mathsf{TSig}}$ and $\mathcal{F}_{\mathsf{Sig}}$, which is required by our protocol Π_{Ex} in Table 2. Note that timings in this table are estimates based on benchmark of a the recent work by Gennaro and Goldfeder [34] for threshold ECDSA (currently the most popular scheme in use by cryptocurrencies) with identifiable abort (which is needed for our protocol).

Total Execution Time. We only implemented and benchmarked the MPC implementation of the C_{compSwap} algorithm since it is clearly going to be the computation and communication related bottleneck when realizing $\mathcal{F}_{\text{Ident}}$ in the way discussed in Sect. 2.3. The only other cryptographic computation of this realization is limited to committing and opening of $O(n(m + s))$ commitments and sampling an equivalent amount of random elements in the MPC computation. Such commitments can be constructed very simply and efficiently in the ROM [17]. In particular in the order of microseconds, when using a standard hash function like SHA-256 to realize the random oracle. Furthermore, we note that besides the realization of $\mathcal{F}_{\text{Ident}}$ and $\mathcal{F}_{\text{TSig}}$ there are no other heavy communication or computation involved in realizing Π_{Ex}, since the other parts is basically straight-line executable business logic.

Taking the above discussion into account, it is easy to see that in a full online execution, the execution C_{compSwap} with no malicious behaviour, will be slower than the time required for computing the threshold signatures[5].

However, we now argue that even with the unoptimized implementation of C_{compSwap} and $\mathcal{F}_{\text{TSig}}$ these are not going to be the bottle-neck in regards to wall-clock execution time in practice. The reason being the time it takes to *finalize* transactions on the ledgers, which is necessary for *any* cross-ledger exchange. A block has been finalized once it has been written to the ledger *and* a certain amount of other blocks have been written afterwards to the same chain. This ensures that one can be reasonably certain that the block with the transaction will not be overwritten, by another, longer branch of blocks. The frequency at which blocks are constructed, and how many should be constructed before a transaction can be considered finalized, depends highly on the specific choice of ledger.

For Bitcoin, a new block is expected to be constructed every 10 min, and a rule of thumb is that 6 further blocks must be written before a transaction can be considered finalized. In case of Cardano, blocks are considered finalized after 10 min. This means that each round of ledger I/O will generally involve a latency of several minutes and hence be the bottleneck in practice.

6   Conclusion

Comparison to Current Solutions. As discussed in Sect. 1, besides our solution, there are generally only two other approaches to cross-chain exchange: either a centralized exchange or using atomic-swaps (*e.g.* as in [13]). Only considering efficiency, even in the case of the centralized exchange, two transactions must be carried out and finalized on the underlying ledgers; one transfer from ledger $\mathcal{L}_a$ to the exchange and one from the exchange to ledger $\mathcal{L}_b$. This means that we can expect a centralized exchange to take an order of tens of minutes to

---

[5] Although we should note that the benchmarks of threshold signatures by Gennaro and Goldfeder [34] are not optimized and run on a single-core consumer laptop whereas our benchmark of C_{compSwap} runs on a powerful AWS instance. We expect that the time required for the threshold signatures can be reduced significantly.

hours before it is has been fully finalized. If a system based on atomic swaps is used, an extra transaction is required, so 3 sequential transactions are used to finalize before the exchange can be considered complete.

When there is no malicious behaviour occurring, our system uses the *optimal* 2 sequential transactions[6] similarly to centralized exchanges. Specifically our system involves the transaction by clients transferring their tokens to the burner addresses and then the transaction of paying out the exchanged tokens. Furthermore, we note that while waiting for the first transaction to finalize the servers are sitting idle. This means that they could *optimistically* leverage this finalization time and start the actual matching computation. If the tokens are not transferred by all clients, the servers will generate refund transactions instead of opening the transactions computed by the private matching. Since the total computation time of Π_{Ex} is less than the finalization time of most blockchains, it means that its execution time will not be noticeable in the time it takes to carry out and finalize a complete exchange. Hence using our protocol will not add any time overhead to the current solutions (centralized or swapping). Furthermore, since nothing (besides the one-time initialization of the server) is written to the ledger, or executed by smart contracts, unless malicious behaviour occurs, it means that there will be no added mining-related cost by our approach. Thus achieving the added distributed security comes with no penalty in price or execution time as long as no malicious behaviour occurs. The only actual cost is what is needed to keep the servers running and the one-time cost of initialization.

Deployment Considerations. In regards to creating a highly usable deployment we note that the clients actually don't need to be involved during the payout phase of the protocol. Instead of having each client $\mathcal{C}_j$ post the signed transaction transferring their exchanged tokens to $\mathsf{vk}_j^{\mathsf{trg}}$ on ledger $\mathcal{L}_j^{\mathsf{trg}}$ themselves, we can simply have one of the honest servers post this transaction on their behalf. This means that they do neither need to wait for all other clients' transfers of source tokens to be finalized, nor for all the servers to finish computing the order-matching. This means that, unless one or more servers are malicious, the only time the clients need to interact with the protocol is during enrollment where they must register at the servers (and receive a signed confirmation). For clients this only involves giving outsourced input to $\mathcal{F}_{\mathsf{Ident}}^{a,b}$, which can be done very efficiently and independently of other clients or the size of the circuit to compute [35]. Thus this is something that can easily be done in the user's browser using a JavaScript web-app that integrates with a user's browser-wallet (e.g. MetaMask for Ethereum), where the server's signed response can be saved in the local web-page cache. Even if some servers act maliciously and the

---

[6] Technically 4 transactions are needed since the servers must put down a deposit to the smart contract, and receive this back at the end. However, the deposit can be reused for an arbitrary amount of executions of exchanges, and we consider this as purely overhead related to system setup. In case of malicious behaviour our protocol uses at most 7 transactions to either complete the exchange or refund the clients and return the honest servers' deposits.

abort branch of the protocol ends up being executed, assuming there is still a single honest server, that honest server could simply act on behalf of the client to ensure they get refunded. This is because all the information the client would need to post to $\mathcal{F}_{\text{SC}}$ is actually constructed and known by all the servers.

Appendix A Smart Contract Functionality $\mathcal{F}_{\text{SC}}$

We now describe the smart contract on a high level, meaning its different states and state transitions. This is to ease understanding, the full description will be presented later. The Smart Contract will have 7 different states init, ready, abort, ok1, ok2, reimburse1, reimburse2 where init is the initial state. State transitions are performed whenever the global clock $\mathcal{F}_{\text{Clock}}$ changes and depending on the messages that are present on the ledger that $\mathcal{F}_{\text{SC}}$ acts upon.

init If a tick happens, then check if all servers signed the same $\text{vk}, \widehat{\text{vk}}_1, \dots, \widehat{\text{vk}}_n$ using their individual $\widehat{\text{sk}}_i$ and that $\mathcal{P}_i$ sent coins(d). If so then change state to ready, otherwise reimburse all servers and stay in init.
ready If a tick happens and a message "done" is present, signed by sk, then reimburse all servers and set the state to init. If a tick happens and a message "abort" is present, signed by a $\widehat{\text{sk}}_i$ that initialized the contract, then change the state to abort.
abort If a tick happens and a message "done" is present, signed by sk, then reimburse all servers and set the state to init. Else, if a tick happens and a message "ok", signed by sk, is present, then change state to ok1. Else, if no such message is present at the tick, then change to reimburse1.

ok1 Call **Test Reveal** on each $\mathcal{F}_{\text{Ident}}^{a,b}$. If no parties J are returned as cheaters by **Test Reveal** then check if for each $\mathcal{P}_i$ and each $\mathcal{F}_{\text{Ident}}^{a,b}$ a message $s_i^{a,b}$ signed by $\widehat{\text{sk}}_i$ is present. If indeed, then verify the output for each $\mathcal{F}_{\text{Ident}}^{a,b}$ using **Verify**. If any of the aforementioned steps fails, then let I_1 be the set of cheating servers.
If $I_1 = \emptyset$ then change the state to ok2. If $I_1 \neq \emptyset$ then identify all the m clients by finding all messages of the form $(\mathcal{C}_j | \mathcal{L}_j^{\text{src}} | \text{am}_j^{\text{src}} | \text{vk}_j^{\text{src}} | \text{vk}_j^{\text{ex}} | \mathcal{L}_j^{\text{trg}} | \text{vk}_j^{\text{trg}})$ that are signed by sk. Furthermore, identify all the transaction ids id_j to burner addresses vk_j^{ex} signed by sk. For each party in I_1 share the deposit among all m clients. Then return the deposit of the parties in $[n] \setminus I_1$ and change the state to init.
ok2 Compute for each $\mathcal{L}_a$ in clear text the values $\text{id}_a, \text{In}_a, \text{Out}_a$ from the outputs of each $\mathcal{F}_{\text{Ident}}^{a,b}$ as well as the client registration data and transaction ids using makeTX. For each $\mathcal{L}_a$ check if each $\mathcal{P}_i$ sent shares of Sig_a signed with $\widehat{\text{sk}}_i$. If so, then check that each share of Sig_a is valid using $\mathcal{F}_{\text{TSig}}$ by running **Share Combination**. If any of the previous steps fails, then let I_2 be the set of cheaters.

Functionality $\mathcal{F}_{SC}$ (Part 1)

$\mathcal{F}_{SC}$ interacts with the global functionalities $\mathcal{F}_{Ident}, \mathcal{F}_{Clock}, \mathcal{F}_{Sig}, \mathcal{F}_{TSig}$. It is parameterized by the compensation q, the maximal number of exchange clients m and the security deposit $d = m \cdot q$. $\mathcal{F}_{SC}$ has an initially empty list $\mathcal{M}$ of messages posted to the authenticated bulletin board and a public state **state** which is initially **init**. It furthermore has the sets $\mathcal{P}$ of servers which is initially empty. Upon each activation $\mathcal{F}_{SC}$ first sends a message (READ, sid) to $\mathcal{F}_{Clock}$. If ν has changed since the last call to $\mathcal{F}_{Clock}$ then it does the following:

state = init: Check if $((vk, \{\widehat{vk}_i\}_{i \in [n]}, \{\mathcal{L}_j\}_{j \in [\ell]}, \{\mathcal{F}_{Ident}^{a,b}\}_{a,b \in [\ell]}^{a<b}), \widehat{vk}_i) \in \mathcal{M}$ for all $i \in [n]$ via $\mathcal{F}_{Sig}$. Furthermore check that each $\mathcal{P}_i$ with key $\widehat{vk}_i$ sent $\text{coins}(d)$. If so then change **state** to **ready** and set $\mathcal{P} = \{\mathcal{P}_1, \ldots, \mathcal{P}_n\}$. If not, for $\mathcal{P}'$ as the parties that provided $\text{coins}(d)$ send $\text{coins}(d)$ to each party in $\mathcal{P}'$ and let **state** = **init**.

state = ready: If $(done, vk) \in \mathcal{M}$ then run $\text{CC}(\emptyset, \emptyset)$ and set **state** to **init**. Else if $(abort, \widehat{vk}_i) \in \mathcal{M}$ for some $\mathcal{P}_i \in \mathcal{P}$ then change **state** to **abort**. Else do not change **state**.

state = abort: If $(done, vk) \in \mathcal{M}$ then run $\text{CC}(\emptyset, \emptyset)$ and set **state** to **init**. Else, if $(ok, vk) \in \mathcal{M}$ then change **state** to **ok1**. Else change **state** to **reimburse1**.

state = ok1: Parse all messages $(C_j | \mathcal{L}_j^{src} | am_j^{src} | vk_j^{src} | vk_j^{ex} | \mathcal{L}_j^{trg} | vk_j^{trg}, vk) \in \mathcal{M}$ (client registrations) and all $(C_j | \overline{id}_j, vk) \in \mathcal{M}$ (transaction ids). Then call **Test Reveal** on each $\mathcal{F}_{Ident}^{a,b}$. Afterwards check if $(s_i^{a,b}, \widehat{vk}_i) \in \mathcal{M}$ for each $\mathcal{P}_i$ and each $\mathcal{F}_{Ident}^{a,b}$ and send (VERIFY, $sid, s_1^{a,b}, \ldots, s_n^{a,b}$) to each $\mathcal{F}_{Ident}^{a,b}$. If all passes, then let $y^{a,b} = \sum_{i \in [n]} s_i^{a,b}$ be the output of $\mathcal{F}_{Ident}^{a,b}$. If any of the aforementioned steps fails, then let I_1 be the set of cheaters.
If $I_1 = \emptyset$ then set **state** to **ok2**, else let $\mathcal{C}$ be the set of clients, run $\text{CC}(I_1, \mathcal{C})$ and change **state** to **init**.

state = ok2: For each ledger $\mathcal{L}_a$ compute $id_a, \text{In}_a, \text{Out}_a$ from $y^{a,b}$ as well as the client registrations and transaction ids using makeTX. Let $vk_{a,1}^{ex}, \ldots, vk_{a,r}^{ex}$ be the source transactions in in_a. For each $\mathcal{L}_a$ check if $((\rho_i^{a,1}, \ldots, \rho_i^{a,r}), \widehat{vk}_i) \in \mathcal{M}$ and send (COMBINE, $sid, id_a | \text{In}_a | \text{Out}_a, \rho_i^{a,c}, vk_{a,c}^{ex}$) to $\mathcal{F}_{TSig}$ for each $c \in [r]$ and $i \in [n]$. If any of the steps fails, then let I_2 be the set of cheaters.
Let $\mathcal{C}$ be the set of clients. If $I_2 = \emptyset$ then run $\text{CC}(\emptyset, \emptyset)$, otherwise run $\text{CC}(I_2, \mathcal{C})$. Finally change **state** to **init**.

state = reimburse1: Change **state** to **reimburse2**.

state = reimburse2: Parse all messages $(C_j | \mathcal{L}_j^{src} | am_j^{src} | vk_j^{src} | vk_j^{ex} | \mathcal{L}_j^{trg} | vk_j^{trg}, vk) \in \mathcal{M}$ (i.e. client registrations) as well as $(\overline{id}_j | \overline{\text{In}}_j | \overline{\text{Out}}_j, vk_j^{src}) \in \mathcal{M}$ (transaction ids) where $\overline{\text{In}}_j = (vk_j^{src}, am_j^{src})$ and $\overline{\text{Out}}_j = (am_j^{src}, vk_j^{ex})$. If there are multiple messages for C_j then ignore C_j.
Compute for C_j the values $id_j, \text{In}_j, \text{Out}_j$ for reimbursement by setting $\text{In}_j = (\overline{id}_j, am_j^{src}), \text{Out}_j = (am_j^{src}, vk_j^{src})$ and id_j as the hash of $\text{In}_j, \text{Out}_j$.
Check if $(\rho_j^i, \widehat{vk}_i) \in \mathcal{M}$ for each C_j and each $\mathcal{P}_i$, then send (COMBINE, $sid, id_j | \text{In}_j | \text{Out}_j, \rho_j^i, vk_j^{ex}$) to $\mathcal{F}_{TSig}$ for each $i \in [n]$. If all values were present on $\mathcal{M}$ and all queries to $\mathcal{F}_{TSig}$ were positive then run $\text{CC}(\emptyset, \emptyset)$ and set **state** to **init**. Otherwise let J be the set of cheaters and $\mathcal{C}$ be the set of all clients. Run $\text{CC}(J, \mathcal{C})$ and set **state** to **init**.

Afterwards it executes the operation and finalizes by sending (UPDATE, sid) to $\mathcal{F}_{Clock}$.

Fig. 10. The stateful smart contract functionality $\mathcal{F}_{SC}$.

Functionality $\mathcal{F}_{\text{SC}}$ (Part 2)

Post: Upon receiving (POST, $sid, m, \text{vk}, \sigma$) from some entity contact the instance of $\mathcal{F}_{\text{Sig}}$ or $\mathcal{F}_{\text{TSig}}$ belonging to vk. If σ verifies for m and vk then send (POST, $sid, m, \text{vk}, \sigma$) to $\mathcal{S}$ and append (m, vk) to the list $\mathcal{M}$.

Read: Upon receiving (READ, sid) from some entity, return $\mathcal{M}$.

Send Deposits: Upon receiving (LOCK-IN, $sid, \text{coins}(d)$) from some entity $\mathcal{P}_i$ containing the d coins of the security deposit send (LOCK-IN, $sid, \text{coins}(d)$) to $\mathcal{S}$. Then if state $=$ init accept the money, otherwise return it to $\mathcal{P}_i$.

Macro CC(punish, $\mathcal{C}$): Let $\text{punish} \subset \mathcal{P}$, $|\mathcal{C}| \le m$ and $\text{reimburse} = \mathcal{P} \setminus \text{punish}$. Send $\text{coins}(d)$ to each party **reimburse** and $\text{coins}(|\text{punish}| \cdot d/|\mathcal{C}|)$ to each party in $\mathcal{C}$.

Fig. 11. The stateful smart contract functionality $\mathcal{F}_{\text{SC}}$.

If $I_2 = \emptyset$ then reimburse all $\mathcal{P}_i$ with their deposit and change the state to init. Otherwise identify all the m clients by finding all client registration data and transaction ids to burner addresses signed by sk. For each party in I_2 share the deposit among all m clients. Then return the deposit of the parties in $[n] \setminus I_2$ and change the state to init.

reimburse1 If a tick happens, then continue to **reimburse2**. Intuitively, during this step all clients that get reimbursed are already fixed so the servers will create the signatures on reimbursement transactions.

reimburse2 If a tick happens, consider all messages provided by each $\mathcal{P}_i$ to $\mathcal{F}_{\text{SC}}$ that are of the form $(\mathcal{C}_j|\mathcal{L}_j^{\text{src}}|\text{am}_j^{\text{src}}|\text{vk}_j^{\text{src}}|\text{vk}_j^{\text{ex}}|\mathcal{L}_j^{\text{trg}}|\text{vk}_j^{\text{trg}})$ that are signed by sk as well as all messages $(\overline{\text{id}}_j|\overline{\text{In}}_j|\overline{\text{Out}}_j, \text{vk}_j^{\text{src}}) \in \mathcal{M}$ (transaction ids) where $\overline{\text{In}}_j = (\text{vk}_j^{\text{src}}, \text{am}_j^{\text{src}})$ and $\overline{\text{Out}}_j = (\text{am}_j^{\text{src}}, \text{vk}_j^{\text{ex}})$. If there are multiple messages for $\mathcal{C}_j$ then ignore $\mathcal{C}_j$

Locally compute for each $\mathcal{C}_j$ the transaction tx_j to reimburse $\mathcal{C}_j$. Therefore set $\text{In}_j = (\overline{\text{id}}_j, \text{am}_j^{\text{src}})$, $\text{Out}_j = (\text{am}_j^{\text{src}}, \text{vk}_j^{\text{src}})$ and set id_j as the hash of both. If each $\mathcal{P}_i^j$ provided ρ_j^i then check using **Share Combination** on $\mathcal{F}_{\text{TSig}}$ that it outputs a valid signature Sig_j on $id_j, \text{In}_j, \text{Out}_j$. If all such Sig_j are valid signatures then reimburse all $\mathcal{P}_i$ and set the state to init. If some signature shares are not valid or some shares ρ_j^i are not present on $\mathcal{F}_{\text{SC}}$ then let J be the set of cheaters. Reimburse all servers $[n] \setminus J$ and distribute the deposit of the parties of J evenly to all $\mathcal{C}_j$. Then set the state to init.

Formalizing the Smart Contract. We use a combined smart contract and public ledger functionality $\mathcal{F}_{\text{SC}}$. It is an extension to $\mathcal{F}_{\text{BB}}$, tailored to be combined with an MPC protocol and similar to the functionality used in [5]. For technical reasons, $\mathcal{F}_{\text{SC}}$ has a hard-coded reference to the publicly verifiable MPC functionality $\mathcal{F}_{\text{Ident}}$ in order to be able to verify outputs. $\mathcal{F}_{\text{SC}}$ is described in Fig. 10 and Fig. 11 and considered as an ordinary UC functionality in our work. Again, this is due to technical limitations of UC, which would not make it possible for the simulator we construct in our security proof to equivocate the necessary outputs.

References

1. Alexandra Institute. FRESCO - a FRamework for Efficient Secure COmputation. https://github.com/aicis/fresco
2. Andrychowicz, M., Dziembowski, S., Malinowski, D., Mazurek, L.: Secure multi-party computations on bitcoin. In: 2014 IEEE Symposium on Security and Privacy. IEEE Computer Society Press, May 2014
3. Badertscher, C., Maurer, U., Tschudi, D., Zikas, V.: Bitcoin as a transaction ledger: a composable treatment. In: Katz, J., Shacham, H. (eds.) CRYPTO 2017. LNCS, vol. 10401, pp. 324–356. Springer, Cham (2017). https://doi.org/10.1007/978-3-319-63688-7_11
4. Baum, C., David, B., Dowsley, R.: A framework for universally composable publicly verifiable cryptographic protocols. Cryptology ePrint Archive, Report 2020/207 (2020). https://eprint.iacr.org/2020/207
5. Baum, C., David, B., Dowsley, R.: Insured MPC: efficient secure computation with financial penalties. In: Bonneau, J., Heninger, N. (eds.) FC 2020. LNCS, vol. 12059, pp. 404–420. Springer, Cham (2020). https://doi.org/10.1007/978-3-030-51280-4_22
6. Baum, C., David, B., Dowsley, R., Nielsen, J.B., Oechsner, S.: CRAFT: composable randomness and almost fairness from time. Cryptology ePrint Archive, Report 2020/784 (2020). https://eprint.iacr.org/2020/784
7. Baum, C., David, B., Frederiksen, T.: P2DEX: privacy-preserving decentralized cryptocurrency exchange. Cryptology ePrint Archive, Report 2021/283 (2021). https://eprint.iacr.org/2021/283
8. Beaver, D., Micali, S., Rogaway, P.: The round complexity of secure protocols (extended abstract). In: 22nd ACM STOC. ACM Press, May 1990
9. Benhamouda, F., Halevi, S., Halevi, T.: Supporting private data on hyperledger fabric with secure multiparty computation. In: IEEE IC2E, pp. 357–363, April 2018
10. Bentov, I., Ji, Y., Zhang, F., Breidenbach, L., Daian, P., Juels, A.: Tesseract: real-time cryptocurrency exchange using trusted hardware. In: ACM CCS 2019. ACM Press, November 2019
11. Bentov, I., Kumaresan, R.: How to use bitcoin to design fair protocols. In: Garay, J.A., Gennaro, R. (eds.) CRYPTO 2014. LNCS, vol. 8617, pp. 421–439. Springer, Heidelberg (2014). https://doi.org/10.1007/978-3-662-44381-1_24
12. Bentov, I., Kumaresan, R., Miller, A.: Instantaneous decentralized poker. In: Takagi, T., Peyrin, T. (eds.) ASIACRYPT 2017. LNCS, vol. 10625, pp. 410–440. Springer, Cham (2017). https://doi.org/10.1007/978-3-319-70697-9_15
13. Binance: Binance DEX Documentation (2020). https://docs.binance.org
14. Bowe, S., Chiesa, A., Green, M., Miers, I., Mishra, P., Wu, H.: ZEXE: enabling decentralized private computation. In: 2020 IEEE Symposium on Security and Privacy. IEEE Computer Society Press, May 2020
15. Bulck, J.V., et al.: Foreshadow: extracting the keys to the intel SGX kingdom with transient out-of-order execution. In: USENIX Security Symposium 2018, pp. 991–1008. USENIX Association (2018)
16. Bünz, B., Agrawal, S., Zamani, M., Boneh, D.: Zether: towards privacy in a smart contract world. In: Bonneau, J., Heninger, N. (eds.) FC 2020. LNCS, vol. 12059, pp. 423–443. Springer, Cham (2020). https://doi.org/10.1007/978-3-030-51280-4_23

17. Camenisch, J., Drijvers, M., Gagliardoni, T., Lehmann, A., Neven, G.: The wonderful world of global random oracles. In: Nielsen, J.B., Rijmen, V. (eds.) EUROCRYPT 2018. LNCS, vol. 10820, pp. 280–312. Springer, Cham (2018). https://doi.org/10.1007/978-3-319-78381-9_11

18. Canetti, R.: Universally composable security: a new paradigm for cryptographic protocols. In: 42nd FOCS. IEEE Computer Society Press, October 2001

19. Canetti, R.: Universally composable signature, certification, and authentication. In: IEEE (CSFW), p. 19. IEEE Computer Society (2004)

20. Canetti, R., Dodis, Y., Pass, R., Walfish, S.: Universally composable security with global setup. In: Vadhan, S.P. (ed.) TCC 2007. LNCS, vol. 4392, pp. 61–85. Springer, Heidelberg (2007). https://doi.org/10.1007/978-3-540-70936-7_4

21. Canetti, R., Gennaro, R., Goldfeder, S., Makriyannis, N., Peled, U.: UC noninteractive, proactive, threshold ECDSA with identifiable aborts. Cryptology ePrint Archive, Report 2021/060 (2021). https://eprint.iacr.org/2021/060

22. Canetti, R., Makriyannis, N., Peled, U.: UC non-interactive, proactive, threshold ECDSA. Cryptology ePrint Archive, Report 2020/492 (2020). https://eprint.iacr.org/2020/492

23. Cartlidge, J., Smart, N.P., Alaoui, Y.T.: Multi-party computation mechanism for anonymous equity block trading: a secure implementation of Turquoise Plato Uncross. Cryptology ePrint Archive, Report 2020/662 (2020). https://eprint.iacr.org/2020/662

24. Cartlidge, J., Smart, N.P., Talibi Alaoui, Y.: MPC joins the dark side. In: ASIACCS 2019. ACM Press, July 2019

25. Choudhuri, A.R., Green, M., Jain, A., Kaptchuk, G., Miers, I.: Fairness in an unfair world: Fair multiparty computation from public bulletin boards. In: ACM CCS 2017. ACM Press, October/November 2017

26. Cleve, R.: Limits on the security of coin flips when half the processors are faulty (extended abstract). In: 18th ACM STOC. ACM Press, May 1986

27. Cramer, R., Damgård, I., Escudero, D., Scholl, P., Xing, C.: SPD $\mathbb{Z}_{2^k}$: efficient MPC mod 2^k for dishonest majority. In: CRYPTO, Part II, 2018. LNCS. Springer, Heidelberg, August 2018

28. Daian, P., et al.: Flash boys 2.0: frontrunning in decentralized exchanges, miner extractable value, and consensus instability. In: 2020 IEEE Symposium on Security and Privacy. IEEE Computer Society Press, May 2020

29. Damgård, I., Escudero, D., Frederiksen, T.K., Keller, M., Scholl, P., Volgushev, N.: New primitives for actively-secure MPC over rings with applications to private machine learning. In: 2019 IEEE Symposium on Security and Privacy. IEEE Computer Society Press, May 2019

30. Damgård, I., Pastro, V., Smart, N., Zakarias, S.: Multiparty computation from somewhat homomorphic encryption. In: Safavi-Naini, R., Canetti, R. (eds.) CRYPTO 2012. LNCS, vol. 7417, pp. 643–662. Springer, Heidelberg (2012). https://doi.org/10.1007/978-3-642-32009-5_38

31. Dziembowski, S., Eckey, L., Faust, S.: FairSwap: how to fairly exchange digital goods. In: ACM CCS 2018. ACM Press, October 2018

32. Escudero, D., Ghosh, S., Keller, M., Rachuri, R., Scholl, P.: Improved primitives for MPC over mixed arithmetic-binary circuits. In: Micciancio, D., Ristenpart, T. (eds.) CRYPTO 2020. LNCS, vol. 12171, pp. 823–852. Springer, Cham (2020). https://doi.org/10.1007/978-3-030-56880-1_29

33. Gągol, A., Kula, J., Straszak, D., Świętek, M.: Threshold ECDSA for decentralized asset custody. Cryptology ePrint Archive, Report 2020/498 (2020). https://eprint.iacr.org/2020/498

34. Gennaro, R., Goldfeder, S.: One round threshold ECDSA with identifiable abort. Cryptology ePrint Archive, Report 2020/540 (2020). https://eprint.iacr. org/2020/540

35. Jakobsen, T.P., Nielsen, J.B., Orlandi, C.: A framework for outsourcing of secure computation. In:Ahn, G., Oprea, A., Safavi-Naini, R. (eds.) ACM CCSW 2014, pp. 81–92. ACM (2014)

36. Katz, J., Maurer, U., Tackmann, B., Zikas, V.: Universally composable synchronous computation. In: Sahai, A. (ed.) TCC 2013. LNCS, vol. 7785, pp. 477–498. Springer, Heidelberg (2013). https://doi.org/10.1007/978-3-642-36594-2_27

37. Kiayias, A., Zhou, H.-S., Zikas, V.: Fair and robust multi-party computation using a global transaction ledger. In: Fischlin, M., Coron, J.-S. (eds.) EUROCRYPT 2016. LNCS, vol. 9666, pp. 705–734. Springer, Heidelberg (2016). https://doi.org/ 10.1007/978-3-662-49896-5_25

38. Knuth, D.E.: The Art of Computer Programming, Sorting and Searching, 2nd edn., vol. 3. Addison-Wesley (1998)

39. Kosba, A.E., Miller, A., Shi, E., Wen, Z., Papamanthou, C.: Hawk: the blockchain model of cryptography and privacy-preserving smart contracts. In: 2016 IEEE Symposium on Security and Privacy. IEEE Computer Society Press, May 2016

40. Kumaresan, R., Bentov, I.: Amortizing secure computation with penalties. In: ACM CCS 2016. ACM Press, October 2016

41. Kumaresan, R., Moran, T., Bentov, I.: How to use bitcoin to play decentralized poker. In: ACM CCS 2015. ACM Press, October 2015

42. Massacci, F., Ngo, C.N., Nie, J., Venturi, D., Williams, J.: FuturesMEX: secure, distributed futures market exchange. In: 2018 IEEE Symposium on Security and Privacy. IEEE Computer Society Press, May 2018

43. Nakamoto, S.: Bitcoin: a peer-to-peer electronic cash system (2008)

44. Selfkey: A Comprehensive List of Cryptocurrency Exchange Hacks 2020. https:// selfkey.org/list-of-cryptocurrency-exchange-hacks/

W-OTS$^+$ Up My Sleeve! A Hidden Secure Fallback for Cryptocurrency Wallets

David Chaum[1], Mario Larangeira[2(✉)], Mario Yaksetig[1,3], and William Carter[1]

[1] xx Network, George Town, Cayman Islands
{david,mario,will}@xx.network
[2] Tokyo Institute of Technology and IOHK, Tokyo, Japan
mario@c.titech.ac.jp, mario.larangeira@iohk.io
[3] University of Porto, Porto, Portugal
mario.yaksetig@fe.up.pt

Abstract. We introduce a new key generation mechanism where users can generate a "back up key", securely nested inside the secret key of a signature scheme.

Our main motivation is that in case of leakage of the secret key, established techniques based on zero-knowledge proofs of knowledge are void since the key becomes public. On the other hand, the "back up key", which is secret, can be used to generate a "proof of ownership", *i.e.*, only the real owner of this secret key can generate such a proof. To the best of our knowledge, this extra level of security is novel, and could have already been used in practice, if available, in digital wallets for cryptocurrencies that suffered massive leakage of account private keys. In this work, we formalize the notion of "Proof of Ownership" and "Fallback" as new properties. Then, we introduce our construction, which is compatible with major designs for wallets based on ECDSA, and adds a W-OTS$^+$ signing key as a "back up key". Thus offering a quantum secure *fallback*. This design allows the hiding of any quantum secure signature key pair, and is not exclusive to W-OTS$^+$. Finally, we briefly discuss the construction of multiple generations of proofs of ownership.

Keywords: Digital currencies · Hash-based signatures · Post-quantum cryptography

1 Introduction

Digital wallets allow users to securely store secret cryptographic keys which can be used to spend cryptocurrency funds. These wallets, and corresponding keys, are becoming increasingly important as hackers attempt to exploit eventual security flaws and, as a result, steal funds controlled by such wallets. In practice, users rely on a few approaches. The most straightforward technique is to resort to secure hardware, *i.e.* hardware wallets [1]. Another popular practice among practitioners is the technique of hot/cold wallets [11], where, briefly, there is a

© Springer Nature Switzerland AG 2021
K. Sako and N. O. Tippenhauer (Eds.): ACNS 2021, LNCS 12726, pp. 195–219, 2021.
https://doi.org/10.1007/978-3-030-78372-3_8

hot wallet permanently connected to the network, typically initiated with the public key and can generate addresses for receiving funds. The cold wallet, on the other hand, stores the secret key and is kept without network connection. This separation ensures that it is harder for attackers to gain access to secret keys as they are kept offline. Despite these security enhanced wallets, we observe that in the case of massive key leakage, including in the cold wallet, any attempt of confirming the ownership of the leaked key is impractical, if possible.

Massive Leaks have Already Happened. We showcase our work by highlighting the hack involving the Trinity wallet [24], which resulted in the theft of roughly 1.5M USD. Trinity, an open-source software wallet which enables users to manage their IOTA tokens, suffered from a hack so severe that the IOTA Foundation decided to halt the coordinator node and, as a result, temporarily stopped the confirmations of all transactions on the network. To perform this attack, the adversary gained the ability to load malicious code into the local Trinity wallet instances running on the computers of the target users and retrieved the secret seeds—along with the encryption passwords—to a malicious server owned by the attacker. The adversary then waited for the release of a new software update, which when installed resulted in overwriting the local cache of each compromised user and cleaned the traces of the exploit. After performing this attack, the adversary effectively gained access to secret keys that were—at least temporarily—on hot storage, resulting in a massive leakage without a practical solution for the users to prove ownership of their secret keys.

On a different threat vector, attacks against cold wallets storing elliptic curve secret keys are believed to be possible with the uprising of quantum computing. Major cryptocurrencies are based heavily on the ECDSA signature scheme. Therefore, an adversary capable of breaking the elliptic curve discrete logarithm problem (ECDLP) can extract the secret keys behind a wallet address, even though such keys never left the cold storage.

Structure in the ECDSA Secret Key. In both attacks mentioned earlier, the target is the secret key, *i.e.* the secret information kept by the wallet. Prior to the leakage, standard technique to prove ownership can be constructed by employing Zero Knowledge Proof of Knowledge (ZKPK) Protocols. The security derives directly from the zero knowledge and soundness properties of ZKPK. However, in the case of a *massive leakage*, any party can generate such proof. Therefore new techniques should be developed.

The main technical challenge is to combine two cryptographic schemes by adding the creation of "some structure" in the ECDSA secret key, which allows for the introduction of some sort of "proof of ownership" that prevents or at least minimizes the damage of situations like the IOTA Hack, while also providing quantum resistance, in the case of the massive leakage. Ideally, this new design should also be compatible with the current address system of cryptocurrencies by not significantly changing the ECDSA design.

We address the issue of guaranteeing backward compatibility with ECDSA based wallets by adding a nested "back up key" to generate a quantum secure "proof of ownership". In other words, we propose a technique to embed a nested private key (in addition to the ordinary private key) to be used only in situations when it is necessary to prove ownership.

1.1   Previous Work: Hash-Based Signatures

We briefly describe hash-based signatures and focus on the one-time use constructions, since these are the ones most closely related to our proposal and offer quantum resistance.

Typically, every signature scheme requires the use of a cryptographic hash function. Hash-based signature schemes rely solely on hash functions and, as a result, do not require any additional cryptographic or computational assumption. Since there are cryptographically-secure hash functions that are considered unfeasible to invert (later we review a more formal definition), users can provide a preimage that serves as proof of ownership of a specific public key.

Lamport [20] proposed a signature scheme that relies only on the security of one-way functions and can be used to sign multiple bits at once. For simplicity, we illustrate the example of the signing of a single bit, where the signer first generates two secret key values (x, y), and publishes the corresponding pair of hash values as the public key $PK = (\mathcal{H}(x), \mathcal{H}(y))$. The signer then releases the secret value x in case the bit to be signed is 0, or releases the secret value y in case the bit is 1. One of the main limitations of this scheme, however, is the fact that it can only produce one-time signatures (OTS).

Shortly after Lamport's publication, Winternitz [21] proposed a scheme known as the Winternitz one-time signature (W-OTS), that allowed the signing of several bits at once as opposed to individual bits. In this scheme, the public key is $\mathcal{H}^w(x)$ instead of the pair $(\mathcal{H}(x), \mathcal{H}(y))$. If the message byte to be signed is, for example, 20, then the signature output is $\mathcal{H}^{20}(x)$, such that $\mathcal{H}^i(x)$ means i nested hashes of x. Moreover, to prevent an attacker from modifying the signature, the signer also releases a checksum value associated with the signed byte. This checksum is designed to prevent the adversary to attempt to produce a forgery by increasing any of the bytes without invalidating the resulting signature.

Hülsing [16] published an upgrade called W-OTS$^+$ that shortens the signatures size and increases the security of the original Winternitz scheme. This construction uses a chaining function in addition to a family of keyed functions, along with the XOR of a random value (or mask) before applying the one-way function to a specific ladder height.

1.2   Our Contribution

We start by defining two new properties we introduce. They are *fallback* and *proof of ownership*. These properties extend the functionality of a signature scheme by (1) allowing, considering a ECDSA scheme, the continued use of a signature scheme despite the leakage of the secret key, albeit using a different scheme (*i.e.* variant of W-OTS$^+$), and (2) prove the ownership of a leaked key, even when it becomes public.

More concretely, regarding (1), in addition to the verification and secret key, the generation algorithm of our constructions also outputs the "back up key" which can be used with the secret key as a separate (quantum secure) signature scheme for the fallback situation. In such situation, our construction is usable for existing wallets, and relies solely on symmetric primitives which, when instantiated with the correct security parameter, are conjectured secure even against adversaries with quantum capabilities or adversaries with access to elliptic curve secret key material stored on hot wallets. Our construction is easily extendable and relevant in a hot/cold wallet setting where the hot wallet—permanently connected to the network—contains the elliptic curve public key and, if needed, the actual elliptic curve key pair. The cold wallet, on the other hand, is kept without any network connection and stores the quantum-secure key pair, including the "back up key".

Regarding (2), we observe that a variant of the W-OTS$^+$ signature scheme nested into the main signature scheme can be used to prove the ownership of an ECDSA secret key. Briefly, by design, the "back up key" is the secret key of the internally nested scheme, *i.e.*, W-OTS$^+$, while the ECDSA secret key is derived from the public key of the W-OTS$^+$ variant. Given that we have an internal signature scheme, the proof of ownership for the, potentially leaked ECDSA secret key, is the W-OTS$^+$ like signature. We emphasize that the combination of two different signature schemes is the main technical challenge of this work, and required a new breakthrough which is the new signature variant we propose: the Extended W-OTS$^+$, *i.e.* eW-OTS$^+$. Note that, likewise we adapt the W-OTS$^+$ signature scheme, other hash based signature schemes can also be adapted in a similar fashion.

The ECDSA secret key is generated by combining the eW-OTS$^+$ verification key ℓ tuple into a L-tree structure, similarly to other existing proposals for other hash based signatures [10]. The resulting value is then treated as the ECDSA secret key, making our practical key generation mechanism especially suited for digital wallets, requiring no change on existing blockchain system designs currently in use. We analyze the security of our construction starting by studying our proposed signature scheme eW-OTS$^+$ in the light of the existing attacks against symmetric cryptographic primitives, including quantum ones as described in [15,23]. Finally, we implemented a prototype with full test coverage and compared our results with reference implementations.

In summary, in this work we:

- introduce new properties for a digital scheme named *fallback* and *proof of ownership*;
- propose a new variant of the W-OTS$^+$ based signature scheme: Extended W-OTS$^+$;
- construct a protocol, named $\mathcal{S}_{leeve}$, for generation and verification of a (single) proof of ownership π and formalize its security based on the Extended W-OTS$^+$;

- report on the results of the experiments of our prototype, which implements the main routines of our construction;
- discuss how to extend our $\mathcal{S}_{leeve}$ construction for multiple proofs of ownership.

We showcase our protocol $\mathcal{S}_{leeve}$ as a tool for a catastrophic scenario as a massive leak of private information. As already happened [24], in order to minimize the damage, the system could be halted, until all the honest users are confirmed. The proof of ownership via $\mathcal{S}_{leeve}$ allows the users to confirm their authenticity, and its addresses, using a *back up key* stored separately (as will be formally introduced later when describing $\mathcal{S}_{leeve}$) and used only in situations like this. Furthermore, it is worth mentioning that although it does not help in the return of the potentially already stolen funds, once the system is stopped, $\mathcal{S}_{leeve}$ allows the quick and safe identification of the honest owners of the addresses.

2 Preliminaries

It is convenient to quickly review the ECDSA construction for digital signature and W-OTS$^+$ signature construction from [16].

Definition 1 (ECDSA). *Given a hash function H, the ECDSA signature scheme is the tuple* (Gen, Sign, Verify), *defined as in Table 1:*

Table 1. ECDSA construction.

Gen(1^λ)	Sign^H(m, sk)	Verify^H(m, vk, σ)
$x \xleftarrow{\$} \mathbb{Z}_p$	$z \leftarrow H(m)$	Parse: $(r, s) \xleftarrow{p} \sigma$
sk $\leftarrow x$	$t \xleftarrow{\$} \mathbb{Z}_p$	If $(r, s) \notin \mathbb{Z}_p$
vk $\leftarrow g^x$	$(e_x, e_y) \leftarrow g^t$	Return 0
return (vk, sk)	$r \leftarrow e_x \mod p$	$w \leftarrow s^{-1}$
	If $r = 0 \mod p$	$z \leftarrow H(m)$
	Pick another t	$u_1 \leftarrow zw \mod p$
	and start again	$u_2 \leftarrow rw \mod p$
	$s \leftarrow t^{-1} \cdot (z + r \cdot \text{sk})$	$(e_x, e_y) \leftarrow g^{u_1} \cdot \text{vk}^{u_2}$
	If $s = 0 \mod p$	If $(e_x, e_y) = (0, 0)$
	Pick another t	Return 0
	and start again	Return $r = e_x \mod p$
	Return $\sigma = (r, s)$	

The W-OTS$^+$ Construction. The Winternitz-OTS$^+$ signature schemes introduced by Hülsing [18] introduces an alternative signature scheme with quantum resistance. Their construction relies on a hash family and a chaining function which we now review.

Definition 2 (Family of Functions). *Given the security and the Winternitz parameters, respectively, $\lambda \in \mathbb{N}$ and $w \in \mathbb{N}, w > 1$, let a family of functions $\mathcal{H}_\lambda$ be $\{h_k : \{0,1\}^\lambda \to \{0,1\}^\lambda | k \in \mathcal{K}_\lambda\}$ with key space $\mathcal{K}_\lambda$.*

Definition 3 (Chaining Function). *Given a family of functions $\mathcal{H}_\lambda$, $x \in \{0,1\}^\lambda$, an iteration counter $i \in \mathbb{N}$, a key $k \in \mathcal{K}_\lambda$, for j λ−bit strings $\mathbf{r} = (r_1, \ldots, r_j) \in \{0,1\}^{\lambda \times j}$ with $j \geq i$, then we have the chaining function as follows*

$$c_k^i(x, \mathbf{r}) = \begin{cases} h_k(c_k^{i-1}(x, \mathbf{r}) \oplus r_i), & 1 \leq i \leq j; \\ x, & i = 0. \end{cases}$$

Additionally, we review the notation for the subset of randomness vector $\mathbf{r} = (r_1, \ldots, r_\ell)$. We denote by $\mathbf{r}_{a,b}$ the subset of $(r_a, \ldots, r_b)$.

Table 2. W-OTS$^+$ construction.

$\mathsf{Gen}_W^k(1^\lambda)$	$\mathsf{Sign}_W^k(\mathsf{m}, \mathsf{sk})$
Pick $(\ell + w - 1)$ λ-bit strings r_i	Compute $\mathsf{m} \to (\mathsf{m}_1, \ldots, \mathsf{m}_{\ell_1})$,
Set $\mathsf{sk}_i \leftarrow r_i$, for $1 \leq i \leq \ell$	for $\mathsf{m}_i \in \{0, \ldots, w-1\}$
Set $\mathsf{sk} = (\mathsf{sk}_1, \ldots, \mathsf{sk}_\ell)$	Compute checksum $C = \sum_{i=1}^{\ell_1}(w-1-\mathsf{m}_i)$,
Set $\mathbf{r} = (r_{\ell+1}, \ldots, r_{\ell+w-1})$	and its base w representation $(C_1, \ldots, C_{\ell_2})$,
Set $\mathsf{vk}_0 = (\mathbf{r}, k)$	for $C_i \in \{0, \ldots, w-1\}$
Set $\mathsf{vk}_i = c_k^{w-1}(\mathsf{sk}_i, \mathbf{r})$, $1 \leq i \leq \ell$	Parse $B = \mathsf{m} \| C$ as $(b_1, \ldots, b_{\ell_1 + \ell_2})$
Set $\mathsf{vk} = (\mathsf{vk}_0, \mathsf{vk}_1, \ldots, \mathsf{vk}_\ell)$	Set $\sigma_i = c_k^{b_i}(\mathsf{sk}_i, \mathbf{r})$, for $1 \leq i \leq \ell_1 + \ell_2$
Return $(\mathsf{sk}, \mathsf{vk})$	Return $\sigma = (\sigma_1, \ldots, \sigma_{\ell_1 + \ell_2})$

$\mathsf{Verify}_W^k(\mathsf{m}, \mathsf{vk}, \sigma)$
Compute $\mathsf{m} \to (\mathsf{m}_1, \ldots, \mathsf{m}_{\ell_1})$,
for $\mathsf{m}_i \in \{0, \ldots, w-1\}$
Compute checksum $C = \sum_{i=1}^{\ell_1}(w-1-\mathsf{m}_i)$,
and the base w representation $(C_1, \ldots, C_{\ell_2})$,
for $C_i \in \{0, \ldots, w-1\}$
Parse $B = \mathsf{m} \| C$ as $(b_1, \ldots, b_{\ell_1 + \ell_2})$
Return 1, if the following equations hold
$\mathsf{vk}_0 = (\mathbf{r}, k)$
$\mathsf{vk}_i = c_k^{w-1-b_i}(\sigma_i, \mathbf{r}_{b_i+1, w-1})$ for $1 \leq i \leq \ell_1 + \ell_2$

Definition 4 (W-OTS$^+$). *Given the security parameter λ, a chaining function c, and $k \leftarrow \mathcal{K}$ from the key space $\mathcal{K}$, the W-OTS$^+$ signature scheme is the tuple $(\mathsf{Gen}_W, \mathsf{Sign}_W, \mathsf{Verify}_W)$, defined as in Table 2:*

The Security of W-OTS$^+$. The standard security notion for digital signature schemes is existential unforgeability under adaptive chosen message attacks (EU-CMA) which is defined using the following experiment. By $\mathsf{Dss}(1^\lambda)$ we denote a digital signature scheme (Dss) with security parameter λ, then we model the security by defining the security experiment $\mathsf{Exp}_{\mathsf{Dss}(1^\lambda)}^{\mathsf{EU\text{-}CMA}}(\mathcal{A})$, as follows:

Experiment $\text{Exp}^{\text{EU-CMA}}_{\text{Dss}(1^\lambda)}(\mathcal{A})$

> (sk, pk) $\longleftarrow$ keygen(1^λ)
>
> $(M^*, \sigma^*) \longleftarrow \mathcal{A}^{\text{Sign}(sk, \cdot)}(\text{pk})$
>
> Let $\{M_i, \sigma_i\}_1^q$ be the query-answer pairs of Sign($sk, \cdot$)
>
> Return 1 iff Verify(pk, M^*, σ^*) = 1 and $M^* \notin \{M_i\}_1^q$

We define the success probability of the adversary $\mathcal{A}$ in the above EU-CMA experiment as

$$\text{Succ}^{\text{EU-CMA}}_{\text{Dss}(1^\lambda)}(\mathcal{A}) = \Pr[\text{Exp}^{\text{EU-CMA}}_{\text{Dss}(1^\lambda)}(\mathcal{A}) = 1].$$

Definition 5 (EU-CMA). *Let* $\lambda, t, q \in \mathbb{N}, t, q = poly(\lambda)$, *Dss a digital signature scheme. We call Dss EU-CMA-secure, if the maximum success probability* $\mathsf{InSec}^{EU\text{-}CMA}(Dss(1^\lambda); t, q)$ *of all possibly probabilistic adversaries A, running in time* $\leq t$, *making at most q queries to* Sign *in the above experiment, is negligible in* λ:

$$\mathsf{InSec}^{EU\text{-}CMA}(Dss(1^\lambda); t, q) = max\ \{Succ^{EU\text{-}CMA}_{Dss(1^\lambda)}(\mathcal{A})\} = negl(\lambda).$$

We note that our construction relies on the W-OTS$^+$ signature scheme, which is EU-CMA secure as long as the number of oracle queries of $\mathcal{A}$ is limited to one (i.e., $q = 1$).

Finally, we review a crucial property for the hash function which is a building block of the W-OTS$^+$ signature scheme.

Definition 6 (Second preimage resistance). *Given a hash function family* $\mathcal{H}_n$, *we define the success probability of an adversary* $\mathcal{A}$ *against the second-preimage resistance of* $\mathcal{H}_n$ *as*

$$Succ^{SPR}_{\mathcal{H}_n}(\mathcal{A}) = Pr[K \xleftarrow{\$} \{0,1\}^k; M \xleftarrow{\$} \{0,1\}^m;$$
$$M' \xleftarrow{\$} \mathcal{A}(K, M) : M' \neq M \wedge H_K(M) = H_K(M')].$$

3 New Properties: Proof of Ownership and Fallback

Our protocol relies on a Digital Signature. We assume there is a generation algorithm $\text{Gen}_\pi(1^\lambda)$ which outputs the pairs of keys, vk and sk, and backup information bk. Whereas the pair is the regular verification key, used for verifying a signature, and the secret-key used for issuing a signature, that allows the issuing of a *ownership proof* π, with the backup information bk, with respect to vk. More concretely, we require adding two extra algorithms, (Proof, Verify-proof), to the tuple (Gen$_\pi$, Sign, Verify), turning into our protocol named $\mathcal{S}_{leeve}$. Given $\text{Gen}_\pi(1^\lambda) \rightarrow (\text{vk}, \text{sk}, \text{bk})$, we have

- Proof(bk, c) $\rightarrow \pi$: it is a PPT algorithm that on input of the backup information bk and the challenge c, it outputs the ownership proof π;

- Verify-proof(vk, sk, π, c) $\rightarrow$ {0, 1}: it is a deterministic algorithm that on input of a public-key vk, secret-key sk, a ownership proof π and a challenge c, it outputs either 0, for an invalid proof, or 1 for a valid one.

We remark that sk is used as a regular secret key with Sign and Verify. Given the earlier formulation, we now introduce the property of *Proof of Ownership*.

Definition 7 (Proof of Ownership). *For any probabilistic polynomial time (PPT) algorithm $\mathcal{A}$, it holds*

$$\Pr[(vk, sk, bk) \leftarrow \mathsf{Gen}_\pi(1^\lambda) : (c^*, \pi^*) \leftarrow \mathcal{A}(sk, vk)$$
$$\wedge \mathsf{Verify\text{-}proof}(vk, sk, \pi^*, c^*) = 1] < negl(\lambda)$$

for all the probabilities are computed over the random coins of the generation and proof verification algorithms and the adversary.

Remark 1 (Prove of knowledge is not enough). Note that an alternative method to prove ownership of a secret-key, fairly straightforward in discrete logarithm based signatures, relies on regular Zero Knowledge Proof of Knowledge Protocol (ZKP), when the signer simply proves the *knowledge* of the secret key. However we argue that, in the case where the secret key is leaked, the security guarantees are voided in such method. On the other hand, the early introduced definition requires a proof of ownership, despite the secret key being already in possession of the adversary, thus showing that *knowledge* of the secret key is not enough.

We now formally introduce the property which allows the permanent switch from the secret key sk, *e.g.* in the case it is hopelessly public, to a brand new "back up secret key" bk, that is, the new, and still protected, secret key is only known to the signer. In addition to the new secret key bk, there is also a brand new signature scheme where the new verification key is the assumed leaked secret key sk.

Remark 2 (Informal meaning of proof). Our earlier definition for Proof of Ownership is formally not a "proof" in the sense of ZKP. For example, it is easy to see we skip completeness and zero-knowledge like security properties. Still following the analogy, our introduced property is equivalent to the ZKP "soundness", and that is enough for our purposes.

Definition 8 (Fallback). *We say that the scheme* (Gen_π, Sign, Verify), *with secret and verification key respectively* sk *and* vk *such that* $\mathsf{Gen}_\pi(1^\lambda) \rightarrow$ (vk, sk, bk), *has fallback if there are sign and verification algorithms* Sign_π *and* Verify_π *such that* sk *and* bk *can be used as verification and secret keys respectively, along with* Sign_π *and* Verify_π *to satisfy Definition 5.*

Remark 3 (Use case for current blockchains-Tranfer of funds). It is worth mention that the current blockhain designs are not compatible with hash based signatures such as W-OTS$^+$. However our design could be used to authenticate to a third party, as, for example, in the case of [24]. Another alternative is to rely on the fallback feature, and the proof of ownership, to transfer the potentially endangered funds to an address or account of a newly created public/private key. Note in such a case, the ECDSA secret key could be exposed since the fund would be securely transferred to a new and safe pair of keys.

4   Protocol Design Overview

Our construction for the Proof of Ownership as presented in Sect. 3 is heavily based on the W-OTS+ Signature Scheme. Before presenting how to construct such proofs, we detail the adaptation of the original construction, described in Definition 4, in order to introduce the Extended W-OTS+ which will be used in combination with ECDSA.

4.1   Adaptation of W-OTS+

Roughly speaking, our construction allows users to generate a quantum secure key pair and, from those values, derive an elliptic curve wallet to be used for cryptocurrency transactions. For simplicity of explanation, we assume the quantum-secure key material to be a W-OTS+ key pair and the elliptic curve wallet to use the ECDSA algorithm. We note, however, that our construction can be easily extended to use other cryptographic primitives.

The L-Tree Data Structure.   We rely on the data structure introduced by Dahmen et al. [10] to keep the W-OTS+ public key. The L-Tree of height h stores 2^h leaves (such that $2^h \geq \ell + 1$, the size of W-OTS+ public key). Each node of the tree is denoted by $y_i[j]$, for node index from left to right is $j = 0, \ldots, 2^i - 1$ and $i = 0, \ldots, h$, and the root is the node $y_0[0]$. The nodes of the tree are computed using a hash function H_x selected from a keyed hash family $\mathcal{H} = \{H_x : \{0,1\}^{2n} \rightarrow \{0,1\}^n\}_{x \in \mathcal{K}}$. On a given level i and node j of the tree, each input is computed by the concatenation of the left and right children nodes outputs, after each was bit wise XORed by the masks $v_i[0]$ and $v_i[1]$, for n-bit strings chosen at uniformly at random. More formally, for $i = h, \ldots, 0$ and $j = 0, \ldots, 2^i - 1$, we have

$$y_i[j] = H_x((y_{i+1}[2j] \oplus v_i[0]) \| (y_{i+1}[2j+1] \oplus v_i[1])).$$

The Typical Combination of W-OTS+ and L-Tree.   Since its introduction in [10], L-Trees have been used in combination with hash based signature schemes [17]. For simplicity, we describe a typical combination between W-OTS+ and L-Tree. Later we adapt this construction to suit our *Extended* W-OTS+ proposal. The L-Tree construction introduces three extra sets of values for the verification key W-OTS$_{vk}^+$, in addition to vk $= (vk_0, vk_1, \ldots, vk_\ell)$ as given by Table 2. They are

- The hash family index x;
- The XOR masks $v_i[0]$ and $v_i[1]$ for $i = 0, \ldots, h$;
- The root value $y_0[0]$.

In order to create a new wallet, a user randomly generates a cryptographicaly secure seed value, to be used to derive the W-OTS$^+$ public seed, the W-OTS$^+$ secret keys $(sk_1, ..., sk_\ell)$, and the hash key x. Once the derivation step is completed, clients use the chaining function to obtain all the W-OTS$^+$ ladder values. The top ladder values are the components of the W-OTS$^+$ public key, which are compressed into a single value using the earlier described L-Trees. Let this value be $L_{v,x}(\text{vk}_0, \text{vk}_1, \ldots, \text{vk}_\ell)$ for the set of h XOR masks and hash family index x.

L-Tree and Extended W-OTS$^+$. We now propose a new construction for W-OTS$^+$, denoted Extended W-OTS$^+$ (eW-OTS$^+$). The motivation of the novel design is to allow the nesting of the W-OTS$^+$ public key into a regular ECDSA secret key, and yet allow the construction of proofs of ownership. This combination of keys will be presented later. The main differences between W-OTS$^+$ and the eW-OTS$^+$ designs are (1) the key generation algorithm incorporates the typical construction with L-Tree earlier described into the key generation, (2) the regular W-OTS$^+$ public key is changed to pk, and (3) the secret key tuple has an extra term, $i.e.$ sk_0, instead of the regular terms $\text{sk}_1, \ldots, \text{sk}_\ell$. eW-OTS$^+$ is introduced because we assume that the nested W-OTS$^+$ public key is in the public domain and, without this extension, any adversary would be able to obtain the ECDSA secret key value by simply hashing the W-OTS$^+$ public key. The full construction is given by Definition 9.

Definition 9 (eW-OTS$^+$). *Given the security parameter λ, a chaining function c, and $k \leftarrow \mathcal{K}$ from the key space $\mathcal{K}$, an unkeyed hash function $\mathcal{H}$, then the eW-OTS$^+$ signature scheme is the tuple* $(\text{Gen}_{eW}, \text{Sign}_{eW}, \text{Verify}_{eW})$, *defined as in Table 3:*

Note that the Extended W-OTS$^+$ construction has as key pair (sk, pk) which differs from the regular construction (sk, vk) of W-OTS$^+$. The reader will certainly notice the need for the notation change in the public key from vk to pk in the next section, when the combination between ECDSA and eW-OTS$^+$ is described and we use both terms.

The ECDSA Key Pair from eW-OTS$^+$. We assume that the elliptic curve wallet is generated in a one-way manner, which means that if the ECDSA wallet is compromised, then the user can prove ownership of the wallet by providing a signature from the eW-OTS$^+$ key pair, which is assumed secure. More formally $\text{pk} = (\text{vk}_0, L, \text{sk}_0)$, as defined in Table 3, is the input in a unkeyed hash function $\mathcal{H}$, resulting in $\mathcal{H}(\text{vk}_0, \mathcal{H}(L, \text{sk}_0))$, which is the ECDSA private key, sk, and can be used to calculate the public key using the trapdoor function of the signature scheme. The ECDSA public and secret key are, respectively, $\text{sk}_{ECDSA} = \mathcal{H}(\text{vk}_0, \mathcal{H}(L, \text{sk}_0))$ and $\text{vk}_{ECDSA} = g^{\mathcal{H}(\text{vk}_0, \mathcal{H}(L, \text{sk}_0))}$. Figure 1 illustrates a simplified diagram of our construction. Typically cryptocurrencies, such

Table 3. Extended W-OTS$^+$ Signature Scheme with the changes from the original W-OTS$^+$ construction (Table 2) highlighted in blue. The changes introduced by our construction are necessary in order to be used in combination with ECDSA signatures.

$\mathsf{Gen}^k_{eW}(1^\lambda)$	$\mathsf{Sign}^k_{eW}(\mathsf{m}, \mathsf{sk})$
Pick $(\ell + w - 1)$ λ-bit strings r_i	Parse $\mathsf{sk} \to (\mathsf{sk}_0, \mathsf{sk}_1, \ldots, \mathsf{sk}_\ell)$
Pick a hash index family x	Parse $\mathsf{sk}_0 \to (v, x)$
Pick h pairs $v = (v_1[0], v_1[1], \ldots, v_h[0], v_h[1])$	Set $\sigma_0 = \mathsf{sk}_0$
$\mathsf{sk}_0 = (v_1[0], v_1[1], \ldots, v_h[0], v_h[1], x)$	Compute $\mathsf{m} \to (\mathsf{m}_1, \ldots, \mathsf{m}_{\ell_1})$,
Set $\mathsf{sk}_i \gets r_i$, for $1 \le i \le \ell$	for $\mathsf{m}_i \in \{0, \ldots, w-1\}$
Set $\mathsf{sk} = (Set\mathsf{sk}_0, \mathsf{sk}_1, \ldots, \mathsf{sk}_\ell)$	Compute checksum $C = \sum_{i=1}^{\ell_1}(w - 1 - \mathsf{m}_i)$,
Set $\mathbf{r} = (r_{\ell+1}, \ldots, r_{\ell+w-1})$	w-base representation $(C_1, \ldots, C_{\ell_2})$,
Set $\mathsf{vk}_0 = (\mathbf{r}, k)$	for $C_i \in \{0, \ldots, w-1\}$
Set $\mathsf{vk}_i = c_k^{w-1}(\mathsf{sk}_i, \mathbf{r})$, $1 \le i \le \ell$	Parse $B = \mathsf{m}\|C$ as $(b_1, \ldots, b_{\ell_1+\ell_2})$
SetSet $L = L_{v,x}(\mathsf{vk}_1, \ldots, \mathsf{vk}_\ell)$	Set $\sigma_i = c_k^{b_i}(\mathsf{sk}_i, \mathbf{r})$, for $1 \le i \le \ell_1 + \ell_2$
Set $\mathsf{pk} = (\mathsf{vk}_0, L, \mathsf{sk}_0)$	Return $\sigma = (\sigma_0, \sigma_1, \ldots, \sigma_{\ell_1+\ell_2})$
Return $(\mathsf{sk}, \mathsf{pk})$	

$\mathsf{Verify}^k_{eW}(\mathsf{m}, \mathsf{pk}, \sigma)$
Parse $\mathsf{pk} \to (\mathsf{pk}_0, \mathsf{pk}_1, \mathsf{pk}_2)$
Parse $\mathsf{pk}_0 \to (\mathbf{r}, k)$
Parse $\sigma \to (\sigma_0, \sigma_1, \ldots, \sigma_{\ell_1+\ell_2})$, $\sigma_0 \to (v, x)$
Compute $\mathsf{m} \to (\mathsf{m}_1, \ldots, \mathsf{m}_{\ell_1})$,
for $\mathsf{m}_i \in \{0, \ldots, w-1\}$
Compute checksum $C = \sum_{i=1}^{\ell_1}(w - 1 - \mathsf{m}_i)$,
and the base w representation $(C_1, \ldots, C_{\ell_2})$,
for $C_i \in \{0, \ldots, w-1\}$
Parse $B = \mathsf{m}\|C$ as $(b_1, \ldots, b_{\ell_1+\ell_2})$
Set $\mathsf{vk}_i = c_k^{w-1-b_i}(\sigma_i, \mathbf{r}_{b_i+1, w-1})$ for $1 \le i \le \ell_1 + \ell_2$
Compute the L-Tree root as $L_{v,x}(\mathsf{vk}_1, \ldots, \mathsf{vk}_{\ell_1+\ell_2})$
Return 1, if the following equations hold
$\mathsf{pk}_1 = L_{v,x}(\mathsf{vk}_1, \ldots, \mathsf{vk}_{\ell_1+\ell_2})$
$\mathsf{pk}_2 = \sigma_0$

as Bitcoin [22], Ethereum [26], Cardano [2] and even general frameworks [19] for wallet address are built by hashing the ECDSA public key. Therefore, to integrate our construction in certain settings, an additional hash of the elliptic curve public key value is necessary, *i.e.* $\mathcal{H}(\mathsf{vk}_{ECDSA})$.

4.2 Ownership Proof Generation and Verification

As described in Sect. 3, the signature scheme that offers Proof of Ownership is a tuple $(\mathsf{Gen}_\pi, \mathsf{Sign}, \mathsf{Verify}, \mathsf{Proof}, \mathsf{Verify\text{-}proof})$, such that $\mathsf{Gen}_\pi(1^\lambda) \to (\mathsf{vk}, \mathsf{sk}, \mathsf{bk})$, $\mathsf{Proof}(\mathsf{bk}, c) \to \pi$ and $\mathsf{Verify\text{-}proof}(\mathsf{vk}, \mathsf{sk}, \pi, c) \to \{0, 1\}$. In order to construct such scheme we combine the ECDSA and eW-OTS$^+$ designs. The generation and verification of signatures are respectively carried by Sign and Verify as regular ECDSA signatures. The proof of ownership is put forth by the eW-OTS$^+$

design via the Proof and Verify-proof algorithms. Put simply, the tuple $(\mathsf{vk}, \mathsf{sk})$ is the regular ECDSA key pair, such that sk is generated from the underpinning eW-OTS$^+$ public key pk. Whereas bk is the eW-OTS$^+$ secret key $(\mathsf{sk}_0, \mathsf{sk}_1, \ldots, \mathsf{sk}_\ell)$ corresponding to pk.

It remains to introduce the Gen_π algorithm to generate the tuple $(\mathsf{vk}, \mathsf{sk}, \mathsf{bk})$.

The Generation of the "back up key". Intuitively, the proof of ownership of the key, requires similar properties of an identification scheme between a prover and a verifier instantiated by a particular signature scheme. In our construction, the identification scheme is based on the earlier introduced eW-OTS$^+$ design. More concretely, given a challenge as a message provided by the verifier, the prover only needs to sign this message with bk. As described earlier, let the ECDSA key pair be $\mathsf{sk} = \mathcal{H}(\mathsf{pk})$, for $\mathsf{pk} = (\mathsf{vk}_0, L, \mathsf{sk}_0)$, and $\mathsf{vk} = g^{\mathcal{H}(\mathsf{vk}_0, \mathcal{H}(L, \mathsf{sk}_0))}$ for an unkeyed hash function $\mathcal{H}$. Therefore the "back up secret key" bk is $(\mathsf{sk}_0, \mathsf{sk}_1, \ldots, \mathsf{sk}_\ell)$, the eW-OTS$^+$ secret-key, is illustrated in Table 3. For completeness, we present the construction of algorithm $\mathsf{Gen}_\pi(1^\lambda) \rightarrow (\mathsf{vk}, \mathsf{sk}, \mathsf{bk})$. Note that in the following construction, the key pair $(\mathsf{vk}, \mathsf{sk})$ can be used as regular signature (*i.e.* for the ECDSA Signature), that is with algorithms (Sign, Verify) as in Table 1.

Generation and Verification of the Proof π. Whereas the regular ECDSA signatures are generated and verified via the pair of algorithms (Sign, Verify) and the keys $(\mathsf{sk}, \mathsf{vk})$ generated via construction Table 4. The proof generation and verification are done via the algorithms for W-OTS$^+$ described by Table 3. More concretely, the algorithm $\mathsf{Proof}^k(\mathsf{bk}, c)$, for a challenge c, is implemented by the algorithm Sign_{eW}, whereas the proof verification Verify-proof$(\mathsf{vk}, \mathsf{sk}, \pi, c)$ is based on an adaptation of the signature verification $\mathsf{Verify}^k_{eW}(\mathsf{pk}, \sigma, \mathsf{m})$. The full description of the procedure is on Table 5.

We argue that the construction can be extended to provide multiple proofs of ownership by adding more eW-OTS$^+$ instances "underneath" the main one presented in Table 4. For the purpose of this work and also for page limitation, it is not necessary to fully describe the algorithms. However we present an informal description of the construction later in Sect. 9.

Practical Considerations. The back up key bk is not necessary to the regular use in combination with the ECDSA scheme, *i.e.* the blockchain use. In order to guarantee a secure and legit use of the bk, that is the generation of proof of ownership in case of a catastrophic leakage, bk should be kept in a separate storage, *i.e.* cold storage.

Table 4. The algorithm Gen_π, likewise the eW-OTS$^+$ construction, adds a L data structure into its procedure, and outputs also the "back up secret key" bk.

$\mathsf{Gen}_\pi^k(1^\lambda)$

Pick uniform random strings $(\ell + w - 1)$ λ-bit strings r_i

Set $\mathsf{bk}_i \leftarrow r_i$, for $1 \leq i \leq \ell$

Pick a hash index family x

Pick n-bit random masks $v_i[0]$ and $v_i[1]$, for $i = 0, \ldots, \log \ell$

Set $\mathsf{bk}_0 = (v_1[0], v_1[1], \ldots, v_{\log \ell}[0], v_{\log \ell}[1], x)$

Set $\mathsf{bk} = (\mathsf{bk}_0, \mathsf{bk}_1, \ldots, \mathsf{bk}_\ell)$

Set $\mathbf{r} = (r_{\ell+1}, \ldots, r_{\ell+w-1})$

Set $\mathsf{vk}_0 = (\mathbf{r}, k)$

Set $\mathsf{vk}_i = c_k^{w-1}(\mathsf{bk}_i, \mathbf{r})$, $1 \leq i \leq \ell$

Set nodes $y_i[j]$ for $j = 0, \ldots, \ell - 1$ and $i = \log \ell, \ldots, 0$ as

$\quad y_{\log \ell}[0] = \mathcal{H}_x(\mathsf{vk}_1), \ldots, y_{\log \ell}[\ell - 1] = \mathcal{H}_x(\mathsf{vk}_\ell)$

$\quad y_i[j] = H_x((y_{i+1}[2j] \oplus v_i[0]) \| (y_{i+1}[2j + 1] \oplus v_i[1]))$

Set $L = y_0[0]$

Set $\mathsf{sk} = (\mathsf{vk}_0, L, \mathsf{bk}_0)$

Set $\mathsf{vk} = g^{\mathcal{H}(\mathsf{vk}_0, \mathcal{H}(L, \mathsf{bk}_0))}$

Return $(\mathsf{sk}, \mathsf{vk}, \mathsf{bk})$

Table 5. The verification of the proof π adapts the verification procedure for eW-OTS$^+$ by adding an extra check on the ECDSA verification key vk.

Verify-proof$(\mathsf{vk}, \mathsf{sk}, c, \pi)$

Parse $\mathsf{sk} \rightarrow (\mathsf{sk}_0, \mathsf{sk}_1, \mathsf{sk}_2)$

Parse $\mathsf{sk}_0 \rightarrow (\mathbf{r}, k)$

Parse $\pi \rightarrow (\pi_0, \pi_1, \ldots, \pi_{\ell_1+\ell_2}), \pi_0 \rightarrow (v, x)$

Compute $c \rightarrow (c_1, \ldots, c_{\ell_1})$,

$\quad$ for $c_i \in \{0, \ldots, w - 1\}$

Compute checksum $C = \sum_{i=1}^{\ell_1}(w - 1 - c_i)$,

$\quad$ and the base w representation $(C_1, \ldots, C_{\ell_2})$,

$\quad$ for $C_i \in \{0, \ldots, w - 1\}$

Parse $B = c \| C$ as $(b_1, \ldots, b_{\ell_1+\ell_2})$

Set $\mathsf{vk}_i = c_k^{w-1-b_i}(\pi_i, \mathbf{r}_{b_i+1,w-1})$ for $1 \leq i \leq \ell_1 + \ell_2$

Compute the L-Tree root as $L = L_{v,x}(\mathsf{vk}_1, \ldots, \mathsf{vk}_{\ell_1+\ell_2})$

Return 1, if the following equations hold

$\mathsf{sk}_1 = L$

$\mathsf{sk}_2 = \pi_0$

$\mathsf{vk} = g^{\mathcal{H}(\mathsf{sk}_0, \mathcal{H}(L, \pi_0))}$

---

5 Ownership, Fallback and eW-OTS$^+$ Security

Here we argue about the properties of our construction for $\mathcal{S}_{leeve}$, providing *Fallback* and generation of *Proof of Ownership*. However, first we describe the security level provided by our design based on the eW-OTS$^+$ construction of Table 3, and we consider it has a security level λ if a successful attack is expected to require on average $2^{\lambda-1}$ evaluations of the used hash function family.

Unforgeability of eW-OTS$^+$. More concretely, we base the security of the extended W-OTS$^+$ on the existential unforgeability of the underlying W-OTS$^+$ signature scheme and the (multi-target) second preimage resistance of the used hash function. Recall that the existential unforgeability under chosen message attack (EU-CMA) for one-time signature schemes is defined when the number of signature queries is limited to 1 [16]. Then we have the following theorem.

Theorem 1. *Given the EU-CMA security of W-OTS$^+$, the Extended W-OTS$^+$ from Table 3 is existentially unforgeable under adaptive chosen message attacks, if $\mathcal{H}_n$ is from a second-preimage resistant hash function family.*

Proof. W-OTS$^+$ uses a family of functions $\mathcal{F}_n : \{f_k : \{0,1\}^n \to \{0,1\}^n | k \in \mathcal{K}_n\}$ with a key space $\mathcal{K}_n$. We know from [16] that, to attack the EU-CMA property, an adversary $\mathcal{A}$ must be able to break the following security level, λ_1, such that $\lambda_1 \geqslant n - \log_2(w^2\ell + w)$.

Alternatively, $\mathcal{A}$ may attempt to subvert the underlying hash function $\mathcal{H}$ we introduce in our construction.

To successfully attack this additional step introduced in the extended W-OTS$^+$ and produce a forged signature, $\mathcal{A}$ must break the second-preimage resistance property of $\mathcal{H}$ and find a colliding $L(\text{W-OTS}_{vk}^+)'$ that matches the target hash output.

We show in Appendix A that the cost of this attack for an n-bit hash is 2^n. Additionally, we know that in a real-world cryptocurrency setting, the adversary has the advantage of being able to perform multi-target attacks on any of the existing d outputs, which results in the following security level of $\lambda_2 \leqslant n_1 - log_2(d)$. Given the above tight bounds, we obtain the security level (λ) of the extended W-OTS$^+$, which is $\lambda \leq min\ \{\lambda_1, \lambda_2\}$.

For simplicity, we assume that $n = n_1$. We, therefore, obtain that the best attack against the extended W-OTS$^+$ construction is the same attack against the original W-OTS$^+$. As a result, if the adversary is able to break the EU-CMA property of the extended W-OTS$^+$, then it can break the unforgeability of the original W-OTS$^+$. Therefore, our construction is no weaker than the original as long as the output of the used hash function $\mathcal{H}$ is $n_1 \geqslant n$. $\square$

Security Regarding Ownership and Fallback. Now we describe the security of our scheme (Gen_π, Sign, Verify, Proof, Verify-proof). Given the eW-OTS$^+$ construction from Definition 9, let Sign_{eW} be the algorithm Proof, Gen_π is given by Table 4, while Verify-proof is given by Table 5, finally Sign and Verify are the ECDSA algorithms for signing and verifying signatures, respectively. For readability, let (Gen_π, Sign, Verify, Proof, Verify-proof) be known as $\mathcal{S}_{leeve}$ (as already mentioned in Sect. 3). Then we can claim the following properties of $\mathcal{S}_{leeve}$.

Corollary 1. *$\mathcal{S}_{leeve}$ generates a single proof of ownership π as per Definition 7.*

Proof. (Sketch) The proof π is an eW-OTS$^+$ signature on a challenge c. Given the security of eW-OTS$^+$ stated by Theorem 1, thereby π generated by $\mathcal{S}_{leeve}$ satisfies Definition 7. □

Now we show that tuple (Gen_π, Sign, Verify), parsed from $\mathcal{S}_{leeve}$ provides a Fallback signature scheme.

Theorem 2. *The tuple (Gen_π, Sign, Verify), derived from $\mathcal{S}_{leeve}$, has the Fallback property as per Definition 8.*

Proof. (Sketch) Following Definition 8, we need to show that there are algorithms Sign_π and Verify_π, such that sk and bk can derive regular verification and secret signatures. By considering the original construction $\mathcal{S}_{leeve}$, we have that $\mathsf{Sign}_\pi = $ Proof and $\mathsf{Verify}_\pi = $ Verify-proof, and this ends the proof. □

6   Applications

We divide this section into two parts. First, we describe a concrete example of how to proceed upon the suspicion of the existence of a successful attack against the computational assumptions that ensure the security of the ECDSA algorithm. Secondly, we introduce different real-world use cases that allow users to prove ownership of their wallet in the event where the ECDSA secret key is leaked, but the $\mathcal{S}_{leeve}$ backup key remains safe.

Hard Fork. If an attacker $\mathcal{A}$ is able to steal the secret keys behind a cryptocurrency wallet, then $\mathcal{A}$ is able to steal all the funds associated with that wallet. Since a $\mathcal{S}_{leeve}$ proof-of-ownership does not convince $\mathcal{A}$ to return the stolen funds, at first glance it may appear that there is no reason to have a fallback mechanism as all these funds are gone.

$\mathcal{S}_{leeve}$ is better suited for situations where the signature scheme associated with the quantum-secure backup can be used as a direct replacement for the original scheme. In a blockchain, this signature transition is only possible by making significant changes in the protocol, which create an alternative blockchain. This process is known as a hard fork. Using our construction, any blockchain can perform a signature scheme transition and allow any user to claim ownership of potentially stolen funds. As quantum algorithms become practical, blockchain platforms can recommend their users to create new wallet addresses using the $\mathcal{S}_{leeve}$ structure such that, when a hard fork is required, any user can produce a proof-of-ownership to transfer the funds to an address containing a new public key.

$\mathcal{S}_{leeve}$ becomes even more applicable in token sales settings where the smart contracts enforce lockup periods to restrict buyers from selling purchased tokens. If there is evidence of a quantum attack against a blockchain, users can utilize the $\mathcal{S}_{leeve}$ construction to prove ownership of potentially compromised tokens and redeem them in an alternative manner while the lockup period is still active, thus ensuring that no theft occurs.

Revoking Wallet Addresses. It is extremely important for users to have the ability to revoke a wallet address they own. Therefore, user Alice should have the ability notify the network that a specific wallet address is to be considered invalid and rejected by the nodes when attempting to make a payment. Alice, in this example, has her ECDSA secret key stolen and revokes her stolen wallet address by creating a proof-of-ownership, using her backup key, to inform the network that her address is compromised and, simultaneously introduce a new wallet address to contain the funds associated with the initial wallet.

Insurance. An insurance company may, for example, need to refund a group of protected customers after a set of ECDSA private keys are leaked and the associated funds stolen. Any user whose key is present in this leak, if in possession of their $\mathcal{S}_{leeve}$ backup key, can remotely prove that they are the true owners of a specific wallet address and prove to the insurance company that they are entitled to the refund. The insurance company knows that an adversary is not able to produce such a forgery unless both keys are compromised.

7   Discussion

In this section we briefly discuss selected issues and analyze open problems as well as some future work challenges.

Fail-Stop Signatures. Traditional digital signatures allow a user Alice to produce signatures such that everyone who knows the public key of the signer Alice can verify such signature. Such signatures are computationally secure for the signer as they can be forged by an adversary with quantum capabilities. Once a signature is forged, it is difficult for the honest signer Alice to convince third parties that she did not produce the forged signature.

Fail-stop signatures [25] solve this problem by offering the signer a method to prove that a forgery took place. After receiving such a proof, the system should be stopped. As a result, the signer is protected from an arbitrarily powerful forgery since all participants, or an eventual system operator, know the signature scheme is broken, and should halt the system.

A possible enhancement for $\mathcal{S}_{leeve}$ is to alter the key generation to support the integration of fail-stop signatures. Instead of generating an ECDSA keypair from a hash-based key, users can generate a fail-stop keypair as this would allow a user to prove that a rogue signature is indeed a forgery and therefore instantiate the backup key to prove the true ownership of a key pair.

Tweakable Hash Functions. In hash-based signature schemes, it is important to use constructions that use security notions such as second-preimage and preimage resistance instead of collision resistance. Different hash-based schemes focus on different ways to achieve these more specific security notions as they substantially enhance the security level of the produced signatures. However, the main idea behind the different constructions to achieve these specific security notions is similar enough that it is possible to create an abstraction, such that it is not necessary to provide a new security analysis for each of the alternatives to move towards (second) preimage resistance.

The work from [5] introduces an abstraction—called tweakable hash functions—which allows protocol designers to unify the description of hash-based signature schemes, separating the exact details of how the scheme computes tree nodes typically used in hash-based constructions. This division allows for the separation of the analysis of the high-level construction from the analysis of how this computation is done. As a result, changing the way nodes are computed in a hash-based signature scheme only requires analyzing the hashing construction as a tweakable hash function.

One optimization we introduce is the use of tweakable hash functions to compress all the W-OTS$^+$ top ladder values into a single root value, which results in a more simplified implementation with better performance.

Cold Storage. Using $\mathcal{S}_{leeve}$ does not necessarily imply that both the ECDSA secret key and the backup key should be stored in different cold storage units. For example, a quantum adversary can gain rogue access to an ECDSA secret key by breaking the discrete log problem using only public information such as the public keys that are present in a blockchain. In this setting, the fallback key remains securely stored and can be freely used by the wallet owner.

To increase the security of $\mathcal{S}_{leeve}$ it is possible, however, to use different storage for the secret key and the backup key to ensure that if a wallet owner moves the ECDSA secret key to a hot wallet, and such a wallet is compromised, then the owner remains protected as the adversary $\mathcal{A}$ should not be able to gain access to the cold wallet containing the $\mathcal{S}_{leeve}$ backup key.

Backwards Compatibility. Ideally, users should be able to use the ideas behind $\mathcal{S}_{leeve}$ to use the seed phrase of a hierarchical deterministic wallet and retroactively prove ownership of a specific wallet address. The feasibility of this remains undefined and represents an interesting future work challenge as it would allow any user to utilize this approach and have the ability to prove ownership of wallet address with guaranteed backwards compatibility with any wallet that supports the use of seed phrases to generate hierarchical deterministic wallets.

We note that our construction preserves the structure of both the ECDSA private and public keys, and if the user actually relies on two different cold storage solutions—one for the ECDSA key and the other for the $\mathcal{S}_{leeve}$ backup key—then it is possible to achieve backwards compatibility as the storage of the ECDSA key pair does not require any particular or different treatment.

To support the $\mathcal{S}_{leeve}$ backup key, however, both the wallets and the blockchain require protocol modifications. Wallets require modification to have the ability to generate hash-based signatures, while the blockchain needs to be modified to have the ability of verifying these hash-based signatures.

Compatibility with Different Post-quantum Signature Schemes. $\mathcal{S}_{leeve}$ is designed in a modular manner that allows the hiding of any quantum secure signature key pair, and is not exclusive to W-OTS$^+$. In this paper, we particularly focus on W-OTS$^+$ as a fallback for ECDSA because it corresponds to the real-world use case that inspired the creation of this construction. Platforms, however, have the flexibility to use different signature schemes accordingly.

Informal Multiple Proofs Construction. The construction introduced in Sect. 4 allows only a single proof. The reason is that eW-OTS$^+$ signature scheme is one-time signature scheme. Here we informally describe a construction to allow the generation of several proofs. The basic change is in the generation of the secret-key tuple $bk_0, bk_1, \ldots, bk_\ell$. Whereas in the previous constructions of Tables 3 and 4 the values in the tuple are picked at random, the extended version computes t tuples, where each set of values $(bk_0^{(j-1)}, bk_1^{(j-1)}, \ldots, bk_\ell^{(j-1)})$ is generated from executing a *Key Derivation Function* (KDF) from the previous tuple $(bk_0^{(j)}, bk_1^{(j)}, \ldots, bk_\ell^{(j)})$, for $j \leq t$. More concretely, $bk_1^{(j-1)} = KDF(L^{(j)})$, and $bk_i^{(j-1)} = KDF(L^{(j)}||salt^{(j-1)}||i)$ for $1 < i \leq \ell$, randomly chosen values $salt^{(j-1)}$ and the L-Tree root value $L^{(j)}$ of the underlying construction *i.e.* eW-OTS$^+$ instance with index j. Thus, for a t-backup key value construction, the generation is as follows:

- Pick $bk_0^{(j)} = (x^{(j)}, v_1^{(j)}[0], v_1^{(j)}[1], \ldots, v_{\log \ell}^{(j)}[0], v_{\log \ell}^{(j)}[1])$, for $1 \leq j \leq t$;
- Pick $vk_0^{(j)} = (r^{(j)}, k^{(j)})$, for $1 \leq j \leq t$, and $(r^{(j)}, k^{(j)})$ chosen as (r, k) in Table 4;
- Pick random values $(bk_1^{(j)}, \ldots, bk_\ell^{(j)})$;

- Given $\mathbf{bk}_0^{(j)}$ and $(\mathbf{bk}_1^{(j)}, \ldots, \mathbf{bk}_\ell^{(j)})$, compute $L^{(j)}$;
- Compute $\mathbf{bk}_1^{(j-1)} = KDF(L^{(i)})$, and $\mathbf{bk}_i^{(j-1)} = KDF(L^{(j)}||salt^{(j-1)}||i)$ for $1 < i \leq \ell, t \geq j \geq 1$ and randomly chosen values $salt^{(j-1)}$.

The intuition is to add $t - 1$ eW-OTS$^+$ constructions "underneath" the upmost one. The public key of the underlying eW-OTS$^+$ instance, generates, via KDF (which can be constructed by a hash function), the secret key of the next (*i.e.* $\mathbf{bk}_1^{(j-1)}$, the last line of the above description).

The verification algorithm for such multiple construction has to take into account in which "level" (from t to 0, in the above description) the signature was generated, and be continually updated on each new signature generation. For comparison, the construction for a single proof only has one level. The "multilevel" p-th proof is of the form

$$\pi = ((\pi_0, \ldots, \pi_{\ell_1 + \ell_2}), (\mathbf{vk}_0^{(1)}, \mathbf{sk}_0^{(1)}, L^{(1)}, salt^{(1)}), \ldots,$$
$$(\mathbf{vk}_0^{(p+1)}, \mathbf{sk}_0^{(p+1)}, L^{(p+1)}, salt^{(p+1)})),$$

for $\mathbf{vk}_0^{(p)} = (v^{(p)}, x^{(p)})$ and $\mathbf{sk}_0^{(p)} = (\mathbf{r}^{(p)}, k^{(p)})$. Thus the verification procedure transverse the underneath structure of eW-OTS$^+$ instances from some point p, *i.e.* the p-th proof, up to the upmost one. Roughly the procedure is as follows:

- Compute $\mathbf{vk}_i^{(p-1)} = c_k^{w-1-b_i}(\pi_i, \mathbf{r}_{b_i+1,w-1}^{(p-1)})$;
- Compute $L^{(p-1)} = L_{v^{(p-1)}, x^{(p-1)}}(\mathbf{vk}_1^{(p-1)}, \ldots, \mathbf{vk}_{\ell_1+\ell_2}^{(p-1)})$.

For $p - 1 < j \leq 1$,

- Compute $\mathbf{sk}_i^{(j)} = KDF(L^{(j-1)}||salt^{(j-1)}||i)$;
- Compute $\mathbf{vk}_i^{(j)} = c_{k^{(j)}}^{w-1}(\mathbf{sk}_i^{(j)}, \mathbf{r}_{b_i+1,w-1}^{(j)})$;
- Compute $L^{(j)} = L_{v^{(j)}, x^{(j)}}(\mathbf{vk}_1^{(j)}, \ldots, \mathbf{vk}_{\ell_1+\ell_2}^{(j)})$,

at this point the verification boils down to the correctness of the value $L = L^{(1)}$ as before.

8 Experimental Results

To validate our results, we implemented a single-threaded prototype in Golang [13].

We note that this implementation does not combine the W-OTS$^+$ public key values using an L-Tree structure. Instead, our implementation uses a tweakable hash function to combine all the W-OTS$^+$ ladder top values into a single root value. Since our construction has a very concrete application, we implemented an additional implementation variant that includes the BIP 39 [6] standard to generate the hidden W-OTS$^+$ fallback from a mnemonic seed. We verified the correctness of this code by comparing it with reference BIP39 implementations [7,14].

We ran our experiments on a 2.8 GHz Quad-Core Intel Core i7 with 16 GB of RAM, running 64-bit macOS 10.15.6. Below, we expose a table containing the corresponding performance of our prototype.

Table 6. Performance metrics of our custom implementation.

Algorithm	Execution time (ms)		
	Gen	Sign	Verify
$\mathcal{S}_{leeve}$	3.87	0.024	1.472
$\mathcal{S}_{leeve}$ w/ BIP39	7.51	0.024	1.472
ECDSA (on secp256r1)	0.77	0.069	0.084

These timings demonstrate that the key generation component of our design is significantly slower than presently used key generation mechanisms. Depending on the protocol instantiation, our key generation is between 5 to 10 times slower than a normal ECDSA key generation algorithm. We highlight, however, that this is an expected result given the amount of additional steps introduced by our construction. We also note that the key generation can be easily accelerated by performing the W-OTS$^+$ ladder calculations in parallel. Regarding key storage, our construction utilizes the same storage space as a normal ECDSA private key. For example, the wallet storage of a Bitcoin secret key would require 256-bits for both the $\mathcal{S}_{leeve}$ construction and for a normal wallet.

9   Conclusion

We proposed $\mathcal{S}_{leeve}$ as a new approach to integrate a quantum-secure fallback inside an elliptic curve private key. The core idea is to have a hidden hash-based signing key pair. The users can show they are the rightful owner of the cryptocurrency secret keys even in the presence of an adversary capable of breaking the elliptic curve discrete logarithm problem, which is not a possibility using any of the existing curve-based cryptocurrency wallets. Moreover in catastrophic scenarios, where a massive leakage has potentially happened, and system is halted, users can show to trusted third parties that they are the correct owners of the wallet.

Along with $\mathcal{S}_{leeve}$, we presented also novel ideas for security guarantees and security analysis, aspiring that they will stimulate additional discussion, and potential improvements in the cryptocurrency wallet research community. As another contribution to the above mentioned discussion, we argue that the $\mathcal{S}_{leeve}$ construction can be changed to scale, in the sense that it can be extended to provide multiples proofs of ownership, $i.e.$ π_i for $t \geq i$ or to provide multiple signatures while in "fallback mode", or even $\mathcal{S}_{leeve}$ can be used combined with Fail-stop Signatures. As a final remark, we recall that although we presented a construction based on W-OTS$^+$ signature scheme, we believe other hash based signature schemes can be adapted in similar fashion.

A   Generic Attacks

The early presented constructions are hash based ones, therefore in this section we present an extensive list of computational complexities of various generic attacks against hash functions, while relating them with our constructions. Later we rely on these complexities to analyse and prove security of our proposed signature scheme.

Preimage Resistance. The adversary $\mathcal{A}$ may obtain a hash digest and attempt to invert the one-way property of the used hash function. Assuming that the inputs are uniform random n-bit values, then this preimage attack costs 2^n in the classical setting. In the post-quantum setting, using Grover's algorithm, this attack costs $2^{n/2}$.

Second Preimage Resistance (SPR). The adversary may instead attempt to find a second preimage of an n-bit message. Assuming a non-compressing hash function, that is, there is at least an n-bit-to-n-bit preimage to hash mapping, then this attack costs 2^n in the classic setting, and $2^{n/2}$ in the post-quantum setting.

Enhanced Target Collision Resistance (eTCR). The notion of eTCR implies that an adversary is allowed to choose a target message M. Upon choosing this target message, $\mathcal{A}$ learns the function $\mathcal{H}_K$ (by learning the key K) and the adversary wins after presenting a new message M' and a (possibly new) key K' such that $H_K(M) = H_{K'}(M')$.

A possible application of the eTCR game in our setting involves the adversary committing to a $L(\text{W-OTS}_{vk}^+)$ public key value and then obtaining the hash function key. There are two ways an adversary may attempt to break the eTCR property of a hash function. First, $\mathcal{A}$ may attempt to obtain a new $L(\text{W-OTS}_{vk}^+)'$ such that $H_K(L(\text{W-OTS}_{vk}^+)) = H_K(L(\text{W-OTS}_{vk}^+)')$. Second, $\mathcal{A}$ may attempt to obtain a new key K' and $L(\text{W-OTS}_{vk}^+)'$ such that $H_K(L(\text{W-OTS}_{vk}^+)) = H_{K'}(L(\text{W-OTS}_{vk}^+)')$.

If $\mathcal{A}$ owns the secret keys corresponding to the colliding $L(\text{W-OTS}_{vk}^+)'$, then $\mathcal{A}$ can forge a proof of ownership of the target wallet. This forgery costs at least 2^n pre-quantum, $2^{n/2}$ post-quantum (Grover's algorithm), and results in the adversary having the ability to prove ownership of an elliptic curve based wallet with a different fallback public key. We highlight, however, that even if the adversary can find a second preimage, it is not guaranteed that it corresponds to a $L(\text{W-OTS}_{vk}^+)'$ actually controlled by $\mathcal{A}$.

Multi-target Attacks. The previous definitions assume an adversary attacking one single target. We assume a hash function with n-bit outputs is used d times and each of these d outputs is publicly posted (*e.g.*, on a blockchain). The adversary $\mathcal{A}$ may, therefore, attempt to invert any of these public d values, which results in an attack complexity of $2^{n-log_2(d)}$ instead of 2^n. In order to show the effectiveness of a multi-target attack, we consider the case where all the secret keys associated with the wallet addresses are publicly exposed and are generated using our hidden key construction.

This setting results in a leakage of approximately 2^{29} target wallet addresses, for example [8,12], which results in an attack complexity cost of 2^{n-29}. Typically, ECDSA secret keys of 256 bits. Therefore, a multi-target attack in the setting we describe results in a direct loss of 29 bits in security, resulting in a cost of 2^{227} instead of 2^{256}. In a post-quantum setting[1], however, the adversary must perform $2^{n/2}/\sqrt{d}$, where $d < 2^{n/3}$.

Decisional Second-Preimage Resistance (DSPR). In [4], Bernstein and Hülsing introduce DSPR, which defines the advantage in deciding, given a random input x, whether x has a second preimage.

An adversary could potentially use this definition to determine in advance whether or not it is worth attacking the SPR (or eTCR) of a hash function. If the DSPR advantage is non-negligible, then the adversary can choose a wallet target, and determine in advance whether or not there is a second-preimage. For example, if there is not a second-preimage associated with a target wallet address, then the adversary can select another target address as opposed to spending unnecessary computational resources trying to find a non-existent value. The paper, however, proves that DSPR is at least as hard to break as preimage resistance (PRE) or second preimage resistance (SPR) for uniform random hash functions from $\{0,1\}^n$ to $\{0,1\}^n$. This results in an attack cost of 2^n in the classical setting, and $2^{n/2}$ in the post-quantum setting.

The authors considered ways to attack DSPR for real hash functions, and concluded that there is no obvious way for a fast attack to achieve any advantage. Consequently, $\mathcal{A}$ cannot take advantage of the DSPR notion to gain any non-negligible advantage in creating forged proof(s)-of-ownership.

---

[1] We highlight the work of Banegas and Bernstein [3] that studies the existing overhead beyond the quantum queries and shows that even in a post-quantum setting, the collision-finding algorithms costs at least $2^{n/2}$, even if it requires a smaller number of queries.

B   Simplified Description of the Construction

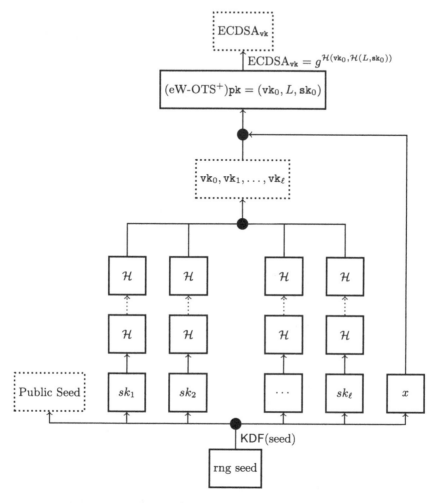

Fig. 1. Hidden key construction for eW-OTS$^+$. The dotted boxes are the potentially public values, while the normal boxes are the secret values. The diagram shows the commonly know as "ladders", *i.e.* the sequence of hash function executions up to the verification values, and "rng seed" generating randomness for the private hash key x.

References

1. Arapinis, M., Gkaniatsou, A., Karakostas, D., Kiayias, A.: A formal treatment of hardware wallets. In: Goldberg, I., Moore, T. (eds.) FC 2019. LNCS, vol. 11598, pp. 426–445. Springer, Cham (2019). https://doi.org/10.1007/978-3-030-32101-7_26

2. Badertscher, C., Gazi, P., Kiayias, A., Russell, A., Zikas, V.: Ouroboros genesis: composable proof-of-stake blockchains with dynamic availability. In: David, L., Mohammad, M., Michael, B., XiaoFeng, W., (eds), ACM CCS 2018: 25th Conference on Computer and Communications Security, Toronto, ON, Canada, 15–19 October 2018, pp. 913–930. ACM Press (2018)

3. Banegas, G., Bernstein, D.J.: Low-communication parallel quantum multi-target preimage search. In: Adams, C., Camenisch, J. (eds.) SAC 2017. LNCS, vol. 10719, pp. 325–335. Springer, Cham (2018). https://doi.org/10.1007/978-3-319-72565-9_16

4. Bernstein, D.J., Hülsing, A.: Decisional second-preimage resistance: when does SPR imply PRE? In: Galbraith, S.D., Moriai, S. (eds.) ASIACRYPT 2019. LNCS, vol. 11923, pp. 33–62. Springer, Cham (2019). https://doi.org/10.1007/978-3-030-34618-8_2

5. Bernstein, D.J., Hülsing, A., Kölb, S., Niederhagen, R., Rijneveld, J., Schwabe, P.: The SPHINCS$^+$ signature framework. In: Cavallaro et al. [9], pp. 2129–2146 (2019)

6. Mnemonic code for generating deterministic keys. https://github.com/bitcoin/bips/blob/master/bip-0039.mediawiki. Accessed 20 Jan 2020

7. Mnemonic code converter. https://iancoleman.io/bip39/. Accessed 20 Jan 2020

8. Study finds less than 40% of btc addresses are economically relevant. https://news.bitcoin.com/study-finds-less-than-40-of-btc-addresses-are-economically-relevant/. Accessed 18 Jan 2020

9. Cavallaro, L., Kinder, J., Wang, X., Katz, J. (eds.): ACM CCS 2019: 26th Conference on Computer and Communications Security. ACM Press (2019)

10. Dahmen, E., Okeya, K., Takagi, T., Vuillaume, C.: Digital signatures out of second-preimage resistant hash functions. In: Buchmann, J., Ding, J. (eds.) PQCrypto 2008. LNCS, vol. 5299, pp. 109–123. Springer, Heidelberg (2008). https://doi.org/10.1007/978-3-540-88403-3_8

11. Das, P., Faust, S., Loss, J.: A formal treatment of deterministic wallets. In: Cavallaro et al. [9], pp. 651–668 (2019)

12. Ethereum unique addresses chart. https://etherscan.io/chart/address. Accessed 18 Sep 2020

13. Implementation of wots up my sleeve. https://github.com/yaksetig/sleeve. Accessed 01 Apr 2021

14. Golang implementation of the bip39 spec. https://godoc.org/github.com/tyler-smith/go-bip39. Accessed 20 Sep 2020

15. Grover, L.K.: A fast quantum mechanical algorithm for database search. In: 28th Annual ACM Symposium on Theory of Computing, Philadephia, PA, USA, 22–24 May 1996, pp. 212–219. ACM Press (1996)

16. Hülsing, A.: W-OTS+ – shorter signatures for hash-based signature schemes. In: Youssef et al. [27], pp. 173–188

17. Hülsing, A., Rijneveld, J., Song, F.: Mitigating multi-target attacks in hash-based signatures. In: Cheng, C.-M., Chung, K.-M., Persiano, G., Yang, B.-Y. (eds.) PKC 2016. LNCS, vol. 9614, pp. 387–416. Springer, Heidelberg (2016). https://doi.org/10.1007/978-3-662-49384-7_15

18. Hutter, M., Schwabe, P.: NaCl on 8-bit AVR microcontrollers. In: Youssef et al. [27], pp. 156–172

19. Karakostas, D., Kiayias, A., Larangeira, M.: Account management in proof of stake ledgers. In: Galdi, C., Kolesnikov, V. (eds.) SCN 2020. LNCS, vol. 12238, pp. 3–23. Springer, Cham (2020). https://doi.org/10.1007/978-3-030-57990-6_1

20. Lamport, L.: Constructing digital signatures from a one-way function. Technical Report SRI-CSL-98, SRI International Computer Science Laboratory (1979)
21. Merkle, R.C.: A certified digital signature. In: Brassard, G. (ed.) CRYPTO 1989. LNCS, vol. 435, pp. 218–238. Springer, New York (1990). https://doi.org/10.1007/0-387-34805-0_21
22. Nakamoto, S.: Bitcoin: a peer-to-peer electronic cash system (2009)
23. Shor, P.W.: Polynomial-time algorithms for prime factorization and discrete logarithms on a quantum computer. SIAM J. Comput. **26**(5), 1484–1509 (1997)
24. Trinity attack incident part 1: Summary and next steps. https://blog.iota.org/trinity-attack-incident-part-1-summary-and-next-steps-8c7ccc4d81e8. Accessed 22 Sept 2020
25. van Heyst, E., Pedersen, T.P.: How to make efficient fail-stop signatures. In: Rueppel, R.A. (ed.) EUROCRYPT 1992. LNCS, vol. 658, pp. 366–377. Springer, Heidelberg (1993). https://doi.org/10.1007/3-540-47555-9_30
26. Wood, G.: Ethereum: a secure decentralised generalised transaction ledger. Ethereum project yellow paper **151**, 1–32 (2014)
27. Youssef, A., Nitaj, A., Hassanien, A.E. (eds.): AFRICACRYPT 2013. LNCS, vol. 7918. Springer, Heidelberg (2013). https://doi.org/10.1007/978-3-642-38553-7

Terrorist Attacks for Fake Exposure Notifications in Contact Tracing Systems

Gennaro Avitabile$^{(\boxtimes)}$, Daniele Friolo, and Ivan Visconti

DIEM, University of Salerno, Fisciano, Italy
{gavitabile,dfriolo,visconti}@unisa.it

Abstract. In this work we show that an adversary can attack the integrity of contact tracing systems based on Google-Apple Exposure Notifications (GAEN) by leveraging blockchain technology. We show that through smart contracts there can be an on-line market where infected individuals interested in monetizing their status can upload to the servers of the GAEN-based systems some keys (i.e., TEKs) chosen by a non-infected adversary. In particular, the infected individual can anonymously and digitally trade the upload of TEKs without a mediator and without running risks of being cheated. This vulnerability can therefore be exploited to generate large-scale *fake* exposure notifications of at-risk contacts with serious consequences (e.g., jeopardizing parts of the health system, affecting results of elections, imposing the closure of schools, hotels or factories).

As main contribution, we design a smart contract with two collateral deposits that works, in general, on GAEN-based systems. We then also suggest the design of a more sophisticated smart contract, using DECO, that could be used to attack in a different way GAEN-based systems (i.e., this second smart contract can succeed even in case GAEN systems are repaired making ineffective the first smart contract).

Our work shows how to realize with GAEN-based systems (in particular with Immuni and SwissCovid), the terrorist attack to decentralized contact tracing systems envisioned by Vaudenay.

Keywords: Contact tracing · GAEN · Smart contracts

1 Introduction

During the COVID-19 pandemic, several governments have decided to use digital contact tracing systems in addition to other practices to contain the spread of SARS-CoV-2. The reason is that digital contact tracing could help in notifying at-risk exposures to individuals that have been in close proximity to people who subsequently tested positive to SARS-CoV-2. This could be very useful especially when the involved individuals do not know each other. If digital contact tracing systems worked perfectly, they would certainly be effective in alerting at-risk individuals who, following some prescribed procedures (e.g., informing

The full version of this work appears in [2].

K. Sako and N. O. Tippenhauer (Eds.): ACNS 2021, LNCS 12726, pp. 220–247, 2021.
https://doi.org/10.1007/978-3-030-78372-3_9

doctors, staying at home in self-quarantine), may significantly limit the spread of the virus. Such systems have been highly recommended by some governments and in some cases (e.g., in Switzerland) an alert received by a contact tracing smartphone application allows to get a test for free.

The most used contact tracing systems rely on Google-Apple Exposure Notifications (GAEN), a feature offered by recent updates of iOS and Android and therefore available on a large fraction of currently used smartphones. These systems are widely used in Europe (e.g., Austria, Belgium, Germany, Ireland, Italy, Poland, Spain, Switzerland) and cross-border compatibility has recently been implemented[1]. Moreover, in the US, several states have adopted GAEN-based systems. GAEN allows to run decentralized contact tracing where there is very low control from governments, and this makes attacks from third parties generally simpler to mount and harder to mitigate.

GAEN-Based Contact Tracing Systems. The approach of GAEN-based contact tracing systems is to use Bluetooth Low Energy (BLE) to detect close proximity contacts among smartphones. Each smartphone broadcasts random pseudonyms via BLE, and this information is received by smartphones in close proximity along with some encrypted metadata. If a citizen is tested positive and decides to notify others, she will upload a set of secret keys named *Temporary Exposure Keys* (we will refer to them as TEKs in the remainder of the paper) corresponding to previous days in which she was presumably contagious. Starting from a TEK, it is possible to generate all the pseudonyms broadcast by a user during a day. The receivers of such pseudonyms will then manage to decrypt the stored metadata to then evaluate a risk factor[2]. The TEKs are disseminated to the users via a back-end server that periodically posts a list of digitally signed TEKs. A detailed description of GAEN can be found at https://covid19.apple.com/contacttracing.

An important point is that GAEN evaluates the reported TEKs if and only if the digital signature verifies successfully under a public key that has been previously communicated by the developers to Apple and Google. Google motivates this requirement saying that it ensures that keys received by the devices are actually from the authorized server and not from malicious third parties[3]. Theoretically, one could also rely on server authentication using TLS, but the use of Content Delivery Networks (CDNs) to disseminate TEKs (e.g., the CDN used by Immuni is operated by Akamai, while the SwissCovid's one is operated by Amazon) requires protection against malicious modifications operated by the CDN itself. Unfortunately, as we will see next, this requirement paves the way for the development of dark economies where TEKs to be uploaded by infected users are traded through smart contracts.

---

[1] EU eHealth Network: European Proximity Tracing. An Interoperability Architecture https://lasec.epfl.ch/people/vaudenay/swisscovid/swisscovid-ana.pdf.

[2] For example, metadata include information useful to estimate the distance among the smartphones which clearly impacts on estimating the risk of a contact.

[3] Google: Exposure Notification Reference Key Server https://google.github.io/exposure-notifications-server/.

False Positives due to Attacks. Since BLE was not originally designed to detect a precise distance among devices, the evaluation of the risk factor is prone to significant errors. To this regard, Leith and Farrell recently evaluated the reliability of BLE for digital contact tracing in several real-world scenarios [12].

While false positives due to BLE limitations in measuring distance can indiscriminately affect all individuals using the smartphone apps, a much more concerning threat allowing to direct false positive alerts to specific targets has been pointed out in prior work (e.g., see [17,23]). Indeed, GAEN-based contact tracing systems[4] can be heavily abused through replay attacks. In this case, the pseudonyms sent by an individual considered at risk (e.g., a person who is taking a test) are transmitted by an adversary to a different location in order to create a fake proximity contact. The attack can have a specific target but can also be performed at large scale. Recently, in [18] Gennaro et al. discussed how the capability of running such attacks at large scale can be used to put a category of citizens in quarantine with the consequence of severely compromising the results of an election. In general, the malicious generation of false positives can be harmful in various ways, the health system can be overloaded of requests that can penalize those citizens who instead are really affected by the virus. A student can cause the complete closure of a school or university and similar attacks can be directed to shops, malls, gyms, post offices, restaurants, factories.

Risks related to replay attacks were already known back in April 2020, and GAEN systems have a pretty large time window (about 2 h)[5] for pseudonyms to be replayed successfully. Nevertheless, governments have so far considered unlikely that such attacks can produce enough damage to cancel out the positive effects of genuine notifications of at-risk contacts. This is could be due to complications involved in the attack. Indeed, an adversary may not want to get herself infected, or it could not be easy to identify, and be in physical proximity with, an individual that soon will report to be infected.

In [24], Vaudenay envisioned the possibility of using smart contracts to realize a *terrorist* attack against decentralized systems, therefore the attack could potentially apply to GAEN-based systems as well. In this case, the attacker would spread on his targets some pseudonyms, subsequently promising through a smart contract a reward to whoever uploads the corresponding keys. Therefore, an infected individual who participates in the contract will cash a reward, and false positive alerts will raise on the smartphones of the targets selected by the terrorist. More details are discussed Sect. 1.2.

1.1 Our Contribution

In this paper, we show that the terrorist attack envisioned by Vaudenay can be concretely mounted against currently deployed GAEN-based contact tracing systems. In particular, we have analyzed its concrete feasibility with respect to

---

[4] Sometimes for brevity we will just say GAEN systems.

[5] Google: Exposure Notification Specification https://blog.google/documents/69/ Exposure_Notification_-_Cryptography_Specification_v1.2.1.pdf.

two systems, such as Immuni [8], used in Italy and SwissCovid [20], used in Switzerland. We expect several other deployed GAEN systems to suffer from the same vulnerabilities.

More generally, our work shows how to attack the integrity of currently deployed GAEN-based contact tracing systems by leveraging blockchain technology. A very alarming side of our contribution is that current systems can be compromised without the need for the attacker to get infected, or to be with high probability in close proximity to individuals that will be soon detected positive and will upload the keys. Our attacks consist of smart contracts to establish a mediator-free market where parties, without knowing each other, without meeting in person and without running risks to be cheated, can abuse exposure notifications procedures of GAEN systems. We give a brief description of the mentioned smart contracts in the following.

Trading TEKs Exploiting Publicly Verifiable Lists of Infected TEKs. As a main contribution we show a smart contract named Take-TEK that allows a buyer (i.e., the adversary willing to spread false positive alerts) to decide the TEKs that will be uploaded by a seller (i.e., the infected individual that is willing to monetize her right to upload TEKs to the servers of the GAEN system). The smart contract requires the buyer to deposit the amount of cryptocurrency (we will call it prize) that he is willing to give to the seller. The seller instead will deposit an amount of cryptocurrency in order to reserve a time slot in which she will try to upload the TEKs. In case she does not manage to complete the upload of the TEKs, the deposit will be assigned to the buyer. The deposit of the seller is therefore useful to make unlikely that a seller tries to prevent other sellers from completing the job. Additionally, we can hide the TEKs so that, even observing all transactions, it is not clear which TEKs have been traded using the smart contract among the many TEKs jointly published by the server of the contact tracing system during a slot.

Take-TEK crucially relies on the server publishing such lists of TEKs along with a signature verifiable with a publicly known public key. We show that the Take-TEK attack can be deployed to generate fake false positive alerts w.r.t. both Immuni and SwissCovid. Indeed, both systems follow strongly the design of GAEN and announce such signed lists of TEKs using ECDSA signatures.

Regardless of Immuni and SwissCovid making available or not their signature public keys, we have successfully extracted the public keys from previously released signatures. Therefore, Take-TEK can be instantiated to attack both (and possibly many more) systems. More details are discussed in Sect. 2.

Trading TEKs Without Publicly Verifiable Signatures: DECO. One might think that realizing the terrorist attack via smart contracts (e.g., Take-TEK) crucially relies on exploiting those signed lists of TEKs under a known (or extractable) public key. At first sight, a fix to such vulnerabilities consists of hiding the public keys and to use a signature scheme such that it is hard to extract the public key from signed messages. However, we show that things are actually more complicated for designers of contact tracing systems. In particular, we show another way to buy/sell TEKs that follows a completely different approach.

The key idea is requiring the seller to prove that a TLS session with the server led to a successful upload of the buyer's TEKs. The only requirements on the communication between smartphone app and server are that 1) both the TEKs and the positive (or negative) outcome of the upload procedure are part of the exchanged application data in the TLS session, and 2) the upload phase consists of just one request made by the client and the response of the sever (e.g., as it is in SwissCovid). At first sight, the attack seems very hard to realize since notoriously TLS produces deniable communication transcripts when it comes to application data (i.e., exchanged messages are only authenticated and not digitally signed). However, we exploit a very recent work of Zhang et al. [30]. They show how to build a fully decentralized TLS oracle, named DECO, for commonly used ciphersuites. Further details are described in Sect. 3.

Remark on the Actual Work Done by our Smart Contracts. Both our smart contracts provide full guarantees to both seller and buyer at the expense of running some cryptographic operations that can obviously produce transaction costs. Nevertheless, if we make an additional optimization based on pragmatism, the expensive computations may happen very rarely in practice. Indeed, we notice that the main computational cost for those smart contracts consists of checking at the very end that the seller has completed the task of uploading TEKs correctly. We observe that a buyer can check that TEKs are published by the server on his own. As a result, he would be satisfied in finding out that the trade has been completed successfully. Therefore, it is natural to expect that the buyer would give his approval to the smart contract to transfer the money to the seller avoiding the execution of expensive computations, and therefore saving transaction costs[6]. Since this behavior would be visible in the wild, the reputation of the buyer would also benefit from such approvals and more sellers would want to run contracts with him. Moreover, a (somewhat irrational) buyer that refuses to speed up the execution of the smart contract would anyway not stop the final transfer of the deposited money to the seller. As a result, the buyer would only get a worse reputation. In conclusion, the expensive work done by our smart contracts belongs to pieces of code that would rarely be executed in practice.

---

[6] Obviously, the smart contract can be adjusted so that, in case the buyer does not give his approval and the seller shows that she completed successfully her part of the contract, the expensive transactions costs due to the lack of help from the buyer are charged to the wallet of the buyer. A simple way to realize this could be asking for an additional deposit made by the buyer which could clearly cover the transaction costs of the seller in case the buyer does not give his approval and the seller shows that she successfully completed the upload procedure.

1.2   Related Work

The design of GAEN is very similar to the low-cost design of DP-3T[7], and thus several vulnerabilities identified in prior work generally apply to both systems. Tang [21] observes that DP-3T is vulnerable to identification attacks and presents an accurate survey about contact tracing systems. In [23], Vaudenay reports both privacy and security issues. The most famous privacy attack is the so-called *Paparazzi* attack. Basically, it is possible through passive antennas to track infected individuals over a certain time window[8] during which pseudonyms are linkable.

Regarding security issues, Vaudenay extensively considers false alert injection attacks, where the adversary manages to raise false alerts on the smartphone apps of targeted victims. Within this category, there are *replay* and *relay* attacks. GAEN is vulnerable to relay attacks and to replay attacks carried out within two hours. Vaudenay in [23] and Pietrzak in [17] proposed, back in April 2020, some solutions to defeat these attacks, but they have not been included neither in DP-3T nor in GAEN designs so far. Baumgärtner et al. [3] provide empirical evidence of the concrete feasibility of both Paparazzi and replay attacks. Pietrzak et al. [1] analyze inverse-sibyl attacks in which multiple adversaries cooperate to use the same pseudonyms. If one of the attackers gets to upload his TEKs, many false alerts may be raised. This attack could be used in combination with either the replay attack or our smart-contract based attacks in order to increase the number of affected targets. Iovino et al. [9] concretely demonstrate the possibility to inject false alerts by replaying released TEKs. In particular, pseudonyms associated with already published TEKs are transmitted to smartphones whose clock is corrupted in order to make them believe these pseudonyms are valid for risk matching. They also show that several apps may publish TEKs that are still valid. These TEKs can be used to generate false alerts without the need of corrupting smartphones' clocks.

Several GAEN-based systems are currently used in the world for digital contact tracing. Vaudenay and Vuagnoux, and later Dehaye and Reardon, extensively evaluated SwissCovid [4,5,25], confirming some vulnerabilities showed in previous works and elucidating new ones.

Finally, another class of attacks leading to false alerts involves bribing. Vaudenay envisions various possibilities for the development of dark economies [24] which could support false alert injection attacks, allowing them to be carried out at very large scales. In particular, the *Lazy Student* attack is connected to replay attacks. It is based on a dark economy where a hunter (i.e., seller) collects pseudonyms of individuals who will likely become infected later on, and deposits them on a smart contract. If the TEKs corresponding to such pseudonyms are uploaded to the server of the contact tracing system, the hunter gets a reward

---

[7] Decentralized Privacy-Preserving Proximity Tracing https://github.com/DP-3T/documents/blob/master/DP3T%20White%20Paper.pdf.

[8] In GAEN, depending on the particular application, this time may amount to up 14 days if the adversary colludes with the authorities, and to one day assuming TEKs are properly mixed and anonymized prior to publication.

paid by a buyer (i.e., the lazy student). If replay attacks are doable, the buyer can use them to make target victims' apps raise false alerts. This dark economy is sustainable only if the smart contract has a way to check that pseudonyms were actually reported to the official server. Another form of dark economy described by Vaudenay is the *terrorist* attack. It involves users reporting pseudonyms that differ from the ones used during the previous days. In fact, in both Immuni and SwissCovid there is no mechanism forcing users to upload genuine TEKs. Again, a TEK could be posted on a smart contract automatically issuing a reward to whoever reports it to the contact tracing system. This purchase may lead to a massive amount of fake notifications, without relying on replay attacks.

On the (Missing) Risk Assessment of the Terrorist Attack. The huge impact of false injection attacks seems to have gone unnoticed or just ignored. In [10] the cybersecurity risks of contact tracing systems are reviewed and compared using a subjective scoring scheme. The report considers injection of false alerts notifications by only mentioning replay attacks or trivial attacks such as recruiting people with symptoms, while the terrorist attack is not even mentioned.

Vaudenay and Vuagnoux expressed these and other concerns in their analysis of SwissCovid [25]. The Swiss National Cyber Security Center (NCSC) answered to their criticism seemingly downplaying those risks. The possible development of dark economies was ignored[9], and a recap table on security issues reports on SwissCovid marks the concerns expressed by Vaudenay as addressed, including false alert injection attacks[10]. Nevertheless, no solution or mitigation to such problems is reported.

Bribing Attacks on Smart Contracts. As we discuss in Sect. 2, our smart contracts make possible to trade TEKs reducing at a minimum the risks related to interacting with a dangerous entity such as a criminal. Bribery attacks on smart contracts for different scenarios have been proposed in the context of bribing miners in Ethereum and Bitcoin [13,15,16,22,26].

2   Trading TEKs in GAEN Systems

The GAEN API has been created to provide an efficient platform for exposure notifications on top of which countries can easily develop digital contact tracing systems. GAEN is supposed to solve various technical problems (e.g., changing BLE MAC address synchronously with the rotation of pseudonyms, keeping BLE

---

[9] Swiss National Cyber Security Center: Security Issue Submission [INR-4434]. Detailed analysis. https://www.melani.admin.ch/dam/melani/de/dokumente/20 20/INR-4434_NCSC_Risk_assessment.pdf.download.pdf/INR-4434_NCSC_Risk_asse ssment.pdf.

[10] Swiss National Cyber Security Center: SwissCovid Proximity Tracing System - Public Security Test, page 8 https://www.melani.admin.ch/dam/melani/de/doku mente/2020/SwissCovid_Public_Security_Test_Current_Findings.pdf.download.pdf/ SwissCovid_Public_Security_Test_Current_Findings.pdf.

advertisements on in background) on a large fraction of available smartphones[11]. At the same time, the API is so inflexible that it forces anyone who is willing to benefit from it to adopt a specific design for contact tracing. What is left in the hand of the developers is merely the creation of the graphical interface, the choice of some parameters and the realization of a server to gather and spread data about infected users and, more importantly, an authentication mechanism to avoid the upload of data by non-infected users.

Whenever a user is tested positive, she is given the right to upload her TEKs to the server so that the other users can be notified a risk of infection. The mechanism can be implemented in different ways. For example, a simple method consists of a code generated by the app that is given first to the health operator in order to activate it on the server. Then, once the server has authorized the code, the app will upload the TEKs along with the code (e.g., Immuni follows this approach). More complex mechanisms may be put in place. However, the attack we show next works for every GAEN-based contact tracing system under some natural assumptions that we will discuss later.

In order to evaluate the contagion risk, GAEN provides appropriate methods that take as input two files containing the last TEKs and the related signature. The matching is not performed if the signature does not verify under a public key previously known to Google and Apple. The first file is named `export.bin` and contains, along with other fields, a list of TEKs belonging to infected users that have decided to perform the upload procedure. Each TEK has also a date attached, which indicates when such TEK was used. The second file, named `export.sig`, contains a digital signature of the file `export.bin`[12]. An example of `export.bin` is reported in Appendix C.

2.1   Take-TEK Smart Contract: Buying/Selling TEKs Uploads

To simplify the description, we will refer to the TEKs file published by the server as a list of pairs of values. In each pair, the first value is a TEK and the second value is the corresponding date of usage date. Let the seller $\mathcal{P}$ be an infected user who would like to monetize her right to upload TEKs, and buyer $\mathcal{B}$ someone who is interested in paying $\mathcal{P}$ in order to upload TEKs of his interest. If the seller can prove she acted as promised, this selling process can be executed remotely remaining automated, anonymous, and scalable. GAEN's design requiring the list of TEKs to be signed makes the verification easy to the smart contract, and greatly facilitates such trades. The trade can be performed using a blockchain capable of executing sufficiently powerful smart contracts (e.g., Ethereum). Such smart contract guarantees that $\mathcal{P}$ gets an economic compensation if and only if $\mathcal{P}$ uploads to the server the TEKs specified by $\mathcal{B}$.

---

[11] Indeed, see the case of UK that tried to develop a system without GAEN but had to give up https://www.bbc.com/news/technology-53095336.

[12] Apple: Setting Up an Exposure Notification Server https://developer.apple.com/documentation/exposurenotification/setting_up_an_exposure_notification_server.
Google: Exposure Key export file format and verification https://developers.google.com/android/exposure-notifications/exposure-key-file-format.

The high-level functioning of the smart contract is as follows. (1) $\mathcal{B}$ creates the smart-contract posting a list of TEKs with the related date, and deposits a prize to be redeemed by a seller. (2) An interested $\mathcal{P}$ also makes a small deposit to declare her intention to upload the TEKs specified by $\mathcal{B}$ (the purpose of this small deposit is explained later). After having made this deposit, (3) $\mathcal{P}$ has a specified amount of time to complete the upload procedure. Before the time runs out, $\mathcal{P}$ must provide a list of TEKs which includes all the pairs (tek, date) specified by $\mathcal{B}$, along with a valid signature under the server's public key. If $\mathcal{P}$ manages to do so, she gets a reward, otherwise both deposits go back to $\mathcal{B}$.

By making a deposit, the seller reserves a time slot during which she can perform the upload. Such deposit protects the buyer from denial of service (DoS) attacks by sellers who actually do not have the right to upload TEKs. Here, as in the remainder of the paper, with the word DoS we mean attacks carried out by fake sellers which prevent honest sellers from participating to the trade.

We name the above smart contract Take-TEK and the attack that leverages the use of this smart contract Take-TEK attack. The time window given to $\mathcal{P}$ must be wide enough to take into account that new TEKs are not continuously released by the server, in fact, several hours may pass between the submission of a TEK and its publication. Obviously, the amounts of both deposits will be significantly higher than transaction fees. A custom software is needed to upload arbitrary TEKs. However, this simple software may be developed even by other entities (not just the buyers), and publicly distributed on the Internet or other sources (e.g., Darknet). Therefore, all the seller would need to do is just running a software on a smartphone/computer; something that is easily doable by a large fraction of the infected citizens willing to gain money[13]. Additionally, the time given to the seller to complete the upload after having been tested positive must be long enough to reserve a slot on the blockchain (i.e., enough to wait that the transaction related to the seller's deposit gets confirmed) and subsequently send the TEKs via the custom software.

Attack Description. $\mathcal{B}$ and $\mathcal{P}$ owns wallets $\mathsf{pk}_{\mathcal{B}}$ and $\mathsf{pk}_{\mathcal{P}}$ respectively. The buyer has no assurance that the seller is actually an infected person, and she is not just a malicious party trying to slow down the buyer's plan. Thus, some collateral must be deposited by $\mathcal{P}$ too. The seller will lose the collateral deposit in case she is not able to prove that she sent the buyer's TEKs to the server S. We use a signature scheme $(\mathsf{Gen}_S, \mathsf{Sign}_S, \mathsf{Ver}_S)$. The protocol description is depicted in Fig. 1 and a brief overview of the main functions follows below.

$\mathtt{Constructor}(\mathbf{T}_{\mathcal{B}}, \mathsf{vk}_S, t, d_{\mathcal{P}})$: It takes as input a set of tuples $\mathbf{T}_{\mathcal{B}} := (\mathsf{tek}_i^{\mathcal{B}}, \mathsf{date}_i^{\mathcal{B}})_{i \in [n]}$ with $n \leq \mathsf{maxteks}$[14], where tek_i is the i-th TEK of the buyer and date_i is the associated date, the verification key vk_S to be used to verify the signature of the TEKs list, a timestamp t, indicating the maximum time

---

[13] COVID-19 by itself caused a global economic crisis which led to lower wages and job losses. More details at https://en.wikipedia.org/wiki/COVID-19_recession.

[14] The maximum number of TEKs that can be uploaded in one shot depends on the particular contact tracing system.

the seller has to provide the correct list and signature, and the collateral value $d_{\mathcal{P}}$ that the seller must deposit.

Deposit(): must be triggered by $\mathcal{B}$ and takes as input a quantity p of coins as the payment for the seller.

Promise(): must be triggered by the seller $\mathcal{P}$ by sending a quantity of collateral deposit $d_{\mathcal{P}}$ as a payment when invoked.

SendTeks($\mathbf{T}_{KS}, \sigma_T$): must be triggered by the seller $\mathcal{P}$ to provide a list of TEKs together with its signature σ_T. Let the list released by the server be $\mathbf{T} = (\text{tek}_i, \text{date}_i)_{i \in [N]}$, where N is the number of published TEKs. It checks that:
  - $\mathbf{T}_{\mathcal{B}} \subseteq \mathbf{T}$ and $\text{Ver}_S(\mathbf{T}, \sigma_{\mathbf{T}}; \text{vk}_S) = 1$.

If the checks passes, $d_{\mathcal{B}}$ coins are transferred to the seller's wallet $\text{pk}_{\mathcal{P}}$.

Take-TEK Attack

We consider two entities: the seller $\mathcal{P}$ and the buyer $\mathcal{B}$, with wallets $\text{pk}_{\mathcal{B}}$ and $\text{pk}_{\mathcal{P}}$ respectively. The protocol works as follows:

1. $\mathcal{B}$ invokes the constructor, taking as input the buyer's TEKs list $\mathbf{T}_{\mathcal{B}}$, the server verification key vk_S that will be used to verify the signed TEKs list, a timestamp t, and a value $d_{\mathcal{P}}$ indicating the minimal amount that $\mathcal{P}$ must deposit in order to participate.
   After having created the contract, $\mathcal{B}$ triggers the function Deposit to deposit the prize p aimed for the seller who uploads $\mathbf{T}_{\mathcal{B}}$ to the server.
2. $\mathcal{P}$ deposits her collateral by triggering the function Promise. Now the seller has at most time t to send a TEKs list $\mathbf{T}$ signed by the server.
3. If $\mathcal{P}$, before time t, triggers the function SendTeks submitting a signed TEKs list $\mathbf{T}$ such that it satisfies conditions $\mathbf{T}_{\mathcal{B}} \subseteq \mathbf{T}$ and $\text{Ver}_S(\mathbf{T}, \sigma_{\mathbf{T}}; \text{vk}_S) = 1$, the collateral deposit $d_{\mathcal{P}}$ of $\mathcal{P}$ and the prize p are transferred to $\mathcal{P}$'s wallet. Otherwise, if t seconds have passed, they are moved to $\mathcal{B}$'s wallet.

Fig. 1. The steps followed by buyer $\mathcal{B}$ and seller $\mathcal{P}$ to carry out the Take-TEK attack.

2.2 On the Practicality of Take-TEK Attack

Various proposed upload authorization mechanisms include manual steps (e.g., SwissCovid uses an authorization code, termed covidcode, which lasts for 24 h) which, in order to function properly, naturally give the seller enough time to perform the steps mentioned in the section above. For example, if a code is communicated to the infected user via a phone call, she should be given a fairly large amount of time to write down the code and insert it in the app later on (the needs of people with disabilities and of elder people must be taken into account). Even systems that have fairly strict requirements on the time by which the upload procedure must be completed should allow for errors and recovery procedures, which may give additional time to the future seller. For example,

Immuni requires that the infected user dictates, via phone call, a code that appears on her device. After that, the user must complete the upload within two minutes. If this does not happen, the procedure must be repeated. Additionally, the system should be tolerant. People should have the opportunity to perform the upload procedure later on if they are unable to do it in that precise moment. It is worth noting that strict requirements on the upload phase reduce users' privacy. A clear example is Immuni, where the medical operator, by checking whether a code has been used or is instead expired, gets to know whether or not the infected user actually uploaded her TEKs.

Implementation. We implemented our results as a smart contract for Ethereum, published it in a public repository[15] and tested it locally. Since Ethereum does not use `ECDSA-SHA256` (i.e., the one used in GAEN) for built-in transaction signature verification, there is the need to use specific solidity smart contract libraries[16] which lead to extra gas usage. Considering the change of 206 dollars per single ETH token on the 20th of July 2020, signature verification costs around 11 dollars (1235000 of gas). In order to compute the full cost, one should add about 0.4 dollars (45000 of gas) for each TEK that is contained in the export.bin file[17]. Note that our smart contract can handle export files large as the maximum data that an Ethereum transaction can handle at most. Details on how to deal with such limitation can be found in Appendix D.

2.3 Subtleties in the Wild

In Sect. 2.1 we gave a high-level overview of how TEKs uploads can be sold safely via blockchains. However, there are some subtleties we overlooked for the sake of simplicity. We first analyze the advantages for adversaries when using automated trade compared to already known attacks. Then, we consider certain problems that arise while trying to concretely mount our attack against deployed GAEN-based contact tracing systems. We also show how these difficulties are easily tackled if very small modifications to our attack are made.

Advantages of Automated Trade (for an Adversary). One might think that malicious injection of fake TEKs is inherent in decentralized contact tracing systems since there is no control over the smartphone used by infected individuals and thus, when the time of the upload comes, the infected person can always use a smartphone belonging to someone else.

While it is true that such simple attacks are very hard to tackle, they have limited impact for at least two main reasons: 1) the buyer must handover his

---

[15] Code available at https://github.com/danielefriolo/TEnK-U.

[16] The one we used for signature verification is available at https://github.com/tdrerup/elliptic-curve-solidity.

[17] The cost of 45000 of gas includes TEK extraction, hashing of the export file for signature verification, checking if the stored TEKs are in the extracted ones. To simplify the gas evaluation, we assume that $\mathcal{B}$ stores only one TEK in the contract.

smartphone to the seller, and this requires physical proximity; 2) sellers and buyers must trust each other since an illegal payment must be performed without being able to rely on justice in case of missing payment or aborted upload of keys. Indeed, even if in need of money, people are generally afraid of dealing with criminals since they may get scammed or threatened. Additionally, the buyer might expose the sellers' identities to the authorities in case he gets arrested or legally persecuted. Equally, the buyer may share the same concern with respect to an unreliable seller. It goes without saying that some citizens are prone to violate the rules[18] when they believe that risks are low compared to the advantages.

As such, attacks involving the exchange of smartphones, or the usage of a malicious app uploading TEKs sent by a criminal contacted directly by the infected citizen, do not scale and their damage may be considered tolerable. Having a mechanism which allows this trade to happen remotely, in anonymity and ensuring no party is cheated, solves all the above problems for parties willing to abuse contact tracing systems. In fact, it provides a framework for large-scale black markets of TEKs. The seller would not feel threatened in any way and could easily earn money, on the other hand, the buyers would benefit from a larger set of users to be in business with, therefore succeeding in many possible attack scenarios. Other systems for black markets based on reputations could also be used, but they are clearly less appealing than the transparency and usability of mediator-free smart contracts.

A Worry-Free Seller. The effectiveness of a digital contact tracing system is strictly related to various factors among which the percentage of active population using them. Appropriate measures should be taken to earn citizens' trust since it is the only way to guarantee broad adoption. With this in mind, the European Commission released a series of recommendations in relation to data protection stating the need of identifying solutions that are the least intrusive and comply with the principle of data minimization [7]. A similar recommendation has been given by the Chaos Computer Club (CCC)[19], the Europe's largest ethical hackers association, which explicitly states that "data which is no longer needed must be deleted". Corona-Warn, the German contact-tracing system, declares to be fully compliant with CCC's guidelines[20]. Many other systems are inspired by similar principles. For example, the Italian system Immuni also declares that data is deleted when no longer needed[21], as well as the Swiss system SwissCovid which also specifies a retention period for the TEKs and the upload authorization codes[22]. In its recommendation to build a verification

---

[18] The infected person also commits a violation by allowing the injection of fake TEKs.

[19] 10 requirements for the evaluation of "Contact Tracing" apps https://www.ccc.de/en/updates/2020/contact-tracing-requirements.

[20] Criteria for the Evaluation of Contact Tracing Apps https://github.com/corona-warn-app/cwa-documentation/blob/ec703906c109bd7c3cc84bc361b7e703b20650ea/pruefsteine.md.

[21] https://github.com/immuni-app/immuni-documentation.

[22] Corona-Warn-App Solution Architecture https://github.com/corona-warn-app/cwa-documentation/blob/master/solution_architecture.md.

server authenticating the uploaded TEKs, Google states that identifiable information should not be associated with uploaded data[23].

The adoption of the above measures ensures that uploaded data do not link to, nor identify a particular individual. This is very important considering that GAEN systems are vulnerable to the Paparazzi attack[24] [23].

Evaluation of Seller's Risks. Considering the above data minimization principles, are the seller and the buyer at risk of being legally persecuted for a trade that may be deemed as illegal? The answer seems to be no. If data is handled as specified above, there would be no way to associate the seller to its uploaded TEKs at a later time. Data exchanged during the attack would also not directly compromise neither the buyer nor the seller[25].

However, there is a problem for a seller who really wants to minimize the chance of getting caught. In fact, since the TEKs proposed by the buyer are posted in clear on the blockchain, authorities may become aware of them and activate ad-hoc procedures monitoring the incriminated TEKs and exploiting the upload authorization process to identify the guilty seller. This, in fact, does not seem to directly contradict the data minimization principle when national security is at stake. If the server getting the TEKs upload monitors the requests (e.g., by storing connection logs) without colluding with the health authority, the seller could be easily incriminated after the TEKs have been detected in the smart contract by just looking at her IP stored together with such request. However, in this case, the usage of an anonymity service like Tor [6] can easily reduce the chance of getting caught. If the authorities are colluding, the upload authorization codes (e.g., the covidcode) may be associated with the identities of infected users, and TEKs could be in turn mapped to a precise individual via such codes. However, by slightly increasing the complexity of the smart contract, such risk may be completely avoided. It suffices for the buyer to encrypt his TEKs with a public key provided by the seller, who then will use a non-interactive zero-knowledge (NIZK) proof system to prove that the TEKs encrypted under the specified public key are indeed contained in the list signed with the server's public key. This requires an additional interaction with the buyer, who has to publish the encrypted TEKs (see Appendix B for more details). Once again, the seller is protected by a timer which assigns her all the deposits if the buyer does not reply.

---

[23] Google: Exposure Notification Verification Server https://developers.google.com/android/exposure-notifications/verification-system.

[24] In *Paparazzi* attack, through passive antennas one can link pseudonyms used by an infected user tracing him over the duration of a TEK or for more days if the TEKs are linked. Therefore leaving open the possibility to link such data to a person's real identity would be extremely incautious.

[25] In this analysis, we refer only to contact tracing system data and messages exchanged via the blockchain during the execution of the attack. We do not take into account border-line situations as, for example, the case where there is only a single infected individual. We also ignore additional information that may help investigators figuring out who the seller is, for example how the money are spent after the trade.

Efficient Ethereum implementations of NIZK proofs (see Appendix A.3) are known in literature, like NIZKs for Σ-protocols [27] or zk-SNARKs [19,31,32].

Even if the buyer decides to claim the authorship of the attack at a later point in time (e.g., as it usually happens for terrorist attacks) by opening the encrypted values on the blockchain to published TEKs, the seller would not be at risk if data was handled according to the principles of data economy and anonymity. Any evidence based on contact tracing data would be a clear indicator that those principles have been violated. This could result in a big disincentive in using the app, since citizens may think (probably rightfully) that data could also be abused for other reasons, perhaps for mass surveillance purposes. Finally, we want to point out that even if several researchers raised the concern about the possible birth of black markets [18,24], we did not find any document related to any contact-tracing system, either issued by governments or national security agencies, which deeply evaluates these risks. To the best of our knowledge, no risk analysis ever mentions to monitor the dark web and blockchains looking for suspicious smart contracts. It goes by itself that if blockchains are not monitored, all extra measures taken in this paragraph to protect the seller are not necessary.

Other Subtleties. There are two other subtleties with limited impact to consider for the actual realization of the attack. We describe them in Appendix E.1 and Appendix E.2 and shortly mention here:

- *Extracting public keys from signatures*: Generally, servers' public keys do not seem to have been made publicly available neither by Google and Apple, nor by the countries which deployed GAEN-based contact tracing systems[26]. However, the signature algorithm used (i.e., ECDSA) allows to retrieve this public key starting from a pair of signed messages.
- *Updates of public keys*: The structure of the `export.bin` file allows for updates of the used digital signature key (see Appendix C). Therefore, it might happen that, after the seller makes the deposit and accepts to upload the buyer's TEK, the server, by coincidence, decides to use a new key which was never used before, thus producing a signature that is not verifiable under the public key posted on the smart contract. However, by making a slight modification to the smart contract, it is possible to handle also this unfortunate event. Moreover, keys have changed very rarely in export files up to now.

3   Connecting Smart Contracts to TLS Sessions

The Take-TEK attack relies on the fact that a digital signature is used to authorize uploads. Additionally, the ability to extract the public key from signed messages may also play a key role. Therefore, one might think that to protect GAEN

---

[26] Once a contact tracing system handles his public key to Google, it can completely rely on GAEN APIs to perform signature verification without storing the public key in clear to the app source code (see https://developers.google.com/android/exposure-notifications/exposure-key-file-format for more details).

systems the public key should remain hidden and the signature scheme should be such that extracting the public key from message-signature pairs is hard. In this way, due to the inability of allowing a smart contract to verify that a TEK is officially in a list of infected TEKs, the attack would fail. However, things are not so easy. The previous smart contract exploited the public verifiability of the signatures because this is what is used in GAEN systems. If a different method is used, it might be abused again. Indeed, we show that TLS oracles can be used to prove to a smart contract that an upload was successfully performed, without relying on signatures of TEKs.

3.1   Decentralized Oracles

Recently, Zhang et al. [30], introduced the concept of Decentralized Oracles. Roughly, an oracle is an entity that can be queried by a client to interact with a TLS server and help the client proving statements about the connection transcript. Previously known oracle constructions rely on trusted/semi-trusted execution environments [29], thus not giving any help in our case. DECO [30] is the first work where a fully-decentralized construction is proposed for specific ciphersuites such as CBC-HMAC and AES-GCM coupled with DH key exchange with ephemeral secrets. We recall that a TLS connection is divided in two parts: a handshake phase where key exchange is performed, and a phase during which the transferred data is encrypted/decrypted by the client/server using the key exchanged in the previous phase. GAEN servers usually accept Elliptic-Curve Diffie-Hellman key Exchange (ECDHE) for the first phase, while for the second phase some servers accept only AES-GCM (e.g., Immuni), whereas others, like SwissCovid's one, accept also CBC-HMAC as a ciphersuite. To guarantee the integrity of data, the plaintext is usually compressed and a MAC on the compressed string is calculated using a key derived from the DH exchanged key.

Decentralized Key-Exchange. We provide below an informal description of the key-exchange in DECO for ECDHE that is called Three Party Handshake (3PHS).

We assume three entities: a prover $\mathcal{P}$, a verifier $\mathcal{V}$ and a server S. $\mathcal{P}$ and $\mathcal{V}$ jointly act as a TLS client. The overall idea of DECO is that the prover and verifier, after performing some two-party computations, compute shares of the exchanged key, while the server computes the entire key without even noticing that $\mathcal{P}$ and $\mathcal{V}$ are two distinct interacting entities.

When using CBC-HMAC, the keys $k_{\mathcal{P}}^{\texttt{MAC}}$, $k_{\mathcal{V}}^{\texttt{MAC}}$ (such that $k_{\mathcal{P}}^{\texttt{MAC}} + k_{\mathcal{V}}^{\texttt{MAC}} = k^{\texttt{MAC}}$) are learned by $\mathcal{P}$ and $\mathcal{V}$ respectively, while $k^{\texttt{Enc}}$ is only known to $\mathcal{P}$. When using AES-GCM, the same key is used for both encryption and MAC, therefore both $\mathcal{P}$ and $\mathcal{V}$ just get a share of it. While $\mathcal{P}$ and $\mathcal{V}$ only learn their secret shares of the key, the server S gets to know both $k^{\texttt{Enc}}$ and $k^{\texttt{MAC}}$.

Let G be an EC group generator. The key exchange phase works as follows:

- $\mathcal{P}$ establishes a TLS connection with the server S.
- When receiving the DH share $Y_{\mathsf{S}} = s_{\mathsf{S}} \cdot G$ from S, $\mathcal{P}$ forwards it to $\mathcal{V}$.

- $\mathcal{V}$ samples a DH secret $s_{\mathcal{V}}$ and sends his DH share $Y_{\mathcal{V}} = s_{\mathcal{V}} \cdot G$ to $\mathcal{P}$.
- $\mathcal{P}$ samples her DH secret $s_{\mathcal{P}}$, calculates her DH share $Y_{\mathcal{P}} = s_{\mathcal{P}} \cdot G$, calculates the combined DH share $Y = Y_{\mathcal{P}} + Y_{\mathcal{V}}$, and sends Y to S.

Finally, S computes the DH exchanged key as $Z = s_{\mathsf{S}} \cdot Y$. $\mathcal{P}$ and $\mathcal{V}$ will compute their secret shares of Z as $Z_{\mathcal{P}} = s_{\mathcal{P}} \cdot Y_{\mathsf{S}}$ and $Z_{\mathcal{V}} = s_{\mathcal{V}} \cdot Y_{\mathsf{S}}$. Note that $Z_{\mathcal{P}} + Z_{\mathsf{S}} = Z$, where $+$ is the EC group operation. Now that $\mathcal{P}$ and $\mathcal{V}$ have secret shares of EC points, they use secure two-party computation (2PC) to evaluate a PRF (that we call TLS-PRF) to derive the keys $k_{\mathcal{P}}^{\mathtt{MAC}}$ and $k_{\mathcal{V}}^{\mathtt{MAC}}$. The authors face and solve several challenges in order to derive keys efficiently via 2PC. We do not cover this part, a more detailed description can be found in [30].

Encrypted Communication. At the end of the 3PHS, $\mathcal{P}$ and $\mathcal{V}$ have to engage in a 2PC protocol to correctly calculate the MAC and the encryption on the plaintext to be sent to the server, without revealing the shares to each other. Privacy of the plaintext is also ensured with respect to $\mathcal{V}$. For CBC-HMAC, the encryption of such plaintext is computed exclusively by $\mathcal{P}$ who holds the encryption key. The authors [30] provide hand-optimized protocols which are much more efficient then the ones obtained by directly applying 2PC techniques. The 2PC protocol for AES-GCM is a lot slower than the one for CBC-HMAC since for AES-GCM $\mathcal{P}$ and $\mathcal{V}$ must cooperate also for the encryption.

Proving Statements. An important feature of DECO is that $\mathcal{P}$, when the communication with S ends, can prove, in zero knowledge, statements on the communication transcript in a clever and efficient way. However, to make their protocol practical for our goal, we do not try to maintain the transcript private. As a result, we will not discuss this part of DECO which can be found in [30]. In the following, we describe how to adapt DECO to our scenario.

3.2   A Smart Contract Oracle

Our goal is to make the smart contract play the role of the DECO verifier. In this way, the smart contract would be able to verify that the intended communication between the seller and the server took place and to reward the seller accordingly. Unfortunately we can not just plug DECO into a smart contract for several reasons. For example, DECO requires to run intensive 2PC related tasks, to sample random values and to maintain a private state[27].

Therefore, we keep running the DECO protocol off-chain but we find a way to connect the DECO run between the prover and the verifier to the state of the smart contract, so that the smart contract will eventually be able to act as an impartial judge punishing the malicious party when a deviation from the prescribed honest behavior is detected. In particular, the seller acts as a prover and the buyer as a verifier, and we guarantee no party is able to cheat (i.e., the seller is paid if and only

---

[27] Keeping a private state inside a smart contract is not possible and computationally intensive operations generate high costs.

if she performs the upload of the requested TEKs) by binding the off-chain execution to the state of the smart contract itself. Furthermore, we guarantee privacy of the messages exchanged between the server and the prover only until their TLS connection is open. After the communication ends, the seller proves that she acted honestly by providing the application-level messages exchanged with the server, along with the corresponding MAC tags w.r.t. the MAC key which is bound to the smart contract. To be more specific, the smart contract freezes a share of the MAC key and the seller has to show a communication transcript (i.e., the messages exchanged with the server and corresponding MAC tags) which is consistent with such share. Privacy of the upload request message to be sent to the server is crucial while the TLS session is open because the verifier may abort the protocol and use the authorization token of the prover to upload data by himself without paying out the promised reward. On the other hand, making the communication public after it took place does not endanger the prover, apart from the considerations made in Sect. 2.3, and makes the verification procedure much more practical. What we need is that the shares of the prover and the verifier are kept private until the end of the protocol, and then revealed to the smart contract, along with other information, for verification and reward paying. In addition, the TLS session timeout should be big enough to allow for the 2PC execution. To this regard, Zhang et al. already verified the practical feasibility of their protocol [30]. Obviously, $\mathcal{P}$ must know how to reach $\mathcal{V}$ to carry out the protocol. To address concerns regarding anonymity, $\mathcal{V}$ may set up a Tor hidden service[28]. Using hidden services may significantly slow down the process, however we found both Immuni and SwissCovid servers to give a generous time out window of two hours[29]. Another point to consider is that upload authorization tokens may have a limited duration. For example, in SwissCovid, the smartphone, by interacting with an appropriate server (different from the TEKs upload server, called CovidCode-Service), exchanges the covid code for a signed JWT token that is valid for 5 min[30]. Then, this token is sent by the smartphone to the server along with the TEKs to complete the upload. Thus, the upload message, containing the TEKs and the authorization token, must be computed and sent to the server within 5 min from the reception of the JWT token. Given the high efficiency of DECO when CBC-HMAC is used, even when bandwidth is limited [14], it is reasonable to think that the attack is feasible in SwissCovid. In Immuni instead, no signed token is used. In fact, the upload must be completed within 2 min after the infected user has communicated the code to the health operator. Therefore, in Immuni the attack would less likely be operative, especially with Tor, given that the slower AES-GCM ciphersuite is required.

Protocol Description. From now on, we refer to the seller and the buyer as prover $\mathcal{P}$ and verifier $\mathcal{V}$ respectively; we denote the server as S. In the following,

---

[28] More on Tor hidden services can be found at https://2019.www.torproject.org/docs/onion-services.

[29] Interestingly, in June the timeout of a TLS session with both Immuni and SwissCovid upload servers was limited to 5 min, but it has been then extended to two hours.

[30] See CovidCode-Service configuration https://github.com/admin-ch/CovidCode-Service/blob/develop/src/main/resources/application-prod.yml.

we explain the detailed attack for the CBC-HMAC ciphersuite. When creating the smart contract, $\mathcal{V}$ also posts the DH share $Y_\mathcal{V} = s_\mathcal{V} \cdot G$ he is willing to use during the 3PHS, along with requested TEKs (and dates).

First, $\mathcal{P}$ transacts on the smart contract to reserve a time slot of duration t_1 by which a DECO protocol run must be performed together with $\mathcal{V}$ and S, and the data needed to redeem the reward must be posted on the smart contract by $\mathcal{P}$. If time t_1 elapses, $\mathcal{P}$ loses her slot. This reservation mechanism is needed to prevent $\mathcal{V}$ from getting back the reward while an honest $\mathcal{P}$ performs the upload of the requested TEKs. In fact, the verifier could also act as a prover and simulate a reward-paying interaction with the server to the smart contract, which would have no mean to distinguish it from a fake one. By adding a reservation mechanism, we are sure a malicious $\mathcal{V}$ cannot play a simulated transcript in the smart contract while honest $\mathcal{P}$ is performing with him the DECO protocol run. Furthermore, since the communication for the upload between the server and the prover consists of just a single query followed by a single response, it is not possible for a cheating verifier to make the timer expire avoiding to pay the prover while at the same time the upload of the TEKs successfully completes. In fact, once $\mathcal{V}$ cooperates with $\mathcal{P}$ to build a valid request, S will reply to $\mathcal{P}$ independently of what $\mathcal{V}$ does, thus giving $\mathcal{V}$ all she needs to redeem the reward.

When executing the 3PHS, $\mathcal{P}$ checks that the value $Y'_\mathcal{V}$ sent by $\mathcal{V}$ during the handshake corresponds to the value $Y_\mathcal{V}$ posted on the smart contract. This prevents $\mathcal{V}$ from providing an erroneous DH share and blaming $\mathcal{P}$ for it. If this is not the case, $\mathcal{P}$ aborts. Since no upload message has been sent to the server yet, no party gains advantage from this operation. If $\mathcal{V}$'s share is correct (i.e., $Y_\mathcal{V} = Y'_\mathcal{V}$), parties engage in the communication with S and jointly compute the MAC (via 2PC as in [30]) on the upload request m_c generated by $\mathcal{P}$. If the connection ends successfully[31], the elected $\mathcal{P}$ posts (only who reserved this slot is allowed to post this message) on the smart contract the following:

- The entire communication transcript, that is (m_c, m_s) together with the MACs (θ_c, θ_s), calculated by the client(s) $\mathcal{P} \leftrightarrow \mathcal{V}$ and the server S.
- The prover's secret $s_\mathcal{P}$.
- The DH share of the server Y_S received during the 3PHS.

Then, the smart contract starts a timer t_2 indicating the maximum time $\mathcal{V}$ has to reveal his secret $s_\mathcal{V}$. In case $\mathcal{V}$ does not do that, the prize is automatically transferred to the seller $\mathcal{P}$. If $\mathcal{V}$ reveals $s_\mathcal{V}$, the smart contract does the following:

- Check that $Y_\mathcal{V} = s_\mathcal{V} \cdot G$ and if not, transfer the prize to $\mathcal{P}$.
- If the check passes, reconstruct the secret Z from $s_\mathcal{V}, s_\mathcal{P}, Y_s$, and apply TLS-PRF to derive the MAC key k^{MAC}.

---

[31] This can be inferred from the communication. For example, as in SwissCovid (see SwissCovid Server Controller: https://github.com/DP-3T/dp3t-sdk-backend/blob/a730a5b276591e5cc8b6c609e2b0ba29c6069eb6/dpppt-backend-sdk/dpppt-backend-sdk-ws/src/main/java/org/dpppt/backend/sdk/ws/controller/GaenController.java), S may reply $\mathcal{P}$ with either a success message such as "200 OK" or an error message.

Now the smart contract has everything it needs to check that the fields inside message m_c (from the prover to the server) are correct (i.e., the buyer's TEK are present), the response message (from the server to the prover) is positive, and that the MACs (θ_c, θ_s) verify w.r.t. k^{MAC}. If all the checks pass, the prize is transferred to $\mathcal{P}$, otherwise $\mathcal{P}$ gains no prize and the deposit is returned back to $\mathcal{V}$.

As mentioned before, $\mathcal{V}$ is not encouraged to provide a different public key w.r.t. the one he used in DECO execution, otherwise $\mathcal{P}$ will just abort. On the other hand, the prover is not able to earn a reward without uploading the promised TEKs. In fact, the probability for the prover to come up with a pair (m'_c, θ'_c) (resp. (m'_s, θ'_s)) that verifies under the key k'^{MAC} derived from $Z' = Z'_{\mathcal{P}} + Z'_{\mathcal{V}}$ with $Z'_{\mathcal{P}} := s'_{\mathcal{P}} \cdot Y'_{\mathsf{S}}$ and $Z_{\mathcal{V}} := s_{\mathcal{V}} \cdot Y'_{\mathsf{S}}$ is negligible due to the fact that $s_{\mathcal{P}}$ is fixed and honestly generated, thus randomizing Z', hence k'^{MAC}.

A Note on DoS Attacks. It is important to prevent DoS attacks run by sellers who actually do not have the right to upload TEKs and end up by just wasting the buyer's precious time. In the previous discussion this protection is not provided: before sending the jointly computed message (m_c, θ_c), the seller can decide to not forward the message to the server. Now, the buyer has to open his commitment to show his secret $s_{\mathcal{V}}$ in order to not lose the prize. As a result, the committed value cannot be used in other runs. To address this issue, the smart contract can be modified to handle multiple sessions. Instead of storing $Y_{\mathcal{V}}$ as a single DH contribute, the buyer stores the root of a Merkle tree. Now, when the seller interacts with the contract to reserve a session, a session id (a simple counter j suffices) is assigned to her: the DH contribute used in the 3HPS will correspond now to the j-th leaf of the Merkle tree. Now, when the buyer has to open his secret $s_{\mathcal{V}}$, he also reveals the path of the Merkle tree from the root to the leaf j. The smart contract will now verify that the contribute is correctly derived from the root by following a path with correct openings. Let us consider a Merkle root committing to 2^k elements, thus allowing the buyer to open as many sessions. For a k large enough, a malicious seller should spend a considerable amount of money in order to reserve all the sessions.

AES-GCM. Carrying out the attack when AES-GCM ciphersuite is required is more involved. A discussion on this is reported in Appendix F.1.

4   Conclusion

In our work we showed that the terrorist attack, previously envisioned by Vaudenay, is concretely realizable against GAEN systems with the aid of cryptographic tools and a blockchain capable of executing smart contracts (e.g., Ethereum). In particular, the Take-TEK attack exploits the fact that the list of infected TEKs, published by the server daily, has always a digital signature attached to it. Such signature allows the smart contract to easily verify that the upload was performed as requested by the terrorist. Even beyond the use of signatures, we have shown a different instantiation of the terrorist attack using DECO. In conclusion, we advise protocol designers not to look at the effects of a specific realization, but to prove the protocol secure against any automated instantiation of a terrorist attack. Our work shows that the power of blockchain technology to trade digital assets is still overlooked even when critical features are digitized.

Acknowledgments. We thank the first author of DECO [30] Fan Zhang for all the clarifications about their paper, Stephen Farrell of the TACT project [11] for his help on how to gather contact tracing data, Serge Vaudenay and Martin Vuagnoux for useful information about the implementation and configuration of SwissCovid. This research is supported by the European Union's Horizon 2020 research and innovation programme under grant agreement No 780477 (project PRIViLEDGE).

A   Tools

A.1   MACs and Signature Schemes

A *Message Authentication Code* consists of a tuple of algorithms (Gen, Tag, Ver) such that

Gen(1^λ): Takes as input the security parameter and outputs a key k in the key space $\mathcal{K}$.

Tag($m; k$): Takes as input a message m in the message space $\mathcal{M}$ and a key k, and outputs a tag θ.

Ver($m, \theta; k$): Takes as input a message m and a key k, and outputs 1 iff θ is a correct tag on m under key k.

It must satisfy the following properties:

- **Completeness:** The probability that Ver($(m, \theta); k$) outputs 1 for an honestly generated tag $\theta \leftarrow$ Tag($m; k$) is 1.
- **Unforgeability:** The probability that an adversary, knowing only challenge message m^* and having access to an oracle giving back tags θ_i on messages $m_i \neq m^*$ (for all $i \in [n]$ with n polynomially bounded in the security parameter), outputs a pair (m^*, θ^*) such that Ver($m^*, \theta^*; k$) $= 1$ is negligible.

A *Signature Scheme* consists of a set of algorithms (Gen, Sign, Ver), such that

Gen(1^λ): Takes as input the security parameter and outputs a pair (sk, vk) sampled from the key space, where sk is the signing key and vk the verification key.

Sign($m; $sk): Takes as input a message m in the message space $\mathcal{M}$ and a signing key sk, and outputs a signature σ_m on that message.

Ver($m, \sigma; $vk): Takes as input a pair (m, σ) and the verification key vk, and outputs 1 if the signature σ correctly verifies under vk.

It must satisfy the following properties:

- **Completeness:** The probability that Ver($(m, \sigma); $vk) outputs 1 for an honestly generated signature $\sigma \leftarrow$ Sign($m; $sk) is 1.

- **Unforgeability:** The probability that an adversary, knowing only the challenge message m^* and having access to an oracle giving back signatures σ_i on messages $m_i \neq m^*$ (for all $i \in [n]$ with n polynomially bounded in the security parameter), outputs a pair (m^*, σ^*) such that $\text{Ver}(m^*, \sigma^*; \text{vk}) = 1$ is negligible.

A.2   Public-Key Encryption Schemes

A Public-Key Encryption Scheme is a tuple of algorithms $(\text{Gen}, \text{Enc}, \text{Dec})$ such that

$\text{Gen}(1^\lambda)$: Takes as input the security parameter, outputs a couple (pk, sk) of keys sampled in the key spaces.

$\text{Enc}(m; \text{pk})$: Takes as input a message m in the message space and a public key pk, and outputs the ciphertext c in the ciphertext space.

$\text{Dec}(c; \text{sk})$: Takes as input a ciphertext c and a secret key, and output a message m'.

A PKE scheme is CPA-Secure if the following properties are satisfied

- **Completeness** The probability that $m = m'$, where $m' \leftarrow \text{Dec}(c; \text{sk})$ with $c \leftarrow_\$ \text{Enc}(m; \text{pk})$ for an honestly generated pair $(\text{pk}, \text{sk}) \leftarrow_\$ \text{Gen}(1^\lambda)$ is 1.
- **CPA-Security** The probability that an attacker, after choosing two messages (m_0, m_1), giving them to a challenger, and receiving back the encryption of one of the two (chosen by the challenger flipping a coin), can distinguish which of the two messages were encrypted, is negligible.

A.3   NIZK Proofs

In a *zero-knowledge proof* system an entity $\mathcal{P}$, called prover, can prove to another entity, called verifier, that an NP-statement x is in some language $\mathcal{L}$ (i.e., there exists at least a witness w such that the relation $\mathcal{R}_\mathcal{L}(x, w)$ for the language $\mathcal{L}$ is satisfied) without revealing a single bit of information on the used witness. Informally, the following properties must be satisfied by a zero-knowledge proof system:

- **Completeness:** The probability that an honest prover $\mathcal{P}$ (i.e. computing the proof by providing a valid (x, w) such that $\mathcal{R}_\mathcal{L}(x, w) = 1$) convinces the verifier $\mathcal{V}$ about the validity of the statement is 1.
- **Soundness:** The probability that a cheating prover convinces the verifier that a statement x is not in the language $\mathcal{L}$ is negligible.
- **Zero Knowledge:** If the statement x is true, the verifier learns no more information other than the fact that the statement is true. This concept is formalized by showing that there exists an efficient simulator that, given only the statement, can produce a protocol transcript that is indistinguishable from a real protocol execution.

A proof is said to be non-interactive when the interaction consists solely on a message sent by the prover to the verifier. A *zero-knowledge proof of knowledge* is a zero-knowledge proof where the prover shows that he actually *knows* a witness for the statement x and this is formalized by showing an efficient extractor that gives a witness in output. When we refer to NIZK proofs throughout the paper we usually intend NIZK proofs of knowledge.

In the random oracle model, both prover and verifier access to a cryptographic hash function that in the security proof is modeled as a random oracle. The simulator for the zero-knowledge property and the extractor for the proof of knowledge property have the power to program the random oracle.

B   Adding Seller's Privacy

As discussed in Sect. 2.3, using publicly posted TEKs is dangerous for the seller due to possible risks of incrimination. This could disincentivize the seller to utilize such smart contract mechanism. To guarantee seller's privacy, in all of our attacks we can enrich our playground by assuming the existence of a CPA-Secure PKE encryption scheme (Gen, Enc, Dec) and a NIZK proof system. The proposed protocols can be modified as follows:

- When the buyer creates the smart contract, he waits that a seller $\mathcal{P}$ is elected before providing his TEKs. When $\mathcal{P}$ is elected, $\mathcal{B}$ posts his TEKs encrypted with $\mathcal{P}$'s public key $\mathsf{pk}_\mathcal{P}$, by triggering an algorithm $\mathsf{SendBuyerTeks}(\mathbf{C}_\mathcal{B})$ where $\mathbf{C}_\mathcal{B} = (c_1, \ldots, c_n)$, with $c_i \leftarrow^\$ \mathsf{Enc}(t_i)$ for each $t_i \in \mathbf{T}_\mathcal{B}$. TEKs are pairs $t_i = (\mathsf{tek}_i, \mathsf{date}_i)$.
- When the signed TEKs list is available, the seller triggers $\mathsf{SendTeks}(\mathbf{T}, \sigma_T, \Pi, \tilde{\mathbf{T}})$, where $\mathbf{T} = (\tilde{t}_1, \ldots, \tilde{t}_N)$ are the published TEKs, σ_T the corresponding signature, and $\Pi = (\pi_1, \ldots, \pi_n)$ is a sequence of proofs in which π_i is a NIZK proof that the prover knows $t_i \leftarrow \mathsf{Dec}(c_i; \mathsf{sk}_\mathcal{P})$ and that at least one element $\tilde{t}_j$ in a subset $\tilde{\mathbf{T}} \subseteq \mathbf{T}$ such that $|\tilde{\mathbf{T}}| > |\mathbf{T}_\mathcal{B}|$ is equal to t_i. The smart contract checks all the proofs, and if all of them verify, transfer the prize to the seller.

Now the only information that an external observer can deduce by looking at the proofs is that all the encrypted buyer's TEKs are indeed inside the list (or in a subset of them). Depending on how the date field is handled it may be also necessary to encrypt it and to prove a slightly more complicated statement. To be sure that an observer cannot pinpoint the buyer's TEKs precisely, it is sufficient that the proofs use as a statement a subset of the published TEKs that contains at least one more TEK w.r.t the buyer's TEKs (proving on a subset and not on the entire list can be beneficial in terms of proof size and efficiency). The only harmful case is when the number of published keys matches with the number of the buyer's keys. We can argue that this condition happens quite rarely, considering that one external more key is sufficient to guarantee buyer's safety, and if GAEN recommendations are followed, a decent amount of keys should be present in the list.

C   GAEN Export Files

An example of an `export.bin` file for Immuni, the Italian contact tracing app is reported below. The meaning of the main fields is commented on the side. The `start_timestamp` and `end_timestamp` are expressed in UTC seconds, `rolling_start_interval_number` is expressed in 10 min increments from UNIX epoch. The `export.sig` contains the digital signature of the `export.bin` file, along with the field `signature_infos`.
The content description of the `export.bin` file follows.

```
start_timestamp: 1591254000 //start of the time window of included keys
end_timestamp: 1591268399 //end of the time window of included keys.
region: "222"  batch_num: 1 batch_size: 1
signature_infos {
verification_key_version: "v1" //version of used verification key
verification_key_id: "222"
signature_algorithm: "1.2.840.10045.4.3.2"
1: "it.ministerodellasalute.immuni"}
keys {
key_data: ".." //base64 encoded TEK
transmission_risk_level: 8
rolling_start_interval_number: 2651616 //date of usage of TEK
rolling_period: 144}...
```

D   Implementation Improvements

As noted in Sect. 2, our smart contract implementation of Take-TEK can handle export files large as the maximum transaction size at most. This limitation can be overcome by making the smart contract accepting the file split in multiple chunks (a transaction for each chunk), and then extracting the keys and verifying the signature by hashing the concatenation of all the stored chunks. A trivial solution to this problem can be to store $n - 1$ chunks in the smart contract, and when the seller sends the n-th chunk, the smart contract performs the concatenation, extracts the keys, and verifies the signature. Unfortunately, storing data in a smart contract is the most expensive operation in terms of gas cost, and storing such a big piece of data in a smart contract state may be too expensive. However, exploiting the Merkle-Damgård construction used by SHA to hash multiple blocks, way less amount of data needs to be stored. Let us define Hash as the hashing algorithm and H_i as the hash of the i-th chunk C_i. TEKs extraction and signature verification in the chunk-based mechanism can be done in the following way:

- The seller divides the export file in different chunks in such a way that, when each chunk is hashed, the hash climbs up to the same level of the Merkle tree of the other hashed chunks.
- When the seller sends a new chunk to the smart contract, the latter extracts all the TEKs contained in the chunk, checks which of the buyer's TEK are present in the chunk and stores this information[32]. After that, it hashes the chunk and stores the hashed value H_i.
- When the last chunk is sent to the smart contract by the seller (together with the signature of the entire export file), the smart contract extracts the last pieces of information, checks if the TEKs contained in the last chunk cover the not yet appeared buyer's TEKs, computes its hash H_n, hashes its concatenation with the previously stored hashed chunks (i.e. it calculates $H_{\mathsf{out}} = \mathtt{Hash}(H_1, \ldots, H_n)$) and triggers the signature verification procedure giving the value H_{out} and the signature file as input.

As can be noticed, the application of the hashing algorithm to the concatenation of the H_is makes the hashing algorithm climbing up to the root of the Merkle tree, thus giving the expected hash of the entire file as output. Now the amount of bits needed to be stored is around $|H| \cdot n = 512 \cdot n$, vs $|C_i| \cdot n$ (usually the maximum transaction size, and so C_i in our case, is around 44 Kbytes in Ethereum).

E   Other Subtleties: Details

E.1   Extracting Public Keys from Signatures

Take-TEK (cfr., Sect. 2.1) requires that the server's public key is known to both the involved parties. This guarantees that the buyer is sure the reward is paid only to sellers who actually upload data to the contact tracing system, and that honest sellers are sure they will be able to satisfy the conditions to be paid, namely obtaining a valid digital signature for reward redemption. A Github issue asking for the public key of the Italian contact tracing app was opened on the 7th of June 2020 and it has still not been addressed at the time of writing. SwissCovid Android app contains a configuration file specifying the production version of the bucket public key (the value BUCKET_PUBLIC_KEY can be found in https://github.com/DP-3T/dp3t-app-android-ch/blob/master/app/backend_certs.gradle) that is used to perform signature verification outside GAEN. Anyway, as we can notice with Immuni, this is not a requirement. One might think that keeping the verification keys secret may prevent attacks as the one of Sect. 2.1. However, it turns out that it is actually not the case. In fact, since GAEN uses ECDSA, starting from a signature and the related message we can recover two candidate public keys, one of which will match the actual one with overwhelming probability. A

---

[32] During the chunk splitting, some TEKs may be cut in half. The smart contract should take care of the first and the last bits of each chunk and reconstruct the missing information.

practical example showing this procedure can be found in [28]. Such message/signature pairs are generally made publicly available and are easily accessible by appropriately querying the server of the specific contact tracing system. Multiple pairs per day may be released. A comprehensive description on how to get this data has been provided by the Testing Apps for COVID-19 Tracing (TACT) project, along with scripts to automate the downloading process [11]. We also practically performed the extraction procedure, successfully extracting the keys for both SwissCovid and Immuni.

E.2   Updates of Public Keys

There is a subtle technical problem with the attack described in Sect. 2.1. The digital signature keys that the server uses may change over time. In fact, as shown in Appendix C, the `export.bin` file includes a field indicating a version for the verification key. This field follows a progressive numeration, that is the first version is termed v1, the second one v2 and so on. This means that the server may change the verification key it uses, perhaps within a set of keys that have been pre-shared with Google and Apple. Therefore, it might happen that, after the seller makes the deposit and accepts to upload the buyer's TEK, the server, by coincidence, decides to use a new key which was never used before, thus producing a signature that is not verifiable under the public key posted on the smart contract.

However, by making a slight modification to the smart contract, it is possible to handle also this unfortunate event. Having realized that she would be unable to redeem the reward, the seller might activate a special recovery condition. After this, the buyer will be able to collect both deposits if and only if he manages to provide a pair of export files which have an `end_timestamp` (cfr., Appendix C) subsequent to the time of the recovery request and verify under the public key originally posted on the smart contract; otherwise the deposits are returned to the original owners. Obviously, enough time should be given to the buyer to provide the export files, similarly to what happens to the seller after her deposit.

This event is certainly very annoying for the seller and might play as disincentive to join the trade, but taking a look at real-world data one realizes that this is a relatively rare event. We considered several countries which are currently using a digital contact tracing system, namely: Italy, Switzerland, Austria, Germany, Ireland, Northern Ireland, Denmark, Latvia, Canada and US Virginia. Until January 13th 2021 (last time we checked), only US Virginia and Italy have switched to the second version of the verification key. In particular, the change to the Italian system dates back to the 15th of June 2020[33] and no modifications have been made since then. Notably, some countries' systems, like Switzerland and Germany's ones, are active from several months now and the verification key has not changed at all. To the best of our knowledge, the criteria by which the verification key should change is not documented anywhere.

---

[33] This change occurred in the 4th export file.

F   Further Notes on Our Smart Contract Oracle

F.1   CBC-HMAC vs AES-GCM

Differently from CBC-HMAC, AES-GCM relies on the same key for both encryption and MACs. The impact of AES-GCM is twofold: 1) more computation is needed to perform the required 2PC to calculate messages from/to the server, due to the AES algorithm itself, 2) the prover does not learn the encryption key after 3PHS, meaning that both encryption and decryption must be done via 2PC as well. On the smart contract side, this difference boils down to a lack of fairness. After V and P have calculated together the upload message and sent it then to S, V could decide not to help the prover to decrypt the server's response. Now, P has no witness in her hands to give to the smart contract in order to prove that she has correctly performed the TEKs upload. As a result, she cannot redeem the prize. The problem can be easily solved by giving to the smart contract the burden of decrypting the server's ciphertext. In our approach, V must commit to his key and open it later. When this happens, the server reconstructs the MAC/encryption key, decrypts the ciphertext, does the necessary checks, and pay the prize to P. The CBC-HMAC version of DECO is way faster then the AES-GCM one. However, looking at practical evaluations made by the authors [14,30] it is reasonable to think that all their solutions may fit in the time window given by contact tracing servers (e.g., 2 h in Immuni and SwissCovid) for the TLS connection, even when hiding V through Tor hidden services. What is less likely is that, in the case of Immuni which uses AES-GCM and requires the upload to be completed within two minutes, the upload request message (m_c, θ_c) is computed and sent to the server in time; especially when the prover and the verifier communicate via Tor.

References

1. Auerbach, B., et al.: Inverse-sybil attacks in automated contact tracing. In: Proceedings of CT-RSA. volume to appear (2021)
2. Avitabile, G., Friolo, D., Visconti, I.: Tenk-u: terrorist attacks for fake exposure notifications in contact tracing systems. IACR Cryptol. ePrint Arch. **2020**, 1150 (2020)
3. Baumgärtner, L., et al.: Mind the GAP: security and privacy risks of contact tracing apps. In: TrustCom 2020, Security Track, pp. 458–467 (2020)
4. Dehaye, P., Reardon, J.: Proximity tracing in an ecosystem of surveillance capitalism. CoRR abs/2009.06077 (2020)
5. Dehaye, P., Reardon, J.: Swisscovid: a critical analysis of risk assessment by swiss authorities. CoRR abs/2006.10719 (2020)
6. Dingledine, R., Mathewson, N., Syverson, P.F.: Tor: the second-generation onion router. In: USENIX, pp. 303–320 (2004)
7. European Commission: Guidance on apps supporting the fight against COVID 19 pandemic in relation to data protection. Official Journal of the European Union (2020). https://eur-lex.europa.eu/legal-content/EN/TXT/PDF/?uri=CELEX:52020XC0417(08)&from=EN

8. Immuni Team: Immuni's high-level description (2020). https://github.com/immuni-app/immuni-documentation. Accessed 23 Aug 2020

9. Iovino, V., Vaudenay, S., Vuagnoux, M.: On the effectiveness of time travel to inject Covid-19 alerts. In: Proceedings of CT-RSA. volume to appear (2021)

10. Legendre, F., Humbert, M., Mermoud, A., Lenders, V.: Contact tracing: an overview of technologies and cyber risks. CoRR abs/2007.02806 (2020). https://arxiv.org/abs/2007.02806

11. Leith, D., Farrell, S.: Testing apps for COVID-19 tracing (TACT) (2020). https://down.dsg.cs.tcd.ie/tact/. Accessed 23 Aug 2020

12. Leith, D.J., Farrell, S.: Coronavirus contact tracing: evaluating the potential of using bluetooth received signal strength for proximity detection. Comput. Commun. Rev. **50**(4), 66–74 (2020)

13. Liao, K., Katz, J.: Incentivizing blockchain forks via whale transactions. In: Brenner, M., et al. (eds.) FC 2017. LNCS, vol. 10323, pp. 264–279. Springer, Cham (2017). https://doi.org/10.1007/978-3-319-70278-0_17

14. Maram, D., et al.: Candid: Can-do decentralized identity with legacy compatibility, sybil-resistance, and accountability. IACR Cryptol. ePrint Arch. **2020**, 934 (2020). https://eprint.iacr.org/2020/934

15. McCorry, P., Hicks, A., Meiklejohn, S.: Smart contracts for bribing miners. In: Zohar, A., et al. (eds.) FC 2018. LNCS, vol. 10958, pp. 3–18. Springer, Heidelberg (2019). https://doi.org/10.1007/978-3-662-58820-8_1

16. Nadahalli, T., Khabbazian, M., Wattenhofer, R.: Timelocked bribing. In: Financial Cryptography. volume to appear (2021)

17. Pietrzak, K.: Delayed authentication: preventing replay and relay attacks in private contact tracing. In: Bhargavan, K., Oswald, E., Prabhakaran, M. (eds.) INDOCRYPT 2020. LNCS, vol. 12578, pp. 3–15. Springer, Cham (2020). https://doi.org/10.1007/978-3-030-65277-7_1

18. Rosario Gennaro, A.K., Krellenstein, J.: Exposure notification system may allow for large-scale voter suppression (2020). https://static1.squarespace.com/static/5e937afbfd7a75746167b39c/t/5f47a87e58d3de0db3da91b2/1598531714869/Exposure_Notification.pdf. Accessed 23 Aug 2020

19. Semaphore Team: Semaphore. https://semaphore.appliedzkp.org/. Accessed 15 Sept 2020

20. Swiss Federal Office of Public Health: New coronavirus: Swisscovid app and contact tracing (2020). https://www.bag.admin.ch/bag/en/home/krankheiten/ausbrueche-epidemien-pandemien/aktuelle-ausbrueche-epidemien/novel-cov/swisscovid-app-und-contact-tracing/datenschutzerklaerung-nutzungsbedingungen.html#-11360452. Accessed 23 Aug 2020

21. Tang, Q.: Privacy-preserving contact tracing: current solutions and open questions. CoRR abs/2004.06818 (2020)

22. Teutsch, J., Jain, S., Saxena, P.: When cryptocurrencies mine their own business. In: Grossklags, J., Preneel, B. (eds.) FC 2016. LNCS, vol. 9603, pp. 499–514. Springer, Heidelberg (2017). https://doi.org/10.1007/978-3-662-54970-4_29

23. Vaudenay, S.: Analysis of DP3T. IACR Cryptol. ePrint Arch. **2020**, 399 (2020)

24. Vaudenay, S.: Centralized or decentralized? the contact tracing dilemma. IACR Cryptol. ePrint Arch. **2020**, 531 (2020)

25. Vaudenay, S., Vuagnoux, M.: Analysis of swisscovid (2020). https://lasec.epfl.ch/people/vaudenay/swisscovid/swisscovid-ana.pdf. Accessed 23 Aug 2020

26. Velner, Y., Teutsch, J., Luu, L.: Smart contracts make bitcoin mining pools vulnerable. In: Brenner, M., et al. (eds.) FC 2017. LNCS, vol. 10323, pp. 298–316. Springer, Cham (2017). https://doi.org/10.1007/978-3-319-70278-0_19

27. Williamson, Z.J.: Aztec (2018). https://github.com/AztecProtocol/AZTEC/blob/master/AZTEC.pdf. Accessed 15 Sept 2020
28. Yang, H.: EC Cryptography Tutorials - Herong's Tutorial Examples. Herong's Tutorial Examples, Herong Yang (2019). https://books.google.it/books?id=4PWKDwAAQBAJ
29. Zhang, F., Cecchetti, E., Croman, K., Juels, A., Shi, E.: Town crier: an authenticated data feed for smart contracts. In: ACM CCS (2016)
30. Zhang, F., Maram, D., Malvai, H., Goldfeder, S., Juels, A.: DECO: liberating web data using decentralized oracles for TLS. In: Ligatti, J., Ou, X., Katz, J., Vigna, G. (eds.) Proceedings of CCS 2020, pp. 1919–1938. ACM (2018)
31. ZkDAI Team: Zkdai (2020). https://github.com/atvanguard/ethsingapore-zk-dai. Accessed 15 Sept 2020
32. ZoKrates Team: Zokrates (2020). https://zokrates.github.io/. Accessed 15 Sept 2020

Digital Signatures

Unlinkable and Invisible γ-Sanitizable Signatures

Angèle Bossuat[1] and Xavier Bultel[2(✉)]

[1] Univ Rennes 1, CNRS, IRISA, Rennes, France
[2] LIFO, INSA Centre Val de Loire, Université d'Orléans, Bourges, France
`xavier.bultel@insa-cvl.fr`

Abstract. Sanitizable signatures (SaS) allow a (single) sanitizer, chosen by the signer, to modify and re-sign a message in a somewhat controlled way, that is, only editing parts (or blocks) of the message that are admissible for modification.

This primitive is an efficient tool, with many formally defined security properties, such as unlinkability, transparency, immutability, invisibility, and unforgeability. An SaS scheme that satisfies these properties can be a great asset to the privacy of any field it will be applied to, *e.g.*, anonymizing medical files.

In this work, we look at the notion of *γ-sanitizable signatures* (γSaS): we take the sanitizable signatures one step further by allowing the signer to not only decide which blocks can be modified, but also how many of them at most can be modified within a single sanitization, setting a limit, denoted with γ. We adapt the security properties listed above to γSaS and propose our own scheme, ULISS (Unlinkable Limited Invisible Sanitizable Signature), then show that it verifies these properties. This extension of SaS can not only improve current use cases, but also introduce new ones, *e.g.*, restricting the number of changes in a document within a certain timeframe.

1 Introduction

One of the main properties of digital signatures is integrity – indeed, it is important that any modification made to a message after it was signed would invalidate said signature.

However, one might wish to modify a signed message without altering its core meaning, for example to anonymize a document, while not wanting (or not being able) to take the time necessary to get the original signer to sign again.

Sanitizable signatures, as introduced in [1] can serve such a purpose by allowing a form of controlled malleability, where a signer will sign a message along with a list of *admissible modifications* with respect to a second entity called the *sanitizer*. That sanitizer will be allowed to re-sign a message, producing a valid signature as long as the message was only modified within the limits defined by the list.

© Springer Nature Switzerland AG 2021
K. Sako and N. O. Tippenhauer (Eds.): ACNS 2021, LNCS 12726, pp. 251–283, 2021.
https://doi.org/10.1007/978-3-030-78372-3_10

The relationship between the signer and the sanitizer will depend on the use case (*e.g.* they can be a boss and their employee, or a service provider and their client) and for this reason the means and content of any communication between those two entities (including credentials used to sign/sanitize) is out of scope of this paper.

A frequent usage example for such a signature scheme would be the anonymization of medical data destined to be analyzed: the name of the patients is – with a high probability – not relevant for the analysis, neither is their email address or phone number; however, it is important to know that the data is authentic, hence the need for it to still be verifiable once it has been anonymized.

However, we do believe that this still leaves too great a latitude to the sanitizer, and that this latitude should be somewhat narrowed down, which is the aim of this work.

Contribution. In this paper, we look at a variant of sanitizable signatures, that we refer to as γ-*Sanitizable Signatures*. This variant restricts the sanitizer to only modify a certain number of blocks at once, a number which is referred to as the *limit*, and denoted with γ. In this variant, even if a signature has been sanitized multiple times, the number of blocks that differ between the *original* message and this one should not be above the limit. When the signer signs the original message, they will thus also set that limit.

We detail some applications for this limit in Sect. 5, all of which are inachievable with regular sanitizable signatures: for example, we show how to use γ-Sanitizable Signatures to limit the number of changes a user can make to their social media profile over a certain period of time, similar to what Facebook currently does with birthdays[1].

This idea of adding a limit was first introduced as an important research problem by Klonowski and Lauks [24] and later applied by Canard and Jambert in [13], but as we detail below in related works, the scheme they proposed satisfies less security properties and is not practical compared to this work. Our first contribution is to adapt the various security properties of sanitizable signatures by taking the limit into account, namely:

Unforgeability: the users cannot produce a valid signature without the secret keys.
Immutability: the sanitizer cannot sanitize on an unauthorized modification.
Transparency: the verifier cannot tell whether a given signature was sanitized or not.
Unlinkability: the verifier cannot link a sanitized signature with its original.
Invisibility: the verifier cannot tell what (or how many) modifications are authorized on a signature without knowledge of any secret key.

In this work, we do not focus on accountability, which ensures that the signer can cancel the transparency *a posteriori*, as this property does not depend on

---

[1] facebook.com/help/563229410363824/.

the limit and achieved for any sanitizable signature scheme by using the generic transformation of [11]. Our second contribution is the scheme ULISS (Unlinkable Limited Invisible Sanitizable Signature), for which we prove all of the above properties in the random oracle model (ROM).

Our Scheme. Our aim when creating ULISS was to build a signature that is originally issued by a signer and that can be modified by the sanitizer, who has to prove that it was done within the authorized limits (*i.e.*, the blocks that were modified are admissible *and the number of blocks that were modified is below the limit*). We also want the resulting signatures to not leak whether they come from the signer or the sanitizer. We focused on the idea that the sanitizer must *prove* that the sanitization was done properly, as allowed, and for this we base our scheme on the use of (non-interactive) zero-knowledge proofs.

The signer first computes commitments pertaining to the authorized modifications and the limit, and signs them, then encrypts some necessary information for the sanitizer. To edit the signature, the sanitizer will retrieve the encrypted data and use it to build some new proofs related to the original commitments, and sign everything (along with the modified message, of course) using the ring signature. Since the information about the modifications and the limit is committed, it cannot be deduced from the signature, which makes ULISS invisible.

Reaching both invisibility and unlinkability is a difficult task; to the best of our knowledge, the scheme presented in Bultel et al. [11] is the only one that achieves these two properties together, thanks to class-equivalence signatures. We use a similar trick for ULISS: a sanitized signature uses the same signed commitments as the original signature. This could be used by an adversary to link these two signatures, however, we use a class-equivalence signature to sign the commitments, which allows the sanitizer to randomize the commitments and the signature in such a way that the messages in the signed commitments are *not* modified.

Related Work. Sanitizable signatures were, as cited above, first introduced by Ateniese et al. [1], proposing applications, among others, in the medical field. This primitive is related to (but should not be confused with) redactable signatures [7], where a sanitizer can erase some parts of the message but not modify it. The security properties were originally presented in [1], but formalized later on by Brzuska et al. in [8] and [9], the latter adding the idea of *unlinkability*. Invisibility was formalized in [12], and invisible constructions are proposed in [12] and [3]. In [11], the authors propose a scheme that is both unlinkable and invisible, using class-equivalent signatures. To the best our knowledge, this scheme is the only one that achieves these two properties together. They also provide a generic way to add accountability on any sanitizable signature scheme, using verifiable ring signatures [10]. Note that these schemes allow the sanitizer modify parts of the message in an unlimited way.

On the other hand, related primitives with a more general application can be used to achieve γ-Sanitizable Signatures, including functional signatures [6] and delegatable functional signatures [2], which allows a user to sign messages that verify some functions or predicate, policy-based signatures [4], where signers are authorized to sign a message if it satisfies some policy, and homomorphic signatures [23]. All of these offer much more variety on what (the equivalent of) the sanitizer can do compared to traditional sanitizable signatures, while being generally much less efficient specifically because of their fine-grained possibilities, using heavy generic primitives (*e.g.*, generic zero-knowledge proofs for garbled boolean circuits or homomorphic encryption). We believe our work lies somewhere in between, offering more control on the sanitizations while remaining practical.

The γ-sanitizable signature schemes were introduced in [24] and revisited by Canard and Jambert in [13], the latter proposing the first security model for γ-sanitizable signatures. To the best of our knowledge, there is no other such scheme in the literature – moreover, these two works are neither invisible nor unlinkable. Adding unlinkability to these schemes is not straightforward, as they use chameleon hashes [25] on modifiable parts of the signatures, which implies that these hashes are the same for both the sanitized signature and the original one. Moreover, adding invisibility does not seem trivial either, as the size of the public parameters of the sanitizer is linear in the limit γ (which must be secret in invisible schemes). Furthermore, the design of the schemes in [13,24] has inherent limitations making them unsuitable for practical applications:

- The signer must use a new public key (of size linear in γ) generated by the sanitizer at each new signature, implying that the signature algorithm is interactive and requires the presence of the sanitizer.
- If the same signature is sanitized several times such that the *total* number of modified parts is greater than γ, then the key of the sanitizer is leaked to anybody, even if the sanitized signatures considered separately are within the limit γ, which drastically restricts the number of sanitizations of a signature.
- To verify that the limit γ is respected on a sanitized signature, the verifier must also have the original signature. However, if the verifier knows the original signature and the original message, sanitizable signatures are useless by design.

For these reasons, we believe that security notions and constructions of γ-Sanitizable Signatures must be revisited, to produce a more *practical* and more *secure* scheme. As explained above, this cannot be achieved by modifying the proposed schemes: we must instead get our inspiration from a regular sanitizable signature scheme that satisfies both unlinkability and invisibility – i.e., [11]. We will show that the cost of introducing a new feature to sanitizable signatures is acceptable, especially since compared to Canard and Jambert's scheme, we obtain a much more practical scheme, and satisfy more security properties.

Outline. This work is organized as follows: in Sect. 2, we present the different cryptographic tools that we use, along with the security definitions, then in Sect. 3 we describe our security model. Our scheme is explained and analysed in Sect. 4. Some applications are presented in Sect. 5. The complete proofs are given in Appendix A for the most technical ones. Due to the page limitation, the less "major", more classical proofs are given in the full version.

2 Cryptographic Tools

In this section, we give or recall the definitions of various cryptographic tools that will be used when building our scheme, or when proving its security properties.

Definition 1 (DDH). *Let $\mathbb{G}$ be a multiplicative group of order p generated from a security parameter λ (with $\lfloor \log(p) \rfloor = \lambda$) with generator g, the* Decisional Diffie-Hellman *(DDH) assumption states that for a, b and c randomly chosen in $\mathbb{Z}_p^*$, it is difficult for a polynomial-time adversary $\mathcal{A}$ to decide whether he has been given $(g^a, g^b, g^{a \cdot b})$ or (g^a, g^b, g^c), i.e., the following function is negligible:*

$$\mathsf{Adv}_{\mathbb{G}}^{DDH}(\lambda) = |\Pr[1 \leftarrow \mathcal{A}(g^a, g^b, g^c)] - \Pr[1 \leftarrow \mathcal{A}(g^a, g^b, g^{a \cdot b})]|.$$

Definition 2 (NIZKP [16]). *A non-interactive zero-knowledge proof (NIZKP) for a language $\mathcal{L}$ is a pair of algorithms (Prove, Verify) such that:*

Prove(s, w): *It outputs a proof π that $s \in \mathcal{L}$ using witness w,*
Verify(s, π): *It checks whether π is a valid proof that $s \in \mathcal{L}$.*

A NIZKP must satisfy the following properties:

Soundness. *No adversary $\mathcal{A}$ (possibly unbounded in time) is such that $\mathcal{A}(\mathcal{L})$ can, with non-negligible probability, output (x, π) where Verify(x, π) = 1 and $x \notin \mathcal{L}$.*
Completeness. *For any statement $s \in \mathcal{L}$ and its witness w, Verify(s, Prove(s, w)) = 1.*
(Perfect) Zero-Knowledge. *The proof π does not leak any information, in other words, there exists a probabilistic polynomial-time (PPT) simulator Sim (which has the ability to program the outputs of the random oracle in the random oracle model) such that Sim(s) follows the same probability distribution as Prove(s, w).*

Definition 3 (2-Ring Signature (2RS) [5]). *A 2-Ring Signature scheme R is a tuple of 4 PPT algorithms defined as follows:*

R.ini(1^λ): *It returns a setup value set.*
R.gen(set): *It returns a pair of public/private keys (pk, sk).*
R.sig(sk, {pk$_0$, pk$_1$}, m): *This algorithm computes a signature σ from the message m using the secret key sk and two public keys (pk$_0$, pk$_1$) (such that sk is the private key corresponding to one of them).*
R.ver({pk$_0$, pk$_1$}, m, σ): *This algorithm returns a bit d.*

A 2RS scheme R is said to be correct if for all (pk$_0$, sk$_0$), (pk$_1$, sk$_1$) output by the algorithm R.gen(set) where set was output by R.ini(1^λ), for any message m, and for $b \in \{0, 1\}$:

$$R.\mathsf{ver}(\{pk_0, pk_1\}, m, R.\mathsf{sig}(sk_b, \{pk_0, pk_1\}, m)) = 1.$$

We use two security notions for 2-Ring Signatures: strong unforgeability, and anonimity, formally defined below.

Definition 4 (Strong Unforgeability). *Let P be a 2-ring signature, then P is strongly unforgeable if for any polynomial-time adversary $\mathcal{A}$, the probability $\Pr[Exp_{P,\mathcal{A}}^{SUF}(\lambda) = 1]$ that $\mathcal{A}$ wins the experiment in Fig. 1 is negligible.*

Definition 5 (Anonymity). *Let P be a 2-ring signature, then P is (perfectly) anonymous if for any polynomial-time adversary $\mathcal{A}$, the probability $\Pr[Exp_{P,\mathcal{A}}^{anon}(\lambda) = 1]$ that $\mathcal{A}$ wins the experiment in Fig. 1 is negligibly close to $1/2$.*

Definition 6 (Equivalence-Class Signature (EQS) [22]). *An Equivalence-Class Signature scheme S on a bilinear group of prime order p generated from a security parameter λ (described as $\mathcal{BG} = (\mathbb{G}_1, \mathbb{G}_2, \mathbb{G}_t, g_1, g_2, g_T, e, q)$) is a tuple of 5 algorithms defined as follows:*

S.ini(1^λ): It returns a setup value set which contains the bilinear group $\mathcal{BG}$.
S.gen(set): It returns a public/private key pair (pk, sk).
S.sig(sk, m): It computes and returns a signature σ on the equivalence class $[m]$ of the message m using the private key sk.
S.ver(pk, σ, m): It verifies the signature σ under the key pk on the equivalence class $[m]$ of the message m.
S.ChRep(pk, σ, m, t): It computes and returns a signature σ' on (the same) equivalence class $[m^t] = [m]$ of message m^t.

An EQS scheme is said to be correct if for all (pk, sk) output by S.gen(set) where set was output by S.ini(1^λ), for any message m, any scalar $t \in \mathbb{Z}_p^*$:

$$S.ver(pk, S.sig(sk, m), m) = 1, \quad and$$
$$S.ver(pk, S.ChRep(pk, S.sig(sk, m), m, t), m^t) = 1$$

Definition 7 (EUF-CMA). *An equivalence-class signature scheme P is said to be existentially unforgeable under chosen message attacks (EUF-CMA) if for any polynomial-time adversary $\mathcal{A}$, the probability $\Pr[Exp_{P,\mathcal{A}}^{EUF\text{-}CMA}(\lambda) = 1]$ that $\mathcal{A}$ wins the EUF-CMA experiment given in Fig. 1 is negligible.*

Definition 8 ((Perfect) Signature Adaptation). *An equivalence-class signature scheme P is said to (perfectly) adapt signatures if, for all tuples (pk, sk, σ, m, t) such that (pk, sk) is a public/private key pair and S.ver(pk, σ, m) = 1, it holds that S.sig(sk, m^t) and S.ChRep(pk, σ, m, t) are identically distributed. Formally, this translates into the fact that for any polynomial-time adversary $\mathcal{A}$, the probability $\Pr[Exp_{P,\mathcal{A}}^{adapt}(\lambda) = 1]$ of winning the adapt experiment given in Fig. 1 is negligibly close to $1/2$.*

Definition 9 (Class-Hiding). *A message space $\mathcal{M} = \mathbb{G}^\ell$ (with $\ell > 1$) of an equivalence-class signature scheme is said to be class-hiding if for all polynomial-time adversary $\mathcal{A}$, the probability $\Pr[Exp_{\mathcal{M},\mathcal{A}}^{class\text{-}hid}(\lambda) = 1]$ of winning the class-hid experiment given in Fig. 1, in which $[m]$ is the equivalence class of m, is negligibly close to $1/2$.*

$\mathbf{Exp}^{\mathsf{SUF}}_{P,\mathcal{A}}(\lambda)$:
set $\leftarrow$ R.ini(1^λ);
$(\mathsf{pk}_0, \mathsf{sk}_0) \leftarrow$ R.gen(set);
$(\mathsf{pk}_1, \mathsf{sk}_1) \leftarrow$ R.gen(set);
$S \leftarrow \{\ \}$;
$(m, \sigma) \leftarrow \mathcal{A}^{\mathsf{R.sig}(\cdot,\{\mathsf{pk}_0,\mathsf{pk}_1\},\cdot)}(\mathsf{pk}_0, \mathsf{pk}_1)$;
if $(m, \sigma) \notin S$ then
return R.ver($\{\mathsf{pk}_0, \mathsf{pk}_1\}, m, \sigma$), else 0;

Oracle R.sig($i, \{\mathsf{pk}_0, \mathsf{pk}_1\}, m$):
$\sigma \leftarrow$ R.sig($\mathsf{sk}_i, \{\mathsf{pk}_0, \mathsf{pk}_1\}, m$);
$S \leftarrow S \cup (m, \sigma)$;
return σ;

$\mathbf{Exp}^{\mathsf{anon}}_{P,\mathcal{A}}(\lambda)$:
$b \overset{\$}{\leftarrow} \{0,1\}$;
set $\leftarrow$ R.ini(1^λ);
$(\mathsf{pk}_0, \mathsf{sk}_0) \leftarrow$ R.gen(set);
$(\mathsf{pk}_1, \mathsf{sk}_1) \leftarrow$ R.gen(set);
$b_* \leftarrow \mathcal{A}^{\mathsf{R.sig}(\mathsf{sk}_b,\{\mathsf{pk}_0,\mathsf{pk}_1\},\cdot)}(\mathsf{pk}_0, \mathsf{pk}_1)$;
return $b = b_*$;

Oracle R.sig($\mathsf{sk}_b, \{\mathsf{pk}_0, \mathsf{pk}_1\}, m$):
return R.sig($\mathsf{sk}_b, \{\mathsf{pk}_0, \mathsf{pk}_1\}, m$);

$\mathbf{Exp}^{\mathsf{EUF\text{-}CMA}}_{P,\mathcal{A}}(\lambda)$:
set $\leftarrow$ S.ini(1^λ);
$(\mathsf{pk}, \mathsf{sk}) \leftarrow$ S.gen(set);
$S \leftarrow \{\ \}$;
$(m, \sigma) \leftarrow \mathcal{A}^{\mathsf{S.sig}(\mathsf{sk},\cdot)}$;
if $(m, \sigma) \notin S$
then return S.ver(pk, m, σ);
else return 0;

Oracle S.sig(sk, m):
$\sigma \leftarrow$ S.sig(sk, m);
$S \leftarrow S \cup (m, \sigma)$;
return σ;

$\mathbf{Exp}^{\mathsf{adapt}}_{P,\mathcal{A}}(\lambda)$:
set $\leftarrow$ S.ini(1^λ);
$(\mathsf{pk}, \mathsf{sk}) \leftarrow$ S.gen(set);
$b_* \leftarrow \mathcal{A}^{\mathsf{S.Ch/Sig}(b,\cdot,\cdot,\cdot,\cdot)}(\mathsf{pk}, \mathsf{sk})$;
if $b_* = b$ then return 1;
else return 0;

Oracle
S.Ch/Sig($b, (\mathsf{sk}, \mathsf{pk}), s, t, m$):
if $b = 0$
then return S.sig(sk, m^t);
return S.ChRep(pk, s, m, t);

$\mathbf{Exp}^{\mathsf{class\text{-}hid}}_{\mathcal{M},\mathcal{A}}(\lambda)$:
$b \overset{\$}{\leftarrow} \{0,1\}$;
set $\leftarrow$ S.ini(1^λ);
$m, m_0 \overset{\$}{\leftarrow} \mathcal{M}^2$;
$m_1 \overset{\$}{\leftarrow} [m]$;
$b_* \leftarrow \mathcal{A}(\mathsf{set}, m, m_b)$;
return $b_* = b$;

$\mathbf{Exp}^{\mathsf{IND\$\text{-}CCA}}_{E,\mathcal{A}}(\lambda)$:
set $\leftarrow$ E.ini(1^λ);
$b \overset{\$}{\leftarrow} \{0,1\}$;
$(\mathsf{pk}, \mathsf{sk}) \leftarrow$ E.gen(set);
$b_* \leftarrow \mathcal{A}^{\mathsf{RREnc}(\mathsf{pk},b,\cdot),\mathsf{Dec}(\mathsf{sk},\cdot)}(\mathsf{pk})$;
return $b = b_*$;

Oracle RREnc(pk, b, m):
if $b = 1$ then return E.enc(pk, m);
$m' \overset{\$}{\leftarrow} \{0,1\}^{|m|}$;
return E.enc(pk, m');

Oracle Dec(sk, c):
if c was output by RRenc
then return $\bot$;
return Dec(sk, c);

Fig. 1. Security experiments and oracles of our cryptographic tools.

Lemma 1 [22]. *A message space $\mathcal{M} = \mathbb{G}^\ell$ is class-hiding if and only if the DDH assumption holds in $\mathbb{G}$.*

Definition 10 (IND\$-CCA). *An encryption scheme $E = (E.ini, E.gen, E.enc, E.dec)$ with security parameter λ is said to be indistinguishable from random under adaptive chosen ciphertext attack (IND\$-CCA) if for any polynomial-time adversary $\mathcal{A}$, the probability $\Pr[\mathsf{Exp}^{\mathsf{IND\$\text{-}CCA}}_{E,\mathcal{A}}(\lambda) = 1]$ that $\mathcal{A}$ wins the experiment in Fig. 1 is negligibly close to 1/2. Note that this notion is equivalent to its more classic version, IND-CCA, in which the adversary must guess which of the two messages sent to the challenger was encrypted.*

3 Security Model

In this section, we define our notion of γ-Sanitizable Signature, as well as the various security properties of our model.

Definition 11 (γ-Sanitizable Signature (γSaS)). *A γ-Sanitizable Signature scheme is a tuple of 6 algorithms defined as follows:*

Init(1^λ): *It returns a setup value set.*
SiGen(set): *It returns a pair of signer public/private keys (pk, sk).*
SaGen(set): *It returns a pair of sanitizer public/private keys ($\mathsf{spk}, \mathsf{ssk}$).*

$\mathsf{Sig}(m, \mathsf{sk}, \mathsf{spk}, \mathrm{ADM}, \gamma)$: *This algorithm computes a signature σ from the message m using the secret key sk, the sanitizer public key spk, the admissible function ADM and the limit γ. Note that we assume that ADM can be efficiently recovered from any signature as in the definition of Fleischhacker et al. [19]. Moreover, for a modification MOD we write that $\mathrm{ADM}(\mathrm{MOD}) = 1$ to signify that the modification is allowed, and for a block number i, we write $i \in \mathrm{ADM}$ to say that the ith block can be modified.*

$\mathsf{San}(m, \mathrm{MOD}, \sigma, \mathsf{pk}, \mathsf{ssk}, \mathsf{spk})$: *Let ADM be the admissible function according to the signature σ. If $\mathrm{ADM}(\mathrm{MOD}) = 1$ and $\mathsf{Ver}(m, \sigma, \mathsf{pk}, \mathsf{spk}) = 1$ then this algorithm returns a signature σ' of the message $m' = \mathrm{MOD}(m)$ using the signature σ, the signer public key pk and the sanitizer public/private key pair $(\mathsf{ssk}, \mathsf{spk})$. Else it returns $\perp$.*

$\mathsf{Ver}(m, \sigma, \mathsf{pk}, \mathsf{spk})$: *It returns a bit b: if the signature σ of m is valid for the two public keys pk and spk then $b = 1$, else $b = 0$. This algorithm is deterministic.*

A γ-SaS is said to be correct if for all set output by $\mathsf{Init}(1^\lambda)$, all Sig and San key pairs $(\mathsf{pk}, \mathsf{sk}), (\mathsf{spk}, \mathsf{ssk})$ output by $\mathsf{SiGen}(set)$ and $\mathsf{SaGen}(set)$, respectively, all admissible functions ADM, limits γ, modifications MOD, messages m, we have:

$$\mathsf{Ver}(m, \mathsf{Sig}(m, \mathsf{sk}, \mathsf{spk}, \mathrm{ADM}, \gamma), \mathsf{pk}, \mathsf{spk}) = 1,$$

and for all σ such that $\mathsf{Ver}(m, \sigma, \mathsf{pk}, \mathsf{spk}) = 1$, and for all σ' output by $\mathsf{San}(m, \mathrm{MOD}, \sigma, \mathsf{pk}, \mathsf{ssk}, \mathsf{spk})$ such that $\sigma' \neq \perp$:

$$\mathsf{Ver}(\mathrm{MOD}(m), \sigma', \mathsf{pk}, \mathsf{spk}) = 1.$$

We now adapt the security properties of sanitizable signatures to fit our notion. In most cases, the limit must be treated in a similar way as the admissible function – however, it is important to consider this additional feature carefully, as it does of course introduce new *trivial* attacks. The detailed meaning and formal definition of each adapted property is given below.

Strong Unforgeability: The (strong) unforgeability property ensures that an adversary cannot create a valid message-signature pair without knowing the corresponding private key (*i.e.*, sk for the signer and ssk for the sanitizer). The adversary has access to the signing oracle and the sanitizing oracle, and must provide a message- signature pair. Of course, the adversary cannot be allowed to trivially win the experiment by sending a pair produced by either of the oracles to the challenger – but can, however, produce a pair containing a message that had been signed by either of the oracles.

Definition 12 (Strong Unforgeability). *Let P be a γSaS of security parameter λ, then P is strongly unforgeable if for any polynomial-time adversary $\mathcal{A}$, the probability $\Pr[\mathsf{Exp}_{ULISS,\mathcal{A}}^{SUF}(\lambda) = 1]$ that $\mathcal{A}$ wins the SUF experiment given in Fig. 2 is negligible.*

Immutability: A γSaS is immutable when no adversary is able to sanitize a signature without the corresponding sanitizer secret key or to sanitize a signature using a modification function that is not admissible (*i.e.*, $\text{ADM}(\text{MOD}) = 0$ or the number of modifications is higher that the limit γ). The adversary has access to a signature oracle.

Definition 13 (Immutability [8]). *Let P be a γSaS. P is Immut-secure (or immutable) when for any polynomial time adversary $\mathcal{A}$, the probability $\Pr[\text{Exp}^{immut}_{ULISS,\mathcal{A}}(\lambda) = 1]$ that $\mathcal{A}$ wins the immut experiment given in Fig. 2 is negligible, where q_{Sig} is the number of calls to the oracle $Sig(\cdot, sk, \cdot, \cdot, \cdot)$, $(m_i, \text{ADM}_i, \gamma_i, spk_i)$ is the ith query to the oracle $Sig(\cdot, sk, \cdot, \cdot, \cdot)$ and σ_i is the corresponding response.*

Transparency: The transparency property guarantees that no adversary is able to distinguish whether a signature is sanitized. In addition to the signature oracle, the adversary has access to a sanitize oracle $San(\cdot, \cdot, \cdot, \cdot, ssk)$. Moreover, the adversary has access to a challenge oracle $Sa/Si(b, pk, spk, sk, ssk, \cdot, \cdot, \cdot, \cdot)$ that depends on a randomly chosen bit b: this oracle signs a given message and sanitizes it, if $b = 0$ then it outputs the original signature, otherwise it outputs the sanitized signature. To succeed in winning the experiment, the adversary must guess b. In order to exclude trivial attacks, we must keep track of the outputs of the challenge oracle. Indeed, the adversary can easily determine whether the Sa/Si called Sig or San by sanitizing the output signature and figuring out how many modifications are allowed. The limit does indeed introduce some new and somewhat tricky trivial attacks for the transparency property. For example, let us consider a message m of length 2, with both blocks being admissible for modifications, and a limit of $\gamma = 1$. The adversary can query Sa/Si with a modification MOD_1 on the first block, then query San on the output with a modification MOD_2 on the second block. If Sa/Si queried Sig, *i.e.*, if the ouput is an original signature on $\text{MOD}_1(m)$, then the modification would be allowed, as $\text{MOD}_1(m)$ and $\text{MOD}_2(\text{MOD}_1(m))$ only have one difference, but if Sa/Si queried San, *i.e.*, if the ouput is a sanitized signature of m on $\text{MOD}_1(m)$, then the sanitization is not allowed, since m and $\text{MOD}_2(\text{MOD}_1(m))$ have two differences.

Definition 14 (Transparency). *Let P be a γSaS. P is Trans-secure (or transparent) when for any polynomial time adversary $\mathcal{A}$, the probability $\Pr[\text{Exp}^{trans}_{ULISS,\mathcal{A}}(\lambda) = 1]$ that $\mathcal{A}$ wins the trans experiment given in Fig. 2 is negligible.*

Unlinkability: The unlinkability property ensures that a sanitized signature cannot be linked with the original one. We consider an adversary that has access to the signature and the sanitize oracles. Moreover, the adversary has access to a challenge oracle $LRSan(b, pk, ssk, spk, \cdot, \cdot)$ that depends on a bit b: this oracle takes as input two signatures σ_0 and σ_1, the two corresponding messages m_0 and m_1 and two modification functions MOD_0 and MOD_1 chosen by the adversary. If the two signatures have the same admissible function ADM, if MOD_0 and MOD_1 are admissible according to ADM and if $\text{MOD}_0(m_0) = \text{MOD}_1(m_1)$ then the challenge oracle sanitizes σ_b using MOD_b and returns it. The goal of the adversary is to guess the bit b. The adversary is allowed to query LRSan on two signatures with different limits, thus to prevent trivial attacks the resulting output will artificially be limited to the smaller of the two. This means that the challenger must keep track of the outputs of all three oracles.

Definition 15 (Unlinkability). *Let P be a γSaS of security parameter λ. P is Unlink-secure (or unlinkable) when for any polynomial time adversary $\mathcal{A}$, the probability $\Pr[\mathsf{Exp}^{unlink}_{ULISS,\mathcal{A}}(\lambda) = 1]$ that $\mathcal{A}$ wins the unlink experiment given in Fig. 2 is negligibly close to 1/2.*

Invisibility: The invisibility property ensures that an adversary who does not know any private key can neither decide whether a block is admissible for modification or not, nor how many blocks can be modified. The adversary we consider has access to the sign oracle, the sanitize oracle, and a left-or-right admissible oracle LRADM that depends on the bit b chosen by the challenger. The adversary will give a message m along with two ADM functions ADM_0, ADM_1 and two γ values γ_0, γ_1 as input to this oracle, which will output a signature with ADM_b as its admissible function, and γ_b as a limit. The adversary will try to guess the value of b. To exclude trivial attacks, we must artificially limit the number of modified blocks to $\min(\gamma_0, \gamma_1)$ on any signature created by LRADM no matter the value of b, and we must also prevent the adversary from querying a sanitization with a MOD function that is admissible by ADM_0 but not by ADM_1 or vice-versa.

Definition 16 (Invisibility). *Let P be a γSaS of security parameter λ, then P is said to be Invis-secure (or invisible) if for any polynomial-time adversary $\mathcal{A}$, the probability $\Pr[\mathsf{Exp}^{invis}_{ULISS,\mathcal{A}}(\lambda) = 1]$ that $\mathcal{A}$ wins the invis experiment given in Fig. 2 is negligibly close to 1/2.*

4   Scheme

We now present our scheme, ULISS, and detail the role of each of its building blocks. We first give an idea of the aim of the centerpiece of our scheme, *i.e.*, the zero-knowledge proofs, and more specifically, their commitments, before giving the formal definition of our scheme, after which we detail the goal of each primitive.

Recall that whoever signs a message must be able to prove that it was done within the authorized bounds. When a message is signed, the signer also computes some *commitments* that will be used in the *zero-knowledge proofs*. Each commitment is a hash of some value concatenated with the public parameters. All commitments are initially elevated to an identical, random exponent x, and signed by the signer. To avoid traceability, the sanitizer will present them elevated to another, random exponent t in each sanitization. This resulting exponent is used as a *witness* in the zero-knowledge proof. The implications of this (change of) exponent are detailed after the definition of our scheme, at the end

$\mathbf{Exp}_{P,\mathcal{A}}^{\mathsf{immut}}(\lambda)$:
set $\leftarrow$ Init(1^λ); (pk, sk) $\leftarrow$ SiGen(set);
$(\mathsf{spk}_*, m_*, \sigma_*) \leftarrow \mathcal{A}^{\mathsf{Sig}(\cdot, \mathsf{sk}, \cdot, \cdot, \cdot)}(\mathsf{pk})$;
if $(\mathsf{Ver}(m_*, \sigma_*, \mathsf{pk}, \mathsf{spk}_*) = 1)$ and $(\forall\, i \in [\![1, q_{\mathsf{Sig}}]\!], (\mathsf{spk}_* \neq \mathsf{spk}_i)$ or $(\forall\, \mathrm{MOD}$ such that $\mathrm{ADM}_i(\mathrm{MOD}) = 1$,
$m_* \neq \mathrm{MOD}(m_i))$ or $D(m_i, m_*) > \gamma_i)$ (where $D(m_i, m_j)$ is the number of different blocks)
then return 1, else return 0;

$\mathbf{Exp}_{P,\mathcal{A}}^{\mathsf{SUF}}(\lambda)$:
set $\leftarrow$ Init(1^λ); (pk, sk) $\leftarrow$ SiGen(set);
(spk, ssk) $\leftarrow$ SaGen(set);
$\mathcal{S} \leftarrow \{\}$;
$\mathcal{O} \leftarrow \{\mathsf{Sig}(\cdot, \mathsf{sk}, \cdot, \cdot, \cdot), \mathsf{San}(\cdot, \cdot, \cdot, \cdot, \mathsf{ssk})\}$;
$(m, \sigma) \leftarrow \mathcal{A}^{\mathcal{O}}(\mathsf{pk}, \mathsf{spk})$;
if $(m, \sigma) \notin \mathcal{S}$
then return $\mathsf{Ver}(m, \sigma, \mathsf{pk}, \mathsf{spk})$, else return 0;

$\mathbf{Exp}_{P,\mathcal{A}}^{\mathsf{invis}}(\lambda)$:
set $\leftarrow$ Init(1^λ); (pk, sk) $\leftarrow$ SiGen(set);
(spk, ssk) $\leftarrow$ SaGen(set);
$b \xleftarrow{\$} \{0,1\}$; $\mathcal{L} \leftarrow []$;
$\mathcal{O} \leftarrow \left\{ \begin{array}{l} \mathsf{Sig}(\cdot, \mathsf{sk}, \cdot, \cdot, \cdot), \mathsf{San}(\cdot, \cdot, \cdot, \cdot, \mathsf{ssk}), \\ \mathrm{LRADM}(b, \mathsf{sk}, \mathsf{spk}, \cdot, \cdot, \cdot) \end{array} \right\}$;
$b' \leftarrow \mathcal{A}^{\mathcal{O}}(\mathsf{pk}, \mathsf{spk})$;
if $(b = b')$ then return 1, else return 0;

$\mathbf{Exp}_{P,\mathcal{A}}^{\mathsf{trans}}(\lambda)$:
set $\leftarrow$ Init(1^λ); (pk, sk) $\leftarrow$ SiGen(set);
(spk, ssk) $\leftarrow$ SaGen(set);
$b \xleftarrow{\$} \{0,1\}$; $\mathcal{L} \leftarrow []$;
$\mathcal{O} \leftarrow \left\{ \begin{array}{l} \mathrm{Sa}/\mathrm{Si}(b, \mathsf{pk}, \mathsf{spk}, \mathsf{sk}, \mathsf{ssk}, \cdot, \cdot, \cdot) \\ \mathsf{Sig}(\cdot, \mathsf{sk}, \cdot, \cdot, \cdot), \mathsf{San}(\cdot, \cdot, \cdot, \cdot, \mathsf{ssk}, \cdot) \end{array} \right\}$;
$b' \leftarrow \mathcal{A}^{\mathcal{O}}(\mathsf{pk}, \mathsf{spk})$;
if $(b = b')$ then return 1, else return 0;

$\mathbf{Exp}_{P,\mathcal{A}}^{\mathsf{unlink}}(\lambda)$:
set $\leftarrow$ Init(1^λ); (pk, sk) $\leftarrow$ SiGen(set);
(spk, ssk) $\leftarrow$ SaGen(set);
$b \xleftarrow{\$} \{0,1\}$; $\mathcal{L} \leftarrow []$;
$\mathcal{O} \leftarrow \left\{ \begin{array}{l} \mathsf{Sig}(\cdot, \mathsf{sk}, \cdot, \cdot, \cdot), \mathsf{San}(\cdot, \cdot, \cdot, \cdot, \mathsf{ssk}, \cdot), \\ \mathrm{LRSan}(b, \mathsf{pk}, \mathsf{ssk}, \mathsf{spk}, \cdot, \cdot) \end{array} \right\}$;
$b' \leftarrow \mathcal{A}^{\mathcal{O}}(\mathsf{pk}, \mathsf{spk})$;
if $(b = b')$ then return 1, else return 0;

immut oracles:
$\mathsf{Sig}(m, \mathsf{sk}, \mathrm{ADM}, \mathsf{spk}, \gamma)$:
return $\mathsf{Sig}(m, \mathsf{sk}, \mathsf{spk}, \mathrm{ADM}, \gamma)$;

invis oracles:
$\mathsf{Sig}(m, \mathsf{sk}, \mathrm{ADM}, \mathsf{spk}, \gamma)$:
return $\mathsf{Sig}(m, \mathsf{sk}, \mathsf{spk}, \mathrm{ADM}, \gamma)$;

$\mathrm{LRADM}(b, \mathsf{sk}, \mathsf{spk}, m, (\mathrm{ADM}_0, \gamma_0), (\mathrm{ADM}_1, \gamma_1))$:
$\sigma \leftarrow \mathsf{Sig}(m, \mathsf{sk}, \mathsf{spk}, \mathrm{ADM}_b, \gamma_b)$;
$\mathcal{L}[\sigma] \leftarrow (m, \min(\gamma_0, \gamma_1), \mathrm{ADM}_0 \cap \mathrm{ADM}_1)$;
return σ;

trans oracles:
$\mathsf{Sig}(m, \mathsf{sk}, \mathrm{ADM}, \mathsf{spk}, \gamma)$:
$\sigma \leftarrow \mathsf{Sig}(m, \mathsf{sk}, \mathsf{spk}, \mathrm{ADM}, \gamma)$;
$\mathcal{L}[\sigma] \leftarrow (m, \gamma)$
return σ;

$\mathsf{San}(m, \mathrm{MOD}, \sigma, \mathsf{pk}, \mathsf{ssk})$:
if $\mathcal{L}[\sigma] = \perp$ then return $\mathsf{San}(m, \mathrm{MOD}, \sigma, \mathsf{pk}, \mathsf{ssk}, \mathsf{spk})$;
$(\bar{m}, \gamma) \leftarrow \mathcal{L}[\sigma]$;
if $D(\bar{m}, \mathrm{MOD}(m)) > \gamma$ then return $\perp$;
$\sigma' \leftarrow \mathsf{San}(m, \mathrm{MOD}, \sigma, \mathsf{pk}, \mathsf{ssk}, \mathsf{spk})$;
$\mathcal{L}[\sigma'] \leftarrow \mathcal{L}[\sigma]$;
returns σ';

unlink oracles:
$\mathsf{Sig}(m, \mathsf{sk}, \mathrm{ADM}, \mathsf{spk}, \gamma)$:
$\sigma \leftarrow \mathsf{Sig}(m, \mathsf{sk}, \mathsf{spk}, \mathrm{ADM}, \gamma)$;
$\mathcal{L}[\sigma] \leftarrow (m, \gamma)$;
return σ;

$\mathsf{San}(m, \mathrm{MOD}, \sigma, \mathsf{pk}, \mathsf{ssk})$:
if $\mathcal{L}[\sigma] = \perp$
then return $\mathsf{San}(m, \mathrm{MOD}, \sigma, \mathsf{pk}, \mathsf{ssk}, \mathsf{spk})$;
$(\bar{m}, \gamma) \leftarrow \mathcal{L}[\sigma]$;
if $D(\mathrm{MOD}(m), \bar{m}) > \gamma$ then return $\perp$;
$\sigma' \leftarrow \mathsf{San}(m, \mathrm{MOD}, \sigma, \mathsf{pk}, \mathsf{ssk}, \mathsf{spk})$;
$\mathcal{L}[\sigma'] \leftarrow \mathcal{L}[\sigma]$;
returns σ';

SUF oracles:
$\mathsf{Sig}(m, \mathsf{sk}, \mathrm{ADM}, \mathsf{spk}, \gamma)$:
$\sigma \leftarrow \mathsf{Sig}(m, \mathsf{sk}, \mathrm{ADM}, \mathsf{spk}, \gamma)$;
$\mathcal{S} = \mathcal{S} \cup (m, \sigma)$;
return σ;

$\mathsf{San}(m, \mathrm{MOD}, \sigma, \mathsf{pk}, \mathsf{ssk})$:
$\sigma' \leftarrow \mathsf{San}(m, \mathrm{MOD}, \sigma, \mathsf{pk}, \mathsf{ssk})$;
$\mathcal{S} = \mathcal{S} \cup (m, \sigma)$;
return σ';

$\mathsf{San}(m, \mathrm{MOD}, \sigma, \mathsf{pk}, \mathsf{ssk})$:
if $\mathcal{L}[\sigma] = \perp$
then return $\mathsf{San}(m, \mathrm{MOD}, \sigma, \mathsf{pk}, \mathsf{ssk}, \mathsf{spk})$;
$(\bar{m}, \gamma, \mathrm{ADM}) \leftarrow \mathcal{L}[\sigma]$;
if $D(\mathrm{MOD}(m), \bar{m}) \leq \gamma$ and $\mathrm{ADM}(\mathrm{MOD}) = 1$
then $\sigma' = \mathsf{San}(m, \mathrm{MOD}, \sigma, \mathsf{pk}, \mathsf{ssk})$;
$\quad \mathcal{L}[\sigma'] = \mathcal{L}[\sigma]$;
$\quad$ return σ';
else return $\perp$;

$\mathrm{Sa}/\mathrm{Si}(b, \mathsf{pk}, \mathsf{spk}, \mathsf{sk}, \mathsf{ssk}, m, \mathrm{ADM}, \mathrm{MOD}, \gamma)$:
if $\mathrm{ADM}(\mathrm{MOD}) = 0$ then return $\perp$;
If $b = 0$ then $\sigma \leftarrow \mathsf{Sig}(\mathrm{MOD}(m), \mathsf{sk}, \mathsf{spk}, \mathrm{ADM}, \gamma)$;
else $\sigma \leftarrow \mathsf{Sig}(m, \mathsf{sk}, \mathsf{spk}, \mathrm{ADM})$;
$\quad \sigma \leftarrow \mathsf{San}(m, \mathrm{MOD}, \sigma, \mathsf{pk}, \mathsf{ssk}, \mathsf{spk})$;
$\mathcal{L}[\sigma] \leftarrow (m, \gamma)$;
returns σ;

$\mathrm{LRSan}(b, \mathsf{pk}, \mathsf{ssk}, \mathsf{spk}, (m_0, \mathrm{MOD}_0, \sigma_0)(m_1, \mathrm{MOD}_1, \sigma_1))$:
for $i \in \{0,1\}$, if $\mathsf{Ver}(m_i, \sigma_i, \mathsf{pk}, \mathsf{spk}) \neq 1$ or $\mathrm{ADM}_0 \neq \mathrm{ADM}_1$
$\quad$ or $\mathrm{ADM}_0(\mathrm{MOD}_0) \neq \mathrm{ADM}_1(\mathrm{MOD}_1)$
$\quad$ or $\mathrm{MOD}_0(m_0) \neq \mathrm{MOD}_1(m_1)$ or $\mathcal{L}[\sigma_i] = \perp$
then return 0;
$(\bar{m}_i, \gamma_i) \leftarrow \mathcal{L}[\sigma_i]$;
for $i \in \{0,1\}$, if $D(\mathrm{MOD}_0(m_0), \bar{m}_0) \leq \gamma_0$
$\quad$ and $D(\mathrm{MOD}_1(m_1), \bar{m}_1) \leq \gamma_1$
then $\sigma' \leftarrow \mathsf{San}(m_b, \mathrm{MOD}_b, \sigma_b, \mathsf{pk}, \mathsf{ssk}, \mathsf{spk})$;
$\quad \mathcal{L}[\sigma'] \leftarrow (\bar{m}_b, \min(\gamma_0, \gamma_1))$;
$\quad$ return σ';
else return $\perp$;

Fig. 2. Security experiments and oracles for γSaS properties.

of this subsection. For simplicity, we omit both the exponent and the public parameters in the following explanation.

Commitments are divided in two categories: those meant to show that only admissible blocks are modified, and those meant to show that the number of modifications is below the limit. For the first kind, they are as follows: if a block i can be modified, then its corresponding commitment is a hash of its index, otherwise it is a hash of its index concatenated with its content. The sanitizer will thus have to show that for each block of the modified message, the commitment is either equal to the hash of the index or the hash of the index concatenated with its content – if at least one unauthorized block was modified, then the sanitizer cannot produce a valid proof. We also add to this batch a commitment of the public parameters, to authenticate them.

The second kind is slightly more intricate: one commitment is the hash of the limit γ, then for each block, the commitment is the concatenation of the index and the content of that block. The sanitizer will have to show that there exists a value v such that the hash of v is equal to the first commitment, and, considering there are n message blocks, at least $n - i$ blocks of the modified message are such that the hash of their index and their content is equal to their corresponding commitment.

Scheme 1 (ULISS). *Let $\mathbb{G}$ be a group of prime order p, and g be a generator of $\mathbb{G}$. Let E be a public key encryption scheme such that $E = (E.ini, E.gen, E.enc, E.dec)$, S be an Equivalence-Class Signature such that $S = (S.ini, S.gen, S.sig, S.ver, S.ChRep)$, R be a 2-Ring Signature scheme such that $R = (R.ini, R.gen, R.sig, R.ver)$, and F and H be two hash functions (of domain $\{0,1\}^*$ and codomain $\mathbb{G}$). Our scheme instantiated with $(\mathbb{G}, E, S, F, H)$ is a γ-sanitizable signature scheme defined by the following algorithms:*

$\mathsf{Init}(1^\lambda)$: *It runs $set_E \leftarrow E.ini(1^\lambda)$, $set_R \leftarrow R.ini(1^\lambda)$ and $set_S \leftarrow S.ini(1^\lambda)$, then it returns the setup $set = (set_E, set_R, set_S)$.*

$\mathsf{SiGen}(set)$: *It parses $set = (set_E, set_R, set_S)$, runs $(pk_S, sk_S) \leftarrow S.gen(set_S)$, $(pk_R, sk_R) \leftarrow R.gen(set_R)$, and returns $(pk, sk) = ((pk_S, pk_R), (sk_S, sk_R))$.*

$\mathsf{SaGen}(set)$: *It parses set, runs $(spk_E, ssk_E) \leftarrow E.gen(set_E)$, $(spk_R, ssk_R) \leftarrow R.gen(set_R)$, and returns $(spk, ssk) = ((spk_E, spk_R), (ssk_E, ssk_R))$.*

$\mathsf{Sig}(m, sk, spk, \mathrm{ADM}, \gamma)$: *It parses sk as (sk_S, sk_R), spk as (spk_E, spk_R) and m as $m_1\|\dots\|m_n$ and sets $pp = pk\|spk$. It picks $x \xleftarrow{\$} \mathbb{Z}_p^*$, sets $V \leftarrow F(pp)^x$ and $C = H(\gamma\|pp)^x$, then for all i in $[n]$:*
 - *It computes $A_i \leftarrow H(i\|m_i\|pp)^x$.*
 - *If $i \in \mathrm{ADM}$, it computes $B_i \leftarrow F(i\|pp)^x$, else it computes $B_i \leftarrow F(i\|m_i\|pp)^x$.*

It then computes the two following proofs:

$$\pi_1 \leftarrow \mathsf{NIZK}\left\{x : \bigwedge_{i=1}^n \left(\begin{matrix} (B_i = F(i\|pp)^x \wedge V = F(pp)^x) \\ \vee (B_i = F(i\|m_i\|pp)^x \wedge V = F(pp)^x) \end{matrix} \right) \right\}$$

$$\pi_2 \leftarrow \mathsf{NIZK}\left\{x : \bigvee_{i=1}^n \left(\begin{matrix} \exists\, J \subseteq [n], (|J| = n - i) \wedge (\forall\, j \in J, \\ (A_j = H(j\|m_j\|pp)^x) \wedge (C = H(i\|pp)^x)) \end{matrix} \right) \right\}$$

Finally, it generates the following values:
- $s \leftarrow \mathsf{S.sig}(sk_S, (A_1, B_1, \ldots, A_n, B_n), C, V)$,
- $e \leftarrow \mathsf{E.enc}(spk_E, (x, (A_i, B_i)_{i \in [n]}, C, V, s))$,
- $r \leftarrow \mathsf{R.sig}(sk_R, \{pk_R, spk_R\}, (m, (A_i, B_i)_{i \in [n]}, C, V, \pi_1, \pi_2, s, e))$,

and returns $\sigma = ((A_i, B_i)_{i \in [n]}, C, V, \pi_1, \pi_2, s, e, r)$.

$\mathsf{San}(m, \mathrm{MOD}, \sigma, \mathsf{pkssk}, \mathsf{spk})$: *This algorithm computes* $m'_1 \| \ldots \| m'_n \leftarrow \mathrm{MOD}(m)$, *sets* $\mathsf{pp} = \mathsf{pk} \| \mathsf{spk}$, *parses* pk *as* (pk_S, pk_R) *and* ssk *as* (ssk_E, ssk_R), *parses* σ *as* $((A_i, B_i)_{i \in [n]}, C, V, \pi_1, \pi_2, s, e, r)$, *picks* $t \xleftarrow{\$} \mathbb{Z}_p^*$, *runs* $(x, (\tilde{A}_i, \tilde{B}_i)_{i \in [n]}, \tilde{C}, \tilde{V}, \tilde{s}) \leftarrow \mathsf{E.dec}(ssk_E, e)$, *sets* $x' = x \cdot t$, $V' = F(\mathsf{pp})^{x'}$ *and* $C' = H(\gamma \| \mathsf{pp})^{x'}$, *and runs* $e' \leftarrow \mathsf{E.enc}(spk_E, (x, (\tilde{A}_i, \tilde{B}_i)_{i \in [n]}, \tilde{C}, \tilde{V}, \tilde{s}))$. *The algorithm verifies that the signatures (s and r) are valid, and verifies that* $\mathrm{ADM}(\mathrm{MOD}) = 1$, *else it aborts. For all i in* $[n]$, *it sets* $A'_i = \tilde{A}_i^t$, $B'_i = \tilde{B}_i^t$, *then it computes the signature* $s' \leftarrow \mathsf{S.ChRep}(pk_S, \tilde{s}, (\tilde{A}_1, \tilde{B}_1, \ldots, \tilde{A}_n, \tilde{B}_n, \tilde{C}, \tilde{V}), t)$. *It then computes the two following proofs:*

$$\pi'_1 \leftarrow \mathrm{NIZK}\left\{x' : \bigwedge_{i=1}^{n}\left(\begin{array}{l}\left(B'_i = F(i \| \mathsf{pp})^{x'} \wedge V' = F(\mathsf{pp})^{x'}\right) \\ \vee \left(B'_i = F(i \| m'_i \| \mathsf{pp})^{x'} \wedge V' = F(\mathsf{pp})^{x'}\right)\end{array}\right)\right\}$$

$$\pi'_2 \leftarrow \mathrm{NIZK}\left\{x' : \bigvee_{i=1}^{n}\left(\begin{array}{l}\exists\, J \subseteq [n], (|J| = n - i) \wedge (\forall\, j \in J, \\ \left(A'_j = H(j \| m'_j \| \mathsf{pp})^{x'}\right) \wedge \left(C' = H(i \| \mathsf{pp})^{x'}\right))\end{array}\right)\right\}$$

Finally, it computes $r' \leftarrow \mathsf{R.sig}(ssk_R, \{pk_R, spk_R\}, (\mathrm{MOD}(m), (A'_i, B'_i)_{i \in [n]}, C', V', \pi'_1, \pi'_2, s', e'))$ *and returns* $\sigma' = ((A'_i, B'_i)_{i \in [n]}, C', V', \pi'_1, \pi'_2, s', e', r')$.

$\mathsf{Ver}(m, \sigma, \mathsf{pk}, \mathsf{spk})$: *It parses* σ *as* $((A_i, B_i)_{i \in [n]}, C, V, \pi_1, \pi_2, s, e, r)$, pk *as* (pk_S, pk_R) *and* spk *as* (spk_E, spk_R), *then if* π_1 *and* π_2 *are valid, and:*
- $\mathsf{S.ver}((A_1, B_1 \ldots, A_n, B_n, C, V), pk_S, s) = 1$,
- $\mathsf{R.ver}((m, (A_i, B_i)_{i \in [n]}, C, V, \pi_1, \pi_2, s, e), \{pk_R, spk_R\}, r) = 1$,

then it returns 1, else 0.

From the definition of the Verify algorithm, we see that the correctness of our scheme relies on the correctness of the NIZKP, as well as the correctness of the 2-Ring Signature and the Equivalence-Class Signature.

Having now introduced all notations, we can give a more in-depth description.

Non-interactive ZKPs. The commitments denoted as V and $\{B_i\}_{i \in [n]}$ are linked to the admissible function, with B_i being the ith block's commitment, and V being the public parameter's commitment. We see that it serves its purpose: the prover must show that for each block (denoted by $\bigwedge_{i=1}^{n}$) in the (modified) message, the corresponding commitment is either equal to the hash of the index, or (denoted by $\vee$) the hash of the index and the content.

The C and $\{A_j\}_{j \in [n]}$ commitments are linked to the limit γ, with C committing the limit and A_j committing the original content of block j. Again, they follow the idea described at the beginning of the section: the prover must show that there is a value $i \in [n]$ (denoted by $\bigvee_{i=1}^{n}$), for which there exists a subset $J \subseteq [n]$ such that $[n] \backslash J$ has a size i, such that i is committed in C, and such that for all indices $j \in J$, the hash of j and the content of block j is equal to A_j. The soundness of these proofs implies the immutability.

Recall that, to compute a sanitization, the sanitizer will generate its own random value t and elevate all commitments to the power of t in order to produce a signature with different commitments, using $x' = x \cdot t$ as its witness in the proofs.

All information about the admissibility or the limits are hidden by the commitments. Since the proofs are zero-knowledge, they do not leak this information to the verifier, which ensures that ULISS is invisible. Moreover, since all the other parts of the signature are computed in the same way by the signer and the sanitizer, ULISS is transparent.

Class-Equivalence Signature. The signer first signs the commitments using a class-equivalence signature. Indeed, as mentioned above, the sanitizer will modify the commitments by elevating them all to the same power, *i.e.*, using different elements from the same equivalence class. Thus, using class-equivalence signature allows the sanitizer to authenticate this change by changing the representative. Thanks to the adaptability, the sanitizer can randomize all the commitments and update the class-equivalence signature accordingly. Since the other parts of the sanitizable signature are re-generated by the sanitizer (the ciphertext, the 2-ring signature, and the proofs), the verifier cannot link the sanitized signature to the original one, making our scheme unlinkable.

Encryption Scheme. Each sanitization will be done on the original commitments and not on the (potentially) sanitized ones. Thus, the signer must include an encryption of the commitments along with the exponent x in the signature. In order for the signatures to remain unlinkable, the sanitizer will re-encrypt the commitments and their exponent when it sanitizes a signature instead of simply keeping the same ciphertext.

2-Ring Signature. The actual signature of the message itself is done with a 2-Ring Signature, which has the interesting property of taking one secret key and two public keys as input, and does not give the information of which public key verifies the signature when it is checked. This allows us to verify the transparency property, as the signer and the sanitizer will input both of their public keys when signing the message, and everything else that was computed, *i.e.*, commitments, proofs, the equivalence-class signature, and the encryption.

Instantiation of the Zero-Knowledge Proofs. ULISS uses two NIZKP for discrete logarithm relations, as detailed above.

Prover P	Verifier V
x	(g_1, g_2, h_1, h_2)

$r \xleftarrow{\$} \mathbb{Z}_p^*$
$R_1 = g_1^r$
$R_2 = g_2^r$ $\xrightarrow{(R_1, R_2)}$ $c \xleftarrow{\$} \mathbb{Z}_p^*$
$z = r + x \cdot c \xleftarrow{\quad c \quad}$
     $\xrightarrow{\quad z \quad}$ If $g_1^z = R_1 \cdot h_1^c$
         and $g_2^z = R_2 \cdot h_2^c$
         then return 1, else 0

Fig. 3. LogEq protocols.

Even if the languages of these proofs seem non-trivial, we show how to efficiently instantiate them without heavy generic zero-knowledge proofs by using specific Schnorr-like protocols only, which guarantees that our signature is practical. We use the interactive proof of two discrete logarithms equality given in [14] by Chaum and Pederson as a building block, which we recall in Fig. 3. We use the technique given in [15] to transform a proof that *an instance belongs to some language* into a proof that *k-out-of-n instances belong to some languages*. This transformation works on sigma protocols, like the Chaum and Pederson proof. The proof π_1 is an AND-proof of n 1-out-of-2 discrete logarithm equality proofs: we can obtain such a proof by performing n 1-out-of-2 discrete logarithm equality proofs separately. Since each discrete logarithm equality uses the same pair of basis/element of the group ($V = F(\text{pp})^x$ in our protocol), the proof that each discrete logarithm is the same x is implicit.

The proof π_2 is a 1-out-of-n proof, where each of the n instances is actually i-out-of-n discrete logarithm equality proof instances, for each i such that $1 \le i \le n$. This proof can be obtained by using the transformation of [15] on the Chaum and Pederson proof twice. We applied the Fiat-Shamir transformation [18], in order to obtain non-interactive versions of these proofs, by using the commitments hash as a challenge.

Performance. We now look at the complexity of π_1 and π_2. More precisely, we study the number of exponentiations performed by the prover and by the verifier, and we deduce the size of the proof by counting the number of group elements. The size of a k-out-of-n proof is n times the size of the original proof, and the verification algorithm requires n times the computation time of the original proof verification. The proof algorithm uses a simulator of the original proof: since the Chaum and Pederson proof is zero-knowledge, there exists at least one simulator that perfectly simulates the proof. We can use the simulator $\text{Sim}(g_1, g_2, h_1, h_2)$ that picks $(c, z) \xleftarrow{\$} (\mathbb{Z}_p^*)^2$, computes $R_1 = g_1^z/h_1^c$ and $R_2 = g_2^z/h_2^c$, and return (R_1, R_2, c, z). The proof algorithm of a k-out-of-n proof requires k times the computation time of the original proof algorithm, and $n - k$ times the computation time of the simulator. We recap the performances of our zero-knowledge proofs in Table 1.

Table 1. NIZKP performance

•	Prove	Verify	Size
Chaum Pederson [14]	2	4	3
k-out-of-n on [14]	$4 \cdot n - 2 \cdot k$	$4 \cdot n$	$3 \cdot n$
π_1	$6 \cdot n$	$8 \cdot n$	$6 \cdot n$
π_2	$3 \cdot n^2 - n$	$4 \cdot n^2$	$3 \cdot n^2$

Scheme Complexity. We use the NIZKPs previously given, the class-equivalence signature presented in Fuchsbauer et al. [20], the Fujisaki-Okamoto CCA-transformation [21] on El Gamal [17] as a Public-Key Encryption, and the Ring-Signature presented in Bultel and Lafourcade [10]. Note that this ring-signature is not the most efficient one, however this scheme is verifiable, meaning it makes our scheme accountable according to the generic transformation given in [11]. We provide the size of our parameters with these choices in Table 2, as well as the number of exponentiations and pairings in Table 3. For the sake of simplicity, we don't differentiate elements of group $\mathbb{G}$ of prime order p where DDH holds, and elements of $\mathbb{Z}_p^*$. The number of message blocks is denoted by n. In average, the computational and size cost of having the limit is a factor n in comparison with [11].

Table 2. Parameter size comparison.

Size of the parameters (group elements)				
Scheme	Sig. sk	Sig. pk	San. sk	San. pk	Signature
ULISS	2	2	2	2	$3n^2 + 10n + 22$
[11]	n + 1	n + 1	2	2	$4n + 18$

Security Proofs. In this section, we list the conditions under which our scheme verifies the security properties defined in Sect. 3. We give brief sketches of the proofs of each theorem, for which complete versions can be found in Appendix A (for Theorems 1, 3, and 5), or in the full version.

Theorem 1 (Strong Unforgeability). *For any underlying strongly unforgeable 2-Ring Signature scheme R, our scheme ULISS is strongly unforgeable.*

Table 3. Complexity comparison.

Complexity (exponentiations and pairings)				
Scheme		Sign	Sanitize	Verify
ULISS	exp	$3n^2 + 9n + 16$	$3n^2 + 7n + 12$	$4n^2 + 8n + 8$
	pairing	0	0	$2n + 5$
[11]	exp	$5n + 13$	$3n + 16$	8
	pairing	0	0	$4n + 6$

Proof. The complete proof is given in Appendix A.1.

We show that if ULISS is not unforgeable, then neither is the 2-Ring Signature Scheme R. This is done by building an adversary $\mathcal{B}$ against the SUF property of R who simulates the experiment for $\mathcal{A}$ by computing everything but signatures from R. $\mathcal{B}$ can simply forward $\mathcal{A}$'s forgery to its challenger.

Theorem 2 (Immutability). *If the underlying class-equivalence signature scheme S is existentially unforgeable under chosen-message attack, and proofs π_1 and π_2 are sound, then our scheme ULISS is immutable.*

Proof. The complete proof is given in the full version.

We show that ULISS is immutable by first listing how $\mathcal{A}$ could win the experiment and then show how (un)likely these events are to occur. In order to produce a sanitized signature that either (1) uses a previously unseen public key spk_*, (2) has modifications on inadmissible blocks, or (3) has too many modifications, the adversary $\mathcal{A}$ must: exploit a collision in the commitments that would match two signatures, if there are none, it must fake the zero-knowledge proofs, and if that is not possible, then it must forge the equivalence-class signature. We thus show how the advantage of $\mathcal{A}$ against the immutability of ULISS is related to these three events.

Theorem 3 (Unlinkability). *If our scheme is strongly unforgeable, and for any IND\$-CCA underlying encryption scheme, any class-hiding and adaptable underlying class-equivalence signature, any zero-knowledge NIZKP, and under the DDH assumption, our scheme ULISS is unlinkable in the random-oracle model.*

Proof. The complete proof is given in Appendix A.2.

The general idea of this proof is to follow a classical game-hops strategy where we replace some elements with random, progressively, to show that the adversary $\mathcal{A}$ cannot distinguish which signature was sanitized if the final result is indistinguishable from random. In the beginning, we ensure the signatures input by $\mathcal{A}$ using the challenger's signer and sanitizer keys are not forgeries, *i.e.*, were computed by the challenger. We then use the IND\$-CCA property of the encryption to replace its input with random, then we use the adaptability of the class-equivalence signature to replace every change of representative (from m to m^t) to a signature (of m^t), breaking that link between a sanitization and its original signature, then we use the zero-knowledge property of the NIZKP to replace them with simulations, in order to afterwards replace the original commitments with random (using DDH), so that we can finally use the class-hiding property of the message space used in the class-equivalence signature to replace the commitments with random in the sanitizations, thus breaking the final relevant link with the original signature.

Theorem 4 (Transparency). *If our scheme ULISS is strongly unforgeable, then for any underlying class-equivalence signature scheme with perfect signature adaptation S, any zero-knowledge NIZKP, any underlying anonymous 2-Ring Signature scheme R, any IND\$-CCA underlying encryption scheme, and under the DDH assumption, ULISS is transparent in the random oracle model.*

Proof. The complete proof is given in the full version.

The idea of this proof is that an adversary $\mathcal{A}$ can either distinguish who signed via the equivalence-class signature S ("is it a signature on m^t, or a change of representative on a signature of m?"), via the commitments ("are these hashes of m or $\text{MOD}(m)$?"), or via the 2-Ring Signature R ("was it signed by pk_R or spk_R?"), or by replacing the signature with a forgery whose properties are the same but whose γ is not artificially controlled by the challenger. If our scheme is strongly unforgeable, if S has perfect signature adaptation, if DDH holds, the proofs are zero-knowledge, if the encryption is IND\$-CCA, and if R is anonymous, then $\mathcal{A}$ cannot answer any of these questions.

The proof first ensures no forgery can happen, then replaces the commitments with random (also replacing the input to the encryption and the NIZKP), then the proof uses a hybrid argument, with experiment 1 (E_1) being the $b = 1$ experiment, then hybrid experiment H which is like E_1 except the 2-Ring signatures are all signed with the signer's key, and experiment 0 (E_0) is the $b = 0$ experiment. Differentiating E_1 from H implies breaking the anonymity of the 2RS, and differentiating H from E_0 implies breaking the perfect adaptation of the class-equivalent signature.

Theorem 5 (Invisibility). *If our scheme ULISS is strongly unforgeable, for any IND\$-CCA underlying encryption scheme, any zero-knowledge NIZKP, and under the DDH assumption, ULISS is invisible in the random oracle model.*

Proof. The complete proof is given in Appendix A.3.

Using the same logic as for the unlinkability, we first ensure that the adversary does not produce and use forgeries, then we progressively replace elements with random and show that the resulting signature is indistinguishable from the real one. The only commitments linked to the limit and the admissible function are C and $\{B_i\}_{i \in [n]}$, thus we first use the IND\$-CCA property of the encryption to replace its input with random, then we replace the zero-knowledge proofs with simulated ones, so that we can ultimately use the DDH property to replace the C and $\{B_i\}_{i \in [n]}$ commitments with random instead of generating them honestly.

5   Application

In this Section, we detail several examples of how γ-Sanitizable Signatures could be used in practice. All scenarios below follow the same basic idea: someone (the signer) wishes to allow another person (the sanitizer) to modify pre-specified blocks of some authenticated data without losing the authentication, but not all of these pre-specified blocks at once. Recall that this limit (the "not *all* allowed blocks at once") is not present in regular SaS, hence the need for γSaS in the following examples.

Medical Data. To keep the usual application on medical data, we believe that it is both important to anonymize – hiding personal information and perhaps uncommon diseases – and censor whatever is irrelevant to the data analysis, while also preventing a too large modification that would allow dishonest results, *e.g.*, linking two unrelated medical conditions. In this example, the signer would be anyone from the medical staff, while someone who is more on the administrative side would be a sanitizer.

In [11], the authors highlight the importance of having both invisibility and unlinkability in sanitizable signature using the following example: a physician signs the medical record of a patient in such a way that the sanitizer can (1) remove the personal information and send the anonymized record for analysis, and (2) remove everything *except* for the personal information, for financing purposes. Unlinkability ensures that the two sanitized signatures cannot be linked, which would mean reconstructing the full medical record. Invisibility maintains secrecy about what has been modified or not, preventing the verifier from assuming anything about the patient's possible pathology. However, without limitation, the sanitizer can modify both medical *and* personal data in the record, and can therefore create just about any false record. Our primitive corrects this flaw: by preventing the sanitizer from modifying more than half of the modifiable parts, we strongly reduce its capacities of generating false records.

Identity Theft. Another (completely different) angle could be usurpation-resistance on websites, mostly social media: some information about a user may change (name, address, phone number, etc.) but usually not all of them at once... unless the user was pretending to be someone else.

Thus, a website moderator could sign a profile with γSaS, allowing a user to modify γ elements at once. After some time has passed since the last modification, the moderator will re-sign the current profile state, allowing the user to change "new" things. This ensures that the profile will remain close to the original even when changes are made.

A similar control is done on Facebook, where you can only change your birthday or the name of your page[2] every once in a while.

Figure 4 explains how our scheme could be used, in a simple case where a user can edit their name and their birthday, *but only one of them each time*, with the moderator re-signing every time t days pass without a modification. In this case, we use a 1SaS scheme (more generally, a γSaS scheme where the user is allowed to modify γ pieces of information). Assume that the information of the user is $\mathsf{info}_0 = $ "name : Alice; bday : 01/01/01". The social media generates the signature

$$\sigma_0 \leftarrow \mathsf{Sig}(\mathsf{info}_0, \mathsf{sk}, \mathsf{spk}, \mathrm{ADM}, 1)$$

to validate Alice's information, where ADM accepts the messages of the form "name : *; bday : *" where * can be replaced by any word. If Alice want to change her name to Bob, she can sanitize σ by computing:

$$\sigma_0' \leftarrow \mathsf{San}(\mathsf{info}_0, \mathrm{MOD}, \sigma_0, \mathsf{pk}, \mathsf{ssk}, \mathsf{spk}),$$

where $\mathrm{MOD}(\mathsf{info}_0) = $ "name : Bob; bday : 01/01/01". The sanitized signature still authenticates the social network, and thanks to the transparency and the unlinkability properties, no user can guess what information has been modified

---

[2] facebook.com/help/271607792873806.

to obtain σ_0', even when having access to σ_0. After t days, the social network generates a new signature on $\mathsf{info}_1 = $ "$\mathtt{name : Alice; bday : 01/01/01}$":

$$\sigma_1 \leftarrow \mathsf{Sig}(\mathsf{info}_1, \mathsf{sk}, \mathsf{spk}, \mathrm{ADM}, 1).$$

Alice can then modify the parameters to further change her profile.

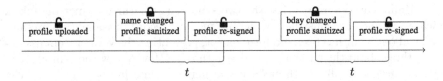

Fig. 4. A timeline of our proposed application.

Contracts. Yet another angle is that of contracts, with a focus on employment contracts. Regulations may differ within a company from branch to branch, compared to what the country's law dictates and what the company's headquarters decide (*e.g.*, in France, trade unions may negotiate with management to obtain better deals, for example on paid leave) and: the director (the signer) could issue and sign a basic contract that can be edited afterwards by the branches (sanitizers), within specified bounds. In this case, we only wish to allow modifications to cover exceptions to the contract while staying as close as possible to the original: SaS are not fine-grained enough to obtain this, which is why we need γSaS.

Takeaway. Ultimately, we simply wish to trust the sanitizer as little as possible: in a broader consideration, we can argue that this limit allows the sanitizer to correct potential mistakes made on a signed document while not being able to act dishonestly, *i.e.*, the signer could write something incorrect at n potential places, but will probably not be wrong more than γ different times.

6   Conclusion

In this work, we looked at an interesting feature for Sanitizable Signatures that we call γ-*Sanitizable Signatures*, which allows to not only control which blocks of a message a sanitizer can modify, but how many of them can be changed at once. We extended the security properties of unlinkability, invisibility, transparency, (strong) unforgeability, and immutability to these γ-Sanitizable Signatures. We proposed our scheme, ULISS, (which stands for Unlinkable Limited Invisible Sanitizable Signature), whose basic building blocks are class-equivalence signatures, 2-ring signatures, and zero-knowledge proofs, and showed that it verifies all of the properties listed above. In the future, we aim to design a scheme as efficient as the ones without limits, *i.e.*, with linear complexity and signature size.

We also intend to work on designing unlinkable and invisible schemes for other restrictions, such as limiting the set of possible messages for each modifiable parts, in a hidden way.

Acknowledgements. We thank Chris Bruska for his very helpful comments and suggestions. This work was supported by the French ANR, grants 16-CE39-0012 (SafeTLS).

A   Complete Proofs

A.1   Proof of Theorem 1

Proof. Let $\mathcal{A}$ be an adversary that wins the strong unforgeability game for ULISS and let $\mathcal{B}$ be an adversary against the strong unforgeability of the underlying 2-Ring Signature R. Let $\mathcal{C}$ be $\mathcal{B}$'s challenger. We show how $\mathcal{B}$ can perfectly simulate the experiment for $\mathcal{A}$ to win its own experiment.

Indeed, to simulate $\mathcal{A}$'s experiment, $\mathcal{B}$ can compute everything on its own (the encryption, the class-equivalence signatures) except for the 2-ring signature.

At the beginning of the experiment, $\mathcal{B}$ generates the necessary key pairs (pk_E, sk_E) and (pk_S, sk_S) to simulate the encryption and the equivalence-class signatures. $\mathcal{B}$ also creates an empty set $\mathcal{S} \leftarrow \{\}$. $\mathcal{C}$ sends (pk_0, pk_1) to $\mathcal{B}$, who can set $\mathsf{pk} \leftarrow (\mathsf{pk}_S, \mathsf{pk}_0)$ and $\mathsf{spk} \leftarrow (\mathsf{pk}_E, \mathsf{pk}_1)$ and send that to $\mathcal{A}$.

Upon receiving a query for a signature (or sanitization) of a message m (or a modified message $\mathrm{MOD}(m)$), $\mathcal{B}$ acts as follows:

$\mathsf{Sig}(\cdot, \mathsf{sk}, \cdot, \cdot, \cdot)$: $\mathcal{A}$ sends $(m, \mathrm{ADM}, \mathsf{spk}, \gamma)$, $\mathcal{B}$ parses m into n blocks, generates $x \xleftarrow{\$} \mathbb{Z}_p^*$, sets $\mathsf{pp} = \mathsf{pk}\|\mathsf{spk}$, then computes $V \leftarrow F(\mathsf{pp})^x$ and $C \leftarrow H(\gamma\|\mathsf{pp})^x$ as well as the $(A_i, B_i)_{i \in [n]}$ and the two proofs π_1 and π_2 as described in Scheme 1.
$\mathcal{B}$ then computes $s \leftarrow \mathsf{S.sig}(\mathsf{sk}_S, (A_i, B_i)_{i \in [n]}, C, V)$ and $e \leftarrow \mathsf{E.enc}(\mathsf{spk}_E, x, (A_i, B_i)_{i \in [n]}, C, V, s)$, and queries $\mathcal{C}$ for $(0, (m, (A_i, B_i)_{i \in [n]}, C, V, \pi_1, \pi_2, s, e))$, receiving s as an answer. $\mathcal{B}$ finally outputs $\sigma \leftarrow ((A_i, B_i)_{[n]}, C, V, \pi_1, \pi_2, s, e, r)$ to $\mathcal{A}$, and adds (m, σ) to $\mathcal{S}$.

$\mathsf{San}(\cdot, \cdot, \cdot, \cdot, \mathsf{ssk})$: $\mathcal{A}$ sends $(m, \mathrm{MOD}, \sigma, \mathsf{pk})$, $\mathcal{B}$ parses $\mathrm{MOD}(m)$ as n blocks, parses σ as $((A_i, B_i)_{[n]}, C, V, \pi_1, \pi_2, s, e, r)$, picks $t \xleftarrow{\$} \mathbb{Z}_p^*$, deciphers e to get $c = x, (\tilde{A}_i, \tilde{B}_i)_{[n]}, \tilde{C}, \tilde{V}, \tilde{s}$ and computes $x' = x \cdot t$, before re-encrypting it as e'. $\mathcal{B}$ then sets $\mathsf{pp} = \mathsf{pk}\|\mathsf{spk}$, computes $V' = F(\mathsf{pp})^{x'}$, $C' = H(\gamma\|\mathsf{pp})^{x'}$, then all A_i' and B_i' as described in Scheme 1, and computes the signature s' as $\mathsf{S.ChRep}(\mathsf{pk}_S, s, (\tilde{A}_i, \tilde{B}_i)_{i \in [n]}, \tilde{C}, \tilde{V}, t)$. $\mathcal{B}$ can then compute the proofs π_1' and π_2' as described in Scheme 1. $\mathcal{B}$ then queries $\mathcal{C}$ for a signature r' as an answer to $(1, (\mathrm{MOD}(m), (A_i', B_i')_{i \in [n]}, C', V', \pi_1', \pi_2', s', e'))$, and finally answers $\mathcal{A}$ with $\sigma' \leftarrow ((A_i', B_i')_{i \in [n]}, C', V', \pi_1', \pi_2', s', e', r')$, adding $(\mathrm{MOD}(m), \sigma')$ to $\mathcal{S}$.

At the end of the experiment, $\mathcal{A}$ will produce a pair (m, σ). If this pair is in $\mathcal{S}$, then $\mathcal{B}$ returns 0, as this is considered a trivial win and thus excluded. Otherwise, $\mathcal{B}$ parses σ as $((A_i, B_i)_{[n]}, C, V, \pi_1, \pi_2, s, e, r)$, sets $\bar{m} = (m, (A_i, B_i)_{[n]}, C, V, \pi_1, \pi_2, s, e))$ and sends $(\bar{m}, r)$ as its answer to $\mathcal{C}$.

Note that the winning conditions for $\mathcal{B}$ and for $\mathcal{A}$ actually coincide: if $(m, (\star, r))$ is in $\mathcal{S}$, then $\mathcal{C}$ has the pair $((m, \star), r)$ in its own set, and vice-versa. There is a direct correspondence between the sets.

To be thorough, let $(m, \sigma) = (m, ((A_i, B_i)_{[n]}, C, V, \pi_1, \pi_2, s, e, r))$ be $\mathcal{A}$'s answer. If there exists $(m, \sigma') = (m, ((A'_i, B'_i)_{[n]}, C', V', \pi'_1, \pi'_2, s', e', r'))$ with $\sigma' \neq \sigma$ in $\mathcal{S}$ (and the corresponding $(\bar{m}_0, r') = ((m, (A'_i, B'_i)_{[n]}, C', V', \pi'_1, \pi'_2, s', e'), r')$ in $\mathcal{C}$'s set), then the pair $(\bar{m}_1, r) = ((m, (A_i, B_i)_{[n]}, C, V, \pi_1, \pi_2, s, e), r)$ that $\mathcal{B}$ forwards to $\mathcal{C}$ can be such that $r = r'$ or $\bar{m}_0 = \bar{m}_1$, but not both, since σ' and σ differ by at least one variable, and thus $(\bar{m}_0, r')$ is not in $\mathcal{C}$'s set.

For the other way around, we apply the same logic to the case where the pair (m', σ) such that $m' \neq m$ is in $\mathcal{S}$ to see that $(\bar{m}_0, r')$ is not in $\mathcal{C}$'s set in this case either. Thus:

$$\mathsf{Adv}^{\mathsf{SUF}}_{\mathsf{ULISS}, \mathcal{A}}(\lambda) \leq \mathsf{Adv}^{\mathsf{SUF}}_{R, \mathcal{B}}(\lambda).$$

A.2   Proof of Theorem 3

Proof. An adversary $\mathcal{A}$ wins the unlinkability experiment by distinguishing which of two signatures σ_0 or σ_1 was sanitized. We exclude trivial ways of winning by asking for *valid* signatures with the same admissible function $\mathrm{ADM}_0 = \mathrm{ADM}_1$, identically admissible modification functions $(\mathrm{ADM}_0(\mathrm{MOD}_0) = \mathrm{ADM}_1(\mathrm{MOD}_1))$, sanitized such that the signed message is identical $(\mathrm{MOD}_0(m_0) = \mathrm{MOD}_1(m_1))$. Note that all calls to H and F are implicitly simulated by a random oracle.

We show that

$$\mathsf{Adv}^{\mathsf{unlink}}_{ULISS, \mathcal{A}}(\lambda) \leq q_{\mathsf{Sig}} q_{\mathsf{LRSan}} \mathsf{Adv}^{\mathsf{class\text{-}hid}}_S(\lambda) + \mathsf{Adv}^{\mathsf{adapt}}_S(\lambda) + \mathsf{Adv}^{\mathsf{IND\$\text{-}CCA}}_E(\lambda)$$
$$+ q_{\mathsf{Sig}}(q_H + q_F) \cdot \mathsf{Adv}^{\mathsf{DDH}}_G(\lambda) + \mathsf{Adv}^{\mathsf{SUF}}_{ULISS}(\lambda).$$

In the following sequence of games, let S_i be the event that $\mathcal{A}$ wins at Game i.

Game 0. This is the original $\mathsf{Exp}^{\mathsf{unlink}}_{ULISS, \mathcal{A}}(\lambda)$ experiment, hence:

$$\mathsf{Adv}^{\mathsf{unlink}}_{ULISS, \mathcal{A}}(\lambda) = \Pr[S_0] - 1/2$$

Game 1. This game is the same as Game 1 except the challenger aborts and returns a random bit if $\mathcal{A}$ queries LRSan on a forgery. Denoting with abort_1 the event that the challenger aborts in this game, we have that

$$\Pr[\mathsf{abort}_1] \leq \mathsf{Adv}^{\mathsf{SUF}}_{ULISS}(\lambda),$$

and since $|\Pr[S_1] - \Pr[S_0]| = \Pr[\mathsf{abort}_1]$,

$$|\Pr[S_1] - \Pr[S_0]| \leq \mathsf{Adv}^{\mathsf{SUF}}_{ULISS}(\lambda).$$

After this game, the adversary can only query LRSan on signatures output by the challenger.

Game 2. This game is identical to Game 1 except the input to the encryption scheme is replaced with random. We claim that:

$$| \Pr[S_2] - \Pr[S_1]| = \mathsf{Adv}_E^{\mathsf{IND\$-CCA}}(\lambda)$$

Proof. We show that if there exists a PPT adversary $\mathcal{A}$ capable of distinguishing between Games 2 and 1 then we can build an adversary $\mathcal{B}$ against the IND\$-CCA security of the encryption scheme.

Let $\mathcal{C}$ be $\mathcal{B}$'s challenger, we show how $\mathcal{B}$ can simulate $\mathcal{A}$'s challenges. At the beginning, $\mathcal{C}$ generates the encryption key pair $(\mathsf{pk}_E, \mathsf{sk}_E)$, picks a bit b, forwards pk_E to $\mathcal{B}$ and whenever $\mathcal{B}$ sends a message m, $\mathcal{C}$ answers with the encryption of a random message if $b = 0$, and with the encryption of m if $b = 1$. $\mathcal{B}$ will embed its challenges into $\mathcal{A}$'s challenges.

$\mathcal{B}$ picks a random bit b'. $\mathcal{B}$ generates key pairs $(\mathsf{pk}_S, \mathsf{sk}_S)$ for the equivalence-class signature S, then two key pairs $(\mathsf{pk}_R, \mathsf{sk}_R)$, $(\mathsf{spk}_R, \mathsf{ssk}_R)$ for the 2-Ring Signature, then sets $(\mathsf{pk}, \mathsf{sk}) \leftarrow ((\mathsf{pk}_S, \mathsf{pk}_R), (\mathsf{sk}_S, \mathsf{sk}_R))$ and $(\mathsf{spk}, \mathsf{ssk}) \leftarrow ((\mathsf{pk}_E, \mathsf{spk}_R), \mathsf{ssk}_R)$. $\mathcal{B}$ then forwards $(\mathsf{pk}, \mathsf{spk})$, to $\mathcal{A}$, sets $\mathcal{L} \leftarrow [\ ]$ to keep track of the limits, $\mathcal{Q} \leftarrow [\ ]$ to keep track of the commitments (indeed, $\mathcal{B}$ won't be able to query $\mathcal{C}$ for decryptions on the challenges), and answers $\mathcal{A}$'s queries as follows:

$\mathsf{Sig}(\cdot, \mathsf{sk}, \cdot, \cdot, \cdot)$: $\mathcal{A}$ sends $(m, \mathrm{ADM}, \overline{\mathsf{spk}}, \gamma)$, $\mathcal{B}$ computes the signature as described in Scheme 1, except if $\overline{\mathsf{spk}} = \mathsf{spk}$, instead of encrypting $c = (x, (A_i, B_i)_{i \in [n]}, C, V)$ itself, it sends c to $\mathcal{C}$ and receives e in exchange, sets $\mathcal{Q}[e] = c$, then continues normally to obtain a signature σ, then sets $\mathcal{L}[\sigma] = (m, \gamma)$, and returns σ.

$\mathsf{LRSan}(b', \mathsf{pk}, \mathsf{ssk}, \mathsf{spk}, \cdot, \cdot)$: on input $((m_0, \mathrm{MOD}_0, \sigma_0)(m_1, \mathrm{MOD}_1, \sigma_1))$, this oracle returns $\perp$ if for $i \in \{0,1\}$, any of the following conditions do not hold: (1) $\mathsf{Ver}(m_i, \sigma_i, \mathsf{pk}, \mathsf{spk}) = 1$, (2) $\mathrm{ADM}_0 = \mathrm{ADM}_1$, (3) $\mathrm{ADM}_0(\mathrm{MOD}_0) = \mathrm{ADM}_1(\mathrm{MOD}_1)$ and (4) $\mathrm{MOD}_0(m_0) = \mathrm{MOD}_1(m_1)$, else it gets $(\overline{m}_i, \gamma_i) \leftarrow \mathcal{L}[\sigma_i]$ for $i \in \{0,1\}$, then if $D(\mathrm{MOD}_0(m_0), \overline{m}_0) \leq \gamma_0$ and $D(\mathrm{MOD}_1(m_1), \overline{m}_1) \leq \gamma_1$, it computes the sanitization of $\sigma_{b'}$:

- $\mathcal{B}$ follows all of the sanitization as described in Scheme 1 to sanitize $\sigma_{b'}$ except for the decryption/encryption; let $e_{b'}$ be the encryption in $\sigma_{b'}$, then $\mathcal{B}$ retrieves $c \leftarrow \mathcal{Q}[e_{b'}]$, queries $\mathcal{C}$ for a new encryption e' of c, then continues normally, producing a sanitized signature σ' using e' as its encryption. finally, $\mathcal{B}$ sets $\mathcal{L}[\sigma'] \leftarrow (\overline{m}_b, \min(\gamma_0, \gamma_1))$, and $\mathcal{Q}[e'] \leftarrow c$, and returns σ',

else it returns $\perp$.

$\mathsf{San}(\cdot, \cdot, \cdot, \cdot, \mathsf{ssk}, \mathsf{spk})$: on input $(m, \mathrm{MOD}, \sigma, \overline{\mathsf{pk}})$, $\mathcal{B}$ gets $(\overline{m}, \gamma) \leftarrow \mathcal{L}[\sigma]$, then if we have $D(\mathrm{MOD}(m), \overline{m}) \leq \gamma$ it computes the sanitization:

- $\mathcal{B}$ computes the sanitized signature normally except for the encryption/decryption; let e be the encryption in σ, if $\overline{\mathsf{pk}} \neq \mathsf{pk}$, then $\mathcal{B}$ queries $\mathcal{C}$ for a decryption of e and obtains c then re-encrypts it to obtain e', else if $\overline{\mathsf{pk}} = \mathsf{pk}$, $\mathcal{B}$ gets $c \leftarrow \mathcal{Q}[e]$ then queries $\mathcal{C}$ on c for an encryption e', setting $\mathcal{Q}[e'] = c$; $\mathcal{B}$ then uses the content of c to follow the steps and compute the sanitized signature σ', then sets $\mathcal{L}[\sigma'] = \mathcal{L}[\sigma]$, and returns σ',

else it returns $\perp$.

At the end of the experiment, $\mathcal{A}$ returns a bit b_*. If $b_* = b'$, then $\mathcal{B}$ returns 1, else it returns 0.

Analysis: If $b = 0$ then $\mathcal{B}$ perfectly simulates Game 2 to $\mathcal{A}$, else it perfectly simulates Game 1. If $\mathcal{B}$ returns 1, it means $\mathcal{A}$ wins ($b_* = b'$), thus :

$$\Pr[\mathcal{B} \to 1|b = 1] = \Pr[b_* = b'|b = 1] = \Pr[\mathcal{A} \text{ wins}|b = 1] = \Pr[S_1]$$
$$\text{and } \Pr[\mathcal{B} \to 1|b = 0] = \Pr[b_* = b'|b = 0] = \Pr[\mathcal{A} \text{ wins}|b = 0] = \Pr[S_2]$$
$$\text{so } |\Pr[S_1] - \Pr[S_2]| = |\Pr[\mathcal{B} \to 1|b = 1] - \Pr[\mathcal{B} \to 1|b = 0]| = \mathsf{Adv}_E^{\mathsf{IND\$-CCA}}(\lambda)$$

After this game, the content of the encryption cannot be used to link the sanitization with the signature.

Game 3. This game is the same as the previous one, except every occurrence of $\mathsf{S.ChRep}(\mathsf{pk}_S, s, m, t)$ is replaced with $\mathsf{S.sig}(\mathsf{pk}_S, m^t)$. We argue that

$$|\Pr[S_3] - \Pr[S_2]| = \mathsf{Adv}_S^{\mathsf{adapt}}(\lambda).$$

Proof. Indeed, we show that if there exists a PPT adversary $\mathcal{A}$ capable of distinguishing between Games 3 and 2, then we can build a PPT adversary $\mathcal{B}$ against the adaptability of the underlying equivalence-class signature, S.

Let $\mathcal{C}$ be $\mathcal{B}$'s challenger. At the beginning of the experiment, $\mathcal{C}$ picks a random bit b and generates a signing key pair $(\mathsf{pk}_S, \mathsf{sk}_S)$, which is sent to $\mathcal{B}$. $\mathcal{B}$ generates the remaining key pairs to complete $(\mathsf{pk}, \mathsf{sk})$ and $(\mathsf{spk}, \mathsf{ssk})$ (*i.e.*, the pairs for the 2-Ring Signature, and the pair for the encryption scheme), and forwards pk and spk to $\mathcal{A}$. $\mathcal{B}$ also picks a random bit b'.

$\mathcal{B}$ answers $\mathcal{A}$'s queries as follows:

$\mathsf{Sig}(\cdot, \mathsf{sk}, \cdot, \cdot, \cdot)$**:** $\mathcal{A}$ sends $(m, \mathrm{ADM}, \bar{\mathsf{spk}}, \gamma)$, $\mathcal{B}$ computes the signature as described in Scheme 1 and returns it, except if $\bar{\mathsf{spk}} = \mathsf{spk}$, instead of encrypting $c = (x, (A_i, B_i)_{i \in [n]}, C, V)$, it encrypts a random string to obtain e, sets $\mathcal{Q}[e] = c$, then continues normally to obtain a signature σ, then sets $\mathcal{L}[\sigma] = (m, \gamma)$, and returns σ.

$\mathsf{LRSan}(b', \mathsf{pk}, \mathsf{ssk}, \mathsf{spk}, \cdot, \cdot)$**:** on input $((m_0, \mathrm{MOD}_0, \sigma_0)(m_1, \mathrm{MOD}_1, \sigma_1))$, this oracle returns $\bot$ if for $i \in \{0, 1\}$, any of the following conditions do not hold: (1) $\mathsf{Ver}(m_i, \sigma_i, \mathsf{pk}, \mathsf{spk}) = 1$, (2) $\mathrm{ADM}_0 = \mathrm{ADM}_1$, (3) $\mathrm{ADM}_0(\mathrm{MOD}_0) = \mathrm{ADM}_1(\mathrm{MOD}_1)$ and (4) $\mathrm{MOD}_0(m_0) = \mathrm{MOD}_1(m_1)$, else it gets $(\bar{m}_i, \gamma_i) \leftarrow \mathcal{L}[\sigma_i]$ for $i \in \{0, 1\}$, then if $D(\mathrm{MOD}_0(m_0), \bar{m}_0) \leq \gamma_0$ and $D(\mathrm{MOD}_1(m_1), \bar{m}_1) \leq \gamma_1$, it computes the sanitization of $\sigma_{b'}$:

  – $\mathcal{B}$ follows all of the sanitization as described in Scheme 1 to sanitize $\sigma_{b'}$ except for the decryption/encryption and the change of representative for the equivalence-class signature s:
  • let $e_{b'}$ be the encryption in $\sigma_{b'}$, then $\mathcal{B}$ retrieves $c \leftarrow \mathcal{Q}[e_{b'}]$, encrypts a random string to obtain e', and sets $c \leftarrow \mathcal{Q}[e']$, then
  • after computing everything else normally (using the content of c), $\mathcal{B}$ queries $\mathcal{C}$ for a signature s' with $((\mathsf{pk}_S, \mathsf{sk}_S), s, ((A_i, B_i)_{i \in [n]}, C, V), t)$,

then $\mathcal{B}$ continues ordinarily, producing a sanitized signature σ' using e' as its encryption and s' as its equivalence-class signature. Finally, $\mathcal{B}$ sets $\mathcal{L}[\sigma'] \leftarrow (\bar{m}_b, \min(\gamma_0, \gamma_1))$, and returns σ',

else it returns $\perp$.

San$(\cdot, \cdot, \cdot, \cdot, \mathsf{ssk}, \mathsf{spk})$: on input $(m, \mathrm{MOD}, \sigma, \bar{\mathsf{pk}})$, if $\bar{\mathsf{pk}} \neq \mathsf{pk}$ it computes the sanitization normally, else $\mathcal{B}$ gets $(\bar{m}, \gamma) \leftarrow \mathcal{L}[\sigma]$, then if $D(\mathrm{MOD}(m), \bar{m}) \leq \gamma$ it computes the sanitization:

- $\mathcal{B}$ computes the sanitized signature as above, *i.e.*, normally except for the decryption/encryption for which it uses $\mathcal{Q}$ and encrypts a random string, respectively, and for the equivalence-class signature, for which it queries $\mathcal{C}$,

else it returns $\perp$.

At the end of the experiment, $\mathcal{A}$ returns a bit b_*: if $b_* = b'$, then $\mathcal{B}$ answers 1 (guessing that $\mathcal{C}$ used S.ChRep), else it answers 0.

Analysis: If $b = 0$ then $\mathcal{B}$ is perfectly simulating Game 3 (every change of representative is actually a new signature), and if $b = 1$ then $\mathcal{B}$ is perfectly simulating Game 2. Using the same justification as in the previous game, we have:

$$|\Pr[S_3] - \Pr[S_2]| = |\Pr[\mathcal{B} \to 1|b=1] - \Pr[\mathcal{B} \to 1|b=0]| = \mathsf{Adv}_S^{\mathsf{adapt}}(\lambda).$$

This game "unlinks" the class-equivalence signature in the sanitization from the one in the original signature.

Game 4. This game is the same as the previous one except that the NIZKPs are faked by the simulator Sim. As the simulator is "perfect", we argue that: $\Pr[S_4] = \Pr[S_3]$.

Proof. Indeed, if there exists a PPT adversary $\mathcal{A}$ capable of distinguishing between Games 4 and 3, then we can build an adversary $\mathcal{B}$ against the zero-knowledge property of the NIZKP π_1, π_2.

Let $\mathcal{C}$ be $\mathcal{B}$'s challenger, we show how $\mathcal{B}$ can simulate $\mathcal{A}$'s challenges. At the beginning, $\mathcal{C}$ picks a random bit b, and $\mathcal{C}$ will answer queries with a fake NIZKP if $b = 0$, and a real one if $b = 1$.

$\mathcal{B}$ generates all key pairs for the encryption E, the 2-Ring Signature scheme R, and the class-equivalence signature scheme S, and forwards the public keys to $\mathcal{A}$. $\mathcal{B}$ picks a random bit b' and embeds its challenges into $\mathcal{A}$'s challenges by answering the queries as follows:

Sig$(\cdot, \mathsf{sk}, \cdot, \cdot, \cdot)$: $\mathcal{A}$ sends $(m, \mathrm{ADM}, \bar{\mathsf{spk}}, \gamma)$, if $\bar{\mathsf{spk}} \neq \mathsf{spk}$, $\mathcal{B}$ computes everything normally, else $\mathcal{B}$ computes the signature as described in the previous game (including adding elements to $\mathcal{L}$ and $\mathcal{Q}$) except instead of computing π_1 and π_2 itself, they are queried from $\mathcal{C}$.

LRSan$(b', \mathsf{pk}, \mathsf{ssk}, \mathsf{spk}, \cdot, \cdot)$: on input $((m_0, \mathrm{MOD}_0, \sigma_0)(m_1, \mathrm{MOD}_1, \sigma_1))$, this oracle returns $\perp$ if for $i \in \{0, 1\}$, any of the following conditions do not hold: (1) $\mathsf{Ver}(m_i, \sigma_i, \mathsf{pk}, \mathsf{spk}) = 1$, (2) $\mathrm{ADM}_0 = \mathrm{ADM}_1$, (3) $\mathrm{ADM}_0(\mathrm{MOD}_0) = \mathrm{ADM}_1(\mathrm{MOD}_1)$ and (4) $\mathrm{MOD}_0(m_0) = \mathrm{MOD}_1(m_1)$, else it gets $(\bar{m}_i, \gamma_i) \leftarrow \mathcal{L}[\sigma_i]$

for $i \in \{0,1\}$, then if $D(\text{MOD}_0(m_0), \bar{m}_0) \leq \gamma_0$ and $D(\text{MOD}_1(m_1), \bar{m}_1) \leq \gamma_1$, it computes the sanitization of $\sigma_{b'}$ as in the previous game (again, including for $\mathcal{L}$ and $\mathcal{Q}$), except it uses $\text{S.sig}((,c)^t)$ instead of $\text{S.ChRep}(c,t)$ to get s', and queries $\mathcal{C}$ for the proofs π_1, π_2 instead of computing them; then finally returns the obtained sanitized signature σ', else it returns $\bot$.

$\text{San}(\cdot, \cdot, \cdot, \cdot, \text{ssk}, \text{spk})$: on input $(m, \text{MOD}, \sigma, \bar{\text{pk}})$, if $\bar{\text{pk}} \neq \text{pk}$, it computes the sanitizations normally, else $\mathcal{B}$ gets $(\bar{m}, \gamma) \leftarrow \mathcal{L}[\sigma]$, then if $D(\text{MOD}(m), \bar{m}) \leq \gamma$ it computes the sanitization as in the previous game (once more, including for $\mathcal{L}$ and $\mathcal{Q}$), except it uses $\text{S.sig}(,i)$nstead of S.ChRep as described for LRSan, and queries $\mathcal{C}$ for the proofs π_1 and π_2, finally returning the obtained sanitized signature σ', else it returns $\bot$.

In the end $\mathcal{A}$ returns a bit b_*, if $b_* = b'$ $\mathcal{B}$ sends 1 to $\mathcal{C}$ (guessing that the proofs are real) else it answers 0.

Analysis: If $b = 0$ then $\mathcal{B}$ is perfectly simulating Game 4 (the proofs are simulated), and if $b = 1$ then $\mathcal{B}$ is perfectly simulating Game 3. Using the same justification as in the previous games, we have: $\Pr[S_4] = \Pr[S_3]$.

After this game, the commitments and the proofs are not linked.

Game 5. This game is the same as the previous one except we replace the commitments with random elements when computing a signature (*i.e.*, when generating them).

We argue that :

$$|\Pr[S_5] - \Pr[S_4]| \leq (q_H + q_F) \cdot \text{Adv}_{\mathbb{G}}^{\text{DDH}}(\lambda),$$

where q_H (resp. q_F) is the number of queries made to the random oracle for hash function H (resp. F).

Proof. First, we propose the definition of *fixed n-DDH*, based on the n-DDH:

Definition 17 (fixed n-DDH). *Let $\mathbb{G}$ be a multiplicative group of prime order q, with g a generator. For an instance $\{(g^a, g^{b_i}, g^{c_b,i})\}_{1 \leq i \leq n}$ such that for $i \in [n]$, $b_i \xleftarrow{\$} \mathbb{Z}_p^*$, and $a \xleftarrow{\$} \mathbb{Z}_p^*$ and $b \xleftarrow{\$} \{0,1\}$ such that $c_{0,i} \xleftarrow{\$} \mathbb{Z}_p^*$ and $c_{1,i} = a \cdot b_i$, the fixed n-DDH problem is guessing b, and the fixed n-DDH assumption states than no PPT algorithm can solve this problem with a non-negligible advantage.*

Lemma 2. *For any $n \in \mathbb{N}$, fixed n-DDH holds under the DDH assumption, with*

$$\text{Adv}_{\mathbb{G}}^{fn\text{-}DDH}(\lambda) \leq n \cdot \text{Adv}_{\mathbb{G}}^{DDH}(\lambda).$$

Proof. The proof of this lemma is given in the full version.

We now show the indistinguishability of Games 5 and 4 using a hybrid argument.

Let q_{Sig} be the number of queries made to the Sig oracle, let H_i be the experiment such that the i first queries to the Sig oracle use honest commitments, and the $q_{\mathsf{Sig}} - i$ last queries use random commitments. Suppose there exists an PPT adversary $\mathcal{A}$ capable of distinguishing H_i from H_{i+1} for $0 \leq i < q_{\mathsf{Sig}}$, then we show how to build an adversary $\mathcal{B}$ against fixed $q_H + q_F$-DDH in $\mathbb{G}$.

Let $\mathcal{C}$ be $\mathcal{B}$'s challenger, we now show how $\mathcal{B}$ simulates $\mathcal{A}$'s challenges. $\mathcal{C}$ starts by picking a random bit b. $\mathcal{C}$ will send $\mathcal{B}$ tuples that will amount into a fixed $(q_H + q_F)$·DDH instance, i.e., tuples of the form $(g, X = g^x, Y = g^y, Z = g^z)$ with a different Y, Z in each tuple. $\mathcal{B}$ generates all necessary keys to build the pair $(\mathsf{pk}, \mathsf{sk})$ for the signer and $(\mathsf{spk}, \mathsf{ssk})$ for the sanitizer, then picks a random bit $b*$, and forwards $(\mathsf{pk}, \mathsf{spk})$ to $\mathcal{A}$. $\mathcal{B}$ also initiates empty lists $\mathcal{L}$ and $\mathcal{Q}$ as above, along with a new list $\mathcal{D}$, to keep track of the DDH queries, and a counter c_{Sig} initated to 0, counting the number of calls to Sig. For clarity, we separate the random oracles by expliciting them, as they are the ones affected by the change:

$H(\cdot)$ (resp. $F(\cdot)$ upon a query u, if $H[u]$ (resp. $F[u]$) exists, $\mathcal{B}$ returns $H[u]$ (resp $F[u]$), else if u is of the form $u'\|\mathsf{pp}$, $\mathcal{B}$ queries $\mathcal{C}$ for a challenge (g, X, Y, Z), sets $H[u] = Y$ (resp. $F[u] = Y$), $\mathcal{D}[Y] = Z$, and returns Y, else it generates a random hash h, set $H[u] = h$ (resp. $F[u] = h$), and returns h.

In the beginning, $\mathcal{B}$ sets $F(\mathsf{pp}) = g$. $\mathcal{B}$ will embed its challenges in $\mathcal{A}$'s challenges by answering its queries as follows:

$\mathsf{Sig}(\cdot, \mathsf{sk}, \cdot, \cdot, \cdot)$: $\mathcal{A}$ sends $(m, \mathrm{ADM}, \bar{\mathsf{spk}}, \gamma)$, if $\bar{\mathsf{spk}} \neq \mathsf{spk}$, then $\mathcal{B}$ computes everything normally, else $\mathcal{B}$ computes the signature as described in the previous game (including adding elements to $\mathcal{L}$ and $\mathcal{Q}$) except it always fakes the NIZKP, and when generating the commitments, it proceeds as follows:
- if $c_{\mathsf{Sig}} \leq i$, it generates the commitments honestly,
- else if $c_{\mathsf{Sig}} = i + 1$, first, $\mathcal{B}$ generates a random t and sets $V = X^t (= (g^x)^t = F(pp)^{xt})$, then for all other commitments, if we denote with u their corresponding input to H or F (e.g., for C, $u = \gamma\|\mathsf{pp}$) then we get a hash $h = F(u)$ (for B_i) or $h = H(u)$ (for A_i and C), and the "actual" commitment is then $\mathcal{D}[h]^t$ (so if $\mathcal{C}$'s bit is 1, the commitment is $Z^t = (Y^x)t = h^{xt}$, otherwise it is random)
- else (so, if $c_{\mathsf{Sig}} > i + 1$), $\mathcal{B}$ generates random commitments,
then $\mathcal{B}$ continues, to obtain a signature σ in the end, which it returns after incrementing c_{Sig}.

$\mathsf{LRSan}(b', \mathsf{pk}, \mathsf{ssk}, \mathsf{spk}, \cdot, \cdot)$: on input $((m_0, \mathrm{MOD}_0, \sigma_0)(m_1, \mathrm{MOD}_1, \sigma_1))$, this oracle returns $\bot$ if for $i \in \{0, 1\}$, any of the following conditions do not hold: (1) $\mathsf{Ver}(m_i, \sigma_i, \mathsf{pk}, \mathsf{spk}) = 1$, (2) $\mathrm{ADM}_0 = \mathrm{ADM}_1$, (3) $\mathrm{ADM}_0(\mathrm{MOD}_0) = \mathrm{ADM}_1(\mathrm{MOD}_1)$ and (4) $\mathrm{MOD}_0(m_0) = \mathrm{MOD}_1(m_1)$, else it gets $(\bar{m}_i, \gamma_i) \leftarrow \mathcal{L}[\sigma_i]$ for $i \in \{0, 1\}$, then if $D(\mathrm{MOD}_0(m_0), \bar{m}_0) \leq \gamma_0$ and $D(\mathrm{MOD}_1(m_1), \bar{m}_1) \leq \gamma_1$, it computes the sanitization of $\sigma_{b'}$ as in the previous game (again, including for $\mathcal{L}$ and $\mathcal{Q}$), returning a sanitized signature σ'; else it returns $\bot$.

$\mathsf{San}(\cdot, \cdot, \cdot, \cdot, \mathsf{ssk}_R, \cdot)$: on input $(m, \mathrm{MOD}, \sigma, \mathsf{pk}, \mathsf{spk})$, $\mathcal{B}$ gets $(\bar{m}, \gamma) \leftarrow \mathcal{L}[\sigma]$, then if $D(\mathrm{MOD}(m), \bar{m}) \leq \gamma$ it computes the sanitization as in the previous game (once more, including for $\mathcal{L}$ and $\mathcal{Q}$), finally returning a sanitized signature σ'; else it returns $\bot$.

In the end $\mathcal{A}$ returns a bit b_*, if $b_* = b'$ $\mathcal{B}$ sends 1 to $\mathcal{C}$ (guessing that the DDH elements are real) else it answers 0.

Analysis: In the case where $b = 1$, as explained in LRSan above, $\mathcal{B}$ simulates H_i. Now if $b = O$, there is no relation between x and the y and z values, and thus the commitments are completely random, simulating H_{i+1}. Hence, following the same logic as in the previous games:

$$|\Pr[\mathsf{H}_{i+1}] - \Pr[\mathsf{H}_i]| = \mathsf{Adv}_{\mathbb{G}}^{f(q_H + q_F)\text{-DDH}}(\lambda) \leq (q_H + q_F) \cdot \mathsf{Adv}_{\mathbb{G}}^{\mathsf{DDH}}(\lambda)$$

Moreover, in $\mathsf{H}_{q_{\mathsf{Sig}}}$ the commitments are done honestly, meaning H_0 is identical to Game 4, and in H_0 all commitments are random, meaning $\mathsf{H}_{q_{\mathsf{Sig}}}$ is identical to Game 5.

Summing the hybrids yields the following inequality:

$$|\Pr[S_5] - \Pr[S_4]| = |\Pr[\mathsf{H}_0] - \Pr[\mathsf{H}_{q_{\mathsf{Sig}}}]|$$
$$\leq q_{\mathsf{Sig}}(q_H + q_F) \cdot \mathsf{Adv}_{\mathbb{G}}^{\mathsf{DDH}}(\lambda)$$

After this game, the commitments are not linked to each other. This step is a necessary setup for the next game.

Game 6. This game is the same as the previous one except the commitments are replaced with random elements when sanitizing a signature.

We argue that:

$$|\Pr[S_6] - \Pr[S_5]| \leq q_{\mathsf{LRSan}} q_{\mathsf{Sig}} \cdot \mathsf{Adv}_S^{\mathsf{class\text{-}hid}}(\lambda),$$

where q_{Sig} is the number of calls to the Sig oracle and q_{LRSan} is the number of calls to the LRSan oracle.

Proof. We show the indistinguishability of Games 6 and 5 using a hybrid argument.

Let H_i be the experiment such that the first i queries to LRSan have honestly computed commitments, while the $q_{\mathsf{LRSan}} - i$ last queries are computed using random commitments.

We show that if there exists a PPT adversary $\mathcal{A}$ capable of distinguishing H_{i+1} from H_i, for $0 \leq i < q_{\mathsf{LRSan}}$, then we can build an adversary $\mathcal{B}$ against the class-hiding property of the message space of S. Let $\mathcal{C}$ be $\mathcal{B}$'s challenger, we now show how $\mathcal{B}$ simulates $\mathcal{A}$'s challenges. $\mathcal{C}$ starts by picking a random bit b. $\mathcal{C}$ will send $\mathcal{B}$ pairs of the form $(C, C') \in (\mathbb{G}^\ell)^2$ such that C' is in the equivalence class of C if $b = 1$, and randomly sampled otherwise. $\mathcal{B}$ generates all necessary keys to build the key pair $(\mathsf{pk}, \mathsf{sk})$ for the signer and $(\mathsf{spk}, \mathsf{ssk})$ for the sanitizer, then picks a random bit b_*, and forwards pk and spk to $\mathcal{A}$. $\mathcal{B}$ also initiates, as before, empty lists $\mathcal{L}$ and $\mathcal{Q}$. It also generates an empty list $\mathcal{T}$ to remember $\mathcal{C}$'s queries, and a counter c_{LRSan} counting the queries to LRSan.

$\mathcal{B}$ will embed its challenges in $\mathcal{A}$'s challenges by answering its queries as follows:

$\mathsf{Sig}(\cdot, \mathsf{sk}, \cdot, \cdot, \cdot)$: $\mathcal{A}$ sends $(m, \mathrm{ADM}, \bar{\mathsf{spk}}, \gamma)$, as usual, if $\bar{\mathsf{spk}} \neq \mathsf{spk}$, $\mathcal{B}$ acts normally, else $\mathcal{B}$ computes the signature as described in the previous game (including adding elements to $\mathcal{L}$ and $\mathcal{Q}$) except when generating the commitments, it queries $\mathcal{C}$ to get a pair (M, M') and uses M as the commitments (which are thus random), to obtain a signature σ in the end, which it returns, and sets $\mathcal{T}[\sigma] = (M, M')$.

$\mathsf{LRSan}(b', \mathsf{pk}, \mathsf{ssk}, \mathsf{spk}, \cdot, \cdot)$: on input $((m_0, \mathrm{MOD}_0, \sigma_0)(m_1, \mathrm{MOD}_1, \sigma_1))$, this oracle returns $\perp$ if for $i \in \{0,1\}$, any of the following conditions do not hold: (1) $\mathsf{Ver}(m_i, \sigma_i, \mathsf{pk}, \mathsf{spk}) = 1$, (2) $\mathrm{ADM}_0 = \mathrm{ADM}_1$, (3) $\mathrm{ADM}_0(\mathrm{MOD}_0) = \mathrm{ADM}_1(\mathrm{MOD}_1)$ and (4) $\mathrm{MOD}_0(m_0) = \mathrm{MOD}_1(m_1)$, else it gets $(\bar{m}_i, \gamma_i) \leftarrow \mathcal{L}[\sigma_i]$ for $i \in \{0,1\}$, then if $D(\mathrm{MOD}_0(m_0), \bar{m}_0) \leq \gamma_0$ and $D(\mathrm{MOD}_1(m_1), \bar{m}_1) \leq \gamma_1$, it computes the sanitization of $\sigma_{b'}$ as in the previous game (again, including for $\mathcal{L}$ and $\mathcal{Q}$), except the commitments are computed as follows, first $\mathcal{B}$ gets $(M, M') \leftarrow \mathcal{T}[\sigma_{b'}]$, then
   - if $c_{\mathsf{LRSan}} \leq i$, it compute the commitments normally, $i.e.$ using M
   - else if $c_{\mathsf{LRSan}} = i + 1$, it generates a random t and uses $(M')^t$, $i.e.$, the elements of M' elevated to the power of t, as the commitments (which will thus be in the class of M if M' also is, otherwise they will be random),
   - else (if $c_{\mathsf{LRSan}} > i + 1$), it computes random commitments,
then finally returns the obtained sanitized signature σ' and sets $\mathcal{T}[\sigma'] = (M, M')$; else it returns $\perp$.

$\mathsf{San}(\cdot, \cdot, \cdot, \cdot, \mathsf{ssk}, \mathsf{spk})$: on input $(m, \mathrm{MOD}, \sigma, \bar{\mathsf{pk}})$, if $\bar{\mathsf{pk}} \neq \mathsf{pk}$, then $\mathcal{B}$ computes the sanitization normally, else $\mathcal{B}$ gets $(\bar{m}, \gamma) \leftarrow \mathcal{L}[\sigma]$, then if $D(\mathrm{MOD}(m), \bar{m}) \leq \gamma$ it computes the sanitization as in the previous game (once more, including for $\mathcal{L}$ and $\mathcal{Q}$), except it computes commitments as described honestly for LRSan, $i.e.$, gets $(M, M') \leftarrow \mathcal{T}[\sigma]$, generates a random t and uses M^t as commitments, finally computing the sanitized signature σ' and returning it, then setting $\mathcal{T}[\sigma'] = (M, M')$; else it returns $\perp$.

In the end $\mathcal{A}$ returns a bit b_*, if $b_* = b'$ $\mathcal{B}$ sends 1 to $\mathcal{C}$ (guessing that the elements are in the same equivalence-class) else it answers 0.

Analysis: If $b = 1$, then $\mathcal{B}$ perfectly simulates H_{i+1}, as explained in LRSan above, since the first $i+1$ queries are answered honestly, else if if $b = 0$, then $\mathcal{B}$ perfectly simulates H_i, as $(M')^t$ is not linked to M and thus the $i+1$st query uses random commitments. Using the same justification as in the previous games, we have:

$$|\Pr[\mathsf{H}_{i+1}] - \Pr[\mathsf{H}_i]| = |\Pr[\mathcal{B} \to 1 | b = 1] - \Pr[\mathcal{B} \to 1 | b = 0]| = q_{\mathsf{Sig}} \mathsf{Adv}_S^{\mathsf{class\text{-}hid}}(\lambda).$$

In H_0 all commitments are computed randomly, which makes it identical to Game 6, and in $\mathsf{H}_{q_{\mathsf{LRSan}}}$ all commitments are honest, which makes it identical to Game 5. Summing the hybrids, we get

$$|\Pr[S_5] - \Pr[S_6]| = |\Pr[\mathsf{H}_{q_{\mathsf{LRSan}}}] - \Pr[\mathsf{H}_0]|$$
$$\leq q_{\mathsf{LRSan}} q_{\mathsf{Sig}} \mathsf{Adv}_S^{\mathsf{class\text{-}hid}}(\lambda)$$

At this point, there is no link between the original signature and its sanitization, that would differentiate the sanitization of σ_0 from that of σ_1, thus the adversary cannot do any better than just guessing. Thus: $\Pr[S_6] = 1/2$.

A.3   Proof of Theorem 5

Proof. Upon querying the LRADM oracle on $(m, (\text{ADM}_0, \gamma_0), (\text{ADM}_1, \gamma_1))$, the adversary $\mathcal{A}$ receives a signature $\sigma = ((A_i, B_i)_{i\in[n]}, C, V, \pi_1, \pi_2, s, e, r)$, on m with ADM_b, γ_b, where b is the challenger's bit. In σ, the C value is directly linked to γ_b, and the B_i values are directly linked to ADM_b. No other value depends on them. The idea of this proof is thus to randomize C and B_i in an indistinguishable way.

We show that:

$$\text{Adv}^{\text{invis}}_{\text{ULISS},\mathcal{A}}(\lambda) \leq \text{Adv}^{\text{SUF}}_{ULISS}(\lambda) + \text{Adv}^{\text{IND\$-CCA}}_E(\lambda) + (q_H + q_F) \cdot \text{Adv}^{\text{DDH}}_G(\lambda),$$

where q_H and q_F are the number of queries to the random oracle simulating H and F, respectively. We follow a logic very similar to the proof for the unlinkability and will thus refer to this proof for the straightforward game hops.

Game 0. This is the original $\text{Exp}^{\text{invis}}_{\text{ULISS},\mathcal{A}}(\lambda)$ experiment, hence:

$$\text{Adv}^{\text{invis}}_{\text{ULISS},\mathcal{A}}(\lambda) = |\Pr[S_0] - 1/2|$$

Game 1. This game is the same as the previous one except the challenger aborts and returns a random bit if $\mathcal{A}$ queries the San oracle on a forged signature.

$$|\Pr[S_1] - \Pr[S_0]| \leq \text{Adv}^{\text{SUF}}_{\text{ULISS},\mathcal{A}}(\lambda).$$

We showed in Appendix A.1 that this is negligible. After this game, all signatures input to San were generated by the challenger. This means, in particular, that $\mathcal{A}$ cannot try to guess if a signature was sanitized or not by trying to "copy" the output of LRADM into a new forged signature to test the limit or admissibility.

Game 2. This game is the same as the previous one, except the challenger replaces the input to the encryption scheme with random. We claim that:

$$|\Pr[S_2] - \Pr[S_1]| \leq \text{Adv}^{\text{IND\$-CCA}}_E(\lambda).$$

Proof. Follows the idea of the proof of Game 2 in the proof of unlinkability, *i.e.*, we construct a secondary adversary $\mathcal{B}$ against IND\$-CCA who injects its challenges by using them as the encryptions in $\mathcal{A}$'s queries to LRADM, and in San if $\mathcal{A}$ wishes to sanitize a signature that was output by LRADM. As in previous proofs, $\mathcal{B}$ must keep track of what should have been encrypted, as it cannot decrypt its challenges.

Game 3. This game is the same as the previous one, except that the NIZKPs are faked by the Simulator. We argue that: $\Pr[S_3] = \Pr[S_2]$.

Proof. Follows the idea of the proof of Game 4 in the proof of unlinkability. We construct a secondary adversary $\mathcal{B}$ against the zero-knowledge property of the NIZKPs. Now, in LRADM and in calls to San for signatures output by LRADM, $\mathcal{B}$ encrypts random messages instead of the commitments, to apply game 2 above, and queries its challenger for the proofs π_1 and π_2.

Game 4. This game is the same as the previous one, except that the commitments that are computed when creating a signature are generated randomly. We argue that:

$$| \Pr[S_4] - \Pr[S_3]| \leq q_{\mathsf{LRADM}}(q_F + q_H) \cdot \mathsf{Adv}_{\mathbb{G}}^{\mathsf{DDH}}(\lambda).$$

Proof. Follows the idea of the proof of Game 5 in the proof of unlinkability. As in that game, we use hybrids, *i.e.* in experiment H_i the first i queries to LRADM have honest commitments and the rest are random, from which we construct an adversary $\mathcal{B}$ against fixed $(q_H + q_F)$-DDH, as defined in Definition 17. Recall that a challenger for $(q_H + q_F)$-DDH outputs tuples $(g, X = g^x, Y_i = g^{y_i}, Z_i = g^{z_i})$ for $i \in [n]$, with the same x every time but a different y_i, and such that either every z_i is equal to $x \cdot y_i$, or they are all random. As in the proof of unlinkability (and transparency), we set $F(\mathsf{pp}) = g$, and $\mathcal{B}$ uses the random oracles as described in these proofs, setting hashes of values ending with pp as the Y_i challenges. In LRADM, as in the unlinkability and transparency, $\mathcal{B}$ will use the Z_i values as commitments in the $i + 1$st query, which will be legit if $\mathcal{B}$'s challenger is giving real DH elements, thus simulating hybrid H_{i+1}, and random otherwise, thus simulating H_i. As all elements of the signatures output by LRADM linked to ADM or γ are random, we have that $\Pr[S_4] = 1/2$.

References

1. Ateniese, G., Chou, D.H., de Medeiros, B., Tsudik, G.: Sanitizable signatures. In: di Vimercati, S.C., Syverson, P., Gollmann, D. (eds.) ESORICS 2005. LNCS, vol. 3679, pp. 159–177. Springer, Heidelberg (2005). https://doi.org/10.1007/11555827_10
2. Backes, M., Meiser, S., Schröder, D.: Delegatable functional signatures. In: Cheng, C.-M., Chung, K.-M., Persiano, G., Yang, B.-Y. (eds.) PKC 2016. LNCS, vol. 9614, pp. 357–386. Springer, Heidelberg (2016). https://doi.org/10.1007/978-3-662-49384-7_14
3. Beck, M.T., et al.: Practical strongly invisible and strongly accountable sanitizable signatures. In: Pieprzyk, J., Suriadi, S. (eds.) ACISP 2017. LNCS, vol. 10342, pp. 437–452. Springer, Cham (2017). https://doi.org/10.1007/978-3-319-60055-0_23
4. Bellare, M., Fuchsbauer, G.: Policy-based signatures. In: Krawczyk, H. (ed.) PKC 2014. LNCS, vol. 8383, pp. 520–537. Springer, Heidelberg (2014). https://doi.org/10.1007/978-3-642-54631-0_30
5. Bender, A., Katz, J., Morselli, R.: Ring signatures: stronger definitions, and constructions without random oracles. In: Halevi, S., Rabin, T. (eds.) TCC 2006. LNCS, vol. 3876, pp. 60–79. Springer, Heidelberg (2006). https://doi.org/10.1007/11681878_4
6. Boyle, E., Goldwasser, S., Ivan, I.: Functional signatures and pseudorandom functions. In: Krawczyk, H. (ed.) PKC 2014. LNCS, vol. 8383, pp. 501–519. Springer, Heidelberg (2014). https://doi.org/10.1007/978-3-642-54631-0_29
7. Brzuska, C., et al.: Redactable signatures for tree-structured data: definitions and constructions. In: Zhou, J., Yung, M. (eds.) ACNS 2010. LNCS, vol. 6123, pp. 87–104. Springer, Heidelberg (2010). https://doi.org/10.1007/978-3-642-13708-2_6

8. Brzuska, C., et al.: Security of sanitizable signatures revisited. In: Jarecki, S., Tsudik, G. (eds.) PKC 2009. LNCS, vol. 5443, pp. 317–336. Springer, Heidelberg (2009). https://doi.org/10.1007/978-3-642-00468-1_18

9. Brzuska, C., Fischlin, M., Lehmann, A., Schröder, D.: Unlinkability of sanitizable signatures. In: Nguyen, P.Q., Pointcheval, D. (eds.) PKC 2010. LNCS, vol. 6056, pp. 444–461. Springer, Heidelberg (2010). https://doi.org/10.1007/978-3-642-13013-7_26

10. Bultel, X., Lafourcade, P.: Unlinkable and strongly accountable sanitizable signatures from verifiable ring signatures. In: Capkun, S., Chow, S.S.M. (eds.) CANS 2017. LNCS, vol. 11261, pp. 203–226. Springer, Cham (2018). https://doi.org/10.1007/978-3-030-02641-7_10

11. Bultel, X., Lafourcade, P., Lai, R.W.F., Malavolta, G., Schröder, D., Thyagarajan, S.A.K.: Efficient invisible and unlinkable sanitizable signatures. In: Lin, D., Sako, K. (eds.) PKC 2019. LNCS, vol. 11442, pp. 159–189. Springer, Cham (2019). https://doi.org/10.1007/978-3-030-17253-4_6

12. Camenisch, J., Derler, D., Krenn, S., Pöhls, H.C., Samelin, K., Slamanig, D.: Chameleon-hashes with ephemeral trapdoors. In: Fehr, S. (ed.) PKC 2017. LNCS, vol. 10175, pp. 152–182. Springer, Heidelberg (2017). https://doi.org/10.1007/978-3-662-54388-7_6

13. Canard, S., Jambert, A.: On extended sanitizable signature schemes. In: Pieprzyk, J. (ed.) CT-RSA 2010. LNCS, vol. 5985, pp. 179–194. Springer, Heidelberg (2010). https://doi.org/10.1007/978-3-642-11925-5_13

14. Chaum, D., Pedersen, T.P.: Wallet databases with observers. In: Brickell, E.F. (ed.) CRYPTO 1992. LNCS, vol. 740, pp. 89–105. Springer, Heidelberg (1993). https://doi.org/10.1007/3-540-48071-4_7

15. Cramer, R., Damgård, I., Schoenmakers, B.: Proofs of partial knowledge and simplified design of witness hiding protocols. In: Desmedt, Y.G. (ed.) CRYPTO 1994. LNCS, vol. 839, pp. 174–187. Springer, Heidelberg (1994). https://doi.org/10.1007/3-540-48658-5_19

16. De Santis, A., Micali, S., Persiano, G.: Non-interactive zero-knowledge proof systems. In: Pomerance, C. (ed.) CRYPTO 1987. LNCS, vol. 293, pp. 52–72. Springer, Heidelberg (1988). https://doi.org/10.1007/3-540-48184-2_5

17. ElGamal, T.: A public key cryptosystem and a signature scheme based on discrete logarithms. IEEE Trans. Inf. Theory **31**, 469–472 (1985)

18. Fiat, A., Shamir, A.: How to prove yourself: practical solutions to identification and signature problems. In: Odlyzko, A.M. (ed.) CRYPTO 1986. LNCS, vol. 263, pp. 186–194. Springer, Heidelberg (1987). https://doi.org/10.1007/3-540-47721-7_12

19. Fleischhacker, N., Krupp, J., Malavolta, G., Schneider, J., Schröder, D., Simkin, M.: Efficient unlinkable sanitizable signatures from signatures with re-randomizable keys. In: Cheng, C.-M., Chung, K.-M., Persiano, G., Yang, B.-Y. (eds.) PKC 2016. LNCS, vol. 9614, pp. 301–330. Springer, Heidelberg (2016). https://doi.org/10.1007/978-3-662-49384-7_12

20. Fuchsbauer, G., Hanser, C., Slamanig, D.: Structure-preserving signatures on equivalence classes and constant-size anonymous credentials. J. Cryptol. **32**(2), 498–546 (2019). https://doi.org/10.1007/s00145-018-9281-4

21. Fujisaki, E., Okamoto, T.: Secure integration of asymmetric and symmetric encryption schemes. In: Wiener, M. (ed.) CRYPTO 1999. LNCS, vol. 1666, pp. 537–554. Springer, Heidelberg (1999). https://doi.org/10.1007/3-540-48405-1_34

22. Hanser, C., Slamanig, D.: Structure-preserving signatures on equivalence classes and their application to anonymous credentials. In: Sarkar, P., Iwata, T. (eds.) ASIACRYPT 2014. LNCS, vol. 8873, pp. 491–511. Springer, Heidelberg (2014). https://doi.org/10.1007/978-3-662-45611-8_26

23. Johnson, R., Molnar, D., Song, D., Wagner, D.: Homomorphic signature schemes. In: Preneel, B. (ed.) CT-RSA 2002. LNCS, vol. 2271, pp. 244–262. Springer, Heidelberg (2002). https://doi.org/10.1007/3-540-45760-7_17

24. Klonowski, M., Lauks, A.: Extended Sanitizable Signatures. In: Rhee, M.S., Lee, B. (eds.) ICISC 2006. LNCS, vol. 4296, pp. 343–355. Springer, Heidelberg (2006). https://doi.org/10.1007/11927587_28

25. Krawczyk, H., Rabin, T.: Chameleon hashing and signatures. In: NDSS (1997)

Partially Structure-Preserving Signatures: Lower Bounds, Constructions and More

Essam Ghadafi[(✉)]

University of the West of England, Bristol, UK

Abstract. In this work we first provide a framework for defining a large subset of pairing-based digital signature schemes which we call Partially Structure-Preserving Signature (PSPS) schemes. PSPS schemes are similar in nature to structure-preserving signatures with the exception that in PSPS schemes messages are scalars from $\mathbb{Z}_p$ instead of being group elements. This class encompasses various existing schemes which have a number of desirable features which makes them an ideal building block for many privacy-preserving cryptographic protocols. Such schemes include the widely-used schemes of Camenisch-Lysyanskaya (CRYPTO 2004) and Pointcheval-Sanders (CT-RSA 2016). We then provide various impossibility and lower bound results for variants of this class. Our results include bounds for the signature and verification key sizes as well as lower bounds for achieving strong unforgeability. We also give a generic framework for transforming variants of PSPS schemes into structure-preserving ones. As part of our contribution, we also give a number of optimal PSPS schemes which may be of independent interest. Our results aid in understanding the efficiency of pairing-based signature schemes and show a connection between this class of schemes and structure-preserving ones.

Keywords: Digital signatures · Bilinear groups · Lower bounds · Structure-preserving

1 Introduction

Digital signatures are a fundamental cryptographic primitive which besides being useful in their own right, they are used as an essential building block for various more complex protocols.

The emergence of pairing-based cryptography has been associated with the introduction of many pairing-based digital signature schemes. One of the extensively used pairing-based signature schemes is that of Camenisch and Lysyanskaya (CL) [16]. The scheme has a number of desirable features which makes it an ideal building block for various privacy-preserving protocols, including group signatures, e.g. [10,16], anonymous credentials, e.g. [16], and direct anonymous attestation, e.g. [20]. Notably, the scheme besides having fully and perfectly randomizable signatures, it is compatible with Pedersen-like commitment schemes

© Springer Nature Switzerland AG 2021
K. Sako and N. O. Tippenhauer (Eds.): ACNS 2021, LNCS 12726, pp. 284–312, 2021.
https://doi.org/10.1007/978-3-030-78372-3_11

[41] and thus it is possible to sign committed messages. A recent improvement to the CL scheme is the Pointcheval and Sanders (PS) scheme [42], which besides enjoying better efficiency and preserving all of its desirable features, it yields constant-size signatures regardless of the size of the message. Despite its relatively young age, the PS scheme has been used in the construction of various protocols. A common feature to the structure of both aforementioned schemes is that the signer is generic, and when viewing the signature components as an exponentiation of the respective group generator to a fraction of polynomials, the denominator polynomials are independent of the message. This is to the contrary of other pairing-based schemes, e.g. [11,12,43,45], which even though are based on non-interactive intractability assumptions, they do not enjoy some of the desirable features of the CL and PS schemes, e.g. the randomizability of the signatures, having a generic signer, the ease of being combined with Pedersen-like commitments, and a short verification key.

The dual-form signature framework [27] was used by [18,27] to obtain (less efficient) variants of some existing schemes, e.g. CL and PS schemes, whose security relies on static intractability assumptions.

Structure-Preserrving Signature (SPS) schemes [4] are also pairing-based signature schemes with the extra requirement that the messages, the verification key and the signatures consist of only source group elements. Verification of signatures in those schemes only involves evaluating Pairing-Product Equations (PPEs) and checking group memberships. Such properties make them compatible with widely-used constructs such as ElGamal encryption [21] and Groth-Sahai proofs [35] and hence they render themselves as a tool for designing cryptographic protocols which dispense with relying on random oracles [22] despite the efficiency degradation. SPS schemes have numerous applications, including group signatures, e.g. [4,38], blind signatures, e.g. [4,24], and anonymous credentials, e.g. [15,23].

A numerous number of SPS schemes have been proposed in the 3 different bilinear groups settings. In the most efficient bilinear group setting, i.e. the Type-3 setting (cf. Sect. 2), existing schemes include [4,5,7,19,29,31,34]. Abe et al. [5] proved that a Type-3 signature must contain at least 3 bilateral elements and require at least 2 PPEs for verification. Optimal SPS schemes rely on security proofs in the generic group model [40,44]. Abe et al. [6] proved that the unforgeability of an optimal Type-3 scheme cannot be based on a non-interactive intractability assumption. Ghadafi [31] showed that by restricting the message space to the set of Diffie-Hellman (DH) pairs (cf. Sect. 2) it is possible to circumvent the lower bound and obtain optimal unilateral signatures consisting of 2 elements. Such variants provide some efficiency gains for some protocols, including direct anonymous attestation [13] and attribute-based signatures [39]. Other constructions for this message space include, e.g. [4,28,29,32,33].

Constructions of SPS schemes relying on non-interactive assumptions include [1–3,8,14,26,36–38]. Chase and Kohlweiss [17] gave a transformation which utilizes pairwise-independent hash functions and the Groth-Sahai proof system [35] to obtain structure-preserving signatures based on standard assumptions from some pairing-based signature schemes for scalar messages. Their transformation is rather costly as it yields signatures consisting of tens of group elements.

Motivation and Our Contribution. While structure-preserving signatures and their efficiency are well studied, other types of pairing-based signature schemes still have some open problems pertaining to their feasibility and bounds for their efficiency are still lacking. For instance, it is not currently known whether efficient strongly unforgeable generic-signer schemes with a similar structure to the CL and PS schemes are possible. Moreover, it is not currently known whether the recent efficient PS scheme is optimal or whether it is possible to improve efficiency while preserving all of its desirable features.

SPS schemes might be less desirable than pairing-based schemes for scalar messages for some applications due to the loss in efficiency. This is particularly the case for applications where relying on random oracles is tolerated, applications requiring a stand-alone signature scheme, or applications not requiring proof systems to hide the message.

Towards a better understanding of the efficiency of pairing-based signature schemes for scalar messages, we first define a framework for capturing a large class of such schemes which we refer to as Partially Structure-Preserving Signature (PSPS) schemes[1]. Other than the messages being scalars from $\mathbb{Z}_p$ rather than source group elements, PSPS schemes have similar properties to structure-preserving signatures, including having a generic signer and signatures and verification keys consisting solely of source group elements. We provide different variants of our definition. More precisely, we define Strongly Partially Structure-Preserving (SPSPS) schemes and Linear-Message Strongly Partially Structure-Preserving (LmSPSPS) schemes. The former requires that the PSPS scheme does not involve the message in the denominator of any of the signature components whereas the latter additionally requires that the message is embedded in the signature components in a linear manner. The CL and PS schemes for example fall into the LmSPSPS class.

We provide various lower bounds and impossibility results for LmSPSPS schemes. More precisely, we prove that existentially unforgeable under random-message attacks (EUF-RMA) schemes must have at least 2 elements in the signature and that strongly existentially unforgeable under chosen-message attacks (sEUF-CMA) schemes must have bilateral signatures consisting of at least 3 elements. Also, we prove that optimal schemes, including one-time schemes, cannot have a verification key consisting of fewer than 2 elements. In essence, this proves that the PS scheme and our new LmSPSPS scheme are optimal in every respect. In Table 1 we summarize our lower bound results for the size of the signature and compare them to those for structure-preserving signatures.

We also construct optimal one-time sEUF-CMA LmSPSPS schemes with one-element signatures and a new optimal EUF-CMA LmSPSPS scheme for a vector of messages. We prove the security of the latter using a new interactive intractability assumption which we show holds in the generic group model. The

---

[1] We remark that such a term was used informally in [31] to refer to SPS schemes where some message components are allowed to be scalar messages.

Table 1. Summary of the lower bounds for $|\sigma|$ in the Type-3 bilinear setting. B stands for bilateral elements whereas U stands for unilateral elements.

Notion	# sign queries	EUF-RMA	sEUF-CMA
LmSPSPS (this work)	1	1	1
	>1	2U	3B
SPS for unilateral messages [5,7]	1	1	1
	>1	3B	3B
SPS for DH pairs [32,33]	1	1	1
	>1	2U	3B

efficiency of our scheme matches that of the PS scheme [42] whose security also relies on an interactive assumption in every respect.

Finally, we show a connection between LmSPSPS schemes and SPS schemes by showing that if a LmSPSPS scheme satisfies an extra requirement which is that the signature and verification key components in either source group are disjoint, which for instance is satisfied by the CL and PS schemes as well as our new scheme, such a scheme automatically yields an analogues SPS scheme where the message space is the set of Diffie-Hellman pairs. The obtained SPS scheme has the same key pair as the original LmSPSPS scheme and is unforgeable in the generic group model. We also show some instantiations of our framework.

Besides being a step closer towards a better understanding of the efficiency of pairing-based signature schemes, our results uncover a link between LmSP-SPS and SPS schemes.

Paper Organization. Some preliminary definitions are in Sect. 2. In Sect. 3 we define PSPS schemes. In Sects. 4 and 5 we present our LmSPSPS constructions. In Sect. 6 we give our transformation from LmSPSPS to SPS schemes and provide example instantiations. Finally, in Sect. 7 we give our feasibility results.

Notation. We write $y = A(x; r)$ when algorithm A on input x and randomness r outputs y. We write $y \leftarrow A(x)$ for the process of setting $y = A(x; r)$ where r is sampled at random. We also write $y \leftarrow S$ for sampling y uniformly at random from a set S. A function $\nu(.) : \mathbb{N} \rightarrow \mathbb{R}^+$ is negligible (in n) if for every polynomial $p(.)$ and all sufficiently large values of n, it holds that $\nu(n) < \frac{1}{p(n)}$. By PPT we mean running in probabilistic polynomial time in the relevant security parameter. We use $[k]$ to denote the set $\{1, \ldots, k\}$ and $[i, k]$ to denote the set $\{i, i+1, \ldots, k\}$. For vectors $\boldsymbol{x}, \boldsymbol{y} \in \mathbb{Z}_p^n$ we denote by $\boldsymbol{x^y}$ the operation $\prod_{i=1}^n x_i^{y_i}$.

2 Preliminaries

In this section we provide some preliminary definitions.

2.1 Bilinear Groups

A bilinear group is a tuple $\mathcal{P} := (\mathbb{G}, \mathbb{H}, \mathbb{T}, p, G, \tilde{H}, e)$ where $\mathbb{G}$, $\mathbb{H}$ and $\mathbb{T}$ are groups of a prime order p, and G and $\tilde{H}$ generate $\mathbb{G}$ and $\mathbb{H}$, respectively. The function e is a non-degenerate bilinear map $e : \mathbb{G} \times \mathbb{H} \longrightarrow \mathbb{T}$. We refer to $\mathbb{G}$ and $\mathbb{H}$ as the source groups whereas we refer to $\mathbb{T}$ as the target group. We will use multiplicative notation for all the groups. To distinguish elements of $\mathbb{H}$ from those of $\mathbb{G}$ we will accent the former with $\tilde{\ }$. We let $\mathbb{G}^{\times} := \mathbb{G}\backslash\{1_{\mathbb{G}}\}$ and $\mathbb{H}^{\times} := \mathbb{H}\backslash\{1_{\mathbb{H}}\}$. We limit our attention to the efficient Type-3 setting [25], where $\mathbb{G} \neq \mathbb{H}$ and there is no efficiently computable homomorphism between the source groups in either direction. We assume an algorithm $\mathcal{BG}$ that on input 1^{κ}, for some security parameter $\kappa \in \mathbb{N}$, outputs a description of a bilinear groups $\mathcal{P}$.

We call a pair $(M, \tilde{N}) \in \mathbb{G} \times \mathbb{H}$ a Diffie-Hellman (DH) pair [4] if it satisfies $e(M, \tilde{H}) = e(G, \tilde{N})$. We denote the set of DH pairs by $\mathcal{DH}$.

2.2 Digital Signatures

A digital signature scheme $\mathcal{DS}$ over a bilinear group $\mathcal{P}$ generated by $\mathcal{BG}$ for a message space $\mathcal{M}$ consists of the following algorithms:

KeyGen($\mathcal{P}$) on input $\mathcal{P}$, it outputs a pair of secret/verification keys (sk, vk).
Sign(sk, m) on input sk and a message $m \in \mathcal{M}$, it outputs a signature σ.
Verify(vk, m, σ) outputs 1 if σ is a valid signature on m w.r.t. vk and 0 otherwise.

Definition 1 (Correctness). *A digital signature scheme $\mathcal{DS}$ over a bilinear group generator $\mathcal{BG}$ is (perfectly) correct if for all $\kappa \in \mathbb{N}$*

$$\Pr\left[\begin{array}{l} \mathcal{P} \leftarrow \mathcal{BG}(1^{\kappa}) \\ (\mathsf{sk}, \mathsf{vk}) \leftarrow \mathsf{KeyGen}(\mathcal{P}) \\ m \leftarrow \mathcal{M} \\ \sigma \leftarrow \mathsf{Sign}(\mathsf{sk}, m) \end{array} : \mathsf{Verify}(\mathsf{vk}, m, \sigma) = 1 \right] = 1.$$

Besides the correctness requirement, we require existential unforgeability.

Definition 2 (Existential Unforgeability). *A digital signature scheme $\mathcal{DS}$ over a bilinear group generator $\mathcal{BG}$ is* Existentially-Unforgeable against adaptive Chosen-Message Attack (EUF-CMA) *if for all $\kappa \in \mathbb{N}$ for all PPT adversaries $\mathcal{A}$, the following is negligible (in κ)*

$$\Pr\left[\begin{array}{l} \mathcal{P} \leftarrow \mathcal{BG}(1^{\kappa}) \\ (\mathsf{sk}, \mathsf{vk}) \leftarrow \mathsf{KeyGen}(\mathcal{P}) \\ (\sigma^*, m^*) \leftarrow \mathcal{A}^{\mathsf{Sign}(\mathsf{sk}, \cdot)}(\mathcal{P}, \mathsf{vk}) \end{array} : \mathsf{Verify}(\mathsf{vk}, m^*, \sigma^*) = 1 \wedge m^* \notin Q_{\mathsf{Sign}} \right],$$

where Q_{Sign} is the set of messages queried to Sign.

Strong Existential Unforgeability against adaptive Chosen-Message Attack (sEUF-CMA) requires that the adversary cannot even output a new signature on a message that was queried to the sign oracle.

A weaker variant of EUF-CMA is *Existential Unforgeability against a Random-Message Attack (EUF-RMA)* in which the sign oracle samples a message uniformly from the message space and returns the message and a signature on it. In one-time signatures, the adversary is restricted to a single signing query.

Sometimes it is desirable that signatures are publicly re-randomizable where there is an algorithm Randomize that on input (vk, m, σ) outputs a new signature σ' on m which is indistinguishable from a fresh signature on the same message.

Structure-Preserving Signatures. Structure-preserving signatures [4] are signature schemes defined over bilinear groups where the messages, the verification key and signatures are all group elements from either or both source groups, and verifying signatures only involves deciding group membership of the signature components and evaluating pairing-product equations (PPEs) of the form of Eq. (1).

$$\prod_i \prod_j e(A_i, \tilde{B}_j)^{c_{i,j}} = 1_{\mathbb{T}}, \tag{1}$$

where $A_i \in \mathbb{G}$ and $\tilde{B}_j \in \mathbb{H}$ are group elements appearing in $\mathcal{P}, m, \text{vk}, \sigma$, whereas $c_{i,j} \in \mathbb{Z}_p$ are constants.

Generic Signer. We refer to a signer that can only decide group membership, evaluate the bilinear map e, compute the group operations in groups $\mathbb{G}, \mathbb{H}$ and $\mathbb{T}$, and compare group elements as a *generic signer*.

3   Partially Structure-Preserving Signatures

In this section we define a class of prime-order pairing-based digital signature schemes which we call Partially Structure-Preserving Signature (PSPS) schemes. Informally, a PSPS scheme is a pairing-based signature scheme for scalar messages from $\mathbb{Z}_p^n$ for $n \geq 1$ where the signature components and verification key contain only source group elements and the signature components are computed by raising source group elements to fraction of polynomials involving the secret key, the messages and the randomness chosen as part of the signing process. We then define 2 variants of PSPS schemes to capture most of the practical schemes existing in the literature. First, we define Strongly Partially Structure-Preserving Signature (SPSPS) schemes which additionally require that the denominator polynomials used in computing the signature components are independent of the messages to be signed. Then we define a variant of SPSPS which we refer to as Linear-Message Strongly Partially Structure-Preserving Signature (LmSP-SPS) schemes which additionally requires that the numerator polynomials are linear in the message to be signed. The latter captures a large class of existing schemes for scalar messages, including variants of the CL and PS schemes.

Definition 3 (Partially Structure-Preserving Signatures). *A digital signature scheme $\mathcal{DS}$ over a bilinear group generator $\mathcal{BG}$ is Partially Structure-Preserving Signature (PSPS) scheme if it satisfies all the following:*

- $\mathcal{BG}(1^\kappa)$ generates a bilinear group description $\mathcal{P} := (\mathbb{G}, \mathbb{H}, \mathbb{T}, p, G, \tilde{H}, e)$.
- The verification key vk consists of $\mathcal{P}$ and source group elements $(\boldsymbol{X}, \boldsymbol{Y}) \in \mathbb{G}^\mu \times \mathbb{H}^{\mu'}$.
- The message space is $\mathcal{M} := \mathbb{Z}_p^n$ for some $n \geq 1$.
- A signature on a message $\boldsymbol{m} \in \mathcal{M}$ is of the form $\sigma := (\boldsymbol{S}, \tilde{\boldsymbol{T}}) \in \mathbb{G}^\nu \times \mathbb{H}^{\nu'}$ which is computed by a generic signer by sampling a vector $\boldsymbol{r} \in \mathbb{Z}_p^{n'}$ (independently of the message $\boldsymbol{m}$) and computing $S_i := G^{\frac{\alpha_i(\mathsf{sk}, \boldsymbol{m}, \boldsymbol{r})}{\alpha_i'(\mathsf{sk}, \boldsymbol{m}, \boldsymbol{r})}}$ and $\tilde{T}_j := \tilde{H}^{\frac{\beta_j(\mathsf{sk}, \boldsymbol{m}, \boldsymbol{r})}{\beta_j'(\mathsf{sk}, \boldsymbol{m}, \boldsymbol{r})}}$ for some formal multivariate polynomials $\alpha_i, \alpha_i', \beta_j, \beta_j' \in \mathbb{F}_p[X_1, \ldots, X_\mu, Y_1, \ldots, Y_{\mu'}, M_1, \ldots, M_n, R_1, \ldots, R_{n'}]$ of total degree bounded by $d(\kappa)$.
- Signature verification involves deciding group membership[2] and evaluating a set of pairing-product equations of the following form:

$$\prod_{i=1}^{\nu} e(S_i, \prod_{j=1}^{\mu'} \tilde{Y}_j)^{\rho_{1,i,j}(\boldsymbol{m})} \prod_{i=1}^{\nu'} e(\prod_{j=1}^{\mu} X_j, \tilde{T}_i)^{\rho_{2,i,j}(\boldsymbol{m})}$$

$$\prod_{i=1}^{\nu} e(S_i, \prod_{j=1}^{\nu'} \tilde{T}_j)^{\rho_{3,i,j}(\boldsymbol{m})} \prod_{i=1}^{\mu} \prod_{j=1}^{\mu'} e(X_i, \tilde{Y}_j)^{\rho_{4,i,j}(\boldsymbol{m})} = Z_\ell, \quad (2)$$

where $\rho_{i,j,k} \in \mathbb{F}_p[M_1, \ldots, M_n]$ are multivariate polynomials of total degree bounded by $d'(\kappa)$ whereas $Z_\ell \in \mathbb{T}$ is a public constant. In the strict sense, one can necessitate that $Z_\ell = 1_\mathbb{T}$.

Definition 4 (Strongly Partially Structure-Preserving Signatures). *A digital signature scheme $\mathcal{DS}$ over a bilinear group generator $\mathcal{BG}$ is Strongly Partially Structure-Preserving Signature (SPSPS) if it is partially structure-preserving and it holds that for all $i \in [\nu]$ and for all $j \in [\nu']$, the polynomials α_i' and β_j' are independent of the message.*

Definition 5 (Linear-Message Strongly Partially Structure-Preserving Signatures). *A digital signature scheme $\mathcal{DS}$ over a bilinear group generator $\mathcal{BG}$ is Linear-Message Strongly Partially Structure-Preserving Signature (LmSP-SPS) if it is strongly partially structure-preserving and it holds that for all $i \in [\nu]$ and for all $j \in [\nu']$, α_i and β_j are linear in $\boldsymbol{M}$, i.e. for all $k \in [n]$, for all $i \in [\nu]$, for all $j \in [\nu']$, the degree of M_k in α_i and β_j is either 0 or 1 and for all $\eta, \eta' \in [n]$ neither of the polynomials contain the monomial $M_\eta M_{\eta'}$.*

We now define a subset of PSPS schemes which we call Disjoint Partially Structure-Preserving Signature (DPSPS) schemes. Informally, a DPSPS scheme is a PSPS scheme where the spans of the sets of fraction of formal polynomials corresponding to the verification key and signature components in the source groups are disjoint.

---

[2] For more generality, we allow membership checks of the forms $S_i \in \mathbb{G}^\times$ and $\tilde{T}_j \in \mathbb{H}^\times$.

Definition 6 (Disjoint Partially Structure-Preserving Signatures). *Let* $\frac{\gamma_{1,i}(\mathbf{SK})}{\gamma'_{1,i}(\mathbf{SK})}$ *for* $i \in [\mu]$ *and* $\frac{\gamma_{2,j}(\mathbf{SK})}{\gamma'_{2,j}(\mathbf{SK})}$ *for* $j \in [\mu']$ *be the fraction of formal polynomials used to compute the verification key* $\boldsymbol{X} \in \mathbb{G}^\mu$ *and* $\boldsymbol{Y} \in \mathbb{H}^{\mu'}$ *(excluding the default source group generators), respectively. We say a signature scheme* $\mathcal{DS}$ *over a bilinear group generator* $\mathcal{BG}$ *is a Disjoint Partially Structure-Preserving Signature (DPSPS) scheme if it is partially structure-preserving and additionally meets the following requirement:*

$$Span\left(\left\{\frac{\gamma_{1,1}(\mathbf{SK})}{\gamma'_{1,1}(\mathbf{SK})}, \ldots, \frac{\gamma_{1,\mu}(\mathbf{SK})}{\gamma'_{1,\mu}(\mathbf{SK})}, \frac{\alpha_1(\mathbf{SK}, \boldsymbol{M}, \boldsymbol{R})}{\alpha'_1(\mathbf{SK}, \boldsymbol{M}, \boldsymbol{R})}, \ldots, \frac{\alpha_\nu(\mathbf{SK}, \boldsymbol{M}, \boldsymbol{R})}{\alpha'_\nu(\mathbf{SK}, \boldsymbol{M}, \boldsymbol{R})}\right\}\right)$$

$$\cap\ Span\left(\left\{\frac{\gamma_{2,1}(\mathbf{SK})}{\gamma'_{2,i}(\mathbf{SK})}, \ldots, \frac{\gamma_{2,\mu'}(\mathbf{SK})}{\gamma'_{2,\mu'}(\mathbf{SK})}, \frac{\beta_1(\mathbf{SK}, \boldsymbol{M}, \boldsymbol{R})}{\beta'_1(\mathbf{SK}, \boldsymbol{M}, \boldsymbol{R})}, \ldots, \frac{\beta_{\nu'}(\mathbf{SK}, \boldsymbol{M}, \boldsymbol{R})}{\beta'_{\nu'}(\mathbf{SK}, \boldsymbol{M}, \boldsymbol{R})}\right\}\right) = \{0\}.$$

We call a LmSPSPS scheme a Disjoint LmSPSPS (DLmSPSPS) scheme if it satisfies the above disjointness requirement. Examples of schemes conforming to this requirement include the PS scheme and our new scheme.

We later show that DLmSPSPS schemes yield equivalent structure-preserving signature schemes for DH pairs. In our transformation, the disjointness requirement ensures that a generic adversary against the SPS scheme cannot feed elements obtained from previous queries to the sign oracle back into the sign oracle since they do not have a matching component in the opposite source group, i.e. they do not form DH pairs. This restricts the messages the SPS adversary can query back into her sign oracle to being constant polynomials, i.e. scalars from $\mathbb{Z}_p$, similarly to the generic adversary against the underlying DLmSPSPS scheme.

4   A New Optimal LmSPSPS Scheme

Here we give a new LmSPSPS scheme for signing a vector $\boldsymbol{m} \in \mathbb{Z}_p^n$. The idea of the new scheme is based on the signature scheme underlying the blind signature scheme in [30]. The efficiency of our scheme matches that of the PS scheme in every respect.

Given the description of a Type-3 bilinear group $\mathcal{P}$ output by $\mathcal{BG}(1^\kappa)$, the scheme is as follows:

- KeyGen($\mathcal{P}$): Select $x, y_1, \ldots, y_{n-1}, z \leftarrow \mathbb{Z}_p^\times$. Set $\tilde{X} := \tilde{H}^x$, $\tilde{Y}_i := \tilde{H}^{y_i}$ for all $i \in [n-1]$ and $\tilde{Z} := \tilde{H}^z$. Set sk $:= (x, y_1, \ldots, y_{n-1}, z)$ and vk $:= (\tilde{X}, \tilde{Y}_1, \ldots, \tilde{Y}_{n-1}, \tilde{Z}) \in \mathbb{H}^{n+1}$.

- Sign(sk, $\boldsymbol{m}$): Select $r \leftarrow \mathbb{Z}_p^\times$ and set $(S_1, S_2) := \left(G^r, G^{\frac{r(x+m_1+\sum_{i=2}^n m_i y_{i-1})}{z}}\right)$.

  The signature is $\sigma := (S_1, S_2) \in \mathbb{G}^{\times 2}$.

- Verify(vk, $\boldsymbol{m}$, σ): Return 1 if $S_1 \neq 1_{\mathbb{G}}$ and $e(S_2, \tilde{Z}) = e(S_1, \tilde{X}\tilde{H}^{m_1} \prod_{i=2}^n \tilde{Y}_{i-1}^{m_i})$ and 0 otherwise.

- Randomize(vk, $\boldsymbol{m}$, σ): Select $r' \leftarrow \mathbb{Z}_p^\times$ and return $\sigma' := \sigma^{r'}$.

4.1   Security of the Scheme

Correctness of the scheme is straightforward and easy to verify. Also, it is easy to verify that the scheme conforms to the requirements of a DLmSPSPS scheme. We now define the following new interactive intractability assumption to which we reduce the unforgeability of the scheme.

Definition 7 *(New PSPS (NPSPS) Assumption).* Let $\mathcal{P} = (\mathbb{G}, \mathbb{H}, \mathbb{T}, p, G, \tilde{H}, e)$ *be the description of a Type-3 bilinear group generated by* $\mathcal{BG}(1^\kappa)$. *Let* $\tilde{X} := \tilde{H}^x$ *and* $\tilde{Y} := \tilde{H}^y$ *for some* $x, y \leftarrow \mathbb{Z}_p^\times$. *Let* $\widehat{\mathcal{O}}_{\tilde{X},\tilde{Y}}(\cdot)$ *be an oracle that when queried on* $m \in \mathbb{Z}_p$, *selects* $r \leftarrow \mathbb{Z}_p^\times$ *and returns the pair* $(G^r, G^{\frac{r(x+m)}{y}}) \in \mathbb{G}^2$. *The NPSPS assumption holds (relative to* $\mathcal{BG}$*) if for all PPT adversaries* $\mathcal{A}$ *given* $(\mathcal{P}, \tilde{X}, \tilde{Y})$ *and unlimited access to* $\widehat{\mathcal{O}}_{\tilde{X},\tilde{Y}}(\cdot)$, *the probability that* $\mathcal{A}$ *outputs a new pair* $(R^*, R^{*\frac{(x+m^*)}{y}}) \in \mathbb{G}^{\times 2}$ *for some* $m^* \in \mathbb{Z}_p$ *which was not queried to* $\widehat{\mathcal{O}}_{\tilde{X},\tilde{Y}}(\cdot)$ *is negligible (in* κ*).*

The following theorem proves that the NPSPS assumption holds in the generic group model.

Theorem 1. *For a generic adversary* $\mathcal{A}$ *which makes* q_G *group operation queries,* q_P *pairing queries and* q_O *queries to the* $\widehat{\mathcal{O}}_{\tilde{X},\tilde{Y}}$ *oracle, the probability that* $\mathcal{A}$ *breaks the NPSPS assumption is* $\mathcal{O}(\frac{q_G^2 + q_P^2 + q_O^2}{p})$ *where p if the prime order of the bilinear group.*

Proof. Let q_O be the number of queries to the $\widehat{\mathcal{O}}_{\tilde{X},\tilde{Y}}$ oracle, q_G be the number of group operation queries and q_P be the number of pairing queries the adversary makes in her game. We first prove that no linear combinations of the formal Laurent polynomials in $\mathbb{Z}_p[R_1, \ldots, R_{q_O}, X, Y^{\pm 1}]$ yields a tuple that constitutes a solution for the underlying NPSPS problem.

In the game, we keep 3 different lists $\mathcal{L}_G$, $\mathcal{L}_H$ and $\mathcal{L}_T$ for the Laurent polynomials corresponding to group elements from groups $\mathbb{G}$, $\mathbb{H}$ and $\mathbb{T}$, respectively. At the end of the game, the total number of (non-constant) Laurent polynomials used is $|\mathcal{L}_G| + |\mathcal{L}_H| + |\mathcal{L}_T| \leq 2 + q_G + q_P + 2q_O$.

Since both elements in the adversary's output (R^*, S^*) are from $\mathbb{G}$, it follows that r^* and s^* can only be constructed using linear combinations of the Laurent polynomials corresponding to elements from $\mathbb{G}$. Thus, we must have that:

$$r^* = a_r + \sum_{i=1}^{q_O} b_{r,i} r_i + \sum_{i=1}^{q_O} c_{r,i} \left(\frac{r_i x}{y} + \frac{r_i m_i}{y} \right)$$

$$s^* = a_s + \sum_{i=1}^{q_O} b_{s,i} r_i + \sum_{i=1}^{q_O} c_{s,i} \left(\frac{r_i x}{y} + \frac{r_i m_i}{y} \right)$$

For the pair $(R^*, S^*) \in \mathbb{G}^{\times 2}$ to be a valid solution, we must have that:

$$s^* y = r^* x + r^* m^* \tag{3}$$

Thus, we must have:

$$a_s y + \sum_{i=1}^{q_O} b_{s,i} r_i y + \sum_{i=1}^{q_O} c_{s,i} \left(r_i x + r_i m_i \right)$$

$$= a_r x + \sum_{i=1}^{q_O} b_{r,i} r_i x + \sum_{i=1}^{q_O} c_{r,i} \left(\frac{r_i x^2}{y} + \frac{r_i m_i x}{y} \right)$$

$$+ \left(a_r + \sum_{i=1}^{q_O} b_{r,i} r_i + \sum_{i=1}^{q_O} c_{r,i} \left(\frac{r_i x}{y} + \frac{r_i m_i}{y} \right) \right) m^*$$

There is no term in y or $r_i y$ on the RHS, so we must have $a_s = 0$, $b_{s,i} = 0$ for all $i \in [q_O]$. Thus, we have:

$$\sum_{i=1}^{q_O} c_{s,i}(r_i x + r_i m_i) = a_r x + \sum_{i=1}^{q_O} b_{r,i} r_i x + \sum_{i=1}^{q_O} c_{r,i}(\frac{r_i x^2}{y} + \frac{r_i m_i x}{y})$$

$$+ \left(a_r + \sum_{i=1}^{q_O} b_{r,i} r_i + \sum_{i=1}^{q_O} c_{r,i}(\frac{r_i x}{y} + \frac{r_i m_i}{y}) \right) m^*$$

There is no term $\frac{r_i x^2}{y}$ on the LHS, so we must have that $c_{r,i} = 0$ for all $i \in [q_O]$. Also, no term in x on the LHS, so we must have that $a_r = 0$. Thus, we have:

$$\sum_{i=1}^{q_O} c_{s,i} \left(r_i x + r_i m_i \right) = \sum_{i=1}^{q_O} b_{r,i} r_i x + \sum_{i=1}^{q_O} b_{r,i} r_i m^*$$

The monomial $r_i x$ implies $c_{s,i} = b_{r,i}$ for all $i \in [q_O]$. Since we must have that that $R^* \in \mathbb{G}^\times$, we must have $r^* \neq 0$ and therefore we must have at least a single value of $c_{s,i} = b_{r,i} \neq 0$. The monomial r_i implies $c_{s,i} m_i = b_{r,i} m^*$ which means $m^* = m_i$ for some i. Thus, the pair (R^*, S^*) is not a valid new pair.

Thus far we have proven that the adversary is unable to symbolically produce a valid tuple for a new scalar. What remains is to bound the probability that the simulation fails. The adversary wins if for any two different Laurent polynomials F and F' in any of the 3 lists evaluate to the same value. Note that the only indeterminate in those Laurent polynomials with a negative power is Y. Thus, for any Laurent polynomial F on any of those 3 lists, we can view F as a fraction of polynomials $F = \frac{F_n}{F_d}$ for some polynomials $F_n \in \mathbb{Z}_p[R_1, \ldots, R_{q_O}, X, Y]$ and $F_d \in \mathbb{Z}_p[Y]$. Note that $\mathbb{Z}_p[Y] \subset \mathbb{Z}_p[R_1, \ldots, R_{q_O}, X, Y]$. Thus, the equality check $F(r_1, \ldots, r_O, x, y, y^{-1}) - F'(r_1, \ldots, r_O, x, y, y^{-1}) = 0$ can be substituted by checking whether $F_n(r_1, \ldots, r_O, x, y) F'_d(y) - F'_n(r_1, \ldots, r_O, x, y,) F_d(y) = 0$. It follows that for $F, F' \in \mathcal{L}_{\mathbb{G}}$ we have $\deg(F_n) \leq 2$ and $\deg(F_d) \leq 1$. Thus, the probability that $F_n(r_1, \ldots, r_O, x, y) F'_d(y) - F'_n(r_1, \ldots, r_O, x, y) F_d(y) = 0$ is $\leq \frac{3}{p}$. For $F, F' \in \mathcal{L}_{\mathbb{H}}$, we have $\deg(F_n) \leq 1$ and $\deg(F_d) = 0$. Thus, the probability that $F_n(r_1, \ldots, r_O, x, y) F'_d(y) - F'_n(r_1, \ldots, r_O, x, y) F_d(y) = 0$ is $\leq \frac{1}{p}$. From this it follows that for $F, F' \in \mathcal{L}_{\mathbb{T}}$ the probability that $F_n(r_1, \ldots, r_O, x, y) F'_d(y) - F'_n(r_1, \ldots, r_O, x, y) F_d(y) = 0$ is $\leq \frac{4}{p}$.

Summing over all choices of F and F' in each case we have that the probability ϵ of the simulation failing for this reason is

$$\epsilon \le \binom{|\mathcal{L}_1|}{2}\frac{3}{p} + \binom{|\mathcal{L}_2|}{2}\frac{1}{p} + \binom{|\mathcal{L}_T|}{2}\frac{4}{p} \le \frac{2(2 + q_G + q_P + 2q_O)^2}{p}.$$

Thus, we have that the probability of the simulation failing is $\mathcal{O}(\frac{q_G^2 + q_P^2 + q_O^2}{p})$. Since by definition we have that q_O, q_G and q_p are all polynomial in κ whereas $\log p \in \Theta(\kappa)$, it follows that the adversary's advantage is negligible. $\square$

The following theorem proves the unforgeability of the scheme.

Theorem 2. *The scheme is EUF-CMA if the NPSPS assumption holds.*

Proof. Let $\mathcal{A}$ be an adversary against the unforgeability of the scheme, we use $\mathcal{A}$ in a blackbox manner to construct an adversary $\mathcal{B}$ against the NPSPS assumption.

Adversary $\mathcal{B}$ gets $(\mathcal{P}, \tilde{X}, \tilde{Y})$ from her game and chooses $y_1, \ldots, y_{n-1}, \alpha_1, \ldots, \alpha_{n-1} \leftarrow \mathbb{Z}_p^\times$ and sets $\tilde{Z} := \tilde{Y}$ and $\tilde{Y}_i := \tilde{Y}^{\alpha_i}\tilde{H}^{y_i}$ for all $i \in [n-1]$. $\mathcal{B}$ initiates $\mathcal{A}$ on $\mathsf{vk} := (\tilde{X}, \tilde{Y}_1, \ldots, \tilde{Y}_{n-1}, \tilde{Z})$. Note that verification key is distributed identically to that of the scheme.

When $\mathcal{A}$ queries the sign oracle on a vector $\boldsymbol{m} \in \mathbb{Z}_p^n$, $\mathcal{B}$ computes $m' := m_1 + \sum_{i=2}^{n} y_{i-1}m_i$ and queries her $\hat{\mathcal{O}}_{\tilde{X},\tilde{Y}}$ oracle on m' to get a tuple $(S_1, S_2) \in \mathbb{G}$. $\mathcal{B}$ computes $S_2' := S_2 S_1^{\sum_{i=2}^{n} \alpha_{i-1}m_i}$ and returns $\sigma := (S_1, S_2')$ to $\mathcal{A}$ as a signature on $\boldsymbol{m}$. This is a valid signature on $\boldsymbol{m}$ w.r.t vk since:

$$e(S_2', \tilde{Z}) = e(S_1^{\frac{x + m_1 + \sum_{i=2}^{n} y_{i-1}m_i}{z}} S_1^{\sum_{i=2}^{n} \alpha_{i-1}m_i}, \tilde{Z})$$

$$= e(S_1^{x + m_1 + \sum_{i=2}^{n} y_{i-1}m_i + z\sum_{i=2}^{n}\alpha_{i-1}m_i}, \tilde{H})$$

$$= e(S_1^{x + m_1 + \sum_{i=2}^{n} (y_{i-1} + \alpha_{i-1}z)m_i}, \tilde{H})$$

$$= e(S_1, \tilde{X}\tilde{H}^{m_1 + \sum_{i=2}^{n}(y_{i-1} + \alpha_{i-1}z)m_i}, \tilde{H})$$

$$= e(S_1, \tilde{X}\tilde{H}^{m_1} \prod_{i=2}^{n} \tilde{Y}_{i-1}^{m_i}).$$

Eventually, when $\mathcal{A}$ halts and outputs her forgery $(\boldsymbol{m}^*, \sigma^*)$, $\mathcal{B}$ computes $m^{*\prime} := m_1^* + \sum_{i=2}^{n} y_{i-1}m_i^*$ and returns $(\sigma^*, m^{*\prime})$ as her output in her game.

It is easy to see that if $\sigma^* = (S_1^*, S_2^*)$ is a signature on the new vector $\boldsymbol{m}^*$ which was not queried to the sign oracle, σ^* is a valid NPSPS tuple on the new scalar $m^{*\prime}$ which $\mathcal{B}$ did not submit to her oracle $\hat{\mathcal{O}}_{\tilde{X},\tilde{Y}}$.

We need to handle the case where $m^* \notin \{m_i\}_{i=1}^q$ but $m^{*\prime} = m_i'$ for some $i \in [q]$ in which case $\mathcal{A}$ wins her game but $\mathcal{B}$ will not be able to break the NPSPS assumption since the returned tuple is not on a new scalar that was not queried to her oracle. Note that $\mathcal{A}$'s view is independent of the y_i's and hence the probability that this event happens is $\leq \frac{q}{p}$ which is negligible. $\square$

5   A New Optimal One-Time sEUF-CMA LmSPSPS Scheme

Here we give an optimal one-time LmSPSPS scheme for a vector of messages with one-element signatures and a verification key of size $n|\mathbb{G}| + |\mathbb{H}|$. The scheme is optimal in every respect.

Given the description of Type-3 bilinear groups $\mathcal{P}$ output by $\mathcal{BG}(1^\kappa)$, the scheme is as follows:

- KeyGen($\mathcal{P}$): Select $x_1, \ldots, x_n, y \leftarrow \mathbb{Z}_p^\times$. Set $\mathsf{sk} := (x_1, \ldots, x_n, y)$, $\mathsf{vk} := (X_1, \ldots, X_n, \tilde{Y}) = (G^{x_1}, \ldots, G^{x_n}, \tilde{H}^y) \in \mathbb{G}^n \times \mathbb{H}$.

- Sign(sk, m): To sign $m \in \mathbb{Z}_p^n$, compute $\sigma = S := G^{\frac{1 + \sum\limits_{i=1}^{n} x_i m_i}{y}}$.

- Verify($\mathsf{vk}, m, \sigma = S$): Return 1 iff $e(S, \tilde{Y}) = e(G \prod\limits_{i=1}^{n} X_i^{m_i}, \tilde{H})$ and 0 otherwise.

Correctness of the scheme is straightforward to verify. We now prove the one-time strong unforgeability of the scheme.

Theorem 3. *The scheme is sEUF-CMA secure in the generic group model.*

Proof. We prove that no linear combinations corresponding to polynomials in the discrete logarithms of the elements the adversary sees correspond to a forgery.

At the start of the game, the only elements in $\mathbb{H}$ the adversary sees are $\tilde{H}$, $\tilde{Y}$, which correspond to the discrete logarithms $1, y$ respectively. Note the sign oracle produces no new elements in $\mathbb{H}$. When queried on a message m, the oracle will return a signature $S = G^{\frac{1 + \sum\limits_{i=1}^{n} x_i m_i}{y}} \in \mathbb{G}$. The forgery $\sigma^* = S^*$ can only be a linear combination of the group elements from $\mathbb{G}$, i.e. a linear combination of $G, S, X_1, \ldots, X_n$. Thus, we have

$$s^* = \alpha_s + \beta_s \frac{(1 + \sum\limits_{i=1}^{n} m_i x_i)}{y} + \sum\limits_{i=1}^{n} \gamma_{s_i} x_i$$

For the forgery to be accepted, (s^*, m^*) has to satisfy $s^* y = 1 + \sum\limits_{i=1}^{n} m_i^* x_i$. Therefore, we must have

$$\left(\alpha_s + \beta_s \frac{(1 + \sum\limits_{i=1}^{n} m_i x_i)}{y} + \sum\limits_{i=1}^{n} \gamma_{s_i} x_i \right) y = 1 + \sum\limits_{i=1}^{n} m_i^* x_i$$

Therefore, we must have

$$\alpha_s y + \beta_s \left(1 + \sum_{i=1}^{n} m_i x_i \right) + \sum_{i=1}^{n} \gamma_{s_i} x_i y = 1 + \sum_{i=1}^{n} m_i^* x_i$$

There is no terms of the form y or $x_i y$ for any $i \in [n]$ on the RHS, so we must have that $\alpha_s = 0$ and $\gamma_{s_i} = 0$ for all $i \in [n]$. Thus, we have that

$$\beta_s + \sum_{i=1}^{n} \beta_s m_i x_i = 1 + \sum_{i=1}^{n} m_i^* x_i$$

The constant term implies that $\beta_s = 1$. The monomial x_i implies that $\beta_s m_i = m_i^*$ from which it follows that we must have that $m_i^* = m_i$ for all $i \in [n]$ which means the forgery can only be the same signature on m the adversary obtained from the sign oracle.

The probability of the simulation failing is $\leq \frac{3(n+2+q_G+q_P)^2}{2p}$, i.e. $\mathcal{O}(\frac{n^2+q_G^2+q_P^2}{p})$. Since by definition we have that n, q_G and q_P are all polynomial in κ whereas $\log p \in \Theta(\kappa)$, it follows that the adversary's advantage is negligible.   □

6   From LmSPSPS Schemes into SPS Schemes

In this section we give a generic framework for transforming any disjoint LmSP-SPS scheme into a structure-preserving scheme for the message space $\mathcal{DH}^n$.

Let $\mathcal{P} := (\mathbb{G}, \mathbb{H}, \mathbb{T}, p, G, \tilde{H}, e)$ be the bilinear group description generated by $\mathcal{BG}$. Let $\mathsf{DLmSPSPS} = \left(\mathsf{KeyGen}, \mathsf{Sign}, \mathsf{Verify}, [\mathsf{Randomize}]\right)$ be a (s)EUF-CMA (resp. (s)EUF-RMA) DLmSPSPS scheme. The following transformation yields a (s)EUF-CMA (resp. (s)EUF-RMA) SPS scheme $\mathsf{SPS} = \left(\mathsf{KeyGen}_{\mathsf{SPS}}, \mathsf{Sign}_{\mathsf{SPS}}, \mathsf{Verify}_{\mathsf{SPS}}, [\mathsf{Randomize}_{\mathsf{SPS}}]\right)$.

- $\mathsf{KeyGen}_{\mathsf{SPS}}(\mathcal{P})$: Run $(\mathsf{sk}, \mathsf{vk}) \leftarrow \mathsf{KeyGen}(\mathcal{P})$. Return $(\mathsf{sk}_{\mathsf{SPS}} := \mathsf{sk}, \mathsf{vk}_{\mathsf{SPS}} := \mathsf{vk})$.
- $\mathsf{Sign}_{\mathsf{SPS}}\left(\mathsf{sk}_{\mathsf{SPS}}, ((M_1, \tilde{M}_1), \ldots, (M_n, \tilde{M}_n))\right)$:
  - Decompose the PPE equations of $\mathsf{DLmSPSPS}$ to the following form:

$$\prod_{i=1}^{\nu} e(S_i, \prod_{j=1}^{\mu'} \tilde{Y}_j)^{a_{i,j,\ell}} \prod_{i=1}^{\nu} \prod_{j=1}^{\mu'} \prod_{k=1}^{n} e(S_i, \tilde{Y}_j)^{a'_{i,j,\ell,k} m_k} \prod_{i=1}^{\nu'} e(\prod_{j=1}^{\mu} X_j, \tilde{T}_i)^{b_{i,j,\ell}}$$

$$\prod_{i=1}^{\nu'} \prod_{j=1}^{\mu} \prod_{k=1}^{n} e(X_j, \tilde{T}_i)^{b'_{i,j,\ell,k} m_k} \prod_{i=1}^{\nu} e(S_i, \prod_{j=1}^{\nu'} \tilde{T}_j)^{c_{i,j,\ell}} \prod_{i=1}^{\nu} \prod_{j=1}^{\nu'} \prod_{k=1}^{n} e(S_i, \tilde{T}_j)^{c'_{i,j,\ell,k} m_k}$$

$$\prod_{i=1}^{\mu} \prod_{j=1}^{\mu'} e(X_i, \tilde{Y}_j)^{d_{i,j,\ell}} \prod_{i=1}^{\mu} \prod_{j=1}^{\mu'} \prod_{k=1}^{n} e(X_i, \tilde{Y}_j)^{d'_{i,j,\ell,k} m_k} = Z_\ell.$$

○ Initialize 2 empty lists E_1 and E_2 of triples representing PPE equations.
○ For each signature component $S_j \in \mathbb{G}$ of DLmSPSPS:
  * Parse S_j as $G^{\displaystyle \frac{\sum\limits_{i=1}^{q} x^{c_{i,j}} y^{c'_{i,j}} r^{c''_{i,j}} \left(a_{i,j} + \sum\limits_{k=1}^{n} d_{i,j,k} m_k\right)}{\sum\limits_{i} b_{i,j} x^{e_{i,j}} y^{e'_{i,j}} r^{e''_{i,j}}}}$.
  * Define the set $\hat{I} \subseteq [q]$ as the subset of indices i where $\exists k \in [n]$ where $d_{i,j,k} \neq 0$ and let $\check{I} := [q] \backslash \hat{I}$. Compute S_j of SPS as:

$$S_j = \left(G^{\sum\limits_{i \in \check{I}} a_{i,j} x^{c_{i,j}} y^{c'_{i,j}} r^{c''_{i,j}}} \prod_{i \in \hat{I}} \prod_{k=1}^{n} M_k^{d_{i,j,k} x^{c_{i,j}} y^{c'_{i,j}} r^{c''_{i,j}}} \right)^{\frac{1}{\sum\limits_{i} b_{i,j} x^{e_{i,j}} y^{e'_{i,j}} r^{e''_{i,j}}}}.$$

○ For each signature component $\tilde{T}_j \in \mathbb{H}$ of DLmSPSPS:
  * Parse $\tilde{T}_j$ as $\tilde{H}^{\displaystyle \frac{\sum\limits_{i=1}^{q} x^{c_{i,j}} y^{c'_{i,j}} r^{c''_{i,j}} \left(a_{i,j} + \sum\limits_{k=1}^{n} d_{i,j,k} m_k\right)}{\sum\limits_{i} b_{i,j} x^{e_{i,j}} y^{e'_{i,j}} r^{e''_{i,j}}}}$.
  * Define the set $\hat{I} \subseteq [q]$ as the subset of indices i where $\exists k \in [n]$ where $d_{i,j,k} \neq 0$ and let $\check{I} := [q] \backslash \hat{I}$. Compute $\tilde{T}_j$ of SPS as:

$$\tilde{T}_j = \left(\tilde{H}^{\sum\limits_{i \in \check{I}} a_{i,j} x^{c_{i,j}} y^{c'_{i,j}} r^{c''_{i,j}}} \prod_{i \in \hat{I}} \prod_{k=1}^{n} \tilde{M}_k^{d_{i,j,k} x^{c_{i,j}} y^{c'_{i,j}} r^{c''_{i,j}}} \right)^{\frac{1}{\sum\limits_{i} b_{i,j} x^{e_{i,j}} y^{e'_{i,j}} r^{e''_{i,j}}}}.$$

○ For each PPE verification equation of DLmSPSPS:
  * For each pairing of the form $e(S_i, \tilde{Y}_j)^{a'_{i,j,\ell,k} m_k}$ where $a'_{i,j,\ell,k} \neq 0$:
    · If $\tilde{Y}_j \neq \tilde{H}$, append (if it does not already exist) $S'_i = M_k^{s_i}$ to $\boldsymbol{S}$, replace the pairing with $e(S'_i, \tilde{Y}_j)^{a'_{i,j,\ell,k}}$ and append (if it does not already exist) the tuple $(S'_i, S_i, \tilde{M}_k)$ to E_1. Note that S_i is independent of the message m_k so knowledge of the discrete logarithm m_k is not required to compute S'_i.
    · Otherwise, replace the above pairing with $e(S_i, \tilde{M}_k)^{a'_{i,j,\ell,k}}$.
  * For each pairing of the form $e(X_i, \tilde{T}_j)^{b'_{i,j,\ell,k} m_k}$ where $b'_{i,j,\ell,k} \neq 0$:
    · If $X_i \neq G$, append (if it does not already exist) $\tilde{T}'_j = \tilde{M}_k^{t_j}$ to $\boldsymbol{T}$, replace the pairing with $e(X_i, \tilde{T}'_j)^{b'_{i,j,\ell,k}}$ and append (if it does not already exist) the tuple $(\tilde{T}'_j, \tilde{T}_j, M_k)$ to E_2. Note that $\tilde{T}_j$ is independent of the message m_k so knowledge of the discrete logarithm m_k is not required to compute $\tilde{T}'_j$.
    · Otherwise, replace the pairing with $e(M_k, \tilde{T}_j)^{b'_{i,j,\ell,k}}$.
  * For each pairing of the form $e(X_i, \tilde{Y}_j)^{d'_{i,j,\ell,k} m_k}$ where $d'_{i,j,\ell,k} \neq 0$:
    · If $X_i = G$, replace the pairing with $e(M_k, \tilde{Y}_j)^{d'_{i,j,\ell,k}}$.
    · If $X_i \neq G$ but $Y_j = \tilde{H}$, replace the pairing with $e(X_i, \tilde{M}_k)^{d'_{i,j,\ell,k}}$.
    · If $X_i \neq G$ and $\tilde{Y}_j \neq \tilde{H}$, append (if it does not already exist) $S_{|\boldsymbol{S}|+1} = M_k^{x_i}$ to $\boldsymbol{S}$, replace the pairing with $e(S_{|\boldsymbol{S}|+1}, \tilde{Y}_j)^{d'_{i,j,\ell,k}}$ and append the tuple $(S_{|\boldsymbol{S}|+1}, X_i, \tilde{M}_k)$ to E_1.

* For each pairing of the form $e(S_i, \tilde{T}_j)^{c'_{i,j,\ell,k} m_k}$ where $c'_{i,j,\ell,k} \neq 0$: Note that by definition m_k cannot appear in the denominator of S_i or $\tilde{T}_j$. Also, we must have that at least one of the signature components is independent of m_k.

  · If S_i is independent of m_k, append (if it does not already exist) $S'_i = M_k^{s_i}$ to $\boldsymbol{S}$, replace the pairing with $e(S'_i, \tilde{T}_j)^{c'_{i,j,\ell,k}}$ and append (if it does not already exist) the tuple $(S'_i, S_i, \tilde{M}_k)$ to E_1.

  · Otherwise, append (if it does not already exist) $\tilde{T}'_j = \tilde{M}_k^{t_j}$ to $\boldsymbol{T}$, replace the pairing with $e(S_i, \tilde{T}'_j)^{c'_{i,j,\ell,k}}$ and append (if it does not already exist) the tuple $(\tilde{T}'_j, \tilde{T}_j, M_k)$ to E_2.

- $\mathsf{Verify}_{\mathsf{SPS}}\left(\mathsf{vk}_{\mathsf{SPS}}, ((M_1, \tilde{M}_1), \ldots, (M_n, \tilde{M}_n)), \sigma_{\mathsf{SPS}}\right)$: Return 1 if all the following holds and 0 otherwise:

  ◦ All modified PPEs of DLmSPSPS verify correctly.
  ◦ For each tuple i in E_1, it holds that: $e(\mathsf{E}_1[i][0], \tilde{H}) = e(\mathsf{E}_1[i][1], \mathsf{E}_1[i][2])$.
  ◦ For each tuple i in E_2, it holds that: $e(G, \mathsf{E}_2[i][0]) = e(\mathsf{E}_2[i][2], \mathsf{E}_2[i][1])$.
  ◦ All signature group membership required by DLmSPSPS verify correctly.
  ◦ $\left((M_1, \tilde{M}_1), \ldots, (M_n, \tilde{M}_n)\right) \in \mathcal{DH}^n$.[3]

Efficiency. What determines the added cost in σ_{SPS} compared to σ is distinct pairings of the form $e(S_i, \tilde{Y}_j)^{a'_{i,j,\ell,k} m_k}$ where $a'_{i,j,\ell,k} \neq 0$ and $Y_j \neq \tilde{H}$, $e(X_i, \tilde{T}_j)^{b'_{i,j,\ell,k} m_k}$ where $b'_{i,j,\ell,k} \neq 0$ and $X_i \neq G$, and $e(S_i, \tilde{T}_j)^{c'_{i,j,\ell,k} m_k}$ where $c'_{i,j,\ell,k} \neq 0$ in the verification equations of the DLmSPSPS scheme. Each distinct pairing of those 3 types adds an extra signature component in $\mathbb{H}$, $\mathbb{G}$, and $\mathbb{G}/\mathbb{H}$ depending on which component is independent of the message, respectively, to σ_{SPS} compared to σ. Also, each distinct pairing of any of those 3 types would add an additional PPE equation involving 2 pairings to the verification overhead of SPS compared to that of DLmSPSPS. Each distinct pairing of the form $e(X_i, \tilde{Y}_j)^{d'_{i,j,\ell,k} m_k}$ where $X_i \neq G$, $\tilde{Y}_j \neq \tilde{H}$ and $d'_{i,j,\ell,k} \neq 0$ incurs an additional signature component in $\mathbb{G}$ and an additional PPE involving 2 pairings. Note that the latter cost is constant for multiple signatures on the same message.

One maintains the same signature size and verification overhead of DLmSPSPS (modulo the cost for verifying the well-formedness of the messages in SPS) when the verification of DLmSPSPS does not involve any pairings of the above forms. Also, it is easy to see that if the original scheme yields randomizable signatures, the same applies to the resultant SPS scheme.

6.1   Example Instantiations

We give some example instantiations of our transformation for the sake of illustration. The first example shown in Fig. 1 shows how to transform our new LmSPSPS scheme into an SPS scheme for a vector of messages which also captures the single-message SPS scheme from [31] as a special case. The second

---

[3] Batch verification techniques, e.g. [9], can speed up this step.

example shown in Fig. 2 shows how to transform the PS scheme [42] into a SPS scheme for a vector of messages which also captures the single-message SPS scheme from [29] as a special case.

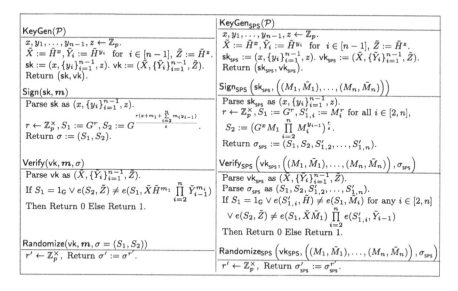

Fig. 1. Transforming our new scheme into a SPS scheme for a vector of messages

6.2 Security

Correctness follows from that of DLmSPSPS and the fact that any added PPE to the verification of the SPS scheme will verify. We now prove the following theorem regarding the unforgeability of the obtained SPS scheme.

Theorem 4. *If DLmSPSPS is (s)EUF-CMA (resp. (s)EUF-RMA), SPS is (s)EUF-CMA (resp. (s)EUF-RMA) in the generic group model.*

Proof. Since DLmSPSPS is unforgeable, it holds that no generic adversary against it can obtain a forgery using linear combinations of the (fraction of) polynomials corresponding to the group elements she sees in the game. We prove that a generic adversary $\mathcal{A}_{\mathsf{SPS}}$ against SPS does not see any additional group elements other than what $\mathcal{A}_{\mathsf{DLmSPSPS}}$ can see in her game and hence it holds that no linear combinations of the (fraction of) polynomials $\mathcal{A}_{\mathsf{SPS}}$ sees leads to a forgery against SPS.

Before the 1st sign query, the group elements $\mathcal{A}_{\mathsf{SPS}}$ sees are the same as those $\mathcal{A}_{\mathsf{DLmSPSPS}}$ can see at the start of her game which include the public key $(\boldsymbol{X}, \tilde{\boldsymbol{Y}}) \in \mathbb{G}^{\mu} \times \mathbb{H}^{\mu'}$. By definition, such a key is disjoint. Now at the first sign query on a valid message vector $\left((M_{1,1}, \tilde{M}_{1,1}), \ldots, (M_{1,n}, \tilde{M}_{1,n})\right)$, it follows that

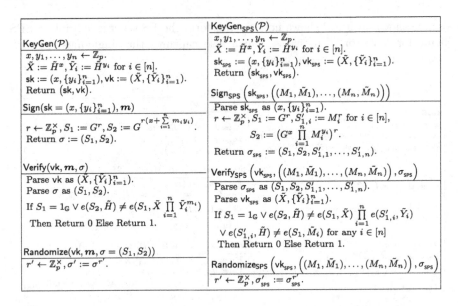

Fig. 2. Transforming the PS scheme [42] into a SPS scheme for a vector of messages

the discrete logarithm $m_{1,i}$ of the message component $(M_{1,i}, \tilde{M}_{1,i})$ for all $i \in [n]$ corresponds to a constant polynomial. The 1st sign query will return a signature of the form $\sigma_1 = (S_1, \tilde{T}_1)$. By definition such a returned signature still conforms to the disjointness requirement and thus such a sign query would not generate any new identical (fractions of polynomials) in groups $\mathbb{G}$ and $\mathbb{H}$ which $\mathcal{A}_{SPS}$ can feed back as a message into a subsequent sign query, i.e. all subsequent sign queries are on message vectors corresponding to constant polynomials.

We now argue that the additional elements $\mathcal{A}_{SPS}$ sees could be obtained by $\mathcal{A}_{DLmSPSPS}$ in her game and hence the former does not have any more advantage over the latter.

- Additional elements of the form $S_i' = M_k^{s_i}$ can be obtained by $\mathcal{A}_{DLmSPSPS}$ by calling her exponentiation oracle for $\mathbb{G}$ to get $S_i^{m_k}$.
- Additional elements of the form $\tilde{T}_i' = \tilde{M}_k^{t_i}$ can be obtained by $\mathcal{A}_{DLmSPSPS}$ by calling her exponentiation oracle for $\mathbb{H}$ to get $\tilde{T}_i^{m_k}$.
- Additional elements of the form $S_j' = M_k^{x_i}$ can be obtained by $\mathcal{A}_{DLmSPSPS}$ by calling her exponentiation oracle for $\mathbb{G}$ to get $X_i^{m_k}$.

Since the SPS forgery must be on a message in $\mathcal{DH}^n$, i.e. the message correspond to a constant polynomials, and DLmSPSPS is unforgeable, it follows that no linear combinations of the group elements $\mathcal{A}_{SPS}$ sees in her game leads to a forgery against SPS. □

7   Impossibility Results

In this section we provide some feasibility results for LmSPSPS schemes.

7.1   A Bound on the Number of Signatures for LmSPSPS Schemes

Here we prove, similarly to the case of structure-preserving signatures proven by Abe et al. [7], that a EUF-RMA LmSPSPS scheme must have for each message superpolynomially many potential signatures.

Theorem 5. *An EUF-RMA LmSPSPS scheme (against $q > 1$ sign queries) must have for each message superpolynomially many potential signatures.*

Proof. We can write the j-th signature component of the ℓ-th signing query as:

$$S_j = G^{\frac{\sum_i x^{c_{i,j}} y^{c'_{i,j}} r_\ell^{c''_{i,j}} (a_{i,j} + \sum_{k=1}^{n} d_{i,j,k} m_k)}{\sum_i b_{i,j} x^{e_{i,j}} y^{e'_{i,j}} r_\ell^{e''_{i,j}}}} \quad \text{or} \quad \tilde{T}_j = \tilde{H}^{\frac{\sum_i x^{c_{i,j}} y^{c'_{i,j}} r_\ell^{c''_{i,j}} (a_{i,j} + \sum_{k=1}^{n} d_{i,j,k} m_k)}{\sum_i b_{i,j} x^{e_{i,j}} y^{e'_{i,j}} r_\ell^{e''_{i,j}}}}$$

for some (fixed) $a_{i,j}, b_{i,j}, d_{i,j,k} \in \mathbb{Z}_p$, $c_{i,j}, e_{i,j} \in \mathbb{Z}_p^\mu$, $c'_{i,j}, e'_{i,j} \in \mathbb{Z}_p^{\mu'}$, $c''_{i,j}, e''_{i,j} \in \mathbb{Z}_p^{n'}$ which are independent of m.

If there are only polynomially many potential signatures for a message vector, there is a polynomial set $\{r_i\}_{i=1}^{\text{poly}(\kappa)}$ from which the randomness vector r is chosen. Thus, with probability $\frac{1}{\text{poly}(\kappa)^2}$ we have that the 2 signatures $\sigma_1 = (S_1, \tilde{T}_1)$ and $\sigma_2 = (S_2, \tilde{T}_2)$ on 2 random messages vectors m_1 and m_2 where $m_1 \neq m_2$, respectively, were produced using the same randomness vector $r_\ell \in \mathbb{Z}_p^{n'}$. Thus, we have that $\sigma^* := \sigma_1^{1-\gamma} \sigma_2^\gamma$ is a valid forgery on the new message vector $m^* = (1-\gamma)m_1 + \gamma m_2$ for any $\gamma \in \mathbb{Z}_p^\times \setminus \{1\}$ and therefore such a scheme is not EUF-RMA secure. □

7.2   Impossibility of LmSPSPS Schemes with One-Element Signatures

Here we prove that an EUF-RMA (aganist $q > 1$ sign queries) LmSPSPS scheme cannot have one-element signatures. However, as we show in Sect. 5, one-time sEUF-CMA LmSPSPS schemes with one-element signatures are possible.

Theorem 6. *An EUF-RMA LmSPSPS scheme (against $q > 1$ sign queries) must have at least 2 elements in the signature.*

Proof. WLOG, let's assume $\sigma = S \in \mathbb{G}$. The proof for the case where $\sigma = \tilde{T} \in \mathbb{H}$ is similar. Since there is only one unknown in the verification equation, i.e. the signature S, it follows that 1 PPE verification equation is sufficient for such a scheme. Thus, the scheme would have a verification equation of the following form:

$$e\left(S, \prod_{j=1}^{\mu'} \tilde{Y}_j^{a_j + \sum_{k=1}^{n} a'_{j,k} m_k}\right) \prod_{i=1}^{\mu} \prod_{j=1}^{\mu'} e(X_i, \tilde{Y}_j)^{d_{i,j} + \sum_{k=1}^{n} d'_{i,j,k} m_k} = Z, \qquad (4)$$

where $a_j, a'_{j,k}, d_{i,j}, d'_{i,j,k} \in \mathbb{Z}_p$ and $Z \in \mathbb{T}$ are public constants. By definition, we must have that for all $k \in [n]$ that $a'_{j,k} = 0$.

Given signatures $\sigma_1^* = S_1$ and $\sigma_2^* = S_2$ on random messages m_1 and m_2 where $m_1 \neq m_2$, respectively, we have that $\sigma^* := \sigma_1^{1-\gamma}\sigma_2^{\gamma}$ is a valid forgery on the message $m^* = (1-\gamma)m_1 + \gamma m_2$ for any $\gamma \in \mathbb{Z}_p^{\times}\backslash\{1\}$. Therefore such a scheme is not EUF-RMA secure against an adversary which makes 2 (random-message) sign queries.   □

7.3 Lower Bounds for sEUF-CMA LmSPSPS Schemes

The following theorem proves that the signatures of a sEUF-CMA LmSP-SPS scheme secure against $q > 1$ sign queries must have bilateral signatures.

Theorem 7. *There is no sEUF-CMA (against $q > 1$ sign queries) LmSP-SPS scheme with unilateral signatures.*

Proof. WLOG let's assume that the signature is of the form $\sigma = S \in \mathbb{G}^{\nu}$. The proof for the case where $\sigma = \tilde{T} \in \mathbb{H}^{\nu'}$ is similar. Such a scheme would have a number of PPE verification equations of the following form:

$$\prod_{i=1}^{\nu} e(S_i, \prod_{j=1}^{\mu'} \tilde{Y}_j)^{\rho_{1,i,j,\ell}(m)} \prod_{i=1}^{\mu} \prod_{j=1}^{\mu'} e(X_i, \tilde{Y}_j)^{\rho_{2,i,j,\ell}(m)} = Z_\ell, \tag{5}$$

where $\rho_{1,i,j,\ell}, \rho_{2,i,j,\ell} \in \mathbb{F}_p[M_1, \ldots, M_n]$ are multivariate polynomials and $Z_\ell \in \mathbb{T}$ are some fixed constants.

By definition, the denominator polynomials used in computing the signature components are independent of the message to be signed. Also, since the signature is unilateral, i.e. the signature components only appear on the LHS of the pairings, the numerator polynomials are linear in the randomness vector r whereas the denominator polynomials are independent of the randomness vector. By Theorem 5 such a scheme must have superpolynomially many potential signatures. By querying the sign oracle twice on any message vector m from the message space, with overwhelming probability we obtain 2 distinct signatures $\sigma_1 = S_1$ and $\sigma_2 = S_2$. We have that $\sigma^* = \sigma_1^{1-\gamma}\sigma_2^{\gamma}$ is with overwhelming probability a new signature on m for any $\gamma \in \mathbb{Z}_p^{\times}\backslash\{1\}$.   □

The following theorem proves that sEUF-CMA LmSPSPS schemes with 2-element bilateral signatures do not exist. This result holds even without the restriction that the message is linear. This sets a lower bound of 3 bilateral elements for such schemes.

Theorem 8. *There is no sEUF-CMA (against $q > 1$ sign queries) LmSP-SPS scheme with 2-element bilateral signatures.*

Proof. The signature is of the form $\sigma = (S, \tilde{T}) \in \mathbb{G} \times \mathbb{H}$ whereas the verification key is of the form $(X, \tilde{Y}) \in \mathbb{G}^{\mu} \times \mathbb{H}^{\mu'}$. As we prove in Lemma 1 in Theorem 9, 1 PPE verification equation is sufficient for a LmSPSPS scheme with 2-element signatures. Therefore, such a scheme would have a PPE verification equation of the following form:

$$e(S, \prod_{j=1}^{\mu'} \tilde{Y}_j)^{a_j} e(\prod_{j=1}^{\mu} X_j, \tilde{T})^{\rho_{2,j}(m)} e(S, \tilde{T})^c \prod_{i=1}^{\mu} \prod_{j=1}^{\mu'} e(X_i, \tilde{Y}_j)^{\rho_{4,i,j}(m)} = Z,$$

where $\rho_{2,j}, \rho_{4,i,j} \in \mathbb{F}_p[M_1, \ldots, M_n]$ are multivariate polynomials, and $a_j, c \in \mathbb{Z}_p$, and $Z \in \mathbb{T}$ are some public constants.

If for all $j \in [\mu']$, $a_j = 0$ and $c = 0$, the verification equation is independent of S and hence by Theorem 6 such a scheme is not secure. Thus, we must have that either for some $j \in [\mu']$ that $a_j \neq 0$ or $c \neq 0$, which we consider below:

- Case $a_j \neq 0$ for some $j \in [\mu']$: Given a signature $\sigma = (S, \tilde{T})$ on a random message m, we compute a new signature on m as $\sigma^* = (S^*, \tilde{T}^*) :=$
  $$\left(S^{\frac{a_j}{a_j + \gamma c}} \prod_{i=1}^{\mu} X_i^{\frac{-\gamma \rho_{2,i}(m)}{a_i + \gamma c}}, \tilde{T}^{\frac{a_j + \gamma c}{a_j}} \prod_{i=1}^{\mu'} Y_i^{\frac{\gamma a_i}{a_j}}\right).$$ We have $\sigma^* \neq \sigma$ for any $\gamma \in \mathbb{Z}_p^\times$.
- Case $a_j = 0$ for all $j \in [\mu']$ and $c \neq 0$: Given a signature $\sigma = (S, \tilde{T})$ on a random message m, we compute a new signature on m as $\sigma^* = (S^*, \tilde{T}^*) :=$
  $$\left(S^{\frac{1}{\gamma}} \prod_{i=1}^{\mu} X_i^{\frac{(1-\gamma)\rho_{2,i}(m)}{\gamma c}}, \tilde{T}^\gamma\right).$$ We have that $\sigma^* \neq \sigma$ for any $\gamma \in \mathbb{Z}_p^\times \setminus \{1\}$.

This concludes the proof. □

7.4 Lower Bounds for the Verification Key of Optimal Schemes

We have seen that an optimal (w.r.t. signature size) EUF-RMA LmSP-SPS scheme must have at least 2 elements in the signature. Here we prove that a scheme with ≤ 2 elements in the signature cannot have a verification key consisting of 1 element even for the case when signing single messages, i.e. when $n = 1$. This sets a lower bound of 2 elements in the verification key for even optimal one-time EUF-RMA schemes. Note some of our proofs below assume that the RHS of the PPE equations in Eq. (4) is $Z_\ell = 1_\mathbb{T}$.[4]

Theorem 9. *There is no EUF-RMA LmSPSPS scheme (against $q \geq 1$ sign queries) with signatures consisting of ≤ 2 elements and one-element verification key.*

Proof. We start by proving the following lemma regarding the number of PPE verification equations required for schemes with 2-element signatures.

Lemma 1. *One PPE verification equation is sufficient for a LmSPSPS scheme with 2-element signatures.*

---

[4] Those proofs also hold if the discrete logarithm of Z_ℓ in the case $Z_\ell \neq 1_\mathbb{T}$ is known.

Proof. If the scheme has 2 PPE equations, both equations must impose non-trivial constraint on the signature components as otherwise they can be reduced to a single equation. Since each PPE equation must involve at least 1 signature component, we have 3 cases:

- Both equations involve both signature components: This means we have 2 quadratic/linear equations in the discrete logarithm of the signature components. Such an equation system have at most 4 distinct solutions implying that there are at most 4 potential signatures for the message vector which contradicts the proof of Theorem 5.
- One equation involves both components whereas the other equation involves one component: In this case, one equation is quadratic/linear involving both signature components, whereas the remaining equation is linear in one of the components. By substituting the value of the signature component in the linear equation into the other equation we end up with one verification equation that is sufficient for verifying the signature.
- Each verification equation involves a single signature component: Since the other constants (the verification key, the public parameters (if any) and the messages) are fixed, we have that each verification equation is a linear equation in one of the signature components, i.e. each equation is a linear equation in one unknown. Thus, there is exactly 1 potential signature for the message vector which contradicts the proof of Theorem 5.   □

The following 4 lemmata complete the proof of the theorem.

Lemma 2. *There is no EUF-RMA SPSPS scheme (against $q \geq 1$ sign queries) with one verification equation and unilateral signatures and a unilateral verification key containing elements from the same source group.*

Proof. Let's consider the case where the signature and the verification key both belong to group $\mathbb{G}$. The proof for the opposite case is similar. The scheme yields a signature $\sigma = (S_1, \ldots, S_\nu) \in \mathbb{G}^\nu$, has a verification key $\mathsf{vk} = (X_1, \ldots, X_\mu) \in \mathbb{G}^\mu$ where WLOG $X_1 = G$, and has a verification equation of the form

$$\prod_{i=1}^{\nu} e(S_i, \tilde{H})^{\rho_{1,i}(m)} \prod_{i=1}^{\mu} e(X_i, \tilde{H})^{\rho_{2,i}(m)} = Z.$$

for some polynomials $\rho_{1,i}$ and $\rho_{2,i}$.

Given a signature $\sigma = (S_1, \ldots, S_\nu)$ on a random message $m \in \mathbb{Z}_p$, we can construct a new forgery $\sigma^* = (S_1^*, \ldots, S_\nu^*)$ on a different message $m^* \neq m$ by fixing some $i \in [\nu]$ and computing let $S_j^* := S_j$ for all $j \in [\nu]\backslash\{i\}$ and

$$S_i^* := \left(S_i^{\rho_{1,i}(m)} \prod_{j \neq i} S_j^{\rho_{1,j}(m) - \rho_{1,j}(m^*)} \prod_{j=1}^{\mu} X_j^{\rho_{2,i}(m) - \rho_{2,i}(m^*)} \right)^{\frac{1}{\rho_{1,i}(m^*)}}. \text{ It is easy to}$$

see that such a forgery is a valid signature on the message m^*.   □

Lemma 3. *There is no one-time EUF-RMA LmSPSPS scheme with one verification equation, one-element signatures and one-element verification key.*

Proof. Note here that we assume that $Z = 1_T$. The case where both the signature and verification key lie in the same group follows from Lemma 2. Assume a scheme has a signature $\sigma = S$, a verification key $\mathsf{vk} = \tilde{Y}$ and a verification equation of the following form:

$$e(S, \tilde{H}^{a_1 + a'_1 m} \tilde{Y}^{a_2 + a'_2 m}) = e(G, \tilde{H}^{b_1 + b'_1 m} \tilde{Y}^{b_2 + b'_2 m}).$$

By definition, we must have that $a'_1 = a'_2 = 0$. Note that we cannot have that $a_1 = a_2 = 0$ as the equation would be independent of the signature, or $b'_1 = b'_2 = 0$ as the equation would be independent of the message.

Given a signature $\sigma = S$ on a random message m, we construct a forgery on $m^* = \gamma m + \frac{(\gamma-1)(b_1 a_2 - a_1 b_2)}{a_2 b'_1 - a_1 b'_2}$ for any $\gamma \in \mathbb{Z}_p \setminus \{1\}$ as $\sigma* = S^* :=$ $G^{\frac{(\gamma-1)(b_1 b'_2 - b'_1 b_2)}{a_2 b'_1 - a_1 b'_2}} S^\gamma$. This is a valid forgery unless $a_2 b'_1 = a_1 b'_2$ which we deal with below:

- Case $a_2 b'_1 = a_1 b'_2 \neq 0$ or $b'_1 = a_1 = 0$: Given a signature $\sigma = S$ on a random message m, we construct a forgery $\sigma^* = S^* := G^\gamma S_1$ on $m^* = m + \frac{\gamma a_2}{b'_2}$ for any $\gamma \in \mathbb{Z}_p^\times$.
- Case $b'_2 = a_2 = 0$: Given a signature $\sigma = S$ on a random message m, we can construct a forgery $\sigma^* = S^* := G^\gamma S_1$ on $m^* = m + \frac{\gamma a_1}{b'_1}$ for any $\gamma \in \mathbb{Z}_p^\times$.   □

Lemma 4. *There is no SPSPS scheme with two-element bilateral signatures and one-element verification key that is secure against a key-only attack.*

Proof. Note here that we assume that $Z = 1_T$. The signature is of the form $\sigma = (S, \tilde{T}) \in \mathbb{G} \times \mathbb{H}$ whereas the verification key is either of the form $\tilde{Y} \in \mathbb{H}$ or $X \in \mathbb{G}$. We prove the first case but the proof for the second case is similar. The scheme has a verification equation of the following form:

$$e(S, \tilde{H}^{\rho_1(m)} \tilde{Y}^{\rho_2(m)}) e(G, \tilde{T})^{\rho_3(m)} e(S, \tilde{T})^{\rho_4(m)} = e(G, \tilde{H}^{\rho_5(m)} \tilde{Y}^{\rho_6(m)}).$$

for some polynomials ρ_i for $i \in [6]$. Given the verification key, we can construct a forgery on any message $m^* \in \mathbb{Z}_p$ by choosing $\gamma \leftarrow \mathbb{Z}_p^\times$ and computing:

$$\sigma^* = (S^*, \tilde{T}^*) := (G^\gamma, \tilde{H}^{\frac{\rho_5(m^*) - \gamma \rho_1(m^*)}{\rho_3(m^*) + \gamma \rho_4(m^*)}} \tilde{Y}^{\frac{\rho_6(m^*) - \gamma \rho_2(m^*)}{\rho_3(m^*) + \gamma \rho_4(m^*)}}).$$

□

Lemma 5. *There is no one-time EUF-RMA LmSPSPS scheme with two-element unilateral signatures and a verification key consisting of one-element from the opposite source group.*

Proof. Note here that we assume that $Z = 1_T$. Let's consider the case where the signature is of the form $\sigma = (S_1, S_2) \in \mathbb{G}^2$ whereas the verification key is of the form $\tilde{Y} \in \mathbb{H}$. The proof for the opposite case is similar. Such a scheme would have a verification equation of the form

$$\prod_{i=1}^{2} e(S_i, \tilde{H}^{a_{i,1} + a'_{i,1} m} \tilde{Y}^{a_{i,2} + a'_{i,2} m}) = e(G, \tilde{H}^{d_1 + d'_1 m} \tilde{Y}^{d_2 + d'_2 m}).$$

By definition, we must have that either $a'_{1,1} = a'_{1,2} = 0$ or $a'_{2,1} = a'_{2,2} = 0$. Let's assume the former case. Note that if $a_{1,1} = a_{1,2} = 0$, the equation is independent of S_1 and hence by Lemma 3 the scheme is not secure against $q \geq 1$ sign queries. Similarly, if $a_{2,1} = a'_{2,1} = a_{2,2} = a'_{2,2} = 0$, the verification equation is independent of S_2 and hence by Lemma 3 it is not secure against $q \geq 1$ sign queries.

Given a signature $\sigma = (S_1, S_2)$ on a random message m, we can construct a new forgery $\sigma = (S_1^*, S_2^*)$ on a new message $m^* \neq m$ by setting $S_1^* := G^{\alpha_{S_1}} S_2^{\beta_{S_1}} S_1$ and $S_2^* := G^{\alpha_{S_2}} S_2^{\beta_{S_2}}$ where

$$\alpha_{S_1} := \frac{(d'_2(a_{2,1} + a'_{2,1}m^*) - d'_1(a_{2,2} + a'_{2,2}m^*))(m^* - m)}{a_{1,2}(a_{2,1} + a'_{2,1}m^*) - a_{1,1}(a_{2,2} + a'_{2,2}m^*)}$$

$$\beta_{S_1} := \frac{(a'_{2,1}a_{2,2} - a_{2,1}a'_{2,2})(m^* - m)}{a_{1,2}(a_{2,1} + a'_{2,1}m^*) - a_{1,1}(a_{2,2} + a'_{2,2}m^*)}$$

$$\alpha_{S_2} := \frac{(a_{1,2}d'_1 - a_{1,1}d'_2)(m^* - m)}{a_{1,2}(a_{2,1} + a'_{2,1}m^*) - a_{1,1}(a_{2,2} + a'_{2,2}m^*)}$$

$$\beta_{S_2} := \frac{a_{1,2}(a_{2,1} + a'_{2,1}m) - a_{1,1}(a_{2,2} + a'_{2,2}m)}{a_{1,2}(a_{2,1} + a'_{2,1}m^*) - a_{1,1}(a_{2,2} + a'_{2,2}m^*)}$$

Thus, we can find a forgery unless $a_{1,2}(a_{2,1} + a'_{2,1}m^*) - a_{1,1}(a_{2,2} + a'_{2,2}m^*) = 0$ for all $m^* \in \mathbb{Z}_p$. We have 2 cases to deal with the above as follows:

- Case $a_{1,1} = a_{2,1} = a'_{2,1} = 0$: Note that as stated earlier, if $a_{1,2} = 0$ or $a_{2,2} = a'_{2,2} = 0$, the verification equation is independent of one of the signature components and hence is not secure. We have 2 cases as follows:
  - Case $d_1 \neq 0$: Give a signature $\sigma = (S_1, S_2)$ on a random message $m \in \mathbb{Z}_p$ satisfying $d_1 + d'_1 m \neq 0$, we have that $\sigma^* = (S_1^*, S_2^*)$ where

$$S_1^* := G^{\frac{-\gamma a_{2,2}(d_1 + d'_1 m^*)}{a_{1,2}d_1}} S_1^{\frac{d_1 + d'_1 m^*}{d_1 + d'_1 m}} \qquad S_2^* := G^\gamma S_2$$

  is a valid forgery on any $m^* \neq m$ satisfying $d_1 + d'_1 m^* \neq 0$ for any $\gamma \in \mathbb{Z}_p^\times$.
  - Case $d_1 = 0$: Given a signature $\sigma = (S_1, S_2)$ on a random message $m \in \mathbb{Z}_p^\times$, we have that $\sigma^* = (S_1^*, S_2^*)$ where

$$S_1^* := G^{\frac{d_2(m - m^*) - \gamma m(a_{2,2} + a'_{2,2}m^*)}{a_{1,2}m}} S_2^{\frac{a_{2,2}(m^* - m)}{a_{1,2}m}} S_1^{\frac{m^*}{m}} \qquad S_2^* := G^\gamma S_2$$

  is a valid forgery on the message $m^* \neq m$ for any $\gamma \in \mathbb{Z}_p^\times$.
- Case $a_{2,2}a_{1,1} = a_{1,2}a_{2,1}$, $a'_{2,2}a_{1,1} = a_{1,2}a'_{2,1}$ and $a_{1,1} \neq 0$: If $a_{1,2} = 0$, we have $a_{2,2} = a'_{2,2} = 0$ and hence we cannot have any of the following cases:
  - $d_2 = d'_2 = 0$: Since verification would be independent of the key $\tilde{Y}$.
  - $a_{2,1} = a'_{2,1} = 0$: Since verification would be independent of S_2.
  - $a'_{2,1} = d'_1 = d'_2 = 0$: Since verification would be independent of m.

  We have that $\sigma^* = (S_1^*, S_2^*)$ where

$$S_1^* := G^{\frac{a_{1,2}\gamma(a_{2,1}d'_1 - a'_{2,1}d_1) + a_{1,1}\left(d_2(a'_{2,1}\gamma - d'_1) + d'_2(d_1 - a_{2,1}\gamma)\right)}{a_{1,1}(a_{1,1}d'_2 - a_{1,2}d'_1)}} \qquad S_2^* := G^\gamma$$

is a valid forgery on $m^* := \frac{a_{1,1}d_2 - a_{1,2}d_1}{a_{1,2}d_1' - a_{1,1}d_2'}$. The forgery is valid unless $a_{1,2}d_1' - a_{1,1}d_2' = 0$. We have 2 cases to deal with this as follows:

○ Case $a_{1,2}d_1' = a_{1,1}d_2' = 0$: Given a signature $\sigma = (S_1, S_2)$ on a random message $m \in \mathbb{Z}_p$, we have that $\sigma^* = (S_1^*, S_2^*)$ where

$$S_1^* := G^{\frac{-\gamma(a_{2,1}+a_{2,1}'m^*)+d_1'(m^*-m)}{a_{1,1}}} S_2^{\frac{a_{2,1}+a_{2,1}'m}{a_{1,1}}} S_1 \qquad\qquad S_2^* := G^\gamma$$

is a valid forgery on any $m^* \neq m$ for any $\gamma \in \mathbb{Z}_p^\times$.

○ Case $a_{1,2}d_1' = a_{1,1}d_2' \neq 0$: Given a signature $\sigma = (S_1, S_2)$ on a random message $m \in \mathbb{Z}_p$, we have that $\sigma^* = (S_1^*, S_2^*)$ where

$$S_1^* := G^{\frac{-\gamma a_{1,2}(a_{2,1}+a_{2,1}'m^*)+d_2'a_{1,1}(m^*-m)}{a_{1,1}a_{1,2}}} S_2^{\frac{a_{2,1}+a_{2,1}'m}{a_{1,1}}} S_1 \qquad\qquad S_2^* := G^\gamma$$

is a valid forgery on any $m^* \neq m$ for any $\gamma \in \mathbb{Z}_p^\times$.

If it is required that $S_i^* \in \mathbb{G}^\times$, we have to additionally handle the case that $d_1 a_{2,1}' = a_{2,1}d_1'$ and $d_2 a_{2,1}' = a_{2,1}d_2'$. Note that we cannot have that $a_{2,1}' = 0$ as otherwise the signature will either be independent of S_2 or m. We have that given a signature $\sigma = (S_1, S_2)$ on a random message $m \in \mathbb{Z}_p^\times$, we have that $\sigma^* = (S_1^*, S_2^*) := (S_1^\gamma, S_2)$ is a valid forgery on any message $m^* = \frac{a_{2,1}(\gamma-1)+a_{2,1}'\gamma m}{a_{2,1}'}$ for any $\gamma \in \mathbb{Z}_p^\times\backslash\{1\}$.   □

This concludes the proof.   □

We have proved that an (optimal) scheme with two-element unilateral signatures must have at least 2 elements in the verification key besides the default source group generators. An intriguing question is whether, similarly to the one-time EUF-CMA scheme we give in Sect. 5, an EUF-RMA scheme with two-element unilateral signatures and a two-element bilateral verification key exists. We answer this question negatively by proving the following theorem. In essence, this means the PS scheme and our new $LmSPSPS$ scheme are optimal w.r.t. the size of the verification key.

Theorem 10. *There is no EUF-RMA (against $q > 1$ sign queries) LmSP-SPS scheme with two-element unilateral signatures and a two-element bilateral verification key.*

Proof. Let's consider a scheme with signatures of the form $\sigma = (S_1, S_2) \in \mathbb{G}^2$ whereas the verification key is of the form $(X, \tilde{Y}) \in \mathbb{G} \times \mathbb{H}$. The proof for the opposite case is similar.

Such a scheme has a PPE verification equation of the form

$$\prod_{i=1}^2 e(S_i, \tilde{H}^{a_{i,1}+a_{i,1}'m}\tilde{Y}^{a_{i,2}+a_{i,2}'m})$$

$$= e(G^{d_{1,1}+d_{1,1}'m}X^{d_{2,1}+d_{2,1}'m}, \tilde{H})e(G^{d_{1,2}+d_{1,2}'m}X^{d_{2,2}+d_{2,2}'m}, \tilde{Y}).$$

By definition, we must have that either $a'_{1,1} = a'_{1,2} = 0$ or $a'_{2,1} = a'_{2,2} = 0$ as otherwise the message features in the denominator polynomial of a signature component. Let's assume WLOG that $a'_{1,1} = a'_{1,2} = 0$ as the other case is similar.

Such a scheme is not secure against an adversary that receives two signatures $\sigma_1 = (S_{1,1}, S_{1,2})$ and $\sigma_2 = (S_{2,1}, S_{2,2})$ on two random distinct messages m_1 and m_2, respectively. We can construct a forgery on a new message $m^* \notin \{m_1, m_2\}$ as follows:

$$\text{Define } A_1 = \begin{bmatrix} a_{2,1} & a_{1,1} \\ a_{2,2} & a_{1,2} \end{bmatrix}, A_2 = \begin{bmatrix} a'_{2,1} & a_{1,1} \\ a'_{2,2} & a_{1,2} \end{bmatrix} \text{ and } A_3 = \begin{bmatrix} a_{2,1} & a'_{2,1} \\ a_{2,2} & a'_{2,2} \end{bmatrix}$$

Let $\alpha := \frac{(|A_1| + |A_2| m_1)(m^* - m_2)}{(|A_1| + |A_2| m^*)(m_1 - m_2)}$ and

$$\beta_{s_{1,1}} := \frac{m_2 - m^*}{m_2 - m_1} \qquad\qquad \beta_{s_{1,2}} := \frac{m_1 - m^*}{m_1 - m_2}$$

$$\gamma_{s_{1,1}} := \frac{|A_3|(m^* - m_2 + (m_2 - m_1)\alpha)}{|A_2|(m_2 - m_1)} \qquad \gamma_{s_{1,2}} := -\gamma_{s_{1,1}}$$

$$\gamma_{s_{2,1}} := \alpha \qquad\qquad \gamma_{s_{2,2}} := -\frac{(|A_1| + |A_2| m_2)(m^* - m_1)}{(|A_1| + |A_2| m^*)(m_1 - m_2)}$$

We have that $\sigma^* = (S_1^* := S_{1,1}^{\beta_{s_{1,1}}} S_{2,1}^{\beta_{s_{1,2}}} S_{1,2}^{\gamma_{s_{1,1}}} S_{2,2}^{\gamma_{s_{1,2}}}, S_2^* := S_{1,2}^{\gamma_{s_{2,1}}} S_{2,2}^{\gamma_{s_{2,2}}})$ is a valid forgery on any message $m^* \in \mathbb{Z}_p \backslash \{m_1, m_2, \frac{-|A_1|}{|A_2|}\}$ satisfying $|A_1| + |A_2| m^* \neq 0$. Thus, we obtain a forgery on a new message unless $|A_2| = 0$ which is dealt with by the following 3 cases:

- Case $a_{1,1} = 0$: We have 2 cases:

  - Case $a_{1,2} = 0$: The verification equation is independent of the signature component S_1 and hence is not secure.
  - Case $a'_{2,1} = 0$: Given signatures $\sigma_1 = (S_{1,1}, S_{1,2})$ and $\sigma_2 = (S_{2,1}, S_{2,2})$ on random messages m_1 and m_2, respectively, we have that $\sigma^* = (S_1^*, S_2^*)$ where

$$S_1^* := S_{1,1}^\gamma S_{2,1}^{1-\gamma} S_{1,2}^{-\frac{a'_{2,2}(\gamma^2 - \gamma)(m_1 - m_2)}{a_{1,2}}} S_{2,2}^{\frac{a'_{2,2}(\gamma^2 - \gamma)(m_1 - m_2)}{a_{1,2}}} \qquad S_2^* := S_{1,2}^\gamma S_{2,2}^{1-\gamma}$$

is a valid forgery on $m^* = \gamma m_1 + (1 - \gamma)m_2$ for any $\gamma \in \mathbb{Z}_p^\times \backslash \{1\}$.

- Case $a'_{2,2} = 0$ and $a_{1,1} \neq 0$: Given signatures $\sigma_1 = (S_{1,1}, S_{1,2})$ and $\sigma_2 = (S_{2,1}, S_{2,2})$ on two random messages m_1 and m_2, respectively, we compute

$$S_1^* := S_{1,1}^\gamma S_{2,1}^{1-\gamma} S_{1,2}^{-\frac{a'_{2,1}(\gamma^2 - \gamma)(m_1 - m_2)}{a_{1,1}}} S_{2,2}^{\frac{a'_{2,1}(\gamma^2 - \gamma)(m_1 - m_2)}{a_{1,1}}} \qquad S_2^* := S_{1,2}^\gamma S_{2,2}^{1-\gamma}$$

We have that $\sigma^* = (S_1^*, S_2^*)$ is a valid forgery on $m^* = \gamma m_1 + (1 - \gamma)m_2$ for any $\gamma \in \mathbb{Z}_p^\times \backslash \{1\}$.

- Case $a'_{2,2}a_{1,1} = a_{1,2}a'_{2,1} \neq 0$: Given signatures $\sigma_1 = (S_{1,1}, S_{1,2})$ and $\sigma_2 = (S_{2,1}, S_{2,2})$ on two distinct random messages m_1 and m_2, respectively, we compute

$$S_1^* := S_{1,1}^{\frac{m_2-m^*}{m_2-m_1}} S_{2,1}^{\frac{m_1-m^*}{m_1-m_2}} S_{1,2}^{-\frac{a'_{2,1}(m^*-m_1)(m^*-m_2)}{a_{1,1}(m_1-m_2)}} S_{2,2}^{\frac{a'_{2,1}(m^*-m_1)(m^*-m_2)}{a_{1,1}(m_1-m_2)}}$$

$$S_2^* := S_{1,2}^{\frac{m_2-m^*}{m_2-m_1}} S_{2,2}^{\frac{m_1-m^*}{m_1-m_2}}$$

We have that $\sigma^* = (S_1^*, S_2^*)$ is a valid forgery on any new message $m^* \in \mathbb{Z}_p \setminus \{m_1, m_2\}$.

This concludes the proof. □

References

1. Abe, M., Ambrona, M., Ohkubo, M., Tibouchi, M.: Lower bounds on structure-preserving signatures for bilateral messages. In: Catalano, D., De Prisco, R. (eds.) SCN 2018. LNCS, vol. 11035, pp. 3–22. Springer, Cham (2018). https://doi.org/10.1007/978-3-319-98113-0_1

2. Abe, M., Chase, M., David, B., Kohlweiss, M., Nishimaki, R., Ohkubo, M.: Constant-size structure-preserving signatures: generic constructions and simple assumptions. In: Wang, X., Sako, K. (eds.) ASIACRYPT 2012. LNCS, vol. 7658, pp. 4–24. Springer, Heidelberg (2012). https://doi.org/10.1007/978-3-642-34961-4_3

3. Abe, M., David, B., Kohlweiss, M., Nishimaki, R., Ohkubo, M.: Tagged one-time signatures: tight security and optimal tag size. In: Kurosawa, K., Hanaoka, G. (eds.) PKC 2013. LNCS, vol. 7778, pp. 312–331. Springer, Heidelberg (2013). https://doi.org/10.1007/978-3-642-36362-7_20

4. Abe, M., Fuchsbauer, G., Groth, J., Haralambiev, K., Ohkubo, M.: Structure-preserving signatures and commitments to group elements. In: Rabin, T. (ed.) CRYPTO 2010. LNCS, vol. 6223, pp. 209–236. Springer, Heidelberg (2010). https://doi.org/10.1007/978-3-642-14623-7_12

5. Abe, M., Groth, J., Haralambiev, K., Ohkubo, M.: Optimal structure-preserving signatures in asymmetric bilinear groups. In: Rogaway, P. (ed.) CRYPTO 2011. LNCS, vol. 6841, pp. 649–666. Springer, Heidelberg (2011). https://doi.org/10.1007/978-3-642-22792-9_37

6. Abe, M., Groth, J., Ohkubo, M.: Separating short structure-preserving signatures from non-interactive assumptions. In: Lee, D.H., Wang, X. (eds.) ASIACRYPT 2011. LNCS, vol. 7073, pp. 628–646. Springer, Heidelberg (2011). https://doi.org/10.1007/978-3-642-25385-0_34

7. Abe, M., Groth, J., Ohkubo, M., Tibouchi, M.: Unified, minimal and selectively randomizable structure-preserving signatures. In: Lindell, Y. (ed.) TCC 2014. LNCS, vol. 8349, pp. 688–712. Springer, Heidelberg (2014). https://doi.org/10.1007/978-3-642-54242-8_29

8. Abe, M., Hofheinz, D., Nishimaki, R., Ohkubo, M., Pan, J.: Compact structure-preserving signatures with almost tight security. In: Katz, J., Shacham, H. (eds.) CRYPTO 2017. LNCS, vol. 10402, pp. 548–580. Springer, Cham (2017). https://doi.org/10.1007/978-3-319-63715-0_19

9. Bellare, M., Garay, J.A., Rabin, T.: Fast batch verification for modular exponentiation and digital signatures. In: Nyberg, K. (ed.) EUROCRYPT 1998. LNCS, vol. 1403, pp. 236–250. Springer, Heidelberg (1998). https://doi.org/10.1007/BFb0054130

10. Bichsel, P., Camenisch, J., Neven, G., Smart, N.P., Warinschi, B.: Get shorty via group signatures without encryption. In: Garay, J.A., De Prisco, R. (eds.) SCN 2010. LNCS, vol. 6280, pp. 381–398. Springer, Heidelberg (2010). https://doi.org/10.1007/978-3-642-15317-4_24

11. Boneh, D., Boyen, X.: Short signatures without random oracles. In: Cachin, C., Camenisch, J.L. (eds.) EUROCRYPT 2004. LNCS, vol. 3027, pp. 56–73. Springer, Heidelberg (2004). https://doi.org/10.1007/978-3-540-24676-3_4

12. Boneh, D., Lynn, B., Shacham, H.: Short signatures from the Weil pairing. J. Cryptol. **17**, 297–319 (2004). https://doi.org/10.1007/s00145-004-0314-9

13. Brickell, E., Camenisch, J., Chen, L.: Direct anonymous attestation. In: ACM CCS. ACM (2004)

14. Camenisch, J., Dubovitskaya, M., Haralambiev, K.: Efficient structure-preserving signature scheme from standard assumptions. In: Visconti, I., De Prisco, R. (eds.) SCN 2012. LNCS, vol. 7485, pp. 76–94. Springer, Heidelberg (2012). https://doi.org/10.1007/978-3-642-32928-9_5

15. Camenisch, J., Dubovitskaya, M., Haralambiev, K., Kohlweiss, M.: Composable and modular anonymous credentials: definitions and practical constructions. In: Iwata, T., Cheon, J.H. (eds.) ASIACRYPT 2015. LNCS, vol. 9453, pp. 262–288. Springer, Heidelberg (2015). https://doi.org/10.1007/978-3-662-48800-3_11

16. Camenisch, J., Lysyanskaya, A.: Signature schemes and anonymous credentials from bilinear maps. In: Franklin, M. (ed.) CRYPTO 2004. LNCS, vol. 3152, pp. 56–72. Springer, Heidelberg (2004). https://doi.org/10.1007/978-3-540-28628-8_4

17. Chase, M., Kohlweiss, M.: A new hash-and-sign approach and structure-preserving signatures from DLIN. In: Visconti, I., De Prisco, R. (eds.) SCN 2012. LNCS, vol. 7485, pp. 131–148. Springer, Heidelberg (2012). https://doi.org/10.1007/978-3-642-32928-9_8

18. Chatterjee, S., Kabaleeshwaran, R.: Rerandomizable signatures under standard assumption. In: Hao, F., Ruj, S., Sen Gupta, S. (eds.) INDOCRYPT 2019. LNCS, vol. 11898, pp. 45–67. Springer, Cham (2019). https://doi.org/10.1007/978-3-030-35423-7_3

19. Chatterjee, S., Menezes, A.: Type 2 structure-preserving signature schemes revisited. In: Iwata, T., Cheon, J.H. (eds.) ASIACRYPT 2015. LNCS, vol. 9452, pp. 286–310. Springer, Heidelberg (2015). https://doi.org/10.1007/978-3-662-48797-6_13

20. Chen, L., Page, D., Smart, N.P.: On the design and implementation of an efficient DAA scheme. In: Gollmann, D., Lanet, J.-L., Iguchi-Cartigny, J. (eds.) CARDIS 2010. LNCS, vol. 6035, pp. 223–237. Springer, Heidelberg (2010). https://doi.org/10.1007/978-3-642-12510-2_16

21. ElGamal, T.: A public key cryptosystem and a signature scheme based on discrete logarithms. IEEE Trans. Inf. Theory **31**(4), 469–472 (1985)

22. Fiat, A., Shamir, A.: How to prove yourself: practical solutions to identification and signature problems. In: Odlyzko, A.M. (ed.) CRYPTO 1986. LNCS, vol. 263, pp. 186–194. Springer, Heidelberg (1987). https://doi.org/10.1007/3-540-47721-7_12

23. Fuchsbauer, G.: Commuting signatures and verifiable encryption. In: Paterson, K.G. (ed.) EUROCRYPT 2011. LNCS, vol. 6632, pp. 224–245. Springer, Heidelberg (2011). https://doi.org/10.1007/978-3-642-20465-4_14

24. Fuchsbauer, G., Hanser, C., Slamanig, D.: Practical round-optimal blind signatures in the standard model. In: Gennaro, R., Robshaw, M. (eds.) CRYPTO 2015. LNCS, vol. 9216, pp. 233–253. Springer, Heidelberg (2015). https://doi.org/10.1007/978-3-662-48000-7_12

25. Galbraith, S., Paterson, K., Smart, N.P.: Pairings for cryptographers. Discrete Appl. Math. **156**, 3113–3121 (2008)

26. Gay, R., Hofheinz, D., Kohl, L., Pan, J.: More efficient (almost) tightly secure structure-preserving signatures. In: Nielsen, J.B., Rijmen, V. (eds.) EUROCRYPT 2018. LNCS, vol. 10821, pp. 230–258. Springer, Cham (2018). https://doi.org/10.1007/978-3-319-78375-8_8

27. Gerbush, M., Lewko, A., O'Neill, A., Waters, B.: Dual form signatures: an approach for proving security from static assumptions. In: Wang, X., Sako, K. (eds.) ASIACRYPT 2012. LNCS, vol. 7658, pp. 25–42. Springer, Heidelberg (2012). https://doi.org/10.1007/978-3-642-34961-4_4

28. Ghadafi, E.: Formalizing group blind signatures and practical constructions without random oracles. In: Boyd, C., Simpson, L. (eds.) ACISP 2013. LNCS, vol. 7959, pp. 330–346. Springer, Heidelberg (2013). https://doi.org/10.1007/978-3-642-39059-3_23

29. Ghadafi, E.: Short structure-preserving signatures. In: Sako, K. (ed.) CT-RSA 2016. LNCS, vol. 9610, pp. 305–321. Springer, Cham (2016). https://doi.org/10.1007/978-3-319-29485-8_18

30. Ghadafi, E.: Efficient round-optimal blind signatures in the standard model. In: Kiayias, A. (ed.) FC 2017. LNCS, vol. 10322, pp. 455–473. Springer, Cham (2017). https://doi.org/10.1007/978-3-319-70972-7_26

31. Ghadafi, E.: More efficient structure-preserving signatures - or: bypassing the type-III lower bounds. In: Foley, S.N., Gollmann, D., Snekkenes, E. (eds.) ESORICS 2017. LNCS, vol. 10493, pp. 43–61. Springer, Cham (2017). https://doi.org/10.1007/978-3-319-66399-9_3

32. Ghadafi, E.: How low can you go? Short structure-preserving signatures for Diffie-Hellman vectors. In: O'Neill, M. (ed.) IMACC 2017. LNCS, vol. 10655, pp. 185–204. Springer, Cham (2017). https://doi.org/10.1007/978-3-319-71045-7_10

33. Ghadafi, E.: Further lower bounds for structure-preserving signatures in asymmetric bilinear groups. In: Buchmann, J., Nitaj, A., Rachidi, T. (eds.) AFRICACRYPT 2019. LNCS, vol. 11627, pp. 409–428. Springer, Cham (2019). https://doi.org/10.1007/978-3-030-23696-0_21

34. Groth, J.: Efficient fully structure-preserving signatures for large messages. In: Iwata, T., Cheon, J.H. (eds.) ASIACRYPT 2015. LNCS, vol. 9452, pp. 239–259. Springer, Heidelberg (2015). https://doi.org/10.1007/978-3-662-48797-6_11

35. Groth, J., Sahai, A.: Efficient non-interactive proof systems for bilinear groups. SIAM J. Comput. **41**(5), 1193–1232 (2012)

36. Jutla, C.S., Roy, A.: Improved structure preserving signatures under standard bilinear assumptions. In: Fehr, S. (ed.) PKC 2017. LNCS, vol. 10175, pp. 183–209. Springer, Heidelberg (2017). https://doi.org/10.1007/978-3-662-54388-7_7

37. Kiltz, E., Pan, J., Wee, H.: Structure-preserving signatures from standard assumptions, revisited. In: Gennaro, R., Robshaw, M. (eds.) CRYPTO 2015. LNCS, vol. 9216, pp. 275–295. Springer, Heidelberg (2015). https://doi.org/10.1007/978-3-662-48000-7_14

38. Libert, B., Peters, T., Yung, M.: Short group signatures via structure-preserving signatures: standard model security from simple assumptions. In: Gennaro, R., Robshaw, M. (eds.) CRYPTO 2015. LNCS, vol. 9216, pp. 296–316. Springer, Heidelberg (2015). https://doi.org/10.1007/978-3-662-48000-7_15

39. Maji, H.K., Prabhakaran, M., Rosulek, M.: Attribute-based signatures. In: Kiayias, A. (ed.) CT-RSA 2011. LNCS, vol. 6558, pp. 376–392. Springer, Heidelberg (2011). https://doi.org/10.1007/978-3-642-19074-2_24

40. Maurer, U.: Abstract models of computation in cryptography. In: Smart, N.P. (ed.) Cryptography and Coding 2005. LNCS, vol. 3796, pp. 1–12. Springer, Heidelberg (2005). https://doi.org/10.1007/11586821_1

41. Pedersen, T.P.: Non-interactive and information-theoretic secure verifiable secret sharing. In: Feigenbaum, J. (ed.) CRYPTO 1991. LNCS, vol. 576, pp. 129–140. Springer, Heidelberg (1992). https://doi.org/10.1007/3-540-46766-1_9

42. Pointcheval, D., Sanders, O.: Short randomizable signatures. In: Sako, K. (ed.) CT-RSA 2016. LNCS, vol. 9610, pp. 111–126. Springer, Cham (2016). https://doi.org/10.1007/978-3-319-29485-8_7

43. Pointcheval, D., Sanders, O.: Reassessing security of randomizable signatures. In: Smart, N.P. (ed.) CT-RSA 2018. LNCS, vol. 10808, pp. 319–338. Springer, Cham (2018). https://doi.org/10.1007/978-3-319-76953-0_17

44. Shoup, V.: Lower bounds for discrete logarithms and related problems. In: Fumy, W. (ed.) EUROCRYPT 1997. LNCS, vol. 1233, pp. 256–266. Springer, Heidelberg (1997). https://doi.org/10.1007/3-540-69053-0_18

45. Waters, B.: Efficient identity-based encryption without random oracles. In: Cramer, R. (ed.) EUROCRYPT 2005. LNCS, vol. 3494, pp. 114–127. Springer, Heidelberg (2005). https://doi.org/10.1007/11426639_7

An Efficient Certificate-Based Signature Scheme in the Standard Model

Guoqiang Wang and Yanmei Cao[✉]

State Key Laboratory of Integrated Service Networks (ISN),
Xidian University, Xi'an 710071, China
gqwang_0@stu.xidian.edu.cn, yanmcao@stu.xidian.edu.cn

Abstract. Certificate-based cryptography optimizes certificate management of the traditional public key infrastructure (PKI) and overcomes the problems of the key escrow and the key distribution in identity-based cryptography (IBC). Currently, many certificate-based signature (CBS) schemes have been proposed in the random oracle model or standard model. However, all existing schemes in the standard model are quietly inefficient. In this paper, we propose an efficient certificate-based signature over bilinear groups in the standard model. Compared with the state-of-the-art constructions in the standard model, the proposed scheme is superior in both communication cost and computational overhead.

Keywords: Certificate-based signature · Standard model · Bilinear pairing.

1 Introduction

In the traditional public key cryptography (PKC) [2], users choose a random string as the public key of their own. Here the public key is unrelated to the identity information of the user, which cause an attack that an adversary can replace user's public key with its own. In order to solve this problem, a trusted Certificate Authority (CA) is introduced by public key infrastructure (PKI) to produce an unforgeable certificate linking the user's public key and identity together for each user. It is not hard to see that certificate management of the CA becomes more and more complex and costly as the number of users increases.

To address the aforementioned problems, Shamir [26] came up with a new concept, named identity-based cryptography (IBC), in 1984. In the identity-based cryptosystem, there exists a trusted party named Private Key Generator (PKG) who generates a private key for the user based on the user's public key, where the public key maybe a phone code or IP address. Obviously, IBC avoids the certificate management problem in PKC [7]. And it can also resist public key replacement attack simultaneously. Nevertheless, new problems of key escrow and key distribution [18] appeared in IBC due to the user trusts the PKG unconditionally. To efficiently reduce the complexity and overhead of certificate management in PKC, and overcome problems of the key escrow and

© Springer Nature Switzerland AG 2021
K. Sako and N. O. Tippenhauer (Eds.): ACNS 2021, LNCS 12726, pp. 313–329, 2021.
https://doi.org/10.1007/978-3-030-78372-3_12

key distribution in IBC, the concepts of certificateless-based cryptography (CLC) [1] and certificate-based cryptography (CBC) [7] were put forward.

In certificateless-based cryptography, there exists a trusted Key Generation Center (KGC) that produces a partial private key and transmits it to the user via a secure channel. The user then obtains a full private key by combining the partial private key from the KGC and the secret key generated by his/her own. Note that the secret key is only known to the user. Therefore, CLC avoids the key escrow problem of IBC and certificate management problem of PKC. However, CLC needs to establish a secure channel to distribute the partial private key. And the schemes in CLC are vulnerable to public key replacement attack.

In certificate-based cryptography, the user first generates his/her own pair of private/public keys, then sends information including public key and user's identity to the CA. Later, the user receives certificate which can be regarded as signature generated by CA with the private key. Note that the certificate in CBC is different from the one in PKC which can be utilized as a part of the user's private key. It is clear that the complexity and costs of certificate management of the CA are efficiently reduced. In addition, this method avoids the problems of key escrow and key distribution in IBC.

Currently, many certificate-based signature schemes have been proposed. In 2004, Kang et al. [12] first introduced the concept of certificate-based signature and gave two CBS schemes in the random oracle. Subsequently, Li et al. [14] presented a secure and efficient CBS scheme in the random oracle model. Huang et al. [10] also proposed a secure scheme in the random oracle. Furthermore, there exist several works focusing on the CBS schemes in the standard model. Liu et al. [18] constructed a CBS scheme in the standard model. Lu and Li [20] proposed a novel CBS scheme in the standard model. In 2017, Zhou and Cui [32] also gave a CBS scheme in the standard model. To our best knowledge, all existing schemes in the standard model are inefficient.

1.1 Our Contribution

In this paper, we focus on constructing a CBS scheme with better efficiency in the standard model. Our contributions can be summarized as follows:

- We present an efficient certificate-based signature scheme in the standard model based on the PS assumption and EPS assumption which are proven to be intractable in the generic group model.
- The proposed scheme satisfies the desired properties of correctness and existential unforgeability under adaptive chosen-message attack. Besides, compared with the state-of-the-art constructions in the standard model, the proposed scheme is superior in both communication cost and computation overhead.

1.2 Related Work

In 2004, Kang et al. [12] introduced the concept of certificate-based signature (CBS) and described the necessary security requirements of certificate-based signature. Additionally, they also proposed two certificate-based signature schemes in the random oracle model. In 2007, Li et al. [14] introduced a new attack called the key replacement attack and pointed out that one of the schemes [12] is insecure against the attack mentioned above. They then redefined the security model of certificate-based signature and designed a secure and efficient CBS scheme in the random oracle model. Liu et al. [18] presented a pairing free CBS scheme in the random oracle model. Later, the scheme in the random oracle model mentioned above was broken by Zhang [30]. After that, Zhang et al. [31] presented an efficient CBS scheme in the random oracle model based on bilinear pairings. In 2009, Wu et al. [28] proposed a generic conversion from an existing secure CLS scheme to a secure CBS scheme and then gave a secure CBS scheme in the random oracle model. Liu et al. [19] constructed a short certificate-based signature (SCBS) scheme in the random oracle. Unfortunately, Cheng et al. [4] pointed out that the scheme [19] was insecure. Concurrently, Li et al. [16] also designed an SCBS scheme in the random oracle model. Hung et al. [11] claimed that the scheme [16] is insecure and then gave an improved scheme. However, the improved scheme [11] was also broken by Kumar and Sharma (see [13]). Wu et al. [27] gave a new CBS scheme under the k-CAA assumption and Inv-CDH assumption in the random oracle model. Ma et al. [21] proposed a new CBS scheme based on the CDH assumption in the random oracle model. Recently, Huang et al. [10] proposed a generic conversion from an existing secure proxy scheme to a secure CBS scheme and then gave a secure CBS scheme in the random oracle model.

Several works focusing on the CBS in the standard model have been found. Liu et al. [18] constructed a CBS scheme in the standard model. Subsequently, Li et al. [15] described a CBS scheme in the standard model based on the CDH assumption. In 2016, Lu and Li [20] further considered a new attack, named malicious-but-passive CA attack. And then they pointed out that several CBS schemes [15,18] in the standard model are insecure against the attack above. Additionally, they also proposed an improved scheme based on CDH assumption in the standard model. Subsequently, Zhou and Cui [32] described an enhanced security model of the CBS which can resist the malicious-but-passive CA attack. They then designed a CBS scheme in the standard model utilizing bilinear pairing. To our best knowledge, all existing CBS schemes in the standard model are insecure or inefficient.

1.3 Organization

The rest of this paper is organized as follows. In Sect. 2, we describe some preliminaries used in this paper. In Sect. 3, we propose an efficient certificate-based signature scheme. In Sect. 4, we provide the security and efficiency analysis of the proposed scheme. Finally, the conclusions are given in Sect. 5.

2   Preliminaries

In this section, we describe some necessary preliminaries used in this paper.

2.1 Bilinear Pairing

Let $\mathbb{G}$, $\hat{\mathbb{G}}$ and $\mathbb{T}$ be multiplicative cyclic groups with prime order p, and let G and $\hat{G}$ be generators of $\mathbb{G}$ and $\hat{\mathbb{G}}$, respectively. The pairing $e : \mathbb{G} \times \hat{\mathbb{G}} \to \mathbb{T}$ is a bilinear one if it satisfies the following properties:

- Bilinearity: $e(G^a, \hat{G}^b) = e(G, \hat{G})^{ab}$ for $\forall a, b \in \mathbb{Z}_p$.
- Non-degeneracy: $e(G, \hat{G}) \neq 1_{\mathbb{T}}$, where $1_{\mathbb{T}}$ is the unit element of $\mathbb{T}$.
- Computability: e is efficiently computable.

If $\mathbb{G} = \hat{\mathbb{G}}$ then the pairing is symmetric, called Type 1 pairing [3,6]. The pairing is asymmetric (Type 2 or 3 pairing) when $\mathbb{G} \neq \hat{\mathbb{G}}$. For Type 2 pairing there exists an efficiently-computable isomorphism $\Psi : \hat{\mathbb{G}} \to \mathbb{G}$. For Type 3 pairing no such isomorphism is known between $\hat{\mathbb{G}}$ and $\mathbb{G}$. Moreover, literature [3] shows that Type 3 pairing is currently the optimal choice in terms of efficiency and security trade-off. Currently, Type 3 pairing is widely utilized in some schemes [5,8,9].

2.2 Intractable Assumptions

In this section, we describe two intractable assumptions which will be utilized in the security analysis of the proposed scheme in this paper.

Definition 1 (PS assumption). *We assume that a* Type 3 *bilinear group is described as* $(\mathbb{G}, \hat{\mathbb{G}}, \mathbb{T}, e, p, G, \hat{G})$, *and let* $\hat{V} = \hat{G}^v$, $\hat{W} = \hat{G}^w$ *for some random scalars* $v, w \in \mathbb{Z}_p$ *where* $\hat{G}$ *is a generator of* $\hat{\mathbb{G}}$. *Let* $\mathcal{O}PS(\cdot)$ *be an oracle on input* $m \in \mathbb{Z}_p$ *that returns a tuple* $(G^r, G^{r(v+mw)})$ *for a random* $r \in \mathbb{Z}_p^*$. *Given* $(\hat{G}, \hat{V}, \hat{W})$ *and unlimited access to this oracle, any adversary can not efficiently generate such a valid tuple for a new scalar* m^*, *not asked to* $\mathcal{O}PS$.

This assumption introduced by Pointcheval and Sanders in [24] has been shown to be intractable in the generic group model. Subsequently, PS assumption is widely utilized in some schemes [17, 22–24, 29, 33].

Definition 2 (EPS assumption). *We assume that a* Type 3 *bilinear group is described as* $(\mathbb{G}, \hat{\mathbb{G}}, \mathbb{T}, e, p, G, \hat{G})$, *and let* $O = G^o, \hat{O} = \hat{G}^o, X = G^x, \hat{X} = \hat{G}^x,$ $\hat{Y} = \hat{G}^y, \hat{Z} = \hat{G}^z$ *for some random scalars* $o, x, y, z \in \mathbb{Z}_p$ *where* $\hat{G}$ *is a generator of* $\hat{\mathbb{G}}$. *Let* $\mathcal{O}PS(\cdot)$ *be an oracle on input* $l \in \mathbb{Z}_p$ *that returns a tuple* $(\alpha_1, \alpha_2) = (G^{r_1}, G^{r_1(y+lz)})$ *for a random* $r_1 \in \mathbb{Z}_p^*$. *Let* $\mathcal{O}EPS(\cdot)$ *be an oracle on input* $(l^*, m) \in \mathbb{Z}_p^2$ *that returns a triple* $(\beta_1, \beta_2, \beta_3) = (G^{r_2}, G^{r_2 r_3}, G^{r_3(r_2(y+l^*z)+o+xm)})$ *for random* $r_2, r_3 \in \mathbb{Z}_p^*$, *where* l^* *is not allowed to access the oracle* $\mathcal{O}PS(\cdot)$. *Given* $(G, \hat{G}, O, \hat{O}, X, \hat{X}, \hat{Y}, \hat{Z})$ *and unlimited access to oracles* $\mathcal{O}PS$ *and* $\mathcal{O}EPS$, *any adversary can not efficiently generate such a valid tuple for a new pair* (l^*, m^*), *not asked to* $\mathcal{O}EPS$.

We show the intractability of the EPS assumption in the general model using the Schwartz-Zipple lemma [25]. Please refer to Appendix A.

2.3 Definition and Security Requirements of CBS

In this section, we provide the formal definition [20,32] and security requirements [28,32] of CBS scheme.

Definition 3 (CBS). *A certificate-based signature scheme is defined by the following five algorithms:*

- **CBS.Setup**(1^λ): It is usually executed by the CA to take a security parameter 1^λ as input, and then outputs a public parameter $Params$ and the CA's master secret key MSK where the private key MSK keeps secret.
- **CBS.UKGen**$(Params, ID)$: It is executed by the user to take the public parameter $Params$ as input and outputs private/public keys (SK_{ID}, PK_{ID}) for the user.
- **CBS.Cert**$(Params, ID, PK_{ID}, MSK)$: It is executed by the CA to take $(Params, ID, PK_{ID}, MSK)$ as input where the identity information ID and the public key PK_{ID} are from the user, and then it outputs a certificate $CERT_{ID}$ for the user.
- **CBS.Sign**$(Params, ID, SK_{ID}, CERT_{ID}, m)$: It is executed by the user to take $(Params, ID, SK_{ID}, CERT_{ID}, m)$ as input and outputs a signature σ on m.
- **CBS.Verify**$(Params, ID, PK_{ID}, m, \sigma)$: It is executed by the verifier to take as input $(Params, ID, PK_{ID}, m, \sigma)$ and outputs 1 meaning the signature passing the verification process or 0 otherwise.

A CBS scheme should satisfy correctness and existential unforgeability under adaptive chosen-message attack (EUF-CMA).

Definition 4 (Correctness). *A CBS scheme is correct if for all* $(Params, MSK) \leftarrow$ ***CBS.UKGen***(1^λ), *all* $(SK_{ID}, PK_{ID}) \leftarrow$ ***CBS.UKGen***$(Params, ID)$, *all* $CERT_{ID} \leftarrow$ ***CBS.Cert***$(Params, ID, PK_{ID}, MSK)$, *all* $\sigma \leftarrow$ ***CBS.Sign***$(Params, ID, SK_{ID}, CERT_{ID}, m)$, *we have that*

$$\textbf{\textit{CBS.Verify}}(Params, ID, PK_{ID}, m, \sigma) = 1.$$

EUM-CMA of CBS. There exist two types of adversaries considered in the existential unforgeability under adaptive chosen-message attack of CBS. One is an uncertified user who has the ability to obtain the object user's private key and replace all user's key pairs, but does not get the object user's certificate. The other one is a malicious-but-passive certifier who has the ability to hold the system master secret key, but can not obtain the target user's private key. We give the existential unforgeability under adaptive chosen-message attack of CBS by describing two games *Game 1* and *Game 2*, where *Game 1* is operated between an uncertified user and a challenger, and *Game 2* is run between a malicious-but-passive certifier and a challenger.

Game 1

Setup. In this stage, the adversary $\mathcal{A}$ obtains public parameter *Params* from the challenger $\mathcal{C}$.

Queries. In this stage, $\mathcal{A}$ issues a number of different queries adaptively as follows.

- **User-Creation oracle** $\mathcal{O}_U$: Given an identity ID. $\mathcal{C}$ first checks whether ID exists in Table T which is maintained by $\mathcal{C}$ and records the already created information of the user's identity and keys. If it does, $\mathcal{C}$ returns corresponding PK_{ID} to $\mathcal{A}$. Otherwise, $\mathcal{C}$ runs algorithm **CBS.UKgen**, generates (SK_{ID}, PK_{ID}), and writes the item (ID, SK_{ID}, PK_{ID}) in Table T. Finally, $\mathcal{C}$ returns PK_{ID} to $\mathcal{A}$.
- **Certificate oracle** $\mathcal{O}_C$: Given an identity ID and public key PK_{ID} existing in table T. $\mathcal{C}$ runs algorithm **CBS.Cert** and returns the corresponding certificate $CERT_{ID}$ to $\mathcal{A}$.
- **Replace public key oracle** $\mathcal{O}_R$: Given an identity ID created and a new key pair (SK'_{ID}, PK'_{ID}). $\mathcal{C}$ searches the item (ID, SK_{ID}, PK_{ID}) in Table T and updates (ID, SK_{ID}, PK_{ID}) with (ID, SK'_{ID}, PK'_{ID}).
- **Private key oracle** $\mathcal{O}_P$: Given an identity ID created. $\mathcal{C}$ searches the item (ID, SK_{ID}, PK_{ID}) in Table T, and returns SK_{ID} associated with ID to $\mathcal{A}$.
- **Signature oracle** $\mathcal{O}_S$: Given a message m, an identity ID. $\mathcal{C}$ checks whether the item (ID, SK_{ID}, PK_{ID}) exists in Table T. If it does, $\mathcal{C}$ returns the signature on m to $\mathcal{A}$ by running algorithm **CBS.Sign**.

Forgery. In this stage, $\mathcal{A}$ forges a signature σ^* on the message m^* under (ID^*, PK_{ID^*}). We say $\mathcal{A}$ wins in *Game 1* when the following conditions are satisfied.

- σ^* passes the validation of **CBS.Verify**.
- ID^* has never been queried to the oracle $\mathcal{O}_C$.
- (m^*, ID^*) has never been queried to the oracle $\mathcal{O}_S$.

Definition 5 (EUF-CMA-1). *A CBS scheme is existentially unforgeable against adaptive chosen message attack in Game 1, if a probability polynomial time (PPT) $\mathcal{A}$ succeeds in the Game 1 with a negligible advantage.*

Game 2

Setup. In this stage, $\mathcal{A}$ executes algorithm **CBS.Setup** to generate $(Params, MSK)$, and gives $(Params, MSK)$ to the challenger $\mathcal{C}$.

Queries. In this stage, $\mathcal{C}$ provides polynomial queries to $\mathcal{A}$. Given the oracles $\mathcal{O}_U$, $\mathcal{O}_P$, and $\mathcal{O}_S$ as defined in *Game 1*.

Forgery. In this stage, $\mathcal{A}$ forges a signature σ^* on the message m^* under (ID^*, PK_{ID^*}). We say $\mathcal{A}$ wins the *Game 2* when the following conditions are satisfied.

- σ^* passes the validation of **CBS.Verify**.

- ID^* has never been queried to the oracle $\mathcal{O}_P$.
- (m^*, ID^*) has never been queried to the oracle $\mathcal{O}_S$.

Definition 6 (EUF-CMA-2). *A CBS scheme is existentially unforgeable against adaptive chosen message attack in Game 2, if a PPT $\mathcal{A}$ succeeds in the Game 2 with a negligible advantage.*

3   An Efficient Certificate-Based Signature Scheme

In this section, we propose an efficient certificate-based signature scheme based on the PS assumption and EPS assumption. Then we give the correctness analysis.

- **CBS.Setup(1^λ):** On input the security parameter 1^λ, the CA first randomly chooses three different multiplicative cyclic groups $\mathbb{G}, \hat{\mathbb{G}}$ and $\mathbb{T}$ with prime order p, where G and $\hat{G}$ are generators of $\mathbb{G}$ and $\hat{\mathbb{G}}$ respectively, and denotes a non-degenerate bilinear mapping $e : \mathbb{G} \times \hat{\mathbb{G}} \to \mathbb{T}$. Then CA selects a collision-resistant hash function $H : \{0,1\}^* \to \mathbb{Z}_p$, and randomly picks four scalars $o, x, y, z \in \mathbb{Z}_p$, computes $O = G^o, \hat{O} = \hat{G}^o, X = G^x, \hat{X} = \hat{G}^x, \hat{Y} = \hat{G}^y, \hat{Z} = \hat{G}^z$, and generates the CA's private key $MSK = (o, x, y, z)$ and public key $MPK = (O, \hat{O}, X, \hat{X}, \hat{Y}, \hat{Z})$. Finally, the CA publishes public parameter $Params = (\mathbb{G}, \hat{\mathbb{G}}, \mathbb{T}, e, p, G, \hat{G}, H, MPK)$.
- **CBS.UKGen($Params, ID$):** On input the public parameter $Params$ and the user's identity information ID. The user selects two random scalars $v, w \in \mathbb{Z}_p$, computes $\hat{V} = \hat{G}^v, \hat{W} = \hat{G}^w$, and then generates private key $SK_{ID} = (v, w)$ and public key $PK_{ID} = (\hat{V}, \hat{W})$.
- **CBS.Cert($Params, ID, PK_{ID}, MSK$):** On input the public parameter $Params$, the user's identity information ID, the user's public key PK_{ID} and the CA's private key MSK. The CA selects a random scalar t, computes $(\alpha_1, \alpha_2) = (G^t, G^{(y+zH(ID||PK_{ID}))t})$, and then sends certificate $CERT_{ID} = (\alpha_1, \alpha_2)$ to the user.
- **CBS.Sign($Params, ID, SK_{ID}, CERT_{ID}, m$):** On input the public parameter $Params$, the user's identity information ID, the user's private key SK_{ID}, the user's certificate $CERT_{ID}$ and a message $m \in \{0,1\}^*$. The user selects a random scalar r and computes $\sigma_1 = G^r$, $\sigma_2 = \alpha_1^r$ and $\sigma_3 = (\alpha_2 O X^{H(m)} G^{v+wH(m)})^r$. The user outputs the signature $\sigma = (\sigma_1, \sigma_2, \sigma_3)$.
- **CBS.Verify($Params, ID, PK_{ID}, m, \sigma$):** On input the public parameter $Params$, the user's identity information ID, the user's public key PK_{ID}, the message m and the signature σ. The verifier checks whether $e(\sigma_3, \hat{G}) = e(\sigma_2, \hat{Y}\hat{Z}^h)e\left(\sigma_1, \hat{O}\hat{X}^{H(m)}\hat{V}\hat{W}^{H(m)}\right)$ where $h = H(ID||PK_{ID})$. If it does, it accepts the signature.

Correctness. The correctness of the proposed scheme follows directly from the equation below.

$$e(\sigma_3, \hat{G}) = e\left(\left(\alpha_2 G^{o+xH(m)+v+wH(m)}\right)^r, \hat{G}\right)$$
$$= e(G^{rt(y+zh)}, \hat{G})e\left(G^{r(o+xH(m)+v+wH(m))}, \hat{G}\right)$$
$$= e(G^{tr}, \hat{G}^{(y+zh)})e\left(G^r, \hat{G}^{o+xH(m)+v+wH(m)}\right)$$
$$= e(\sigma_2, \hat{Y}\hat{Z}^h)e\left(\sigma_1, \hat{O}\hat{X}^{H(m)}\hat{V}\hat{W}^{H(m)}\right)$$

where $h = H(ID\|PK_{ID})$.

4   Security and Efficiency Analysis

In this section, we provide the security and efficiency analysis of the proposed scheme.

4.1   Security Analysis

Theorem 1. *The proposed CBS scheme is existentially unforgeable against adaptive chosen message attack in Game 1 if the EPS assumption holds.*

Proof. Suppose there exists a PPT $\mathcal{A}$ who breaks the existential unforgeability of the proposed CBS scheme in *Game 1* with a non-negligible advantage ε, then we can build an adversary $\mathcal{C}$ to solve the EPS assumption with a non-negligible advantage $Adv_{\mathcal{C}}$.

Assume that $\mathcal{A}$ can carry out at most q_U user-creation queries, q_C certificate queries, q_P private key queries, q_R replace public key queries and q_S signature queries. Let $\mathcal{O}PS(\cdot)$ and $\mathcal{O}EPS(\cdot)$ be oracles defined in the EPS assumption, $\mathcal{C}$ can access them polynomially many times and is given $(\mathbb{G}, \hat{\mathbb{G}}, \mathbb{T}, e, p, G, \hat{G}, O, \hat{O}, X, \hat{X}, \hat{Y}, \hat{Z})$, $\mathcal{C}$ works as follows.

Setup. $\mathcal{C}$ sets $MPK = (O, \hat{O}, X, \hat{X}, \hat{Y}, \hat{Z})$ and chooses a collision-resistant hash function $H: \{0,1\}^* \rightarrow \mathbb{Z}_p$. $\mathcal{C}$ outputs $Params = (\mathbb{G}, \hat{\mathbb{G}}, \mathbb{T}, e, p, G, \hat{G}, H, MPK)$ to $\mathcal{A}$.

Suppose that an index π is randomly selected from $\{1, ..., q_U\}$ by $\mathcal{C}$.

Queries. $\mathcal{A}$ issues a number of different queries adaptively as follows.

- $\mathcal{O}_U$: Given an identity ID_i. $\mathcal{C}$ first checks whether the ID_i has been created and written in the table T maintained by $\mathcal{C}$, which is used to record the user's identity information and key pair and initially empty. If it does, $\mathcal{C}$ returns PK_{ID_i} of ID_i to $\mathcal{A}$. Otherwise, $\mathcal{C}$ executes algorithm **CBS.UKgen** to produce key pair $(SK_{ID_i}, PK_{ID_i}) = ((v_{ID_i}, w_{ID_i}), (\hat{V}_{ID_i}, \hat{W}_{ID_i}))$ belonging to ID_i. $\mathcal{C}$ puts $(ID_i, SK_{ID_i}, PK_{ID_i})$ into table T and returns PK_{ID_i} to $\mathcal{A}$.
- $\mathcal{O}_C$: Given an identity ID_i created.

- $ID_i \neq ID_\pi$. $\mathcal{C}$ first computes $H(ID_i||PK_{ID_i})$ and then accesses the oracle $\mathcal{OPS}$ to generate a valid tuple $(\alpha_1, \alpha_2) = \left(G^r, G^{r(y+H(ID_i||PK_{ID_i})z)}\right)$. Finally, $\mathcal{C}$ returns it to $\mathcal{A}$.
- $ID_i = ID_\pi$. $\mathcal{C}$ aborts.
- $\mathcal{O}_P$: Given an identity ID_i created. $\mathcal{C}$ first searches the table T to get the private key (v_{ID_i}, w_{ID_i}), and then returns it to $\mathcal{A}$.
- $\mathcal{O}_R$: Given identity ID_i existing in table T and a valid key pair (SK'_{ID_i}, PK'_{ID_i}). $\mathcal{C}$ first searches the table T to find out the item $(ID_i, SK_{ID_i}, PK_{ID_i})$, and then updates it with $(ID_i, SK'_{ID_i}, PK'_{ID_i})$.
- $\mathcal{O}_S$: Given an identity ID_i existing in table T and a message m.
  - $ID_i \neq ID_\pi$. $\mathcal{C}$ first accesses the oracle $\mathcal{OPS}$ and obtains a valid tuple on (ID_i, PK_{ID_i}). Then it searches the table T to find out the item $(ID_i, SK_{ID_i}, PK_{ID_i})$. Finally, $\mathcal{C}$ generates a signature by using the algorithm **CBS.Sign** and returns it to $\mathcal{A}$.
  - $ID_i = ID_\pi$. $\mathcal{C}$ first accesses the oracle $\mathcal{OEPS}(\cdot)$ to get a valid tuple $(\beta_1, \beta_2, \beta_3)$ on the pair $(H(ID_\pi||PK_{ID_\pi}), H(m))$. Then it searches the table T and obtains item $(ID_\pi, v_{ID_\pi}, w_{ID_\pi}, \hat{V}_{ID_\pi}, \hat{W}_{ID_\pi})$. Finally, $\mathcal{C}$ computes $\sigma_1 = \beta_1, \sigma_2 = \beta_2, \sigma_3 = \beta_3 \beta_1^{v_{ID_\pi} + w_{ID_\pi} H(m)}$ and returns $\sigma = (\sigma_1, \sigma_2, \sigma_3)$ to $\mathcal{A}$.

Forgery. $\mathcal{A}$ outputs a forged signature $\sigma^* = (\sigma_1^*, \sigma_2^*, \sigma_3^*)$ on (ID^*, PK_{ID^*}, m^*). If $ID^* \neq ID_\pi$, $\mathcal{C}$ aborts. Otherwise, $\mathcal{C}$ computes

$$\beta_3^* = \left(\frac{\sigma_3^*}{\sigma_1^{* v_{ID^*} + H(m^*) w_{ID^*}}} \right) = G^{r^*((y+H(ID^*||PK_{ID^*})z)t^* + o + xH(m^*))}$$

and outputs a new valid tuple $(\beta_1^* = \alpha_1^*, \beta_2^* = \alpha_2^*, \beta_3^*)$ on the pair $(H(ID^*||PK_{ID^*}), H(m^*))$ not asked the oracle $\mathcal{OEPS}$. It is clear that $\mathcal{C}$ breaks the EPS assumption.

Now we estimate the successful advantage of $\mathcal{C}$. In order to complete the simulation without aborting, the following conditions should be satisfied.

- In all certificate queries, $ID_i \neq ID_\pi$;
- In the forgery phase, $ID^* = ID_\pi$.

The probability of ID_π selected by $\mathcal{A}$ in the forgery phase is $1/q_U$. The probability of $ID_i \neq ID_\pi$ in the certificate queries is $(1 - q_C/q_U)$. Thus, we can draw the conclusion that the successful advantage of $\mathcal{C}$ is

$$Adv_\mathcal{C} \geq \frac{\varepsilon(q_U - q_C)}{q_U^2},$$

which is non-negligible. Therefore, the proposed CBS scheme is existentially unforgeable against adaptive chosen message attack in *Game 1* if the EPS assumption holds.

Theorem 2. *The proposed CBS scheme is existentially unforgeable against adaptive chosen message attack in Game 2 if the PS assumption holds.*

Proof. Suppose there exists a PPT $\mathcal{A}$ who breaks the existential unforgeability of the proposed CBS scheme in *Game 2* with a non-negligible advantage ε. Then we can build an adversary $\mathcal{C}$ to solve the PS assumption with a non-negligible advantage $Adv_{\mathcal{C}}$.

Assume that $\mathcal{A}$ can carry out at most q_U user-creation queries, q_P private key queries and q_S signature queries. Let $\mathcal{OPS}(\cdot)$ be oracles defined in the PS assumption, $\mathcal{C}$ can access them polynomially many times and is given $(\mathbb{G}, \hat{\mathbb{G}}, \mathbb{T}, e, p, G, \hat{G}, \hat{V}, \hat{W})$. $\mathcal{C}$ works as follows.

Setup. Given a Type 3 bilinear group described as $(\mathbb{G}, \hat{\mathbb{G}}, \mathbb{T}, e, p, G, \hat{G})$. $\mathcal{A}$ randomly selects scalars $o, x, y, z \in \mathbb{Z}_p$, sets $MSK = (o, x, y, z)$, and computes $MPK = (O, \hat{O}, X, \hat{X}, \hat{Y}, \hat{Z}) = (G^o, \hat{G}^o, G^x, \hat{G}^x, \hat{G}^y, \hat{G}^z)$. It then chooses a collision-resistant hash function $H: \{0,1\}^* \to \mathbb{Z}_p$ at random. Finally, $\mathcal{A}$ publishes $Params = (\mathbb{G}, \hat{\mathbb{G}}, \mathbb{T}, e, p, G, \hat{G}, H, MPK)$, and sends $MSK = (o, x, y, z)$ to $\mathcal{C}$.

Assume that an index π is randomly selected from $\{1, ..., q_U\}$ by $\mathcal{C}$.

Queries. $\mathcal{A}$ issues a number of different queries adaptively as follows.

- $\mathcal{O}_U$: Given an identity ID_i. $\mathcal{C}$ first checks whether the ID_i has been created and written in the table T maintained by $\mathcal{C}$, which is used to record the user's identity information and key pair and initially empty. If it does, $\mathcal{C}$ returns PK_{ID_i} of ID_i to $\mathcal{A}$. Otherwise, $\mathcal{C}$ performs the following procedures and returns PK_{ID_i} to $\mathcal{A}$.
  - $ID_i \neq ID_\pi$. $\mathcal{C}$ executes algorithm **CBS.UKgen** to produce key pair $(SK_{ID_i}, PK_{ID_i}) = ((v_{ID_i}, w_{ID_i}), (\hat{V}_{ID_i}, \hat{W}_{ID_i}))$ belonging to ID_i. $\mathcal{C}$ puts $(ID_i, SK_{ID_i}, PK_{ID_i})$ into the table T and returns PK_{ID_i} to $\mathcal{A}$.
  - $ID_i = ID_\pi$. $\mathcal{C}$ puts $(ID_\pi, \bot, (\hat{V}_{ID_\pi}, \hat{W}_{ID_\pi}))$ into the table T and returns $(\hat{V}_{ID_\pi}, \hat{W}_{ID_\pi})$ to $\mathcal{A}$.
- $\mathcal{O}_P$: Given an identity ID_i created.
  - $ID_i \neq ID_\pi$. $\mathcal{C}$ first searches the table T to get the private key (v_{ID_i}, w_{ID_i}), and then returns it to $\mathcal{A}$.
  - $ID_i = ID_\pi$. $\mathcal{C}$ aborts.
- $\mathcal{O}_S$: Given a ID_i existing in table T and a message m.
  - $ID_i \neq ID_\pi$. $\mathcal{C}$ searches the table T to obtain the item $(ID_i, SK_{ID_I}, PK_{ID_i})$. Then it executes algorithms **CBS.Cert** and **CBS.Sign** to generate the signature on the pair (ID_i, m) and returns it to $\mathcal{A}$.
  - $ID_i = ID_\pi$. $\mathcal{C}$ first accesses the oracle $\mathcal{OPS}$ to generate a valid tuple $(\alpha_1, \alpha_2) = (G^r, G^{r(v+wH(m))})$ on the message m. Then it computes the signature $\sigma_1 = \alpha_1, \sigma_2 = \alpha_1^t, \sigma_3 = \alpha_1^{t(y+H(ID_\pi||PK_{ID_\pi})z)+o+xH(m)}\alpha_2$ and returns $(\sigma_1, \sigma_2, \sigma_3)$ to $\mathcal{A}$.

Forgery. $\mathcal{A}$ outputs a forged signature $\sigma^* = (\sigma_1^*, \sigma_2^*, \sigma_3^*)$ on (ID^*, PK_{ID^*}, m^*). If $ID^* \neq ID_\pi$, $\mathcal{C}$ aborts. Otherwise, $\mathcal{C}$ computes

$$\alpha_2^* = \left(\frac{\sigma_3^*}{\sigma_1^{*o+xH(m^*)}\sigma_2^{*y+H(ID^*||PK_{ID^*})z}} \right) = G^{(v_{ID^*}+H(m^*)w_{ID^*})r^*}$$

and outputs a new valid tuple $(\alpha_1^* = \sigma_1^*, \alpha_2^*)$ on the new scalar $H(m^*)$ not asked the oracle $\mathcal{OPS}$. It is clear that $\mathcal{C}$ breaks the PS assumption.

Now we estimate the successful advantage of $\mathcal{C}$. In order to complete the simulation without aborting, the following conditions should be satisfied.

- In all private key queries, $ID_i \neq ID_\pi$;
- In the forgery phase, $ID^* = ID_\pi$.

The probability of ID_π selected by $\mathcal{A}$ is $1/q_U$. The probability of $ID_i \neq ID_\pi$ in the private key queries is $(1 - q_P/q_U)$. Thus, we can draw the conclusion that the successful advantage of $\mathcal{C}$ is

$$Adv_\mathcal{C} \geq \frac{\varepsilon(q_U - q_P)}{q_U^2},$$

which is non-negligible. Therefore, the proposed CBS scheme is existentially unforgeable against adaptive chosen message attack in *Game 2* if the PS assumption holds.

4.2 Efficiency Analysis

In this subsection, we compare the proposed CBS scheme with the schemes [20, 32] in the communication cost and computation overhead.

Communication Cost. We provide the communication cost comparison of the three schemes above in Table 1, where n is the output length of collision-resistant hash function in [20, 32]. For the sake of simplicity, we denote by PK system public parameter, by PK public key of user. We denote the size of the signature as Sig.Size, the size of the certificate as Cert.Size. Moreover, let $\mathbb{G}_1$, $\mathbb{G}_2$ be two groups belonging to Type 1 pairing. And let $|G_1|$, $|G_2|$, $|G|$ and $|\hat{G}|$ be the size of the group element in $\mathbb{G}_1$, $\mathbb{G}_2$, $\mathbb{G}$ and $\hat{\mathbb{G}}$, respectively.

Table 1. Comparison of communication cost

Scheme	PP	PK	Sig.Size	Cert.Size
Scheme [20]	$(n + 6)|G_1| + |G_2|$	$3|G_1| + |G_2|$	$3|G_1|$	$2|G_1|$
Scheme [32]	$(n + 3)|G_1|$	$4|G_1|$	$3|G_1|$	$2|G_1|$
Our scheme	$3|G| + 5|\hat{G}|$	$2|\hat{G}|$	$3|G|$	$2|G|$

Compared with the schemes [20, 32], the proposed scheme is superior in the communication cost. Specifically, the size of PP in the proposed scheme is independent of parameter n which only requires 3 group element in $\mathbb{G}$ and 5 group elements in $\hat{\mathbb{G}}$. Moreover, the size of PK in the proposed scheme is reduced to 2 group elements in $\hat{\mathbb{G}}$.

Computation Overhead. We give the computation overhead comparison of the three schemes above in Table 2, where n is the output length of collision-resistant hash function in [20,32]. We respectively use Cert, Sign and Verify to denote the algorithms of issuing certificate, signature and verification. We denote by M_1 a multiplication operation in $\mathbb{G}_1$, by M_2 a multiplication operation in $\mathbb{G}_2$, by $M_{\mathbb{G}}$ a multiplication operation in $\mathbb{G}$, by $M_{\hat{\mathbb{G}}}$ a multiplication operation in $\hat{\mathbb{G}}$, by $M_{\mathbb{T}}$ a multiplication operation in $\mathbb{T}$, by E_1 an exponentiation operation in $\mathbb{G}_1$, by E_2 an exponentiation operation in $\mathbb{G}_2$, by $E_{\mathbb{G}}$ an exponentiation operation in $\mathbb{G}$, by $E_{\hat{\mathbb{G}}}$ an exponentiation operation in $\hat{\mathbb{G}}$, by P_1 a Type 1 pairing operation, by P_2 a Type 3 pairing operation.

Table 2. Comparison of computation overhead

Scheme	Cert	Sign	Verify
Scheme [20]	$(n+1)M_1 + 3E_1$	$(n+3)M_1 + 6E_1$	$(n+2)M_1 + 3M_2 + E_1 + E_2 + 7P_1$
Scheme [32]	$(n+1)M_1 + 3E_1$	$M_1 + 4E_1$	$nM_1 + 3M_2 + 7P_1$
Our scheme	$2E_{\mathbb{G}}$	$3M_{\mathbb{G}} + 5E_{\mathbb{G}}$	$4M_{\hat{\mathbb{G}}} + M_{\mathbb{T}} + 3E_{\hat{\mathbb{G}}} + 3P_2$

Compared with the schemes [20,32], the proposed scheme requires lower computation overhead. More precisely, it is obvious that the computation complexity of the phases of Cert and Verify in the proposed scheme is independent of parameter n. And the proposed scheme is more efficient than [20] in the phase of Sign. Furthermore, note that fewer number of operations are performed in the phase of **Sign** of the scheme [32], but overall all algorithms of the proposed scheme mentioned above require less computational overhead than the scheme [32].

5   Conclusion

In this paper, we propose an efficient certificate-based signature scheme in the standard model based on the PS assumption and EPS assumption. We then show that the proposed scheme achieves the desired security properties. Finally, compared with the state-of-the-art constructions in the standard model, the proposed scheme is superior in both communication cost and computation overhead.

Acknowledgment. This work is supposed by the National Cryptography Development Fund (No. MMJJ20180110).

A   Appendix

Theorem 3. *The EPS assumption holds in the general bilinear group model: after q $\mathcal{OPS}$ oracle queries, k $\mathcal{OEPS}$ oracle queries and q_G group-oracle queries, no adversary can generate a valid tuple for a new pair with probability greater than $2(6 + 2q + 3k + q_G)^2/p$.*

Let $(\mathbb{G}, \hat{\mathbb{G}}, \mathbb{T}, e, p, G, \hat{G})$ be a Type 3 bilinear group, where G and $\hat{G}$ are generators of $\mathbb{G}$ and $\hat{\mathbb{G}}$, respectively. Let $O = G^o, \hat{O} = \hat{G}^o$, $X = G^x$, $\hat{X} = \hat{G}^x$, $\hat{Y} = \hat{G}^y$, $\hat{Z} = \hat{G}^z$ for some random scalars $o, x, y, z \in \mathbb{Z}_p$. Let $r_{1,i} \in \mathbb{Z}_p^*$ be the scalar such that the ith oracle answer from $\mathcal{OPS}(\cdot)$ on scalar l_i is answered by $(\alpha_{1,i} = G^{r_{1,i}}, \alpha_{2,i} = G^{r_{1,i}(y+l_i z)})$. Let $r_{2,j}, r_{3,j} \in \mathbb{Z}_p^*$ be the scalars such that the jth oracle answer from $\mathcal{OEPS}(\cdot)$ on pair (l^*, m_j) is answered by $(\beta_{1,j} = G^{r_{2,j}}, \beta_{2,j} = G^{r_{2,j}r_{3,j}}, \beta_{3,j} = G^{r_{2,j}((y+l^*z)r_{3,j}+o+xm_j)})$. Note that l^* is not allowed to access the oracle $\mathcal{OPS}(\cdot)$.

In the following, we associate group elements with polynomials whose formal variables are the above unknown scalars: $o, x, y, z, r_{1,1}, ..., r_{1,q}, r_{2,1}, ..., r_{2,k}$, $r_{3,1}, ..., r_{3,k}$, with first all the inputs available to the adversary: $\hat{O} = \hat{G}^o$, $\hat{X} = \hat{G}^x$, $\hat{Y} = \hat{G}^y$, $\hat{Z} = \hat{G}^z$ in $\hat{\mathbb{G}}$, $O = G^o$ $X = G^x$ in $\mathbb{G}$, $(\alpha_{1,i}, \alpha_{2,i}) = (G^{r_{1,i}}, G^{r_{1,i}(y+l_i z)})$ for $i = 1, ..., q$, and $(\beta_{1,j}, \beta_{2,j}, \beta_{3,j}) = (G^{r_{2,j}}, G^{r_{2,j}r_{3,j}}, G^{r_{2,j}((y+l^*z)r_{3,j}+o+xm_j)})$ for $j = 1, ..., k$ in $\mathbb{G}$. We must first prove that an adversary $\mathcal{A}$ is unable to symbolically produce a new valid tuple, and then that an accidental validity is quite unlikely.

For the output tuple $(\beta_1^*, \beta_2^*, \beta_3^*) = (G^{r_2^*}, G^{r_2^* r_3^*}, G^{r_2^*((y+l^*z)r_3^*+o+xm^*)})$ on a new pair (l^*, m^*), since $(G^{r_2^*}, G^{r_2^* r_3^*}, G^{r_2^*((y+l^*z)r_3^*+o+xm^*)})$ are elements in $\mathbb{G}$, they can just be combinations of previous tuples $(\alpha_{1,i}, \alpha_{2,i}), (\beta_{1,j}, \beta_{2,j}, \beta_{3,j}), G, O$ and X (without any help from elements in $\hat{\mathbb{G}}$): they have been built with queries to the oracle of internal law in $\mathbb{G}$, and so we know $((u_{1,i}, v_{1,i}, u_{2,i}, v_{2,i}, v_{3,i}, u_{3,i})_i$, $(a_{1,j}, b_{1,j}, c_{1,j}, a_{2,j}, b_{2,j}, c_{2,j}, a_{3,j}, b_{3,j}, c_{3,j})_j, (w_1, w_2, w_3), (w_1', w_2', w_3'), (w_1'', w_2'', w_3'')) \in \mathbb{Z}_p^{6q+9k+9}$ such that:

$$G^{r_2^*} = \beta_1^* = G^{w_1} O^{w_1'} X^{w_1''} \prod_{i=1}^{q} \alpha_{1,i}^{u_{1,i}} \alpha_{2,i}^{v_{1,i}} \prod_{j=1}^{k} \beta_{1,j}^{a_{1,j}} \beta_{2,j}^{b_{1,j}} \beta_{3,j}^{c_{1,j}},$$

$$G^{r_2^* r_3^*} = \beta_2^* = G^{w_2} O^{w_2'} X^{w_2''} \prod_{i=1}^{q} \alpha_{1,i}^{u_{2,i}} \alpha_{2,i}^{v_{2,i}} \prod_{j=1}^{k} \beta_{1,j}^{a_{2,j}} \beta_{2,j}^{b_{2,j}} \beta_{3,j}^{c_{2,j}},$$

$$G^{s^*} = \beta_3^* = G^{w_3} O^{w_3'} X^{w_3''} \prod_{i=1}^{q} \alpha_{1,i}^{u_{3,i}} \alpha_{2,i}^{v_{3,i}} \prod_{j=1}^{k} \beta_{1,j}^{a_{3,j}} \beta_{2,j}^{b_{3,j}} \beta_{3,j}^{c_{3,j}},$$

and thus

$$r_2^* = w_1 + o w_1' + x w_1'' + \sum_{i=1}^{q}(u_{1,i} r_{1,i} + v_{1,i}(r_{1,i}(y + l_i z)))$$

$$+ \sum_{j=1}^{k}(a_{1,j} r_{2,j} + b_{1,j} r_{2,j} r_{3,j} + c_{1,j}(r_{2,j} r_{3,j}(y + l^* z) + r_{2,j}(o + m_j x)))$$

$$r_2^* r_3^* = w_2 + o w_2' + x w_2'' + \sum_{i=1}^{q} (u_{2,i} r_{1,i} + v_{2,i}(r_{1,i}(y + l_i z)))$$

$$+ \sum_{j=1}^{k} (a_{2,j} r_{2,j} + b_{2,j} r_{2,j} r_{3,j} + c_{2,j}(r_{2,j} r_{3,j}(y + l^* z) + r_{2,j}(o + m_j x)))$$

$$s^* = w_3 + o w_3' + x w_3'' + \sum_{i=1}^{q} (u_{3,i} r_{1,i} + v_{3,i}(r_{1,i}(y + l_i z)))$$

$$+ \sum_{j=1}^{k} (a_{3,j} r_{2,j} + b_{3,j} r_{2,j} r_{3,j} + c_{3,j}(r_{2,j} r_{3,j}(y + l^* z) + r_{2,j}(o + m_j x)))$$

The validity of the new tuple implies that $s^* = r_2^* r_3^* (y + l^* z) + r_2^*(o + m^* x)$, which leads to:

$$w_3 + o w_3' + x w_3'' + \sum_{i=1}^{q} (u_{3,i} r_{1,i} + v_{3,i}(r_{1,i}(y + l_i z)))$$

$$+ \sum_{j=1}^{k} (a_{3,j} r_{2,j} + b_{3,j} r_{2,j} r_{3,j} + c_{3,j}(r_{2,j} r_{3,j}(y + l^* z) + r_{2,j}(o + m_j x)))$$

$$= y(w_2 + o w_2' + x w_2'' + \sum_{i=1}^{q} (u_{2,i} r_{1,i} + v_{2,i}(r_{1,i}(y + l_i z)))$$

$$+ \sum_{j=1}^{k} (a_{2,j} r_{2,j} + b_{2,j} r_{2,j} r_{3,j} + c_{2,j}(r_{2,j} r_{3,j}(y + l^* z) + r_{2,j}(o + m_j x))))$$

$$+ l^* z (w_2 + o w_2' + x w_2'' + \sum_{i=1}^{q} (u_{2,i} r_{1,i} + v_{2,i}(r_{1,i}(y + l_i z)))$$

$$+ \sum_{j=1}^{k} (a_{2,j} r_{2,j} + b_{2,j} r_{2,j} r_{3,j} + c_{2,j}(r_{2,j} r_{3,j}(y + l^* z) + r_{2,j}(o + m_j x))))$$

$$+ (o + m^* x)(w_1 + o w_1' + x w_1'' + \sum_{i=1}^{q} (u_{1,i} r_{1,i} + v_{1,i}(r_{1,i}(y + l_i z)))$$

$$+ \sum_{j=1}^{k} (a_{1,j} r_{2,j} + b_{1,j} r_{2,j} r_{3,j} + c_{1,j}(r_{2,j} r_{3,j}(y + l^* z) + r_{2,j}(o + m_j x))))$$

For the two multivariable polynomials to be equal, the same monomials should appear on both sides:

- no constant term on the right, so $w_3 = 0$;
- no term in $r_{1,i}$ on the right, $u_{3,i} = 0$ for all i;

- no term in $r_{2,j}$ nor $r_{2,j}r_{3,j}$ on the right, $a_{3,j} = b_{3,j} = 0$ for all j;
- no monomials of degree 4 on the left, so $c_{1,j} = c_{2,j} = 0$ for all j;
- no term in y, yo, yx, $y^2r_{1,i}$ and $yr_{2,j}$ on the left, so $w_2 = w_2' = w_2'' = 0$, $v_{2,i} = 0$ for all i, $a_{2,j} = 0$ for all j;
- no term in o^2, ox, $or_{1,i}$, $or_{1,i}y$ and $or_{2,j}r_{3,j}$ on the left, so $w_1' = w_1'' = 0$, $u_{1,i} = v_{1,i} = 0$ for all i, $b_{1,j} = 0$ for all j:

$$w_3'o + w_3''x + \sum_{i=1}^{q}(v_{3,i}r_{1,i}(y + l_iz)) + \sum_{j=1}^{k}(c_{3,j}(r_{2,j}r_{3,j}(y + l^*z) + r_{2,j}(o + m_jx)))$$

$$= w_1o + w_1xm^* + \sum_{i=1}^{q}(u_{2,i}(r_{1,i}(y + l^*z))) + \sum_{j=1}^{k}(b_{2,j}(r_{2,j}r_{3,j}(y + l^*z))$$

$$+ a_{1,j}r_{2,j}(o + m^*x)).$$

The monomial o implies $w_3' = w_1$, the monomial x implies $w_3'' = w_1m^*$. The monomials $r_{1,i}y$ imply $v_{3,i} = u_{2,i}$ for all i, and the monomials $r_{1,i}z$ imply $v_{3,i}l_i = u_{2,i}l^*$ for all i. Since $l_i \neq l^*$ for all i, so $v_{3,i} = u_{2,i} = 0$ for all i. The monomials $r_{2,j}r_{3,j}y$ imply $c_{3,j} = b_{2,j}$ for all j, the monomials $r_{2,j}o$ imply $c_{3,j} = a_{1,j}$ for all j, and the monomials $r_{2,j}x$ imply $c_{3,j}m_j = a_{1,j}m^*$ for all j. Since $r_2^*r_3^* \neq 0$, so there is at least one $b_{2,j} = c_{3,j} = a_{1,j} \neq 0$, and then $m^* = m_i$. Therefore, the tuple is not for a new pair which means that an adversary is unable to symbolically produce a valid tuple for a new pair.

Now, we evaluate the probability for an accidental validity: the same value is output by two different polynomials involved in the answers to the oracle. Note that the elements generated by the oracle and the public elements are associated with polynomials of degree at most 3 and 1, thus polynomials generated by querying to the different group oracle are of degree at most 4. We denote the maximum number of group-oracle queries by q_G. There are at most $2q+6+3k+q_G$ polynomials and at most $(2q+6+3k+q_G)^2/2$ pairs of distinct polynomials could evaluate to the same value. By the Schwartz-Zippel lemma, the probability of such an event occurs is $\leq 2(6 + 2q + 3k + q_G)^2/p$ which is negligible.

References

1. Al-Riyami, S.S., Paterson, K.G.: Certificateless public key cryptography. In: Laih, C.-S. (ed.) ASIACRYPT 2003. LNCS, vol. 2894, pp. 452–473. Springer, Heidelberg (2003). https://doi.org/10.1007/978-3-540-40061-5_29
2. Batten, L.M.: Public Key Cryptography. Applications and Attacks. Wiley-Blackwell, Hoboken (2016)
3. Chatterjee, S., Menezes, A.: On cryptographic protocols employing asymmetric pairings - the role of ψ revisited. Discret. Appl. Math. **159**(13), 1311–1322 (2011)
4. Cheng, L., Xiao, Y., Wang, G.: Cryptanalysis of a certificate-based on signature scheme. Procedia Eng. **29**, 2821–2825 (2012)
5. Fuchsbauer, G., Hanser, C., Slamanig, D.: Structure-preserving signatures on equivalence classes and constant-size anonymous credentials. J. Cryptol. **32**(2), 498–546 (2019)

6. Galbraith, S.D., Paterson, K.G., Smart, N.P.: Pairings for cryptographers. Discret. Appl. Math. **156**(16), 3113–3121 (2008)

7. Gentry, C.: Certificate-based encryption and the certificate revocation problem. In: Biham, E. (ed.) EUROCRYPT 2003. LNCS, vol. 2656, pp. 272–293. Springer, Heidelberg (2003). https://doi.org/10.1007/3-540-39200-9_17

8. Ghadafi, E.: Efficient round-optimal blind signatures in the standard model. In: Kiayias, A. (ed.) FC 2017. LNCS, vol. 10322, pp. 455–473. Springer, Cham (2017). https://doi.org/10.1007/978-3-319-70972-7_26

9. Ghadafi, E.: More efficient structure-preserving signatures - or: bypassing the type-III lower bounds. In: Foley, S.N., Gollmann, D., Snekkenes, E. (eds.) ESORICS 2017. LNCS, vol. 10493, pp. 43–61. Springer, Cham (2017). https://doi.org/10.1007/978-3-319-66399-9_3

10. Huang, R., Huang, Z., Chen, Q.: A generic conversion from proxy signatures to certificate-based signatures. J. Internet Technol. **22**(1), 209–217 (2021)

11. Hung, Y., Huang, S., Tsen, Y.: A short certificate-based signature scheme with provable security. Inf. Technol. Control. **45**(3), 243–253 (2016)

12. Kang, B.G., Park, J.H., Hahn, S.G.: A certificate-based signature scheme. In: Okamoto, T. (ed.) CT-RSA 2004. LNCS, vol. 2964, pp. 99–111. Springer, Heidelberg (2004). https://doi.org/10.1007/978-3-540-24660-2_8

13. Kumar, P., Sharma, V.: Insecurity of a secure certificate-based signature scheme. In: ICACCCN 2018, pp. 371–373. IEEE (2018). https://doi.org/10.1109/ICACCCN.2018.8748312

14. Li, J., Huang, X., Mu, Y., Susilo, W., Wu, Q.: Certificate-based signature: security model and efficient construction. In: Lopez, J., Samarati, P., Ferrer, J.L. (eds.) EuroPKI 2007. LNCS, vol. 4582, pp. 110–125. Springer, Heidelberg (2007). https://doi.org/10.1007/978-3-540-73408-6_8

15. Li, J., Huang, X., Mu, Y., Susilo, W., Wu, Q.: Constructions of certificate-based signature secure against key replacement attacks. J. Comput. Secur. **18**(3), 421–449 (2010)

16. Li, J., Huang, X., Zhang, Y., Xu, L.: An efficient short certificate-based signature scheme. J. Syst. Softw. **85**(2), 314–322 (2012)

17. Liu, D., Alahmadi, A., Ni, J., Lin, X., Shen, X.: Anonymous reputation system for IIoT-enabled retail marketing atop PoS blockchain. IEEE Trans. Ind. Inform. **15**(6), 3527–3537 (2019)

18. Liu, J.K., Baek, J., Susilo, W., Zhou, J.: Certificate-based signature schemes without pairings or random oracles. In: Wu, T.-C., Lei, C.-L., Rijmen, V., Lee, D.-T. (eds.) ISC 2008. LNCS, vol. 5222, pp. 285–297. Springer, Heidelberg (2008). https://doi.org/10.1007/978-3-540-85886-7_20

19. Liu, J.K., Bao, F., Zhou, J.: Short and efficient certificate-based signature. In: Casares-Giner, V., Manzoni, P., Pont, A. (eds.) NETWORKING 2011. LNCS, vol. 6827, pp. 167–178. Springer, Heidelberg (2011). https://doi.org/10.1007/978-3-642-23041-7_17

20. Lu, Y., Li, J.: Improved certificate-based signature scheme without random oracles. Inf. Secur. **10**(2), 80–86 (2016)

21. Ma, X., Shao, J., Zuo, C., Meng, R.: Efficient certificate-based signature and its aggregation. In: Liu, J.K., Samarati, P. (eds.) ISPEC 2017. LNCS, vol. 10701, pp. 391–408. Springer, Cham (2017). https://doi.org/10.1007/978-3-319-72359-4_23

22. Ni, J., Lin, X., Zhang, K., Shen, X.: Privacy-preserving real-time navigation system using vehicular crowdsourcing. In: VTC Fall 2016, pp. 1–5. IEEE (2016). https://doi.org/10.1109/VTCFall.2016.7881177

23. Ni, J., Zhang, K., Yu, Y., Lin, X., Shen, X.S.: Privacy-preserving smart parking navigation supporting efficient driving guidance retrieval. IEEE Trans. Veh. Technol. **67**(7), 6504–6517 (2018)
24. Pointcheval, D., Sanders, O.: Short randomizable signatures. In: Sako, K. (ed.) CT-RSA 2016. LNCS, vol. 9610, pp. 111–126. Springer, Cham (2016). https://doi.org/10.1007/978-3-319-29485-8_7
25. Schwartz, J.T.: Fast probabilistic algorithms for verification of polynomial identities. J. ACM **27**(4), 701–717 (1980)
26. Shamir, A.: Identity-based cryptosystems and signature schemes. In: Blakley, G.R., Chaum, D. (eds.) CRYPTO 1984. LNCS, vol. 196, pp. 47–53. Springer, Heidelberg (1985). https://doi.org/10.1007/3-540-39568-7_5
27. Wu, L., Zhang, Y., Ren, Y., He, D.: Efficient certificate-based signature scheme for electronic commerce security using bilinear pairing. J. Internet Technol. **18**(5), 1159–1166 (2017)
28. Wu, W., Mu, Y., Susilo, W., Huang, X.: Certificate-based signatures: new definitions and a generic construction from certificateless signatures. In: Chung, K.-I., Sohn, K., Yung, M. (eds.) WISA 2008. LNCS, vol. 5379, pp. 99–114. Springer, Heidelberg (2009). https://doi.org/10.1007/978-3-642-00306-6_8
29. Yu, Y., Zhao, Y., Li, Y., Du, X., Wang, L., Guizani, M.: Blockchain-based anonymous authentication with selective revocation for smart industrial applications. IEEE Trans. Ind. Inform. **16**(5), 3290–3300 (2020)
30. Zhang, J.: On the security of a certificate-based signature scheme and its improvement with pairings. In: Bao, F., Li, H., Wang, G. (eds.) ISPEC 2009. LNCS, vol. 5451, pp. 47–58. Springer, Heidelberg (2009). https://doi.org/10.1007/978-3-642-00843-6_5
31. Zhang, Y., Li, J., Wang, Z., Yao, W.: A new efficient certificate-based signature scheme. Chin. J. Electron. **24**(4), 776–782 (2015)
32. Zhou, C., Cui, Z.: Certificate-based signature scheme in the standard model. Inf. Secur. **11**(5), 256–260 (2017)
33. Zhu, L., Li, M., Zhang, Z., Qin, Z.: ASAP: an anonymous smart-parking and payment scheme in vehicular networks. IEEE Trans. Dependable Secur. Comput. **17**(4), 703–715 (2020)

Embedded System Security

SnakeGX: A Sneaky Attack Against SGX Enclaves

Flavio Toffalini[1]([✉]), Mariano Graziano[2], Mauro Conti[3], and Jianying Zhou[1]

[1] Singapore University of Technology and Design, Singapore, Singapore
flavio.toffalini@mymail.sutd.edu.sg, jianying_zhou@sutd.edu.sg
[2] Cisco Systems, Inc., Vimercate, Italy
magrazia@cisco.com
[3] University of Padua, Padua, Italy
conti@math.unipd.it

Abstract. Intel Software Guard eXtension (SGX) is a technology to create enclaves (*i.e.,* trusted memory regions) hardware isolated from a compromised operating system. Recently, researchers showed that unprivileged adversaries can mount code-reuse attacks to steal secrets from enclaves. However, modern operating systems can use memory-forensic techniques to detect their traces. To this end, we propose SnakeGX, an approach that allows stealthier attacks with a minimal footprint; SnakeGX is a framework to implant a persistent backdoor in legitimate enclaves. Our solution encompasses a new architecture specifically designed to overcome the challenges SGX environments pose, while preserving their integrity and functionality. We thoroughly evaluate SnakeGX against StealthDB, which demonstrates the feasibility of our approach.

Keywords: SGX · TEE · Code-reuse attacks

1 Introduction

Intel Software Guard eXtention (SGX) is a trusted computing technology that enables the creation of restricted user-space memory regions, called *enclaves* [34]. When digitally-signed, an enclave is a Trusted Execution Environment (TEE) that hardware-supported microcode isolates. This design, coupled with a full encryption of an enclave's content, provides advanced protection mechanisms and a trusted communication channel between the enclave and the host—the main application the enclave belongs to.

The success of SGX stems from its strict threat model. The attacker model—the Iago attacker [15]—considers the OS malicious: one can thus tamper with applications, modify their behavior, exfiltrate sensitive information, and so on. In this context, SGX disallows kernel- and user-space code to manipulate enclave memory pages, thus guaranteeing integrity and confidentiality in the presence of any Iago attacker.

K. Sako and N. O. Tippenhauer (Eds.): ACNS 2021, LNCS 12726, pp. 333–362, 2021.
https://doi.org/10.1007/978-3-030-78372-3_13

The strong isolation introduced by SGX stimulated researchers and practitioners to develop new attacks vectors [14,23,27,29]. Among them, an interesting research line is to exploit memory-corruption errors inside the enclave code and run one-shot code-reuse attacks to steal enclave secrets (*e.g.*, cryptographic keys) [40]. Recently, we observed many solutions that identify such flaws in enclaves [17,44] and new code-reuse techniques tailored for SGX [12,27]. First, Lee et al. discussed Dark-ROP [27] that combines a colluded OS and oracles to identify gadgets for return-oriented programming (ROP) [40]. An advanced technique was proposed by Biondo et al. with Guard's Dilemma [12] that does not require the assistance of the OS to perform the attack. In this scenario, however, the authors did not consider an OS that may employ existing memory forensic techniques to identify the intrusions [22,25,32,42]. For instance, in case of external intrusion into a remote server running SGX enclaves, the adversary is also interested in reducing the amount of traces left; otherwise, analysts may detect the intrusion and act consequently. This is even more critical in case the enclave secret changes and the adversary has to repeat the attack many times. Consequently, we pose a new research question:

Can we carry out an attack against SGX enclaves without being noticed by an healthy Operating System?

We answer this question with a new approach that pushes further the stealthiness of code-reuse attacks in non-compromised OSs. Our intuition is to implant a permanent payload inside the target enclave as a backdoor, thus exploiting the SGX protections to avoid inspection. Our strategy definitely overcomes the limitations of the state-of-the-art; the adversary does not need to repeat the attack and we minimize the traces left. We implement our intuition in SnakeGX, a framework to implant data-only backdoors in legitimate enclaves. We build on the concept of data-only malware [46] but extend it with a novel architecture to adhere to the strict requirements of SGX environments.

Contrary to prior one-shot attacks [12,27], our backdoor acts as an additional secure function (Sect. 5), which is: (i) **persistent** in the context of the enclave, (ii) **stateful** as it maintains an internal state, (iii) **interactive** with the host by means of seamless context switches. Core to this is the identification of a design flaw that affects the Intel SGX Software Development Kit (SDK) and allows an attacker to trigger arbitrary code in enclaves (Sect. 4).[1] SnakeGX facilitates the creation of versatile backdoors concealed in enclaves that evade memory forensic analysis by inheriting all the benefits SGX provides. Our aim is to raise awareness of TEEs—and SGX in particular—and how attackers may abuse that, which requires the community to reason more on the need of monitoring systems and advanced forensic techniques for SGX.

We evaluate the properties of SnakeGX against StealthDB [45], an open-source project that implements an encrypted database on top of SGX enclaves. In particular, StealthDB uses dynamically generated AES keys to protect the database's fields, thus urging the need of multiple one-shot attacks. SnakeGX exfiltrates the keys upon the verification of specific conditions with a minimum

---

[1] We reported the flawed behavior to Intel, which acknowledged it.

footprint. Our evaluation focuses on three aspects of SnakeGX (Sect. 6). First, we illustrate our use-case: we show how SnakeGX achieves its goals while preserving the original functionality of the enclave. Second, we measure and compare the stealthiness of SnakeGX against the state-of-the-art. Finally, we discuss possible countermeasures.

In summary, we make the following contributions:

- We propose SnakeGX, a framework built around an Intel SGX SDK design flaw (Sect. 4), and a novel architecture designed to create persistent, stateful, and interactive data-only malware for SGX (Sect. 5).
- We demonstrate the feasibility of SnakeGX on a real-world open source project.[2]
- We measure and compare the attack footprint with current SGX state-of-the-art techniques (Sect. 6).

2 Background

In this section, we illustrate the technical background for SGX (Sect. 2.1) and discuss code-reuse attacks applied to SGX enclaves (Sect. 2.2).

2.1 SGX Overview

The Intel SGX technology provides secure containers that execute so-called *secure functions* in an isolated context, thereby shielding them from tampering and monitoring attempts. These containers, properly known as enclaves, are the core of SGX programming patterns; they are digitally signed at compile time and represent the building blocks on which SGX achieves attestation.

SGX achieves a strong isolation by implementing a fine-grain memory access control at Memory Management Unit (MMU) level. These checks are implemented by using microcode and thus hardware assistant. This strategy allows SGX to validate memory access independently by the Operating System (OS). At enclave boot time, the OS sets enclave page permission. If those permissions differ from enclave signature, the microcode will raise an exception. Also, the kernel cannot change the page permission at run-time since microcode performs a double-check. Therefore, SGX ensures that the enclave is loaded as intended. This means that classic hacking strategies, which aim at setting a page as executable, are not useful against SGX. Some researchers exploited enclave misconfigurations to load a shellcode [12], but this is not the standard case. Since we cannot load custom code in an enclave, we opted for code-reuse programming (like ROP) [13]. This strategy allows us to re-use code already in memory without breaking enclave attestation.

In Fig. 1, we depict two basic interaction mechanisms between enclave and host process: synchronous and asynchronous. The synchronous interaction is implemented by two new leaf functions: EENTER and EEXIT. This interaction

---

[2] SnakeGX's source code is available at https://github.com/tregua87/snakegx.

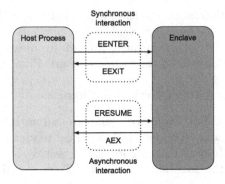

Fig. 1. The two types of enclave interaction, the pair `EENTER` and `EEXIT` are used in the synchronous interaction, while the pair `AEX` and `ERESUME` are used in the asynchronous one.

Table 1. `ENCLU` registers specification for x86 64bit.

Instr. leaf	RAX	RBX	RCX
EENTER	0x02	TCS	AEP
ERESUME	0x03	TCS	AEP
EEXIT	0x04	Target address	

is used to invoke secure functions within the enclave. The asynchronous one, instead, handles enclave exceptions (both software and hardware) and it is represented by an Asynchronous Enclave Exit (`AEX`). When an `AEX` happens, the exception is first thrown to the host (*i.e.,* to an Asynchronous Exit Pointer – `AEP`) that will examine the exception in the untrusted memory. The `AEP` can, eventually, resume the enclave execution through the leaf function `ERESUME`. Finally, the enclave can decide whether to internally manage the exception or interrupt the secure function execution.

The leaf functions described so far are implemented by using the real opcode `ENCLU`, that is available only in user-space. In x86 64bit, which is the platform we refer, we can execute `EENTER`, `ERESUME`, or `EEXIT` by calling `ENCLU` and setting CPU registers as described in Table 1.

Reading Table 1, we notice that `EENTER` and `ERESUME` require a Thread Control Structure (TCS) address as an input. A TCS is a structure that represents a thread in SGX programming pattern. This means that the threading policy is handled by the untrusted memory. `EEXIT`, instead, requires only a virtual-address as a target address in register `rbx`. This address contains the next instruction to execute inside the host process after the control leaves the enclave. `EENTER` and `ERESUME` can be used only by the host process in user-space, while `EEXIT` works only from inside the enclave.

2.2   Code-Reuse Attacks for SGX

In this section, we discuss code-reuse attacks techniques applied to the SGX realm and relative limitations.

Generally speaking, a code-reuse payload [12,27] requires specific structures that point to code inside the enclave (*i.e.,* gadgets). However, SGX does not allow an adversary to arbitrary write these structures inside an enclave. To achieve the intrusion, there are two strategies from the literature: (i) inject the entire payload inside the victim enclave as a malicious input buffer [27], or (ii) maintain the payload in the untrusted memory and tamper with the `rsp` register to point to the payload (*i.e.,* stack-pivoting) [12]. In both cases, the adversary has to maintain a copy of the payload in the untrusted memory. This enables an analyst to use known memory forensic techniques [22,25,32,42] to detect the payload, whose precision strictly depends on the amount of traces in memory. Furthermore, the adversary has to create new payloads every time she performs an attack, *i.e.,* a one-shot payload gets corrupted after being triggered [46]. These limitations increase the risk of being detected. Therefore, minimizing the amount of data in memory improves the probability of success of an intrusion. We achieve this goal with the installation of a permanent backdoor inside the enclave, thus avoiding the need of new attacks and evading the detection as well. In this way, SnakeGX makes stealthier and more sophisticated attacks than previous one-shot ones.

3   Threat Model and Assumptions

In this section, we first describe our threat model. Then, we perform a preliminary analysis to measure the widespread of our assumptions over real SGX open-source projects.

Threat Model. One of the differences between SnakeGX and the previous one-shot code-reuse works is in the threat model. Advanced code-reuse techniques require an unprivileged attacker [12]. However, a non-compromised host can identify the presence of an adversary in the system memory (Sect. 2.2). Therefore, we have to consider three players in our scenarios: the attacker, the victim enclave, and the host. Below, we list their requirements, respectively.

Attacker Capabilities. In our scenario, the attacker is highly motivated and has the following assumptions:

– **The enclave contains a memory corruption vulnerability.** The adversary is aware of a memory corruption error (*e.g.,* a buffer overflow) in the target enclave. This error can be exploited to take control of the enclave itself. Having a memory-corruption is an assumption already taken by similar works [12,27]. This is even more likely in projects that use SGX as a sub-system container [10,11,39,43]. Such projects host out-of-the-box software and, therefore, enclaves inherit their vulnerabilities.
– **A code-reuse technique.** SnakeGX does not require any specific code-reuse techniques (*e.g.,* ROP, JOP, BROP, SROP) as long as this enables the

attacker to take control of the enclave execution. For the sake of simplicity, we use the term *chain* to indicate a generic code-reuse payload (*e.g.,* a ROP-chain).

- **Knowledge of victim enclave memory layout.** The attacker can infer the memory layout by inspecting the victim address-space. It is also possible to leak memory information from within the enclave, as also assumed in [12].
- **Adversary Location.** In our scenario, the adversary resides in user-space. SnakeGX will reduce the adversary footprint, thus evading standard memory forensic techniques [22,25,32,42], whose effectiveness relies on the amount of traces left in memory (see Sect. 2.2).

Enclaves Capabilities. These are the assumptions for the enclave:

- **Legitimate enclaves.** The system contains one or more running enclaves. It is possible to exploit enclaves based on both SGX 1.0 or 2.0.
- **Intel SGX SDK usage.** The victim enclave should be implemented by using the standard Intel SGX Software Development Kit (SDK), we tested our approach with all the SDK versions currently available.[3] This is a reasonable assumption since the Intel SGX SDK provides a framework for developing applications on different OSs: Linux and Windows.
- **Multi-threading.** This is not strictly required, but the victim enclave should have at least two threads for a more general approach. The rationale behind this requirement is that the proposed implementation may disable a trusted thread [2] and in case of a single-thread application this is a problem. An enclave without free threads cannot process secure functions, thus attracting the analysts attention. We might partially ease this requirement with the introduction of SGX 2.0. However, multi-thread enclaves are a reasonable assumption since different open-source projects use already this feature [6,8, 43,45,49] and SGX-based applications are growing in complexity.

Host Capabilities. This is the assumption for the host:

- **Memory Inspection.** The host can inspect the processes memory and use standard approaches to detect traces of previous or ongoing attacks [22,25, 32,42].

We extend the threat model of previous works [12] by assuming the host can perform memory forensic analysis. Therefore, an adversary has the need of hiding her presence in the machine and minimizing the interactions with the victim enclave.

Preliminary Analysis of Assumptions. We collected a set of 27 stand-alone SGX open-source projects from an online hub [9] to investigate the correctness of our assumptions (see full list in Appendix D). The results show that among the 27 projects, 24 of them were based on the Intel SGX SDK, while others were

---

[3] At the time of writing, the last SDK version is 2.9.

developed with Graphene [43], Open Enclave SDK [28], or contained mocked enclaves. From the Intel SGX SDK based projects, we counted 31 enclaves in total, among which 24 were multi-threading (77%). This preliminary analysis indicates that our threat model fulfills real scenarios. Furthermore, we discuss the porting of SnakeGX over SDKs other than the Intel one in Sect. 7.

4   Intel SGX SDK Design Limitation

SnakeGX can trigger a payload inside the enclave without the need of repeating a new attack. This feature is challenging because the enclave has a fixed entry point, thus an adversary cannot activate arbitrary code inside the enclave from the untrusted memory. SnakeGX achieves this goal through a design error that affects all the SGX Software Development Kit (SDK) versions released by Intel. In this section, we make a deep analysis of the Intel SGX SDK in order to highlight these issues and propose possible mitigation.

4.1   SDK Overview

SGX specifications define only basic primitives for creating and interacting with an enclave. Thus, Intel also provides an SDK that helps building SGX-based applications. The Intel SGX SDK contains a run-time library that is composed by two parts: an untrusted run-time library (uRts) that is contained in the host process, and a trusted run-time library (tRts) that is contained in the enclave. Specifically, uRts handles operations like multi-threading, while tRts manages secure functions dispatching and context-switch.

The Intel SGX SDK exposes a set of APIs that are built on top of the leaf functions described in Sect. 2. ECALL, ERET, OCALL, and ORET are the most important APIs for SnakeGX. Figure 2 shows the interaction between the host process and the enclave. At the beginning, the host process invokes a secure function by using an ECALL, which is implemented by means of an EENTER (Fig. 2, step 1). When a secure function is under execution, it may need to interact with the OS (e.g., for writing a file). Since a secure function cannot directly invoke syscalls, Intel SGX SDK uses additional functions that reside in the untrusted memory (i.e., called outside functions). A secure function can invoke an outside function by using an OCALL (Fig. 2, point 2), that performs two steps: (i) save the enclave state, and (ii) pass the control to the outside function. More precisely, OCALL first saves the secure function state by using a dedicate structure called ocall_context, which we deeply analyze in Sect. 4.2. Then, OCALL uses the EEXIT leaf function to switch the context back to the uRts, that finally dispatches the actual outside function. Once an outside function ends, the control passes back to the secure function by using an ORET (Fig. 2, point 3). Since SGX does not allow to trigger arbitrary code from the untrusted memory (i.e., the enclave entry point is fixed), the Intel SGX SDK implements ORET as a special secure function (whose index is −2) that follows the standard ECALL specifications. As we discuss in the next sessions, ORET has the ability of activating

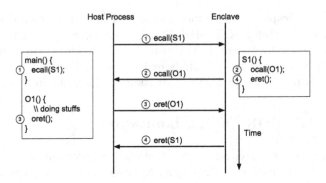

Fig. 2. Example of interaction between host process and enclave by using the Intel SGX SDK. The host process invokes the secure function S1 from the main function (ECALL). S1 function invokes O1 (OCALL), and this latter returns to S1 (ORET). Finally, S1 returns back to the main function (ERET).

arbitrary portion of code in an enclave. Normally, the ORET restores the state previously stored by the OCALL. Once the ORET is done, the secure function can continue its execution, and finally, invoke an ERET to terminate (Fig. 2, point 4).

4.2 OCALL Context Setting

The ocall_context is the structure that holds the enclave state once an OCALL is invoked. The way in which the structure is set slightly differs between Intel SGX SDK before and after version 2.0. In this discussion, we consider the case of the Intel SGX SDK greater than 2.0. However, a similar approach can be also applied to previous versions.

New ocall_contextes are located on top of the stack, as shown in Fig. 3, moreover, the new structures should follow a specific setting. In particular, three ocall_context fields should be tuned:

- pre_last_sp must point to a previous ocall_context or to the stack base address. This needs to handle a chain of nested ECALLs, which are basically ECALLs performed by an outside function.
- ocall_ret is used from SDK 2.0 to save extended process state [7]. More precisely, the system allocates a xsave_buff pointed by ocall_ret. This buffer must be located after the new ocall_context.
- rbp must point to a memory location that contains the new frame pointer and the return address, consecutively. This is because the asm_oret() function will use this structure as epilogue [12].

It is important to underline that SGX does not validate ocall_context integrity. Therefore, an attacker that takes control of an enclave may craft a fake ocall_context. This problem has been existing in all SDK version available so far. In the next section, we discuss why this is an underestimated problem and what threats can lead to.

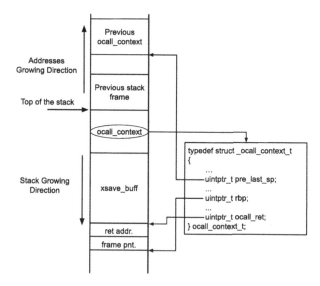

Fig. 3. Example of `ocall_context` disposition in an enclave stack, the fields point to structures within the stack itself in a precise order.

4.3 Exploiting an ORET as a Trigger

`ORET` is the only secure function that can trigger arbitrary code in an enclave. Therefore, an adversary enabled to abusing this function has also privileged access to the enclave itself. To understand why it is possible, we analyze the pseudo-code in Fig. 4, which shows the `do_oret()` secure function implementation. Essentially, `do_oret()` extracts the thread-local storage (TLS) from the current thread (Line 6). The TLS contains information of the last `ocall_context` saved. After some formal controls (Line 8), the `ocall_context` structure is used to restore the secure function execution through the `asm_oret()` function (Line 15). The formal checks performed by `do_oret()` over the previous `ocall_context` are quite naive. There are three basic requirements: (i) the `ocall_context` must be within the current stack space, (ii) the `ocall_context` must contain a constant (hard-coded) magic number, and (iii) the `pre_last_sp` must point before the actual `ocall_context`.

After the previous analysis, we realized that the Intel SGX SDK has no strict mechanisms to verify the integrity of an `ocall_context`. In other words, any `ocall_context` that fulfills the previous conditions can be used to restore any context in an enclave. First steps in this direction were explored by previous works [12], which exploited `asm_oret()` simply to control the processor registers in a one-shot code-reuse attack. However, we want to push further the limitation of the Intel SGX SDK and show which consequences these issues can lead to. In fact, SnakeGX uses a combination of `ORET` and tampered `ocall_context`es to restore arbitrary *chains* inside the enclave without performing further exploits. In particular, SnakeGX abuses of this flaw for two reasons: (i) as a trigger to

```
1  sgx_status_t do_oret()
2  {
3    // TLS structure
4    tls = get_thread_data();
5    // last ocall_context structure
6    ocall_context = tls->last_sp;
7
8    if (!formal_requirements(ocall_context))
9      return SGX_ERROR_UNEXPECTED;
10
11   // set TLS to point to previous ocall_context
12   tls->last_sp = ocall_context->pre_last_sp;
13
14   // restore last ocall_context
15   asm_oret(ocall_context);
16
17   // in the normal execution
18   // the control should not reach this point
19   return SGX_ERROR_UNEXPECTED;
20 }
```

Fig. 4. Simplified do_oret() pseudo-code.

activate a custom payload hidden inside the enclave; (ii) for the payload to perform a reliable context-switch between host and enclave. Therefore, crafting malicious ocall_contextes leads to the possibility of implanting backdoor in a trusted enclave without tampering the enclave code itself. As such, the backdoor is shielded by the SGX features by design. Moreover, the fact of using a single ORET to trigger the backdoor reduces the interactions required by a weak adversary for new attacks. We discuss technical details in Sect. 5 and show our proof-of-concept (PoC) in Sect. 6.

4.4 Mitigation

There are many strategies to improve the ocall_context integrity. A pure software solution could be computing an encrypted hash of ocall_context when it is generated. The hash might be appended as an extra field to the structure. Another approach, instead, could be encrypting the entire structure itself. However, pure software mitigation can be potentially bypassed by any code-reuse attack. Once the attacker gains control of the enclave, she can basically revert or fake any encrypted processes. A stronger solution could be introducing dedicated leaf functions that manage the generation and consumption of ocall_contextes. For instance, during an OCALL, the enclave might use a dedicated leaf function that creates an ocall_context and saves a copy (*i.e.*, an hash) in a memory location out of the attacker control (similar to TCS or SECS pages [18]). An ORET, then, should use another leaf function that performs extra checks and validate the integrity of the ocall_context. This solution might raise the bar for attacks, but it has two important drawbacks: (i) it forces Intel to re-thinking the SGX structures at low level, (ii) it leaves less freedom to developers that want to adapt the Intel SGX SDK to their own needs (*e.g.,* to customize or introduce new structures). After this consideration, we believe this issue would last for long before being fixed. We reported this limitation to Intel that is reviewing its memory corruption protections.

5   SnakeGX

SnakeGX is the first framework that facilitates the implanting of persistent, stateful, and interactive backdoors inside SGX enclaves. The framework design is challenging because we want to preserve the original enclave functionality and configuration. Even though SGX 2.0 encompasses run-time page permissions setting [3], an unexpected configuration may attract analysts attention (*i.e.,* the host can read the enclave page permissions). On the contrary, our solutions purely rely on code-reuse techniques that do not affect the enclave functionality and configuration. To the best of our knowledge, no previous works on SGX code-reuse attacks never addressed these challenges. We also recall we assume two conditions: (i) the target enclave has to be built with the Intel SGX SDK, and (ii) it contains at least one exploitable memory-corruption vulnerability (*e.g.,* a stack-based buffer overflow).

5.1   Overview

The backdoor implanting is composed by three main phases: (i) enclave memory analysis, (ii) installation phase, and (iii) payload triggering.

Enclave Memory Analysis. In this phase, the attacker has to achieve two goals: (i) inspect the process memory layout to identify enclave elements, and (ii) find a suitable location to install SnakeGX. Since SGX does not implement any memory layout randomization, an adversary can easily inspect the victim process memory by only using user-space privileges (*e.g.,* the enclave pages are assigned to a virtual device called *isgx* in Linux environments). Moreover, we target enclaves made with the Intel SGX SDK that follow the Enclave Linear Address Range (ELRANGE) [18]. As a result, an adversary with solely user-space privileges can obtain: (i) the enclave base address, (ii) the size, and (iii) the enclave trusted thread locations. In Sect. 5.2, we discuss how to obtain a reliable memory location.

Payload Installation. The installation phase is a one-shot attack that exploits an enclave vulnerability and uses a code-reuse technique for installing the payload. This attack has to achieve three goals: (i) copy the payload inside an enclave (*e.g.,* the *chain* and the fake `ocall_context`), (ii) set a hook to trigger the payload, (iii) resume the normal application behavior. These three goals make this phase quite critical for three reasons. First, either enclave and host process have to remain available after the payload installation, or else we have to re-start the enclave. Second, the enclave behavior does have not to change, or else the host should realize the attack. Finally, we have to remove the payload in the untrusted memory, or else it could be detected. This phase can be implemented by using any current code-reuse attacks for SGX enclaves [12,27].

Payload Triggering. After the installation phase, the adversary only needs to trigger an ORET to activate the payload (Sect. 5.3). This allows an external adversary to activate the payload without attacking the enclave from scratch. The payload contains the logic for interacting with the OS and the enclave. To achieve persistence, we design a generic architecture that fits the SGX realm (Sect. 5.4). Moreover, since the payload can potentially leave the enclave, we designed a generic context-switch mechanism that enables the payload to keep control over the enclave (Sect. 5.5).

5.2 Getting a Secure Memory Location

We employ a trusted thread as backdoor location because it allows us to abuse the design error described in Sect. 4. If an enclave does not have any available trusted thread, SnakeGX can still work by stealing one of the available threads. In this case, the target application may notice some degradation of the performances. However, the system does not raise any exception because it is not possible to determinate the real cause. In this way, we can take control of an enclave trusted thread without affecting enclave functionality. These properties are SGX specific and were not considered in previous code-reuse works.

Un-releasing a Trusted Thread. This technique is based on a misbehaviour of the thread binding mechanisms in the uRts library. Once a secure function is invoked through the Intel SGX SDK, the uRts searches a free trusted thread and marks it as *busy*. Then, the trusted thread is released when the secure function ends. However, an attacker can exploit a secure function and leaves the enclave skipping the *releasing* phase in the uRts. As a result, the trusted thread remains *busy* and it will never be assigned to future executions, in this way it is stolen. The strategy of this technique is composed by two phases: (i) invoking and exploiting a secure function, then (ii) exiting from the enclave (*e.g.,* by using EEXIT) and skipping the *releasing* of the trusted thread. This approach requires the enclave has at least two trusted threads, otherwise the application might realize that the enclave is unavailable. We use this approach for our PoC.

Making a New Thread. SGX 2.0 and recent versions of the Intel SGX SDK allow creating trusted threads at run-time. Therefore, an attacker may force the enclave to create a new trusted thread without tampering with the pool. However, this approach should be used wisely, otherwise unexpected trusted threads may attract the analyst attention, thus affecting the stealthiness of SnakeGX.

5.3 Set a Payload Trigger

We design our trigger on top of the Intel SGX SDK flaw highlighted in Sect. 4. We assume that an attacker has already gained control of an enclave by means of a code-reuse attack. Moreover, either the payload and the trigger must be tuned for the trusted thread under attack.

To install the trigger, the adversary has to mimic an OCALL such that the next ORET will activate the backdoor (*i.e.*, a *chain*) instead of resuming the execution of a secure function. To achieve this goal, the adversary has to perform three main operations: (i) set a fake ocall_context on the stack that satisfies the formal requirements as described in Sect. 4.2; (ii) call the function save_xregs() (which is contained in tRts) to save extended process features, the function should take as an argument the xsave_buff location of the fake ocall_context previously copied; (iii) call the function update_ocall_lastsp() (which is contained in tRts) by passing the pointer to the fake ocall_context. This function will set TLS last_sp to the fake ocall_context, thus simulating an OCALL.

This setting allows us to resume the payload execution by performing an ORET on the attacked trusted thread. More precisely, asm_oret() will restore the context previously installed and it will activate the first gadget. By default, ocall_context does not perform a pivot (*i.e.*, it does not set the rsp register). To bypass this issue, we used a pivot gadget that is contained in asm_oret() function itself: mov rsp, rbp; pop rbp; ret. This gadget is present in any SDK version released so far, so it is a generic technique for SGX backdoors. We observed the same gadget also in Windows tRts. Therefore, the first instruction triggered by the fake ocall_context is a pivot gadget. Then, we set the rbp to point to a fake stack inside the stolen thread. In this way, the ORET always pivots to the fake stack that contains the actual payload. Notice that this mechanism just pivots to the fake address indicated by the fake ocall_context (*i.e.*, rbp). As such, an attacker only needs one fake ocall_context that pivots to a fixed location. Then, she can just copy different fake stacks to the same location to activate different payloads.

5.4   Backdoor Architecture

Figure 5 shows the payload architecture that we adopted for SnakeGX. This solution allows us to achieve payload persistence in an SGX enclave by only using the stack address space. By default, the Intel SGX SDK sets the stack size at 40 KB, therefore, we design SnakeGX to fit this size. For the sake of simplicity, we describe the switching mechanism in Sect. 5.5.

As underlined in [46], classic code-reuse attacks (*e.g.*, ROP) are designed to be one-shot. After executing a *chain*, it may be destroyed due to gadgets side effects. Therefore, we need a location to keep a backup of the structures used. According to this consideration, we split the stack address memory in four sections:

Fake Frame. SnakeGX requires a dedicated location for installing an ocall_context. This structure is used to either perform the payload trigger and the context-switch (see Sect. 4). These features are crucial to implement a persistent backdoor in the SGX realm since classic techniques cannot be used.

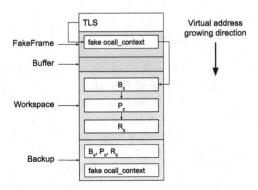

Fig. 5. Trusted thread stack after SnakeGX installation. The memory is split in four areas: FakeFrame, buffer, workspace, and backup. Moreover, the stack contains copies of B_c, P_c, and R_c.

Buffer. This area contains temporary variables that are used by payloads. For instance, our PoC stores the previous data exfiltrated (see Sect. 6).

Workspace. The fake frame previously installed is tuned to pivot the execution to this location. Generally speaking, any payload is coped here before being executed.

Backup. This location contains a copy of all the structures needed by SnakeGX to work properly. After the SnakeGX installation, this location should not be overwritten.

Since the *chains* used may be destroyed after payload execution, we need a mechanism that brings SnakeGX to the initial state after the payload has been executed. More precisely, it has to make the payload available for future invocations. To achieve this goal, we use three *chains*: Boot Chain (B_c), Payload Chain (P_c), and Reset Chain (R_c). Each of them is formed by a fake stack that is maintained in the backup zone and moved in the workspace on demand:

Boot Chain (B_c). This is the first chain that is triggered by the hook, its duties are: (i) copy P_c and R_c into the workspace, and (ii) pivot to P_c. This chain is usually quite short.

Payload Chain (P_c). This contains the actual payload and is strictly enclave dependent. When the payload ends, it just pivots to R_c.

Reset Chain (R_c). This *chain* resets the payload inside the enclave and makes it ready for the next calls without the need of the installation phase. This is achieved with the following operations: (i) copy B_c into workspace, (ii) copy the `ocall_context` in the fake frame, (iii) set TLS to point to `ocall_context`.

After the execution of R_c, SnakeGX can be triggered again by a new ORET. The loop boot-payload-reset *chain*, along the architecture shown in Fig. 5, is a simple framework that can be used by the adversaries to design their customized payload for SnakeGX.

5.5   Context-Switch

To allow SnakeGX to interact with the host OS, while maintaining the enclave control, we need to perform three operations: (S1) temporarily copy part of the payload outside, (S2) leave the enclave, and (S3) resume the execution inside the enclave. The first two operations are relatively simple: the Intel SGX SDK already provides standard routines (*e.g.*, memcpy) to move data outside the enclave. Moreover, it is possible to pivoting outside the enclave by abusing the EEXIT opcode (Sect. 2). On the contrary, resuming the enclave execution requires SnakeGX to invoke an EENTER opcode. However, it is not possible to arbitrarily jump inside an enclave (*i.e.*, the entry point is fixed). Therefore, we abuse again of the Intel SGX SDK deign error described in Sect. 4.

To perform the context-switch, we split the payload in three chains, called outside-chain (O_c), payload-one (P_1), and payload-two (P_2). O_c is the part of the payload copied in the untrusted memory, while P_1 and P_2 remain inside the enclave. During the context-switch, we execute P_1, O_c, and P_2, consequently. More precisely, once P_1 requires to interact with the host, it performs (S1) to prepare the O_c activation, installs a fake frame (Sect. 5.4), and prepares P_2 in the workspace. At this point, P_1 can perform (S2): leave the enclave and pivot to O_c. When the operations in untrusted memory are terminated, O_c only needs to run an ORET that will activate P_2 (S3). Finally, P_2 can clean the traces left by O_c and continue the backdoor execution. It is possible to perform many context-switch by tuning the payload accordingly.

6   Experimental Evaluation

We evaluate the real impact of our framework against StealthDB [45], an open-source project that leverages on the SGX technology. We opted for StealthDB because it is a generic representation of our scenario, as we describe in Sect. 6.1. We split our evaluation in three parts: (i) a technical discussion of our use-case (Sect. 6.2), (ii) a measurement of the traces left (Sect. 6.3), and (iii) a discussion about the countermeasures (Sect. 6.4).

6.1   StealthDB

StealthDB [45] is a plugin for PostgreSQL [20] that uses Intel SGX enclaves to implement an encrypted database. This project is the ideal use-case for SnakeGX: StealthDB lifetime is bounded to PostgreSQL, thus we can rely on its enclaves as a secure save point for storing the payload and launching the attacks.

StealthDB uses a single SGX enclave to handle encrypted fields and operations that are performed inside the enclave itself. In this way, the database can securely save encrypted fields on disk, while the plain values are handled only inside the enclave. The encryption algorithm is AES-CTR with keys 128 bits long. These keys are sealed on the disk through the standard SGX features. A user can define multiple keys that are loaded on-demand inside the enclave, however, the StealthDB enclave maintains in memory only a single key at a time.

In this scenario, one-shot state-of-the-art techniques require multiple interactions to obtain all the keys. This approach leaves more copies of the payload in the memory, thus increasing the risk of being detected. Even if an adversary manages to obtain all the sealed keys, she still has to perform new attacks whenever a new key is generated. SnakeGX is able to understand when a new key is loaded and performs the exfiltration steps accordingly. In this way, the attacker transparently hides and activates complex logic that resides inside a trusted enclave.

6.2   Use-Case Discussion

In this section, we discuss the properties of our PoC payload and some implementation details. For more technical details about our payload see Appendix A. Our setup is composed by an application that loads StealthDB enclave and performs the attacks. We extracted the gadgets for the *chains* by running ROPGadget [1] on the compiled enclave. As our threat model details in Sect. 3, we introduced a memory corruption vulnerability in StealthDB to simplify the payload delivery. We developed our data-only malware for SGX in a host OS running Linux with kernel 4.15.0 and Intel SGX SDK version 2.9.

We composed our PoC of three steps. First, the application starts and loads the enclave. Second, we exploit the enclave vulnerability and implant the payload. Third, we alternatively invoke normal secure functions and the backdoor. This shows that SnakeGX does not alter the normal enclave functionality. Once the backdoor is triggered, SnakeGX exfiltrates the keys only when the condition is satisfied. Without using SnakeGX, the adversary has to perform many attacks to achieve the same goal, which potentially leaves traces for an analyst. Moreover, SnakeGX avoids the burden of crafting new payloads at each exfiltration.

The Payload. Our payload shows three important features: (i) persistence, (ii) internal state, and (iii) context-switch. More precisely, the payload exfiltrates a key if and only if it changes. This is crucial in our threat model (Sect. 3), which assumes a non-compromised host, thus the attacker has to reduce unuseful actions. In fact, all the payload structures are kept inside the enclave, and an adversary only needs to trigger an ORET against the compromised thread. Once activated, the payload is able to self-check its status, and in case, leak the key. The payload is composed by three *chains*:

- P_1 is the first payload to be activated. It checks if the key changed, and in case activates the exfiltration.
- O is the outside-chain that actually exfiltrates the key. It is temporary copied in the untrusted memory by P_1.
- P_2 is the second payload that is triggered by O after the exfiltration. The purpose of P_2 is to wipe out all the temporary structures previously copied in the untrusted memory, *i.e.*, O and the key.

From an external analyzer, all the structures (*i.e.*, P_1, P_2, and O) are always contained in the enclave when the payload is not activated. The only *chain* temporary copied outside is O, but P_2 cleans its traces. Moreover, to activate the payload, the attacker only needs to trigger an ORET instead of preparing complex code-reuse attacks. In Sect. 6.3, we measure and compare the traces of SnakeGX *w.r.t.* the state-of-the-art attacks.

Chains Composition. Our payload maintains an internal state and interacts with the host. To handle the state, the payload is able to perform a conditional pivoting by comparing the current key and a copy of the last key exfiltrated [40]. The conditional chain is implemented in P_1. Once the key changes, P_1 will pivot to a *chain* that performs the exfiltration. Otherwise, the payload will pivot to another *chain* that simply resumes the normal enclave behavior. We describe the gadgets used to perform conditional pivoting in Appendix B. The interaction with the OS, instead, requires two types of *chains*: some that run inside the enclave (*i.e.*, P_1 and P_2), and others that run outside (*i.e.*, O). Table 2 shows some statistics about *chains* composition. The *chains* inside the enclave are entirely composed by gadgets from the tRts. More precisely, P_1 and P_2 invokes 27 and 13 functions such as memcpy(), and update_ocall_lastsp(), respectively. In terms of memory, P_1 and P_2 occupy 2816 and 1232 byes, respectively. The chain O, instead, is composed by classic gadgets from libc. More precisely, O is composed by 20 small standard gadgets. The internal ecosystem of tRts, and the libc in Linux systems, provide enough gadgets and functions to create useful payloads. We describe the gadgets used for these *chains* in Appendix C.

Table 2. Statistics of the gadgets used for the payload.

Chain	# fnc/sys	# gadgets	Size [B]
P_1	27	23	2816
P_2	13	7	1232
O	4	20	312
Sum	44	50	4360

6.3   Trace Measurements

We analyze our PoC and measure the advantages SnakeGX introduces. We recall that our threat model assumes a weak adversary which has no control of the host, and therefore, she has to improve her stealthiness. To perform the same goal of our PoC by using state-of-the-art one-shot attacks [12], an attacker has to leave in the untrusted memory around 4 KB of structures (*i.e.*, P_1, P_2 and O). These traces can be found by using previous results already shown in the literature [22,25,32,42]. Moreover, their identification results even simpler since they use peculiar structures such as sgx_exception_info_t (see Appendix A). On the contrary, SnakeGX requires only one ORET to trigger the payload. In particular, our PoC implements an ORET by using only 4 gadgets and leaving a negligible footprint of 56 byes in memory. As a result, the trigger used by SnakeGX is able to activate payloads arbitrary complex by leaving a minimal footprint.

6.4   Countermeasures

SnakeGX poses new challenges for forensic investigators and backdoor analysts as well as for experienced reverse engineers. The current state-of-the-art tools cannot detect and dissect this new threat. It is necessary to develop new tools and techniques for the detection and possibly the prevention of threats affecting SGX and similar technologies. Here, we discuss some possible directions for the detection that can be used to observe the presence of SnakeGX in a system. Moreover, we analyze how the current state-of-the-art defenses can mitigate our attack and which future research lines can be taken. This is not a comprehensive study and we leave this part for future work. We hope this research paves the way for new works in the malware analysis field.

Memory Forensic Analysis. SnakeGX is an infector of legitimate enclaves and is by definition stealthier. This means that any form of memory forensics is no more possible. The memory of the enclave cannot be inspected. As explained in Sect. 2, SGX makes impossible to read memory pages that belong to an enclave. Any attempts at reading such pages will result in a fake value 0xFF. Another possible approach is to use new attacks based on microcode flaws [14] or fault injections [29] to dump an enclave content. Alternatively, it is possible to use side-channel attacks to infer specific enclave manipulations, as discussed in [31]. It should also be pointed out that it is still possible to retrieve uRts information. For instance, we could compare the number of trusted threads in uRts and the number of trusted threads in the ELRANGE structure. An inconsistency will bring to clues regarding the state of that enclave.

Sandboxes. Recently, researchers proposed sandboxes to reduce the interaction of a malware-enclave and the system [48]. These solutions are designed for systems that cannot assess the origin of an enclave beforehand, thus they do not trust it. These defenses can, in principle, reduce the attack surface of SnakeGX. However, since we target only systems that host known and trusted enclaves, we do not expect sandboxes in place. In the worst case, we can still detect the presence of a sandbox by probing the process (*i.e.,* through a syscall) and interrupt the attack.

Syscalls Trace. Even though the payload is hidden from reading, it is still possible to analyze the syscall interaction of the outside-chains. This approach has been extensively studied and it is quite common in the field of malware analysis. Researchers may design a tracer and superficially focus on the interaction with the enclave. For instance, this tool may spot that SnakeGX generated a file operation that did not appear in previous interactions. In this way, analysts can infer the behaviour of the code inside the enclave.

Control Flow Integrity Checks. Control Flow Integrity checks (CFI) are strong weapons already used in standard programs to mitigate code-reuse attacks. Such mechanisms rely on different strategies to force a program to execute only valid paths at run-time. In the current enclave implementation, the system relies on classic stack canary to avoid buffer overflow. However, Lee et al. [27] discussed a technique to bypass such protection. Other non-standard systems, such as SGX Shield [39], implement a custom CFI to mitigate these issues. However, Biondo et al. [12] managed to bypass their protection too. So far, there are not effective defenses against code-reuse attacks in the context of enclaves. This approach might raise the bar for attackers who would attempt to deploy SnakeGX or to perform code-reuse attacks in general.

Detecting Fake Structures. SnakeGX exploits the possibility to craft fake structures that are used in critical tRts functions, *i.e.,* ocall_context. We deeply analyzed this issues and proposed mitigation strategies in Sect. 4.4.

7   Discussion

Here, we discuss various aspects of SnakeGX generalization.

7.1   SnakeGX Portability

The current implementation of SnakeGX is based on a specific version of the Intel SGX SDK, for a specific application and operating system. In this section, we study the portability of our PoC and show the approach is generic and can be easily adapted to other SDKs and OSs. Recently, new SGX frameworks were released on the market, or research prototypes, to provide an abstraction layer that simplifies the enclave development. In particular, projects such as Open Enclave [28], Google Asylo [21], and SGX Shield [11] use the standard Intel SGX SDK to perform host interaction (*i.e.,* OCALL/ORET), thus inheriting the same limitations described in Sect. 4. From our point of view, we can implant SnakeGX in any enclave developed with these frameworks if they follow our threat model assumptions (Sect. 3). We also analyzed the Intel SGX SDK for Windows, in which we found and tested the same flaw described in our work. Finally, the standard tRts libraries contain all the gadgets used in our PoC. In general, SnakeGX can potentially affect enclaves developed on different SDKs as long as: (i) they are abstraction layers of the Intel SGX SDK, or (ii) they use a host interaction that relies on unprotected structures like ocall_context. In this paper, we proposed an instance of SnakeGX targeting StealthDB on Linux. However, the idea is generic and the persistence, stateful, and context-switch properties can be found and achieved also in other OSs and popular SDKs based on the Intel one.

7.2   Persistence Offline

SnakeGX maintains persistence in memory as long as the host enclave is loaded. This is similar to what Vogl et al. [46] have shown with "Chuck". In their proof of concept they achieved persistence on the running system. Their ROP rootkit did not survive after reboot. In our scenario, SnakeGX may achieve a more complete persistence by exploiting the sealing mechanism. In this case, the malicious payload would not be affected if the enclave is restarted. This sealing mechanism is a common SGX practice. It saves the enclave state (*i.e.,* its data) before the enclave shuts down. If the victim enclave has a loophole in the restoring phase, this could be exploited to inject SnakeGX again after a reboot. However, this is strictly enclave-dependent and therefore we did not include in our discussion and it is left for the future.

7.3   SnakeGX 32bit

In this paper, we designed our PoC for 64bit architectures. However, Intel SGX supports also 32bit code to run in enclaves. From our point of view, the main difference between 32bit and 64bit is the calling convention. Therefore, the techniques we discussed and used for SnakeGX are still valid and can be easily ported to 32bit applications.

8   Related Work

SnakeGX combines properties from different research areas. Here, we discuss the difference with classic malware-enclaves works (Sect. 8.1), memory corruption errors (Sect. 8.2) and data-only- malware (Sect. 8.3).

8.1   Enclaves as Malware

SnakeGX implants a malware (*i.e.,* a backdoor) in a legit enclave. Researchers already investigated SGX isolation properties as malware container in previous works [4,5,19,33,36–38]. However, all these approaches require the introduction of a new enclave in the system. The main issue of this approach is that an unexpected enclave can be detected and, consequently, attract analysts' attentions. On the contrary, SnakeGX hides its presence in a running and legitimate enclave thus proposing a new approach for malware-enclave.

Nguyen et al. [30] proposed EnGarde, which is an enclave loader that checks whether the enclave matches a set of predefined policies in order to avoid loading potentially dangerous code. In this way, it is no more possible to introduce a new malicious enclave in the system. However, once an enclave is loaded, it follows standard SGX specification and SnakeGX can take control of it if its assumptions are satisfied.

To mitigate malware-enclaves, Weiser et at. introduced SGXJail [48], which is the first sandbox for untrusted enclaves. In their scenario, the authors assume that a malicious enclave is developed on purpose and then deployed in a machine without being inspected (*e.g.,* the enclave is shipped as encrypted). Once installed, the malicious enclave can launch several attacks, *e.g.,* leak information, compromise the host. SGXJail restricts the enclave interaction by mean of a sandboxed process with a very narrowed number of syscalls enabled. In principle, the design of SGXJail reduces the attack surface of SnakeGX. However, since we attack only trusted enclaves (*i.e.,* enclaves that were verified beforehand), we consider reasonable not to assume sandboxes in place. In addition, we can implement a sandbox detection to avoid the infection, *i.e.,* we can probe the host process by running specific syscalls during the installation phase and, in case, interrupt the attack.

8.2 Memory Corruption

SGX applications are not immune to flaws that may lead to memory corruption attacks. In this scenario, the attacker can use classic exploitation techniques. However, it is important to underline that the SGX isolation by default complicates the exploitation phase. In this hostile environment, Lee et al. [27] developed Dark-ROP, a technique to gain information about the enclave to build a successful attack. The work of Lee et al. [27] forces a victim enclave to crash and restart many times to look up the gadgets and build the ROP-chains. Their strategy is reasonable since they assume the entire host as compromised, and therefore, the adversary has no need to hide its presence. An optimized strategy has been proposed by Biondo et al. [12], in which they assume a non-compromised host. The goal of Biondo is to gain control of the enclave in a single iteration. However, as we discussed in Sect. 6.3, the strategy of Biondo leaves a certain amount of traces that can be detected. SnakeGX, instead, improves its stealthiness by permanently injecting a backdoor in the enclave. As a result, SnakeGX just needs an ORET to activate payloads arbitrary complex. This increases the stealthiness of our attack in case of a non-compromised host. To achieve our goal, we overcame new challenges, such as persistence in an enclave by solely using code-reuse attacks and expanding the data-only malware model by proposing new techniques. To the best of our knowledge, these novel challenges have not been discussed and solved for SGX technology before.

Other works in the literature investigated memory integrity mechanisms for SGX enclaves. Dmitrii et al. implemented SGXBounds [26]. This tool instruments enclave code to mitigate memory corruption errors. Unfortunately, SGXBounds has been developed only for SCONE [10], which is a project that enforces Docker containers by using small enclaves. Schuster et al. describe VC3 [35], which is a Map-Reduce framework based on SGX. Since VC3 takes custom software as an input, the authors developed a set of static-code checks to limit memory corruption issues. To reduce memory corruptions flaws, Wang et al. [47] described a Rust environment for SGX. However, as underlined by the authors, even with a framework written in a safe programming language we cannot solve all the memory corruption issues. Shih et al. [41] proposed T-SGX, which reduces the amount of information gathered from enclave crashes and limited the impact of attacks like Dark-ROP. SnakeGX, however, is a generic framework that can rely on any code-reuse attack for SGX enclaves. For instance, Van Bulck et al. [44] conducted a systematic study of the memory errors in the SGX run-time libraries and they found several flaws in different projects. Cloosters et al. [17] proposed TeeRex, an automatic analyzer for memory corruption errors in enclaves. All these defensive works show a limitation in the SGX design. This technology shields all the threats from the outside but has almost no protections to harden a flawed application running inside the enclave. Unfortunately, all the proposed defensive solutions are not ready for a real production deployment and do not entirely solve the problem. In many cases they can be bypassed and, at the moment, there are code-reuse attacks [12,27] able to disarm standard and additional SGX memory-integrity mechanisms.

8.3   Data-Only Malware

Data-only malware is any malicious payload that does not introduce or change any existing code into the system [46]. Data-only malware are based on code-reuse techniques such as ROP and JOP, and can hijack the control flow of the target application. This is possible by exploiting a vulnerability and crafting a specific payload. The payload implementing the malicious functionality is usually "one-shot". The first data-only malware proposed by Hund et al. [24] and Chen et al. [16] managed to bypass state-of-the-art protections and they were based on ROP and JOP techniques, respectively. However, both works lack of persistence. This means that if the attacker wants to repeat the same action, she needs to exploit again the same vulnerability. The concept of persistence for data-only malware and more in general for code-reuse attacks has been discussed and solved by Vogl et al. [46] for the x86 architecture. They proposed "Chuck" the first persistent data-only (ROP) rootkit. However, the solutions used in Chuck cannot be transparently adapted to the SGX realm, and therefore, we expanded their work and introduced novel techniques to have a data-only malware for SGX. Our contributions are described in Sect. 5.

9   Conclusion

Recent code-reuse attacks against SGX enclaves can exfiltrate secrets without depending on compromised OSs. This scenario opens new possibilities in which the OS can inspect the memory and identify the intrusion as well. Furthermore, analyzing the state-of-the-art of code-reuse techniques for SGX, we realized that current memory-forensic results can find traces of the attack.

With this in mind, we proposed a new stealthy code-reuse attack that minimizes its presence against a healthy OS. Our intuition is to implant a backdoor inside the victim enclave. Consequently, an adversary just needs a minimal trigger without repeating the attack from scratch. We implemented our idea in SnakeGX, which is a framework to install backdoors in SGX enclaves that behave like additional secure functions. SnakeGX extends and adapts to the strict SGX environment the concepts of data-only malware [46]. In particular, SnakeGX has a reliable context-switch mechanism based on a newly discovered design error of the Intel Software Development Kit for SGX, which we reported to Intel.

We evaluated our findings against StealthDB, an open-source project that implements an encrypted database. Our experiments show that we can reduce the memory footprint of the payload while preserving the enclave functionality. Our proof-of-concept is publicly available for the community.[4]

Acknowledgments. We would thank Lorenzo Cavallaro and Fabio Pierazzi for the fruitful discussions and insights. We would also thank the anonymous reviewers for their valuable comments.

A   Code-Reuse Technique

To show the feasibility of SnakeGX, we choose for our proof-of-concept the technique described by Biondo et al. [12]. This means that SnakeGX uses ROP. However, as stated in Sect. 3, SnakeGX does not rely on a specific technique, but it does require one to control its behavior. Moreover, we adapted their approach to work on the Intel SGX SDK newer versions.

In the original approach, the authors exploited `asm_oret()` and `continue_execution()` functions. More precisely, they crafted a set of fake frame in order to create a loop between these functions. In the x64 architecture, the first four function parameters are passed by registers. Therefore, the authors used `asm_oret()` for setting `continue_execution()` registers pointing to a controlled structure. However, as also Biondo underlined, it is more complicated to use `asm_oret()` for SDK 2.0. This is why in our approach we substituted `asm_oret()` with a *glue gadget*. This might be any gadget that sets the input register for the `continue_execution()` function. Since we developed our proof-of-concept for Linux 64bit, `continue_execution()` expects the first argument (*i.e.*, a `sgx_exception_info_t` address) in the `rdi` register. This is achievable by using a classic `pop rdi` gadget. Windows, instead, follows a different calling convention and `continue_execution()` expects an `ocall_context` address shifted by 8 byes in the `rcx` register. Therefore we used a `pop rcx` as a *glue gadget*. In our evaluation, we found `pop rdi` and `pop rcx` gadgets in the Intel SGX SDK version for Linux and Windows, respectively.

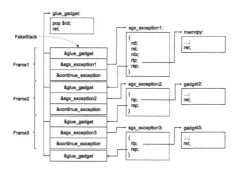

Fig. 6. Chain used in the proof-of-concept of SnakeGX.

---

[4] SnakeGX's source code is available at https://github.com/tregua87/snakegx.

Figure 6 describes our code-reuse technique. The attacker crafts a fake stack that can reside inside or outside the enclave, we used both approaches. The fake stack is composed by frames, one of which contains in order: (i) a *glue gadget* address, (ii) a fake `sgx_exception_info_t` address, (iii) the `continue_execution()` address. Once the first *glue gadget* is triggered, it will set rdi (or rcx in Windows) register pointing to the fake `sgx_exception_info_t` structure. Then, the `continue_execution()` will set registers according to `sgx_exception_info_t` and it will also pivot to the actual gadget. Since `continue_execution()` allows us to control all general registers, we can easily invoke another function instead of a simple gadget (*e.g.*, `memcpy` in Frame 1). Finally, the gadget will return at the beginning of the next frame. At this point, the CPU will trigger a new *glue gadget* and the attack continues.

Our technique is more flexible compared to the one described by Biondo. By using a *glue gadget*, we can easily drive `continue_execution()` without relying on other SDK functions that might change in future versions.

B   Conditional Chain

Conditional ROP-chain, the chain is triggered by using `sgx_exception_info_t` structure that configures the initial registers (see Appendix A). The SP register is perturbed if the value of `&lastKey` differs from the value of `&key` in order to pivot a true or a false ROP-chain, respectively.

```
1   /// we set the following registers through
2   /// a sgx_exception_info_t structure:
3   /// rdi = &lastKey; last key exfiltrated
4   /// rax = &key; current key loaded
5   /// rdx = #offset; to pivot to the false ROP-chain
6   /// rcx = &true-chain; address of the true ROP-chain
7   mov eax, dword ptr [rax] ; ret
8   mov rdi, qword ptr [rdi + 0x68] ; ret
9   cmp eax, edi ; sete al ; movzx eax, al ; ret
10  neg eax ; ret
11  and eax, edx ; ret
12  add rax, rcx ; ret
13  xchg rax, rsp ; ret
14  // 0x80 nops for padding
15  // beginning of true ROP-chain
16  pop rdi ; ret
17  // context to pivot to the ROP-chain that implements the
        true branch
18  &context_true
19  // address of continue_execution function
20  &continue_execution
21  // beginning of false ROP-chain
22  pop rdi ; ret
23  // context to pivot to the ROP-chain that implements the
        false branch
```

```
24    &context_false
25    // address of continue_execution function
26    &continue_execution
```

C   Context-Switch Chain

Details of the `sgx_exception_info_t` structures used to leak the key and to switch outside the enclave. The structures are used according to the techniques described in Appendix A.

```
1   /* ...previous sgx_exception_info_t structures... */
2   // leaks the key outside the enclave
3   // memcpy(key, buff)
4   ctxPc[2].cpu_context.rsi = &key; // address of the key
5   ctxPc[2].cpu_context.rdi = &buff; // memory regions where
        leaking the key
6   ctxPc[2].cpu_context.rdx = KEY_LENGTH; // length of the key
7   ctxPc[2].cpu_context.rip = &memcpy;
8   // prepares the next boot chain in the workspace
9   // memcpy(boot_chain, workspace)
10  ctxPc[3].cpu_context.rdi = &workspace; // workspace address
11  ctxPc[3].cpu_context.rdx = sizeof(boot_chain);
12  ctxPc[3].cpu_context.rsi = &boot_chain_backup;
13  ctxPc[3].cpu_context.rip = &memcpy;
14  // set the fake OCALL frame in the enclave
15  // memcpy(fake_frame, enclave)
16  ctxPc[4].cpu_context.rdi = &fake_frame;
17  ctxPc[4].cpu_context.rdx = sizeof(fake_frame);
18  ctxPc[4].cpu_context.rsi = &fake_frame_backup;
19  ctxPc[4].cpu_context.rip = &memcpy;
20  // saves CPU extended states for asm_oret
21  // save_xregs(xsave_buffer)
22  ctxPc[5].cpu_context.rdi = &xsave_buffer;
23  ctxPc[5].cpu_context.rip = &save_xregs;
24  // sets the trusted thread as it is performing an OCALL
25  // update_ocall_lastsp(fake_frame)
26  ctxPc[6].cpu_context.rdi = fake_frame;
27  ctxPc[6].cpu_context.rip = &update_ocall_lastsp;
28  // pivots to the outside-chain
29  // eenclu[exit] -> outside_chain
30  ctxPc[7].cpu_context.rax = 0x4; // EEXIT
31  ctxPc[7].cpu_context.rsp = &outside_chain_stack;
32  ctxPc[7].cpu_context.rbx = &outside_chain_first_gadget;
33  ctxPc[7].cpu_context.rip = &enclu;
```

Details of the outside ROP-chains used to resume payload inside the enclave.

```
1 /* ... previous gadgets for shipping the password remotely
      ... */
2 // gadgets to resume payload within the enclave
3 pop rax ; ret
4 0x2 // EENTER
5 pop rbx ; ret
6 &tcs_address
7 pop rdi ; ret // rdi = −2 −> ORET
8 0xfffffffffffffffe // −2
9 pop rcx ; ret // for async exit handler
10 &Lasync_exit_pointer
11 &enclu_urts
```

D   Preliminary Analysis of Assumptions

Table 3 contains a list of 27 stand-alone SGX projects extracted from [9]. For each project, we indicate their category, if it used the Intel SGX SDK, the number of trusted threads for each enclave of the project, and a note. We also list details for each enclave, if the project contains many. We counted 24 out of 27 projects developed on top of Intel SGX SDK, two projects use alternative SDKs (*i.e.*, Open Enclave SDK [28] and Graphene [43]), while one contains a simulated enclave. Among the projects based on the Intel SGX SDK, we counted a total of 31 enclaves, and 24 out of 31 are multi-threading (77%).

Table 3. SGX open-source projects extracted from [9].

Category/Project	Intel SGX SDK	# of threads
Blockchain		
teechain	✓	10
private-data-objects	✓	10
	✓	1
	✓	2
fabric-secure-chaincode	✓	10
	✓	8
eevm	Open Enclave SDK [28]	
lucky	Based on a mock SGX implementation	
node-secureworker	✓	1
town-crier	✓	10
	✓	10
	✓	1
	✓	6
bolos-enclave	✓	1
Machine learning framework		
gbdt-rs	✓	1
bi-sgx	✓	1
slalom	✓	4
Applications		
sgxwallet	✓	16
sgx-tor	✓	10
	✓	10
obscuro	✓	50
channel-id-enclave	✓	10
sfaas	✓	3
phoenix	Graphene [43]	
posup	✓	4
tresorsgx	✓	10
Private Key/Passphrase Management		
sgx-kms	✓	8
keystore	✓	1
safekeeper-server	✓	10
Database		
talos	✓	50
opaque	✓	10
stealthdb	✓	10
sgx_sqlite	✓	10
shieldstore	✓	8

References

1. ROPgadget - gadgets finder and auto-roper. https://github.com/JonathanSalwan/ROPgadget (2011). Accessed Mar 2020
2. Intel® software guard extensions (intel®sgx) - developer guide (2013). https://download.01.org/intel-sgx/linux-2.1.3/docs/Intel_SGX_Developer_Guide.pdf. Accessed June 2020
3. Intel® software guard extensions programming reference (2013). https://software.intel.com/sites/default/files/managed/48/88/329298-002.pdf. Accessed June 2020
4. Thoughts on intel's upcoming software guard extensions (part 1) (2013). http://theinvisiblethings.blogspot.com/2013/08/thoughts-on-intels-upcoming-software.html. Accessed Nov 2018
5. Thoughts on intel's upcoming software guard extensions (part 2) (2013). http://theinvisiblethings.blogspot.com/2013/09/thoughts-on-intels-upcoming-software.html. Accessed Nov 2018
6. Technology preview: private contact discovery for signal (2017). https://signal.org/blog/private-contact-discovery/. Accessed Nov 2018
7. Intel architecture instruction set extensions programming reference (2018). https://software.intel.com/sites/default/files/managed/b4/3a/319433-024.pdf?_ga=1.118002441.1853754838.1418826886. Accessed Nov 2018
8. SGX-Tor (2018). https://github.com/kaist-ina/SGX-Tor. Accessed Nov 2018
9. Awesome SGX open source projects (2019). https://github.com/Maxul/Awesome-SGX-Open-Source. Accessed June 2020
10. Arnautov, S., et al.: SCONE: secure linux containers with intel SGX. In: 12th USENIX Symposium on Operating Systems Design and Implementation (OSDI 2016), pp. 689–703. USENIX Association, Savannah (2016). https://www.usenix.org/conference/osdi16/technical-sessions/presentation/arnautov
11. Baumann, A., Peinado, M., Hunt, G.: Shielding applications from an untrusted cloud with haven. ACM Trans. Comput. Syst. (TOCS) 33(3), 8 (2015)
12. Biondo, A., Conti, M., Davi, L., Frassetto, T., Sadeghi, A.R.: The guard's dilemma: efficient code-reuse attacks against intel SGX. In: Proceedings of 27th USENIX Security Symposium (2018)
13. Bletsch, T.: Code-reuse attacks: new Frontiers and defenses. Ph.D. thesis (2011). aAI3463747
14. Bulck, J.V., et al.: Foreshadow: extracting the keys to the intel SGX kingdom with transient out-of-order execution. In: 27th USENIX Security Symposium (USENIX Security 2018), pp. 991–1008. USENIX Association, Baltimore, August 2018. https://www.usenix.org/conference/usenixsecurity18/presentation/bulck
15. Checkoway, S., Shacham, H.: Iago attacks: why the system call API is a bad untrusted RPC interface. SIGARCH Comput. Archit. News 41(1), 253–264 (2013). https://doi.org/10.1145/2490301.2451145. http://doi.acm.org/10.1145/2490301.2451145
16. Chen, P., Xing, X., Mao, B., Xie, L.: Return-oriented rootkit without returns (on the x86). In: Soriano, M., Qing, S., López, J. (eds.) ICICS 2010. LNCS, vol. 6476, pp. 340–354. Springer, Heidelberg (2010). https://doi.org/10.1007/978-3-642-17650-0_24
17. Cloosters, T., Rodler, M., Davi, L.: TeeRex: discovery and exploitation of memory corruption vulnerabilities in SGX enclaves. In: 29th USENIX Security Symposium (USENIX Security 20). USENIX Association, Boston, August 2020. https://www.usenix.org/conference/usenixsecurity20/presentation/cloosters

18. Costan, V., Devadas, S.: Intel SGX explained. IACR Cryptology ePrint Archive **2016**, 86 (2016)
19. Davenport, S., Ford, R.: SGX: the good, the bad and the downright ugly. Virus Bulletin, p. 14 (2014)
20. Drake, J.D., Worsley, J.C.: Practical PostgreSQL. O'Reilly Media Inc., Sebastopol (2002)
21. Google: Asylo (2018). https://github.com/google/asylo. Accessed Mar 2020
22. Graziano, M., Balzarotti, D., Zidouemba, A.: ROPMEMU: a framework for the analysis of complex code-reuse attacks. In: Proceedings of the 11th ACM on Asia Conference on Computer and Communications Security, ASIA CCS 2016, pp. 47–58. ACM, New York (2016). https://doi.org/10.1145/2897845.2897894. http://doi.acm.org/10.1145/2897845.2897894
23. Hähnel, M., Cui, W., Peinado, M.: High-resolution side channels for untrusted operating systems. In: 2017 USENIX Annual Technical Conference (USENIX ATC 2017), pp. 299–312. USENIX Association, Santa Clara (2017). https://www.usenix.org/conference/atc17/technical-sessions/presentation/hahnel
24. Hund, R., Holz, T., Freiling, F.C.: Return-oriented rootkits: bypassing kernel code integrity protection mechanisms. In: USENIX Security Symposium, pp. 383–398 (2009)
25. Kittel, T., Vogl, S., Kirsch, J., Eckert, C.: Counteracting data-only malware with code pointer examination. In: Bos, H., Monrose, F., Blanc, G. (eds.) RAID 2015. LNCS, vol. 9404, pp. 177–197. Springer, Cham (2015). https://doi.org/10.1007/978-3-319-26362-5_9
26. Kuvaiskii, D., et al.: SGXBOUNDS: memory safety for shielded execution. In: Proceedings of the Twelfth European Conference on Computer Systems, EuroSys 2017, pp. 205–221. ACM, New York (2017). https://doi.org/10.1145/3064176.3064192. http://doi.acm.org/10.1145/3064176.3064192
27. Lee, J., et al.: Hacking in darkness: return-oriented programming against secure enclaves. In: USENIX Security, pp. 523–539 (2017)
28. Microsoft: Open enclave SDK (2019). https://openenclave.io/sdk/. Accessed Mar 2020
29. Murdock, K., Oswald, D., Garcia, F.D., Van Bulck, J., Gruss, D., Piessens, F.: Plundervolt: software-based fault injection attacks against intel SGX. In: Proceedings of the 41st IEEE Symposium on Security and Privacy (S&P 2020) (2020)
30. Nguyen, H., Ganapathy, V.: EnGarde: mutually-trusted inspection of SGX enclaves. In: 2017 IEEE 37th International Conference on Distributed Computing Systems (ICDCS), pp. 2458–2465, June 2017. https://doi.org/10.1109/ICDCS.2017.35
31. Oleksenko, O., Trach, B., Krahn, R., Silberstein, M., Fetzer, C.: Varys: protecting SGX enclaves from practical side-channel attacks. In: 2018 USENIX Annual Technical Conference (USENIX ATC 2018), pp. 227–240. USENIX Association, Boston (2018). https://www.usenix.org/conference/atc18/presentation/oleksenko
32. Polychronakis, M., Keromytis, A.D.: ROP payload detection using speculative code execution. In: 2011 6th International Conference on Malicious and Unwanted Software, pp. 58–65. IEEE (2011)
33. van Prooijen, J.: The design of malware on modern hardware. Technical report (2016)
34. Rozas, C.: Intel® software guard extensions (Intel® SGX) (2013)
35. Schuster, F., et al: VC3: trustworthy data analytics in the cloud using SGX. In: 2015 IEEE Symposium on Security and Privacy (SP), pp. 38–54. IEEE (2015)

36. Schwarz, M., Lipp, M.: When good turns evil: Using intel SGX to stealthily steal bitcoins. Black Hat Asia (2018)
37. Schwarz, M., Weiser, S., Gruss, D.: Practical enclave malware with intel SGX. CoRR abs/1902.03256 (2019). http://arxiv.org/abs/1902.03256
38. Schwarz, M., Weiser, S., Gruss, D., Maurice, C., Mangard, S.: Malware guard extension: using SGX to conceal cache attacks. In: Polychronakis, M., Meier, M. (eds.) DIMVA 2017. LNCS, vol. 10327, pp. 3–24. Springer, Cham (2017). https://doi.org/10.1007/978-3-319-60876-1_1
39. Seo, J., et al.: SGX-shield: enabling address space layout randomization for SGX programs. In: NDSS (2017)
40. Shacham, H.: The geometry of innocent flesh on the bone: Return-into-libc without function calls (on the x86). In: Proceedings of the 14th ACM Conference on Computer and Communications Security, pp. 552–561, CCS 2007. ACM, New York (2007). https://doi.org/10.1145/1315245.1315313. http://doi.acm.org/10.1145/1315245.1315313
41. Shih, M.W., Lee, S., Kim, T., Peinado, M.: T-SGX: eradicating controlled-channel attacks against enclave programs. In: Proceedings of the 2017 Annual Network and Distributed System Security Symposium (NDSS), San Diego, CA (2017)
42. Stancill, B., Snow, K.Z., Otterness, N., Monrose, F., Davi, L., Sadeghi, A.-R.: Check my profile: leveraging static analysis for fast and accurate detection of ROP gadgets. In: Stolfo, S.J., Stavrou, A., Wright, C.V. (eds.) RAID 2013. LNCS, vol. 8145, pp. 62–81. Springer, Heidelberg (2013). https://doi.org/10.1007/978-3-642-41284-4_4
43. Che Tsai, C., Porter, D.E., Vij, M.: Graphene-SGX: a practical library OS for unmodified applications on SGX. In: 2017 USENIX Annual Technical Conference (USENIX ATC 2017), pp. 645–658. USENIX Association, Santa Clara (2017). https://www.usenix.org/conference/atc17/technical-sessions/presentation/tsai
44. Van Bulck, J., Oswald, D., Marin, E., Aldoseri, A., Garcia, F.D., Piessens, F.: A tale of two worlds: assessing the vulnerability of enclave shielding runtimes. In: Proceedings of the 2019 ACM SIGSAC Conference on Computer and Communications Security, pp. 1741–1758. ACM (2019)
45. Vinayagamurthy, D., Gribov, A., Gorbunov, S.: StealthDB: a scalable encrypted database with full SQL query support. In: Proceedings on Privacy Enhancing Technologies 2019(3) (2019)
46. Vogl, S., Pfoh, J., Kittel, T., Eckert, C.: Persistent data-only malware: function hooks without code. In: NDSS (2014)
47. Wang, H., et al.: Towards memory safe enclave programming with rust-SGX. In: Proceedings of the 2019 ACM SIGSAC Conference on Computer and Communications Security, pp. 2333–2350. ACM (2019)
48. Weiser, S., Mayr, L., Schwarz, M., Gruss, D.: SGXJail: defeating enclave malware via confinement. In: 22nd International Symposium on Research in Attacks, Intrusions and Defenses (RAID 2019), pp. 353–366. USENIX Association, Chaoyang District, Beijing, September 2019. https://www.usenix.org/conference/raid2019/presentation/weiser
49. yerzhan7: Sgx_sqlite. https://github.com/yerzhan7/SGX_SQLite. Accessed Jan 2019

Telepathic Headache: Mitigating Cache Side-Channel Attacks on Convolutional Neural Networks

Hervé Chabanne[1,2], Jean-Luc Danger[2], Linda Guiga[1,2(✉)], and Ulrich Kühne[2]

[1] Idemia, Paris, France
{herve.chabanne,linda.guiga}@idemia.com
[2] Télécom Paris, Paris, France
{herve.chabanne,jean-luc.danger,linda.guiga,
ulrich.kuhne}@telecom-paris.com

Abstract. Convolutional Neural Networks (CNNs) are the target of several side-channel attacks aiming at recovering their parameters and hyper-parameters. Attack vectors include monitoring of the cache, power consumption analysis and execution time measurements. These attacks often rely on the knowledge of a certain – large – set of hyper-parameters among which the victim model lies. The goal of the potential attacker is then to reduce that search space or even deduce the correct architecture. One such attack, Cache Telepathy by Yan et al., monitors access to a common matrix multiplication algorithm, GeMM (Generalized Matrix Multiply), in order to determine the victim model's hyper-parameters. In this paper, we propose to change the order in which the computations are made and add randomness to the said computations in order to mitigate Cache Telepathy. The security analysis of our protection shows that the Cache Telepathy attack on a protected VGG-16 has an increased search space: from 16 to 2^{22}.

Keywords: Side-channel attack · CNN protection · Model extraction

1 Introduction

Thanks to their high accuracy and performance, Deep Neural Networks (DNNs) are applied to an increasing number of tasks. Among those are image processing [16] and game playing [24]. They are now overly present in our daily lives, for instance in mobile phones [14]. The NN models implemented on those mobile devices require long training and a careful selection of their architecture in order to achieve a high accuracy. The resulting architecture and parameters of those trained models therefore constitute intellectual property.

However, NNs are the target of several reverse-engineering attacks. In those, the attacker aims at recovering the target NN's architecture and/or parameters [4–6,11–13,15,28,31]. While [6,15] are cryptographic attacks and [28] is based on equation-solving, most attacks are side-channel ones. Side-channel

© Springer Nature Switzerland AG 2021
K. Sako and N. O. Tippenhauer (Eds.): ACNS 2021, LNCS 12726, pp. 363–392, 2021.
https://doi.org/10.1007/978-3-030-78372-3_14

attacks rely on information leakages due to the implementation of an algorithm rather than the algorithm itself. For instance, an attacker can observe memory access patterns [27], the cache [11,12,31] or power and electromagnetic traces [4] and infer secret information from those collected traces.

The knowledge of the architecture can make launching other attacks – such as adversarial ones [20] or membership inference ones [18] – easier [22]. Once the architecture is available, the parameters can also be deduced by possible attackers, either through side-channel attacks [13] or through equation solving [6,15,28].

Protecting the architecture of such NN models is therefore paramount both to protect the intellectual property and to avoid making other attacks easier.

The architecture of a model is mainly comprised of its number of layers, layer types, connections and activation functions. Cache Telepathy [31] targets the cache behavior of the GeMM (Generalized Matrix Multiply) algorithm in order to recover those *hyper-parameters*. Most Machine Learning (ML) frameworks, such as TensorFlow [1] or PyTorch [21] use this algorithm to compute certain layers on CPUs. The number of GeMM operations in the computations, as well as the sizes of the matrices involved provide sensitive information about the target NN.

In this paper, we aim at limiting the information leaked through this attack vector. Since the leakage observed is due to the layers being computed sequentially, we propose to reorder independent neuron computations to make the Cache Telepathy attack harder.

As in Cache Telepathy [31], we consider an attacker who has a black-box access to a model in a Machine Learning as a Service (MLaaS) context, and aims at recovering its architecture. The attacker's only prior knowledge is a family of possible architectures for the targeted model, called the *search space*. The attacker shares the same cache as the process running the model and her only possibility is to monitor the cache. This can for instance be achieved by inducing the victim to install a malicious chrome add-on [12]. Thus, we consider a software attack, as Cache Telepathy does not apply to the hardware context.

Even if nowadays many computations are carried out on GPUs, some recent MLaaS platforms such as Amazon's SageMaker [3] allow CPU computations for inference, as mentioned in [31].

Our contributions are as follows:

- We propose a way of reordering neuron computations. We compute blocks of neurons instead of complete layers at a time.
- We explain how to add randomness to the order of the computations.
- We carry out the Cache Telepathy attack with and without our protection and discuss our methodology. In particular, we analyze the added security and show its practicability regarding its overhead in terms of performances.

After detailing the background and related works in Sect. 2 and Sect. 3, we detail our reordering strategy in Sect. 4. We then explain how to add randomness to the computing order in Sect. 5. We discuss our results, limitations and the security of our strategy in Sect. 7. Finally, Sect. 8 concludes.

2   Background

2.1   NNs

Neural Networks (NNs) are algorithms trained to recognize patterns. They can be represented as graphs where the nodes are the *neurons* and the edges are the *weights*. The weights are values that change over the course of the training so as to solve an optimization problem.

NNs are usually comprised of several layers, which can be of various types.

– Fully connected (FC) layers: A neuron's value is equal to the sum of the previous layer's neurons multiplied by the corresponding weights. A *bias* is generally added to the value. Thus, for an input $X = x_{1 \leq i \leq m}$, weights $W = w_{1 \leq i \leq n, 1 \leq j \leq m}$ and biases $\beta = \beta_{1 \leq i \leq n}$, an FC layer computes:

$$O_i = \sum_{k=1}^{m} w_{i,k} \times x_k + \beta_i \implies O = W \cdot X + \beta$$

– Convolutional layers: These layers operate a convolution between one – or several – filter(s) and the input. For a given filter $F_{1 \leq i \leq k, 1 \leq j \leq k}$, input $x_{1 \leq i \leq n, 1 \leq j \leq n}$ and a bias β the output is computed as follows:

$$O_{i,j} = \sum_{l=1}^{k} \sum_{h=1}^{k} w_{i+l,j+h} \times x_{l,h} + \beta$$

– Pooling layers: They consider the output by blocks, and take one significant value for each block. Their goal is to reduce the dimensionality of the input. One common pooling layer is the max pooling: they take the maximum among all block values.

Each layer is followed by a nonlinear *activation* function. It activates or deactivates neurons depending on some criteria. For instance, $ReLU(x) = max(0, x)$ deactivates negative neurons.

Convolutional and FC layers can be rewritten as a matrix multiplication. This is what many ML frameworks, such as TensorFlow [1], do to compute them when executing on CPUs. Figure 1 shows how a convolutional layer is transformed into a matrix multiplication. Each row in the filter matrix F_i corresponds to one filter. Each column in the input matrix R_i corresponds to one convolutional window of the size of the filter.

2.2   GeMM

The matrix multiplication in FC and convolutional layers is computed using Goto's GeMM algorithm [9]. The latter efficiently divides the input matrices in smaller blocks so that the computations completely fill the cache. As in [31], let us consider the OpenBLAS library. In OpenBLAS, the algorithm makes use of three interesting functions: `itcopy`, `oncopy` and `kernel`. The pattern of appearance of these three functions is highly correlated with the dimensions of the matrices involved in the matrix multiplication. Thus, monitoring these three functions is enough for an attacker to recover the matrices' dimensions.

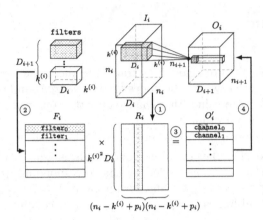

Fig. 1. Convolutional layer into matrix multiplication. I_i is layer i's input, R_i its reshaped form. O_i and O_i' are the layer's output and its reshaped form. D_i is layer i's number of input channels. $k^{(i)}$ is layer i's filter size.

2.3 Flush and Reload Attack [32]

The goal of cache attacks is to determine whether a target function has been accessed within a certain period of time.

The cache is a small but fast memory space used to store the recently accessed data. If a process tries to access d, the CPU will first search the cache for it. If it is found in the cache, this is a *cache hit*. If it is not there, this is a *cache miss*, and the processor needs to access the much larger and slower main memory.

This difference in the time necessary to return the data d can be exploited by attackers to monitor certain sensitive addresses, such as those of `itcopy`, `oncopy` and `kernel`. Let d denote the target address. The Flush and Reload attack then consists in the three following steps:

1. Flush the address from the cache.
2. Wait for a certain period of time t_{wait}, to enable the victim to access d if it needs to.
3. Access the address, and measure the access time t_{access}.

If t_{access} is lower than a certain threshold T, then d was already in the cache when the attacker accessed it. Thus, the victim accessed it during step 2. If t_{access} is greater than T, then the victim did not access d during step 2. If T and t_{wait} are selected properly, this method enables a potential attacker to recover the number of times d was accessed, as well as when it was accessed.

2.4 Cache Telepathy Attack

The authors of [31] exploit the sequence of appearance of `itcopy`, `oncopy` and `kernel` in Goto's algorithm to recover the matrix sizes in GeMM computations. This provides a potential attacker with the filter, input and output sizes of a given layer. Thus, an attacker can proceed as follows:

1. Determine the number of layers by counting the matrix multiplications.
2. For each multiplication, recover the `itcopy`, `oncopy` and `kernel` pattern.
3. Deduce the filter, input and output sizes m, thanks to the observed patterns.
4. Determine the connections between layers thanks to the input and output sizes.

Even though the architecture can usually not be recovered in its entirety as multiple options for the sizes and connections remain possible, this method can still significantly reduce the search space for the target architecture.

To achieve this, the attacker needs to count the matrix multiplications and monitor the loops, by observing the cache, and carrying out a Flush and Reload attack for instance. The authors of Cache Telepathy [31] explain that common ML frameworks' backends rely on linear algebra libraries such as OpenBLAS, Intel MKL and Eigen. They launched their attack on both OpenBLAS and MKL, as they work in a very similar way. In the OpenBLAS library, they observe the pattern formed by the functions `itcopy`, `oncopy` and `kernel` to count the number of matrix multiplications and deduce the matrix sizes. In this paper, we only considered the OpenBLAS case. But the similarities bewteen MKL and OpenBLAS lead us to believe that our protection would work similarly on the MKL library.

3   Related Work

Reordering for Hardware Acceleration: Several papers propose to modify the way convolutional layers are generally computed, with the aim of accelerating CNN computations on hardware devices. The authors of [23] consider each neuron individually, and compute its value as soon as it is ready. Indeed, in convolutional layers, only a small window of values from the previous layer is used to compute a given neuron. In [23], a buffer in layer i stores the values as they arrive in a sequential order. Once enough values arrive to compute a neuron, it executes the computation and sends the value to the following layer. The scheme is described in Fig. 2.

The authors of [2] consider computing CNN layers in a similar fashion. The aim of [2] and [23] is to limit the bandwidth necessary to make NN computations, by only loading on chip the necessary values. It also enables a parallelization of some computations.

As the following sections will explain it, we consider a similar approach as [23] and [2], but outside of the hardware context. Furthermore, our goal is not to accelerate the computations but to protect them from architecture extraction attacks.

Security: [29] also considers the computations in NNs in a different order, but their goal is to run the victim NNs in Trusted Execution Environments (TEEs). Since TEEs have a limited memory space, all weights and inputs cannot be loaded at once. Therefore, they partition the target NNs in three different ways

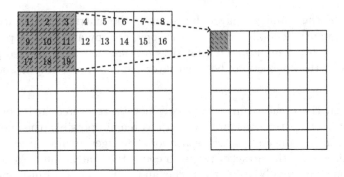

Fig. 2. The blue neurons from convolutional layer i (left) are the ones needed to compute the green neuron in layer $i + 1$ (right), when layer i's filter size is 3. (Color figure online)

(per layer, within a layer and branched partitioning) when loading them into the TEEs.

Some papers [7,8,19] also aim at protecting NNs from architecture extraction attacks. [7] considers a hardware masking approach to protect neuron computations against power-based side-channel attacks. In the latter, the attacker runs the victim NN and measures its power traces in order to recover the architecture [4]. By masking the hardware computations, the authors of [7] aim at making the power traces leakage free. [19] and [8] mitigate memory access pattern attacks. In memory access pattern attacks, the attacker observes which memory locations have been accessed in order to deduce (part of) the NN's architecture [13]. The authors of [19] and [8] randomize memory access patterns in order to mitigate the aforementioned attacks. To the extent of our knowledge, no paper has considered protections against cache-based side-channel attacks on CNNs yet.

In this paper, we mix two ideas: the interleaving of layers presented in [23] and the block multiplications as in GeMM. We apply them to the software level rather than the hardware one. We also have a different aim: while existing approaches [2,23] applied the interleaving of layers for efficiency, we applied it for security purposes. As detailed in Sect. 5, we also added a randomization element. This mix of the two ideas along with the randomization led us to some experimental results showing our idea does thwart the Cache Telepathy attack (see Sect. 7).

4   Reordering Computations: The Convolutional Case

In this paper, our goal is to mitigate cache attacks targeting the GeMM computations during the inference phase of a victim CNN. We consider out of scope other side-channel vectors such as power consumption or memory access patterns. Furthermore, our proposed method concerns convolutional and maxpooling layers. Even though Cache Telepathy also targets FC layers, we will see in Sect. 7.1 that our approach still mitigates the attack.

4.1   Convolutional Layer

The protection we propose is based on two observations:

First, the sequential execution of layers enables a potential attacker to determine the depth of an NN. Indeed, the depth directly results from the number of observed matrix multiplications.

Second, the hyper-parameters of a given layer can be deduced by a potential attacker because each layer is executed as a whole before moving on to the next one.

Therefore, a depth-first computation should improve the security of an NN. In CNNs, several neurons in a layer i can be executed before layer $i - 1$ has been fully computed. Indeed, a neuron only requires a window of values from the previous layer, as described in Fig. 2.

Based on these observations, we propose to compute layers in a depth-wise fashion. But instead of computing a neuron in layer i as soon as all necessary neurons in layer $i - 1$ are ready, we wait for a block of neurons in layer i to be ready before starting the execution. With this method, we aim at making layer computations overlap, without being restricted to computing one neuron at a time.

Let us detail our proposed method. Our goal is to make the computations of several layers overlap. We start executing layer $i + 1$ before the execution of layer i is over. The GeMM algorithm is thoroughly optimized, and makes sure the entire cache is used for large matrix multiplications. Making one neuron computation at a time – to execute neurons as soon as enough data is available – would lead to too much overhead. Thus, a balance needs to be reached between the added overhead and the number of subdivisions of matrix multiplications.

Let us first consider the case of convolutional layers. Let layer i be a convolutional one, with $n_k^{(i)}$ filters of size $k^{(i)} \times k^{(i)}$. Let R denote the reshaped matrix – as in Fig. 1 – of the input I (of size $n \times n$). For an example of a standard way to reshape the input, see Appendix C, Fig. 8. Let F denote the $n_k^{(i)} \times (k^{(i)} \cdot k^{(i)})$ matrix where each row is a flattened filter.

Here, our goal is to compute the matrix multiplication $F \times R$ by blocks. Every time a block A of neurons in matrix R is ready, we multiply A with the corresponding filter blocks in F. Let us detail how this is achieved.

If there is no padding, the reshaped matrix R has dimensions $(k^{(i)^2} \cdot n_k^{(i)}) \times (n - k^{(i)} + 1)^2$. Let $B \in \mathbb{N}$. R is divided in N non-overlapping blocks $\{R_{B_l}\}_{1 \leq l \leq N}$ of size $B \times B$. There are $W^{(i)} := \left\lceil \frac{(n - k^{(i)} + 1)^2}{B} \right\rceil$ blocks R_B width-wise and $H^{(i)} := \left\lceil \frac{k^{(i)} \times k^{(i)}}{B} \right\rceil$ blocks height-wise, corresponding to a total of $N^{(i)} := \left\lceil \frac{(n - k^{(i)} + 1)^2}{B} \right\rceil \times \left\lceil \frac{k^{(i)} \times k^{(i)}}{B} \right\rceil$ blocks R_B.

Each such block R_{B_r} needs to be multiplied by filter blocks F_{B_r} of size $n_k^{(i)} \times B$. We can further divide F_{B_r} into $M_r^{(i)}$ blocks $\{F_{b_{r,l}}\}_{1 \leq l \leq M_r^{(i)}}$ of size

$B \times B$. If $n_k^{(i)}$ is not a multiple of B, we pad the last block $F_{b_{M_r^{(i)}}}$. Thus, each block R_B needs to be multiplied by $M_r^{(i)} := \left\lceil \frac{n_k^{(i)}}{B} \right\rceil$ filter blocks.

Once the layer receives all the values in the $r-th$ block R_{B_r} from the previous layer, all the multiplications $\{R_{B_r} \times F_{b_{r,j}}\}_{1 \le j \le M_r^{(i)}}$ are computed. The results are added to those of the other R_B blocks involving the same columns in R. Since there are $H^{(i)}$ blocks R_B height-wise, $H^{(i)}$ matrix multiplications are required to compute one neuron for layer $i + 1$. Since, moreover, computations are made with sub-matrices of sizes $B \times B$, B neurons are computed at a time.

Let us note that GeMM computations are more efficient when matrix sizes are multiples of 32 [9]. Thus, the default block size should be a multiple of 32 as well. Moreover, the number of computations is correlated with the block sizes: if we increase the block size, there are fewer matrix multiplications. But the efficiency of the computations also depends on the cache size, the various layers' input sizes and the padding added. It is therefore important to tailor the block size to the architecture's hyperparameters. Furthermore, taking into account the matrix sizes in each layer is important: if the block sizes are too large, no overlap can occur between a convolutional layer and the following one. Thus, block sizes need to be adapted to the architecture at hand.

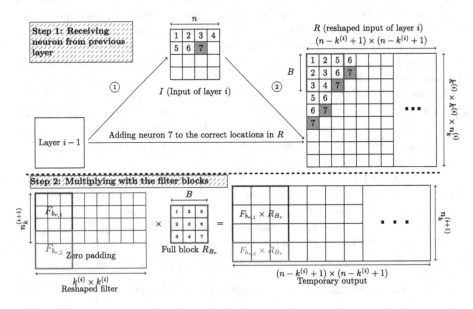

Fig. 3. Process for a layer of size 4×4 receiving values from the previous layer. The block size is $B = 3$ and the filter's width and height are equal to 3.

Figure 3 summarizes the process for one convolutional layer. In Step 1, layer $i - 1$ sends neuron 7 to layer i, which adds it in the reshaped matrix R.

Algorithm 1: add_elts: Receive elements from the previous layer, and compute ready blocks

---

input : Block size B. Arrays A_C, B_C. Value v to add. Accumulator acc

1   L = get_indices_reshaped_input(v) /* Gets indices where v needs to be added. */
2   **for** $i \in L$ **do**
3   b_c = get_block_index(i); /* Gets index of the layer block i belongs to. */
4   B_C[b_c] += 1;
5   **if** $B\_C[b\_c] = B \times B$ **then**
       /* If the block is now full */
6   filter_blocks = get_associated_filter_blocks(b_c) ;
7   **for** $F \in$ *filter_blocks* **do**
8   R = compute_sgemm(F, b_c);
         /* Send values to next layer. */
9   accumulator_handler(B, A_C, B_C, acc, R, get_next_layer());
10   **endfor**
11   **end**
12 **endfor**

Algorithm 2: accumulator_handler: Add computed elements and send computed neurons to the next layer

---

input : Block size B. Arrays A_C, B_C. Array acc. Matrix of computed values R. Pointer to the next layer: next_layer

/* acc stores the current values of the layer's elements. A_C is used to check whether a value in acc is ready. B_C is used to check whether a block is ready. R is the result of a matrix multiplication. */

1   indices = get_indices_acc(R)
2   n = len(R)
3   **for** $i = 0$ **to** n **do**
4   acc[indices[i]] += R[i];
5   A_C[indices[i]] += 1;
6   f_c = get_full_ac(indices[i], B); /* Gets the number of matrix multiplications necessary to have a correct value in acc[indices[i]] */
7   **if** $A\_C[indices[i]] == f\_c$ **then**
8   next_layer→add_elts(indices[i], A_C, B_C);
9   **end**
10 **endfor**

Since neuron 7 fills the red block R_{B_r}, a matrix multiplication can occur. Step 2 corresponds to the multiplications with the blue and green filter blocks $\{F_{b_{r,j}}\}_{j \in \{1,2\}}$. The results are added to the output matrix (O' in Fig. 1). A value in the output matrix is only correct when the associated column in R is fully computed.

Algorithms 1 and 2 provide the pseudo-code for our method. Algorithm 1 receives a list of elements from layer $i-1$ and checks whether a block R_{B_r} is full (line 5). If it is the case, it computes $\{F_{b_{r,j}} \times R_{B_r}\}_{1 \le j \le M_r}$ (using compute_sgemm, line 10) whether layer $i-1$'s execution is over or not. It sends the temporary values to layer i by calling Algorithm 2: accumulator_handler (lines 7–10). Algorithm 2 takes those output elements, adds them to the correct locations in $R^{(i)}$ (lines 1–4) and checks whether a neuron is completely computed (line 7). If it is the case, it sends the result to layer $i+1$.

4.2 Dealing with Pooling Layers

Pooling layers need to be dealt with differently. The reason why is twofold: first, in such layers, the various channels are managed independently. Filter sizes are small, resulting in a small height for reshaped matrices. It is therefore more practical to consider blocks width-wise only. Second, no GeMM multiplication is involved in the computation. They are therefore not the target of the cache attack considered.

However, executing a pooling computation introduces overhead in between block computations. This leaks some information to a potential attacker and she might determine the number of multiplications required to obtain one column in the reshaped pooling input. This provides the attacker with a small range of possible hyper-parameter values. If the victim waits for several columns in the reshaped pooling layer to be ready before starting the execution, the range of possible hyper-parameter values increases, making it harder for an attacker to recover the correct architecture. It is therefore important to also consider a blocked computation for layers without GeMM computations, such as pooling ones.

We propose to adapt the methodology described in Sect. 4.1 to pooling layers. We still compute several neurons at once. But here, we wait for multiple entire columns to be completed instead of blocks. Moreover, we deal with the various channels independently. We consider a pooling layer i with a window size of $k^{(i)} \times k^{(i)}$. Let $B \in \mathbb{N}$. Given the maxpooling layer's input I of size $n \times n$, let R (of size $k^{(i)^2} \times (\frac{n}{k^{(i)}})^2$) be its reshaping. We divide R into $N^{(i)} := \left\lceil \frac{(n/k^{(i)})^2}{B} \right\rceil$ blocks $\{R_{B_r}\}_{1 \leq r \leq N^{(i)}}$ width-wise. Whenever all of block R_{B_r}'s values are ready – i.e. whenever they were relayed by the previous layer –, the computation can be executed for that block. This results in B neurons that need to be passed on to the following layer.

5 Randomization of Block Sizes

Computing the matrix multiplications by blocks as explained in Sect. 4 helps mitigate the attack at hand, as the attacker only recovers a set of possible hyper-parameter values. However, it is still possible to increase that range of values, by injecting randomness in the block sizes.

5.1 Improving Security Through Randomization

So far, within a layer i, all block sizes were identical. Having different block sizes within a layer provides more entropy in the number of multiplications per layer (see Sect. 7.1 for a more detailed analysis of the protection's security).

Let us first consider the convolutional case. When the architecture of the target NN is created, we generate two arrays tw and th of random block sizes. The first array corresponds to the number of columns of each block, while the second corresponds to the number of rows of each block. tw[1] returns the index

---

Algorithm 3: `full_computation`: Full computation with random

---

input : Model's input I. Arrays A_C, B_C. Block size B
1 For each convolutional layer, generate random arrays W (block widths) and H (block heights)
2 **for** *input blocks* i_b **do**
3   filter_blocks = get_associated_filters(i_b);
4   **for** $F \in$ *filter_blocks* **do**
5   R = compute_sgemm(F, i_b);
6   accumulator_handler(B, A_C, B_C, acc, R, get_next_layer());
7   **endfor**
8 **endfor**

---

of the column at which the $l-th$ block width-wise starts, and th[j] returns the index at which the $j-th$ block height-wise starts. A block with coordinates (l, j) therefore has th[l]−th[l-1] rows and tw[j]−tw[j-1] columns. Appendix C provides an example of such a subdivision.

In that scenario, the blocks in the same column have the same width, and those in the same row have the same height. To prevent an attacker from using this, we can zero-pad the blocks right before each multiplication to turn the rectangle blocks into squares. Thus, each block is a square of size max(*width, height*), where *width* and *height* are the block's original width and height. This way, the blocks in a same row or in a same column can have different block sizes.

As explained in Sect. 4.2, the reshaped pooling matrices cannot be divided height-wise due to their small height. Therefore, only one array of random block sizes is created, to divide the matrix width-wise.

In the random case, Algorithm 1 needs to be updated to take into account the height and width of the considered block. Only lines 5 and 6 in Algorithm 1 change. Before the loop on line 5, we get the correct block width and height thanks to the generated arrays tw and th. These are then provided to accumulator_handler.

Algorithm 3 is the full computation. For all input elements, the function computes the GeMM multiplications (line 5) and sends them, one by one, to the accumulator handler (line 6). This is enough to start the whole process.

6   Full Scheme

Let us now clearly state the steps of our proposed countermeasure, that we call *Telepathic Headache*.

1. For each convolutional layer: Generate two arrays of block sizes, for the width and the height. Possible block sizes need to fulfill two conditions:
   (a) Not too large: it would defeat the purpose of the countermeasure, as we need an overlapping of layers. For instance, $B \leq n$ where n is the input size. But higher B values are often possible.
   (b) Not too small: it would lead to too much overhead (for instance, $B > 1$).
2. For each pooling layer: Generate an array of width-wise block sizes. Block sizes need to fulfill the two previous conditions as well.

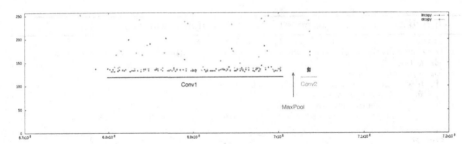

(a) Unprotected case. The layers are executed sequentially. We observe a large matrix multiplication corresponding to $Conv1$, a latency for the max pooling layer and a smaller, matrix multiplication corresponding to $Conv2$.

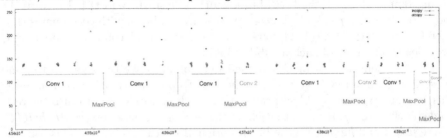

(b) Protected case. Block sizes are between 32 and 38. Each group of points corresponds to one multiplication. 5 multiplications from $Conv1$ are executed, then there is a latency for one max pooling computation, then another 4 multiplications from $Conv1$, etc. We see that $Conv1$, $MaxPool$ and $Conv2$ interleave.

Fig. 4. Flush and Reload on an unprotected (a) and a protected (b) architecture with two convolutional layers (filter size: 3×3) separated by a max pooling layer (window size: 2×2). The y-axis corresponds to the number of clock cycles it takes to access the correct cache line. The x-axis indicates the time elapsed since the beginning of the experiment.

3. Start the first layer computations.
4. If a block in layer i is full, compute the matrix multiplications.
5. If the previous computations lead to at least one neuron being completely computed, send the value to layer $i + 1$ and pursue computations in layer $i + 1$ if possible.
6. Repeat steps 4 and 5 until all values have been computed.

   Steps 1 and 2 are part of the architecture creation, and are only executed once for a given model. Generating the new, protected architecture only once per model and user prevents a potential attacker from carrying out statistical attacks.

   Let us further detail the way we deal with convolutional GeMM computations in step 4. Let R_{B_r} be a full block in layer i, and w and h be its corresponding width and height respectively. As explained in Sect. 4.1, each R_{B_i} is associated with filter blocks $\{F_{b_{r,j}}\}_{1 \leq j \leq M_r^{(i)}}$. $M_r^{(i)}$ multiplications $F_{b_{r,l}} \times R_{B_r} \ \forall 0 \leq l \leq M_r^{(i)}$

are computed. The output of those multiplications are sent to the next layer. Since R_{B_r}'s columns are only subcolumns from the reshaped input R's columns, the outputs computed are only partial results. The results for all height-wise input blocks need to be summed in order for some neurons to be ready in the following layer.

Figure 4 shows that contrary to a normal execution, our protection leads to an overlap of layer computations.

7   Results

7.1   Security Analysis

We consider an attacker whose goal is to recover the architecture of a target CNN. The list of hyper-parameters to recover is therefore:

- Number and types of layers, and connections between layers.
- Filter sizes for convolutional layers and window sizes for pooling ones.
- Input and output sizes.
- Padding.

The authors of Cache Telepathy restrict the possible target architectures to a search space. The latter is built thanks to the following assumptions:

- In convolutional layers with filter size $k \times k$, we have that: $k \in \{1, ..., 11\}$.
- The padding p is such that $p \leq k$.
- In each layer, the number of output channels is such that: n_{out} is a multiple of 64 and $n_{out} \leq 64 \times 32$.

We make the same assumptions in this paper.

As explained in Sect. 2, the attackers in Cache Telepathy monitor GeMM computations in order to recover those hyper-parameters. The number of convolutional layers in the target CNN is equal to the number of matrix multiplications. Filter sizes are deduced from the sizes of the matrices involved in the multiplications. The possibilities for padding values and pooling sizes are restricted thanks to constraints on the dimensions of each layer.

The Flush+Reload attack on GeMM functions (as explained in Sect. 2) along with these assumptions enable the attacker in [31] to limit the search space to a very small set of possible architectures. For instance, for the VGG-16 architecture [25], the Cache Telepathy attack reduces the search space from over 5.4×10^{12} possible architectures to 16.

Let us consider layers 4 (*Conv4*), 5 (*Conv5*) and 6 (*MaxPool*) of VGG-16. They are two convolutional layers followed by a max pooling layer. *Conv4* and *Conv5* have input size $n \times n = 112 \times 112$. Let $k^{(i)} \times k^{(i)}$ denote *Convi*'s filter size. In our case, $k^{(4)} = k^{(5)} = 3$. The input size is the same in both layers because a padding of two ($p = 1$) is applied in both directions to *Conv4*'s output. *Conv4* has $in_4 = 64$ input channels and $out_4 = 128$ output channels. *Conv5* has $in_5 = out_5 = 128$ input and output channels (see Fig. 5).

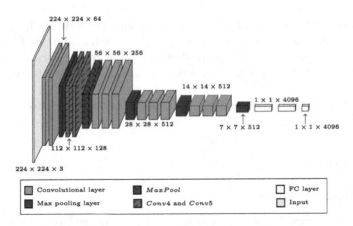

Fig. 5. VGG-16 architecture. The sizes mentioned in the figure are the input sizes of the layers in the form: (input width × input height × number of channels).

The reshaped input image R_4 for $Conv4$ has width $W^{(4)} = (n + 2 \cdot p - k^{(4)} + 1)^2 = 112 \times 112$ and height $H^{(4)} = k^{(4)} \times k^{(4)} \times in_4 = 576$. The reshaped filter matrix F_4 for $Conv4$ has width $F_W^{(4)} = H^{(4)} = k^{(4)} \times k^{(4)} \times in_4 = 576$ and height $F_H^{(4)} = out_4 = 128$.

A potential attacker is assumed to know n and in_4. This is a reasonable assumption, since the input size is known to an attacker who can query the target model. Furthermore, for simplicity, let us assume that the attacker knows that layers are sequentially connected.

Recovering the Unprotected Architecture with Cache Telepathy: By monitoring GeMM multiplications, the attacker in Cache Telepathy can identify the two convolutional layers, as each corresponds to one matrix multiplication. Moreover, the lack of a max pooling layer in between the two layers is identified through timing analysis. Indeed, a max pooling layer incurs a time overhead between GeMM operations. The attacker also determines the matrix sizes. This directly provides her with $out_4 = in_5$ and $H^{(4)}$. Since $H^{(4)} = k^{(4)} \times k^{(4)} \times in_4$ and in_4 is known, the attacker can deduce $k^{(4)}$. The attacker also directly observes that $n' = (n + 2 \cdot p - k^{(4)} + 1)^2$. Since the attacker now knows n and $k^{(4)}$, she can easily recover $p = \frac{\sqrt{n'} - n + k^{(4)} - 1}{2}$. $MaxPool$'s window size is determined to be 2 by comparing the input and output sizes of the pooling layer.

Thus, monitoring GeMM computations enables an attacker to find: the number of convolutional layers by counting the GeMM operations; the input and output shapes (including channels) of $Conv4$ and $Conv5$ thanks to the matrix sizes; the filter sizes for the two layers thanks to the matrix sizes.

In short, the attacker manages to recover all the hyper-parameters of $Conv4$ and $Conv5$.

Protected Case, When Convolutional Layers Can be Distinguished: Let us now study the impact of our protection on those two convolutional layers. The attacker has at her disposal the same information as before. Once again, the goal is to recover the hyper-parameters of $Conv4$ and $Conv5$. By launching Cache Telepathy, the attacker is able to recover all matrix sizes in the GeMM multiplications. In our case, the layers are not executed sequentially but in blocks of various sizes, and depth-wise. This means that as soon as a block of values – of random size, as explained in Sect. 5 – in layer i is ready, it is executed, regardless of whether layer $i - 1$ has finished its execution. Thus, the layers interleave, as shown in Fig. 4.

Because the order of multiplications is changed and the layers are not executed sequentially, the attacker knows neither the number of layers nor which layer a matrix multiplication belongs to. However, an attacker can detect a pooling layer computation, since it incurs a latency between multiplications. Therefore, she can determine the number of multiplications required for the first blocked max pooling computation to occur. We should also bear in mind that several architectures have multiple consecutive convolutional layers [17,25].

For a clearer explanation, we first focus on the unlikely case where the attacker can observe a change of layer (and therefore identify the first $Conv5$ operation). Let us note that we believe this case to be mainly hypothetical. For it to hold, there should be a notable latency in between convolutional layers. The said latency should also be different from the overhead incurred by maxpooling layers. We present this scenario for pedagogical purposes. In Appendix A, we compute the number $tot^{4,5}$ of multiplications in $Conv4$ required to start computing $Conv5$ depending on the block sizes B. We use that analysis to then compute, in Appendix B, the number of multiplications necessary for the first block in $MaxPool$ to get executed.

Let us first consider $tot^{4,5}$. Because each block size is random, we can compute a range of possible values for $tot^{4,5}$ by considering the two extreme cases, where $B_{min} = 32$ and $B_{max} = 64$.

$$tot_{B,B}^{4,5} = \left(\sum_{q=0}^{b-1} H_q^{(4)} \times M_r^{(4)} \right) + \left\lceil \frac{ch}{B} \right\rceil \times H_b^{(4)} \tag{1}$$

where b is the number of the block (width-wise) containing the last element we need to compute in $Conv4$; $H_j^{(4)}$ is the number of filters height-wise in $Conv4$, for width-wise block j; $M_q^{(4)}$ is the number of filters associated to block q; ch is the channel of element (B, B) in $Conv5$'s input (see Appendix A for details).

Here, we have: $tot^{4,5} \in [74, 292]$. This range of values can be obtained because we know the padding, input and output shapes, and filter sizes. A potential attacker, however, only knows the number of input channels and the input shape.

The remaining question is whether the range of values for different filter and padding sizes overlap. If it is the case, then an attacker cannot differentiate between the various hyper-parameter values. Let us suppose, for simplicity, that $k = k^{(4)} = k^{(5)}$ and compute all the possible values for $tot_{x,y}^{4,5}$ $((x'_{min}, y'_{min}) = (32, 32)$ and $(x'_{max}, y'_{max}) = (64, 64))$, given out_4, out_5 and in_5. Table 1 shows the resulting values.

Table 1. Maximal and minimal number of multiplications depending on the filter size, when the attacker can distinguish between convolutional layers.

$k^{(4)}$	1	2	3	4	5	6	7	8	9	10	11
$tot^{4,5}_{x'_{min},y'_{min}}$	2	8	306	928	1,400	4,896	5,488	7,168	6,480	8,000	6,776
$tot^{4,5}_{x'_{max},y'_{max}}$	1	4	9	16	25	36	49	64	324	400	242

If $k = 1$, $tot^{4,5} \in [1,2]$. If $k = 2$, $tot^{4,5} \in [4,8]$ and so on. Because of those ranges, if an attacker manages to recover $tot^{4,5}$, she can determine whether $k = 1$ or $k = 2$. However, the ranges for $k > 2$ overlap, meaning that for a given $tot^{4,5}$, she has at least two possibilities for k. In our architecture, we have that $tot^{4,5} \in [74, 292]$. An attacker observing this number only knows that $9 > k > 2$. This multiplies by 6 the number of possible architectures for that set of layers. There are 13 convolutional layers in VGG-16. If we extrapolate and assume we have 6 possibilities for each layer, the reduced search space is multiplied by 6^{13}. This is an overevaluation of the added uncertainty. But we see that because of the overlapping, we have at least two possibilities per layer for the filter value, when there was previously no uncertainty. This leads to a multiplication of the search space by at least 2^{13}. Let us note that it represents a high increase in the search space, as recovering the correct architecture then requires training all of the remaining possibilities. In [31], the authors reduced the search space for VGG-16 to 16 possibilities. With our protection, we can increase it to 2^{17}.

Furthermore, this computation does not provide the attacker with the padding, as she does not know the full output size, resulting in an even larger search space.

Protected Case, When an Attacker Can Only See Max Pooling Layers: In reality, as stated before, it is difficult for an attacker to differentiate between convolutional layers. This means that $tot^{4,5}$ is not observable, and the attacker can only recover the number of multiplications required to reach the following max pooling layer $MaxPool$. We therefore need to compute $tot^{4,6}$. If we denote (x, y) the last element in the first $MaxPool$ block B, and (x', y') the last element in $Conv5$ that needs to be computed for B to be ready, then: $tot^{4,6}_{x,y} = tot^{4,5}_{x',y'} + tot^{5,6}_{x,y}$.

This time, we consider the possible ranges of $tot^{4,6}$, given that in_5 and out_5 are not available to the attacker. The results are shown in Table 2.

Table 2. Maximal and minimal number of multiplications depending on the filter size, when the attacker cannot distinguish between convolutional layers.

$k^{(4)}$	1	2	3	4	5	6	7	8	9	10	11
$tot^{4,6}_{x_{min},y_{min}}$	$>9 \cdot 10^6$	$>10 \cdot 10^6$	$>10 \cdot 10^6$	$>11 \cdot 10^6$	$>11 \cdot 10^6$	$>12 \cdot 10^6$	$>13 \cdot 10^6$	$>15 \cdot 10^6$	$>19 \cdot 10^6$	$>28 \cdot 10^6$	$>54 \cdot 10^6$
$tot^{4,6}_{x_{max},y_{max}}$	42	42	44	44	46	48	54	64	80	116	226

All $k^{(4)}$ values are possible. The attacker cannot determine $k^{(4)}$, $k^{(5)}$ or $k^{(6)}$. In all cases, we have at least 2 possibilities for each of the filter sizes. Since there are 18 max pooling and convolutional layers in VGG-16, we can extrapolate once again and say that our protection could lead to a multiplication of the search space by 2^{18}. This leads to a reduced search space of 2^{22}. Let also remind the reader that $k^{(4)}$ and $k^{(5)}$ can actually differ, making a potential attacker's life even harder.

7.2   Performance Evaluation

Experimental Platform. We launch our experiments on a DELL work station OptiPlex 7040 with a 4-core Intel Core i7 processor and three levels of cache of sizes, respectively, 32 KB, 256 KB and 8192 KB. Our experiments are carried out using Debian 4.19.152-1.

Performance. Let us consider a perfect attacker, who can recover the Flush and Reload traces without any noise. To simulate this, we use the GNU Debugger (GDB) to log all calls to `itcopy` and `oncopy`, along with the cycles at which they were called. Figure 6a shows such a simulation of an unprotected model.

(a) Simulation of a Flush and Reload attack on `itcopy` and `oncopy` patterns of an unprotected model.

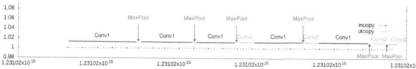

(b) Simulation of a Flush and Reload attack on `itcopy` and `oncopy` patterns of a protected model.

Fig. 6. Simulation of Flush and Reload on an unprotected (a) and a protected (b) model. The model considered has 2 convolutional layers separated by a max pooling one. Block sizes are between 32 and 38 in (b).

Once again, we can see in Fig. 6 that the layers' traces are interleaved, and it is difficult for an attacker to distinguish between the various layers.

Let us now consider our protection's overhead. Note that we do note take the creation of the architecture into account here, as it only needs to be executed once, rather than at each inference computation. We consider three architectures in our experiments. In all cases, there is only 1 input and output featuremap, the convolutional filter size is 3×3, the pooling window size is 2×2 and there is no padding. The architectures are as follows:

1. Conv – MaxPool – Conv – MaxPool (arch1)
2. Conv – MaxPool – Conv (arch2)
3. Conv – Conv (arch3).

We average the execution time over 1,000 runs for several input sizes, as shown in Table 3. The time overhead depends heavily on the architecture's depth, the input size, the layer types and the block sizes. The case $B = 1$ in Table 4 is included to show the importance of correctly selecting the minimal block size. The high overhead incurred in the case where one neuron is computed at a time confirms our assertion in Sect. 4.1, stating that considering one neuron at a time would take too long. Let us now consider the case $B = 32$. In some cases, such as arch2 with input shape $1 \times 20 \times 20$, the randomized protection has almost the same execution time as a normal execution. We believe that the higher overhead in arch3 is due to the lack of maxpooling layers: this leads to higher input sizes for the convolutional layers, and convolutional layers take naturally longer to compute than maxpooling. Let us remind the reader that we did not use common frameworks such as PyTorch [21] or TensorFlow [1], as explained in Sect. 7.4. Moreover, because the GeMM operation is operated on a very low level and ensures an optimally filled cache, it is very efficient. It is not the case for our high-level block subdivisions and multiplications. Thus, since common ML frameworks are heavily optimized, and so is the GeMM operation, we believe that the worst case in Table 3 being 8 times more time consuming than an unprotected operation is reasonable, and the time overhead could be improved a lot with further optimization. This is especially the case since we compare our implementation's execution time to a standard, highly optimized, Keras – with TensorFlow as a backend – one. Furthermore, despite the incurred overhead, we believe that our countermeasure is a first important step towards a secure real time execution.

Table 3. Execution times for three different architectures, depending on the type of protection added. In all cases, the block size is $B = 32$.

Input shape	Protection type	arch1		arch2		arch3	
$1 \times 28 \times 28$	None	/	/	842 μs	1	606 μs	1
	Blocks, no random	/	/	1634 μs	×1.94	4966 μs	×8.19
	Blocks, random	/	/	1714 μs	×2.04	4995 μs	×8.24
$1 \times 22 \times 22$	None	698 μs	1	610 μs	1	764 μs	1
	Blocks, no random	904 μs	×1.30	927 μs	×1.52	2340 μs	×3.06
	Blocks, random	1004 μs	×1.44	989 μs	×1.62	2391 μs	×3.13
$1 \times 20 \times 20$	None	/	/	635 μs	1	542 μs	1
	Blocks, no random	/	/	745 μs	×1.17	1718 μs	×3.17
	Blocks, random	/	/	816 μs	×1.29	1765 μs	×3.26

Table 4. Execution times for three different architectures, depending on the block size considered. We compare the case $B = 1$ to the case $B = 32$ to show how crucial it is to select the correct block size. In all cases, we consider the random protection.

Block size	Input shape	arch1	arch2	arch3
1	$1 \times 28 \times 28$	/	2539 µs	50198 µs
	$1 \times 22 \times 22$	1047 µs	1006 µs	13923 µs
	$1 \times 20 \times 20$	/	842 µs	9406 µs
32	$1 \times 28 \times 28$	/	1714 µs	4995 µs
	$1 \times 22 \times 22$	1004 µs	989 µs	2391 µs
	$1 \times 20 \times 20$	/	816 µs	1765 µs

7.3 Discussion

Our approach is similar to [2] and [23] in the sense that we obtain the value of some neurons in layer $i+1$ before the execution of layer i is done. But besides the fact that we do not consider a hardware context, our suggestion differs in that we introduce randomization in the computation of neurons: we do not compute the value of a neuron as soon as enough elements are ready. Rather, we compute them in a random way determined at the creation of the architecture. Moreover, our goal is different: we aim at increasing the security by mitigating cache attacks based on the GeMM computations during an NN inference.

One limitation in our method is the pooling layer. Indeed, because its execution differs from that of convolutional layers, and no GeMM is applied, a potential attacker can detect when an execution switches between a convolutional layer and a pooling one. As shown in Sect. 7.1, however, our methodology still mitigates Cache Telepathy in architectures with pooling layers. We believe that architectures such as Fully Convolutional Networks (FCN) [17], which have several consecutive convolutional layers, could make the architecture almost completely leakage free.

The overhead induced depends on the block sizes and the model's depth. Balancing security of the protection – linked to the random block sizes – and the incurred overhead is however possible, as the said overhead is still manageable. We also believe that a better optimization of our implementation should reduce the observed overhead.

Even if our protection targets Cache Telepathy specifically, we believe it could be used against other side-channel attacks such as CSI [4], DeepRecon [12] or How to 0wn NAS [11]. Both CSI [4] and How to 0wn NAS [11] mention that reordering would indeed be a countermeasure to their method. CSI [4] bases its attack on the sequential nature of NNs. It proceeds layer by layer to find the number of neurons and the weights in each layer. In each layer, and for each multiplication $w \cdot x$ (where w is the weight and x is an input value), the attacker makes two hypotheses: either this multiplication takes place in layer i, or it takes place in layer $i + 1$. If the layers are not computed sequentially, then the hypotheses no longer make sense, as the multiplication could take place at a later layer. In the case of [11], layers as a whole are targeted. Indeed, specific functions corresponding to specific layers are monitored. Thus, splitting the layers would prevent them from targeting the pre-existing functions.

7.4 Scope and Limitations

Let us now discuss the scope and limitations of our countermeasure.

First of all, because the proposed approach needs to compute layers in a non-sequential order, it does not apply to FC layers, even though Cache Telepathy targets them as well. Indeed, these layers require all neurons from the previous layer to be computed before they can start their execution. We therefore limit our countermeasure to CNNs. However, as CNNs are now widely used in various fields such as the medical one [30], image processing [14] or game playing [24], our countermeasure can still apply to many commonly used architectures [10,25,26].

Second, as in the Cache Telepathy paper [31], we place ourselves in the CPU context. Indeed, as mentioned in [12], monitoring GeMM functions requires them to be in the same instruction line in the cache for the victim and the attacker. They therefore need to run on the CPU. As mentioned in Sect. 1, several popular MLaaS frameworks [3] provide CPU computations for inference.

Third, instead of using high-level, highly optimized frameworks such as TensorFlow [1] or PyTorch [21], we wrote our own implementation in C++. Indeed, we required more freedom when writing code, as commonly used functions in those frameworks apply to entire layers, when we needed to deal with neurons individually. Moreover, using C++ still enabled us to apply GeMM, which is the target of the attacker. This C++ implementation – necessarily less optimized than common ML frameworks – partially explains the overhead observed in Table 3 in Sect. 7.2.

Finally, as detailed in Sect. 7.2, our goal is to mitigate the Cache Telepathy attack by preventing an attacker from getting a tractable search space for the victim model's architecture. Thus, even though not all leakages are eliminated, an attacker still cannot recover the correct architecture without training over 2^{17} architectures, which is not feasible in a reasonable period of time.

8 Conclusion

In this paper, we introduce Telepathic Headache, a protection against cache-based attacks targeting the GeMM algorithm used by most ML frameworks to implement fully connected and convolutional layers in a CPU setting. To achieve this protection, we mix layers by computing neurons depth-wise, as soon as certain random-sized blocks of values in a layer are ready.

The security analysis of our method shows a multiplication by at least 2^{18} of the reduced search space obtained by Cache Telepathy on VGG-16. This makes our protection effective against the Cache Telepathy attack. The methodology we introduce could also be effective against other timing attacks such as DeepRecon and electromagnetic-based side-channel attacks such as CSI.

Further work could include a deeper analysis of the overhead incurred and how to limit it depending on the architecture. In the future, we can also study the effectiveness of our defense against other reverse-engineering attacks.

Acknowledgments. We would like to thank for all the insightful remarks and suggestions made to our article after its submission. They helped us to improve it a lot.

A   Protected Case: When the Attacker can Distinguish between Convolutional Layers

As explained in Sect. 7, we consider layers 4 ($Conv4$), 5 ($Conv5$) and 6 ($MaxPool$) in a VGG-16 architecture [25] (depicted in Fig. 5). $Conv4$ and $Conv5$ are computed according to the process in Fig. 1. In that process, inputs I_4 and I_5 are reshaped into R_4 and R_5 respectively. Let us note that in order to have an output size equal to the input size, the input needs to be padded. We consider I_4 and I_5 to be the padded inputs. Their shape is $(64, 114, 114)$ and $(128, 114, 114)$ respectively. Let $O^{(j)}$ denote the reshaped output of layer j – i.e. the output of the layer's matrix multiplication.

Let $H^{(4)} = \{H_1^{(4)}, ..., H_t^{(4)}\}$ be the number of blocks height-wise for each width-wise column of blocks. Let us denote $w^{(4)} = \{w_1^{(4)}, ..., w_{t'}^{(4)}\}$ – respectively $h^{(4)} = \{h_1^{(4)}, ..., h_t^{(4)}\}$ – the sizes of the blocks width-wise – respectively height-wise. These are determined as described in Sect. 5. Further, let $\{M_{i,j}^{(4)}\}_{1 \leq i \leq t, 1 \leq t'}$ denote the number of filter blocks associated with each of $Conv4$'s input blocks. The reshaped filters are F_4 and F_5 respectively. The blocks we consider are submatrices in $R_{4,5}$ and $F_{4,5}$. R_4 and R_5 both have width $W_{4,5} = 112 \times 112$. R_4 has height $3 \times 3 \times 64$ while R_5 has height $3 \times 3 \times 128$.

In our case, each block has size between 32×32 and 64×64. Let (x_b, y_b) be the coordinates of the last element in the first block in R_5. If we take the minimal block size, then $(x_{\min}, y_{\min}) = (32, 32)$. In the case of the maximal block size, $(x_{\max}, y_{\max}) = (64, 64)$.

Let $tot_{x,y}^{i,j}$ denote the number of matrix multiplications in layer i required so that the element (x, y) in R_j is ready. Since our goal is to determine the number of multiplications in $Conv4$ necessary to have the first block in $Conv5$ ready, we actually need to compute $tot_{x_b,y_b}^{4,5}$. We will consider block size extremes to give a range of values for $tot_{x_b,y_b}^{4,5}$:

$$tot_{x_{\max},y_{\max}}^{4,5} \leq tot_{x_b,y_b}^{4,5} \leq tot_{x_{\min},y_{\min}}^{4,5}$$

In order to compute that value, we need to find the coordinates of element $e = (x, y)$ in I_5 rather than R_5. Indeed, this will provide us with the blocks that need to be computed in $Conv4$ to obtain e.

First, let us find which input channel ch element e belongs to. Because of the way R_5 is obtained, we have that:

$$ch = \left\lfloor \frac{x}{k^{(4)} \times k^{(4)}} \right\rfloor$$

Thus:

$$ch_{e_{\min}} = \left\lfloor \frac{32}{k^{(4)} \times k^{(4)}} \right\rfloor = 3$$

$$ch_{e_{\max}} = \left\lfloor \frac{64}{k^{(4)} \times k^{(4)}} \right\rfloor = 7$$

where $e_{\min} = (x_{\min}, y_{\min})$ and $e_{\max} = (x_{\min}, y_{\min})$ indicate the maximal and minimal block sizes respectively.

Let us now find the coordinates (row, col) of element e in channel ch. Let $n' = n+2{\cdot}p = 114$ be the padded input width and height. With an input of shape (n', n'), a convolution results in an output of size $(n' - k^{(4)} + 1, n' - k^{(4)} + 1) = (n, n)$ here. Because of the way I_5 is reshaped, each column in R_5 is a $k^{(5)} \times k^{(5)}$ window in I_5. Thus,

$$row = \left\lfloor \frac{y}{n} \right\rfloor + \left\lfloor \frac{x \mod (k^{(5)} \times k^{(5)})}{k^{(5)}} \right\rfloor$$

$$col = y \mod n + (x \mod (k^{(5)} \times k^{(5)})) \mod k^{(5)}$$

As mentioned before, these coordinates include the padding. We need to remove said padding to find out how many computations from the previous layer need to have been made. If (row, col) does not correspond to a padding value, we have:

$$row_{unpadded} = row - p$$

$$col_{unpadded} = col - p$$

If $row < p$ with $ch = 0$, then no value from the previous layer needs to be computed for the first block to be executed. This results in $tot_{x,y}^{4,5} = 0$. The same goes for $row = p$, $ch = 0$ and $col < p$.

If (x, y) is a padding value outside of the two previous cases, then we consider the previous non-padding value in I_5. This corresponds to:

$$row_{unpadded} = row - 1$$

$$col_{unpadded} = n'$$

Indeed, we then need to take the last (non-padding) element in the previous row.

With $(x_{\min}, y_{\min})$ and $(x_{\max}, y_{\max})$, we have that:

$$row_{\min} = \left\lfloor \frac{32}{112} \right\rfloor + \left\lfloor \frac{32 \mod (3 \times 3)}{3} \right\rfloor = 2$$

$$col_{\min} = 32 \mod 112 + (32 \mod (3 \times 3)) \mod 3 = 34$$

$$row_{\max} = \left\lfloor \frac{64}{112} \right\rfloor + \left\lfloor \frac{64 \mod (3 \times 3)}{3} \right\rfloor = 0$$

$$col_{\max} = 64 \mod 112 + (64 \mod (3 \times 3)) \mod 3 = 65$$

Because $e_{\max} = (x_{\max}, y_{\max})$ is in the first row of I_5, it corresponds to a padding element. However, not all elements in that block stem from padding elements. Instead, we can take the last non-padding element in the previous channel. We therefore need to consider channel $ch'_{e_{\max}} = ch_{e_{\max}} - 1 = 6$. We also need to select the last element of the (3×3) input window, meaning:

$$row'_{\max} = 2$$
$$col'_{\max} = 66$$

We then remove the padding from $e_{\min} = (x_{\min}, y_{\min})$ so as to find the coordinates in $Conv4$'s output. This gives us:

$$row'_{\min} = 1$$
$$col'_{\min} = 33$$
$$ch'_{e_{\min}} = 3$$
$$row'_{\max} = 2$$
$$col'_{\max} = 66$$
$$ch'_{e_{\max}} = 6$$

These are the coordinates of the last element we need in the output of $Conv4$. The coordinates c of that element in the said output are:

$$c_{\min} = (ch'_{e_{\min}}, row'_{\min} \times n + col'_{\min}) = (3, 145)$$
$$c_{\max} = (ch'_{e_{\max}}, row'_{\max} \times n + col'_{\max}) = (6, 290)$$

We now have enough information to compute $tot_e^{4,5}$.

Let $b = \arg\min_{b'} \left(\sum_{q=0}^{b'} w_1 \geq c \right)$. b is the number of the block width-wise containing c. For each block number $b' < b$, we need to multiply all the blocks height-wise with their associated block filters, meaning $H_{b'}^{(4)} \times M_{b'}^{(4)}$ multiplications for each block b'. For b, we need to compute all the height-wise block multiplications up to the block containing ch. This is equal to: $\left\lceil \frac{ch}{h_1^{(4)}} \right\rceil \times H_b^{(4)}$.

The full formula is then:

$$tot_e^{1,2} = \left(\sum_{q=0}^{b-1} H_q^{(4)} \times M_q^{(4)} \right) + \left\lceil \frac{ch}{h_1^{(4)}} \right\rceil \times H_b^{(4)} \tag{2}$$

We can apply that to e_{max} and e_{min}, considering constant block shapes of either $(32, 32)$ for e_{min} or $(64, 64)$ for e_{max}:

$$b_{e_{min}} = \left\lceil \frac{145}{32} \right\rceil = 5 \tag{3}$$

$$H_{q,min}^{(4)} = \left\lceil \frac{3 \times 3 \times 64}{32} \right\rceil = 18 \; \forall q \leq b \tag{4}$$

$$M_{q,min}^{(4)} = \left\lceil \frac{128}{32} \right\rceil = 4 \; \forall q \leq b \tag{5}$$

$$\left\lceil \frac{ch_{e'_{min}}}{32} \right\rceil \times H_{b,min}^{(4)} = 4 \tag{6}$$

$$tot_{e_{min}}^{4,5} = b_{e_{min}} \times H_q^{(4)} \times M_q^{(4)} + \left\lceil \frac{ch_{e'_{min}}}{32} \right\rceil \times H_b^{(4)} \tag{7}$$

$$= 292 \tag{8}$$

$$b_{e_{max}} = \left\lceil \frac{290}{64} \right\rceil = 5 \tag{9}$$

$$H_{max}^{(4)} = H_{q,max}^{(4)} = \left\lceil \frac{3 \times 3 \times 64}{64} \right\rceil = 9 \; \forall q \leq b \tag{10}$$

$$M_{max}^{(4)} = M_{q,max}^{(4)} = \left\lceil \frac{128}{64} \right\rceil = 2 \tag{11}$$

$$\left\lceil \frac{ch_{e'_{max}}}{64} \right\rceil \times H_{b,max}^{(4)} = 2 \tag{12}$$

$$tot_{e_{max}}^{4,5} = (b_{e_{max}} - 1) \times H_{max}^{(4)} \times M_{max}^{(4)} + \left\lceil \frac{ch_{e'_{max}}}{64} \right\rceil \times H_{b,max}^{(4)} \tag{13}$$

$$= 74 \tag{14}$$

Thus, the total number of matrix multiplications required for one block in $Conv5$ to be ready ranges between 74 and 292 depending on the block sizes. This range of values can be obtained because we know the padding and filter sizes. A potential attacker, however, does not have access to this information. She only knows the number of input channels and the input shape.

Table 5. Maximal and minimal number of multiplications depending on the filter size, when the attacker can distinguish between convolutional layers.

$k^{(4)}$	1	2	3	4	5	6	7	8	9	10	11
$tot_{x'_{min}, y'_{max}}^{4,5}$	2	8	306	928	1,400	4,896	5,488	7,168	6,480	8,000	6,776
$tot_{x'_{max}, y'_{min}}^{4,5}$	1	4	9	16	25	36	49	64	324	400	242

Let us compute all the possible values for $tot_{x,y}^{1,2}$ $(x'_{min}, y'_{min}) = (32, 32)$ and $(x'_{max}, y'_{max}) = (64, 64)$, given out_4, out_5 and in_5 and depending on $k^{(4)} = k^{(5)}$. Table 5 shows the resulting values.

B   Protected Case: When the Attacker Cannot Distinguish Between Convolutional Layers

Since the attacker cannot distinguish between convolutional layers, we need to compute $tot^{4,6}$. If we denote (x, y) the last element in the first $MaxPool$ block R_B, and (x', y') the last element in $Conv5$ that needs to be computed for R_B to be ready, then: $tot_{x,y}^{4,6} = tot_{x',y'}^{4,5} + tot_{x,y}^{5,6}$. In our case, $MaxPool$ has window size $k^{(6)} = 2$, and does not require any padding. Furthermore, all channels need to be computed at once in the pooling case. Thus, the coordinates of (x, y) in the output of $Conv5$ are:

$$row = \left\lfloor \frac{k^{(6)} \cdot y}{n} \right\rfloor + \left\lfloor \frac{x}{k^{(6)}} \right\rfloor$$

$$col = \left(y \mod \frac{n}{k^{(6)}} \right) \times k^{(6)} + x \mod k^{(6)}$$

$$c = row \times n + col$$

We also have that $b = \arg\min_{b'} \left(\sum_{q=0}^{b'} w_1 \geq c \right)$. Applying it to our case for $(x_{min}, y_{min}) = (32, 32)$ and $(x_{max}, y_{max}) = (64, 64)$, we have:

$$row_{min} = \left\lfloor \frac{2 \cdot 32}{112} \right\rfloor + \left\lfloor \frac{32}{2} \right\rfloor \qquad\qquad = 16$$

$$col_{min} = \left(32 \mod \frac{112}{2} \right) \times 2 + 32 \mod 2 \qquad = 64$$

$$c_{min} = row \times 112 + col \qquad\qquad\qquad = 1856$$

$$b_{min} = \left\lceil \frac{c_{min}}{32} \right\rceil \qquad\qquad\qquad\qquad = 58$$

$$row_{max} = \left\lfloor \frac{2 \cdot 64}{112} \right\rfloor + \left\lfloor \frac{64}{2} \right\rfloor \qquad\qquad = 33$$

$$col_{max} = \left(64 \mod \frac{112}{2} \right) \times 2 + 64 \mod 2 \qquad = 16$$

$$c_{max} = row \times 112 + col \qquad\qquad\qquad = 3712$$

$$b_{max} = \left\lceil \frac{c_{max}}{64} \right\rceil \qquad\qquad\qquad\qquad = 58$$

In $O^{(5)}$, we need the element with coordinates $(ch, B \cdot b)$ where ch is the last filter of $Conv5$, since $MaxPool$ requires all channels to be completed. That element requires element $(x', y') = (in_5 \times k^{(5)} \times k^{(5)}, B \cdot b)$ in $I^{(5)}$. Indeed, the column number in $O^{(5)}$ and $I^{(5)}$ must be the same. Furthermore, the whole column must be computed, which is why $x' = in_5 \times k^{(5)} \times k^{(5)}$. Thus, the previous formulas directly provide us with (x', y'):

$$(x'_{min}, y'_{min}) = (in_5 \times k^{(5)} \times k^{(5)} - 1, 32 \cdot b_{min}) \qquad = (128 \times 9 - 1, 1856)$$

$$(x'_{max}, y'_{max}) = (in_5 \times k^{(5)} \times k^{(5)} - 1, 64 \cdot b_{max}) \qquad = (128 \times 9 - 1, 3712)$$

Thus, given $Conv5$ has 128 input and output channels:

$$H^{(5)}_{min} = \left\lceil \frac{128 \times 9 - 1}{32} \right\rceil \qquad = 36$$

$$H^{(5)}_{max} = \left\lceil \frac{128 \times 9 - 1}{64} \right\rceil \qquad = 18$$

$$M^{(5)}_{min} = \left\lceil \frac{128}{32} \right\rceil \qquad = 4$$

$$M^{(5)}_{max} = \left\lceil \frac{128}{64} \right\rceil \qquad = 2$$

$$tot^{5,6}_{32,32} = b_{min} \times H^{(5)}_{min} \times M^{(5)}_{min} \qquad = 8352$$

$$tot^{5,6}_{64,64} = b_{max} \times H^{(5)}_{max} \times M^{(5)}_{max} \qquad = 2088$$

Here, we have $H^{(5)} \times M^{(5)}$ for width-wise block b as well because the whole b-th block width-wise needs to be computed, as well as all channels.

Applying the same process as previously to compute $tot^{4,5}_{e_{min}}$ and $tot^{4,5}_{e_{max}}$, we have:

$$tot^{4,5}_{x'_{min},y'_{min}} = 4338$$

$$tot^{4,5}_{x'_{max},y'_{max}} = 1053$$

Thus, we have:

$$tot^{4,6}_{x'_{min},y'_{min}} = tot^{5,6}_{x_{min},y_{min}} + tot^{4,5}_{in_5 \times k^{(5)} \times k^{(5)}, e_{min} \cdot b_{min}} \qquad = 12690$$

$$tot^{4,6}_{x'_{max},y'_{max}} = tot^{5,6}_{x_{max},y_{max}} + tot^{4,5}_{in_5 \times k^{(5)} \times k^{(5)}, e_{max} \cdot b_{max}} \qquad = 3141$$

Thus, the total number of multiplications for one $MaxPool$ block to be ready ranges between $3,141$ and $12,690$ in the set of layers we study from the VGG-16 architecture.

Once again, the attacker does not know $k^{(4)}, k^{(5)}, k^{(6)}$ or the padding values. For each layer, $k^{(i)} \in \{1, ..., 11\}$. We also suppose, like before, that $k^{(4)} = k^{(5)}$. The padding p between $Conv4$ and $Conv5$ (the only one that intervenes in the computations) is such that $p < k^{(4)}$. We get tables of possible values depending on $k^{(4)} = k^{(5)}$, p and $k^{(6)}$. As before, we take the maximum and minimal values over all possible p. Table 6 considers the range of $tot^{4,6}$ depending on $k^{(4)}$.

Table 6. Maximal and minimal number of multiplications depending on the filter size, when the attacker cannot distinguish between convolutional layers but knows out_4, in_5 and out_5.

$k^{(4)}$	1	2	3	4	5	6	7	8	9	10	11
$tot^{4,6}_{x_{min},y_{min}}$	2,712	10,976	24,912	44,800	70,600	102,528	141,120	185,856	237,168	295,200	360,096
$tot^{4,6}_{x_{max},y_{max}}$	126	504	1,134	1,984	3,100	4,464	5,978	7,808	9,882	12,000	14,520

Once again, the ranges for all possible $tot^{4,6}$ values overlap, making it harder for the attacker to determine the architecture. In our case, we had $tot^{4,6} \in [3141, 12041]$. An attacker could therefore only deduce that $1 < k^{(4)} < 11$. The range can be further deduced depending on the value actually observed, but there are at least two filter size values in every case. Furthermore, for most $k^{(6)}$ values, $2 < k^{(4)} < 10$.

So far, we had assumed, for simplicity, that the number of input and output channels are known for all layers. But it is generally not the case. Taking this last fact into account, the possible $tot^{4,6}$ values are given in Table 7.

Table 7. Maximal and minimal number of multiplications depending on the filter size, when the attacker cannot distinguish between convolutional layers.

$k^{(4)}$	1	2	3	4	5	6
$tot^{4,6}_{x_{min},y_{min}}$	$>9.6 \cdot 10^6$	$>10.5 \cdot 10^6$	$>10 \cdot 10^6$	$>11 \cdot 10^6$	$>11 \cdot 10^6$	$>12 \cdot 10^6$
$tot^{4,6}_{x_{max},y_{max}}$	42	42	44	44	46	48
$k^{(4)}$	7	8	9	10	11	
$tot^{4,6}_{x_{min},y_{min}}$	$>13.4 \cdot 10^6$	$>15.8 \cdot 10^6$	$>19.2 \cdot 10^6$	$>28.3 \cdot 10^6$	$>54.7 \cdot 10^6$	
$tot^{4,6}_{x_{max},y_{max}}$	54	64	80	116	226	

C   Reshaping

See Fig. 7 and Fig. 8.

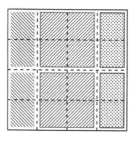

Fig. 7. Example of a subdivision of a reshaped input

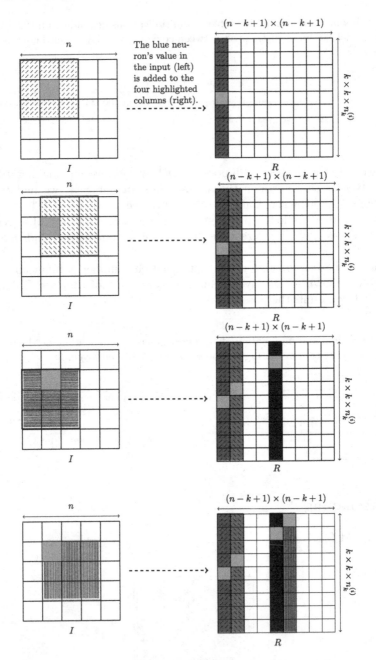

Fig. 8. Reshaping the input to turn a convolution into a matrix multiplication. The input size is $n \times n$ and the filter size is $k \times k$.

References

1. Abadi, M., et al.: TensorFlow: a system for large-scale machine learning. In: 12th USENIX Symposium on Operating Systems Design and Implementation (OSDI 2016), pp. 265–283 (2016)
2. Alwani, M., Chen, H., Ferdman, M., Milder, P.A.: Fused-layer CNN accelerators. In: MICRO, pp. 22:1–22:12. IEEE Computer Society (2016)
3. Amazon: Sagemaker ML InstanceTypes (2018). https://aws.amazon.com/sagemaker/pricing/instance-types/
4. Batina, L., Bhasin, S., Jap, D., Picek, S.: CSI NN: reverse engineering of neural network architectures through electromagnetic side channel. In: USENIX Security Symposium, pp. 515–532. USENIX Association (2019)
5. Breier, J., Jap, D., Hou, X., Bhasin, S., Liu, Y.: SNIFF: reverse engineering of neural networks with fault attacks. CoRR abs/2002.11021 (2020)
6. Carlini, N., Jagielski, M., Mironov, I.: Cryptanalytic extraction of neural network models. In: Micciancio, D., Ristenpart, T. (eds.) CRYPTO 2020. LNCS, vol. 12172, pp. 189–218. Springer, Cham (2020). https://doi.org/10.1007/978-3-030-56877-1_7
7. Dubey, A., Cammarota, R., Aysu, A.: MaskedNet: a pathway for secure inference against power side-channel attacks. CoRR abs/1910.13063 (2019)
8. Dubey, A., Cammarota, R., Aysu, A.: BoMaNet: Boolean masking of an entire neural network. CoRR abs/2006.09532 (2020)
9. Goto, K., van de Geijn, R.A.: Anatomy of high-performance matrix multiplication. ACM Trans. Math. Softw. 34(3), 12:1–12:25 (2008)
10. He, K., Zhang, X., Ren, S., Sun, J.: Deep residual learning for image recognition. In: 2016 IEEE Conference on Computer Vision and Pattern Recognition, CVPR 2016, Las Vegas, NV, USA, 27–30 June 2016, pp. 770–778. IEEE Computer Society (2016). https://doi.org/10.1109/CVPR.2016.90
11. Hong, S., Davinroy, M., Kaya, Y., Dachman-Soled, D., Dumitras, T.: How to own the NAS in your spare time. In: ICLR. OpenReview.net (2020)
12. Hong, S., et al.: Security analysis of deep neural networks operating in the presence of cache side-channel attacks. CoRR abs/1810.03487 (2018)
13. Hua, W., Zhang, Z., Suh, G.E.: Reverse engineering convolutional neural networks through side-channel information leaks. In: DAC, pp. 4:1–4:6. ACM (2018)
14. Apple Inc.: Face id security. White paper (2017)
15. Jagielski, M., Carlini, N., Berthelot, D., Kurakin, A., Papernot, N.: High-fidelity extraction of neural network models. CoRR abs/1909.01838 (2019)
16. Krizhevsky, A., Sutskever, I., Hinton, G.E.: ImageNet classification with deep convolutional neural networks. In: NIPS, pp. 1106–1114 (2012)
17. Long, J., Shelhamer, E., Darrell, T.: Fully convolutional networks for semantic segmentation. In: CVPR, pp. 3431–3440. IEEE Computer Society (2015)
18. Long, Y., et al.: Understanding membership inferences on well-generalized learning models. CoRR abs/1802.04889 (2018)
19. Mondal, A., Srivastava, A.: Energy-efficient design of MTJ-based neural networks with stochastic computing. ACM J. Emerg. Technol. Comput. Syst. 16(1), 7:1–7:27 (2020)
20. Papernot, N., McDaniel, P.D., Jha, S., Fredrikson, M., Celik, Z.B., Swami, A.: The limitations of deep learning in adversarial settings. In: EuroS&P, pp. 372–387. IEEE (2016)
21. Paszke, A., et al.: PyTorch: an imperative style, high-performance deep learning library. In: Wallach, H., Larochelle, H., Beygelzimer, A., d' Alché-Buc, F., Fox, E.,

Garnett, R. (eds.) Advances in Neural Information Processing Systems, vol. 32, pp. 8024–8035. Curran Associates, Inc. (2019). http://papers.neurips.cc/paper/9015-pytorch-an-imperative-style-high-performance-deep-learning-library.pdf

22. Ren, K., Zheng, T., Qin, Z., Liu, X.: Adversarial attacks and defenses in deeplearning. Engineering **6**(3), 346–360 (2020). https://doi.org/10.1016/j.eng.2019.12.012. https://www.sciencedirect.com/science/article/pii/S209580991930503X

23. Shafiee, A., et al.: ISAAC: a convolutional neural network accelerator with in-situ analog arithmetic in crossbars. In: ISCA, pp. 14–26. IEEE Computer Society (2016)

24. Silver, D., et al.: Mastering the game of go without human knowledge. Nature **550**(7676), 354–359 (2017)

25. Simonyan, K., Zisserman, A.: Very deep convolutional networks for large-scale image recognition. In: ICLR (2015)

26. Szegedy, C., Vanhoucke, V., Ioffe, S., Shlens, J., Wojna, Z.: Rethinking the inception architecture for computer vision. In: 2016 IEEE Conference on Computer Vision and Pattern Recognition, CVPR 2016, Las Vegas, NV, USA, 27–30 June 2016, pp. 2818–2826. IEEE Computer Society (2016). https://doi.org/10.1109/CVPR.2016.308

27. Tople, S., Grover, K., Shinde, S., Bhagwan, R., Ramjee, R.: Privado: practical and secure DNN inference. CoRR abs/1810.00602 (2018)

28. Tramèr, F., Zhang, F., Juels, A., Reiter, M.K., Ristenpart, T.: Stealing machine learning models via prediction apis. CoRR abs/1609.02943 (2016)

29. VanNostrand, P.M., Kyriazis, I., Cheng, M., Guo, T., Walls, R.J.: Confidential deep learning: executing proprietary models on untrusted devices. CoRR abs/1908.10730 (2019)

30. Yamashita, R., Nishio, M., Do, R.K.G., Togashi, K.: Convolutional neural networks: an overview and application in radiology. Insights Imaging **9**(4), 611–629 (2018). https://doi.org/10.1007/s13244-018-0639-9

31. Yan, M., Fletcher, C.W., Torrellas, J.: Cache telepathy: leveraging shared resource attacks to learn DNN architectures. In: USENIX Security Symposium, pp. 2003–2020. USENIX Association (2020)

32. Yarom, Y., Falkner, K.: FLUSH+RELOAD: a high resolution, low noise, L3 cache side-channel attack. In: USENIX Security Symposium, pp. 719–732. USENIX Association (2014)

Efficient FPGA Design of Exception-Free Generic Elliptic Curve Cryptosystems

Kiyofumi Tanaka[1](✉), Atsuko Miyaji[1,2], and Yaoan Jin[2]

[1] School of Information Science, Japan Advanced Institute of Science
and Technology, 1–1 Asahidai, Nomi, Ishikawa 923–1292, Japan
kiyofumi@jaist.ac.jp
[2] Graduate School of Engineering, Osaka University, Suita, Osaka 565–0871, Japan
miyaji@comm.eng.osaka-u.ac.jp, jin@cy2sec.comm.eng.osaka-u.ac.jp

Abstract. Elliptic curve cryptography (ECC) is one of promising cryptosystems in embedded systems as it provides high security levels with short keys. Scalar multiplication is a dominating and time-consuming process that ensures security in ECC. We implement hardware modules for generic ECC over 256-bit prime fields on field-programmable gate array (FPGA). The key points in our design are (1) secure and exception-free for any scalar with less memory usage, (2) long-bit modular arithmetic modules utilizing today's advanced and high-performance programmable logic and considering balance between the modules in terms of propagation delay, (3) parallelism extraction inside each elliptic curve point computation as well as between the point computations, and (4) efficient hardware–software co-processing facilitated by application interfaces between a processing core and hardware modules. The evaluation results demonstrate that our design achieves the best performance to existing FPGA designs without using a table for generic ECC.

Keywords: Elliptic curve cryptosystem · Complete addition · Exception-free · FPGA

1 Introduction

Elliptic curve cryptography (ECC) is one of promising cryptosystems in embedded systems as it provides high security levels with short keys. Therefore, ECC is becoming a mainstream cryptosystem in embedded systems where memory resources are constrained. However, the use of ECC still requires considerable processing time as well as memory, especially for software in embedded systems with constrained processing speed. Hardware acceleration is a promising option to reduce the overhead of software processing.

The dominant computation of ECCs is scalar multiplication, which computes kP for an elliptic curve point P and a scalar k. Thus, the security and efficiency of the scalar multiplication are paramount. To implement scalar multiplication, several types of coordinates for elliptic curves exist (such as affine, Jacobian, or

© Springer Nature Switzerland AG 2021
K. Sako and N. O. Tippenhauer (Eds.): ACNS 2021, LNCS 12726, pp. 393–414, 2021.
https://doi.org/10.1007/978-3-030-78372-3_15

Projective). To be secure against simple power analysis (SPA), these coordinates need to be combined with secure scalar multiplication algorithms without any branch instruction such as Joye's RL algorithm [17].

Recently, more advanced security notion of *exception free* is introduced [32], where scalar multiplication should work for any scalar k including $k = 0$. Since complete addition (CA) formulae can work in the same formulae of addition and doubling formulae [32], combining with Joye's RL algorithm is secure against SPA and exception-free for any scalar k. Although various ECC FPGA implementations have been proposed so far [6–8,12–14,22,26], any of them neither employs CA formulae nor satisfies exception-free secure. They fail to execute a case that the MSB of k is equal to 0 as well as $k = 0$. However, CA formulae uses three coordinates of X, Y, and Z to represent an elliptic curve point and, thus, it is far from less memory. Recently, another approach to use exception-free affine coordinate, which is a combination of affine and extended affine coordinates, is proposed [16]. Combining exception-free affine coordinates with improved Joye's RL algorithm is secure against SPA for any scalar k. Importantly, exception-free affine coordinates can represent an elliptic curve point by two coordinates, which can work with less memory compared with combination of CA formulae and Joye's RL algorithm. To give high performance of the scalar multiplication while keeping the resistance to SPA, one of simple ways is to focus on a specified elliptic curve such as NIST P-256 [14], which chooses an affine coordinate for the reason of less memory and works efficiently on only NIST P-256. However, their design cannot be applied to any other elliptic curves. For universal usage, an important point is *generic* elliptic curve design, which provides an architecture available to any elliptic curve over a finite field. Another strategy to give the high-performance is to use a precomputation table such as window methods [25,30]. However, it requires additional memory. For example, the implementation in [24] can work on a generic elliptic curve and is secure against SPA and exception-free. However, since it is based on window methods, it needs additional memory of points.

In this paper, we aim at efficient hardware–software FPGA design of generic ECC with less-memory which is secure against SPA and satisfies exception-free for $\forall k$. Especially, we focus on system-on-chip (SoC) type of FPGA device. Compared to conventional FPGA devices with programmable logic only, SoC FPGA device provides a tightly coupled system so that data transfer between a processor core and a programmable logic part is performed at high speeds. We implement EC point computations as hardware modules by making complete use of advanced and high-performance programmable logic in today's FPGA devices. Software processing performs scalar multiplication by invoking each hardware module when needed. In real-time applications, EC scalar multiplication processing shorter than 1 ms is highly desirable as many control tasks use a period less than or equal to 1 ms [34]. Our design achieves this requirement by utilizing high-performance resources in today's FPGA devices. To the best of our knowledge, our accelerator performs secure and exception-free scalar multiplications faster than any FPGA implementations for a generic ECC without any table over 256-bit prime fields [6, 7, 12–14, 22, 26].

This paper is organized as follows. First, we summarize basic notion of elliptic cryptosystems in Sect. 2. Then, we describe related works in Sect. 3. Subsequently, we clarify our targets in Sect. 4. We describe the details of our design in Sect. 5. Experimental results are shown in Sect. 6. We conclude our work in Sect. 7.

2   Operations in Elliptic Curve Cryptography

2.1   Addition Formulae on Elliptic Curve

Elliptic curve cryptography (ECC), which was proposed in the 1980s [19, 29], is a public-key cryptography system, and its cipher strength depends on the difficulty of the elliptic curve discrete logarithm problem. This section describes our target elliptic curve and addition formulae.

We target the elliptic curve E over a prime field $\mathbb{F}_p (p > 3)$ expressed by the following short Weierstrass form:

$$E/\mathbb{F}_p : y^2 = x^3 + ax + b \ \ (a, b \in \mathbb{F}_p, 4a^3 + 27b^2 \neq 0)$$

For a set of points on this curve and a point at infinity, $\mathcal{O}$, the addition is geometrically defined. In the affine coordinate system, for a point $P_1 = (x_1, y_1)$ and a point $P_2 = (x_2, y_2)$ $(P_1 \neq P_2)$, point addition, $P_3 = (x_3, y_3) = P_1 + P_2$, is calculated as follows:

$$x_3 = (\frac{y_2 - y_1}{x_2 - x_1})^2 - x_1 - x_2$$

$$y_3 = (\frac{y_2 - y_1}{x_2 - x_1})(x_1 - x_3) - y_1$$

Similarly, point doubling, $P_3 = 2P_1$, is defined as follows:

$$x_3 = (\frac{3x_1^2 + a}{2y_1})^2 - 2x_p$$

$$y_3 = (\frac{3x_1^2 + a}{2y_1})(x_1 - x_3) - y_1$$

Compared to the formulae for other projective coordinate systems, the above calculation of the affine coordinate system is desirable in terms of memory usage. As the variables in the above formulae (x_1, y_2, and so on) are multi-bit data (longer than 32- or 64-bit) and P_3 must be an element in $\mathbb{F}_p$, multi-bit modular addition (subtraction), multi-bit modular multiplication, and multi-bit modular inversion for division are required. Performing multi-bit division directly would involve high computational complexity. Instead, an inverse element should be obtained and multiplied.

2.2 Scalar Multiplication

While processing encryption and decryption in elliptic curve cryptography systems, multiplication of a point on the elliptic curve and scalar dominates the total computation cost. Scalar multiplication can be performed by applying point addition and point doubling in Sect. 2.1. The simplest approach is to use a binary method [10]: variables R and Q, initialized to $\mathcal{O}$ and P, respectively, are prepared. A scalar value in binary is scanned from the least significant bit to the most significant bit (or in the opposite direction). When the corresponding bit is zero, Q is updated by $2Q$. Otherwise, Q is updated by $2Q$ after R is updated by $R + Q$. (For the opposite scanning direction, R is updated by addition after Q is updated by doubling.) The final R is the result of scalar multiplication, kP.

In the above method, the execution time of a loop iteration varies according to the value of the corresponding bit. That is, it performs only point doubling, or both point addition and point doubling. This indicates that the method is vulnerable to simple power analysis (SPA) attacks that exploit energy dissipation measured and infer the input value [20]. To alleviate this problem, Joye's m-ary Ladder [17] was proposed by reforming the binary method, where the computation in an iteration is made uniform. This uniformity is achieved by transforming each digit in the m-ary expression of the scalar into a nonzero form such that an addition and a m-times multiplication are executed every time. However, it is not completely secure against SPA, as there can be exceptional addition with $\mathcal{O}$ in the processing of point addition on the affine coordinates.

To solve the problem of exceptional addition with $\mathcal{O}$, Jin et al. proposed the New 1-bit 2-ary Right-to-Left Powering Ladder [16]. This algorithm does not involve exceptional addition by avoiding initialization with $\mathcal{O}$ in the above-mentioned method. In addition, the algorithm is extended to the New 2-bit 2-ary Right-to-Left Powering Ladder, where the main loop is unrolled such that processing for every two bits in k is done in an iteration. In the iteration, affine double-quadruple [23] is used to obtain double and quadruple values, with only one inversion computation involved. As a result, the combination of loop unrolling and affine double-quadruple reduces the amount of computation in the main loop.

To reduce the amount of hardware resources required, our target algorithm is the above-mentioned New 1-bit 2-ary Right-to-Left Powering Ladder, rather than the 2-bit derivation. We implement a scalar multiplication accelerator by analyzing dataflow in point addition and point doubling and extracting full parallelism in the algorithm, as well as fully utilizing advanced and high-performance FPGA logic resources.

3   Related Work

In this section, we review several FPGA implementations of scalar multiplication. FPGA implementations over prime fields are classified into specific-prime-field and general-prime-field. The examples of the former are observed in

[2, 9, 26, 27, 33]. The use of specific primes enables fast modular reduction, leading to division replaced by a series of additions and subtractions; however, it has some inflexibility, where the accelerators are limited to supporting specific prime fields, for example, the NIST primes, i.e., generalized Merssene primes. In contrast, implementations over general prime fields provide considerable flexibility in terms of selecting a prime number, p, and they can be applied to various applications such as digital signature generation and key agreement. Some examples of FPGA implementations over general-prime-fields include [6, 7, 12–14, 22].

Another perspective is regarding the choice of coordinate system. One is an affine coordinate system, and the other is a projective or Jacobian coordinate system. The former has the advantage of smaller memory usage than the latter with an additional axis of coordinates, leading to a smaller number of registers in FPGA resources. However, inversion calculation is required for every point addition and doubling over affine coordinates, whereas it is performed once at the end of scalar multiplication over projective or Jacobian coordinates. In this study, because we prioritize the flexibility of prime fields and memory/hardware resource usage, we focus on FPGA designs for scalar multiplication over general prime fields and affine coordinates.

Ghosh et al. proposed an FPGA implementation that performs point addition and point doubling in parallel [6]. This parallelism is naive and common in various hardware implementations. For modular multiplication, their interleaved multiplication algorithm takes $k+1$ cycles, where k is the bit length of p, i.e., 257 cycles when 256-bit p is assumed. Similarly, the modular multipliers in [12, 13, 22] used similar algorithms and took at least k cycles. As modular multiplication is one of the main calculations in EC scalar multiplication, the cycles taken by these implementations result in long computation time for scalar multiplication. In contrast, our implementation of modular multiplication described in Sect. 5, which utilizes DSP modules embedded in FPGA devices, takes 28 cycles with 256-bit p, leading to a much faster execution of EC scalar multiplication. Today's FPGA devices include high-performance embedded DSP modules. Using them is better than constructing complicated multipliers with programmable logic based on look-up tables and long-delayed wiring.

Javeed et al. used a modular multiplier that includes a radix-8 Booth encoded multiplier with iterative addition and reduction modulo p of partial products [14]. Although this modular multiplier reduces the execution cycles compared with the above-mentioned modular multipliers, it still requires 88 cycles for 256-bit p, whereas our implementation requires only 28 cycles. In addition, the cascaded adders structure in [14] makes the critical path long, thereby preventing the clock frequency from improving.

In the implementations in [26, 33] (which are dedicated to NIST P-256 prime fields), redundant signed digit (RSD) arithmetic is used, where multi-bit addition can be performed without carry propagation at the expense of additional FPGA resource areas. In contrast, our implementation of addition/subtraction simply utilizes fast carry logic in today's FPGA slices and achieves one-cycle addition/subtraction with 256-bit operands at over 200 MHz. Similar to the use of DSP modules, we can expect that using fast carry logic yields faster and smaller adders than RSD-based adders.

Considering the use in embedded systems, the amount of hardware required for EC accelerators is important. The accelerator in [7] saves on hardware by sharing hardware resources among different finite-field modular arithmetic operations and among EC point computations at the sacrifice of parallelism inside point addition and doubling. In contrast, our implementation decouples multi-bit arithmetic units from EC point computations to reuse arithmetic units between point computations that are serially processed while duplicating the arithmetic units to extract full parallelism inside each point computation and among point computations running in parallel.

Unlike the above-mentioned designs, some implementations use projective or Jacobian coordinate systems. The use of these coordinate systems eliminates division in every EC point addition/doubling at the cost of increased storage space, accelerating scalar multiplication. The implementations in [8,24] are examples. These designs can be applicable to real-time applications since they achieve less than 1 ms of processing for scalar multiplication, whereas all the designs in affine coordinates mentioned above take more than 2 ms. Our objective is to achieve less than 1 ms of processing for scalar multiplication in the affine coordinate system to satisfy the performance and cost requirements in various real-time applications.

4   Target Algorithm and Modular Arithmetics

4.1   Algorithms for Scalar Multiplication

Algorithm 1 proposed in [16] computes a scalar multiplication with a point, P, on the elliptic curve and an integer scalar, k, and outputs $Q = kP$. This algorithm has two important features. First, an affine coordinate is used to reduce the memory usage. Second, it satisfies *secure generality* (i.e., it can operate on any input scalar k). To achieve secure generality, this algorithm does not include exceptional initialization or exceptional computation and is thus secure against a side-channel attack (SCA). Therefore, we choose this algorithm.

The algorithm comprises three parts: initialization, main loop, and final correction. The initialization starts with $R[0] =\leftarrow -P$ and $R[1] \leftarrow P$ in Steps 1 and 2, respectively, avoiding exceptional initialization with $\mathcal{O}$ and exceptional computation $\mathcal{O} + P$ in the main loop while leaving the computation for adjustment, $+2R[1]$, in Step 10 in the final correction. Steps 3 and 4 perform affine point doubling and affine point addition, respectively, and help in avoiding exceptional computations, $P + P$ or $P - P$. The extra computations are adjusted in the final correction. The main loop from Steps 5 to 8 dominates the execution time of scalar multiplication. In each iteration, affine point addition and affine point doubling are performed in Steps 6 and 7, respectively.

After the main loop, the final correction is performed. This is one of the important security-enhanced parts. They introduced extended affine point addition and doubling that can execute exceptional computation such as $P - P$ and

Algorithm 1. New 1-bit 2-ary Rright-to-Left Powering Ladder (Algorithm 7 in [16])

Input: $P \in E(\mathbb{F}_q)$, $k = \sum_{i=0}^{l-1} k_i 2^i$, $k \in [0, N]$
Output: $Q = kP$

    Initialization
1: $R[0] \leftarrow -P$
2: $R[1] \leftarrow P$
3: $A \leftarrow 2P$
4: $R[k_0] \leftarrow R[k_0] + A$

    Main Loop
5: **for** $i = 1$ to $l - 1$ **do**
6:     $R[k_i] \leftarrow R[k_i] + A$
7:     $A \leftarrow 2A$
8: **end for**

    Final Correction
9: $R[k_0] \leftarrow R[k_0] - P$
10: $A \leftarrow (-A + R[0]) +_E 2_E R[1]$
11: **return** A

$2P = \mathcal{O}$. In Step 9, an affine point addition is applied to $R[k_0]$ and the complement of P. The conventional affine coordinates are used in Steps 1 to 9. In contrast, in Step 10, while affine point addition, $-A + R[0]$, is computed using conventional affine coordinates, extended affine point doubling is applied to $R[1]$, described by $2_E R[1]$. Finally, these two results are added by an extended affine point addition ($+_E$ in Step 10). Extended affine point addition and extended affine point doubling are used to avoid exceptional computations. Details regarding the extended affine point addition and affine point doubling can be found in [16]. Importantly, our elegant FPGA design does not increase the FPGA resource usage as arithmetic calculators in the extended affine point addition and doubling are shared with other point computations.

4.2 Modular Arithmetic

Elliptic curve (EC) point computations comprise multi-bit modular arithmetic: addition, subtraction, multiplication, and inversion. Modular addition (subtraction) is a combination of multi-bit addition (subtraction) and conditional subtraction (addition) for the residue. In our implementation, subtraction (addition) for the residue is performed only when it is indispensable. Each addition or subtraction is performed without the residue, thereby reducing the computation complexity at the expense of additional most-significant bits. After several additions/subtractions, subtraction or addition for the residue is applied to reduce the value to the field range.

    For modular multiplication, we use the Montgomery multiplication algorithm [31] that involves multi-bit additions/subtractions and multi-bit multiplications.

Several algorithms, such as the Karatsuba method [18], are candidates for multi-bit multiplications. We adopt a simple method for the parallel generation of partial products as the operand length is at most 264 bits. For inversion calculation, a constant binary extended GCD algorithm [3] is selected, wherein the shift and subtraction operations are performed in each iteration, while the number of iterations is constant.

5   Design and Implementation

Our method offers programmability (i.e., application programming interfaces) in designing an accelerator for scalar multiplications such that higher-layer EC cryptography protocols such as ECDH and ECDSA [4] can invoke the hardware accelerator when required. EC point computations along with modular/multi-bit arithmetic calculators are provided as hardware modules, whereas the control sequence among the modules is provided via software processing, which achieves hardware–software co-processing for scalar multiplication. Current tightly coupled SoC-type FPGA devices facilitate fast communication between processor cores and FPGA modules, thereby making hardware–software co-processing efficient.

5.1   Design of Arithmetic Units

Based on the directions mentioned in the previous section, we designed and implemented the following arithmetic units in hardware description language (VHDL): multi-bit adder, multi-bit subtractor, multi-bit multiplier, modular Montgomery multiplier, and modular inversion calculator.

Multi-bit Adder/Subtracter. While our ECC system targets 256-bit elements over the prime field $\mathbb{F}_p$ with 256-bit p, 260-bit adders and subtractors are implemented since 260-bit temporary data emerge internally as the result of postponed residue operations. In addition, a 520-bit adder is required inside Montgomery multipliers, wherein multi-bit multiplication generates 520-bit operands. Furthermore, a 264-bit subtractor is used in Montgomery multipliers. These adders and subtracters are designed to output the results in one clock cycle, as current FPGA devices include fast carry logic and can achieve one-cycle 520-bit addition at over 200 MHz. Simple '+' operators in the HDL source files generate these calculators.

Multi-bit Multiplier. In the process of Montgomery multiplications, 264-bit × 264-bit multiplications are performed. Our multi-bit multiplier generates a multiplication result in four clock cycles, as depicted in Fig. 1. In the first cycle, the 2's complement values are obtained when the operands are negative. In the second and third cycles, each 264-bit operand is divided into two 132-bit segments, and 132-bit × 132-bit multiplications in parallel generate partial products. For these multiplications, embedded multipliers in the target device, DSP48E2 [36], which perform 27-bit × 18-bit multiplication, are allocated through logic synthesis in the FPGA design tool Vivado [37]. Finally, in the fourth cycle, the summation of the partial products as well as the 2's complement operation, if necessary, yields a multiplication result. Simple * and + operators are used in the HDL source files for partial multiplication and addition, respectively.

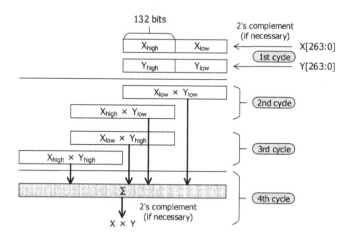

Fig. 1. 264-bit × 264-bit multiplier.

Multi-bit Modular Montgomery Multiplier. The algorithm of our modular multiplication is based on the Montgomery reduction technique. The designed Montgomery multiplier receives two 260-bit input data, x_1 and x_2, and generates a 260-bit result, z, through two 520-bit additions, two 264-bit subtractions, and six 264-bit × 264-bit multiplications. These calculations are performed serially since no parallelism is inherent in the Montgomery multiplication algorithm. The dataflow for Montgomery multiplication is shown in Fig. 2. In Steps 1, 2, 3, 6, 7, and 8, the above-mentioned multi-bit multiplier is used. Each multiplication process takes four cycles. In Steps 4 and 9, a multi-bit adder is used in one cycle. Subtraction is performed for residue calculation in Steps 5 and 10. A total of 28 cycles are used for processing.

Multi-bit Modular Inversion Calculator. An inversion calculator is designed such that it inputs a 260-bit data and outputs a 256-bit result that is the corresponding inverse element over a prime field. The calculation is based on the binary extended GCD algorithm [28], wherein one subtraction or two subtractions in parallel along with one-bit shift operations (insignificant delay) are conditionally performed in each loop iteration. Considering that the operands are 260-bit data and that, in contrast, 520-bit additions are performed in one

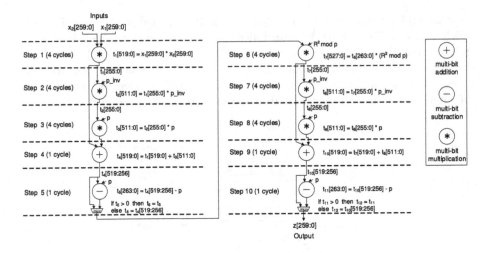

Fig. 2. Dataflow in Montgomery multiplication.

clock cycle in the Montgomery multiplier, our strategy is to unroll two consecutive iterations so that two subtractions are serially performed in one clock cycle. As a result, it executes half the number of iterations compared with the original algorithm and spends half of the clock cycles.

Figure 3(a) shows the pseudocode of the original binary extended GCD algorithm. The variables u, v, B, and D are used in the computation. According to their values, shift, subtraction, or subtraction and shift operations are applied. The shift operations are performed without combinational logic in the hardware implementation, as they are achieved simply by connecting wires appropriately, whereas the subtractions are performed by subtractors. In contrast, in our inversion algorithm, shown in Fig. 3(b), two consecutive iterations in the original algorithm are unrolled and executed in an iteration. Additional variables—$u0$, $v0$, $B0$, and $D0$—hold the temporal results of the first part that are then used in the second part. This unrolling technique causes two subtractions, at most, to be cascaded in an iteration. For example, two subtractions in lines (A) and (B) in Fig. 3(b) are serially executed, when u, v, $u0$, and $v0$ are odd, $u \geq v$, and $u0 \geq v0$. These cascaded subtractions are within one clock-cycle delay in our implementation. In addition, six subtractors are implemented and reused, whereas 12 subtractions are to be executed in the algorithm.

The number of iterations in the original binary extended GCD algorithm depends on the input data. As a measure against side-channel attacks, dummy iterations are added after completing the calculation until it reaches a predefined upper bound, so that the execution time is fixed regardless of the input data. In addition, random calculations are performed in dummy iterations to maintain the energy dissipation. As the predefined upper bound, we use 742 for a 256-bit prime field, which is the theoretical upper bound for the binary extended GCD algorithm [3]. This leads to an execution time of $742/2 = 371$ clock cycles for the main loop in the algorithm.

```
# Initialization
u <= p;   # field modulus
v <= x;   # input data
B <= 0;  D <= 1;

# Main loop
while ( u > 0 ) do
  if ( u is even ) then
    u <= u >> 1;   # 1-bit right shift
    if ( B is even ) then
      B <= B >> 1;
    else
      B <= (B – p) >> 1;
    end if;
    v <= v;  D <= D;
  elsif ( v is even ) then
    v <= v >> 1;
    if ( D is even ) then
      D <= D >> 1;
    else
      D <= (D – p) >> 1;
    end if;
    u <= u;  B <= B;
  elsif ( u >= v ) then
    u <= u – v;  B <= B – D;
    v <= v;       D <= D;
  else
    v <= v – u;  D <= D – B;
    u <= u;       B <= B;
  end if;

end while;   # D is final output
```

(a) Original inversion algorithm

```
# Initialization
u <= p;   # field modulus
v <= x;   # input data
B <= 0;  D <= 1;

# Main loop
while ( u > 0 ) do
# Corresponding to 1st iteration
  if ( u is even ) then
    u0 <= u >> 1;   # 1-bit right shift
    if ( B is even ) then
      B0 <= B >> 1;
    else
      B0 <= (B – p) >> 1;
    end if;
    v0 <= v;  D0 <= D;
  elsif ( v is even ) then
    v0 <= v >> 1;
    if ( D is even ) then
      D0 <= D >> 1;
    else
      D0 <= (D – p) >> 1;
    end if;
    u0 <= u;  B0 <= B;
  elsif ( u >= v ) then
    u0 <= u – v;  B0 <= B – D; · · · · (A)
    v0 <= v;       D0 <= D;
  else
    v0 <= v – u;  D0 <= D – B;
    u0 <= u;       B0 <= B;
  end if;
```

```
# Corresponding to 2nd iteration
  if ( u0 = 0 ) then
    u <= u0;  v <= v0;  B <= B0;  D <= D0;
  else   # u0 > 0
    if ( u0 is even ) then
      u <= u0 >> 1;
      if ( B0 is even ) then
        B <= B0 >> 1;
      else
        B <= (B0 – p) >> 1;
      end if;
      v <= v0;  D <= D0;
    elsif ( v0 is even ) then
      v <= v0 >> 1;
      if ( D0 is even ) then
        D <= D0 >> 1;
      else
        D <= (D0 – p) >> 1;
      end if;
      u <= u0;  B <= B0;
    elsif ( u0 >= v0 ) then
      u <= u0 – v0;  B <= B0 – D0; · · · · (B)
      v <= v0;        D <= D0;
    else
      v <= v0 – u0;  D <= D0 – B0;
      u <= u0;        B <= B0;
    end if;
  end if;

end while;   # D is final output
```

(b) Revised algorithm with unrolling

Fig. 3. Inversion algorithms.

5.2 Design of EC Point Computation Modules and Parallelism

Based on the directions mentioned in the previous section, we designed and implemented the following EC point computation modules: affine point addition module (PADD), affine point doubling module (PDBL), extended affine point addition module (EXA_PADD), and extended affine point doubling module (EXA_PDBL).

EC Point Computation Modules. PADD, PDBL, EXA_PADD, and EXA_PDBL modules are composed of the aforementioned arithmetic units (adders/subtractors, Montgomery multipliers, and inversion calculators) with predefined control sequences. The data are transmitted between the arithmetic units via 260-bit temporary registers. To achieve parallel processing between the EC point computation modules, as described later, the designed system is equipped with six temporary registers: one of them is occupied by the PADD module, the other two are shared by the PADD and EXA_PADD modules, and the remaining three are shared by the PDBL, EXA_PDBL, and EXA_PADD modules.

Figures 4(a) and (b) show the dataflow in PADD and PDBL, respectively, and Figs. 5(a) and (b) show the dataflow in EXA_PADD and EXA_PDBL, respectively. Parallel processing contributes not only to high-performance processing, but also to resistance to SPA, as it makes power analysis more difficult than in sequential processing. The system utilizes two types of parallelism: intra-module and inter-module parallelism. In terms of the former, parallelism inside

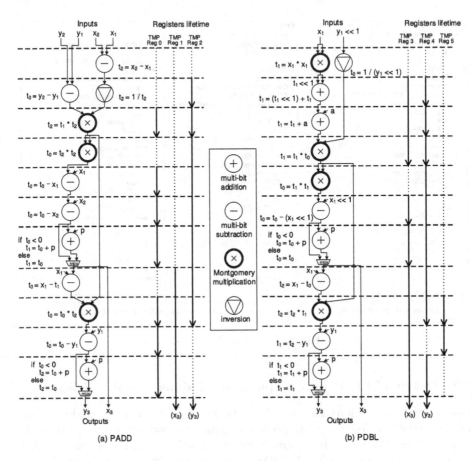

Fig. 4. Dataflow in (a) PADD and (b) PDBL.

EXA_PADD is described as an example. Analyzing the dataflow and considering the processing time of each arithmetic unit offers the possibility of parallel execution among arithmetic. In Fig. 5(a), during the inversion processing, addition, subtraction, and three Montgomery multiplications can be processed and completed. The same strategy is applied to the other EC point computation modules (PADD, PDBL, and EXA_PDBL), although the amount of parallelism extracted is small for them. After scheduling the arithmetic units and allocating registers, the number of necessary temporary registers is known. That is, three registers are necessary for PADD, PDBL, and EXA_PDBL, whereas five registers are necessary for EXA_PADD.

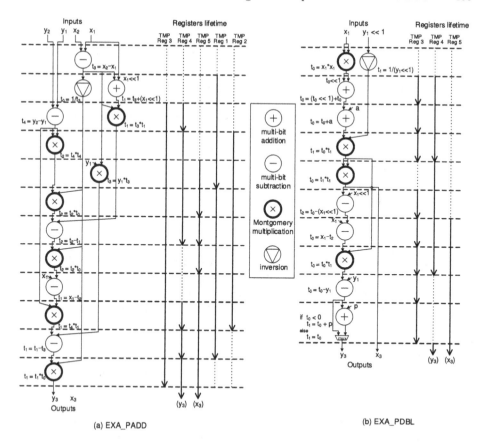

Fig. 5. Dataflow in (a) EXA_PADD and (b) EXA_PDBL.

After intra-module parallelism is fixed, inter-module parallelism is established. In the main loop of Algorithm 1, an affine point addition (Step 6) and affine point doubling (Step 7) are executed. The latter does not have read-after-write dependency with the former. Therefore, affine point doubling can be executed in parallel with the preceding affine point addition. Affine point doubling has a write-after-read relation with the affine point addition in terms of A, that is, update of A by affine point doubling has to be performed after the affine point addition reads it. This is solved by introducing synchronization mechanisms, as described in the next subsection. In addition to this parallelism, at Step 10 in the final correction, affine point addition and extended affine point doubling are processed in parallel. Considering the inter-module parallel processing and the number of temporary registers required by each EC point computation module, the temporary registers are efficiently shared between modules as mentioned above. As a result, the introduction of the two extended affine point computations does not require additional registers. Thus, enhancing security for exceptional addition can be done with no additional registers.

5.3 APIs for Inter-module Parallelism and Synchronization

To achieve parallel processing and synchronization between EC point computation modules, the software procedures shown in Table 1 are implemented. These APIs enable our efficient hardware–software co-processing.

For each EC point computation module, the corresponding Start_*() procedure invokes the hardware module and finishes (or returns to the caller) asynchronously, i.e., without waiting for the completion of the hardware operation. In contrast, when End_*() is called, it waits for the completion of the corresponding hardware processing. As affine point doubling has a write-after-read relation with the affine point addition in the main loop, its result is not directly written in the corresponding buffers (described later) but written in the temporary registers. The execution of Sync_PDBL() moves the result to the target buffer.

Using these procedures, the main loop of Algorithm 1 is written in C language, as in Fig. 6. With the use of the APIs described above, PDBL and PADD run in parallel. Here, Start_*() procedures have parameters for EC point data. For Start_PDBL(), the buffer identifier "2" is specified since Buffer[2] contains an EC point A. Similarly, for Start_PADD(), the buffer identifiers "2" and "ki" are specified so that Buffer[ki] is updated by Buffer[2] + Buffer[ki]. In contrast, Sync_PDBL() is accompanied by the destination buffer identifier "2" so that the temporary register value is copied to Buffer[2].

In addition to the parallelism between affine point doubling and affine point addition, affine point addition and extended affine point doubling can run in parallel in Step 10 of Algorithm 1. Considering these chances of parallelism, resource sharing for temporary registers and arithmetic units is performed. The possible combinations of EC point computations for parallel processing are a pair of PADD and PDBL and a pair of PADD and EXA_PDBL. Each EC point computation module uses a set of an adder, a subtractor, a Montgomery multiplier, and an inversion calculator. To reduce the total hardware amount, a set of arithmetic units is shared between PADD and EXA_PADD and another set is

Table 1. Application Programming Interfaces (APIs).

Procedure	Action
Start_PADD()	Invokes PADD
End_PADD()	Waits for completion of PADD
Start_PDBL()	Invokes PDBL
End_PDBL()	Waits for completion of PDBL
Sync_PDBL()	Stores the result of PDBL in buffers
Start_EXA_PADD()	Invokes EXA_PADD
End_EXA_PADD()	Waits for completion of EXA_PADD
Start_EXA_PDBL()	Invokes EXA_PDBL
End_EXA_PDBL()	Waits for completion of EXA_PDBL

```
for ( i = 1; i < l; i ++ ) {
    Start_PDBL( 2 );       /* TMP_Reg = 2 * Buffer[2] */

    ki = (k >> i) & 0x1;
    Start_PADD( 2, ki );  /* Buffer[ki] = Buffer[2] + Buffer[ki]; */
    End_PADD();

    End_PDBL()
    Sync_PDBL( 2 );        /* writing TMP_Reg in Buffer[2] */
}
```

Fig. 6. Software code of main loop in Algorithm 1.

shared between PDBL and EXA_PDBL (Fig. 7). Similarly, temporary registers TMP-Reg 1 and TMP-Reg 2 can be shared between PADD and EXA_PADD, and TMP-Regs 3 to 5 are shared between PDBL, EXA_PDBL, and EXA_PADD.

5.4 System Structure

The designed ECC system was implemented in Xilinx Zynq UltraScale+ MPSoC ZU7EV device [39]. Figure 7 depicts the system structure, including the designed arithmetic units and EC point computation modules. A Cortex-A53 core in the processing system (PS) executes software code at a clock frequency of 500 MHz.

EC point computation modules with arithmetic units are implemented in programmable logic (PL), working at a clock frequency of 214.286 MHz[1]. In the figure, the multi-bit adder, subtractor, multiplier, Modular Montgomery multiplier, and inversion calculator are depicted as ADD, SUB, MUL, MONT_MUL, and INVERSE, respectively. Each EC point computation module includes a control register and a status register. PS software calls Start_*() procedure, which writes an invocation signal as well as buffer identifiers in the control register. Similarly, it calls End_*() and reads from the status register to recognize the completion of module processing. The control and status registers are memory-address-mapped and accessed via conventional load/store instructions[2].

Data transfer between PS and PL is performed through a high-speed on-chip bus (AXI), and the unit of transfer is 64 bits. EC point data are transferred via four global buffers (Buffer[0–3] in the figure). These buffers are memory-address-mapped and accessed by conventional load/store instructions. Each buffer contains point data (256 bits × 2) on the elliptic curve. Each EC point computation module uses buffers specified by the control register. During computation, the temporary registers (TMP-Regs 0 to 5 in the figure) are used to store the results of the arithmetic units.

---

[1] Phase Locked Loop (PPL) in the device generates 214.286 MHz by 33.3 MHz × 90/14.

[2] As ARM processors use relaxed memory models, memory barrier (DMB) instructions must be properly inserted to guarantee access order to the control and status registers.

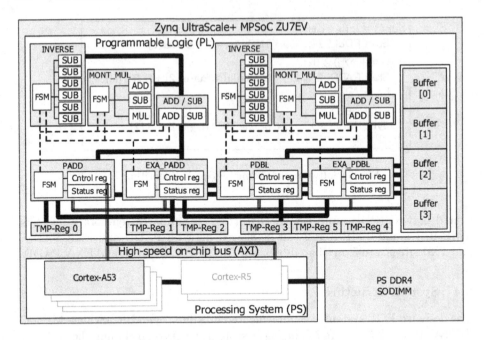

Fig. 7. System structure for Algorithm 1.

5.5 Execution Cycles

Table 2 shows the execution clock cycles of the arithmetic units, EC point computation modules, and scalar multiplication. Our design gives constant execution times for all the computation modules. PADD and PDBL take almost the same number of cycles, leading to balanced parallel processing in the main loop.

The execution cycles for scalar multiplication are 120 403, corresponding to 0.562 ms at the clock frequency in our implementation, that is, 214.286 MHz. These cycles do not include software execution, such as API procedures and operands transfer. The total execution time of the hardware–software co-processing is described in the next section.

6   Analysis

This section presents the evaluation results in terms of performance and hardware-resource usage. Table 3 compares our designs with the other existing FPGA designs for generic ECC over 256-bit prime fields described in Sect. 3. As the FPGA devices used are different in terms of their generations, the table includes, in the right-most column, the processing time normalized to 200-MHz processing for reference. It also compares them from the point of view of security of exception-free for any k and usage of pre-computation tables.

Table 2. Execution clock cycles of arithmetic units, EC point computation modules, and scalar multiplication.

Arithmetic unit	Cycles
ADD/SUB	1
MUL	4
MONT_MUL	28
INVERSE	372

EC point computation module	Cycles
PADD	463
PDBL	461
EXA_PADD	488
EXA_PDBL	460

Scalar multiplication	Cycles
PDBL×1 + PADD×258 + EXA_PADD×1	120,403

6.1 Execution Time

The designed ECC system was synthesized and implemented with Xilinx Vivado v2019.2. The processing time of the ECC scalar multiplication was measured on a ZCU104 evaluation board [38]. Software with Linux 4.14.0 runs on the processor (Cortex-A53) in PS at 500 MHz. The software code is written in C language and compiled using gcc 6.3.0 with -O4 option. The elapsed time was obtained using the gettimeofday() library function. The elapsed time includes not only the hardware processing time but also the software processing time.

For comparison, software-only processing, "Soft," that executes Algorithm 1 using GNU Multiple Precision Arithmetic Library (GMP) Version 6.1.2 [1] is prepared. Our proposed system of processing with hardware modules is "w/HW." Another implementation is "w/HW-auto," equipped with an auto loop mechanism, where the main loop sequence is automatically processed in the hardware (without Start/End_PADD/PDBL()) to mitigate the overhead of PS-from/to-PL communication/synchronization.

For our implementations (Soft, w/HW, and w/HW-auto), the average processing time of scalar multiplication for 1000 pairs of (k, P) is presented in Table 3. Soft takes 7.943 ms, which is not fast enough for various real-time applications. In contrast, the execution time of w/HW is 0.742 ms, which is approximately 11 times faster than Soft. In addition, w/HW-auto takes 0.575 ms, which is 23% faster than w/HW and 14 times faster than Soft. This result implies that the overhead of invoking hardware and recognizing its completion, i.e., writing to/reading from control/status registers, is non-negligible.

Table 3 shows that our design is the fastest among the existing FPGA implementations without a precomputation table. Let us compare our design with [24], which uses 15 points for a pre-computation table. Thanks to the pre-computation table, it can reduce the number of point additions to 71 from the original 256. Nevertheless, our design is comparable to it, although processing executes 256 point additions and doublings without pre-computation table, each of which involves inversion calculation. This indicates that the number of clock cycles to be taken by our design is sufficiently low. In other words, our design achieves

Table 3. Comparison of scalar multiplication over arbitrary 256-bit prime fields.

Design	Exception free (any k)	Pre-comp. Table (# points)	Device	Area	Frequency (MHz)	Time (ms)	Time at 200 MHz (ms)
Soft (GMP)	Yes	No	Cortex-A53	N/A	500	7.943	–
This work							
w/HW			Zynq	6.3K slices		0.742	0.795
w/HW-auto	Yes	No	UltraScale+	(42K LUTs)	214.286	0.575	0.626
				+ 256 DSPs			
[22] (2019)	No	No	Virtex-7	5.4K slices	124.2	3.730	2.316
[13] (2018)	No	No	Virtex-4	9.4K slices	20.44	29.840	3.050
[12]	No	No	Kintex-7	11.3K slices	121.5	3.270	1.987
[14] (2016)	No	No	Virtex-6	(No report)	70	2.800	0.980
			Virtex-4	1.3K slices	40	5.000	1.000
			Virtex-4	(no report)	54	6.260	1.690
[7] (2011)	No	No	Virtex-II Pro	12K slices (20K LUTs)	36	9.380	1.688
[6] (2009)	No	No	Virtex-4	20K slices (34K LUTs)	43.32	7.700	1.668
[24] (2013)	Yes	Yes (15 pts)	Virtex-5	1.7K slices (4.2K LUTs) + 37 DSPs	291	0.380	0.553
[8] (2010)	No	No	Stratix II	9K ALMs + 96 DSPs	157.2	0.680	0.534

more efficient processing per cycle. Therefore, we conclude that our ECC system should be based on a highly efficient digital logic design.

The performance gain of our designs is attributed to the high performance in inverse calculation and utilization of intra-/inter-module parallelism. Table 4 shows the performances of several high-performance designs for modular inversion over 256-bit prime fields. All implementations, including our design, in the table are based on the extended Euclidean algorithm or its variants. This means that the processing time of these implementations depends on the input values. Their processing times in Table 4 are from the corresponding literature, which are regarded as the average execution times. In contrast, our implementation of inversion, "Ours w/ UB" in the table, shows the execution time of inversion with the upper bound mentioned in Sect. 5.1, which is the fixed execution time, whereas "Ours w/o UB", which is for reference, corresponds to the average execution time when the upper-bounded loop execution is not applied. The table shows that our designed inversion calculator is the fastest among the recently published designs.

Table 4. Performance of modular inversion over 256-bit prime fields.

Design	Device	Area	Frequency (MHz)	Time (μs)	Time at 200 MHz (μs)
Ours w/o UB	Zynq	6,926 LUTs	214.286	1.279	1.370
Ours w/UB	UltraScale+			1.736	1.860
[21] (2019)	Virtex-7	1,069 slices	168.560	2.013	1.697
[5] (2018)	Virtex-7	617 slices	144.011	2.220	1.599
[11] (2015)	Virtex-7	1,480 slices	146.380	2.329	1.705
[15] (2016)	Virtex-6	4,758 LUTs	151.000	3.391	2.560

6.2 FPGA Resources

Table 3 and Table 4 include the information of FPGA resources (Area) occupied by each design. As the FPGA devices used are different from design to design, directly comparing their sizes is difficult. For example, the UltraScale+ architecture has a slice structure containing eight 6-input look-up tables (LUTs), whereas a slice in Virtex-6/7 has four 6-input LUTs, or Virtex-4 has 4-input LUTs. Nevertheless, the proposed system seems to occupy more resources than the others. However, the size is sufficiently practical since the area information of our implementation reported in Table 3 is not only for scalar multiplication processing but also for all other components including the high-speed on-chip bus and the DDR4 DIMM controller, and the total hardware can be accommodated using low-price FPGA devices such as a Xilinx Artix-7 XC7A200T that comprises 134 600 LUTS and 740 DSPs [35].

7 Conclusion

We have investigated various methods for efficient FPGA implementations of scalar multiplication on elliptic curve cryptosystems over any prime field. Our design makes the most of the advanced and high-performance programmable logic in today's FPGA devices and extracts the full parallelism inherent in the algorithms. Our proposed hardware–software coprocessing outperforms the existing FPGA implementations for generic ECC over 256-bit prime fields without a pre-computation table and is also secure against SPA and exception-free for any scalar. The processing time result of 0.575 ms shows that our design could be applicable to any real-time embedded system.

Acknowledgments. This work was supported by enPiT (Education Network for Practical Information Technologies) at MEXT, Innovation Platform for Society 5.0 at MEXT, and JSPS KAKENHI Grant Number JP21H03443.

References

1. https://gmplib.org/
2. Alrimeih, H., Rakhmatov, D.: Fast and flexible hardware support for ECC over multiple standard prime fields. IEEE Trans. Very Large Scale Integr. (VLSI) Syst. **22**(12), 2661–2674 (2014)
3. Bernstein, D.J., Yang, B.-Y.: Fast constant-time GCD computation and modular inversion. IACR Trans. Cryptogr. Hardw. Embedded Syst. **2019**(3), 340–398 (2019)
4. Blake, I., Seroussi, G., Smart, N.: Elliptic Curves in Cryptography. Cambridge University Press, Cambridge (1999)
5. Dong, X., Zhang, L., Gao, X.: An efficient FPGA implementation of ECC modular inversion over F'_{256}. In: Proceedings International Conference on Cryptography, Security and Privacy, pp. 29–33 (2018)
6. Ghosh, S., Alam, M., Chowdhury, D.R., Guputa, I.S.: Parallel crypto-devices for GF(p) elliptic curve multiplication resistant against side channel attacks. Comput. Electr. Eng. **35**(2), 329–338 (2009)
7. Ghosh, S., Mukhopadhyay, D., Roychowdhury, D.: Petrel: power and timing attack resistant elliptic curve scalar multiplier based on programmable GF(p) arithmetic unit. IEEE Trans. Circ. Syst. **58**(8), 1798–1812 (2011)
8. Guillermin, N.: A high speed coprocessor for elliptic curve scalar multiplications over $\mathbb{F}_p$. In: Proceedings of International Conference on Cryptographic Hardware and Embedded Systems, pp. 48–64 (2010)
9. Güneysu, T., Paar, C.: Ultra high performance ECC over NIST primes on commercial FPGAs. In: Oswald, E., Rohatgi, P. (eds.) CHES 2008. LNCS, vol. 5154, pp. 62–78. Springer, Heidelberg (2008). https://doi.org/10.1007/978-3-540-85053-3_5
10. Hankerson, D., Menezes, A.J., Vanstone, S.: Guide to Elliptic Curve Cryptography. Springer, New York (2004). https://doi.org/10.1007/b97644
11. Hossain, M.S., Kong, Y.: High-performance FPGA implementation of modular inversion over $\mathbb{F}_{256}$ for elliptic curve cryptography. In: Proceedings of IEEE International Conference on Data Science and Data Intensive Systems, pp. 169–174 (2015)
12. Hossain, M.S., Kong, Y., Saeedi, E., Vayalil, N.C.: High-performance elliptic curve cryptography processor over NIST prime fields. IET Comput. Digit. Tech. **11**(1), 33–42 (2017)
13. Hu, X., Zheng, X., Zhang, S., Cai, S., Xiong, X.: A low hardware consumption elliptic curve cryptographic architecture over GF(p) in embedded application. Electronics **7**(7), 13p (2018)
14. Javeed, K., Wang, X.: FPGA based high speed SPA resistant elliptic curve scalar multiplier architecture. Int. J. Reconfig. Comput. **2016**(5), 1–10 (2016)
15. Javeed, K., Wang, X.: Low latency flexible FPGA implementation of point multiplication on elliptic curves over GF(p). Int. J. Circuit Theory Appl. **45**(2), 214–228 (2016)
16. Jin, Y., Miyaji, A.: Secure and compact elliptic curve cryptosystems. In: Jang-Jaccard, J., Guo, F. (eds.) ACISP 2019. LNCS, vol. 11547, pp. 639–650. Springer, Cham (2019). https://doi.org/10.1007/978-3-030-21548-4_36
17. Joye, M.: Highly regular m-Ary powering ladders. In: Jacobson, M.J., Rijmen, V., Safavi-Naini, R. (eds.) SAC 2009. LNCS, vol. 5867, pp. 350–363. Springer, Heidelberg (2009). https://doi.org/10.1007/978-3-642-05445-7_22

18. Karatsuba, A.A., Ofman, Y.: Multiplication of multidigit numbers on automata. Soviet Phys. Doklady **7**(7), 595–596 (1963)

19. Koblitz, N.: Elliptic curve cryptosystems. Math. Comput. **48**, 203–209 (1987)

20. Kocher, P.C.: Timing attacks on implementations of Diffie-Hellman, RSA, DSS, and other systems. In: Koblitz, N. (ed.) CRYPTO 1996. LNCS, vol. 1109, pp. 104–113. Springer, Heidelberg (1996). https://doi.org/10.1007/3-540-68697-5_9

21. Kudithi, T., Sakthivel, R.: An efficient hardware implementation of finite field inversion for elliptic curve cryptography. Int. J. Innov. Technol. Explor. Eng. **8**(9), 827–932 (2019)

22. Kudithi, T., Sakthivel, R.: High-performance ECC processor architecture design for IoT security applications. J. Supercomput. **75**(1), 447–474 (2019). https://doi.org/10.1007/s11227-018-02740-2

23. Le, D.-P., Nguyen, B.P.: Fast point quadrupling on elliptic curves. In: Proceedings of Symposium on Information and Communication Technology, pp. 218–222 (2012)

24. Ma, Y., Liu, Z., Pan, W., Jing, J.: A high-speed elliptic curve cryptographic processor for generic curves over GF(p). In: Proceedings of International Conference on Selected Areas in Cryptography, pp. 421–437 (2013)

25. Mamiya, H., Miyaji, A., Morimoto, H.: Secure elliptic curve exponentiation against RPA, ZRA, DPA, and SPA. IEICE Trans. Fundam. Electron. Commun. Comput. Sci. **89-A**(8):2207–2215 (2006)

26. Marzouqi, H., Al-Qutayri, M., Salah, K., Saleh, H.: A 65 nm ASIC based 256 NIST prime field ECC processor. In: Proceedings of IEEE 59th International Midwest Symposium on Circuits and Systems, pp. 1–4 (2016)

27. Marzouqi, H., Al-Qutayri, M., Salah, K., Schinianakis, D., Stouraitis, T.: A high-speed FPGA implementation of an RSD-based ECC processor. IEEE Trans. Very Large Scale Integr. (VLSI) Syst. **24**(1), 151–164 (2016)

28. Menezes, A.J., van Oorschot, P.C., Vanstone, S.A.: Handbook of Applied Cryptography. CRC Press, Boca Raton (1996)

29. Miller, V.S.: Use of elliptic curves in cryptography. In: Williams, H.C. (ed.) CRYPTO 1985. LNCS, vol. 218, pp. 417–426. Springer, Heidelberg (1986). https://doi.org/10.1007/3-540-39799-X_31

30. Möller, B.: Parallelizable elliptic curve point multiplication method with resistance against side-channel attacks. In: Chan, A.H., Gligor, V. (eds.) ISC 2002. LNCS, vol. 2433, pp. 402–413. Springer, Heidelberg (2002). https://doi.org/10.1007/3-540-45811-5_31

31. Montgomery, P.L.: Modular multiplication without trial division. Math. Comput. **44**(170), 519–521 (1985)

32. Renes, J., Costello, C., Batina, L.: Complete addition formulas for prime order elliptic curves. In: Fischlin, M., Coron, J.-S. (eds.) EUROCRYPT 2016. LNCS, vol. 9665, pp. 403–428. Springer, Heidelberg (2016). https://doi.org/10.1007/978-3-662-49890-3_16

33. Shylashree, N., Sridhar, V., Patawardhan, D.: FPGA based efficient elliptic curve cryptosystem processor for NIST 256 prime field. In: Proceedings of IEEE Region 10 Conference, pp. 194–199 (2016)

34. Wu, X., Chouliaras, V., Goodall, R.: An application-specific processor hard macro for real-time control. In: Proceedings of IEEE International SOC Conference, pp. 369–372 (2004)

35. Xilinx, Inc.: 7 Series FPGAs Data Sheet: Overview, DS180 (v2.6)
36. Xilinx, Inc.: UltraScale Architecture DSP Slice User Guide, UG579 (v1.10)
37. Xilinx, Inc.: Vivado Design Suite User Guide, Synthesis UG901 (v2020.1)
38. Xilinx, Inc.: ZCU104 Evaluation Board User Guide, UG1267 (v1.1)
39. Xilinx, Inc.: Zynq UltraScale+ MPSoC Data Sheet: Overview, DS891 (v1.8)

Lattice Cryptography

Access Control Encryption from Group Encryption

Xiuhua Wang, Harry W. H. Wong, and Sherman S. M. Chow[(✉)] [iD]

Department of Information Engineering, The Chinese University of Hong Kong,
Shatin, N.T., Hong Kong
xhwang@link.cuhk.edu.hk, {whwong,sherman}@ie.cuhk.edu.hk

Abstract. Access control encryption (ACE) enforces both read and
write permissions. It kills off any unpermitted subliminal message channel via the help of a sanitizer who knows neither of the plaintext, its
sender and receivers, nor the access control policy. This work aims to
solve the open problem left by the seminal work of Damgård *et al.*
(TCC 2016), namely, "to construct practically interesting ACE from
noisy, post-quantum assumptions such as LWE." We start with revisiting group encryption (GE), which allows anyone to encrypt to a certified
group member, whom remains anonymous unless the opening authority
decided to reveal him/her. We propose: 1) the notion of sanitizable GE
(SGE), with specific changes for non-interactive proof, 2) the notion of
traceable ACE (tACE), which helps damage control by tracing after-
the-fact if some secret were leaked unluckily, 3) a generic construction of
(t)ACE for equality policy (ACE-EP) from SGE, 4) a generic construction of ACE for general policy from ACE-EP, 5) a lattice-based instantiation of SGE, which comes with 6) a simple mechanism for checking
that the randomness of ciphertexts can span the randomness space.

Keywords: Access control encryption · Group encryption ·
Lattice-based encryption · Learning with error · Post-quantum
security · Chosen-ciphertext security · Sanitization · Traceability

1 Introduction

Sensitive data should not propagate arbitrarily without restriction; encryption
techniques can enforce access control over the read but not write permissions.
Meanwhile, enforcing control over who can write to whom is equally important.
Consider a CEO who worries about leaking any strategic plan to arbitrary staff
(*e.g.*, interns), say, via a malware-infected program s/he used for processing the
related sensitive data. Note that digital signatures do not help since the recipient
of the sensitive data can ignore any verification. Even worse, the data can be sent
via a subliminal means, *e.g.*, embedding it as the randomness of a ciphertext.

Sherman S. M. Chow is supported by General Research Fund (Project Numbers: CUHK
14210217 and CUHK 14209918) from Research Grant Council, Hong Kong.

K. Sako and N. O. Tippenhauer (Eds.): ACNS 2021, LNCS 12726, pp. 417–441, 2021.
https://doi.org/10.1007/978-3-030-78372-3_16

It seems necessary to have a *sanitizer* to "monitor" the traffic for enforcing access control, especially over the write permissions. Ideally, the sanitization process should be "blindfolded," *i.e.*, without the need to know who the sender is, who the recipient is, and what the access control policy is. Such an idea is formalized by Damgård, Haagh, and Orlandi [12] as access control encryption (ACE).

1.1   Designs from Two Ends of a Spectrum, and Open Problems

Sanitizing a ciphertext blindfolded is not an easy task. Damgård *et al.* [12] proposed two constructions. They first started with ACE for a single user (1-ACE) from standard (*e.g.*, decisional Diffie-Hellman) assumptions. To make it a fully-fledged ACE scheme, *i.e.*, supporting the *general policy* $\mathsf{P} : \{0,1\}^\ell \times \{0,1\}^\ell \to \{0,1\}$ which sender $\mathsf{ID}_s \in \{0,1\}^\ell$ can write to receiver $\mathsf{ID}_r \in \{0,1\}^\ell$ if and only if $\mathsf{P}(\mathsf{ID}_s, \mathsf{ID}_r) = 1$, it runs 2^ℓ parallel copies of 1-ACE, making both the master public key and the ciphertext $O(2^\ell)$-long. This is not only for hiding the intended reader but also for a uniform treatment in sanitization without knowing who the writer is. They also proposed a construction that offers $\mathsf{poly}(\ell)$ efficiency, yet, it relies on a sanitizable variant of general-purpose functional encryption (FE) [6]. While FE for limited functionality (mostly inner-product) can be efficient, general-purpose FE is much more powerful and less efficient. Damgård *et al.* instantiated it with indistinguishability obfuscation.

Follow-up works mostly fall into two extremes: using practically-inefficient techniques to construct a regular ACE scheme, or practically-efficient techniques to construct an ACE scheme with limited functionality. Kim and Wu [18] built an ACE scheme from FE for randomized functionality (rFE) [2] and predicate-encryption (PE). Sanitization uses an FE key to create a PE ciphertext. Although the FE scheme can be instantiated by the LWE (learning-with-error) assumption, expressing the encryption algorithm of PE as a circuit is not that efficient. For the second paradigm, Fuchsbauer *et al.* [13] proposed a generic construction and a pairing-based construction for *equality policy* (ACE-EP), *i.e.*, the receiver is the sender. They also proposed to use many ACE-EP instances for interval membership policy, which is useful, albeit still not general.

A concurrent work by Wang and Chow [26] does not fall into the above two categories. In some sense, their generic construction can be considered as a "dual" of our proposed approach here. However, most of its building blocks, specifically structure-preserving signatures and broadcast encryption, are more "pairing-friendly," meaning that lattice-based instantiations are still limited now.

One of the open problems left by Damgård *et al.* in their original work [12] is as follows: "*to construct practically interesting ACE from noisy, post-quantum assumptions such as LWE*" and they commented that "*the challenge here is that it always seems possible for a malicious sender to encrypt with just enough noise that any further manipulation by the sanitizer makes the decryption fail.*"

Tan *et al.* [25] use Gentry–Sahai–Waters fully-homomorphic encryption [14] to instantiate 1-ACE. Their 2^ℓ-extension still suffers from $O(2^\ell)$ ciphertext size. The scheme of Kim and Wu [18] still relies on a general-purpose rFE scheme for arbitrary functions (albeit it can be LWE-based). Both fail to close the above open problem. Furthermore, both require the sanitizer to have a *private sanitization key*. Removing this requirement is also left as an open problem by Kim and Wu [18]. In this work, we ask ourselves a bigger question: *"Can we achieve the best of both worlds, i.e., using practically interesting lattice-based building blocks to build a general-policy ACE scheme, supporting keyless sanitization?"*

1.2 Viewing ACE Through the Lens of Group Encryption (GE)

Recurrent research activities in the cryptography community include identifying similarities and differences between primitives and connecting them if possible (*e.g.*, [11]). Our starting point is group encryption (GE), introduced by Kiayias Tsiounis, and Yung [17]. GE is like public-key encryption (PKE). Anyone can encrypt to a certified group member. GE shares one basic feature of ACE, which is hiding who can decrypt a given ciphertext. In normal circumstances, this group member remains anonymous. When needed, an opening authority can reveal him/her. These features make GE an attractive primitive for privacy-preserving applications [17], *e.g.*, filtering encrypted traffic or "oblivious retriever storage systems" [10]. There are a few existing GE schemes [3,8,21]. Notably, Libert *et al.* [20] proposed a lattice-based scheme (to be adapted by this paper).

However, GE falls short as ACE in many regards, notably the writing permission control: 1) Anyone can encrypt (no policy enforcement). 2) It does not feature a sanitization algorithm that randomizes a ciphertext (still without the need to know who can decrypt). It also falls short in terms of the reading permission control: 3) It encrypts to a single reader (not for the general policy).

The first two features can be added generically. Recall that an encryptor in GE first retrieves the public key of the intended receiver and its certificate issued by the group manager (GM) as a signature. The ciphertext contains a zero-knowledge proof of the certificate. By viewing the decryptor in GE also as the encryptor, we get ACE-EP. Sanitization, roughly, can be done by randomizing the ciphertext based on this hidden public key "accordingly" (which turns out to be tricky, see below). Indeed, these tricks are just rediscovery of the generic ACE-EP construction of Fuchsbauer *et al.* [13], who also mentioned, "A similar concept had previously been introduced in [15][1]." We do not claim any novelty of extending GE with sanitizability [15]. What we deem important is that revisiting this conceptual connection allows us to borrow the existing results in lattice-based GE to solve our problems in ACE, forming the starting point of this work.

1.3 Sanitizable Group Encryption for Sanitization in ACE

We first describe what sanitizable group encryption (SGE) is and how its sanitizability is defined. Similar to how sanitizable PKE [13] (SPKE, see Sect. 3.3)

---

[1] Izabachene *et al.* [15] proposed mediated traceable anonymous encryption that predates ACE. The mediator is essentially the sanitizer here. Like GE, it is a PKE scheme, and hence the missing feature is the enforcement of who can write. Their scheme design shares conceptual similarity with the 1-ACE scheme [12].

extends PKE, SGE extends GE with a San algorithm sanitizing ciphertexts. San essentially randomizes its input ciphertext without knowing the public key of its intended receipt. We expect *sanitizability*, which requires sanitized versions of an *adversarially generated* ciphertext and honest encryption of a random message remain computationally (instead of statistically [12]) indistinguishable. This definition is a variant of the subliminal-channel freeness of mediated traceable anonymous encryption [15] and similar to the no-write rule requirement of ACE.

With the working mechanisms of ACE-EP and SGE as outlined above, this paper starts with a generic construction of ACE-EP from any SGE. As a by-product, we obtain traceable ACE, with traceability analogous to the anonymity revocation of SGE, which traces the information (leakage) flow.

1.4   Meaningful Chosen-Ciphertext Security Under Sanitizability

It would be nice if there is a generic upgrade from any GE to SGE. However, the development of GE emphasizes security against chosen-ciphertext attacks (CCA) [3,8,20,21]. A CCA-secure GE is unsanitizable by definition. For example, the lattice-based GE construction of Libert *et al.* [20] (the scheme we will modify) uses the transformation of Canetti, Halevi, and Katz (CHK) [7] to achieve CCA security. Encryption starts by picking a one-time signature key. The verification key is attached to the *label* of an underlying encryption that is secure against chosen-plaintext attacks (CPA-secure), such that no one can modify the label. The whole ciphertext is then signed by this one-time key, intuitively providing the integrity needed by CCA security. However, the label for tightly coupling the signature key with the ciphertext forms a convenient channel for a malicious writer that the sanitizer cannot easily randomize/sanitize.

This illustrates why most ACE literature did not consider CCA security. Notably, Badertscher, Matt, and Maurer [4] formulate a meaningful CCA security notion for ACE that protects the integrity of unsanitized ciphertexts. Consider a non-CCA-secure scheme and an attacker without any write permission. By capturing *only one* ciphertext before it reached the sanitizer, the attacker might be able to maul it to encrypt an arbitrary message and write to whomever the original creator is authorized to. Their CCA notion prevents such attacks.

Similarly, our SGE notion aims for such a flavor of CCA security. Following the generic GE construction of El Aimani and Joye [3], we propose a generic SGE construction from a CPA-secure, key private, and sanitizable PKE scheme that still features a "compatible" public ciphertext validity check. Roughly, similar to the trick of Badertscher *et al.*, the ciphertext produced by our SGE scheme allows the sanitizer to easily check (for CCA security) and drop the "validity tag." Any potential subliminal channel formed by this tag will be completely killed off, while the remaining parts can be sanitized.

1.5   Challenges in Sanitization

The property we stipulated above, namely, *"rerandomizability without knowing the underlying public key,"* turns out to be non-trivial to achieve in lattices.

Although rerandomization can be done by applying similar tricks of the existing ACE-EP construction via additive homomorphism, there is a mismatch in the threat models. In normal PKE usage, the encryptor has no intention to use imperfect randomness, while it is completely the opposite case for ACE, in which a malicious encryptor is motivated to establish a subliminal channel. To the best of our knowledge, no existing lattice-based PKE scheme is proven sanitizable.

To prevent the encryptor from cheating, *i.e.*, crafting a ciphertext c such that even an honest rerandomization of c will not result in a perfectly rerandomized ciphertext, we propose an efficient technique to detect such kind of adversarial behavior. At a high level, the vectors of randomness are required to be linearly independent to span the whole randomness space, so the sanitizer can use it to fully rerandomize a ciphertext. To filter out the randomness that fails to span the whole space, we leverage the lemma for rank relation of matrix multiplication for a ciphertext component formed by a multiplication between the public key and the randomness. This structure is not readily available, and we need to adapt an existing LWE-based scheme (see Footnote 4). The underlying sanitization technique requires a dedicated analysis, which may own independent interest.

1.6   Efficient ACE for General Policy from ACE for Equality Policy

Finally, we propose a generic upgrade extending an ACE for equality policy to a general-policy scheme for 2^ℓ users. Our crucial observation is to strategically manage the credentials, which does not require 2^ℓ-repetition of an underlying ACE scheme [12]. We still set the "legitimate decryptor" as the sender itself as in ACE for equality policy. Instead of granting the decryption key to the sender, we grant the decryption key to all the users that this particular sender can encrypt to. In this way, we obtain an ACE scheme for general policy, featuring constant-size ciphertexts, but at the cost of a decryption key that can be as long as the maximum number of senders a particular user can receive messages from.

1.7   Putting It Altogether

Our instantiation mostly uses the building blocks underlying the lattice-based GE scheme of Libert *et al.* [20], but with two major changes as explained above. We replace the underlying encryption scheme with a modified version of Regev's LWE encryption [23], in which we build an efficient detection technique for confirming if its ciphertext "spans." For CCA security, we use the Naor–Yung transformation [22,24]. This leads to our lattice-based construction of SGE. With our generic transformation, we get a lattice-based ACE scheme for general policy, featuring keyless sanitization and constant-size ciphertexts. It provides a solution to two open problems: one from Damgård *et al.* [12] since it does not use *general-purpose* FE for circuits, and another from Kim and Wu [18] that asks for a general-policy ACE scheme with public sanitizer key (which rules out FE-based sanitization [12,18]). It is also the second in the ACE literature that features CCA security. Like other LWE-based schemes, it is also post-quantum secure.

Organization. Section 2 recalls the definitions of ACE. Section 3 defines the SGE notion and presents our generic SGE construction. We upgrade it to ACE-EP and ultimately general-policy ACE in Sect. 4. Finally, Sect. 5 presents our SGE instantiation from lattices, which leads to our general-policy ACE.

2   Access Control Encryption with Keyless Sanitization

2.1   Definition

ACE is defined by the following probabilistic polynomial-time (PPT) algorithms.

- Setup$(1^\lambda, P) \to$ pp: This algorithm takes the security parameter λ and a policy $P : \{0,1\}^\ell \times \{0,1\}^\ell \to \{0,1\}$ as input. It outputs the public parameter pp, which includes the message space $\mathcal{M}$ and two ciphertext spaces $\mathcal{C}$ and $\mathcal{C}'$.
- MKGen(pp) $\to$ (mpk, msk): This algorithm takes pp as input. It outputs a master public-secret key pair (mpk, msk). We assume mpk is an implicit input for all algorithms below.
- EKGen$(msk, ID_i) \to ek_{ID_i}$: This algorithm takes the master secret key msk and an identity $ID_i \in \{0,1\}^\ell$ as input. It outputs an encryption key ek_{ID_i}.
- DKGen$(msk, ID_j) \to dk_{ID_j}$: This algorithm takes the master secret key msk and an identity $ID_j \in \{0,1\}^\ell$ as input. It outputs a decryption key dk_{ID_j}.
- Enc$(ek, M) \to c$: This algorithm takes an encryption key ek and a message M as input. It outputs a ciphertext $c \in \mathcal{C}$.
- San$(c) \to c'$: This algorithm transforms an incoming ciphertext $c \in \mathcal{C}$ into a sanitized ciphertext $c' \in \mathcal{C}' \cup \{\bot\}$. We only consider keyless sanitization.
- Dec$(dk, c') \to M$: The algorithm takes a decryption key dk and a ciphertext $c \in \mathcal{C}'$ as input. It outputs a message $M \in \mathcal{M} \cup \{\bot\}$.

For all $M \in \mathcal{M}$ and $ID_i, ID_j \in \{0,1\}^\ell$ with $P(ID_i, ID_j) = 1$, an ACE scheme is correct if: $\Pr[Dec(dk_{ID_j}, San(Enc(ek_{ID_i}, M))) \neq M] \leq negl(\lambda)$ where pp $\leftarrow$ Setup$(1^\lambda, P)$, (mpk, msk) $\leftarrow$ MKGen(pp), $ek_{ID_i} \leftarrow$ EKGen(msk, ID_i), and $dk_{ID_j} \leftarrow$ DKGen(msk, ID_j). The probability space is over the coin flips of all the algorithms.

2.2   Security

ACE is for enforcing two access-control rules: the *no-read rule* and the *no-write rule*. Most existing works [12,13,18,25] consider them under only CPA-based definitions, where the adversary is given access to the oracles for encryption, encryption-key generation, and decryption-key generation. Badertscher et al. [4] consider a CCA-based definition with a malicious insider who can maul an honestly-generated and unsanitized ACE ciphertext into a carrier for sending a message to a receiver that is forbidden by the policy otherwise. Even though ACE needs to assume an operational environment where ciphertexts must be routed through the sanitizer before reaching their final destination, it does not assume that no one can eavesdrop and maul them before reaching the sanitizer.

Instead of a typical decryption oracle, Badertscher *et al.* proposed an oracle that first sanitizes the ciphertext then decrypts it, *i.e.*, a sanitize-then-decrypt oracle. If an ACE scheme remains CCA-secure in this sense, no one can maul an unsanitized ciphertext. Note that the CCA protection does not extend to a sanitized ciphertext. Also, in practice, the sanitizer can sign on the sanitized ciphertexts and publish them on a public bulletin board for (anonymous) retrieval.

Let $\mathcal{ACE} = (\mathsf{Setup}, \mathsf{MKGen}, \mathsf{EKGen}, \mathsf{DKGen}, \mathsf{Enc}, \mathsf{San}, \mathsf{Dec})$ be an ACE scheme for policy $\mathsf{P} : \{0,1\}^\ell \times \{0,1\}^\ell \to \{0,1\}$ over a message space $\mathcal{M}$. For a security parameter λ and a random bit b drawn from a fair coin flip, the general experiment $\mathsf{Exp}_{\mathcal{ACE}, \mathcal{A}}(\lambda)$ for a PPT adversary $\mathcal{A}$ starts with the challenger sampling $\mathsf{pp} \leftarrow \mathsf{Setup}(1^\lambda, \mathsf{P})$ and $(\mathsf{mpk}, \mathsf{msk}) \leftarrow \mathsf{MKGen}(\mathsf{pp})$. Then $\mathsf{Exp}_{\mathcal{ACE}, \mathcal{A}}(\lambda)$ diverges into no-read rule experiment $\mathsf{Exp}_{\mathcal{ACE}, \mathcal{A}}^{\mathsf{NoRead}}(\lambda)$ or no-write experiment $\mathsf{Exp}_{\mathcal{ACE}, \mathcal{A}}^{\mathsf{NoWrite}}(\lambda)$ with a different challenge oracle and a different set of training oracles as below.

- $\mathcal{O}^{\mathsf{Enc}}(M, \mathsf{ID}_i) \to c$: On input $M \in \mathcal{M}$ and a sender identity $\mathsf{ID}_i \in \{0,1\}^\ell$, the encryption oracle outputs $c \leftarrow \mathsf{Enc}(\mathsf{EKGen}(\mathsf{msk}, \mathsf{ID}_i), M)$.
- $\mathcal{O}^{\mathsf{SanEnc}}(M, \mathsf{ID}_i) \to c'$: On input a message $M \in \mathcal{M}$ and a sender identity $\mathsf{ID}_i \in \{0,1\}^\ell$, it outputs $c' \leftarrow \mathsf{San}(\mathsf{Enc}(\mathsf{EKGen}(\mathsf{msk}, \mathsf{ID}_i), M))$.
- $\mathcal{O}^{\mathsf{EKGen}}(\mathsf{ID}_i) \to \mathsf{ek}_{\mathsf{ID}_i}$: On input a sender identity $\mathsf{ID}_i \in \{0,1\}^\ell$, the encryption key generation oracle outputs $\mathsf{ek}_{\mathsf{ID}_i} \leftarrow \mathsf{EKGen}(\mathsf{msk}, \mathsf{ID}_i)$.
- $\mathcal{O}^{\mathsf{DKGen}}(\mathsf{ID}_j) \to \mathsf{dk}_{\mathsf{ID}_j}$: On input a receiver identity $\mathsf{ID}_j \in \{0,1\}^\ell$, the decryption key generation oracle outputs $\mathsf{dk}_{\mathsf{ID}_j} \leftarrow \mathsf{DKGen}(\mathsf{msk}, \mathsf{ID}_j)$.
- $\mathcal{O}^{\mathsf{Dec}}(\mathsf{ID}_j, c) \to M$: With a receiver identity $\mathsf{ID}_j \in \{0,1\}^\ell$ and an unsanitized ciphertext $c \in \mathcal{C}$, it outputs $M \leftarrow \mathsf{Dec}(\mathsf{DKGen}(\mathsf{msk}, \mathsf{ID}_j), \mathsf{San}(c))$.
- $\mathcal{O}^{\mathsf{NoRead}}((M_0, M_1), (\mathsf{ID}_0, \mathsf{ID}_1)) \to c_b$: This is the challenge oracle for the no-read experiment. On input a pair of messages $(M_0, M_1) \in \mathcal{M} \times \mathcal{M}$ and a pair of sender indices $(\mathsf{ID}_0, \mathsf{ID}_1) \in \{0,1\}^\ell \times \{0,1\}^\ell$, the challenger responds with $c_b \leftarrow \mathsf{Enc}(\mathsf{EKGen}(\mathsf{msk}, \mathsf{ID}_b), M_b)$.
- $\mathcal{O}^{\mathsf{NoWrite}}(c, \mathsf{ID}^*) \to c_b$: This is the challenge oracle for the no-write experiment. On input an unsanitized ciphertext $c \in \mathcal{C}$ and a sender identity $\mathsf{ID}^* \in \{0,1\}^\ell$, it sets $c_0^* \leftarrow c$. Then the challenger samples $M^* \leftarrow \mathcal{M}$, computes $c_1^* \leftarrow \mathsf{Enc}(\mathsf{EKGen}(\mathsf{msk}, \mathsf{ID}^*), M^*)$, and responds with $c_b \leftarrow \mathsf{San}(c_b^*)$.

$\mathcal{A}$ outputs a bit $b' \in \{0,1\}$ as the output of the experiment at the end.

Definition 1 (No-Read Rule). *$\mathcal{A}$ wins the no-read game with $\mathcal{O}^{\mathsf{Enc}}$, $\mathcal{O}^{\mathsf{EKGen}}$, $\mathcal{O}^{\mathsf{DKGen}}$, $\mathcal{O}^{\mathsf{Dec}}$, and $\mathcal{O}^{\mathsf{NoRead}}$ if $b' = b$, $|M_0| = |M_1|$, for all queries $\mathsf{ID}_j \in \{0,1\}^\ell$ that $\mathcal{A}$ makes to the $\mathcal{O}^{\mathsf{DKGen}}$, $\mathsf{P}(\mathsf{ID}_0, \mathsf{ID}_j) = \mathsf{P}(\mathsf{ID}_1, \mathsf{ID}_j) = 0$, and c_b has never been queried to $\mathcal{O}^{\mathsf{Dec}}$. ACE satisfies the no-read rule if for all PPT $\mathcal{A}$, the advantage for $\mathcal{A}$ to win the no-read game is $\mathsf{Adv}^{\mathcal{A}} = \Pr[\mathcal{A} \text{ wins } \mathsf{Exp}_{\mathcal{ACE}, \mathcal{A}}^{\mathsf{NoRead}}(\lambda)] - \frac{1}{2} \leq \mathsf{negl}(\lambda)$.*

The adversary can compromise the sanitizer under the above definition since the challenge ciphertext is not sanitized, and our ACE notion does not have any sanitizer key. The no-read rule ensures payload privacy, *i.e.*, no unintended receivers can learn anything about the message. It also guarantees (outsider) sender anonymity, which holds against any coalition of receivers that cannot decrypt the challenge ciphertext. This definition is weaker than requiring sender anonymity to hold even against an adversary who can decrypt the ciphertext.

Definition 2 (No-Write Rule). *Given the oracles of* $\mathcal{O}^{\mathsf{SanEnc}}$, $\mathcal{O}^{\mathsf{EKGen}}$, $\mathcal{O}^{\mathsf{DKGen}}$, $\mathcal{O}^{\mathsf{Dec}}$, *and* $\mathcal{O}^{\mathsf{NoWrite}}$, $\mathcal{A}$ *wins the no-write game if* $b' = b$, $\mathsf{San}(c) \neq \bot$, *and:*

- *The adversary* $\mathcal{A}$ *makes at most one query²* *to the challenge oracle* $\mathcal{O}^{\mathsf{NoWrite}}$.
- *For all identities* $\mathsf{ID}_i \in \{0,1\}^\ell$ *that* $\mathcal{A}$ *submits to* $\mathcal{O}^{\mathsf{EKGen}}$ *prior to its challenge and all identities* $\mathsf{ID}_j \in \{0,1\}^\ell$ *that* $\mathcal{A}$ *submits to* $\mathcal{O}^{\mathsf{DKGen}}$, $\mathsf{P}(\mathsf{ID}_i, \mathsf{ID}_j) = 0$.

We say that an ACE scheme satisfies the no-write rule if for all PPT adversary $\mathcal{A}$, *the advantage of* $\mathcal{A}$ *is* $\mathsf{Adv}^{\mathcal{A}} = \Pr[\mathcal{A}\ wins\ \mathsf{Exp}^{\mathsf{NoWrite}}_{\mathcal{ACE},\mathcal{A}}(\lambda)] - \frac{1}{2} \leq \mathsf{negl}(\lambda)$.

The *no-write rule* means that a sender can only encrypt to receivers permitted by the policy. Even an adversary can somehow embed in a ciphertext some subliminal information, it will be killed off after sanitization. Likewise, this property should hold even when multiple senders and receivers collude.

Sender Policy and Message Policy. The formulation of Kim and Wu [18] additionally considers "fine-grained sender policy" with the access control policy also governs the messages a sender can send. This policy is embedded in and authorized via the encryption key. They also suggested that an encryption key for multiple policies over the message can be supported in a straightforward manner by granting the sender multiple certified encryption keys.

In this paper, we consider a variant definition that the message policy can be *ad hoc*, *i.e.*, the sender can create ciphertexts encrypting different messages satisfying different relations to any legitimate receiver. This flexibility has (seemingly inherent) implications on privacy and the no-write rule since the sanitizer needs to know about the relation and cannot "sanitize" the relation.

2.3 Traceable ACE

To obtain traceable ACE (tACE), we equip the traceability feature via two algorithms below, and with Enc algorithm now takes, besides the user encryption key ek, also an input of opening-authority public key tpk for the tracing feature.

- $\mathsf{TKGen}(\mathsf{pp}) \to (\mathsf{tpk}, \mathsf{tsk})$: This algorithm takes as input the public parameter pp and outputs the tracer public/secret key pair $(\mathsf{tpk}, \mathsf{tsk})$.
- $\mathsf{Trace}(\mathsf{tsk}, c') \to \mathsf{ID}$: This algorithm takes the input of the tracer secret key tsk and a sanitized ciphertext $c' \in \mathcal{C}'$. It outputs the sender identity ID of c'.

Tracing the sender can be desirable in the context of ACE since we can locate which user has his/her machine compromised that tried to leak information. One may consider an alternative formulation that traces the receiver.

Here, we only consider a primitive form of tracing that recovers a user identity ID associated with a ciphertext [15]. Akin to traceable signatures [16], one could consider using a user-specific trapdoor for ID to check [1] whether ID is associated with a ciphertext [21] or to trace [9] all ciphertexts associated with a specific ID.

---

² A standard hybrid argument shows that security against an adversary that makes a single challenge query implies security against one that makes multiple such queries.

Traceability Correctness and Soundness. For all $M \in \mathcal{M}$ and $\mathsf{ID}_i \in \{0,1\}^\ell$, $\mathsf{pp} \leftarrow \mathsf{Setup}(1^\lambda, \mathsf{P})$, $(\mathsf{mpk}, \mathsf{msk}) \leftarrow \mathsf{MKGen}(\mathsf{pp})$, $(\mathsf{tpk}, \mathsf{tsk}) \leftarrow \mathsf{TKGen}(\mathsf{pp})$, and $c \leftarrow \mathsf{Enc}(\mathsf{EKGen}(\mathsf{msk}, \mathsf{ID}_i), M)$, *traceability correctness* means $\Pr[\mathsf{Trace}(\mathsf{tsk}, \mathsf{San}(c)) \neq \mathsf{ID}_i] \leq \mathsf{negl}(\lambda)$. The probabilities are taken over the randomness of all algorithms.

A tACE scheme has *traceability soundness* if, for any PPT adversary $\mathcal{A}$ who queries to $\mathcal{O}^{\mathsf{EKGen}}$ and outputs a ciphertext c, the advantage for $\mathcal{A}$ to win, defined to be $\Pr[\mathsf{ID} \notin \mathcal{Q}^{\mathsf{EKGen}} | \mathsf{Trace}(\mathsf{tsk}, \mathsf{San}(c)) = \mathsf{ID}]$, is negligible, where $\mathcal{Q}^{\mathsf{EKGen}}$ denotes the set of queries to $\mathcal{O}^{\mathsf{EKGen}}$, *i.e.*, c should not trace to an uncompromised user.

3 Sanitizable Group Encryption

3.1 Syntax of Sanitizable Group Encryption

A sanitizable group encryption scheme consists of the following algorithms.

- $\mathsf{Setup}(1^\lambda) \to \mathsf{pp}$: On input a security parameter λ, this probabilistic algorithm outputs the public parameter pp as an implicit input of what follows.
- $(\mathsf{G}_r, \mathsf{Sample}_{\mathcal{R}})$: On input of λ, G_r generates the key pair $(\mathsf{pk}_{\mathcal{R}}, \mathsf{sk}_{\mathcal{R}})$ of the relation $\mathcal{R}$ concerning a message M one might want to prove about. $\mathsf{sk}_{\mathcal{R}}$ can be empty if $\mathcal{R}$ is publicly sampleable. We assume there is a PPT algorithm that can check if $(\mathsf{pk}_{\mathcal{R}}, \mathsf{sk}_{\mathcal{R}})$ is a valid output of G_r. On input of $(\mathsf{pk}_{\mathcal{R}}, \mathsf{sk}_{\mathcal{R}})$, $\mathsf{Sample}_{\mathcal{R}}$ produces (x, M) where x is an instance and M is a witness for $\mathcal{R}$.
- $\mathsf{KeyGen}_E(\mathsf{pp}) \to (\mathsf{pk}_E, \mathsf{sk}_E)$: This algorithm outputs the key pair $(\mathsf{pk}_E, \mathsf{sk}_E)$ of the entity E in the system. E can either be the group manager GM, the opening authority OA, or a group member u identified by ID.
- $\mathsf{Join}(\mathsf{sk}_{\mathsf{GM}}, \mathsf{pk}_{\mathsf{GM}}, \mathsf{pk}_{\mathsf{ID}}) \to \mathsf{cert}_{\mathsf{pk}_{\mathsf{ID}}}$: This algorithm outputs a certificate $\mathsf{cert}_{\mathsf{pk}_{\mathsf{ID}}}$ on public key $\mathsf{pk}_{\mathsf{ID}}$ and stores $(\mathsf{ID}, \mathsf{pk}_{\mathsf{ID}}, \mathsf{cert}_{\mathsf{pk}_{\mathsf{ID}}})$ in a directory db.
- $\mathsf{Vfcert}(\mathsf{pk}_{\mathsf{GM}}, \mathsf{pk}_{\mathsf{ID}}, \mathsf{cert}_{\mathsf{pk}_{\mathsf{ID}}})$: It verifies the validity of $\mathsf{cert}_{\mathsf{pk}_{\mathsf{ID}}}$ for $\mathsf{pk}_{\mathsf{ID}}$.
- $\mathsf{Enc}(\mathsf{pk}_{\mathsf{GM}}, \mathsf{pk}_{\mathsf{OA}}, \mathsf{pk}_{\mathsf{ID}}, \mathsf{cert}_{\mathsf{pk}_{\mathsf{ID}}}, (\mathsf{pk}_{\mathcal{R}}, x,) \, M) \to c$: On input the respective public key $\mathsf{pk}_{\mathsf{GM}}$, $\mathsf{pk}_{\mathsf{OA}}$, and $\mathsf{pk}_{\mathsf{ID}}$ of GM, OA, and a group member certified by $\mathsf{cert}_{\mathsf{pk}_{\mathsf{ID}}}$, and optionally a relation $\mathsf{pk}_{\mathcal{R}}$ with a public value x, it returns a ciphertext c of the plaintext M, which $(x, M) \in \mathcal{R}$ is supposed to hold.
- $\mathsf{Vf}(\mathsf{pk}_{\mathsf{GM}}, \mathsf{pk}_{\mathsf{OA}}, (\mathsf{pk}_{\mathcal{R}}, x,) \, c) \to \{0, 1\}$: It outputs 1 if c is valid; 0 otherwise.
- $\mathsf{San}(c) \to c'$: On input a valid ciphertext c, this algorithm outputs its sanitization c' (or a rejection symbol $\perp$).
- $\mathsf{Dec}(\mathsf{sk}_{\mathsf{ID}}, c') \to M$: On input the private key $\mathsf{sk}_{\mathsf{ID}}$ and a sanitized ciphertext c', this algorithm decrypts c' and outputs the message M (or $\perp$).
- $\mathsf{Open}(\mathsf{sk}_{\mathsf{OA}}, c') \to \mathsf{pk}_{\mathsf{ID}}$: On input the private key $\mathsf{sk}_{\mathsf{OA}}$ of OA and a sanitized ciphertext c', this algorithm recovers from c' the public key $\mathsf{pk}_{\mathsf{ID}}$.

Similar to the application scenario of ACE, we consider SGE ciphertexts to be (verified and) sanitized before reaching the final destination. This explains why our Dec and Open algorithms only work on sanitized ciphertexts. One might consider an alternative definition that they also work on unsanitized ciphertexts.

Our SGE formulation is kept as non-interactive as possible. Instead of having an explicit Prove algorithm/protocol in the prior GE formulation, the ciphertext produced by Enc contains a non-interactive proof. Existing schemes can indeed be formulated in this setting, some at the cost of using Fiat–Shamir heuristics. Also, the Join protocol is reduced to a pair of algorithms that the GM uses the algorithm Join to sign on a given public key for generating a certificate on it[3], which the user can then run Vfcert to verify its validity. This helps to simplify the security definitions. We remark that the security definition for existing non-interactive GE schemes [8, 21] still separates the proof from the ciphertext.

Correctness. We require for an SGE scheme, the correctness game Corr defined in Fig. 1 returns 1 with overwhelming probability.

Experiment $\mathsf{Exp}^{\mathsf{Corr}}(\lambda)$

$1 : \mathsf{pp} \leftarrow \mathsf{Setup}(1^\lambda); (\mathsf{pk}_\mathcal{R}, \mathsf{sk}_\mathcal{R}) \leftarrow \mathsf{G}_r(1^\lambda); (x, M) \leftarrow \mathsf{Sample}_\mathcal{R}(\mathsf{pk}_\mathcal{R}, \mathsf{sk}_\mathcal{R});$

$2 : (\mathsf{pk}_{\mathsf{GM}}, \mathsf{sk}_{\mathsf{GM}}) \leftarrow \mathsf{KeyGen}_{\mathsf{GM}}(\mathsf{pp}); (\mathsf{pk}_{\mathsf{OA}}, \mathsf{sk}_{\mathsf{OA}}) \leftarrow \mathsf{KeyGen}_{\mathsf{OA}}(\mathsf{pp});$

$3 : \mathsf{cert}_{\mathsf{pk}_{\mathsf{ID}}} \leftarrow \mathsf{Join}(\mathsf{sk}_{\mathsf{GM}}, \mathsf{pk}_{\mathsf{GM}}, \mathsf{pk}_{\mathsf{ID}});$

$4 : c \leftarrow \mathsf{Enc}(\mathsf{pk}_{\mathsf{GM}}, \mathsf{pk}_{\mathsf{OA}}, \mathsf{pk}_{\mathsf{ID}}, \mathsf{cert}_{\mathsf{pk}_{\mathsf{ID}}}, (\mathsf{pk}_\mathcal{R}, x,) M); c' \leftarrow \mathsf{San}(c);$

$5 : \mathsf{cond}_1 \leftarrow \mathsf{Vf}(\mathsf{pk}_{\mathsf{GM}}, \mathsf{pk}_{\mathsf{OA}}, (\mathsf{pk}_\mathcal{R}, x,) c);$

$6 : \mathsf{cond}_2 \leftarrow (\mathsf{pk}_{\mathsf{ID}} = \mathsf{Open}(\mathsf{sk}_{\mathsf{OA}}, c'));$

$7 : \mathsf{cond}_3 \leftarrow (M = \mathsf{Dec}(\mathsf{sk}_{\mathsf{ID}}, c'));$

$8 : \text{Return } (\mathsf{cond}_1 = \mathsf{cond}_2 = \mathsf{cond}_3 = 1).$

Fig. 1. Experiment for the correctness of SGE

3.2   Security Model of Sanitizable Group Encryption

In the following, we assume the adversary $\mathcal{A}$ is stateful. By maintaining the state information state, $\mathcal{A}$ becomes aware of at which stage it is.

Message Indistinguishability (IND). An SGE scheme meets the IND-CCA notion if the success probability of any PPT adversary $\mathcal{A}$ to distinguish among encryptions of a chosen message and of a random message is at most negligibly better (in parameter λ) than $\frac{1}{2}$ in the experiment Ind in Fig. 2a, where the oracles are defined as below.

- $\mathcal{O}_\mathcal{L}^{\mathsf{Join}^*}()$ is a stateful oracle that simulates executions for honest users who request to join the group. It maintains as state information an initially empty list $\mathcal{L}$. For its i-th invocation, the simulator executes $(\mathsf{pk}_{\mathsf{ID}_i}, \mathsf{sk}_{\mathsf{ID}_i}) \leftarrow$

---

[3] The public key can be proven valid by an external mechanism (e.g., via any proof-of-possession mechanism over its secret key). Our final goal is to reduce ACE to GE. In ACE, each public key is generated by a trusted key generator, and hence it suffices.

$\mathsf{KeyGen}_\mathsf{u}(\mathsf{pp})$, sends it to the adversary, which responds with $\mathsf{cert}_{\mathsf{pk}_{\mathsf{ID}_i}}$. The output $(\mathsf{pk}_{\mathsf{ID}_i}, \mathsf{sk}_{\mathsf{ID}_i}, \mathsf{cert}_{\mathsf{pk}_{\mathsf{ID}_i}})$ of the user is stored in $\mathcal{L}$ if the $\mathsf{Join}()$-executing $\mathcal{A}$ provides a valid certificate $\mathsf{cert}_{\mathsf{pk}_{\mathsf{ID}_i}}$.

- $\mathcal{O}^{\mathsf{Dec}}_{\neg(\mathsf{ID}^*, c_b)}(\mathsf{ID}, c_i)$ is a stateless decryption oracle. On input a ciphertext c_i, it runs $M' \leftarrow \mathsf{Dec}(\mathsf{sk}_{\mathsf{ID}}, \mathsf{San}(c_i))$ and returns M' if $(\mathsf{ID}, c_i) \neq (\mathsf{ID}^*, c_b)$.
- $\mathcal{O}^{\mathsf{RoR}}_b(\mathsf{pk}_{\mathsf{ID}}, \mathsf{pk}_\mathcal{R}, x, M)$ is a real-or-random challenge oracle that is only queried once. For a bit b, it samples a random plaintext M_0 uniformly from $\mathcal{M}$, and sets $M_1 = M$. It returns $c_b \leftarrow \mathsf{Enc}(\mathsf{pk}_{\mathsf{GM}}, \mathsf{pk}_{\mathsf{OA}}, \mathsf{pk}_{\mathsf{ID}}, \mathsf{cert}_{\mathsf{pk}_{\mathsf{ID}}}, (\mathsf{pk}_\mathcal{R}, x,) M_b)$.

Experiment $\mathsf{Exp}^{\mathsf{Ind}}_\mathcal{A}(\lambda)$	Experiment $\mathsf{Exp}^{\mathsf{Ano}}_\mathcal{A}(\lambda)$
$1 : \mathsf{pp} \leftarrow \mathsf{Setup}(1^\lambda);$	$1 : \mathsf{pp} \leftarrow \mathsf{Setup}(1^\lambda);$
$2 : (\mathsf{pk}_{\mathsf{GM}}, \mathsf{pk}_{\mathsf{OA}}, \mathsf{state}) \leftarrow \mathcal{A}(\mathsf{pp});$	$2 : (\mathsf{pk}_{\mathsf{OA}}, \mathsf{sk}_{\mathsf{OA}}) \leftarrow \mathsf{KeyGen}_{\mathsf{OA}}(\mathsf{pp});$
$3 : (\mathsf{pk}_{\mathsf{ID}^*}, \mathsf{cert}_{\mathsf{pk}_{\mathsf{ID}^*}}, \mathsf{pk}_\mathcal{R}, x, M, \mathsf{state})$	$3 : (\mathsf{pk}_{\mathsf{GM}}, \mathsf{state}) \leftarrow \mathcal{A}(\mathsf{pp}, \mathsf{pk}_{\mathsf{OA}});$
$\quad \leftarrow \mathcal{A}^{\mathcal{O}^{\mathsf{Join}^*}_\mathcal{L}(), \mathcal{O}^{\mathsf{Dec}}_{\neg(\mathsf{ID}^*, c_b)}(\cdot, \cdot)}(\mathsf{state});$	$4 : (\{\mathsf{pk}_{\mathsf{ID}_d}, \mathsf{cert}_{\mathsf{pk}_{\mathsf{ID}_d}}\}_{d \in \{0,1\}}, \mathsf{pk}_\mathcal{R}, x, M,$
$4 : \mathsf{If}\ ((\mathsf{pk}_{\mathsf{ID}^*}, \cdot, \mathsf{cert}_{\mathsf{pk}_{\mathsf{ID}^*}}) \notin \mathcal{L}) \vee$	$\quad \mathsf{state}) \leftarrow \mathcal{A}^{\mathcal{O}^{\mathsf{Open}}_{\neg c_b}(\mathsf{sk}_{\mathsf{OA}}, \cdot)}(\mathsf{state});$
$\quad ((x, M) \notin \mathcal{R})\ \mathsf{then\ return}\ 0;$	$5 : \mathsf{If}\ (\mathsf{Vfcert}(\mathsf{pk}_{\mathsf{GM}}, \mathsf{pk}_{\mathsf{ID}_0}, \mathsf{cert}_{\mathsf{pk}_{\mathsf{ID}_0}}) = 0) \vee$
$5 : b \leftarrow \{0,1\}; c_b \leftarrow \mathcal{O}^{\mathsf{RoR}}_b(\mathsf{pk}_{\mathsf{ID}^*}, \mathsf{pk}_\mathcal{R}, x, M);$	$\quad (\mathsf{Vfcert}(\mathsf{pk}_{\mathsf{GM}}, \mathsf{pk}_{\mathsf{ID}_1}, \mathsf{cert}_{\mathsf{pk}_{\mathsf{ID}_1}}) = 0) \vee$
$6 : b^* \leftarrow \mathcal{A}^{\mathcal{O}^{\mathsf{Join}^*}_\mathcal{L}(), \mathcal{O}^{\mathsf{Dec}}_{\neg(\mathsf{ID}^*, c_b)}(\cdot, \cdot)}(c_b, \mathsf{state});$	$\quad ((x, M) \notin \mathcal{R})\ \mathsf{then\ return}\ 0;$
$7 : \mathsf{If}\ (b = b^*)\ \mathsf{then\ return}\ 1\ \mathsf{else\ return}\ 0.$	$6 : \mathsf{ch} \leftarrow (\{\mathsf{pk}_{\mathsf{ID}_d}, \mathsf{cert}_{\mathsf{pk}_{\mathsf{ID}_d}}\}_{d \in \{0,1\}}, \mathsf{pk}_\mathcal{R}, x);$
(a)	$7 : b \leftarrow \{0,1\}; c_b \leftarrow \mathcal{O}^{\mathsf{Ano}}_b(\mathsf{pk}_{\mathsf{GM}}, \mathsf{ch}, M);$
	$8 : b^* \leftarrow \mathcal{A}^{\mathcal{O}^{\mathsf{Open}}_{\neg c_b}(\mathsf{sk}_{\mathsf{OA}}, \cdot)}(c_b, \mathsf{state});$
	$9 : \mathsf{If}\ (b = b^*)\ \mathsf{then\ return}\ 1\ \mathsf{else\ return}\ 0.$
	(b)

Fig. 2. Experiments for (2a) IND-CCA and (2b) ANO-CCA notions of SGE

Anonymity. The formal definition of anonymity against chosen-ciphertext attacks (ANO-CCA) is as follows. The notion is met if the success probability of any PPT adversary $\mathcal{A}$ is at most negligibly better than $\frac{1}{2}$. We introduce the following oracles and the game Ano in Fig. 2b.

- $\mathcal{O}^{\mathsf{Open}}_{\neg c_b}(\mathsf{sk}_{\mathsf{OA}}, \cdot)$ returns $\mathsf{Open}(\mathsf{sk}_{\mathsf{OA}}, \mathsf{San}(c))$ on input of a ciphertext $c \neq c_b$,
- $\mathcal{O}^{\mathsf{Ano}}_b(\mathsf{pk}_{\mathsf{GM}}, \{\mathsf{pk}_{\mathsf{ID}_d}, \mathsf{cert}_{\mathsf{pk}_{\mathsf{ID}_d}}\}_{d \in \{0,1\}}, \mathsf{pk}_\mathcal{R}, x, M)$ is a challenge oracle that is only queried once. It returns $c_b \leftarrow \mathsf{Enc}(\mathsf{pk}_{\mathsf{GM}}, \mathsf{pk}_{\mathsf{OA}}, \mathsf{pk}_{\mathsf{ID}_b}, \mathsf{cert}_{\mathsf{pk}_b}, (\mathsf{pk}_\mathcal{R}, x,) M)$.

Soundness. In a soundness attack, $\mathcal{A}$ creates adaptively the intended group of receivers communicating with the genuine GM. $\mathcal{A}$ is successful if it can output a ciphertext c and a chosen $\mathsf{pk}_\mathcal{R}$ such that (1) c is not in the valid ciphertext space denoted by $\mathcal{C}^{\mathsf{pk}_{\mathsf{GM}}, \mathsf{pk}_{\mathsf{OA}}, \mathsf{db}, \mathsf{pk}_\mathcal{R}, x} = \{\mathsf{Enc}(\mathsf{pk}_{\mathsf{GM}}, \mathsf{pk}_{\mathsf{OA}}, \mathsf{pk}_{\mathsf{ID}}, \mathsf{cert}_{\mathsf{pk}_{\mathsf{ID}}}, (\mathsf{pk}_\mathcal{R}, x,) M) :$

$((x, M) \in \mathcal{R}) \wedge (\mathsf{pk}_{\mathsf{ID}} \in \mathsf{db}) \wedge \mathsf{Vfcert}(\mathsf{pk}_{\mathsf{GM}}, \mathsf{pk}_{\mathsf{ID}}, \mathsf{cert}_{\mathsf{pk}_{\mathsf{ID}}}) = 1\}$, and (2) opening c results in a public key that does not belong to any group member.

An SGE scheme is sound if, for any PPT $\mathcal{A}$, the experiment $\mathsf{Exp}_{\mathcal{A}}^{\mathsf{Sound}}(\lambda)$ outputs 1 with negligible probability. We introduce the following oracle and the game Sound in Fig. 3a.

- $\mathcal{O}_{\mathsf{db}}^{\mathsf{Join}}(\mathsf{sk}_{\mathsf{GM}}, \mathsf{pk}_{\mathsf{GM}}, \cdot)$ is a stateful oracle that simulates GM and maintains db storing each registered public key $\mathsf{pk}_{\mathsf{ID}}$ along with its certificate $\mathsf{cert}_{\mathsf{pk}_{\mathsf{ID}}}$.

Experiment $\mathsf{Exp}_{\mathcal{A}}^{\mathsf{Sound}}(\lambda)$

1 : $\mathsf{pp} \leftarrow \mathsf{Setup}(1^\lambda)$;
   $(\mathsf{pk}_{\mathsf{GM}}, \mathsf{sk}_{\mathsf{GM}}) \leftarrow \mathsf{KeyGen}_{\mathsf{GM}}(\mathsf{pp})$;
   $(\mathsf{pk}_{\mathsf{OA}}, \mathsf{sk}_{\mathsf{OA}}) \leftarrow \mathsf{KeyGen}_{\mathsf{OA}}(\mathsf{pp})$;

2 : $(\mathsf{pk}_{\mathcal{R}}, x, c)$
   $\leftarrow \mathcal{A}^{\mathcal{O}_{\mathsf{db}}^{\mathsf{Join}}(\mathsf{sk}_{\mathsf{GM}}, \mathsf{pk}_{\mathsf{GM}}, \cdot)}(\mathsf{pp}, \mathsf{pk}_{\mathsf{GM}}, \mathsf{pk}_{\mathsf{OA}}, \mathsf{sk}_{\mathsf{OA}})$;

3 : If $\mathsf{Vf}(\mathsf{pk}_{\mathsf{GM}}, \mathsf{pk}_{\mathsf{OA}}, (\mathsf{pk}_{\mathcal{R}}, x,) c) = 0$
   then return 0;

4 : $\mathsf{cond}_1 = (\mathsf{Open}(\mathsf{sk}_{\mathsf{OA}}, \mathsf{San}(c)) \notin \mathsf{db})$;

5 : $\mathsf{cond}_2 = (c \notin C^{\mathsf{pk}_{\mathsf{GM}}, \mathsf{pk}_{\mathsf{OA}}, \mathsf{db}, \mathsf{pk}_{\mathcal{R}}, x})$;

6 : Return $(\mathsf{cond}_1 \vee \mathsf{cond}_2)$.

(a)

Experiment $\mathsf{Exp}_{\mathcal{A}}^{\mathsf{wSan}}(\lambda)$

1 : $\mathsf{pp} \leftarrow \mathsf{Setup}(1^\lambda)$;

2 : $(\mathsf{pk}_{\mathsf{GM}}, \mathsf{pk}_{\mathsf{OA}}, \mathsf{state}) \leftarrow \mathcal{A}(\mathsf{pp})$;

3 : $(\mathsf{pk}_{\mathsf{ID}^*}, \mathsf{cert}_{\mathsf{pk}_{\mathsf{ID}^*}}, \mathsf{pk}_{\mathcal{R}}, x, c, \mathsf{state})$
   $\leftarrow \mathcal{A}^{\mathcal{O}_{\mathcal{L}}^{\mathsf{Join}^*}(), \mathcal{O}_{\neg(\mathsf{ID}^*, c)}^{\mathsf{Dec}}(\cdot, \cdot)}(\mathsf{state})$;

4 : If $(\mathsf{pk}_{\mathsf{ID}^*}, \cdot, \mathsf{cert}_{\mathsf{pk}_{\mathsf{ID}^*}}) \notin \mathcal{L}$ then return 0;

5 : $b \leftarrow \{0, 1\}; c_b \leftarrow \mathcal{O}^{\mathsf{wSan}}(\mathsf{pk}_{\mathcal{R}}, \mathsf{sk}_{\mathcal{R}}, c)$;

6 : $b^* \leftarrow \mathcal{A}^{\mathcal{O}_{\mathcal{L}}^{\mathsf{Join}^*}(), \mathcal{O}_{\neg(\mathsf{ID}^*, c)}^{\mathsf{Dec}}(\cdot, \cdot)}(c_b, \mathsf{state})$;

7 : If $(b = b^*)$ then return 1 else return 0.

(b)

Fig. 3. Experiments for the (3a) Soundness and (3b) Sanitizability of SGE

Sanitizability. Sanitizability requires that sanitization of two ciphertexts, one given by the adversary and the other randomly picked from the ciphertext space, cannot be distinguished as long as the adversary has no decryption key that decrypts any one of the ciphertexts. An SGE scheme is sanitizable if, for any PPT $\mathcal{A}$, the experiment $\mathsf{Exp}_{\mathcal{A}}^{\mathsf{wSan}}(\lambda)$ outputs 1 with negligible probability. With the two oracles $\mathcal{O}_{\mathcal{L}}^{\mathsf{Join}^*}()$ and $\mathcal{O}_{\neg(\mathsf{ID}^*, c)}^{\mathsf{Dec}}(\mathsf{ID}, c_i)$ introduced in Fig. 2a, we introduce an additional oracle below and the game wSan in Fig. 3b.

- $\mathcal{O}^{\mathsf{wSan}}(\mathsf{pk}_{\mathcal{R}}, \mathsf{sk}_{\mathcal{R}}, c) \rightarrow c_b$ is a real-or-random challenge oracle that is only queried once, It aborts if $\mathsf{Vf}(\mathsf{pk}_{\mathsf{GM}}, \mathsf{pk}_{\mathsf{OA}}, \mathsf{pk}_{\mathcal{R}}, x, c) = 0$. For a bit b, it first sets $c_0^* \leftarrow c$ and runs $(x, M^*) \leftarrow \mathsf{Sample}_{\mathcal{R}}(\mathsf{pk}_{\mathcal{R}}, \mathsf{sk}_{\mathcal{R}})$ to sample M^* uniformly from $\mathcal{M}$ under the constraint that $(x, M^*) \in \mathcal{R}$. It then computes $c_1^* \leftarrow \mathsf{Enc}(\mathsf{pk}_{\mathsf{GM}}, \mathsf{pk}_{\mathsf{OA}}, \mathsf{pk}_{\mathsf{ID}}, \mathsf{cert}_{\mathsf{pk}_{\mathsf{ID}}}, (\mathsf{pk}_{\mathcal{R}}, x,) M^*)$ and returns $c_b \leftarrow \mathsf{San}(c_b^*)$.

3.3 Sanitizable Public-Key Encryption

Let $\mathcal{E} = (\mathsf{Setup}, \mathsf{KeyGen}, \mathsf{Enc}, \mathsf{San}, \mathsf{Dec})$ be a key-private sanitizable PKE scheme. We omit to repeat the standard definitions of correctness, key privacy, and CPA security here [13]. Sanitizability requires any adversary generating two pairs of message and randomness $(M_0, r_0), (M_1, r_1)$ cannot distinguish the random bit b when given a sanitized ciphertext $\mathsf{San}(\mathsf{Enc}(\mathsf{pk}, M_b; r_b))$, where $\mathsf{Enc}(\mathsf{pk}, M; r)$ refers to using r as its internal randomness.

3.4   Generic SGE Construction

We construct SGE by adapting the generic GE construction of El Aimani and Joye [3]. In a nutshell, the membership certificate is a signature. To create a GE ciphertext, the message and the public key are encrypted in two ciphertexts, and the validity of the certificate and well-formedness of the GE ciphertext are proven by non-interactive zero-knowledge (NIZK) proof. To achieve CCA security, they use tag-based public-key encryption with label and employ the CHK transform. A one-time signature verification key is put as the label, which is not sanitizable.

Instead of the CHK transform, we use the Naor–Yung technique [22, 24] to upgrade from CPA- to CCA-security. At a high level, two "component" ciphertexts, both encrypting the same message, are proven to be so via non-malleable NIZK. To simulate the decryption oracle, the reduction knows the decryption key for one of the two PKE instances, and hence decryption is trivial. The challenge ciphertext can be simulated via simulation soundness of NIZK, which ensures that the adversary has no advantage even if the simulated NIZK for the challenge query is for a wrong statement, and can easily be achieved via, $e.g.$, Fiat–Shamir heuristic. With this approach, we can achieve a CCA-security definition akin to that of ACE we defined in Sect. 2.2, following the prior definition [4]. Namely, the sanitizer first checks the well-formedness of the ciphertexts, drops the proof and the redundant ciphertext, and then performs rerandomization.

Let $\Sigma = (\mathsf{Gen}, \mathsf{Sign}, \mathsf{Vf})$ be a signature scheme that is existentially unforgeable against chosen-message attacks (EUF-CMA). Let h be a collision-resistant hash function from the public-key space to the message space of $\mathcal{E}$. With an NIZK proof system, an SGE scheme is constructed as follows.

- $\mathsf{Setup}(1^\lambda) \to \mathsf{pp}$: This algorithm runs the setup algorithms (if any) for the building blocks and outputs all the public parameters as pp. Let $\mathcal{R}$ be a relation with a key pair $(\mathsf{pk}_\mathcal{R}, \mathsf{sk}_\mathcal{R})$ for sampling pairs $(x, M) \in \mathcal{R}$.
- $\mathsf{KeyGen}_{\mathsf{GM}}(\mathsf{pp}) \to (\mathsf{pk}_{\mathsf{GM}}, \mathsf{sk}_{\mathsf{GM}})$: This key generation algorithm for the group manager outputs $(\mathsf{pk}_{\mathsf{GM}}, \mathsf{sk}_{\mathsf{GM}})$, which is set to be $(\Sigma.\mathsf{pk}, \Sigma.\mathsf{sk}) \leftarrow \Sigma.\mathsf{Gen}(1^\lambda)$.
- $\mathsf{KeyGen}_{\mathsf{OA}}(\mathsf{pp}) \to (\mathsf{pk}_{\mathsf{OA}}, \mathsf{sk}_{\mathsf{OA}})$: It runs $\mathcal{E}.\mathsf{KeyGen}(1^\lambda)$, which output the pairs $(\mathcal{E}.\mathsf{pk}_{\mathsf{OA}}, \mathcal{E}.\mathsf{sk}_{\mathsf{OA}})$ and $(\mathcal{E}.\mathsf{pk}_{\mathsf{OA}}^*, \mathcal{E}.\mathsf{sk}_{\mathsf{OA}}^*)$. It returns $((\mathcal{E}.\mathsf{pk}_{\mathsf{OA}}, \mathcal{E}.\mathsf{pk}_{\mathsf{OA}}^*), \mathcal{E}.\mathsf{sk}_{\mathsf{OA}})$.
- $\mathsf{KeyGen}_{\mathsf{u}}(\mathsf{pp}) \to (\mathsf{pk}_{\mathsf{ID}}, \mathsf{sk}_{\mathsf{ID}})$: It runs $\mathcal{E}.\mathsf{KeyGen}(1^\lambda)$ twice. Let the outputs be $(\mathcal{E}.\mathsf{pk}_{\mathsf{ID}}, \mathcal{E}.\mathsf{sk}_{\mathsf{ID}})$ and $(\mathcal{E}.\mathsf{pk}_{\mathsf{ID}}^*, \mathcal{E}.\mathsf{sk}_{\mathsf{ID}}^*)$. It outputs $((\mathcal{E}.\mathsf{pk}_{\mathsf{ID}}, \mathcal{E}.\mathsf{pk}_{\mathsf{ID}}^*), \mathcal{E}.\mathsf{sk}_{\mathsf{ID}})$.
- $\mathsf{Join}(\mathsf{sk}_{\mathsf{GM}}, \mathsf{pk}_{\mathsf{GM}}, \mathsf{pk}_{\mathsf{ID}}) \to \mathsf{cert}_{\mathsf{pk}_{\mathsf{ID}}}$: It runs $\mathsf{cert}_{\mathsf{pk}_{\mathsf{ID}}} \leftarrow \Sigma.\mathsf{Sign}(\mathsf{sk}_{\mathsf{GM}}, \mathsf{pk}_{\mathsf{ID}})$ and returns $\mathsf{cert}_{\mathsf{pk}_{\mathsf{ID}}}$ to user ID. GM also stores $(\mathsf{pk}_{\mathsf{ID}}, \mathsf{cert}_{\mathsf{pk}_{\mathsf{ID}}})$ in db.
- $\mathsf{Vfcert}(\mathsf{pk}_{\mathsf{GM}}, \mathsf{pk}_{\mathsf{ID}}, \mathsf{cert}_{\mathsf{pk}_{\mathsf{ID}}})$: It outputs $\Sigma.\mathsf{Vf}(\mathsf{pk}_{\mathsf{GM}}, \mathsf{pk}_{\mathsf{ID}}, \mathsf{cert}_{\mathsf{pk}_{\mathsf{ID}}})$.
- $\mathsf{Enc}(\mathsf{pk}_{\mathsf{GM}}, \mathsf{pk}_{\mathsf{OA}}, \mathsf{pk}_{\mathsf{ID}}, \mathsf{cert}_{\mathsf{pk}_{\mathsf{ID}}}, (\mathsf{pk}_\mathcal{R}, x,) \ M) \to c$: It firstly generates $c_M \leftarrow \mathcal{E}.\mathsf{Enc}(\mathcal{E}.\mathsf{pk}_{\mathsf{ID}}, M)$, $c_M^* \leftarrow \mathcal{E}.\mathsf{Enc}(\mathcal{E}.\mathsf{pk}_{\mathsf{ID}}^*, M)$, $c_{\mathsf{OA}} \leftarrow \mathcal{E}.\mathsf{Enc}(\mathcal{E}.\mathsf{pk}_{\mathsf{OA}}, h(\mathsf{pk}_{\mathsf{ID}}))$, and $c_{\mathsf{OA}}^* \leftarrow \mathcal{E}.\mathsf{Enc}(\mathcal{E}.\mathsf{pk}_{\mathsf{OA}}^*, h(\mathsf{pk}_{\mathsf{ID}}))$, and a non-malleable NIZK proof π for:

$$(x, M) \in \mathcal{R}, \qquad \Sigma.\mathsf{Vf}(\mathsf{pk}_{\mathsf{GM}}, \mathsf{cert}_{\mathsf{pk}_{\mathsf{ID}}}, \mathsf{pk}_{\mathsf{ID}}) = 1,$$
$$c_M \leftarrow \mathcal{E}.\mathsf{Enc}(\mathcal{E}.\mathsf{pk}_{\mathsf{ID}}, M), \qquad c_M^* \leftarrow \mathcal{E}.\mathsf{Enc}(\mathcal{E}.\mathsf{pk}_{\mathsf{ID}}^*, M),$$
$$c_{\mathsf{OA}} \leftarrow \mathcal{E}.\mathsf{Enc}(\mathcal{E}.\mathsf{pk}_{\mathsf{OA}}, h(\mathsf{pk}_{\mathsf{ID}})), \qquad c_{\mathsf{OA}}^* \leftarrow \mathcal{E}.\mathsf{Enc}(\mathcal{E}.\mathsf{pk}_{\mathsf{OA}}^*, h(\mathsf{pk}_{\mathsf{ID}}))$$

with statement $(\mathsf{pk}_{\mathsf{GM}}, \mathsf{pk}_{\mathsf{OA}}, \mathsf{pk}_{\mathcal{R}}, x)$ and witness $(M, \mathsf{coins}, \mathsf{pk}_{\mathsf{ID}}, \mathsf{cert}_{\mathsf{pk}_{\mathsf{ID}}})$, and coins denotes the randomness used in all invocations of $\mathcal{E}.\mathsf{Enc}()$ above. It outputs $c = (c_M, c_M^*, c_{\mathsf{OA}}, c_{\mathsf{OA}}^*, \pi)$. Note that $(\mathsf{pk}_{\mathcal{R}}, x)$ can be optional.

- $\mathsf{Vf}(\mathsf{pk}_{\mathsf{GM}}, \mathsf{pk}_{\mathsf{OA}}, (\mathsf{pk}_{\mathcal{R}}, x,) c) \to \{0, 1\}$: For $c = (c_M, c_M^*, c_{\mathsf{OA}}, c_{\mathsf{OA}}^*, \pi)$, it verifies the NIZK proof π, and outputs 1 if the proof is accepted, 0 otherwise.
- $\mathsf{San}(c) \to c'$: It calls Vf on c and returns $\bot$ if it is invalid. It then parses c into $(c_M, c_M^*, c_{\mathsf{OA}}, c_{\mathsf{OA}}^*)$, and outputs $c' = (\mathcal{E}.\mathsf{San}(c_M), \mathcal{E}.\mathsf{San}(c_{\mathsf{OA}}))$.
- $\mathsf{Dec}(\mathsf{sk}_{\mathsf{ID}}, c') \to M$: Parsing $c' = (c_M', c_{\mathsf{OA}}')$, it returns $M \leftarrow \mathcal{E}.\mathsf{Dec}(\mathsf{sk}_{\mathsf{ID}}, c_M')$.
- $\mathsf{Open}(\mathsf{sk}_{\mathsf{OA}}, c') \to \mathsf{pk}_{\mathsf{ID}}$: It parses $c' = (c_M', c_{\mathsf{OA}}')$, runs $h^* \leftarrow \mathcal{E}.\mathsf{Dec}(\mathsf{sk}_{\mathsf{OA}}, c_{\mathsf{OA}}')$, then looks up at db and outputs the public key $\mathsf{pk}_{\mathsf{ID}}$ such that $h(\mathsf{pk}_{\mathsf{ID}}) = h^*$.

The following theorems assert the security of our generic construction.

Theorem 1. *Our SGE scheme satisfies IND-CCA security if $\mathcal{E}$ is IND-CCA-secure, Σ is EUF-CMA-secure, and NIZK is zero-knowledge proof-of-knowledge.*

Theorem 2. *Our SGE scheme satisfies ANO-CCA anonymity if $\mathcal{E}$ is ANO-CCA-anonymous, Σ is EUF-CMA-secure, and NIZK is zero-knowledge proof-of-knowledge.*

Theorem 3. *Our SGE scheme satisfies soundness if Σ is EUF-CMA-secure and NIZK is zero-knowledge proof-of-knowledge.*

Theorem 4. *Our SGE scheme satisfies sanitizability if Σ is EUF-CMA-secure, $\mathcal{E}$ is key-private and sanitizable, and NIZK is zero-knowledge proof-of-knowledge.*

The proofs for the first three mostly follow those for the generic GE construction of El Aimani and Joye [3]. The proof for the sanitizability mostly follows that for the no-write rule of the generic ACE construction of Fuchsbauer et al. [13]. Their details are deferred to the full version.

4   ACE from Sanitizable Group Encryption

4.1   Our Generic Construction of (t)ACE-EP

Using an SGE scheme, we can construct a (t)ACE scheme for the equality policy, i.e., $\mathsf{P}(\mathsf{ID}_i, \mathsf{ID}_j) = 1$ iff $\mathsf{ID}_i = \mathsf{ID}_j$ as follows. Setup of (t)ACE includes Setup of SGE. $(\mathsf{G}_r, \mathsf{Sample}_{\mathcal{R}})$ is optional. ACE, by default, does not expect the message as a witness of some relation. However, incorporating so means that we can also enforce what kind of messages (even) a legitimate sender can send (cf., [18]).

The key generator takes the roles of GM of SGE. It generates keys for users in the system by calling KeyGen_u and Join to generate the public/secret key pair and create a certificate on the public key sequentially. To support sender tracing, the key generator stores $(\mathsf{ID}, \mathsf{pk}_{\mathsf{ID}}, \mathsf{cert}_{\mathsf{pk}_{\mathsf{ID}}})$ in a directory db.

For access control, any sender of (t)ACE should be a group member in SGE. The group member keeps the certificate $\mathsf{cert}_{\mathsf{pk}_{\mathsf{ID}}}$ on $\mathsf{pk}_{\mathsf{ID}}$ returned from GM privately as the encryption key for proving the write permission and keeps $\mathsf{sk}_{\mathsf{ID}}$ as the decryption key for exercising the read permission. During encryption, the sender calls the algorithm Enc of SGE to generate a ciphertext consists of an NIZK proof for the following relation: (1) the anonymous decryptor is a group member, (2) the payload message is encrypted under the public key of that decryptor, and for tACE (3) the hash of the public key of the decryptor is encrypted in a ciphertext attached which is decryptable by the secret tracing key. The ciphertext is sent to the sanitizer. If the sanitizer accepts the proof embedded inside the ciphertext, it sanitizes the ciphertext and broadcasts it. Finally, the receiver calls the algorithm Dec of SGE to decrypt. The tracer can call the algorithm Open of SGE to search for the corresponding ID if the need arises.

Let $\mathcal{GE} = (\mathsf{Setup}, (\mathsf{G}_r, \mathsf{Sample}_{\mathcal{R}}), \mathsf{KeyGen}_{\mathsf{GM}}, \mathsf{KeyGen}_{\mathsf{OA}}, \mathsf{KeyGen}_{\mathsf{u}}, \mathsf{Join}, \mathsf{Vfcert}, \mathsf{Enc}, \mathsf{Vf}, \mathsf{San}, \mathsf{Dec}, \mathsf{Open})$ be an SGE scheme. Our (t)ACE scheme for equality policy, or (t)ACE-EP, is constructed as follows.

- $\mathsf{Setup}(1^\lambda, \mathsf{P}) \to \mathsf{pp}_{\mathcal{ACE}}$: With security parameter λ and the policy P, this algorithm runs $\mathsf{pp} \leftarrow \mathcal{GE}.\mathsf{Setup}(1^\lambda)$ and returns $\mathsf{pp}_{\mathcal{ACE}} = \mathsf{pp}$.
- $\mathsf{MKGen}(\mathsf{pp}_{\mathcal{ACE}}) \to (\mathsf{mpk}, \mathsf{msk})$: It runs $(\mathsf{pk}_{\mathsf{GM}}, \mathsf{sk}_{\mathsf{GM}}) \leftarrow \mathcal{GE}.\mathsf{KeyGen}_{\mathsf{GM}}(\mathsf{pp})$ and returns master public/secret key tuple as $(\mathsf{mpk}, \mathsf{msk}) = (\mathsf{pk}_{\mathsf{GM}}, \mathsf{sk}_{\mathsf{GM}})$.
- $\mathsf{TKGen}(\mathsf{pp}_{\mathcal{ACE}}) \to (\mathsf{tpk}, \mathsf{tsk})$: It runs $(\mathsf{pk}_{\mathsf{OA}}, \mathsf{sk}_{\mathsf{OA}}) \leftarrow \mathcal{GE}.\mathsf{KeyGen}_{\mathsf{OA}}(\mathsf{pp})$ and returns $(\mathsf{tpk}, \mathsf{tsk}) = (\mathsf{pk}_{\mathsf{OA}}, \mathsf{sk}_{\mathsf{OA}})$.
- $\mathsf{EKGen}(\mathsf{msk}, \mathsf{ID}_i) \to \mathsf{ek}_{\mathsf{ID}_i}$: With the input of ID_i, it first calls $(\mathsf{pk}_{\mathsf{ID}_i}, \mathsf{sk}_{\mathsf{ID}_i}) \leftarrow \mathcal{GE}.\mathsf{KeyGen}_{\mathsf{u}}(\mathsf{pp})$ then $\mathsf{cert}_{\mathsf{pk}_{\mathsf{ID}_i}} \leftarrow \mathcal{GE}.\mathsf{Join}(\mathsf{sk}_{\mathsf{GM}}, \mathsf{pk}_{\mathsf{GM}}, \mathsf{pk}_{\mathsf{ID}_i})$ (and stores in a directory db $(\mathsf{ID}, \mathsf{pk}_{\mathsf{ID}_i}, \mathsf{cert}_{\mathsf{pk}_{\mathsf{ID}_i}})$ for tracing). Finally, $\mathsf{ek}_{\mathsf{ID}_i} = (\mathsf{pk}_{\mathsf{ID}_i}, \mathsf{cert}_{\mathsf{pk}_{\mathsf{ID}_i}})$.
- $\mathsf{DKGen}(\mathsf{msk}, \mathsf{ID}_j) \to \mathsf{dk}_{\mathsf{ID}_j}$: For a receiver with identity ID_j, this algorithm returns $\mathsf{sk}_{\mathsf{ID}_j}$ that has been generated by $\mathsf{EKGen}(\mathsf{msk}, \mathsf{ID}_i)$. In practice, the key generator can use a pseudorandom function output of ID_j as the randomness used by $\mathcal{GE}.\mathsf{KeyGen}_{\mathsf{u}}(\mathsf{pp})$ within $\mathsf{EKGen}(\mathsf{msk}, \mathsf{ID}_i)$. It outputs $\mathsf{dk}_{\mathsf{ID}_j} = \mathsf{sk}_{\mathsf{ID}_j}$.
- $\mathsf{Enc}(\mathsf{ek}_{\mathsf{ID}_i}, \mathsf{tpk}, M) \to c$: Using an encryption key $\mathsf{ek}_{\mathsf{ID}_i} = (\mathsf{pk}_{\mathsf{ID}_i}, \mathsf{cert}_{\mathsf{pk}_{\mathsf{ID}_i}})$, possibly with a tracer public key $\mathsf{tpk} = \mathsf{pk}_{\mathsf{OA}}$ (in tACE), this algorithm encrypts a message M via $c \leftarrow \mathcal{GE}.\mathsf{Enc}(\mathsf{pk}_{\mathsf{GM}}, \mathsf{pk}_{\mathsf{OA}}, \mathsf{pk}_{\mathsf{ID}_i}, \mathsf{cert}_{\mathsf{pk}_{\mathsf{ID}_i}}, M)$, or $c \leftarrow \mathcal{GE}.\mathsf{Enc}(\mathsf{pk}_{\mathsf{GM}}, \mathsf{pk}_{\mathsf{OA}}, \mathsf{pk}_{\mathsf{ID}}, \mathsf{cert}_{\mathsf{pk}_{\mathsf{ID}}}, \mathsf{pk}_{\mathcal{R}}, x, M)$ if the message policy with respect to $(\mathsf{pk}_{\mathcal{R}}, x)$ where $(x, M) \in \mathcal{R}$ is also enforced.
- $\mathsf{San}(c) \to c'$: Output $c' \leftarrow \mathcal{GE}.\mathsf{San}(c)$ if $\mathsf{Vf}(\mathsf{pk}_{\mathsf{GM}}, \mathsf{pk}_{\mathsf{OA}}, c)$ returns true; $\bot$ otherwise. If the policy also mandates $(x, M) \in \mathcal{R}$, San takes additional inputs of $(\mathsf{pk}_{\mathcal{R}}, x)$ and runs $\mathsf{Vf}(\mathsf{pk}_{\mathsf{GM}}, \mathsf{pk}_{\mathsf{OA}}, \mathsf{pk}_{\mathcal{R}}, x, c)$ instead.
- $\mathsf{Dec}(\mathsf{dk}_{\mathsf{ID}_j}, c') \to M$: On input a ciphertext c' and secret key $\mathsf{dk}_{\mathsf{ID}_j} = \mathsf{sk}_{\mathsf{ID}_j}$, this algorithm runs $M \leftarrow \mathcal{GE}.\mathsf{Dec}(\mathsf{sk}_{\mathsf{ID}_j}, c')$, which either returns M or $\bot$.
- $\mathsf{Trace}(\mathsf{tsk}, c') \to \mathsf{ID}$: On input a ciphertext c' and the tracing secret key tsk, it runs $\mathsf{pk}_{\mathsf{ID}} \leftarrow \mathcal{GE}.\mathsf{Open}(\mathsf{sk}_{\mathsf{OA}}, c')$ and returns ID by looking up stored db.

The correctness of this (t)ACE-EP scheme directly follows from the correctness of the SGE scheme $\mathcal{GE}$. Since the SGE does not require any sanitizer key, the sanitization of our construction is done without any sanitizer key as well.

The proofs for correctness and security are mostly straightforward since sanitizable group encryption and (traceable) access control encryption are almost equivalent, modulo to the terminologies. They are deferred to the full version.

4.2 Extension to General Policy

Similar to the scheme of Fuchsbauer et al. [13], this (t)ACE-EP construction can also be extended to support range policies and a disjunction clause over them, with both the ciphertext size and decryption key size being $\mathsf{poly}(\ell)$.

Beyond the above policies, we show that (t)ACE-EP can be extended to support general policy. Our intuition is as follows. For a receiver ID_j, the system generates the decryption key $\mathsf{sk}_{\mathsf{ID}_i}$ of the (t)ACE-EP scheme for each ID_i where $\mathsf{P}(\mathsf{ID}_i, \mathsf{ID}_j) = 1$, i.e., receiver ID_j holds a set of decryption keys $\{\mathsf{dk}_{\mathsf{ID}_i}\}_{\mathsf{P}(\mathsf{ID}_i,\mathsf{ID}_j)=1}$.

Let $(t)\mathcal{ACE}_{\mathsf{eq}}$ = (Setup, MKGen, (TKGen), EKGen, DKGen, Enc, San, Dec, (Trace)) be an (t)ACE-EP scheme for $\mathsf{P}_{\mathsf{eq}}(\mathsf{ID}_i, \mathsf{ID}_j) = 1$ iff $\mathsf{ID}_i = \mathsf{ID}_j$. We construct out (t)ACE scheme for general policy by changing the DKGen and Dec algorithms (all other algorithms remain unchanged).

- DKGen(msk, ID_j) $\rightarrow$ $\mathsf{dk}_{\mathsf{ID}_j}$: With the input of msk and an identity ID_j, for any identities ID_i with predicate $\mathsf{P}(\mathsf{ID}_i, \mathsf{ID}_j) = 1$, this algorithm computes $\mathsf{dk}_{\mathsf{ID}_i} \leftarrow \mathcal{ACE}_{\mathsf{eq}}.\mathsf{DKGen}(\mathsf{msk}, \mathsf{ID}_i)$ and returns the set $\{\mathsf{dk}_{\mathsf{ID}_i}\}_{\mathsf{P}(\mathsf{ID}_i,\mathsf{ID}_j)=1}$ as the decryption key for receiver ID_j.
- Dec(dk, c) $\rightarrow$ M: With the input of a ciphertext c' and decryption key $\mathsf{dk}_{\mathsf{ID}_j} = \{\mathsf{dk}_{\mathsf{ID}_i}\}_{\mathsf{P}(\mathsf{ID}_i,\mathsf{ID}_j)=1}$, this algorithm decrypts c' using each $\mathsf{dk}_{\mathsf{ID}_i}$. It outputs the message M if one of the decryptions succeeds, $\perp$ otherwise.

Our method needs not to replicate the whole cryptosystem for 2^ℓ copies [12]. The ciphertext size of our ACE scheme for the general policy is the same as the underlying (t)ACE-EP scheme, which is $O(1)$. The encryption key size remains the same as the underlying, i.e., $O(1)$ too. The decryption key size is bounded by the maximum number of senders any user can receive messages from (denoted by $s_{\max}$). Theoretically speaking, this can still be as long as 2^ℓ when a particular user can receive from all other users. In practice, we can always heuristically assign a special identity to this kind of users to reduce the key size. Table 1 compares the size of the parameters of interests for our general-policy ACE instantiation (from ACE-EP) and the existing one (from 1-ACE [12, §3]).

Note that this scheme only achieves sender anonymity against outsiders. In other words, a legitimate decryptor can learn information about who the sender is. This matches the level of Kim–Wu ACE [18]. As argued [18], it suffices for all application scenarios originally envisioned [12].

Table 1. Comparison of key size and ciphertext (Ctxt.) sizes

Instantiations from different building blocks	Enc. Key	Dec. Key	Ctxt.	San. Key
General-policy ACE from 1-ACE [12, §3]	$O(2^\ell)$	$O(1)$	$O(2^\ell)$	$O(2^\ell)$
General-policy ACE from ACE-EP (This work)	$O(1)$	$O(s_{\max})$	$O(1)$	Nil

5   Lattice-Based Access Control Encryption

To achieve our final goal, we adapt Libert *et al.* [20]'s lattice-based GE scheme, which is not sanitizable due to a non-randomizable tag. We thus disassemble it and replace its encryption scheme with a new lattice-based SPKE scheme.

5.1   Lattice Background

We quickly review some preliminaries in lattice-based cryptography. We cite a special version of the leftover hash lemma [23], which argues the indistinguishability from a uniform distribution. For our scheme, we consider $\mathbb{Z}_q^n$ as the Abelian group $\mathbb{G}$ and $m = 2n \log q$ be the maximum number of samples to be summed up.

Theorem 5 ([23]). *Let $\mathbb{G}$ be some finite Abelian group and let k be some integer. For any m elements $g_1, \ldots, g_m \in \mathbb{G}$, consider the statistical distance between the uniform distribution on $\mathbb{G}$ and the distribution given by the sum of a random subset of $g_1, \ldots, g_m$. The expectation of this statistical distance over a uniform choice of $g_1, \ldots, g_m \in \mathbb{G}$ is at most $\sqrt{|\mathbb{G}|/2^m}$. In particular, the probability that this statistical distance is more than $\sqrt[4]{|\mathbb{G}|/2^m}$ is at most $\sqrt[4]{|\mathbb{G}|/2^m}$.*

The decisional-LWE problem asks to distinguish samples from a perturbed linear system and random elements from the uniform distribution.

Definition 3 (Decisional Learning with Error [23]**).** *Let $\mathbb{Z}_q$ be the ring of integers modulo a positive integer q, and $\mathbb{Z}_q^n$ be the set of n-vectors over $\mathbb{Z}_q$. Given a probability distribution χ over $\mathbb{Z}$, a positive integer n, and a positive integer q of size dependent on n, the goal of learning with error $\mathsf{LWE}_{q,\chi}$ is to distinguish between the sample $(\mathbf{a}, \mathbf{b})$ from distribution $A_{\mathbf{s},\chi}$, defined as $b = \mathbf{a}\mathbf{s} + e$ with $e \leftarrow \chi$ for some uniform secret $\mathbf{s} \leftarrow \mathbb{Z}_q^n$ and $(\mathbf{a}, \mathbf{u})$ is sampled (via oracle accesses) from a uniform distribution on $\mathbb{Z}_q^n \times \mathbb{Z}_q$ for randomly sampled $\mathbf{a}$.*

Definition 4 (Noise Sample Space [23]**).** *For $\alpha \in (0, 1)$ and a prime q, let Ψ_α denote the distribution over $\mathbb{Z}_q$ of the random variable $\lfloor qX \rceil \bmod q$, where X is a normal random variable with mean 0 and standard deviation $\alpha/2\sqrt{\pi}$.*

Specifically, if the noise added to the perturbed linear system being an amplified-then-quantized Gaussian noise (as mentioned in the above definition of noise sample space), one can apply the following theorem to reduce the hardness of LWE to existing lattice problems, which helps us to decide the parameters.

Theorem 6 (Regev's Reduction [23]**).** *For* $\alpha \in (0,1)$ *and prime* q, *if there exists an efficient, possibly quantum, algorithm for deciding the* $(\mathbb{Z}_q, n, \Psi_\alpha)$-*LWE problem for* $\alpha q > 2\sqrt{n}$, *then there is an efficient quantum algorithm for approximating the shortest independent vector problem and the gap shortest vector problem, to within* $\tilde{O}(n/\alpha)$ *factors in* ℓ_2 *norm, in the worst case.*

5.2 Lattice-Based Sanitizable Encryption

We start with Regev's encryption scheme based on the LWE problem [23]. It features ciphertext indistinguishability, meaning that an honestly generated ciphertext is indistinguishable from a random element in the ciphertext space, which implies key privacy. Sanitization relies on encryption of 0 as *randomizers*. When the randomizers form a basis for spanning the randomness space of Regev's scheme, the ciphertext can be rerandomized by adding a random subset-sum of the randomizers. This requires additive homomorphism. However, the noise accumulates after homomorphic evaluations. We thus change the parameters of the scheme such that the evaluation correctness (decryption correctness of an evaluated ciphertext) holds for a bounded number of additions. Namely, we scale up the modulo size to increase the noise tolerance of decryption.

This sanitization technique assumes an honest encryptor to prepare linearly independent randomness components, which mismatches the threat model that randomness is adversarially picked. We address this by a specific structure of the randomizer that allows us to check the rank of the randomizer, which implies the rank of the underlying randomness used by the randomizer.

Denote matrix and vector by bold capital and small letter, respectively; our SPKE scheme (Setup, KeyGen, Enc, Dec, San) is as follows.

- Setup$(1^\lambda) \to$ pp: Set $n = O(\lambda)$, prime $q = \tilde{O}(n) > 16m(m+1)$, $m = 2n \log q$, $k = \text{poly}(n)$. The probability distribution χ is taken to be Ψ_α, with $\alpha = 1/(\sqrt{m}\omega(\sqrt{\log n}))$. Sample $\bar{\mathbf{A}} \leftarrow \mathbb{Z}_q^{n \times m}$ and compute $r_{\bar{\mathbf{A}}} = \text{Rank}(\bar{\mathbf{A}})$. Output pp $= (q, n, m, k, \chi, \bar{\mathbf{A}}, r_{\bar{\mathbf{A}}})$.
- KeyGen(pp) $\to$ (pk, sk): Sample $\mathbf{s} \in \mathbb{Z}_q^n$ and $\mathbf{e} \leftarrow \chi^m$. Compute $\mathbf{b} = \bar{\mathbf{A}}^\mathsf{T}\mathbf{s} + \mathbf{e} \in \mathbb{Z}_q^m$. Output (pk, sk) $= (\mathbf{b}, \mathbf{s})$.
- Enc(pk, $\mathbf{m}$) $\to$ $\mathbf{c}$: Given $\mathbf{m} \in \{0,1\}^k$, sample $\mathbf{R_m} \leftarrow \{0,1\}^{k \times m}$ and linearly independent $\mathbf{R_r} \leftarrow \{0,1\}^{m \times m}$. Set $\mathbf{c_m} = (\mathbf{R_m}\bar{\mathbf{A}}^\mathsf{T}, \mathbf{R_m}\mathbf{b} + \mathbf{m} \cdot \lfloor q/2 \rfloor) \in \mathbb{Z}_q^{(k+1) \times n}$ and $\mathbf{c_r} = (\mathbf{R_r}\bar{\mathbf{A}}^\mathsf{T}, \mathbf{R_r}\mathbf{b}) \in \mathbb{Z}_q^{(m+1) \times n}$. Output $\mathbf{c} = (\mathbf{c_m}, \mathbf{c_r})$.
- Dec(sk, $\mathbf{c}'$) $\to$ $\mathbf{m}$: We suppose $\mathbf{c}'$ has been sanitized by San. Parse $\mathbf{c}' = (\mathbf{c}_0, \mathbf{c}_1)$. Set $\mathbf{m}' = \mathbf{c}_1 - \mathbf{c}_0\mathbf{s} \bmod q$. For each entry i of $\mathbf{m}'$, say $\mathbf{m}'_i$, set $\mathbf{m}_i = 0$ if $\mathbf{m}'_i$ is closer to 0 than $\lfloor q/2 \rfloor$. Otherwise, set $\mathbf{m}_i = 1$. Output $\mathbf{m}$.
- San(c) $\to$ $\mathbf{c}'$: Parse $\mathbf{c} = ((\mathbf{c}_{m,0}, \mathbf{c}_{m,1}), (\mathbf{c}_{r,0}, \mathbf{c}_{r,1}))$. Check if $\text{Rank}(\mathbf{c}_{r,0}) = r_{\bar{\mathbf{A}}}$, output $\perp$ if it is not. Otherwise, sample $\mathbf{R} \in \{0, \pm 1\}^{k \times m}$ and output $\mathbf{c}' = (\mathbf{c}_{m,0} + \mathbf{R}\mathbf{c}_{r,0}, \mathbf{c}_{m,1} + \mathbf{R}\mathbf{c}_{r,1}) \in \mathbb{Z}_q^{(k+1) \times n}$.

Correctness. The decryption correctness of sanitized ciphertext largely follows the original scheme [23] and by scaling up the modulo q by $m+1$ times to preserve the correctness after the additions done by San. Decryption outputs

$$\begin{aligned}
\mathbf{c}_1 - \mathbf{c}_0\mathbf{s} &= (\mathbf{c}_{\mathbf{m},1} + \mathbf{R}\mathbf{c}_{r,1}) - (\mathbf{c}_{\mathbf{m},0} + \mathbf{R}\mathbf{c}_{r,0})\mathbf{s} \\
&= (\mathbf{R}_\mathbf{m}\mathbf{b} + \mathbf{m} \cdot \lfloor q/2 \rfloor + \mathbf{R}\mathbf{R}_r\mathbf{b}) - (\mathbf{R}_\mathbf{m}\bar{\mathbf{A}}^\mathsf{T} + \mathbf{R}\mathbf{R}_r\bar{\mathbf{A}}^\mathsf{T})\mathbf{s} \\
&= (\mathbf{R}_\mathbf{m} + \mathbf{R}\mathbf{R}_r)(\mathbf{b} - \bar{\mathbf{A}}^\mathsf{T}\mathbf{s}) + \mathbf{m} \cdot \lfloor q/2 \rfloor \\
&= (\mathbf{R}_\mathbf{m} + \mathbf{R}\mathbf{R}_r)\mathbf{e} + \mathbf{m} \cdot \lfloor q/2 \rfloor.
\end{aligned}$$

Since $\mathbf{R}_\mathbf{m}$, $\mathbf{R}$ and $\mathbf{R}_r$ are binary matrices, the absolute value of entries in $\mathbf{R}'\mathbf{e}$ for $\mathbf{R}' = \mathbf{R}_\mathbf{m} + \mathbf{R}\mathbf{R}_r$ is upper bounded by $(m+1)\sum_{i=1}^m e_i$, where e_i is the i-th entry of vector $\mathbf{e}$. To recover $\mathbf{m}$, we need to show that the entry of $\mathbf{R}'\mathbf{e}$ is upper bounded by $q/16$; in other words, $\sum_{i=1}^m e_i$ is upper bounded by $q/16(m+1)$.

By the definition of Ψ_α, $e_i = \lfloor qx_i \rceil \bmod q$, where x_i's are independent normal variables with mean 0 and variances α^2. Note that $\sum_{i=1}^m e_i$ is at most $m/2 \leq q/32$ away from $\sum_{i=1}^m qx_i \bmod q$. It suffices to show that $|\sum_{i=1}^m qx_i \bmod q| \leq q/16(m+1)$ with high probability. Since x_i's are independent, $|\sum_{i=1}^m x_i \bmod q|$ is distributed as a normal variable with mean 0 and standard deviation $\sqrt{m} \cdot \alpha \leq 1/\omega(\sqrt{\log n})$. Thus, by the tail inequality on normal variables, the probability that the absolute value of the entry in $\mathbf{R}'\mathbf{e}$ greater than $q/16$ is negligible.

Security. The proof mostly follows the existing [23]. We sketch its two hybrids.

The first hybrid game shows that a "well-formed" public key is indistinguishable from a random element based on the decisional-LWE assumption (Definition 3). By this assumption, replacing the component of the public key $\mathbf{b}$ (the LWE instance) with a random element $\mathbf{u}$ is indistinguishable.

The second hybrid game shows that a ciphertext is statistically indistinguishable from a random element by the leftover hash lemma (Theorem 5). Since the ciphertext $(\mathbf{r}^\mathsf{T}\bar{\mathbf{A}}^\mathsf{T}, \mathbf{r}^\mathsf{T}\mathbf{u})$ is a random subset-sum of $(\bar{\mathbf{A}}^\mathsf{T}, \mathbf{u})$ as $\mathbf{r} \in \{0,1\}^m$, it is statistically indistinguishable from a uniform distribution. It completes our argument for indistinguishability from random.

Sanitizability. Although checking for uniformly-sampled randomizer is difficult, one can check whether the randomizers are linearly independent (for randomness space being a vector) instead so that the randomizers always span the whole randomness space. Recall that one of the components of the ciphertext is $\mathbf{c}_{r,0} = \mathbf{R}_r\bar{\mathbf{A}}^\mathsf{T}$, we leverage the following lemma for the rank of matrix multiplication in linear algebra to check whether the randomness $\mathbf{R}_r$ is linearly independent or not.[4] Given m-dimensional square matrix $\mathbf{R}$ and $(n \times m)$-dimensional matrix $\mathbf{A}$, if $\mathbf{R}$ is full rank, $\mathsf{Rank}(\mathbf{R}\mathbf{A}^\mathsf{T}) = \mathsf{Rank}(\mathbf{A}^\mathsf{T})$. Hence, if

---

[4] We remark that the dual version of our sanitizable encryption scheme has no such efficient machinery (which explains our choices). Although randomly adding randomizer to payload-part can still rerandomize its randomness, "linearly independence" is not well-defined (the randomness space is $\mathbb{Z}_q^n$ but it needs $n \log q$ linearly independent vectors to rerandomize, where linear independence means none of the samples is a *subset-sum* of the other samples), and checking seems to have the same complexity as the NP-complete subset-sum problem. Also, the corresponding ciphertext component to be checked is perturbed by noise, which ruins the structure.

$\mathsf{Rank}(\mathbf{c}_{r,0}) = \mathsf{Rank}(\bar{\mathbf{A}}^{\mathsf{T}})$, it implies that $\mathbf{R}_r$ is full rank (linearly independent), and the corresponding randomizers can be used to span the whole randomness space. For example, sanitization changes the randomness from $\mathbf{R}_m$ to $\mathbf{R}_m + \mathbf{R}\mathbf{R}_r$.

For the indistinguishability of sanitized ciphertexts from a random element in the space of sanitized ciphertexts because of the changes in randomness space (from binary to integer), an appropriate version of the leftover hash lemma can be used. In its proof [23, Sect. 5], selecting a subset-sum or an integer combination of the basis vector does not affect the argument.

Verifiable Encryption. We show the proof system [20] for the ciphertext's well-formedness of our SPKE scheme. The ciphertext is transformed into a linear relation in the form of $\mathbf{P} \cdot \mathbf{x} = \mathbf{v}$, where witness $\mathbf{x}$ has the same Hamming weight for 0 and 1. Consider the payload-part of a single-bit encryption $\mathbf{c}_m = (\mathbf{r}_m \bar{\mathbf{A}}^{\mathsf{T}}, \mathbf{r}_m \mathbf{b} + m \cdot \lfloor q/2 \rfloor)$ as an example. One can trivially extend to the multi-bit version as in our scheme since the matrix witness can be formulated as a single vector by concatenating the columns of the matrix one-by-one. Also, the randomizer $\mathbf{c}_r$ is an encryption of 0. By matrix arrangement (joining two relations via an "AND" relation), the well-formedness of the whole ciphertext is guaranteed. Consider the relation:

$$\mathcal{R} = \{((\mathbf{c}_{m,0}, \mathbf{c}_{m,1}, \bar{\mathbf{A}}), (\mathbf{r}_m, \mathbf{b})) :$$
$$\mathbf{c}_{m,0} = \mathbf{r}_m \bar{\mathbf{A}}^{\mathsf{T}} \wedge \mathbf{c}_{m,1} = \mathbf{r}_m \mathbf{b} + m \cdot \lfloor q/2 \rfloor \wedge \mathbf{r}_m \in \{0,1\}^m \wedge m \in \{0,1\}\}.$$

With the techniques of Libert et al. [20], the quadratic relation $\mathbf{c}_{m,1} = \mathbf{r}_m \mathbf{b} + m \cdot \lfloor q/2 \rfloor$ boils down to $(\mathbf{c}_{m,1} = \mathbf{qz} + m \cdot \lfloor q/2 \rfloor) \wedge (\mathbf{z} = \mathsf{expand}^{\otimes}(\mathbf{r}_m, \mathsf{vdec}_{m,q}(\mathbf{b})))$, where $\mathsf{expand}^{\otimes}$ is a function that exhausts all possibilities of two binary vectors, one obtained from the binary decomposition function vdec, and $\mathbf{z} \in \{0,1\}^{4m^2 \log q}$ such that $\mathbf{qz} = \mathbf{r}_m \mathbf{b}$. Hence, we have

$$\mathbf{P} = \begin{bmatrix} \mathbf{A} & \mathbf{0}^{n \times m} & \mathbf{0} & 0 & 0 \\ 0 & 0 & \mathbf{q} & \lfloor q/2 \rfloor & 0 \end{bmatrix}, \qquad \mathbf{x} = \begin{bmatrix} \mathbf{r}_m \\ \mathbf{r}_m^c \\ \mathbf{z} \\ m \\ m^c \end{bmatrix}, \qquad \mathbf{v} = \begin{bmatrix} \mathbf{c}_{m,0} \\ \mathbf{c}_{m,1} \end{bmatrix},$$

with $\mathbf{z} = \mathsf{expand}^{\otimes}(\mathbf{r}_m, \mathsf{vdec}_{m,q}(\mathbf{b}))$ as an additional part to be verified. Within $\mathbf{x}$, $\mathbf{r}_m^c$ is a padding (complement) to make the concatenation of $\mathbf{r}_m$ and $\mathbf{r}_m^c$ having the same Hamming weight for 0 and 1. The term $\mathbf{m}^c$ is for similar usage.

5.3   Lattice-Based Sanitizable Group Encryption

With our generic ACE construction from any SGE, it remains to instantiate our generic SGE construction. We mostly adopt the building blocks of Libert et al. [20], i.e., the signature scheme $\Sigma = (\mathsf{Setup}, \mathsf{KeyGen}, \mathsf{Sign}, \mathsf{Vf})$ based on the short-integer-solution assumption they used [5,19] (its detailed description [20, Appendix A.1] is not repeated here) and their techniques in zero-knowledge arguments for matrix-vector relations, but with the encryption scheme replaced by our SPKE scheme $\mathcal{E} = (\mathsf{Setup}, \mathsf{KeyGen}, \mathsf{Enc}, \mathsf{San}, \mathsf{Dec})$.

We omitted $(\mathsf{G}_r, \mathsf{Sample}_\mathcal{R})$ and the related inputs and steps of Enc below since they are independent of the cryptosystem. The encryptor can add the NIZK proof for the desired relation, $e.g.$, for inhomogeneous SIS [20], if needed.

- $\mathsf{Setup}(1^\lambda) \to \mathsf{pp}$:
  1. Run $\mathcal{E}.\mathsf{pp} \leftarrow \mathcal{E}.\mathsf{Setup}(1^\lambda)$ and $\Sigma.\mathsf{pp} \leftarrow \Sigma.\mathsf{Setup}(1^\lambda)$.
  2. Pick two random matrices $\mathbf{F}, \mathbf{F}^* \leftarrow \mathbb{Z}_q^{n \times m \log q}$, which will be used to hash a user public key from $\mathbb{Z}_q^{m \log q}$ to $\mathbb{Z}_q^n$.
  3. Set matrix $\mathbf{H}_{n,q} \in \mathbb{Z}_q^{n \times \bar{m}}$ such that for any $\mathbf{x} \in \mathbb{Z}_q^n$, $\mathbf{x} = \mathbf{H}_{n,q} \cdot \mathsf{vdec}_{n,q}(\mathbf{x})$, and $\mathsf{vdec}_{n,q} : \mathbb{Z}_q^n \to \{0,1\}^{\bar{m}}$ is an injective vector-decomposition function [20, Sect. 3.1].

  Output $\mathsf{pp} = (\mathcal{E}.\mathsf{pp}, \Sigma.\mathsf{pp}, \mathbf{F}, \mathbf{F}^*)$.
- $\mathsf{KeyGen}_{\mathsf{GM}}(\mathsf{pp}) \to (\mathsf{pk}_{\mathsf{GM}}, \mathsf{sk}_{\mathsf{GM}})$: Output $(\mathsf{pk}, \mathsf{sk}) \leftarrow \Sigma.\mathsf{KeyGen}(1^\lambda)$.
- $\mathsf{KeyGen}_{\mathsf{OA}}(\mathsf{pp}) \to (\mathsf{pk}_{\mathsf{OA}}, \mathsf{sk}_{\mathsf{OA}})$:
  1. Run $\mathcal{E}.\mathsf{KeyGen}(1^\lambda)$ for twice to get $(\mathcal{E}.\mathsf{pk}_{\mathsf{OA}}, \mathcal{E}.\mathsf{sk}_{\mathsf{OA}})$ and $(\mathcal{E}.\mathsf{pk}_{\mathsf{OA}}^*, \mathcal{E}.\mathsf{sk}_{\mathsf{OA}}^*)$.
  2. Output $((\mathcal{E}.\mathsf{pk}_{\mathsf{OA}}, \mathcal{E}.\mathsf{pk}_{\mathsf{OA}}^*), \mathcal{E}.\mathsf{sk}_{\mathsf{OA}})$.
- $\mathsf{KeyGen}_u(\mathsf{pp}) \to (\mathsf{pk}_{\mathsf{ID}}, \mathsf{sk}_{\mathsf{ID}})$:
  1. Run $\mathcal{E}.\mathsf{KeyGen}(1^\lambda)$ for twice to get $(\mathcal{E}.\mathsf{pk}_{\mathsf{ID}}, \mathcal{E}.\mathsf{sk}_{\mathsf{ID}})$ and $(\mathcal{E}.\mathsf{pk}_{\mathsf{ID}}^*, \mathcal{E}.\mathsf{sk}_{\mathsf{ID}}^*)$.
  2. Output $((\mathcal{E}.\mathsf{pk}_{\mathsf{ID}}, \mathcal{E}.\mathsf{pk}_{\mathsf{ID}}^*), \mathcal{E}.\mathsf{sk}_{\mathsf{ID}})$.
- $\mathsf{Join}(\mathsf{sk}_{\mathsf{GM}}, \mathsf{pk}_{\mathsf{GM}}, \mathsf{pk}_{\mathsf{ID}}) \to \mathsf{cert}_{\mathsf{pk}_{\mathsf{ID}}}$:
  1. Parse $\mathsf{pk}_{\mathsf{ID}}$ as $(\mathcal{E}.\mathsf{pk}_{\mathsf{ID}}, \mathcal{E}.\mathsf{pk}_{\mathsf{ID}}^*)$ and compute a single hash value of them: $\mathbf{h}_{\mathsf{ID}} = \mathbf{F} \cdot \mathsf{vdec}_{m,q}(\mathcal{E}.\mathsf{pk}_{\mathsf{ID}}) + \mathbf{F}^* \cdot \mathsf{vdec}_{m,q}(\mathcal{E}.\mathsf{pk}_{\mathsf{ID}}^*) \in \mathbb{Z}_q^n$.
  2. Output $\mathsf{cert}_{\mathsf{pk}_{\mathsf{ID}}} \leftarrow \Sigma.\mathsf{Sign}(\mathsf{sk}_{\mathsf{GM}}, \mathbf{h}_{\mathsf{ID}})$ and store $(\mathsf{pk}_{\mathsf{ID}}, \mathsf{cert}_{\mathsf{pk}_{\mathsf{ID}}})$ in db.
- $\mathsf{Vfcert}(\mathsf{pk}_{\mathsf{GM}}, \mathsf{pk}_{\mathsf{ID}}, \mathsf{cert}_{\mathsf{pk}_{\mathsf{ID}}})$: Output $\Sigma.\mathsf{Vf}(\mathsf{pk}_{\mathsf{GM}}, \mathsf{pk}_{\mathsf{ID}}, \mathsf{cert}_{\mathsf{pk}_{\mathsf{ID}}})$.
- $\mathsf{Enc}(\mathsf{pk}_{\mathsf{GM}}, \mathsf{pk}_{\mathsf{OA}}, \mathsf{pk}_{\mathsf{ID}}, \mathsf{cert}_{\mathsf{pk}_{\mathsf{ID}}}, (\mathsf{pk}_\mathcal{R}, x,) \ \mathsf{m}) \to \mathbf{c}$: To encrypt $\mathbf{m} \in \{0,1\}^m$,
  1. Parse $\mathsf{pk}_{\mathsf{OA}}$ as $(\mathcal{E}.\mathsf{pk}_{\mathsf{OA}}, \mathcal{E}.\mathsf{pk}_{\mathsf{OA}}^*) = (\mathbf{b}_{\mathsf{OA}}, \mathbf{b}_{\mathsf{OA}}^*)$.
  2. Parse $\mathsf{pk}_{\mathsf{ID}}$ as $(\mathcal{E}.\mathsf{pk}_{\mathsf{ID}}, \mathcal{E}.\mathsf{pk}_{\mathsf{ID}}^*) = (\mathbf{b}_{\mathsf{ID}}, \mathbf{b}_{\mathsf{ID}}^*)$.
  3. Compute the hash value $\mathbf{h}_{\mathsf{ID}} = \mathbf{F} \cdot \mathsf{vdec}_{m,q}(\mathcal{E}.\mathsf{pk}_{\mathsf{ID}}) + \mathbf{F}^* \cdot \mathsf{vdec}_{m,q}(\mathcal{E}.\mathsf{pk}_{\mathsf{ID}}^*)$.
  4. Compute the ciphertexts $\mathbf{c_m} \leftarrow \mathcal{E}.\mathsf{Enc}(\mathcal{E}.\mathsf{pk}_{\mathsf{ID}}, \mathbf{m})$, $\mathbf{c_m^*} \leftarrow \mathcal{E}.\mathsf{Enc}(\mathcal{E}.\mathsf{pk}_{\mathsf{ID}}^*, \mathbf{m})$, $\mathbf{c}_{\mathsf{OA}} \leftarrow \mathcal{E}.\mathsf{Enc}(\mathcal{E}.\mathsf{pk}_{\mathsf{OA}}, \mathsf{vdec}_{n,q}(\mathbf{h}_{\mathsf{ID}}))$, and $\mathbf{c}_{\mathsf{OA}}^* \leftarrow \mathcal{E}.\mathsf{Enc}(\mathcal{E}.\mathsf{pk}_{\mathsf{OA}}^*, \mathsf{vdec}_{n,q}(\mathbf{h}_{\mathsf{ID}}))$.
  5. Generate the non-interactive proof π with witnesses:
     - for signature verification: $[\mathbf{d}_1^\mathsf{T} || \mathbf{d}_2^\mathsf{T} || \tau[1] \cdot \mathbf{d}_2^\mathsf{T} || \cdots || \tau[l] \cdot \mathbf{d}_2^\mathsf{T}]^\mathsf{T}$, $\mathbf{b}, \mathbf{b}^*, \mathbf{r}$,
     - for vector decomposition: $\mathbf{w} = \mathsf{vdec}_{n,q}(\mathbf{D}_0 \cdot \mathbf{r} + \mathbf{D}_1 \cdot \mathbf{h})$, $\mathbf{h} = \mathsf{vdec}_{n,q}(\mathbf{h}_{\mathsf{ID}})$,
     - for encryption of message: $\mathbf{R_m}, \mathbf{b}, \mathbf{m}, \mathbf{R}_{\mathbf{m},r}, \mathbf{R}_{\mathbf{m}}^*, \mathbf{b}^*, \mathbf{R}_{\mathbf{m},r}^*$,
     - for encryption of hash of public key: $\mathbf{R}_{\mathsf{OA}}, \mathbf{h}_{\mathsf{ID}}, \mathbf{R}_{\mathsf{OA},r}, \mathbf{R}_{\mathsf{OA}}^*, \mathbf{R}_{\mathsf{OA},r}^*$,
     in the following relations:
     - $\Sigma.\mathsf{Vf}(\mathsf{pk}_{\mathsf{GM}}, \mathsf{cert}_{\mathsf{pk}_{\mathsf{ID}}}, \mathsf{pk}_{\mathsf{ID}}) = 1$ with $(\mathbf{A}, \mathbf{A}_0, \dots, \mathbf{A}_l, \mathbf{D}, \mathbf{D}_0, \mathbf{D}_1)$ from $\mathsf{pk}_{\mathsf{GM}}$ and $(\tau, \mathbf{d}, \mathbf{r})$ from $\mathsf{cert}_{\mathsf{pk}_{\mathsf{ID}}}$:

$$\mathbf{u} = [\mathbf{A}|\mathbf{A}_0|\cdots|\mathbf{A}_l] \cdot [\mathbf{d}_1^\mathsf{T}||\mathbf{d}_2^\mathsf{T}||\tau[1]\mathbf{d}_2^\mathsf{T}||\cdots||\tau[l]\mathbf{d}_2^\mathsf{T}]^\mathsf{T} + (-\mathbf{D}) \cdot \mathbf{w} \bmod q,$$
$$0 = \mathbf{H}_{n,q} \cdot \mathbf{w} + (-\mathbf{D}_0) \cdot \mathbf{r} + (-\mathbf{D}_1) \cdot \mathbf{h} \bmod q$$
$$0 = \mathbf{H}_{m,q} \cdot \mathbf{h} + (-\mathbf{F}) \cdot \mathsf{vdec}_{m,q}(\mathbf{b}) + (-\mathbf{F}^*) \cdot \mathsf{vdec}_{m,q}(\mathbf{b}^*) \bmod q.$$

- $c_m \leftarrow \mathcal{E}.\mathsf{Enc}(\mathcal{E}.\mathsf{pk}_{ID}, m)$ and $c_m^* \leftarrow \mathcal{E}.\mathsf{Enc}(\mathcal{E}.\mathsf{pk}_{ID}^*, m)$ with (b, b^*) from public key pk_{ID} and $(R_m, R_{m,r}, R_m^*, R_{m,r}^*)$ as the randomness:

$$
\begin{aligned}
c_{m,0} &= R_m \bar{A}^\mathsf{T}, & c_{m,1} &= R_m b + m \cdot \lfloor q/2 \rfloor, \\
c_{m,r,0} &= R_{m,r} \bar{A}^\mathsf{T}, & c_{m,r,1} &= R_{m,r} b, \\
c_{m,0}^* &= R_{OA}^* \bar{A}^\mathsf{T}, & c_{m,1}^* &= R_m^* b^* + m \cdot \lfloor q/2 \rfloor, \\
c_{m,r,0}^* &= R_{m,r}^* \bar{A}^\mathsf{T}, & c_{m,r,1}^* &= R_{m,r}^* b^*.
\end{aligned}
$$

- $c_{OA} \leftarrow \mathcal{E}.\mathsf{Enc}(\mathcal{E}.\mathsf{pk}_{OA}, h)$ and $c_{OA}^* \leftarrow \mathcal{E}.\mathsf{Enc}(\mathcal{E}.\mathsf{pk}_{OA}^*, h)$ with $h = \mathsf{vdec}_{n,q}(h_{ID})$, (b_{OA}, b_{OA}^*) from pk_{OA} and $(R_{OA}, R_{OA,r}, R_{OA}^*, R_{OA,r}^*)$ as the randomness:

$$
\begin{aligned}
c_{OA,0} &= R_{OA} \bar{A}^\mathsf{T}, & c_{OA,1} &= R_{OA} b_{OA} + h \cdot \lfloor q/2 \rfloor, \\
c_{OA,r,0} &= R_{OA,r} \bar{A}^\mathsf{T}, & c_{OA,r,1} &= R_{OA,r} b_{OA}, \\
c_{OA,0}^* &= R_{OA}^* \bar{A}^\mathsf{T}, & c_{OA,1}^* &= R_{OA}^* b_{OA}^* + h \cdot \lfloor q/2 \rfloor, \\
c_{OA,r,0}^* &= R_{OA,r}^* \bar{A}^\mathsf{T}, & c_{OA,r,1}^* &= R_{OA,r}^* b_{OA}^*.
\end{aligned}
$$

Some witnesses are transformed to binary representation, which fits with the existing proof for the linear system [20] that uses binary witness.

6. Output the ciphertext $c = (c_m, c_m^*, c_{OA}, c_{OA}^*, \pi)$.

- $\mathsf{Vf}(\mathsf{pk}_{GM}, \mathsf{pk}_{OA}, \mathsf{pk}_{\mathcal{R}}, x, c)$: Return the verification result of proof π against c.
- $\mathsf{San}(c) \rightarrow c'$: Call Vf over c and output $\perp$ if it is invalid; otherwise, parse $c = (c_m, c_m^*, c_{OA}, c_{OA}^*, \pi)$ and output $(\mathcal{E}.\mathsf{San}(c_m), \mathcal{E}.\mathsf{San}(c_{OA}))$.
- $\mathsf{Dec}(\mathsf{sk}_{ID}, c') \rightarrow m$: Parse c' as (c_m', c_{OA}') and output $m \leftarrow \mathcal{E}.\mathsf{Dec}(\mathsf{sk}_{ID}, c_m')$.
- $\mathsf{Open}(\mathsf{sk}_{OA}, c') \rightarrow \mathsf{pk}_{ID}$: Parse c' as (c_m', c_{OA}') and run $h \leftarrow \mathcal{E}.\mathsf{Dec}(\mathsf{sk}_{ID}, c_{OA}')$. Compute $h^* = H_{m,q} \cdot h$ and search for the public key hashes to the value h^* by $F \cdot \mathsf{vdec}_{m,q}(\cdot) + F^* \cdot \mathsf{vdec}_{m,q}(\cdot)$. Output the corresponding public key pk_{ID}; or $\perp$ if it is not found.

Optimization. Instantiating our generic construction as above is not optimized. Specifically, for the ciphertexts marked with $*$, i.e., $c_{m,r}^*$ and $c_{OA,r}^*$, their randomizer components are redundant because these ciphertexts are not sanitized at San but simply dropped instead. One can remove these randomizers from the ciphertexts, which also reduces the size of the witness.

Furthermore, the randomizers for encryption of m for a user and $\mathsf{vdec}_{n,q}(h_{ID})$ for OA can be shared by using only single randomness R as a witness instead of two $R_{m,r}, R_{OA,r}$. Specifically, $c_{m,r,0}$ and $c_{OA,r,0}$ can be shared, i.e., $c_{m,r}$ and $c_{OA,r}$ are changed into $(c_r = R_r \bar{A}^\mathsf{T}, c_{m,r} = R_r b, c_{OA,r} = R_r b_{OA})$, with San algorithm inputs $(c_r, c_{m,r})$ for c_m and $(c_r, c_{OA,r})$ for c_{OA} as randomizers.

Concerns with Subliminal Channel over Error. One may concern that the error term may form a subliminal channel, as mentioned in the open problem of Damgård et al. [12]. We briefly explain how our construction prevents it. First, the public key is certified that the error term there cannot be changed. Second, our encryption algorithm by itself does not need any other noises (beyond the involvement of the public key). Third, if the adversary tries to introduce an error term to the ciphertext, it will fail the proof verification.

Our sanitization mechanism critically relies on homomorphism. As argued before, a sanitized ciphertext of our construction, which is a homomorphically-evaluated HE ciphertext, remains a random element in the ciphertext space to any adversary without the decryption key. The noise analysis of lattice-based encryption schemes, *e.g.*, for breaking circuit privacy, is not applicable here since it requires the knowledge of the decryption key.

6   Concluding Remarks

We connect two seemingly related but different primitives, namely, access control encryption and group encryption. We borrowed the wisdom from the group encryption literature and proposed a new access control encryption scheme. Together with our sanitization technique for LWE-based encryption, we provide a candidate solution to the open problem left by Damgård in their seminal work in access control encryption, namely, a practically interesting access control encryption scheme from noisy, post-quantum assumptions, instead of using heavyweight tools such as indistinguishability obfuscation or fully homomorphic encryption.

While we slightly optimized our instantiation (compared to the existing lattice-based group encryption scheme), there is still room for improvement, especially for the delicate proof techniques. For practical efficiency, our suggestion is to use the latest access control encryption scheme of Wang and Chow [26], which comes with timing figures for a prototype implementation (and appears to be adaptive secure in the random oracle model, or selective secure in the common reference string model by replacing Fiat–Shamir proof with ZK non-interactive succinct argument of knowledge). A long-term research problem is to improve the efficiency of cryptosystems with resiliency to potential quantum computers.

References

1. Abe, M., Chow, S.S.M., Haralambiev, K., Ohkubo, M.: Double-trapdoor anonymous tags for traceable signatures. Int. J. Inf. Sec. **12**(1), 19–31 (2013)
2. Agrawal, S., Wu, D.J.: Functional encryption: deterministic to randomized functions from simple assumptions. In: Coron, J.-S., Nielsen, J.B. (eds.) EUROCRYPT 2017. LNCS, vol. 10211, pp. 30–61. Springer, Cham (2017). https://doi.org/10.1007/978-3-319-56614-6_2
3. El Aimani, L., Joye, M.: Toward practical group encryption. In: Jacobson, M., Locasto, M., Mohassel, P., Safavi-Naini, R. (eds.) ACNS 2013. LNCS, vol. 7954, pp. 237–252. Springer, Heidelberg (2013). https://doi.org/10.1007/978-3-642-38980-1_15

4. Badertscher, C., Matt, C., Maurer, U.: Strengthening access control encryption. In: Takagi, T., Peyrin, T. (eds.) ASIACRYPT 2017. LNCS, vol. 10624, pp. 502–532. Springer, Cham (2017). https://doi.org/10.1007/978-3-319-70694-8_18

5. Böhl, F., Hofheinz, D., Jager, T., Koch, J., Striecks, C.: Confined guessing: new signatures from standard assumptions. J. Cryptol. **28**(1), 176–208 (2014). https://doi.org/10.1007/s00145-014-9183-z

6. Boneh, D., Sahai, A., Waters, B.: Functional encryption: definitions and challenges. In: Ishai, Y. (ed.) TCC 2011. LNCS, vol. 6597, pp. 253–273. Springer, Heidelberg (2011). https://doi.org/10.1007/978-3-642-19571-6_16

7. Canetti, R., Halevi, S., Katz, J.: Chosen-ciphertext security from identity-based encryption. In: Cachin, C., Camenisch, J.L. (eds.) EUROCRYPT 2004. LNCS, vol. 3027, pp. 207–222. Springer, Heidelberg (2004). https://doi.org/10.1007/978-3-540-24676-3_13

8. Cathalo, J., Libert, B., Yung, M.: Group encryption: non-interactive realization in the standard model. In: Matsui, M. (ed.) ASIACRYPT 2009. LNCS, vol. 5912, pp. 179–196. Springer, Heidelberg (2009). https://doi.org/10.1007/978-3-642-10366-7_11

9. Chow, S.S.M.: Real traceable signatures. In: Jacobson, M.J., Rijmen, V., Safavi-Naini, R. (eds.) SAC 2009. LNCS, vol. 5867, pp. 92–107. Springer, Heidelberg (2009). https://doi.org/10.1007/978-3-642-05445-7_6

10. Chow, S.S.M., Fech, K., Lai, R.W.F., Malavolta, G.: Multi-client oblivious RAM with poly-logarithmic communication. In: Moriai, S., Wang, H. (eds.) ASIACRYPT 2020. LNCS, vol. 12492, pp. 160–190. Springer, Cham (2020). https://doi.org/10.1007/978-3-030-64834-3_6

11. Chow, S.S.M., Roth, V., Rieffel, E.G.: General certificateless encryption and timed-release encryption. In: Ostrovsky, R., De Prisco, R., Visconti, I. (eds.) SCN 2008. LNCS, vol. 5229, pp. 126–143. Springer, Heidelberg (2008). https://doi.org/10.1007/978-3-540-85855-3_9

12. Damgård, I., Haagh, H., Orlandi, C.: Access control encryption: enforcing information flow with cryptography. In: Hirt, M., Smith, A. (eds.) TCC 2016-B. LNCS, vol. 9986, pp. 547–576. Springer, Heidelberg (2016). https://doi.org/10.1007/978-3-662-53644-5_21

13. Fuchsbauer, G., Gay, R., Kowalczyk, L., Orlandi, C.: Access control encryption for equality, comparison, and more. In: Fehr, S. (ed.) PKC 2017. LNCS, vol. 10175, pp. 88–118. Springer, Heidelberg (2017). https://doi.org/10.1007/978-3-662-54388-7_4

14. Gentry, C., Sahai, A., Waters, B.: Homomorphic encryption from learning with errors: conceptually-simpler, asymptotically-faster, attribute-based. In: Canetti, R., Garay, J.A. (eds.) CRYPTO 2013. LNCS, vol. 8042, pp. 75–92. Springer, Heidelberg (2013). https://doi.org/10.1007/978-3-642-40041-4_5

15. Izabachène, M., Pointcheval, D., Vergnaud, D.: Mediated traceable anonymous encryption. In: Abdalla, M., Barreto, P.S.L.M. (eds.) LATINCRYPT 2010. LNCS, vol. 6212, pp. 40–60. Springer, Heidelberg (2010). https://doi.org/10.1007/978-3-642-14712-8_3

16. Kiayias, A., Tsiounis, Y., Yung, M.: Traceable signatures. In: Cachin, C., Camenisch, J.L. (eds.) EUROCRYPT 2004. LNCS, vol. 3027, pp. 571–589. Springer, Heidelberg (2004). https://doi.org/10.1007/978-3-540-24676-3_34

17. Kiayias, A., Tsiounis, Y., Yung, M.: Group encryption. In: Kurosawa, K. (ed.) ASIACRYPT 2007. LNCS, vol. 4833, pp. 181–199. Springer, Heidelberg (2007). https://doi.org/10.1007/978-3-540-76900-2_11

18. Kim, S., Wu, D.J.: Access control encryption for general policies from standard assumptions. In: Takagi, T., Peyrin, T. (eds.) ASIACRYPT 2017. LNCS, vol. 10624, pp. 471–501. Springer, Cham (2017). https://doi.org/10.1007/978-3-319-70694-8_17

19. Libert, B., Ling, S., Mouhartem, F., Nguyen, K., Wang, H.: Signature schemes with efficient protocols and dynamic group signatures from lattice Assumptions. In: Cheon, J.H., Takagi, T. (eds.) ASIACRYPT 2016. LNCS, vol. 10032, pp. 373–403. Springer, Heidelberg (2016). https://doi.org/10.1007/978-3-662-53890-6_13

20. Libert, B., Ling, S., Mouhartem, F., Nguyen, K., Wang, H.: Zero-knowledge arguments for matrix-vector relations and lattice-based group encryption. In: Cheon, J.H., Takagi, T. (eds.) ASIACRYPT 2016. LNCS, vol. 10032, pp. 101–131. Springer, Heidelberg (2016). https://doi.org/10.1007/978-3-662-53890-6_4

21. Libert, B., Yung, M., Joye, M., Peters, T.: Traceable group encryption. In: Krawczyk, H. (ed.) PKC 2014. LNCS, vol. 8383, pp. 592–610. Springer, Heidelberg (2014). https://doi.org/10.1007/978-3-642-54631-0_34

22. Naor, M., Yung, M.: Public-key cryptosystems provably secure against chosen ciphertext attacks. In: ACM Symposium on Theory of Computing (STOC), pp. 427–437 (1990)

23. Regev, O.: On lattices, learning with errors, random linear codes, and cryptography. In: Symposium on Theory of Computing (STOC), pp. 84–93 (2005)

24. Sahai, A.: Non-malleable non-interactive zero knowledge and adaptive chosen-ciphertext security. In: ACM Symposium on Foundations of Computer Science (FOCS), pp. 543–553 (1999)

25. Tan, G., Zhang, R., Ma, H., Tao, Y.: Access control encryption based on LWE. In: ACM ASIA Public-Key Cryptography@AsiaCCS, pp. 43–50 (2017)

26. Wang, X., Chow, S.S.M.: Cross-domain access control encryption: arbitrary-policy, constant-size, efficient. In: IEEE Symposium on Security and Privacy (S&P), pp. 388–401 (2021)

Password Protected Secret Sharing from Lattices

Partha Sarathi Roy[1]([⊠]), Sabyasachi Dutta[2], Willy Susilo[1],
and Reihaneh Safavi-Naini[2]

[1] Institute of Cybersecurity and Cryptology, School of Computing and Information
Technology, University of Wollongong, Northfields Avenue,
Wollongong, NSW 2522, Australia
{partha,wsusilo}@uow.edu.au

[2] Department of Computer Science, University of Calgary, 2500 University Drive,
Calgary, NW T2N 1N4, Canada
{sabyasachi.dutta,rei}@ucalgary.ca

Abstract. A password protected secret sharing (PPSS) allows a user to
store shares of a secret on a set of L servers, and use a single password
to authenticate itself to any subset of k servers at a later time to access
the shares and reconstruct the secret. Security of PPSS ensures that a
coalition of up to $k-1$ servers cannot reveal any information about the
secret message or the password. A related primitive is threshold password authenticated key exchange protocol (TPAKE) that allows a user
to establish individual authenticated shared secret keys with members of
a subset of k out of L servers, using a single password. These primitives
are well motivated, with applications such as secure storage of secret
keys, and secure group communication using passwords for authentication. In this paper, we give the first construction of these primitives that
provide post-quantum security. We prove security of our constructions
in concurrent setting, and in the standard model, reducing security to
the decisional LWE problem.

Keywords: Password authentication · Secret sharing · LWE

1 Introduction

Secure storage of secret keys on mobile devices is increasingly becoming com-
monplace for applications such as issuing transactions or accessing resources.
This however has the risk of device getting lost or compromised, and the secret
becoming unrecoverable or falling in the hand of others. To provide protection against these threats one can use secret sharing to generate and store the
shares of the secret on multiple cloud servers, and reconstruct the secret on the
device when needed. This however requires the user to authenticate herself to
the clouds, requiring individual secrets or passwords to be used to authenticate to each cloud. This however results in a new problem of secure storage or
remembering multiple secrets.

© Springer Nature Switzerland AG 2021
K. Sako and N. O. Tippenhauer (Eds.): ACNS 2021, LNCS 12726, pp. 442–459, 2021.
https://doi.org/10.1007/978-3-030-78372-3_17

Password protected secret sharing schemes (PPSS), proposed by Bagherzandi et al. [3], provides an elegant solution to this problem by allowing the user to store the shares of the secret on L clouds such that any subset of k out of the L clouds can be used to recover the secret, while authentication to clouds requires a single human memorizable password. This makes the system highly usable. Security of PPSS has been considered in passive and active case where in the former case protection is against offline password attacks and collusion of the server, and in the latter case also includes arbitrary tampering and modifications of protocol messages by malicious servers and network attackers.

PPSS is closely related to a previously studied cryptographic primitive known as threshold password authenticated key exchange (TPAKE), proposed by Mackenzie et al. [15], where the goal of the user is to establish individual authenticated shared keys with each of the k clouds out of a set of L clouds. TPAKE extend two party password authenticated key exchange (PAKE) [4] to multiuser setting. Bagherzandi et al. [3] show that one can use a TPAKE to construct a PPSS, and vice versa. All known constructions of TPAKE [1,8,15,21] however require interaction among servers, while PPSS constructions in [3] and the follow-up works in [2,5,6,12–14] do not require server to server interactions.

1.1 Our Contributions

We propose the first PPSS scheme that is quantum-safe in the sense that it relies on a hard problem for which efficient quantum algorithms are not known. Our construction starts with the general approach of Bagherzandi et al. [3] but using cryptographic primitives that are quantum safe, but requires significant redesign of the protocol because of the properties of the primitives. First, we design a basic scheme secure against semi-honest adversary assuming secure channel, that is based on the hardness of decisional learning with error problem (dLWE) and prove its security in the standard model, and then extend it to the full malicious adversary case. The main building block of the proposed protocols is an additive homomorphic encryption with bounded number of multiplications and a threshold decryption protocol. The basic PPSS protocol uses fully homomorphic encryption scheme (FHE) by Gentry, Sahai and Waters (GSW)[1] [11] (see Sect. 2.2 for an overview of the scheme). Using this encryption scheme instead of ElGamal scheme used in Bagherzandi et al.'s work, requires redesign of their basic protocol. Further, to provide security against malicious adversaries without assuming secure channels between the user and the servers, we need to ensure that compromised servers are not able to convince a user to construct a wrong secret message and also transcript of the protocol cannot be used for off-line attacks. Our proposed PPSS protocol provides security against malicious adversaries, and provides strong security in the sense that in addition to the transcript of the protocol, adversary also receives a bit indicating whether the local output of a user instance has output some secret message or a rejection symbol "$\perp$".

---

[1] Throughout the paper, we will denote FHE of [11] by GSW scheme. The acronym is the authors' initials.

Construction of strongly secure PPSS against malicious adversary enables the first lattice-based construction of TPAKE using the efficient generic conversion of [3].

1.2 Overview of Our Technique

Our lattice-based constructions of PPSS protocol follows the general structure of Bagherzandi et al. [3] where to store a secret message M with servers and use a password pw to recover it, the user encrypts M and the password pw, and distributes among the servers the secret key of the encryption scheme using Shamir's secret sharing [20]. The user only need to memorize the password and there is no other secret information. To recover the secret message, the user triggers a distributed decryption process using only the password and public parameter(s). We also follow the same design rationale to construct lattice-based PPSS.

A challenge of using lattice-based schemes is that the existing group homomorphic encryption schemes [10,18] do not support re-randomization of the secret key which is a crucial technique used in [3]. To overcome the difficulty and to construct strongly secure PPSS against malicious adversaries without assuming secure channel, we take advantage of fully homomorphic encryption scheme of Gentry-Sahai-Waters (GSW) [11] to compute over ciphertexts.

PPSS consists of two algorithms: initialization Init and recovery Rec. The Init algorithm is performed by a user $\mathbf{U}$ and the Rec algorithm consists of two interactive algorithms User (performed by $\mathbf{U}$) and Server (performed by server $\mathbf{S_j}$). Let the secret message $M \in \{0,1\}^{\log q}$ and the password pw belongs to dictionary $\mathbf{D}$ which is hashed into $\mathbb{Z}_q$ using a collision-resistant hash function H. For $(H(\mathsf{pw}), M) \in \mathbb{Z}_q \times \{0,1\}^{\log q}$, the initialization algorithm $\mathbf{Init}(\mathsf{pw}, M)$ runs the key generation algorithm of GSW to output $(\mathbf{A} \in \mathbb{Z}_q^{\mathbf{m} \times (\mathbf{n+1})}, \mathbf{v} \in \mathbb{Z}_q^{\mathbf{N}})$ as GSW key-pair and secret share the vector $\mathbf{v}$: $\{\mathbf{sh}_i\}_{i=1}^{L} \xleftarrow{(k,L)}$ ShamirShare($\mathbf{v}$) among servers using (k, L) secret sharing [20].

$\mathbf{Init}(\mathsf{pw}, M)$ outputs public parameters st_0 which contain public-key of the GSW scheme ($\mathbf{A}$), collision-resistant hash function (H), GSW encryptions of $H(\mathsf{pw})$ (viz. $\mathbf{C_{pw}}$) and message M (viz. $\mathbf{C}_M$); and private information of servers $\mathsf{st}_i \leftarrow \mathbf{sh}_i$. The recovery algorithm $\mathbf{Rec}(\tilde{\mathsf{pw}}, \mathsf{st}_0, \mathsf{st}_{i \in \mathcal{Q}})$ is a 3-round protocol. Servers initiate Rec by sending encryptions of random elements (viz. $\mathbf{C}_{R_j}$'s for random R_j's) to the user. The user then replies to every server with a fresh encryption of her password $\mathbf{C_{\tilde{pw}}}$ and the set of all encryptions of random elements $\{\mathbf{C}_{R_j}\}$. Each of the servers compute the encryption $\mathbf{CF_j}$ of $\sum_j R_j(\tilde{\mathsf{pw}} - \mathsf{pw}) + M$ from the ciphertexts, obtained from the user during the protocol and from the public state st_0, utilizing the capability of computing over ciphertexts provided by the underlying FHE and sends $\mathbf{CF_j} \cdot \mathbf{sh_j}$ to the user. A linear combination of these quantities performed by the user reveals M to her.

The encryptions $\mathbf{C}_{R_j}$'s mask the encryption of password in such a way that the offline dictionary attack can be withstood. This basic PPSS protocol is secure in the semi-honest setting assuming secure channel (private and authenticated channel) between the user and each server. However, this basic protocol cannot be easily extended to provide security guarantees in the presence of malicious parties and without assuming the existence of secure channels.

This basic PPSS protocol is secure in semi-honest setting, and assuming secure channel (private and authenticated channel) between the user and each server. To provide security against malicious adversaries and in the absence of secure channels, Bagherzandi et al. [3] exploit the secret key re-randomization technique of El-Gamal encryption scheme, and use non-interactive simulation-sound zero-knowledge proofs (SS-NIZK). In lattice based setting, to provide strong security in the absence of secure channels, we replace secret key re-randomization property of encryption with the homomorphic properties of the GSW encryption scheme, and to protect against adversarial tampering of protocol messages, use a lattice-based EUF-CMA signature that will be instantiated using [7].

In the following we describe how we modify the steps of our basic protocol to provide security against malicious adversary without any secure channel. As in the basic protocol, each participating server initiates Rec by sending an encryption of a random element viz. $\mathbf{C}_{R_j}$ to the user as the first step. However, now $\mathbf{C}_{R_j}$'s can be modified by a malicious adversary to remove the random masking of encryption of password. Therefore we let the servers sign their corresponding $\mathbf{C}_{R_j}$'s using a lattice-based EUF-CMA signature that can be instantiated using [7] to protect against such modifications. That is why the user includes the signing keys of servers in their secret states st_i's, and includes all the corresponding verification keys into st_0. In the basic protocol, the user is supposed to reply with an encryption of her password with fresh randomness. However, a malicious user may re-randomize the encrypted password stored in st_0 which will ultimately prove her as a legitimate user. To resist this attack, we force the user to forward fresh encryption of password. To this end, the legitimate user generates another GSW key pair $(\bar{\mathbf{A}}, \bar{\mathbf{v}})^2$ during the Init and append the public key $\bar{\mathbf{A}}$ in st_0. User needs to encrypt the same password, using $\mathbf{A}$ and $\bar{\mathbf{A}}$ with the same randomness and sends the two encryptions along with the "proof" of same randomness. User also sends an encryption $\mathbf{C}_X$ with respect to the public key $\mathbf{A}$ of a random element X.

Verification of use of the same randomness is possible by a non-interactive simulation-sound zero-knowledge proof (SS-NIZK) for which we need lattice-based SS-NIZK. Recently, Peikert et al. [17, Theorem 5.4] proposed non-interactive zero-knowledge proof system for any NP language based on the hardness of decisional LWE. Generic conversion proposed by Sahai [19] transform any ordinary non-interactive zero-knowledge proof system into SS-NIZK. Thus, we have SS-NIZK based on the hardness of decisional LWE, which can be used in the proposed protocol. After verifying, through SS-NIZK, that the user has honestly generated fresh encryptions of her password using same randomness, each of the

---

[2] It is worth mentioning that the secret key $\bar{\mathbf{v}}$ does not play any role at any point during the execution of Rec. Thus user neither requires $\bar{\mathbf{v}}$ to be shared and stored among the servers nor to keep it with her - she can delete $\bar{\mathbf{v}}$ after executing the Init.

servers compute encrypted information $\mathbf{CF_j}$ of $\sum_j R_j(\tilde{\mathsf{pw}} - \mathsf{pw}) + M + X$ and sends $\mathbf{CF_j} \cdot \mathbf{sh_j}$ to the user to facilitate threshold decryption of the secret M. Of course, each of the servers has to sign $\mathbf{CF_j} \cdot \mathbf{sh_j}$ to prevent any modification by an adversary. Here, $\mathbf{sh_j}$ denotes the Shamir share of secret key $\mathbf{v}$ of the j-th server. In the end, the user can simply compute a linear sum of $\mathbf{CF_j} \cdot \mathbf{sh_j}$ to retrieve $M + X$ and then remove X to obtain M. Note that, an eavesdropper also can retrieve $M + X$ from $\mathbf{CF_j} \cdot \mathbf{sh_j}$'s but since X was randomly chosen, the secret message M is perfectly hidden from the eavesdropper.

One last point to address is that malicious server(s) may try to convince the user with a different message $M' \neq M$. The user signs the secret message M during Init phase using EUF-CMA signature to output σ. Finally, the user encrypts $M\|\sigma$ instead of just encrypting M. At the end of the recovery phase, the user checks the veracity of the recovered secret message by the verification key of signature, which ensures *soundness*. As a consequence, the user needs to add the verification key of the user's signature in $\mathsf{st_0}$ during the execution of Init.

1.3   Related Works

Bagherzandi et al. [3] proposed the first password protected secret sharing scheme (PPSS) in the PKI model. They also showed how to generically transform a PPSS scheme into a TPAKE scheme. This generic transformation successfully removed the need for server-to-server communication for authenticating a user in a TPAKE protocol. Moreover, their security model does not relax the power of a network adversary – the adversary remains as powerful as the TPAKE adversary. In their scheme, secret data m is encrypted as $(g^r, y^r \cdot m)$ using ElGamal encryption and the user password pw is encrypted using a lifted ElGamal $(g^r, y^r \cdot h^{\mathsf{pw}})$ and both are made public. The secret key (the strong secret) x of ElGamal is secret shared among the servers. The security of Bagherzandi et al.'s PPSS is defined through any PPT adversary's inability to distinguish between two instantiations of the protocol run with two adversarially chosen messages and a uniformly chosen (outside adversary's view) password pw from the dictionary space. In summary, the adversary does not have any non-negligible advantage to attack the system – the best it can do is to perform online attack which is always inherently present in any password based secure systems. Security of the proposed scheme is based on DDH assumption and in the concurrent security model.

Camenisch et al. [6] proposed a universally composable security definition for the two-server case in the public-key setting. Their instantiation is secure under the hardness of DDH problem in the random oracle model. Jarecki et al. [12] put forward a scheme *without* PKI authentication in the reconstruction such that the reconstruction procedure takes a single round (two messages) between a user and each server. Indistinguishability based definition of PPSS security in the crs model is proposed in their paper. The scheme guarantees that the user is able to recover her shared secret data in the single protocol instance as long as it has unobstructed communication with at least k honest servers and if $2k - 1 \leq n$. The construction makes use of a verifiable oblivious pseudorandom function

(VOPRF) to achieve this property. The follow up work by Jarecki et al. [13] improves the performance of [12]. Their protocol relaxed the verifiable property of the OPRF, giving up the ability to discard incorrect computations during interactions with servers. Finally, Jarecki et al. [14] used a universally composable threshold oblivious pseudorandom functions to produce PPSS in the crs model.

Among other important works, Abdalla et al. [2] studied general methodologies to ensure robustness in PPSS reconstruction and Camenisch et al. [5] discussed proactive security for distributed password verification and can be applied to PPSS also.

However, none of the schemes presented so far are secure in the post-quantum world – almost all of them are instantiated based on the hardness of the Diffie-Hellman assumption and its variants.

2   Preliminaries

We denote the sets of real numbers and the integers by $\mathbb{R}$ *and* $\mathbb{Z}$ respectively. We denote column-vectors by lower-case bold letters (e.g. $\mathbf{b}$), so row-vectors are represented via transpositions (e.g. $\mathbf{b}^T$). Matrices are denoted by upper-case bold letters and we sometimes treat a matrix $\mathbf{X}$ interchangeably with its corresponding ordered set representation of column vectors $\{\mathbf{x}_1, \mathbf{x}_2, \ldots\}$. We use $\mathbf{I}$ for the identity matrix and $\mathbf{0}$ for the zero matrix, where the dimension will be clear from the contexts. We use $[*|*]$ to denote concatenation of vectors or matrices of matching dimensions and $\langle ., .\rangle$ to denote inner product of two vectors of same dimension. We denote the shares of a (k, L) threshold Shamir secret sharing [20] of a vector $\mathbf{v}$ by $\{\mathbf{sh}_i\}_{i=1}^{L} \xleftarrow{(k,L)} \mathsf{ShamirShare}(\mathbf{v})$, where each coordinate of $\mathbf{sh}_i$ is share of corresponding coordinate of $\mathbf{v}$. A negligible function is denoted by $\mathsf{negl}(n)$. The *statistical distance* between two distributions $\mathbf{X}$ and $\mathbf{Y}$ over a finite or countable domain Ω is defined as $\frac{1}{2}\sum_{w\in\Omega} |\mathsf{Pr}[\mathbf{X} = w] - \mathsf{Pr}[\mathbf{Y} = w]|$.

We now state some important concepts and notations from Gentry et al. [11] which are required for our proposed constructions. Let $\mathbf{a}, \mathbf{b} \in \mathbb{Z}_q^k$, $\ell = \lfloor \log q \rfloor + 1$, and $N = k\ell$. $\mathsf{BitDecomp}(\mathbf{a})$ denotes the N-dimensional vector $(a_{1,0}, .., a_{1,\ell-1}, \ldots, a_{k,0}, \ldots, a_{k,\ell-1})$, where $a_{i,j}$ is the j-th bit in a_i's binary representation where bits are ordered from least significant to most significant. For $\mathbf{a}' = (a_{1,0}, \ldots, a_{1,\ell-1}, \ldots, a_{k,0}, \ldots, a_{k,\ell-1})$, let $\mathsf{BitDecomp}^{-1}(\mathbf{a}') = (\sum_{j=0}^{l-1} 2^j \cdot a_{1,j}, \ldots, \sum_{j=0}^{l-1} 2^j \cdot a_{k,j})$ be the inverse of $\mathsf{BitDecomp}$. Note that the inverse function $\mathsf{BitDecomp}^{-1}$ remains well-defined even when the input is not a $0/1$ vector. For N-dimensional $\mathbf{a}'$ define, $\mathsf{Flatten}(\mathbf{a}') = \mathsf{BitDecomp}(\mathsf{BitDecomp}^{-1}(\mathbf{a}'))$, to be an N-dimensional vector with $0/1$ entries. When $\mathbf{X}$ is a matrix, $\mathsf{BitDecomp}(\mathbf{X})$, $\mathsf{BitDecomp}^{-1}$, or $\mathsf{Flatten}(\mathbf{X})$ denotes the matrix formed by applying the corresponding operation to each row of $\mathbf{X}$ separately. Finally, let $\mathsf{Powersof2}(\mathbf{b}) = (b_1, 2b_1, \ldots, 2^{\ell-1}b_1, \ldots, b_k, 2b_k, \ldots, 2^{\ell-1}b_k)$ denotes an N-dimensional vector obtained from $\mathbf{b} \in \mathbb{Z}_q^k$. Following are two useful facts from [11] required for our constructions:

- $\langle \mathsf{BitDecomp}(\mathbf{a}), \mathsf{Powersof2}(\mathbf{b}) \rangle = \langle \mathbf{a}, \mathbf{b} \rangle$.
- For any N-dimensional $\mathbf{a}'$,
  $\langle \mathbf{a}', \mathsf{Powersof2}(\mathbf{b}) \rangle = \langle \mathsf{BitDecomp}^{-1}(\mathbf{a}'), \mathbf{b} \rangle = \langle \mathsf{Flatten}(\mathbf{a}'), \mathsf{Powersof2}(\mathbf{b}) \rangle$.

2.1 Lattices

A *lattice* Λ is a discrete additive subgroup of $\mathbb{R}^m$. Specifically, a lattice Λ in $\mathbb{R}^m$ with basis $\mathbf{B} = [\mathbf{b}_1 | \cdots | \mathbf{b}_n] \in \mathbb{R}^{m \times n}$, where each $\mathbf{b}_i$ is written in column form, is defined as $\Lambda := \{\sum_{i=1}^{n} \mathbf{b}_i x_i | x_i \in \mathbb{Z} \ \forall i = 1, \dots, n\} \subseteq \mathbb{R}^m$. We call n the rank of Λ and if $n = m$ we say that Λ is a full rank lattice. The dual lattice Λ^* is the set of all vectors $\mathbf{y} \in \mathbb{R}^m$ satisfying $\langle \mathbf{x}, \mathbf{y} \rangle \in \mathbb{Z}$ for all vectors $\mathbf{x} \in \Lambda$. If $\mathbf{B}$ is a basis of an arbitrary lattice Λ, then $\mathbf{B}^* = \mathbf{B}(\mathbf{B}^T\mathbf{B})^{-1}$ is a basis for Λ^*. For a full-rank lattice, $\mathbf{B}^* = \mathbf{B}^{-T}$. We refer to $\widetilde{\mathbf{B}}$ as a Gram-Schmidt orthogonalization of $\mathbf{B}$.

In this paper, we mainly consider full rank lattices containing $q\mathbb{Z}^m$, called q-ary lattices, defined as the following, for a given matrix $\mathbf{A} \in \mathbb{Z}_q^{n \times m}$ and $\mathbf{u} \in \mathbb{Z}_q^n$.

$$\Lambda_q(\mathbf{A}) := \{\mathbf{z} \in \mathbb{Z}^m : \exists \, \mathbf{s} \in \mathbb{Z}_q^n \ s.t. \ \mathbf{z} = \mathbf{A}^T\mathbf{s} \bmod q\}.$$
$$\Lambda_q^{\perp}(\mathbf{A}) := \{\mathbf{z} \in \mathbb{Z}^m : \mathbf{A}\mathbf{z} = 0 \bmod q\}.$$
$$\Lambda_q^{\mathbf{u}}(\mathbf{A}) := \{\mathbf{z} \in \mathbb{Z}^m : \mathbf{A}\mathbf{z} = \mathbf{u} \bmod q\} = \Lambda_q^{\perp}(\mathbf{A}) + \mathbf{x} \ for \ \mathbf{x} \in \Lambda_q^{\mathbf{u}}(\mathbf{A}).$$

Gaussian on Lattices: Let $\Lambda \subseteq \mathbb{Z}^m$ be an integer lattice. For a vector $\mathbf{c} \in \mathbb{R}^m$ and a positive parameter $\sigma \in \mathbb{R}$, define: $\rho_{\mathbf{c},\sigma}(\mathbf{x}) = \exp\left(\pi \frac{\|\mathbf{x}-\mathbf{c}\|^2}{\sigma^2}\right)$ and $\rho_{\mathbf{c},\sigma}(\Lambda) = \sum_{\mathbf{x} \in \Lambda} \rho_{\mathbf{c},\sigma}(\mathbf{x})$, where $\|\mathbf{x} - \mathbf{c}\|$ denotes the regular euclidean distance between vectors. The discrete Gaussian distribution over Λ with center $\mathbf{c}$ and parameter σ is $\mathcal{D}_{\mathbf{c},\sigma}(\Lambda)(\mathbf{y}) = \frac{\rho_{\mathbf{c},\sigma}(\mathbf{y})}{\rho_{\mathbf{c},\sigma}(\Lambda)}, \forall \mathbf{y} \in \Lambda$.

Learning With Errors (LWE) [18]: The Learning with Errors (LWE) problem was introduced by Regev [18]. We define the decisional version of LWE, the security of our schemes are based on this hardness assumption.

Definition 1 (Decisional LWE (dLWE)). *Consider a prime integer q, positive integers n, m and a noise distribution χ over $\mathbb{Z}_q$. Suppose $\mathbf{B} \xleftarrow{\$} \mathbb{Z}_q^{n \times m}$, $\mathbf{s} \xleftarrow{\$} \mathbb{Z}_q^n$, $\mathbf{b} \xleftarrow{\$} \mathbb{Z}_q^m$ and $\mathbf{e} \xleftarrow{\$} \chi^m$ are sampled. The $\mathsf{dLWE}_{n,m,q,\chi}$ problem is to distinguish the following two distributions:*

$$(\mathbf{B}, \mathbf{B}^T\mathbf{s} + \mathbf{e}) \quad and \quad (\mathbf{B}, \mathbf{b}).$$

The noise distribution χ is said to be B-bounded if its support is in $[-B, B]$. We denote by $\chi_{max}(< q)$ to be the bound on the noise distribution χ. The difficulty of the problem is measured by the ratio q/χ_{max}. This ratio is always bigger than 1 and the smaller it is the harder the dLWE problem.

Lemma 1 ([18]). *Let n, m, q, χ be such that the $\mathsf{dLWE}_{n,m,q,\chi}$ holds. Let $\mathbf{R} \xleftarrow{\$} \mathbb{Z}_q^{N \times m}$, $\mathbf{A} = [\mathbf{B}^T\mathbf{s} + \mathbf{e} | \mathbf{B}] \in \mathbb{Z}_q^{m \times (n+1)}$, where $\mathbf{B} \xleftarrow{\$} \mathbb{Z}_q^{n \times m}$, $\mathbf{s} \xleftarrow{\$} \mathbb{Z}_q^n$, and $\mathbf{e} \xleftarrow{\$} \chi^m$ are sampled. Then the joint distribution $(\mathbf{A}, \mathbf{R} \cdot \mathbf{A})$ is computationally indistinguishable from uniform over $\mathbb{Z}_q^{m \times (n+1)} \times \mathbb{Z}_q^{N \times (n+1)}$.*

2.2 The GSW Scheme [11]

We briefly summarize the encryption scheme of GSW which we need for our constructions.

SetUp(1^λ):

- Let χ be a χ_{max}-bounded distribution for which dLWE$_{n,m,q,\chi}$ is hard, where n is an integer, $q = poly(n)$ large enough prime power, and $m = \Theta(n \log q)$. Let $params = (n, q, \chi, m)$ and $N = (n + 1) \cdot (\lfloor \log q \rfloor + 1)$. For convenience, we will assume that q is power of 2.

KeyGen($Params$):

- Sample $\mathbf{t} \leftarrow \mathbb{Z}_q^n$, and set $\mathbf{s} = (1, -t_1, \ldots, -t_n) \in \mathbb{Z}_q^{n+1}$.
  Let $\mathbf{v} = \mathsf{Powersof2}(\mathbf{s}) \in \mathbb{Z}_q^N$.
- Sample $\mathbf{B} \leftarrow \mathbb{Z}_q^{m \times n}$, and $\mathbf{e} \leftarrow \chi^m$. Compute $\mathbf{b} = \mathbf{B} \cdot \mathbf{t} + \mathbf{e}$ and set $\mathbf{A} = [\mathbf{b}|\mathbf{B}] \in \mathbb{Z}_q^{m \times (n+1)}$.
- Output $(pk, sk) = (\mathbf{A}, \mathbf{v})$.

Enc($Params, pk, M$): On input a message $M \in \mathbb{Z}_q$, sample $\mathbf{R}_M \leftarrow \{0, 1\}^{N \times m}$ and compute ciphertext $\mathbf{C}$ as follows:

$$\mathbf{C} = \mathsf{Flatten}\left(M \cdot \mathbf{I}_N + \mathsf{BitDecomp}(\mathbf{R}_M \cdot \mathbf{A})\right) \in \mathbb{Z}_q^{N \times N}.$$

Dec($Params, sk, \mathbf{C}$): On input a ciphertext $\mathbf{C}$ and $sk = \mathbf{v}$, compute

$$\mathbf{C} \cdot \mathbf{v} = M \cdot \mathbf{v} + small.$$

Observe that first $\lfloor \log q \rfloor$ coefficients of $\mathbf{v}$ are $1, 2, \cdots, 2^{\lfloor \log q \rfloor - 2}$, and therefore if $\mathbf{C} \cdot \mathbf{v} = M \cdot \mathbf{v} + small$, then the first $\lfloor \log q \rfloor - 1$ coefficients of $\mathbf{C} \cdot \mathbf{v}$ are $M \cdot \mathbf{g} + small$, where $\mathbf{g} = (1, 2, \cdots, 2^{\lfloor \log q \rfloor - 2})$. Recover $LSB(M)$, least-significant-bit of M, from $M \cdot 2^{\lfloor \log q \rfloor - 2} + small$, then recover the next-least-significant-bit from $(M - LSB(M)) \cdot 2^{\lfloor \log q \rfloor - 3} + small$, and so on.

2.3 Non-interactive Simulation-Sound Zero-Knowledge Proofs

To assure that protocol messages are well-formed we use simulation-sound non-interactive zero-knowledge (SS-NIZK) proofs. To construct our lattice-based PPSS, we need lattice-based SS-NIZK. Recently, Peikert et al. [17, Theorem 5.4] proposed non-interactive zero-knowledge proof system for any NP language based on the hardness of dLWE. Generic conversion proposed by Sahai [19] transform any ordinary non-interactive zero-knowledge proof system into SS-NIZK. Thus, we now have SS-NIZK based on the hardness of dLWE.

Loosely speaking, a NIZK proof system for language $\mathcal{L}$ is a triplet of algorithms, prover $\mathcal{P}$ which produces a proof π on input a statement instance x, witness ω and public parameters PP; verifier $\mathcal{V}$ which accepts or rejects on input (PP, x, π); and a simulator $\mathcal{S}$ which outputs a (simulated) proof on the input PP and x. We briefly recall that for a $(T_S, q_P, \epsilon_{ZK}, \epsilon_{SS})$ SS-NIZK, there is a simulator algorithm $\mathcal{S}$ running in time T_S which answers up to q_P prover queries with simulated proofs on statements of adversary's choice (which can include false statements) such that (1) the statistical difference between the view of an interaction with $\mathcal{S}$ and an interaction with the real prover is at most ϵ_{ZK}, and (2) the probability that any adversary interacting with $\mathcal{S}$ outputs a correct proof on a new false statement, i.e. a for a statement different from those for which it receives simulated proof from $\mathcal{S}$, is at most ϵ_{SS}.

We need such proofs for the language $\mathcal{L}_U^{sto}$ corresponding to the one protocol message from User to Servers (see Sect. 3.2) parameterized by public parameters $st_0 \leftarrow \{\mathbf{A}, \bar{\mathbf{A}}, H, \mathbf{C}_{pw}, \mathbf{C}_M, \{Ver_i\}_{i=1}^L\}$, where

$\mathcal{L}_U^{sto} = \{(\mathbf{C}_{\tilde{pw}}, \bar{\mathbf{C}}_{\tilde{pw}}) \in \mathbb{Z}_q^{N \times N} \mid \exists\ (H_{\tilde{pw}}, \mathbf{R}_{\tilde{pw}}) \in \mathbb{Z}_q \times \{0,1\}^{N \times m}$ where $\mathbf{C}_{\tilde{pw}} =$ Flatten$(H_{\tilde{pw}} \cdot \mathbf{I}_N + $ BitDecomp$(\mathbf{R}_{\tilde{pw}} \cdot \mathbf{A}))$ & $\bar{\mathbf{C}}_{\tilde{pw}} = $ Flatten$(H_{\tilde{pw}} \cdot \mathbf{I}_N + $ BitDecomp$(\mathbf{R}_{\tilde{pw}} \cdot \bar{\mathbf{A}}))$.

2.4   Password Protected Secret Sharing (PPSS)

We follow the definition of Bagherzandi et al. [3] for password protected secret sharing (PPSS). A PPSS scheme is a protocol involving a user $\mathbf{U}$, and L servers $(\mathbf{S}_1, \ldots, \mathbf{S}_L)$. The scheme is a tuple (Init, Rec), where Init(pw, M) is an initialization algorithm (followed by $\mathbf{U}$) which on inputs pw from a dictionary $\mathbf{D}$ and secret message M from message space $\mathbf{M}$ outputs st $= (st_0, st_1, \ldots, st_L)$, where st_0 are public parameters and st_i is the private state of server $\mathbf{S}_i$; Rec consists of two interactive algorithms – User($\tilde{pw}, st_0$) followed by user $\mathbf{U}$ on its password $\tilde{pw}$ along with public parameters st_0 and Server(st_i) is followed by $\mathbf{S}_i$ on input its secret state st_i.

Definition 2 ((k, L)-Password Protected Secret Sharing [3]). *A (k, L)-PPSS scheme for secret message space $\mathbf{M}$, and dictionary $\mathbf{D}$ is a tuple (Init, Rec) involves user $\mathbf{U}$ and L servers $\mathbf{S}_1, \ldots, \mathbf{S}_L$:*

- st $\longleftarrow$ Init(pw, M): *On input a secret message $M \in \mathbf{M}$ and password pw $\in \mathbf{D}$ outputs st $= (st_0, st_1, \ldots, st_L)$, where st_0 is public parameters/state and st_i is the private state of server $\mathbf{S}_i$.*
- $M'/\perp \longleftarrow$ Rec($\tilde{pw}, st_0, st_{i \in \mathcal{Q}}$): *Rec is an interactive protocol between user $\mathbf{U}$ and a subset of k servers indexed by $\mathcal{Q} \subset \{1, \ldots, L\}$ such that*
  - $M'/\perp \longleftarrow$ User($\tilde{pw}, st_0$): *On input a password $\tilde{pw} \in \mathbf{D}$ and st_0, outputs $M'/\perp$. User is an interactive protocol followed by $\mathbf{U}$.*
  - Server(st_0, st_i): *Server is an interactive protocol, followed by $\mathbf{S}_i$, runs on input (st_0, st_i). Server algorithm has no local output.*

Definition 3 (Correctness). *If honest user $\mathbf{U}$ interacts with k or more uncorrupted servers then it must reconstruct the same secret message M that was input of Init; i.e., for any $M \in \mathbf{M}$, any pw $\in \mathbf{D}$ with st $\longleftarrow$ Init(pw, M) and $M' \longleftarrow$ Rec(pw, $st_0, st_{i \in \mathcal{Q}}$), we have $M = M'$.*

In this paper, we consider the reconstruction process Rec to be performed among the user and exactly k many servers.

The security of a (k, L)-PPSS scheme as described in Bagherzandi et al. [3], is defined in terms of adversary's advantage in distinguishing between two PPSS instances initialized with two different secret messages (M_0, M_1), where the adversary can access the public parameters st_0, the private states $\{\mathsf{st}_i\}_{i \in \mathcal{F}}$ of a set of servers $\mathcal{F}$ with $|\mathcal{F}| = k - 1$ it corrupts, and has concurrent oracle access to instances of the User and Server algorithms executing on inputs defined by the Init algorithm.

Definition 4 (Security). *A (k, L)-PPSS scheme on dictionary D and secret message space $\mathbf{M}$ is said to be $(L, k, \mathsf{Time}, q_U, q_S, \epsilon)$-secure if for any $M_0 \neq M_1 \in \mathbf{M}$, and any probabilistic algorithm $\mathcal{A}$ with running time Time which interacts with at most q_U user and q_S server sessions, it must hold that*

$$|p_0 - p_1| \leq \left\lfloor \frac{q_S}{|D|} \right\rfloor + \epsilon,$$

where $p_b := \Pr[1 \leftarrow \mathcal{A}^{\mathsf{User}^\diamond(\mathsf{pw},\mathsf{st}_0),\mathsf{Server}^\diamond(\mathsf{st}_0,\{\mathsf{st}_i\}_{i \in \mathcal{F}})}(M_b, \mathsf{st}_0, \{\mathsf{st}_i\}_{i \in \mathcal{F}})]$ for a random $\mathsf{pw} \in \mathbf{D}$ and $\mathsf{st} \leftarrow \mathsf{Init}(\mathsf{pw}, M_b)$. Here, $\mathsf{User}^\diamond(\mathsf{pw}, \mathsf{st}_0)$ is an oracle which allows $\mathcal{A}$ to interact with any number of $\mathsf{User}(\mathsf{pw}, \mathsf{st}_0)$ instances concurrently; $\mathsf{Server}^\diamond(\mathsf{st}_0, \{\mathsf{st}_i\}_{i \in \mathcal{F}})$ is an oracle which allows $\mathcal{A}$ to interact with any number of $\mathsf{Server}(\mathsf{st}_0, \{\mathsf{st}_i\}_{i \in \mathcal{F}})$ instances concurrently. Note that, in addition to protocol transcript, we let $\mathcal{A}$ learn a bit which indicates whether $\mathsf{User}(\mathsf{pw}, \mathsf{st}_0)$ instance locally outputs some secret s or it locally outputs a rejection sign $\bot$.

Note 1. We consider the strong security notion of PPSS. If we do not allow the adversary to obtain a bit corresponding to the local output of the user instance then a weak-secure model of PPSS is captured [3].

Definition 5 (Soundness). *A PPSS scheme on dictionary $\mathbf{D}$ and secret message space $\mathbf{M}$ is δ-sound if for any $(M, \mathsf{pw}, \tilde{\mathsf{pw}}) \in \mathbf{M} \times \mathbf{D} \times \mathbf{D}$ and $\mathsf{User}(\tilde{\mathsf{pw}}, \mathsf{st}_0)$ interacting with $\mathcal{A}(M, \mathsf{pw}, \tilde{\mathsf{pw}}, \mathsf{st})$, $\Pr[M' \notin \{M, \bot\}] < \delta$, where st is output by $\mathsf{Init}(\mathsf{pw}, M)$ and M' is output by $\mathsf{User}(\tilde{\mathsf{pw}}, \mathsf{st}_0)$. We define weak soundness in the same way but restricting $\tilde{\mathsf{pw}}$ to $\tilde{\mathsf{pw}} = \mathsf{pw}$.*

3   Password Protected Secret Sharing (PPSS)

In this section, we present our constructions of (k, L)-PPSS. First, we describe a basic PPSS scheme secure against semi-honest adversaries assuming secure channel(s) between user and server(s). We then extend the basic protocol to have security against malicious adversaries without assuming any secure channel.

3.1 (k, L)-PPSS Secure Against Semi-Honest Adversaries Assuming Secure Channel

We set the parameters as the following:

- Let χ be a χ_{max}-bounded distribution for which $\mathsf{dLWE}_{n,m,q,\chi}$ is hard, where n is an integer, $q = poly(n)$ large enough prime power, and $m = \Theta(n \log q)$. For convenience, we will assume that q is power of 2.
- Let $N = (n+1) \cdot (\lfloor \log q \rfloor + 1)$.

The proposed PPSS consists of the following algorithms:

$\mathsf{Init}(\mathsf{pw}, M)$: On input a secret message $M \in \mathbb{Z}_q$ and password $\mathsf{pw} \in \mathbf{D}$,

1. Run KeyGen of GSW:
   - Sample $\mathbf{t} \leftarrow \mathbb{Z}_q^n$, and set $\mathbf{s} = (1, -t_1, \ldots, -t_n) \in \mathbb{Z}_q^{n+1}$.
   - Let $\mathbf{v} = \mathsf{Powersof2}(\mathbf{s}) \in \mathbb{Z}_q^N$.
   - Sample $\mathbf{B} \leftarrow \mathbb{Z}_q^{m \times n}$, and $\mathbf{e} \leftarrow \chi^m$.
   - Compute $\mathbf{b} = \mathbf{B} \cdot \mathbf{t} + \mathbf{e}$ and set $\mathbf{A} = \begin{bmatrix} \mathbf{b} | \mathbf{B} \end{bmatrix} \in \mathbb{Z}_q^{m \times (n+1)}$.
2. Choose *collision resistant hash function* $H : \{0,1\}^* \rightarrow \mathbb{Z}_q$. Compute $H_{\mathsf{pw}} = H(\mathsf{pw})$.
3. Run Enc of GSW to encrypt $H_{\mathsf{pw}} \in \mathbb{Z}_q$ and $M \in \mathbb{Z}_q$:
   - Sample $\mathbf{R}_{\mathsf{pw}}, \mathbf{R}_M \leftarrow \{0,1\}^{N \times m}$.
   - Compute

$$\mathbf{C}_{\mathsf{pw}} = \mathsf{Flatten}\,(H_{\mathsf{pw}} \cdot \mathbf{I}_N + \mathsf{BitDecomp}(\mathbf{R}_{\mathsf{pw}} \cdot \mathbf{A})) \in \mathbb{Z}_q^{N \times N};$$
$$\mathbf{C}_M = \mathsf{Flatten}\,(M \cdot \mathbf{I}_N + \mathsf{BitDecomp}(\mathbf{R}_M \cdot \mathbf{A})) \in \mathbb{Z}_q^{N \times N}.$$

4. Compute $\{\mathbf{sh}_i\}_{i=1}^L \xleftarrow{(k,L)} \mathsf{ShamirShare}(\mathbf{v})$.
5. Output $\mathsf{st} = (\mathsf{st}_0, \mathsf{st}_1, \ldots, \mathsf{st}_L)$, where $\mathsf{st}_0 \leftarrow \{\mathbf{A}, H, \mathbf{C}_{\mathsf{pw}}, \mathbf{C}_M\}$ is the public parameters, and $\mathsf{st}_i \leftarrow \mathbf{sh}_i$ is the secret state of server $\mathbf{S_i}$ for $i = 1, \ldots, L$.

$\mathbf{Rec}(\tilde{\mathsf{pw}}, \mathsf{st}_0, \mathsf{st}_{i \in \mathcal{Q}})$: On input st_0 and secret states st_i of k many servers indexed by $\mathcal{Q}$ and password $\tilde{\mathsf{pw}} \in \mathbf{D}$, perform the following steps:

- Server 1: Server $\mathbf{S}_j$ (for every $j \in \mathcal{Q}$) performs the following steps:
  1. Randomly choose $R_j \in \mathbb{Z}_q$ and run Enc of GSW to encrypt R_j:
     - Sample $\mathbf{R_{S}}_j \leftarrow \{0,1\}^{N \times m}$.
     - Compute

$$\mathbf{C}_{R_j} = \mathsf{Flatten}\,\left(R_j \cdot \mathbf{I}_N + \mathsf{BitDecomp}(\mathbf{R_{S}}_j \cdot \mathbf{A})\right) \in \mathbb{Z}_q^{N \times N}.$$

  2. Sends $\mathbf{C}_{R_j}$ to the user $\mathbf{U}$.

- User 1: User $\mathbf{U}$ with input $\tilde{\mathsf{pw}}$ (possibly equal to pw) and st_0 performs the following steps:
  1. Compute $H_{\tilde{\mathsf{pw}}} = H(\tilde{\mathsf{pw}})$ and run Enc of GSW to encrypt $H_{\tilde{\mathsf{pw}}}$:
     - Sample $\mathbf{R}_{\tilde{\mathsf{pw}}} \leftarrow \{0,1\}^{N \times m}$ and compute

$$\mathbf{C}_{\tilde{\mathsf{pw}}} = \mathsf{Flatten}\,(H_{\tilde{\mathsf{pw}}} \cdot \mathbf{I}_N + \mathsf{BitDecomp}(\mathbf{R}_{\tilde{\mathsf{pw}}} \cdot \mathbf{A})) \in \mathbb{Z}_q^{N \times N}.$$

  2. Compute $\lambda_j = \frac{\prod_{i \neq j}(-ID_i)}{\prod_{i \neq j}(ID_j - ID_i)} \mod q$. Here ID_j denotes server ID of j-th server session, where $ID_j \in \mathcal{Q} \subseteq \{1, \ldots, L\}$ and $|\mathcal{Q}| = k$.

3. Send $(\mathbf{C}_{\widetilde{pw}}, \{\mathbf{C}_{\tilde{R}_j}, \lambda_j\}_{j \in \mathcal{Q}})$ to $\{\mathbf{S}_j\}_{j \in \mathcal{Q}}$.

- Server 2: Server $\mathbf{S}_j$ (for all $j \in \mathcal{Q}$) proceeds as follows:
  1. Compute
  $$\mathbf{CF}_j = \left(\sum_{i \in \mathcal{Q}\setminus\{j\}} \mathbf{C}_{\tilde{R}_i} + \mathbf{C}_{R_j}\right) \cdot \mathbf{C}_{\widetilde{pw}} - \left(\sum_{i \in \mathcal{Q}\setminus\{j\}} \mathbf{C}_{\tilde{R}_i} + \mathbf{C}_{R_j}\right) \cdot \mathbf{C}_{pw} + \mathbf{C}_M.$$
  2. Compute $\mathbf{W}_j = \lambda_j \mathbf{CF}_j \cdot \mathbf{sh}_j$.
  3. Send $\mathbf{W}_j$ to the user $\mathbf{U}$.

- User 2: User $\mathbf{U}$ proceeds as follows:
  1. Computes $\sum_{i \in \mathcal{Q}} \lambda_i \cdot \mathbf{CF}_i \cdot \mathbf{sh}_i$, and outputs M.

Correctness and Security. In this section, we analyze the correctness and security of the above PPSS.

Theorem 1 (Correctness). *The above scheme with parameters proposed in Sect. 3.1 is correct.*

Proof. When all the servers and user are honest, all the $\mathbf{CF}_i$ of User2 round are same, say, $\mathbf{CF}$. Hence, $\sum_{i \in \mathcal{Q}} \lambda_i \cdot \mathbf{CF}_i \cdot \mathbf{sh}_i = \mathbf{CF} \cdot (\sum_{i \in \mathcal{Q}} \lambda_i \mathbf{sh}_i) = \mathbf{CF} \cdot \mathbf{v}$ (by Lagrange's interpolation). Correctness of the above scheme now follows from the correctness of decryption algorithm of GSW scheme. □

We note that in the above scheme, the eavesdropping attack is warded off by the assumption of secure channels. Moreover, offline attack is resisted due to the masking of $\widetilde{pw}$ by the random element $\sum_{i \in \mathcal{Q}} R_i$. Hence, the security follows from the security of FHE [11] and secret sharing scheme [20]. We have the following theorem, the security proof of which follows from the proof technique of Theorem 4 with proper restrictions.

Theorem 2. *The above construction is secure against semi-honest adversary, according to the Definition 4, assuming secure channel and the hardness of the* dLWE$_{n,m,q,\chi}$.

3.2 (k, L)-PPSS Secure Against Malicious Adversaries

We set the parameters as follows:

- Let χ be a χ_{max}-bounded distribution for which dLWE$_{n,m,q,\chi}$ is hard, where n is an integer, $q = poly(n)$ large enough prime power, and $m = \Theta(n \log q)$. For convenience, we will assume that q is power of 2.
- Let $N = (n + 1) \cdot (\lfloor \log q \rfloor + 1)$.

The proposed PPSS consists of the following algorithms:

Init(pw, M): On input a secret message $M \in \mathbb{Z}_q$ and password pw $\in \mathbf{D}$, perform the following steps:

1. Generate EUF-CMA Signature algorithm [7] $\{(\mathsf{Sig}_i, \mathsf{Ver}_i)\}_{i=1}^{L}$.
2. Run KeyGen of GSW:
   - Sample $\mathbf{t} \leftarrow \mathbb{Z}_q^n$, and set $\mathbf{s} = (1, -t_1, \dots, -t_n) \in \mathbb{Z}_q^{n+1}$.
   - Let $\mathbf{v} = \mathsf{Powersof2}(\mathbf{s}) \in \mathbb{Z}_q^N$.
   - Sample $\mathbf{B} \leftarrow \mathbb{Z}_q^{m \times n}$, and $\mathbf{e} \leftarrow \chi^m$.
   - Compute $\mathbf{b} = \mathbf{B} \cdot \mathbf{t} + \mathbf{e}$ and set $\mathbf{A} = [\mathbf{b}|\mathbf{B}] \in \mathbb{Z}_q^{m \times (n+1)}$.
3. Independently run KeyGen of GSW i.e. choose $\bar{t}, \bar{\mathbf{B}}, \bar{\mathbf{e}}$ and construct $\bar{\mathbf{A}} = [\bar{\mathbf{b}}|\bar{\mathbf{B}}] \in \mathbb{Z}_q^{m \times (n+1)}$.
4. Choose *collision resistant hash function* $H : \{0,1\}^* \to \mathbb{Z}_q$. Compute $H_{\mathsf{pw}} = H(\mathsf{pw})$.
5. Run Enc of GSW to encrypt H_{pw} and M with respect to $\mathbf{A}$:
   - Sample $\mathbf{R}_{\mathsf{pw}}, \mathbf{R}_M \leftarrow \{0,1\}^{N \times m}$.
   - Compute

$$\mathbf{C}_{\mathsf{pw}} = \mathsf{Flatten}\,(H_{\mathsf{pw}} \cdot \mathbf{I}_N + \mathsf{BitDecomp}(\mathbf{R}_{\mathsf{pw}} \cdot \mathbf{A})) \in \mathbb{Z}_q^{N \times N};$$
$$\mathbf{C}_M = \mathsf{Flatten}\,(M \cdot \mathbf{I}_N + \mathsf{BitDecomp}(\mathbf{R}_M \cdot \mathbf{A})) \in \mathbb{Z}_q^{N \times N}.$$

6. Compute $\{\mathbf{sh}_i\}_{i=1}^{L} \xleftarrow{(k,L)} \mathsf{ShamirShare}(\mathbf{v})$.
7. Output $\mathsf{st} = (\mathsf{st}_0, \mathsf{st}_1, \dots, \mathsf{st}_L)$, where $\mathsf{st}_0 \leftarrow \{\mathbf{A}, \bar{\mathbf{A}}, H, \mathbf{C}_{\mathsf{pw}}, \mathbf{C}_M, \{\mathsf{Ver}_i\}_{i=1}^{L}\}$, and $\{\mathsf{st}_i \leftarrow \{\mathbf{sh}_i, \mathsf{Sig}_i\}\}_{i=1}^{L}$.

Rec($\tilde{\mathsf{pw}}, \mathsf{st}_0, \mathsf{st}_{i \in \mathcal{Q}}$): On input st_0 and secret states st_i of k many servers indexed by $\mathcal{Q}$ and password $\tilde{\mathsf{pw}} \in \mathbf{D}$, perform the following steps:

– Server 1: Server $\mathbf{S}_j$ (for each $j \in \mathcal{Q}$) performs the following steps:
   1. Randomly choose $R_j \in \mathbb{Z}_q$ and run Enc of GSW to encrypt R_j w.r.t $\mathbf{A}$:
      - Sample $\mathbf{R}_{\mathbf{S}_j} \leftarrow \{0,1\}^{N \times m}$
      - Compute

$$\mathbf{C}_{R_j} = \mathsf{Flatten}\,(R_j \cdot \mathbf{I}_N + \mathsf{BitDecomp}(\mathbf{R}_{\mathbf{S}_j} \cdot \mathbf{A})) \in \mathbb{Z}_q^{N \times N}.$$

   2. Compute $\mathsf{Sig}_j(\mathbf{C}_{R_j})$.
   3. Send $\mathbf{C}_{R_j}$ and $\mathsf{Sig}_j(\mathbf{C}_{R_j})$ to the user $\mathbf{U}$.

– User 1: User $\mathbf{U}$ does the following:
   1. Check $\{\mathsf{Ver}_i(\mathsf{Sig}_i(\mathbf{C}_{\tilde{R}_i})) = accept \text{ or } reject\}_{i \in \mathcal{Q}}$.
      - If any $\mathsf{Ver}_i(\mathsf{Sig}_i(\mathbf{C}_{\tilde{R}_i})) \neq accept$ for $i \in \mathcal{Q}$, send $\perp$ to $\{\mathbf{S}_j\}_{j \in \mathcal{Q}}$.
   2. Otherwise,
      (a) Compute $H_{\tilde{\mathsf{pw}}} = H(\tilde{\mathsf{pw}})$ and randomly choose $X \in \mathbb{Z}_q$. Run Enc of GSW to (*i*) encrypt $H_{\tilde{\mathsf{pw}}}$ with respect to $\mathbf{A}$ and $\bar{\mathbf{A}}$ with the same randomness $\mathbf{R}_{\tilde{\mathsf{pw}}}$ and (*ii*) encrypt X with respect to $\mathbf{A}$.

- Sample $\mathbf{R}_{\tilde{p}\tilde{w}}, \mathbf{R}_X \leftarrow \{0, 1\}^{N \times m}$.
- Compute

$$\mathbf{C}_{\tilde{p}\tilde{w}} = \mathsf{Flatten}\,(H_{\tilde{p}\tilde{w}} \cdot \mathbf{I}_N + \mathsf{BitDecomp}(\mathbf{R}_{\tilde{p}\tilde{w}} \cdot \mathbf{A})) \in \mathbb{Z}_q^{N \times N};$$

$$\bar{\mathbf{C}}_{\tilde{p}\tilde{w}} = \mathsf{Flatten}\,(H_{\tilde{p}\tilde{w}} \cdot \mathbf{I}_N + \mathsf{BitDecomp}(\mathbf{R}_{\tilde{p}\tilde{w}} \cdot \bar{\mathbf{A}})) \in \mathbb{Z}_q^{N \times N};$$

$$\mathbf{C}_X = \mathsf{Flatten}\,(X \cdot \mathbf{I}_N + \mathsf{BitDecomp}(\mathbf{R}_X \cdot \mathbf{A})) \in \mathbb{Z}_q^{N \times N}.$$

(b) Compute $\lambda_j = \frac{\prod_{i \neq j}(-ID_i)}{\prod_{i \neq j}(ID_j - ID_i)}$ mod q where ID_j denotes server ID of j-th server session, where $ID_j \in \mathcal{Q} \subseteq \{1, \dots, L\}$ and $|\mathcal{Q}| = k$.

(c) Compute $\{\pi_j \leftarrow \mathcal{P}[\mathcal{L}_U^{\mathsf{sto}}]((\mathbf{C}_{\tilde{p}\tilde{w}}, \bar{\mathbf{C}}_{\tilde{p}\tilde{w}}), (H_{\tilde{p}\tilde{w}}, \mathbf{R}_{\tilde{p}\tilde{w}}))\}_{j \in \mathcal{Q}}$.

(d) Send $(\mathbf{C}_{\tilde{p}\tilde{w}}, \bar{\mathbf{C}}_{\tilde{p}\tilde{w}}, \mathbf{C}_X, \pi_j, \{\mathbf{C}_{\tilde{R}_j}, \mathsf{Sig}_j(\mathbf{C}_{\tilde{R}_j}), \lambda_j\}_{j \in \mathcal{Q}})$ to $\{\mathbf{S}_j\}_{j \in \mathcal{Q}}$.

- Server 2: Server $\mathbf{S}_j$ (for all $j \in \mathcal{Q}$) proceeds as follows:
    1. Check $\{\mathsf{Ver}_i(\mathsf{Sig}_i(\mathbf{C}_{\tilde{R}_i})) = accept \text{ or } reject\}_{i \in \mathcal{Q}}$.
        - If any $\mathsf{Ver}_i(\mathsf{Sig}_i(\mathbf{C}_{\tilde{R}_i})) \neq accept$ for $i \in \mathcal{Q}$, send $\perp$ to user $\mathbf{U}$.
    2. If $\mathcal{V}[\mathcal{L}_U^{\mathsf{sto}}]((\mathbf{C}_{\tilde{p}\tilde{w}}, \bar{\mathbf{C}}_{\tilde{p}\tilde{w}}), (H_{\tilde{p}\tilde{w}}, \mathbf{R}_{\tilde{p}\tilde{w}})) = reject$, send $\perp$ to user $\mathbf{U}$.
    3. Otherwise,
        - compute

$$\mathbf{CF}_j = \left(\textstyle\sum_{i \in \mathcal{Q} \backslash \{j\}} \mathbf{C}_{\tilde{R}_i} + \mathbf{C}_{R_j}\right) \cdot \mathbf{C}_{\tilde{p}\tilde{w}} - \left(\textstyle\sum_{i \in \mathcal{Q} \backslash \{j\}} \mathbf{C}_{\tilde{R}_i} + \mathbf{C}_{R_j}\right) \cdot \mathbf{C}_{\mathsf{pw}} + (\mathbf{C}_M + \mathbf{C}_X)$$

 - compute $\mathbf{W}_j = \lambda_j \mathbf{CF}_j \cdot \mathbf{sh}_j$
 - compute $\mathsf{Sig}_j(\mathbf{W}_j)$
    4. Send $(\mathbf{W}_j, \mathsf{Sig}_j(\mathbf{W}_j))$ to the user $\mathbf{U}$.

- User 2: User $\mathbf{U}$ performs the following steps:
    1. If receive $\perp$ from any server $\mathbf{S}_i$ (for $i \in \mathcal{Q}$) then output $\perp$.
    2. Check $\{\mathsf{Ver}_i(\mathsf{Sig}_i(\mathbf{W}_i)) = accept \text{ or } reject\}_{i \in \mathcal{Q}}$.
        - If any $\mathsf{Ver}_i(\mathsf{Sig}_i(\mathbf{W}_i)) \neq accept$ for $i \in \mathcal{Q}$, output $\perp$.
    3. Otherwise,
        - compute $\sum_{i \in \mathcal{Q}} \mathbf{W}_j = \sum_{i \in \mathcal{Q}} \lambda_i \mathbf{CF}_i \cdot \mathbf{sh}_i$ to retrieve $M + X$.
        - output $M = (M + X) - X$.

Correctness and Security. We now analyze the correctness and security of the above PPSS.

Theorem 3 (Correctness). *The above scheme with parameters proposed in Sect. 3.2 is correct.*

Proof. When all the servers and user are honest, all the $\mathbf{CF}_i$ of User2 round are same, say, $\mathbf{CF}$. Hence, $\sum_{i \in \mathcal{Q}} \lambda_i \cdot \mathbf{CF}_i \cdot \mathbf{sh}_i = \mathbf{CF} \cdot (\sum_{i \in \mathcal{Q}} \lambda_i \mathbf{sh}_i) = \mathbf{CF} \cdot \mathbf{v}$ (by Lagrange's interpolation). So, by the decryption algorithm of GSW scheme, user will get M. $\square$

Theorem 4. *The above construction is secure against malicious adversary, according to the Definition 4, assuming the hardness of* $\mathsf{dLWE}_{n,m,q,\chi}$.

Proof. Let $\mathcal{A}$ be an algorithm followed by an adversary attacking the PPSS scheme, running in time T, accessing at most q_U user and q_S server sessions, and corrupting servers $\{\mathbf{S}_i\}_{i \in \mathcal{F}}$ for some set $\mathcal{F}$ such that $|\mathcal{F}| = k-1$. The proof follows by sequence of games. Let $p^i = \Pr[1 \leftarrow (\mathcal{A} \Longleftrightarrow \mathsf{Game}_i)]$.

Game 0: Game_0 models the interaction of $\mathcal{A}$ with the PPSS scheme. For convenience, we will assume following modification: $\mathcal{A}$ can engage in at most q_S sessions but it is up to $\mathcal{A}$ to decide which servers will be involved in these sessions. We handle this in the security game by creating q_S distinct sessions for each server, thus $n \cdot q_S$ total sessions, even though a q_S-limited adversary will utilize only q_S of them.

Game 1: Game_0 and Game_1 are similar apart from following exception: in Game_0, $\mathbf{sh}_i$'s are (k, L)-secret-sharing of a random value of $\mathbb{Z}_q^N$ whereas in Game_1 $\mathbf{sh}_i$'s are (k, L)-secret-sharing of $\mathbf{0} \in \mathbb{Z}_q^N$. Therefore unless $\mathcal{A}$ knows k shares, the view of $\mathcal{A}$ in Game_1 is identical to its view in Game_0. Now, $\mathcal{A}$ gets to know $k-1$ shares of $\mathbf{v}$ simply by corrupting $k-1$ servers. However server queries could possibly leak information about $\mathbf{sh}_i$'s from $\mathbf{W}_j$. But in any server query, if adversary does not use the legitimate password, $\mathbf{W}_j$ is masked with a random value in both Game_0 and Game_1. Thus, the maximum number of $\mathbf{sh}_i$ that is effectively used by the adversary in either game is $k-1$. Hence, Game_0 and Game_1 are identical in the view of adversary which follows from the perfect secrecy of [20].

Game 2: Game_1 and Game_2 are similar apart from following exception: in Game_2, User$^\circ$ chooses a random diagonal matrix from $\mathbb{Z}_q^{N \times N}$ and a random matrix from $\{0,1\}^{N \times m}$, and computes $\mathbf{C}_{\tilde{p}\tilde{w}}$ and $\bar{\mathbf{C}}_{\tilde{p}\tilde{w}}$ using $\mathbf{A}$ and $\bar{\mathbf{A}}$, respectively; replies with $\mathbf{C}_{\tilde{p}\tilde{w}}$ and $\bar{\mathbf{C}}_{\tilde{p}\tilde{w}}$ in each of q_u sessions. Server$^\circ$ follows Game_1. As $\mathbf{C}_{\tilde{p}\tilde{w}}$ and $\bar{\mathbf{C}}_{\tilde{p}\tilde{w}}$ are output of GSW [11], the view of $\mathcal{A}$ in Game_2 is computationally indistinguishable to its view in Game_0, i.e., $|p^1 - p^2| = q_u \cdot (\epsilon_{\mathsf{GSW}} + \epsilon_{\mathsf{Sig}} + \epsilon_{\mathsf{SS}})$, since we have to add the probability ϵ_{Sig} that some signature sent to the each user session is not verified for some $\mathsf{Sig}_j(\mathbf{C}_{\bar{\mathbf{R}}_j})$ and we have to add the probability ϵ_{SS} that some $(\mathbf{C}_{\tilde{p}\tilde{w}}, \bar{\mathbf{C}}_{\tilde{p}\tilde{w}})$ sent to the each user session is not verified to be of the form $(\mathsf{Flatten}(H_{\tilde{p}\tilde{w}} \cdot \mathbf{I_N} + \mathsf{BitDecomp}(\mathbf{R}_{\tilde{p}\tilde{w}} \cdot \mathbf{A})), \mathsf{Flatten}(H_{\tilde{p}\tilde{w}} \cdot \mathbf{I_N} + \mathsf{BitDecomp}(\mathbf{R}_{\tilde{p}\tilde{w}} \cdot \bar{\mathbf{A}}))$.

Game 3: Game_2 and Game_3 are similar apart from following exception: in Game_3, Server$^\circ$ replies a random value from $\mathbb{Z}_q^{N \times N}$ as $\mathbf{CF}_j$, in each of $n \cdot q_s$ sessions. User$^\circ$ follows Game_2. Due to the security of GSW, $\mathbf{CF}_j$ is pseudorandom. Hence, the view of $\mathcal{A}$ in Game_3 is computationally indistinguishable to its view in Game_2, i.e., $|p^2 - p^3| = n \cdot q_s \cdot (\epsilon_{\mathsf{GSW}} + \epsilon_{\mathsf{Sig}})$, since we have to add the probability ϵ_{Sig} that all signature sent to the each server session is not verified for some $\mathsf{Sig}_j(\mathbf{C}_{\bar{\mathbf{R}}_j})$.

Game 4: Game_3 and Game_4 are similar apart from following exception: in Game_4, $\mathbf{A}$ is always chosen as a random element of $\mathbb{Z}_q^{m \times (n+1)}$ in **Init** phase.

It remains to show that Game_3 and Game_4 are computationally indistinguishable for a PPT adversary, which we do by giving a reduction from the dLWE problem.

Reduction to dLWE: Suppose $\mathcal{A}$ has non-negligible advantage in distinguishing Game_3 and Game_4. We use $\mathcal{A}$ to construct an dLWE algorithm $\mathcal{B}$. The simulator $\mathcal{B}$ uses the adversary $\mathcal{A}$ to solve dLWE in the following way:
Given access to dLWE instance $(\mathbf{B}^*, \mathbf{b}^*)$ over $\mathbb{Z}_q^{n \times m} \times \mathbb{Z}_q^m$, we can transform it to $\mathbf{A}^* = \left[\mathbf{b}^* | \mathbf{B}^* \right] \in \mathbb{Z}_q^{m \times (n+1)}$. Replace $\mathbf{A}$ by $\mathbf{A}^*$ in **Init** phase. If $\mathbf{A}^*$ is random element from $\mathbb{Z}_q^{m \times (n+1)}$, then the view of $\mathcal{A}$ is exactly same as Game_4. If $\mathbf{A}^*$ follows dLWE distribution, then the view of $\mathcal{A}$ is exactly same as Game_3. Hence, $\mathcal{B}$'s advantage in solving dLWE is the same as $\mathcal{A}$'s advantage in distinguishing Game_3 and Game_4, as required. This completes the proof. □

Soundness: The PPSS protocol described in Sect. 3.2 satisfies the correctness property (*see* Definition 3) and strong security property (*see* Definition 4). However, the malicious server(s) may try to convince a honest user to output a wrong secret message $M' \neq M$ by sending manipulated or ill-formed ciphertexts during the protocol described in Sect. 3.2. To protect against such malicious attacks, or in other words, to achieve soundness (*see* Definition 5) the user signs the secret message M during Init phase using EUF-CMA signature to obtain σ and encrypts the concatenation $M \| \sigma$ instead of just encrypting M. At the end of the recovery phase, the user checks the veracity of the recovered secret message by the verification key of signature. As a consequence, the user needs to add the verification key Ver_U of the user's signature in st_0 during the execution of Init. With this modification, the resulting scheme is δ-sound, where $\delta = \epsilon_{\mathsf{Sig}}$ is the forgery probability of $(\mathsf{Sig}_U, \mathsf{Ver}_U)$.

Note that to encrypt $M \| \sigma$ using GSW, we first need to encode the concatenated value. One possible encoding technique is to use *trapdoor hash function* of [9]. □

3.3 Constructing Lattice Based **TPAKE** from **PPSS**

We briefly describe a generic conversion of the PPSS protocol into a TPAKE which was proposed by Bagherzandi et al. [3] in the PKI model. The conversion required three primitives - a strongly secure PPSS protocol, a CCA secure encryption scheme and an EUF-CMA signature scheme. However, the generic conversion could not be instantiated to achieve post quantum security due to the absence of strongly secure quantum safe PPSS scheme. Our lattice based strongly secure PPSS construction removes the obstacle and enables us to have an instantiation of TPAKE in quantum safe platform.

We recall that in a TPAKE protocol, a user establishes (symmetric) keys in a secure manner with a "threshold" number of servers by authenticating herself to the servers. Moreover, the authentication of the user is performed jointly by a threshold number of servers on the basis of a password that was chosen by the user during the initial set up phase.

In the generic conversion of a PPSS into a TPAKE, the user chooses a CCA secure lattice based encryption scheme [16] (based on the hardness of dLWE problem), generates the public key and secret key pair (pk, sk), runs the Init procedure of PPSS with secret message sk and password pw and includes pk into the public state st_0. During the Rec procedure of PPSS (Sect. 3.2), every server $\mathbf{S_j}$ which does not abort the process (i.e., in step Server 2 the servers have successfully verified the well-formedness of ciphertexts of the password computed by the user), randomly chooses a key k_j, signs the key with the EUF-CMA Signature of [7] to produce σ_j, encrypts (k_j, σ_j) with pk to output e_j and sends e_j to the user along with $\mathbf{W}_j$. Suppose the local output of the user is sk' in a particular PPSS instance. If $sk' = \bot$ then the user sets $k_j = \bot$ and aborts the process, otherwise user decrypts e_j to obtain (k_j, σ_j) and verifies whether σ_j is a valid signature of k_j. If yes, then the user locally outputs k_j as its common secret key with server $\mathbf{S_j}$.

The EUF-CMA signatures and CCA encryption scheme guarantee that no network adversary can re-route messages from a session in which honest players are involved, or modify them in any manner, which implies in particular that all the User sessions are independent of each other.

4   Conclusion

The existing literature on PPSS does not have any treatment on post-quantum security, which leaves a research gap. In this paper, we construct a lattice-based PPSS to fill this gap. Our construction assumes PKI and supports concurrent execution against quantum adversaries in the standard model. As an important consequence, we successfully achieved the first quantum-safe construction of a TPAKE, by a generic transformation, which resolves a long standing open problem.

References

1. Abdalla, M., Chevassut, O., Fouque, P.-A., Pointcheval, D.: A simple threshold authenticated key exchange from short secrets. In: Roy, B. (ed.) ASIACRYPT 2005. LNCS, vol. 3788, pp. 566–584. Springer, Heidelberg (2005). https://doi.org/10.1007/11593447_31
2. Abdalla, M., Cornejo, M., Nitulescu, A., Pointcheval, D.: Robust password-protected secret sharing. In: Askoxylakis, I., Ioannidis, S., Katsikas, S., Meadows, C. (eds.) ESORICS 2016. LNCS, vol. 9879, pp. 61–79. Springer, Cham (2016). https://doi.org/10.1007/978-3-319-45741-3_4
3. Bagherzandi, A., Jarecki, S., Saxena, N., Lu, Y.: Password-protected secret sharing. In: CCS 2011, pp. 433–444 (2011)
4. Bellovin, S.M., Merritt, M.: Encrypted key exchange: password-based protocols secure against dictionary attacks. In: IEEE Computer Society Symposium on Research in Security and Privacy, pp. 72–84 (1992)
5. Camenisch, J., Lehmann, A., Neven, G.: Optimal distributed password verification. In: CCS 2015, pp. 182–194 (2015)

6. Camenisch, J., Lysyanskaya, A., Neven, G.: Practical yet universally composable two-server password-authenticated secret sharing. In: CCS 2012, pp. 525–536 (2012)

7. Cash, D., Hofheinz, D., Kiltz, E., Peikert, C.: Bonsai trees, or how to delegate a lattice basis. In: Gilbert, H. (ed.) EUROCRYPT 2010. LNCS, vol. 6110, pp. 523–552. Springer, Heidelberg (2010). https://doi.org/10.1007/978-3-642-13190-5_27

8. Di Raimondo, M., Gennaro, R.: Provably secure threshold password-authenticated key exchange. In: Biham, E. (ed.) EUROCRYPT 2003. LNCS, vol. 2656, pp. 507–523. Springer, Heidelberg (2003). https://doi.org/10.1007/3-540-39200-9_32

9. Döttling, N., Garg, S., Ishai, Y., Malavolta, G., Mour, T., Ostrovsky, R.: Trapdoor hash functions and their applications. In: Boldyreva, A., Micciancio, D. (eds.) CRYPTO 2019. LNCS, vol. 11694, pp. 3–32. Springer, Cham (2019). https://doi.org/10.1007/978-3-030-26954-8_1

10. Gentry, C., Peikert, C., Vaikuntanathan, V.: Trapdoors for hard lattices and new cryptographic constructions. In: STOC 2008, pp. 197–206 (2008)

11. Gentry, C., Sahai, A., Waters, B.: Homomorphic encryption from learning with errors: conceptually-simpler, asymptotically-faster, attribute-based. In: Canetti, R., Garay, J.A. (eds.) CRYPTO 2013. LNCS, vol. 8042, pp. 75–92. Springer, Heidelberg (2013). https://doi.org/10.1007/978-3-642-40041-4_5

12. Jarecki, S., Kiayias, A., Krawczyk, H.: Round-optimal password-protected secret sharing and T-PAKE in the password-only model. In: Sarkar, P., Iwata, T. (eds.) ASIACRYPT 2014. LNCS, vol. 8874, pp. 233–253. Springer, Heidelberg (2014). https://doi.org/10.1007/978-3-662-45608-8_13

13. Jarecki, S., Kiayias, A., Krawczyk, H., Xu, J.: Highly-efficient and composable password-protected secret sharing (or: How to protect your bitcoin wallet online). In: EuroS&P 2016, pp. 276–291. IEEE (2016)

14. Jarecki, S., Kiayias, A., Krawczyk, H., Xu, J.: TOPPSS: cost-minimal password-protected secret sharing based on threshold OPRF. In: Gollmann, D., Miyaji, A., Kikuchi, H. (eds.) ACNS 2017. LNCS, vol. 10355, pp. 39–58. Springer, Cham (2017). https://doi.org/10.1007/978-3-319-61204-1_3

15. MacKenzie, P., Shrimpton, T., Jakobsson, M.: Threshold password-authenticated key exchange. In: Yung, M. (ed.) CRYPTO 2002. LNCS, vol. 2442, pp. 385–400. Springer, Heidelberg (2002). https://doi.org/10.1007/3-540-45708-9_25

16. Micciancio, D., Peikert, C.: Trapdoors for lattices: simpler, tighter, faster, smaller. In: Pointcheval, D., Johansson, T. (eds.) EUROCRYPT 2012. LNCS, vol. 7237, pp. 700–718. Springer, Heidelberg (2012). https://doi.org/10.1007/978-3-642-29011-4_41

17. Peikert, C., Shiehian, S.: Noninteractive zero knowledge for NP from (plain) learning with errors. In: Boldyreva, A., Micciancio, D. (eds.) CRYPTO 2019. LNCS, vol. 11692, pp. 89–114. Springer, Cham (2019). https://doi.org/10.1007/978-3-030-26948-7_4

18. Regev, O.: On lattices, learning with errors, random linear codes, and cryptography. J. ACM (JACM) **56**(6), 1–40 (2009)

19. Sahai, A.: Non-malleable non-interactive zero knowledge and adaptive chosen-ciphertext security. In: 40th Annual Symposium on Foundations of Computer Science (Cat. No. 99CB37039), pp. 543–553. IEEE (1999)

20. Shamir, A.: How to share a secret. Commun. ACM **22**(11), 612–613 (1979)

21. Yi, X., Hao, F., Chen, L., Liu, J.K.: Practical threshold password-authenticated secret sharing protocol. In: Pernul, G., Ryan, P.Y.A., Weippl, E. (eds.) ESORICS 2015. LNCS, vol. 9326, pp. 347–365. Springer, Cham (2015). https://doi.org/10.1007/978-3-319-24174-6_18

Efficient Homomorphic Conversion Between (Ring) LWE Ciphertexts

Hao Chen[1], Wei Dai[2], Miran Kim[3], and Yongsoo Song[2(✉)]

[1] Facebook, Cambridge, USA
[2] Microsoft Research, Redmond, USA
{wei.dai,yongsoo.song}@microsoft.com
[3] Ulsan National Institute of Science and Technology, Ulsan, Republic of Korea
mirankim@unist.ac.kr

Abstract. In the past few years, significant progress on homomorphic encryption (HE) has been made toward both theory and practice. The most promising HE schemes are based on the hardness of the Learning With Errors (LWE) problem or its ring variant (RLWE). In this work, we present new conversion algorithms that switch between different (R)LWE-based HE schemes to take advantage of them. Specifically, we present and combine three ideas to improve the key-switching procedure between LWE ciphertexts, transformation from LWE to RLWE, as well as packing of multiple LWE ciphertexts in a single RLWE encryption. Finally, we demonstrate an application of building a secure channel between a client and a cloud server with lightweight encryption, low communication cost, and capability of homomorphic computation.

Keywords: Homomorphic encryption · Learning with Errors · Key switching

1 Introduction

In recent years, there have been remarkable advances in cryptographic primitives for secure computation without compromising data privacy. Specifically, homomorphic encryption (HE) [28] has been considered as one of the most attractive solutions due to its conceptual simplicity and efficiency. HE is a cryptosystem which supports arithmetic operation on encrypted data, so that any computational task can be outsourced to a public cloud while data provider does not need to either perform a large amount of work or stay online during the protocol execution. In addition, the concrete efficiency of HE has been improved rapidly by theoretic and engineering optimizations [4,15,41]. Recent studies demonstrated that this technology shows reasonable performance in real-world tasks such as biomedical analysis and machine learning [20,33,34].

Currently, all the best-performing HE schemes, such as BGV [8], BFV [6,23], TFHE [18] and CKKS [16], are based on the hardness of Learning with Errors (LWE) or its ring variant (RLWE). In particular, ring-based HE systems have

© Springer Nature Switzerland AG 2021
K. Sako and N. O. Tippenhauer (Eds.): ACNS 2021, LNCS 12726, pp. 460–479, 2021.
https://doi.org/10.1007/978-3-030-78372-3_18

shown remarkable performance in real-world applications due to the efficient use of the ciphertext packing technique [43]. Each HE scheme has its own pros and cons, but it has been relatively less studied how to take advantage of various HE schemes by converting ciphertexts of different types [5].

Our Contribution. In this paper, we provide a toolkit to transform (R)LWE-based ciphertexts and generate another ciphertext under a new key or of a different structure. Specifically, we present three conversion methods: (1) to perform a new key-switching (KS) operation between LWE ciphertexts; (2) to transform an LWE ciphertext into an RLWE-based ciphertext; and (3) to merge multiple LWE ciphertexts into a single RLWE ciphertext. The first two conversions (from LWE to LWE/RLWE) have quasi-linear complexity $\tilde{O}(N)$ where N denotes the dimension of (R)LWE. The last packing algorithm is a generalization of LWE-to-RLWE conversion which achieves a better amortized complexity. Our algorithms are almost optimal in the sense that their complexities are quasi-linear with respect to the size of input ciphertext(s). Moreover, there is no reduction of ciphertext level (modulus) because all building blocks (e.g. homomorphic automorphism) are depth-free. The proposed methods have wide applications in the literature: For example, our KS algorithm can replace the old KS method in the FHEW and TFHE schemes [18,22], and our LWEs-to-RLWE packing method can improve the performance of [5,10] which present a hybrid framework between different HE schemes. In addition, the proposed methods can be easily generalized to design better key-switching methods between (R)LWE ciphertexts with different dimensions, or more generally, Module LWE [8,35] based schemes with different parameters.

Finally, we present experimental results to show that our techniques achieve better asymptotic and concrete performance than previous methods. Moreover, we provide a secure outsourcing solution of storage and computation to a cloud with low communication cost. A client encrypts data via an LWE-based symmetric encryption on a lightweight device. On receiving LWE ciphertexts, the public server transforms or packs them into RLWE encryptions to provide better functionality for homomorphic arithmetic. Compared to prior works based on block or stream ciphers [3,9,21,27,37], our approach has advantages in terms of flexibility, functionality and efficiency.

Technical Overview. Let N be the dimension and q the modulus of an LWE problem. An LWE ciphertext with secret $\mathbf{s} \in \mathbb{Z}^N$ is of the form $(b, \mathbf{a}) \in \mathbb{Z}_q^{N+1}$ and its *phase* is defined as $\mu = b + \langle \mathbf{a}, \mathbf{s} \rangle \pmod{q}$. Typically, the phase is a noisy encoding of some underlying plaintext. Performing homomorphic operations on a ciphertext will increase this noise and thus the phase will be changed, but as long as the noise is below a given threshold, the underlying plaintext is preserved. Similarly, in the case of RLWE over $R = \mathbb{Z}[X]/(X^N + 1)$ and its residue ring $R_q = R/qR$, the phase of an RLWE ciphertext $(b, a) \in R_q^2$ of secret s is defined as $\mu = b + as \pmod{q}$.

Suppose that we are given some ciphertexts of a cryptosystem (which is not necessarily an HE scheme) and wish to publicly transform them into ciphertexts of another HE scheme for secure computation. In general, this task can be done by evaluating the decryption circuit of the initial cryptosystem using an HE system if a homomorphically encrypted secret key is given. Furthermore, the conversion can be more efficient if input ciphertexts are encrypted by an LWE-based cryptosystem because it suffices to homomorphically evaluate the phase, instead of performing the full decryption which usually includes expensive (non-arithmetic) operations such as bit extraction or rounding [12,26].

We remark that this approach can be still inefficient in some cases. For example, if we aim to convert an LWE encryption $(b, \mathbf{a}) \in \mathbb{Z}_q^{N+1}$ under secret $\mathbf{s} \in \mathbb{Z}^N$ into an RLWE ciphertext, the secret key owner should generate and publish an RLWE 'encryption' of $\mathbf{s}$ as the evaluation key, and the conversion can be done by computing the LWE phase $\mu = b + \langle \mathbf{a}, \mathbf{s} \rangle$ homomorphically over an RLWE-based HE system. In fact, the evaluation key consists of N key-switching keys from individual $\mathbf{s}[i]$ to the RLWE secret and the conversion requires N RLWE KS operations. Consequently, the total complexity grows quadratically with the security parameter. The techniques we present in this work do not follow the existing framework of the phase evaluation.

Our first idea is to embed elements of $\mathbb{Z}_q^N$ or $\mathbb{Z}_q$ into R_q. Given an LWE ciphertext $(b, \mathbf{a}) \in \mathbb{Z}_q^{N+1}$ of the phase $\mu_0 = b + \langle \mathbf{a}, \mathbf{s} \rangle$, we consider the RLWE ciphertext $\mathsf{ct} = (b, a) \in R_q^2$ for $a = \sum_{i \in [N]} \mathbf{a}[i] \cdot X^i$ and the secret $s = \sum_{i \in [N]} \mathbf{s}[i] \cdot X^{-i} \in R$. The ciphertext ct is not a completely valid RLWE ciphertext but its phase $\mu = b + as \pmod{q}$ contains $\mu_0 = \mu[0]$ in its constant term. We use this idea to accelerate the KS procedure between LWE ciphertexts. For another LWE secret $\mathbf{s}'$, we first perform a RLWE KS procedure from s to $s' = \sum_{i \in [N]} \mathbf{s}'[i] \cdot X^{-i}$. Then the phase of the output ciphertext is approximately equal to μ in R, so it is enough to extract an LWE ciphertext from the ciphertext.

Our second algorithm is an efficient conversion from LWE to RLWE. In the example above, the RLWE ciphertext ct cannot be directly used for further homomorphic computation because the phase μ contains invalid values in its coefficients except the constant term. We observe that the *field trace* function $\mathrm{Tr}_{K/\mathbb{Q}}$ of the number field $K = \mathbb{Q}[X]/(X^N + 1)$ zeroizes all the monomials X^i for $0 \neq i \in [N]$ but keeps the constant term (scaled by a factor of N). We homomorphically evaluate the trace function to obtain an RLWE ciphertext whose phase is approximately equal to the constant polynomial $N \cdot \mu_0$ (the extra factor N can be easily removed). To minimize the conversion complexity, we present a recursive algorithm that includes only $\log N$ automorphism evaluations, based on the tower of number fields. Furthermore, our algorithm reduces the number of key-switching keys to $\log N$ compared to N of the previous method.

Finally, we present a packing algorithm that takes at most N LWE ciphertexts as the input and returns a single RLWE ciphertext. Suppose that we are given $n \leq N$ input ciphertexts of phases $\mu_j \in \mathbb{Z}_q$. A naive solution is to perform our LWE-to-RLWE conversion on each LWE ciphertext and adds up the output RLWE ciphertexts into a single ciphertext, which requires $n \log N$ homomorphic automorphisms. We can improve the complexity by performing the FFT-style ciphertext packing algorithm. The first step is a tree-based algorithm which generates an RLWE ciphertext of phase $\mu \in R_q$ such that $\mu[(N/n) \cdot j] \approx n \cdot \mu_j$

Table 1. Computational costs (number of scalar operations) and storage (number of $\mathbb{Z}_q$ elements to store a switching key) of conversion algorithms. N denotes the dimension of (R)LWE, n denotes the number of input LWE ciphertexts to be packed in an RLWE ciphertext, and d denotes the gadget decomposition degree.

Type	Previous works [17,39]		This work	
	Complexity	Storage	Complexity	Storage
LWE-to-LWE	$O(dN^2)$	dN^2	$O(dN \log N)$	$2dN$
LWE-to-RLWE	$O(dN^2)$	$2dN^2$	$O(dN \log^2 N)$	$2dN \log N$
nLWEs-to-RLWE	$O(dN^2 \log N)$	$2dN^2$	$O(dN \log N(n+ \log(N/n)))$	$2dN \log N$

for all $j \in [n]$, i.e., it collects the phases μ_j's in an element $\sum_{j\in[n]} \mu_j \cdot Y^j$ of $K_n = \mathbb{Z}[Y]/(Y^n + 1)$. In the following step, we evaluate the field trace Tr_{K/K_n} to annihilate the useless coefficients $\mu[i]$ for $(N/n) \nmid i$ and finally return an RLWE ciphertext of phase $\approx N \cdot \sum_{j\in[n]} \mu_j \cdot Y^j$. The whole process requires $(n-1) + \log(N/n)$ homomorphic automorphisms, so we achieve an amortized complexity of $< 1 + n^{-1} \cdot \log N$ automorphisms per an LWE ciphertext.

Related Works. In [25,26], the authors presented a method to switch the underlying field of HE ciphertexts. In these works, *ciphertexts* were taken as the input of the trace function to reduce the dimension of the base ring dynamically during computation purely for efficiency reasons. Meanwhile, in our LWE(s)-to-RLWE algorithm, we utilize the trace function in a totally different way for a different purpose. We homomorphically evaluate the field trace on *plaintexts* (phases) to generate a valid RLWE ciphertext over a larger ring R_q from LWE ciphertexts over $\mathbb{Z}_q$.

It has been studied in [17,39] how to convert multiple LWE ciphertexts into a single RLWE ciphertext. Given n LWE ciphertexts $\{(b_j, \mathbf{a}_j)\}_{j\in[n]}$, it vertically stacks the i-th entries of all ciphertexts in a polynomial by $b = \sum_{j\in[n]} b_j \cdot X^j$ and $a_i = \sum_{j\in[n]} \mathbf{a}_j[i] \cdot X^j$ for $i \in [N]$. Then it homomorphically evaluates $b + \sum_i a_i \cdot s_i$ over an RLWE-based HE scheme. Different from our packing algorithm, this method has a fixed complexity of N RLWE KS operations, independently from the number n of input ciphertexts. This implies that it needs to pack $\Omega(N)$ many ciphertexts to achieve minimal amortized complexity.

Boura et al. [5] presented various transformations between ciphertexts of different RLWE-based HE schemes. Our work is in an orthogonal direction to [5] as we aim to switch the secret key or change the type of ciphertexts (e.g. LWE, RLWE) while preserving their phases (encoded plaintexts). In addition, the performance of [5] can be improved by replacing the underlying KS methods by our conversion algorithms.

Cheon and Kim [13] considered converting an ElGamal-like public key encryption scheme to an HE scheme. This involves evaluating the decryption circuit homomorphically, which consumes at least 10 levels, while our approach is almost depth-free.

In Table 1, we provide the performance of previous works and analyze the computational costs of our algorithms. Our LWE-to-RLWE conversion consists of several iterations in which we evaluate an automorphism and add the resulting ciphertext to the original input. There have been proposed a few algorithms [11, 12, 14, 31] which are technically similar to our conversion algorithm. However, to the best of our knowledge, this is the first study to reinterpret and apply this building block to the KS (conversion) of HE ciphertexts.

Recently, Gentry and Halevi [24] and Brakerski et al. [7] presented a new framework that compresses multiple HE ciphertexts into a single ciphertext with the nearly optimal rate of $1 - o(1)$. Our approach solves an associated but fundamentally different problem. In our application, we could build a lightweight and low-latency communication from the client to the cloud because fresh ciphertexts are high-rate and extremely small. However, they should be packed or converted into an RLWE ciphertext before computation. Meanwhile, previous works [7,24] aim to compress HE ciphertexts after computation and thereby minimize the communication cost from the cloud to the client.

2   Background

We denote vectors in bold, e.g. $\mathbf{u}$, and the i-th entry of a vector $\mathbf{u}$ will be denoted by $\mathbf{u}[i]$. For simplicity, we identify $\mathbb{Z} \cap (-q/2, q/2]$ as a set of representatives of $\mathbb{Z}_q$ and write the index set $[N] = \{0, 1, \ldots, N - 1\}$. For a finite set S, $U(S)$ denotes the uniform distribution on S.

2.1   Cyclotomic Field

Let $\zeta = \exp(\pi i / N)$ for a power-of-two integer N. We denote by $K = \mathbb{Q}(\zeta)$ the $2N$-th cyclotomic field and $R = \mathbb{Z}[\zeta]$ the ring of integers of K. We will identify K (resp. R) with $\mathbb{Q}[X]/(X^N + 1)$ (resp. $\mathbb{Z}[X]/(X^N + 1)$) with respect to the map $\zeta \mapsto X$. The residue ring of R modulo an integer q is denoted by $R_q = R/qR$. For $a, b \in \mathbb{Z}$ (or R, R_q), we informally write $a \approx b \pmod{q}$ if $a = b + e$ for some small $e \in \mathbb{Z}$ (or R).

An element of K (resp. R, R_q) can be uniquely represented as a polynomial of degree less than N with coefficients in $\mathbb{Q}$ (resp. $\mathbb{Z}$, $\mathbb{Z}_q$). The i-th coefficient of a polynomial $a(X)$ will be denoted by $a[i]$. We use the map $\iota : \mathbf{a} \mapsto \sum_{i \in [N]} \mathbf{a}[i] \cdot X^i$ to identify a polynomial and the vector of its coefficients.

2.2   (Ring) Learning with Errors

Given the dimension N, modulus q and error distribution ψ over $\mathbb{Z}$, the LWE distribution with secret $\mathbf{s} \in \mathbb{Z}^N$ is a distribution over $\mathbb{Z}_q^{N+1}$ which samples $\mathbf{a} \leftarrow U(\mathbb{Z}_q^N)$ and $e \leftarrow \psi$, and returns $(b, \mathbf{a}) \in \mathbb{Z}_q^{N+1}$ where $b = \langle \mathbf{a}, \mathbf{s} \rangle + e \pmod{q}$.

The (decisional) LWE assumption of parameter (N, q, χ, ψ) is that it is computationally infeasible to distinguish the LWE distribution of a secret $\mathbf{s} \leftarrow \chi$ from the uniform distribution $U(\mathbb{Z}_q^{N+1})$.

The RLWE problem [36] is a variant of LWE which has been widely used to design HE schemes, e.g. [8,16,18,23]. The key s is chosen from the key distribution χ over R, and an RLWE sample $(b, a) \in R_q^2$ by sampling random a and noise e from $U(R_q)$ and the error distribution ψ over R and computing $b = as + e$ (mod q). The RLWE assumption with parameter (N, q, χ, ψ) is that the RLWE distribution of a secret $s \leftarrow \chi$ and $U(R_q^2)$ are computationally indistinguishable.

2.3 Gadget Decomposition

Let q be an integer and $\mathbf{g} = (g_0, \ldots, g_{d-1})$ be an integral vector. A *gadget decomposition* [38], denoted by $\mathbf{g}^{-1} : \mathbb{Z}_q \to \mathbb{Z}^d$, is a map satisfying $\langle \mathbf{g}^{-1}(a), \mathbf{g} \rangle = a$ (mod q) for all $a \in \mathbb{Z}_q$. We can naturally extend its domain and define $\mathbf{g}^{-1} : R_q \to R^d$ by $a = \sum_{i \in [N]} a_i \cdot X^i \mapsto \sum_{i \in [N]} \mathbf{g}^{-1}(a_i) \cdot X^i$.

The base (digit) decomposition [6,8] and prime decomposition [4,15] are typical examples. This technique has been widely used to control the noise growth during homomorphic computation such as key-switching, which will be described in the next section.

2.4 Key Switching

We describe a well known KS method for RLWE ciphertexts. The goal of KS procedure is to transform a ciphertext into another ciphertext under a different secret key while approximately preserving its phase.

- KSKeyGen($s \in R, s' \in R$) : Sample $\mathbf{k}_1 \leftarrow U(R_q^d)$ and $\mathbf{e} \leftarrow \chi^d$. Compute $\mathbf{k}_0 = -s' \cdot \mathbf{k}_1 + s \cdot \mathbf{g} + \mathbf{e}$ (mod q) and return the KS key $\mathbf{K} = [\mathbf{k}_0 | \mathbf{k}_1] \in R_q^{d \times 2}$.

- KeySwitch(ct; $\mathbf{K}$) : Given an RLWE ciphertext ct $= (c_0, c_1) \in R_q^2$ and a KS key $\mathbf{K} \in R_q^{d \times 2}$, compute and return the ciphertext ct$' = (c_0, 0) + \mathbf{g}^{-1}(c_1) \cdot \mathbf{K}$ (mod q).

Roughly speaking, a KS key consists of d RLWE 'encryptions' of $s \cdot g_i$ under s', i.e., $\mathbf{K} \cdot (1, s') \approx s \cdot \mathbf{g}$ (mod q). For an RLWE ciphertext ct $\in R_q^2$ and a KS key $\mathbf{K} \leftarrow$ KSKeyGen(s, s'), the output ct$' \leftarrow$ KeySwitch(ct; $\mathbf{K}$) satisfies that

$$\langle ct', (1, s') \rangle = c_0 + \mathbf{g}^{-1}(c_1) \cdot \mathbf{K} \cdot (1, s')$$
$$= c_0 + \langle \mathbf{g}^{-1}(c_1), s \cdot \mathbf{g} + \mathbf{e} \rangle = \langle ct, (1, s) \rangle + e_{ks} \quad (\text{mod } q) \quad (1)$$

for the KS noise $e_{ks} = \langle \mathbf{g}^{-1}(c_1), \mathbf{e} \rangle \in R$.

2.5 Galois Group and Evaluation of Automorphisms

We recall that $K \geq Q$ is a Galois extension and its Galois group Gal($K/\mathbb{Q}$) consists of the automorphisms $\tau_d : \zeta \mapsto \zeta^d$ for $d \in \mathbb{Z}_{2N}^\times$, the invertible residues modulo $2N$. The automorphisms $\tau_d \in \mathrm{Gal}(K/\mathbb{Q})$ gives some distinctive functionalities to the HE system. For example, many of RLWE-based schemes such as BGV [8], BFV [6,23] and CKKS [16] utilize the Discrete Fourier Transform (DFT) to encode multiple plaintext values in a single polynomial, so that the slots of a ciphertext can be permuted by evaluating an automorphism.

We describe a well-known method to homomorphically evaluate an automorphism $\tau_d : a(X) \rightarrow a(X^d)$.

- $\mathsf{AutoKeyGen}(d \in \mathbb{Z}_{2N}^\times; s \in R)$: Run $\mathbf{A}_d \leftarrow \mathsf{KSKeyGen}(\tau_d(s), s)$.

- $\mathsf{EvalAuto}\left(\mathsf{ct} \in R_q^2, d \in \mathbb{Z}_{2N}^\times; \mathbf{A}_d\right)$: Given a ciphertext $\mathsf{ct} = (c_0, c_1) \in R_q^2$, an integer $d \in \mathbb{Z}_{2N}^\times$ and an automorphism key $\mathbf{A}_d$, compute and return the ciphertext $\mathsf{ct}' \leftarrow \mathsf{KeySwitch}\left((\tau_d(c_0), \tau_d(c_1)); \mathbf{A}_d\right)$.

Security. The homomorphic automorphism algorithm is a simple application of KS, so its security basically relies on the hardness of RLWE for $\mathsf{KSKeyGen}$. Moreover, an additional circular security assumption should be made because $\mathbf{A}_d$ is a special encryption of $\tau_d(s)$ with secret s.

Correctness. Suppose that $\mathsf{ct} \in R_q^2$ is an RLWE ciphertext such that $\mu = \langle \mathsf{ct}, (1, s) \rangle \pmod{q}$ and $\mathbf{A}_d \leftarrow \mathsf{AutoKeyGen}(d; s)$ is an automorphism key. Then the output ciphertext $\mathsf{ct}' \leftarrow \mathsf{EvalAuto}(\mathsf{ct}, d; \mathbf{A}_d)$ satisfies that

$$\langle \mathsf{ct}', (1, s) \rangle \approx \langle (\tau_d(c_0), \tau_d(c_1)), (1, \tau_d(s)) \rangle = \tau_d\left(\langle \mathsf{ct}, (1, s) \rangle\right) = \tau_d(\mu) \pmod{q},$$

from the property of $\mathsf{KeySwitch}$.

In the rest of this paper, we simply write $\mathsf{EvalAuto}(\mathsf{ct}, d; \mathbf{A}_d) = \mathsf{EvalAuto}(\mathsf{ct}, d)$ by assuming that an automorphism key $\mathbf{A}_d \leftarrow \mathsf{AutoKeyGen}(d; s)$ is properly generated and implicitly taken as input of the $\mathsf{EvalAuto}$ algorithm. We remark that homomorphic automorphism has almost the same complexity as the KS procedure because the computation of $\tau_d(c_i)$ is very cheap.

3   Conversion Algorithms

This section presents core ideas and their application to efficient conversion between HE ciphertexts of different secret keys or algebraic structures.

3.1   Functionality of Automorphisms on Coefficients

We examine how the elements of $\mathrm{Gal}(K/\mathbb{Q})$ act on the coefficients of an input polynomial. Let us define the sets $I_k = \left\{i \in [N] : 2^k \,\|\, i\right\}^1$ for $0 \leq k < \log N$ and $I_{\log N} = \{0\}$. Then, the index set $[N]$ can be written as the disjoint union $\bigcup_{0 \leq k \leq \log N} I_k$. We are interested in how the automorphism $\tau_d(\cdot)$ acts on the monomials for $d = 2^\ell + 1$, $1 \leq \ell \leq \log N$. We note that the map $i \mapsto i \cdot d$

---

[1] $2^k \,\|\, i$ if and only if $2^k \,|\, i$ and $2^{k+1} \nmid i$.

(mod N) is a signed permutation on I_k, i.e., if $i \in I_k$, then $\tau_d(X^i) = \pm X^j$ for some $j \in I_k$. In particular, we see that

$$\tau_d(X^i) = X^i \quad \text{for} \quad i \in \bigcup_{k > \log N - \ell} I_k,$$

$$\tau_d(X^i) = -X^i \quad \text{for} \quad i \in I_{\log N - \ell}. \tag{2}$$

In other words, the map $\mu \mapsto \mu + \tau_d(\mu)$ doubles the coefficients $\mu[i]$ if $2^{\log N - \ell + 1} \mid i$, but zeroizes the coefficients $\mu[i]$ if $2^{\log N - \ell} \| i$.

3.2   LWE to LWE

Let $(b, \mathbf{a}) \in \mathbb{Z}_q^{N+1}$ be an LWE ciphertext under a secret $\mathbf{s} \in \mathbb{Z}^N$ with phase $\mu_0 = b + \langle \mathbf{a}, \mathbf{s} \rangle \pmod q$. We aim to design an efficient LWE-to-LWE conversion, which replaces the secret of the ciphertext into another secret $\mathbf{s}' \in \mathbb{Z}^N$ while almost preserving the phase μ_0.

Our first idea is to embed $\mathbb{Z}_q^N$ and $\mathbb{Z}_q$ into R_q to utilize the ring structure. We consider the two polynomials

$$a := \iota(\mathbf{a}) = \sum_{i \in [N]} \mathbf{a}[i] \cdot X^i \in R_q,$$

$$s := \tau_{-1} \circ \iota(\mathbf{s}) = \sum_{i \in [N]} \mathbf{s}[i] \cdot X^{-i} \in R,$$

and we define the polynomial pair $\mathsf{ct} = (b, a) \in R_q^2$. We remark that ct can be viewed as an RLWE ciphertext with secret s satisfying $\langle \mathsf{ct}, (1, s) \rangle [0] = (b + as)[0] = \mu_0$, i.e., its phase $\mu = \langle \mathsf{ct}, (1, s) \rangle \pmod q$ of ct stores $\mu[0] = \mu_0$ in the constant term but all other coefficients, $\mu[i]$ for $0 \neq i \in [N]$, have no valid values.

Though ct is not a valid RLWE ciphertext, we can still apply the KS algorithm. If we perform the KS procedure from s to $s' = \tau_{-1} \circ \iota(\mathbf{s}')$, then the output ciphertext also includes a valid value in its constant term from the property of KS. Finally, we can extract an LWE ciphertext with secret $\mathbf{s}'$.

- LWE-to-LWE $((b, \mathbf{a}), \mathbf{K})$: Given an LWE ciphertext $(b, \mathbf{a}) \in \mathbb{Z}_q^{N+1}$ and a KS key $\mathbf{K} \in R_q^{L \times 2}$, set the RLWE ciphertext $\mathsf{ct} \leftarrow (b, a) \in R_q^2$ where $a = \iota(\mathbf{a})$. Compute $\mathsf{ct}' = (b', a') \leftarrow \mathsf{KeySwitch}(\mathsf{ct}, \mathbf{K}) \in R_q^2$ and let $a' = \iota^{-1}(a')$. Return the ciphertext $(b'[0], \mathbf{a}') \in \mathbb{Z}_q^{N+1}$.

Correctness. We claim that, if $\mathbf{K} \leftarrow \mathsf{KSKeyGen}(s, s')$ is a KS key from s to s', then $(b'[0], \mathbf{a}')$ is an LWE ciphertext under $\mathbf{s}'$ whose phase is approximately equal to the phase of $(b, \mathbf{a})$ under $\mathbf{s}$. It can be shown by

$$b'[0] + \langle \mathbf{a}', \mathbf{s}' \rangle = (b' + a's')[0] \approx (b + as)[0] = b + \langle \mathbf{a}, \mathbf{s} \rangle \pmod q,$$

where the approximate equality is derived from the property of KeySwitch (see Eq. (1)).

Algorithm 1. Homomorphic Evaluation of the Trace Function (EvalTr$_{N/n}$)

Input: ciphertext ct $= (b, a) \in R_q^2$, a power-of-two integer $n \leq N$.

1: ct$'$ $\leftarrow$ ct
2: **for** $k = 1$ to $\log(N/n)$ **do**
3:     ct$'$ $\leftarrow$ ct$'$ + EvalAuto(ct$'$; $2^{\log N - k + 1} + 1$)
4: **return** ct$'$ $\in R_q^2$

3.3 LWE to RLWE

Our next goal is to design a conversion algorithm from LWE to RLWE. As explained above, if we set an RLWE ciphertext $(b, a = \iota(\mathbf{a})) \in R_q^2$ from an LWE ciphertext $(b, \mathbf{a}) \in \mathbb{Z}_q^{N+1}$, then its phase has the valid value only in the constant term. Hence, the key question is how to annihilate useless coefficients of μ except the constant term $\mu[0]$ to generate a valid RLWE ciphertext.

We remark that the *field trace* $\mathrm{Tr}_{K/\mathbb{Q}} : K \to \mathbb{Q}$, $a \mapsto \sum_{\tau \in \mathrm{Gal}(K/\mathbb{Q})} \tau(a)$ has the required property, i.e., $\mathrm{Tr}_{K/\mathbb{Q}}(1) = N$ and $\mathrm{Tr}_{K/\mathbb{Q}}(X^i) = 0$ for all $0 \neq i \in [N]$. Therefore, conversion from LWE into RLWE can be done by evaluating the field trace homomorphically. A naive solution is to evaluate each automorphism $\tau(\cdot)$ and add up all the resulting ciphertexts, and therefore it requires N KS operations. We now describe a recursive algorithm that uses an algebraic structure of cyclotomic fields for reducing the conversion complexity. To be precise, for the tower of finite fields $K = K_N \geq K_{N/2} \geq \cdots \geq K_1 = \mathbb{Q}$, where K_n denotes the $(2n)$-th cyclotomic field for a power-of-two integer n, the field trace can be expressed as a composition $\mathrm{Tr}_{K/\mathbb{Q}} = \mathrm{Tr}_{K_2/K_1} \circ \cdots \circ \mathrm{Tr}_{K_N/K_{N/2}}$ of $\log N$ field traces and each Galois group $\mathrm{Gal}(K_{2^\ell}/K_{2^{\ell-1}})$ has a (unique) nontrivial element $\tau_{2^\ell+1}|_{K_{2^\ell}}$ for $\ell = 1, \ldots, \log N$. Therefore, the evaluation of $\mathrm{Tr}_{K_{2^\ell}/K_{2^{\ell-1}}}$ requires only one homomorphic rotation.

See Algorithm 1 for a description of homomorphic trace evaluation Tr_{K_N/K_n} for any power-of-two integer $n \leq N$. We use the parameter $n = 1$ in the following LWE-to-RLWE conversion algorithm.

- LWE-to-RLWE $\left((b, \mathbf{a}) \in \mathbb{Z}_q \times \mathbb{Z}_q^N \right)$: Set the RLWE ciphertext ct $\leftarrow (b, a) \in R_q^2$ where $a = \iota(\mathbf{a})$. Then, run Algorithm 1 and return the ciphertext ct$'$ $\leftarrow$ EvalTr$_{N/1}$(ct) $\in R_q^2$.

The phase of the input LWE ciphertext $(b, \mathbf{a})$ is multiplied by N by the trace evaluation. We will explain in the next section how to remove the constant N by adding a pre-processing step.

Correctness. We will prove the correctness of Algorithm 1 for an arbitrary $n \leq N$. Let $\mu = \langle \mathrm{ct}, (1, s) \rangle \pmod{q}$ be the phase of an input ct. We inductively show that the phase $\mu' = \langle \mathrm{ct}', (1, s) \rangle \pmod{q}$ satisfies

$$\mu' \approx \mathrm{Tr}_{K_N/K_{N/2^k}}(\mu) = 2^k \cdot \sum_{2^k | i \in [N]} \mu[i] \cdot X^i \pmod{q} \tag{3}$$

at iteration k. For the base case $k = 0$, the statement is trivially true since $\mu' = \mu$. Now we assume that (3) is true for $k - 1$. In the next k-th iteration, we evaluate the map $\mu' \mapsto \mu' + \tau_d(\mu')$ for $d = 2^{\log N - k + 1} + 1$. We recall from (2) that $\tau_d(X^i) = X^i$ for $2^k \mid i \in [N]$ and $\tau_d(X^i) = -X^i$ for $i \in [N]$ such that $2^{k-1} \parallel i$. From the induction hypothesis,

$$\mu' \approx 2^{k-1} \cdot \sum_{2^{k-1} \mid i} \mu[i] \cdot X^i$$

$$= 2^{k-1} \cdot \sum_{2^k \mid i} \mu[i] \cdot X^i + 2^{k-1} \cdot \sum_{2^{k-1} \parallel i} \mu[i] \cdot X^i \quad (\mathrm{mod}\ q),$$

$$\tau_d(\mu') \approx 2^{k-1} \cdot \sum_{2^k \mid i} \mu[i] \cdot X^i - 2^{k-1} \cdot \sum_{2^{k-1} \parallel i} \mu[i] \cdot X^i \quad (\mathrm{mod}\ q),$$

and thereby $\mu' + \tau_d(\mu') \approx 2^k \cdot \sum_{2^k \mid i} \mu[i] \cdot X^i$. Finally, we obtain

$$\mu' \approx \mathrm{Tr}_{K_N/K_n}(\mu) = (N/n) \cdot \sum_{(N/n) \mid i \in [N]} \mu[i] \cdot X^i \quad (\mathrm{mod}\ q)$$

after $k = \log(N/n)$ iterations. We remark that the noise does not blow up much during the evaluation since $\tau_d(\cdot)$ preserves the size of elements in R.

The correctness of LWE-to-RLWE is directly derived from this result with a parameter $n = 1$. Given an RLWE encryption $\mathsf{ct} = (b, a)$, we homomorphically compute the field trace $\mathrm{Tr}_{K_N/\mathbb{Q}}$ and the phase $\mu' = \langle \mathsf{ct}', (1, s) \rangle$ of the output ciphertext is approximately equal to $\mathrm{Tr}_{K_N/\mathbb{Q}}(b + as) = N \cdot (b + as)[0] = N \cdot (b + \langle \mathbf{a}, \mathbf{s} \rangle)$, as desired.

3.4 LWEs to RLWE

An LWE ciphertext has a phase in $\mathbb{Z}_q$, which can store only one scalar message, so our LWE-to-RLWE conversion algorithm aims to generate an RLWE ciphertext whose phase μ contains an approximate value of an initial LWE phase in its constant term. However, in general, an RLWE ciphertext can store at most N scalars in the coefficients of its phase. So a natural question is how to efficiently merge multiple LWE ciphertexts into a single RLWE ciphertext.

Suppose that we are given n LWE ciphertexts $\{(b_j, \mathbf{a}_j)\}_{j \in [n]}$ for some $n = 2^\ell \le N$ and let $\mu_j \in \mathbb{Z}_q$ be the phase of $(b_j, \mathbf{a}_j)$ under the same secret $\mathbf{s} \in \mathbb{Z}^N$. A naive answer for the question above is to run $\mathsf{ct}'_j \leftarrow \mathsf{LWE\text{-}to\text{-}RLWE}\,((b_j, \mathbf{a}_j)) \in R_q^2$ for all $j \in [n]$ and take their linear combination $\mathsf{ct}' = \sum_{j \in [n]} \mathsf{ct}'_j \cdot Y^j$ for $Y = X^{N/n}$. Then the phase of ct' is approximately equal to $N \cdot \sum_{j \in [n]} \mu_j \cdot Y^j$, which is an element of the ring of integers of K_n. However, this method is not optimal in terms of both complexity and noise growth.

In this section, we present a generalized version of our previous algorithm which takes multiple LWE encryptions as input and returns a single RLWE ciphertext. This conversion consists of two phases: packing and trace evaluation. The first step (Algorithm 2) is an FFT-style algorithm which merges $n = 2^\ell$

Algorithm 2. Homomorphic Packing of LWE Ciphertexts (PackLWEs)

1: **input** ciphertexts $\mathsf{ct}_j = (b_j, a_j) \in R_q^2$ for $j \in [2^\ell]$
2: **if** $\ell = 0$ **then**
3:     **return** $\mathsf{ct} \leftarrow \mathsf{ct}_0$
4: **else**
5:     $\mathsf{ct}_{even} \leftarrow \mathsf{PackLWEs}\left(\{\mathsf{ct}_{2j}\}_{j \in [2^{\ell-1}]}\right)$
6:     $\mathsf{ct}_{odd} \leftarrow \mathsf{PackLWEs}\left(\{\mathsf{ct}_{2j+1}\}_{j \in [2^{\ell-1}]}\right)$
7:     $\mathsf{ct} \leftarrow \left(\mathsf{ct}_{even} + X^{N/2^\ell} \cdot \mathsf{ct}_{odd}\right) + \mathsf{EvalAuto}\left(\mathsf{ct}_{even} - X^{N/2^\ell} \cdot \mathsf{ct}_{odd}, 2^\ell + 1\right)$
8:     **return** ct

---

multiple RLWE ciphertexts into one. The phase μ of an output ciphertext stores the constant terms of input phases in its coefficients $\mu[i]$ for $(N/n) \mid i$. All valid values are now packed into an element of R_n, so in the next step, we use the idea of the previous section to evaluate the field trace Tr_{K_N/K_n} and zeroize useless coefficients.

- $\mathsf{LWEs\text{-}to\text{-}RLWE}\left(\{(b_j, \mathbf{a}_j)\}_{j \in [n]}\right)$: Given $n = 2^\ell$ LWE ciphertexts $(b_j, \mathbf{a}_j) \in \mathbb{Z}_q^{N+1}$, do the following:

1. Set $\mathsf{ct}_j \leftarrow (b_j, a_j) \in R_q^2$ for each $j \in [n]$ where $a_j = \iota(\mathbf{a}_j)$.
2. Run Algorithm 2 to get $\mathsf{ct} \leftarrow \mathsf{PackLWEs}\left(\{\mathsf{ct}_j\}_{j \in [n]}\right)$.
3. Compute and return the ciphertext $\mathsf{ct}' \leftarrow \mathsf{EvalTr}_{N/n}(\mathsf{ct})$.

The packing algorithm and the subsequent field trace evaluation for $n = 2^\ell$ ciphertexts require $(n-1)$ and $\log(N/n)$ homomorphic automorphisms, respectively. Hence the total complexity of $\mathsf{LWEs\text{-}to\text{-}RLWE}$ is $(n-1) + \log(N/n) < n + \log N$ automorphisms, yielding an amortized complexity less than $(1 + n^{-1} \cdot \log N)$ automorphisms per an input LWE ciphertext. We remark that this conversion algorithm achieves the asymptotically optimal amortized complexity ($O(1)$ automorphisms) when $n = \Omega(\log N)$. Similar to the LWE-to-RLWE conversion, the phase of input ciphertexts are multiplied by the factor of N which can be removed by a pre-processing step described below.

Correctness. We first show the correctness of our packing algorithm. For $j \in [2^\ell]$, let ct_j be input ciphertexts of Algorithm 2 such that $\mu_j = \langle \mathsf{ct}_j, (1, s) \rangle [0]$ (mod q). For the output ciphertext $\mathsf{ct} \leftarrow \mathsf{PackLWEs}\left(\{\mathsf{ct}_j\}_{j \in [2^\ell]}\right)$, we claim that its phase satisfies

$$\mu\left[(N/2^\ell) \cdot j\right] \approx 2^\ell \cdot \mu_j \quad (\text{mod } q) \quad \text{for all} \quad j \in [2^\ell]. \tag{4}$$

We again use the induction on $\ell \geq 0$. The base case $\ell = 0$ is trivial since $\mu[0] = \mu_0$. Suppose that our statement is true for some $0 \leq \ell - 1 < \log N$. For 2^ℓ input ciphertexts, Algorithm 2 first divides them into two groups of size $2^{\ell-1}$ and runs $\mathsf{PackLWEs}$ twice (in lines 5 and 6). From the induction hypothesis, the output ciphertexts $\mathsf{ct}_{even}, \mathsf{ct}_{odd}$ have phases μ_{even}, μ_{odd} such that

$$\mu_{even}\left[(N/2^{\ell-1})\cdot j\right] \approx 2^{\ell-1}\cdot\mu_{2j} \pmod{q},$$
$$\mu_{odd}\left[(N/2^{\ell-1})\cdot j\right] \approx 2^{\ell-1}\cdot\mu_{2j+1} \pmod{q},$$

for all $j \in [2^{\ell-1}]$. Then, we compute and return the ciphertext ct whose phase is

$$\mu \approx (\mu_{even} + X^{N/2^{\ell}}\cdot\mu_{odd}) + \tau_d\left(\mu_{even} - X^{N/2^{\ell}}\cdot\mu_{odd}\right)$$
$$= \mu'_{even} + X^{N/2^{\ell}}\cdot\mu'_{odd},$$

for $\mu'_{even} = \mu_{even} + \tau_d(\mu_{even})$ and $\mu'_{odd} = \mu_{odd} + \tau_d(\mu_{odd})$, which satisfies that

$$\mu'_{even}\left[(N/2^{\ell})\cdot(2j)\right]\approx 2^{\ell}\cdot\mu_{2j}, \quad \mu'_{even}\left[(N/2^{\ell})\cdot(2j+1)\right]\approx 0 \pmod{q},$$
$$\mu'_{odd}\left[(N/2^{\ell})\cdot(2j)\right]\approx 2^{\ell}\cdot\mu_{2j+1}, \quad \mu'_{odd}\left[(N/2^{\ell})\cdot(2j+1)\right]\approx 0 \pmod{q}$$

for all $j \in [2^{\ell-1}]$. Therefore, their linear combination $\mu = \mu'_{even} + X^{N/2^{\ell}}\cdot\mu'_{odd}$ has coefficients $\mu\left[(N/2^{\ell})\cdot j\right]\approx 2^{\ell}\cdot\mu_j$ for all $j \in [2^{\ell}]$, as desired.

Now let us discuss the LWEs-to-RLWE algorithm. After running the packing algorithm, the phase μ of ct $\leftarrow$ PackLWEs $(\{ct_j\}_{j\in[n]})$ has $n\cdot\mu_j$ in its coefficients $\mu[i]$ such that $(N/n) \mid i$. So we homomorphically evaluate the field trace Tr_{K_N/K_n} on the ciphertext ct to zeroize all other coefficients. It follows from the property of Algorithm 1 that the final output ct' $\leftarrow$ EvalTr$_{N/n}$(ct) satisfies

$$\langle ct', (1, s)\rangle \approx \mathrm{Tr}_{K_N/K_n}(\mu) = (N/n)\cdot\sum_{(N/n)|i\in[N]}\mu[i]\cdot X^i$$

$$\approx (N/n)\cdot\sum_{j\in[n]}(n\cdot\mu_j)\cdot X^{(N/n)\cdot j} = N\cdot\sum_{j\in[n]}\mu_j\cdot Y^j \pmod{q}$$

where $Y = X^{N/n}$, as desired.

Removing the Leading Term. Let $\{ct_j\}_{j\in[n]}$ be n LWE input encryptions of our LWEs-to-RLWE algorithm and ct' the output RLWE ciphertext. We denote their phases by $\mu_j = \langle ct_j, (1, s)\rangle \pmod{q}$ and $\mu' = \langle ct', (1, s)\rangle \pmod{q}$, respectively. As shown in their correctness proofs, our algorithms converting one or more LWE encryptions into an RLWE ciphertext introduce the additional term N into the phase of output RLWE ciphertext.

We present a pre-processing technique to remove this constant. We multiply the constant $N^{-1} \pmod{q}$ to the input LWE ciphertexts so that their phases μ_j are also multiplied by the same factor. If we run the same algorithm on the ciphertexts of phases $N^{-1}\cdot\mu_j \pmod{q}$, then the leading term N is naturally cancelled out and the phase of the output RLWE ciphertext will be approximately equal to $N\cdot\sum_{j\in[n]}(N^{-1}\cdot\mu_j)\cdot Y^j = \sum_{j\in[n]}\mu_j\cdot Y^j$, as desired.

We note that this method is depth-free and does not incur extra noise growth. It requires the ciphertext modulus q to be co-prime to the dimension N, but it is not a strong assumption in practice[2].

---

[2] The ciphertext modulus q is usually set to be a product of primes 1 modulo $2N$ so that we can utilize an efficient Number Theoretic Transformation (NTT) for polynomial arithmetic in R_q.

Further Computation on a Packed Ciphertext. In a plaintext level, our conversion algorithm computes the function $\mathbb{Z}_q^n \to R_q$, $(\mu_j)_{j\in[n]} \mapsto \sum_{j\in[n]} \mu_j \cdot Y^j$, which is not a multiplicative homomorphism. However, it is often required to pack multiple values in plaintext slots, instead of coefficients, so that parallel computation (e.g. element-wise addition or multiplication) is allowed over an encrypted vector of plaintexts.

It has been studied in several researches about HE bootstrapping [12,14,26, 32] how to represent values from coefficients to slots and vice versa. In the case of BGV, BFV or CKKS, the transformation can be done by evaluating the encoding or decoding functions of the underlying scheme, which are expressed as linear transformations over plaintext vectors. We do not consider it here because this coefficients-to-slots conversion is scheme-dependent. Moreover, its computational cost is cheaper than the main part, so that the total/amortized complexities do not change much even if we add this extra step at the end.

4 Implementation

4.1 Experimental Results

We provide a proof-of-concept implementation to show the performance of our conversion algorithms. Our source code is developed in C++ by modifying Microsoft SEAL version 3.5.1 [42]. All experiments are performed on a desktop with an Intel Core i7-4770K CPU running a single thread at 3.50 GHz, compiled with Clang 9.0.0 (-O3)[3].

We set the secret distribution as the uniform distribution over the set of ternary polynomials in R coefficients in $\{0, \pm1\}$. Each coefficient/entry of (R)LWE error is drawn according to the discrete Gaussian distribution centered at zero with standard deviation $\sigma = 3.2$. The selected parameter sets provide at least 128-bit of security level according to the LWE estimator [2] and HE security standard white paper [1].

Table 2 presents timing results and noise growth of our conversion algorithms. The ciphertext moduli q of three parameter sets are products of 2, 4, and 8 distinct primes, respectively. We use an RNS-friendly decomposition method [4] and exploit an efficient NTT in order to optimize the basic polynomial arithmetic. As discussed in Sect. 3.4, the LWEs-to-RLWE conversion algorithm achieves a better amortized running time as the number n of input LWE ciphertexts increases. For comparison, we implemented the old KS method using the same parameter sets and decomposition method, and it took 203ms and 1628ms when $(N, \log q) = (2^{12}, 72)$ and $(2^{13}, 174)$, respectively, compared to 1.0ms and 4.8ms of our method. We refer the reader to Appendix A which provides noise analysis of our conversion algorithms. The noise variances of the LWE-to-LWE and LWE(s)-to-RLWE conversions are $O(N)$ and $O(N^3)$, respectively, which align very well with our experimental results.

---

[3] Currently, our source repository is private to keep the anonymity, but we will make it public in the final version.

Table 2. Concrete performance of our conversion algorithms measured by total running time (amortized timing per ciphertext) and noise growth (an upper bound on the bit size of coefficients of conversion errors). n stands for the number of input LWE ciphertexts.

$(N, \log q)$	n	$(2^{12}, 72)$		$(2^{13}, 174)$		$(2^{14}, 389)$	
		Total (Amortized)	Noise	Total (Amortized)	Noise	Total (Amortized)	Noise
LWE to LWE	-	1.03 ms	7	4.81 ms	8	27.1 ms	10
LWE to RLWE	-	11.2 ms	18	57.7 ms	21	361 ms	23
LWEs to RLWE	2	11.4 ms (5.70 ms)	18	58.7 ms (29.4 ms)	21	364 ms (182 ms)	23
	8	16.8 ms (2.10 ms)	20	83.2 ms (10.4 ms)	22	492 ms (61.5 ms)	24
	32	45.0 ms (1.41 ms)	20	209 ms (6.53 ms)	22	1168 ms (36.5 ms)	24

We did not specify the underlying HE scheme or its plaintext space as the performance of our conversion algorithms depends only on the parameters N, $\log q$ and n. Since the bit-size of a conversion noise is only $O(\log N)$ bits, the rest of the space can be used to store a plaintext or be left empty to provide more homomorphic functionality after conversion. For example, if we use the BFV scheme with the second parameter set $(N, \log q) = (2^{13}, 174)$, then our conversion algorithms work correctly as long as the bit-size of its plaintext modulus is ≤ 152.

4.2 Lightweight Communication with Homomorphic Functionality

HE is a useful cryptographic technology for secure outsourced computation on the cloud, however, its applications have some common issues in practice. Since HE schemes are comparably expensive, a client must have enough memory and computing power. Moreover, the ciphertext expansion rate can be reasonably small only when we pack a large number of values in a single RLWE ciphertext. Therefore, the total communication cost may blow up much when the client sends a small amount of information.

To mitigate this issue, Naehrig et al. [40] came up with a blueprint that the client sends data, encrypted by a light-weight symmetric encryption scheme, as well as a homomorphically encrypted secret key of the cryptosystem. Then, the cloud homomorphically evaluates its decryption circuit to get homomorphically encrypted data. In this scenario, the main challenge is to construct a symmetric encryption with low communication cost (expansion rate) and conversion complexity. After the first attempt by Gentry et al. [27] which evaluated the AES-128 circuit using the BGV scheme, there has been a line of studies (e.g. LowMC [3], Kreyvium [9], FLIP [37], Rasta [21]) to design HE-friendly symmetric encryption schemes. These block/stream ciphers made progresses in communication cost and encryption time, but the transformation of ciphertexts results in a considerable computational overhead on the cloud side.

In this work, we present a new solution that the client uses an LWE-based symmetric encryption on the edge device. On receiving the LWE ciphertexts, the cloud transforms them into RLWE encryptions using our conversion algorithm. In addition, we adapt the idea of Coron et al. [19] to reduce the size of LWE ciphertexts and communication cost. To be precise, a symmetric key LWE encryption of secret s is of the form $(b, \mathbf{a}) \in \mathbb{Z}_q^{N+1}$ for a random vector $\mathbf{a} \leftarrow U(\mathbb{Z}_q^N)$ and $b = -\langle \mathbf{a}, \mathbf{s} \rangle + \mu \pmod q$ where μ is the phase from the input which is a randomized encoding of the plaintext. Since the second component $\mathbf{a}$ is purely random over $\mathbb{Z}_q^N$, we can modify the encryption algorithm such that it samples a seed se and takes it as the input of a pseudo-random number generator $f : \{0,1\}^* \rightarrow \mathbb{Z}_q^N$ to generate $\mathbf{a} = f(\mathsf{se})$. As a result, a ciphertext can be represented as a pair (b, se), and this variant remains semantically secure in the random oracle model. Moreover, when a client sends multiple LWE ciphertexts to the cloud, the same seed can be reused by computing the random part of the i-th ciphertext by $\mathbf{a}_i = f(\mathsf{se}; i)$. Hence, the communication cost per an LWE ciphertext is only $\log q$ bits.

Our approach has advantages in computational efficiency compared to prior works based on block/stream ciphers. Prior works have several minutes' latency for the transformation (e.g. 4.1, 63.1, 29.3, 0.65 and 15.2 min of AES-128, LowMC v1, Kreyvium, FLIP, and Rasta, respectively[4]), and have to collect a number of ciphertexts to achieve the minimal amortized complexity. Meanwhile, our method has significantly better conversion latency and amortized timings (several milliseconds), and enables a smooth trade-off between them via the packing algorithm. As discussed in Sect. 3.4, it requires to collect only $\Omega(\log N)$ LWE ciphertexts to obtain a nearly optimal amortized complexity.

Our method is generic in the sense that it preserves the phases of input ciphertexts approximately regardless of the type of HE schemes or a plaintext space. Therefore, it is allowed to use the BGV/BFV scheme with a non-binary plaintext space, or CKKS for approximate computation. Moreover, we provide a flexible parameter setting that enables us to achieve an almost optimal expansion rate of $1 + o(1)$ even when a client sends only a small amount of information at a time. For example, as shown in Table 2, the expansion rate can be reduced down to $174/(174 - 21) \approx 1.14$ or $389/(389 - 23) \approx 1.06$ when $(N, \log q) = (2^{13}, 174)$ or $(2^{14}, 389)$, respectively.

Acknowledgments. The work of Kim was supported by the Settlement Research Fund (No. 1.200109.01) of UNIST (Ulsan National Institute of Science and Technology).

A   Noise analysis

The key switching procedure described in Sect. 2.4 is the only source of an extra noise during our conversion algorithms. Recall that the key-switching procedure

---

[4] These performance benchmarks are taken from Table 10 in [21].

KeySwitch($\mathsf{ct} = (c_0, c_1); \mathbf{K}$) introduces the noise $e_{ks} = \langle \mathbf{g}^{-1}(c_1), \mathbf{e} \rangle$ where $\mathbf{e}$ is the noise of the KS key $\mathbf{K}$. We make a heuristic assumption (which has been widely used in HE researches, e.g. [17,27,30]) such that a KS noise behaves as if its coefficients are sampled independently from a Gaussian distribution with a fixed variance, which will be denoted by V_{ks}. For a random variable $a = \sum_{i \in [N]} a_i \cdot X^i$ over R, we denote by $\mathsf{Var}(a)$ the maximum among the variances of its coefficients $\{\mathsf{Var}(a_i) : 0 \le i < N\}$.

In practice, we need to specify the gadget decomposition method to compute V_{ks}. For example, suppose that the ciphertext modulus $q = \prod_{0 \le i < d} q_i$ is a product of relatively co-prime integers and the gadget decomposition is defined as $R_q \to \prod_{i \in [d]} R_{q_i}, a \mapsto \mathbf{g}^{-1}(a) = (a \pmod{q_i})_{0 \le i < d}$[5]. Then, the coefficients of $e_{ks} = \langle \mathbf{g}^{-1}(c_1), \mathbf{e} \rangle$ have the common variance $V_{ks} \le \frac{1}{12} N \sigma^2 \cdot \sum_{i \in [d]} q_i^2$ where σ^2 is the variance of RLWE error distribution.

A.1   LWE to LWE

Technically, our LWE-to-LWE conversion includes only one KS procedure between RLWE ciphertexts and then we extract an LWE ciphertext from the output ciphertext. As shown in the correctness proof in Sect. 3.2, the additional noise in the final LWE ciphertext is equal to the constant term of the KS noise, whose variance is V_{ks}.

A.2   LWE to RLWE

We will analyze the noise of homomorphic trace evaluation ($\mathsf{EvalTr}_{N/n}$ in Algorithm 1) since the LWE-to-RLWE conversion is a special case where $n = 1$.

We showed that if $\mu = b + as \pmod{q}$ is the phase of the input ciphertext ct, then the phase of ct' is $\mathsf{Tr}_{K_N/K_{N/2^k}}(\mu) + e_k$ for some error e_k after k iterations. We will estimate the variance of e_k using the induction on k.

If $k = 0$, we have $e_0 = 0$. For $1 \le k \le \log(N/n)$, we denote by $e'_k \in R$ the additional noise from the homomorphic automorphism at the k-th iteration. Then, we get $e_k = e_{k-1} + \tau_d(e_{k-1}) + e'_k$ for $d = 2^{\log N - k + 1} + 1$ and its variance is bounded by $\mathsf{Var}(e_k) \le 4 \cdot \mathsf{Var}(e_{k-1}) + V_{ks}$. Therefore, the noise of the output ciphertext from Algorithm 1 is bounded by $\mathsf{Var}(e_k) \le (1 + 4 + \cdots + 4^{k-1}) \cdot V_{ks} \le \frac{1}{3} ((N/n)^2 - 1) \cdot V_{ks}$.

Our LWE-to-RLWE algorithm is the case of $n = 1$ (or equivalently $k = \log N$) which returns a ciphertext whose phase is $\mathsf{Tr}_{K/\mathbb{Q}}(\mu) + e_{\log N}$ for some $e_{\log N}$ such that $\mathsf{Var}(e_{\log N}) \le \frac{1}{3}(N^2 - 1) \cdot V_{ks}$.

A.3   LWEs to RLWE

We first analyze the noise growth of Algorithm 2. We showed that if $\{\mathsf{ct}_j = (b_j, a_j)\}_{j \in [2^\ell]}$ are the input RLWE ciphertexts such that $\mu_j = (b_j + a_j \cdot s)[0]$,

---

[5] This method is called the prime decomposition which is widely used in the construction of RNS-friendly HE schemes such as [4,29,34,42].

then the phase μ of output ciphertext satisfies that $\mu[(N/2^\ell) \cdot j] = 2^\ell \cdot \mu_j + e_{\ell,j}$ (mod q) for all $j \in [2^\ell]$ and for some $e_{\ell,j} \in \mathbb{Z}$. If $\ell = 0$, then there is no extra noise from the packing algorithm. In the case of $\ell > 0$, we divide the input ciphertexts into two groups and run the packing algorithm on each subgroup separately. Suppose that the phases of ct_{even} and ct_{odd} satisfy

$$\mu_{even}[(N/2^{\ell-1}) \cdot j] = 2^{\ell-1} \cdot \mu_{2j} + e_{\ell-1,2j} \quad (\text{mod } q),$$

$$\mu_{odd}[(N/2^{\ell-1}) \cdot j] = 2^{\ell-1} \cdot \mu_{2j+1} + e_{\ell-1,2j+1} \quad (\text{mod } q)$$

for some errors $e_{\ell-1,2j}, e_{\ell-1,2j+1} \in \mathbb{Z}$. Let $e'_\ell(X)$ be the additional noise from the evaluation of automorphism $\mathsf{EvalAuto}(\mathsf{ct}_{even} - X^{N/2^\ell} \cdot \mathsf{ct}_{odd}, 2^\ell + 1)$ and $e'_{\ell,j}$ the $(N/2^\ell) \cdot j$-th coefficient of $e'_\ell(X)$ for $j \in [2^\ell]$. Then, we get a relation $e_{\ell,j} = 2e_{\ell-1,j} + e'_{\ell,j}$ between errors from the equation $\mu = \mu'_{even} + X^{N/2^\ell} \cdot \mu'_{odd} + e'_\ell(X)$ for all $j \in [2^\ell]$. Since $e'_{\ell,j}$ has a fixed variance V_{ks} for all ℓ and j, we have $\mathsf{Var}(e_{\ell,j}) = 4 \cdot \mathsf{Var}(e_{\ell-1,j}) + V_{ks}$. Finally, we use the induction on ℓ and show that $\mathsf{Var}(e_{\ell,j}) = (1 + 4 + \cdots + 4^{\ell-1}) \cdot V_{ks} = \frac{1}{3}(n^2 - 1) \cdot V_{ks}$ when $n = 2^\ell$.

In our LWEs-to-RLWE conversion, the packing algorithm is followed by the trace evaluation $\mathsf{EvalTr}_{N/n}$ whose noise growth is analyzed above. Hence, the phase of the output ciphertext from the LWEs-to-RLWE conversion satisfies that $\mu = (N/n) \cdot \left(\sum_{j \in [n]} (n\mu_j + e_{\ell,j}) \cdot X^{(N/n) \cdot j} \right) + e_k(X)$ (mod q) where e_k denotes the noise from trace evaluation and $k = \log(N/n)$. Therefore, the variance of total noise $(N/n) \cdot \left(\sum_{j \in [n]} e_{\ell,j} \cdot X^{(N/n) \cdot j} \right) + e_k(X)$ is bounded by $(N/n)^2 \cdot \mathsf{Var}(e_{\ell,j}) + \mathsf{Var}(e_k) \leq \frac{1}{3}(N^2 - 1) \cdot V_{ks}$.

References

1. Albrecht, M., et al.: Homomorphic encryption security standard. Technical Report, HomomorphicEncryption.org, Toronto, November 2018
2. Albrecht, M.R., Player, R., Scott, S.: On the concrete hardness of learning with errors. J. Math. Cryptol. 9(3), 169–203 (2015)
3. Albrecht, M.R., Rechberger, C., Schneider, T., Tiessen, T., Zohner, M.: Ciphers for MPC and FHE. In: Oswald, E., Fischlin, M. (eds.) EUROCRYPT 2015. LNCS, vol. 9056, pp. 430–454. Springer, Heidelberg (2015). https://doi.org/10.1007/978-3-662-46800-5_17
4. Bajard, J.-C., Eynard, J., Hasan, M.A., Zucca, V.: A full RNS variant of FV like somewhat homomorphic encryption schemes. In: Avanzi, R., Heys, H. (eds.) SAC 2016. LNCS, vol. 10532, pp. 423–442. Springer, Cham (2017). https://doi.org/10.1007/978-3-319-69453-5_23
5. Boura, C., Gama, N., Georgieva, M., Jetchev, D.: Chimera: combining ring-LWE-based fully homomorphic encryption schemes. J. Math. Cryptol. 14(1), 316–338 (2020)
6. Brakerski, Z.: Fully homomorphic encryption without modulus switching from classical GapSVP. In: Safavi-Naini, R., Canetti, R. (eds.) CRYPTO 2012. LNCS, vol. 7417, pp. 868–886. Springer, Heidelberg (2012). https://doi.org/10.1007/978-3-642-32009-5_50

7. Brakerski, Z., Döttling, N., Garg, S., Malavolta, G.: Leveraging linear decryption: Rate-1 fully-homomorphic encryption and time-lock puzzles. In: Hofheinz, D., Rosen, A. (eds.) TCC 2019. LNCS, vol. 11892, pp. 407–437. Springer, Cham (2019). https://doi.org/10.1007/978-3-030-36033-7_16

8. Brakerski, Z., Gentry, C., Vaikuntanathan, V.: (Leveled) fully homomorphic encryption without bootstrapping. In: Proceedings of ITCS, pp. 309–325. ACM (2012)

9. Canteaut, A., et al.: Stream ciphers: a practical solution for efficient homomorphic-ciphertext compression. J. Cryptol. **31**(3), 885–916 (2018)

10. Carpov, S., Gama, N., Georgieva, M., Troncoso-Pastoriza, J.R.: Privacy-preserving semi-parallel logistic regression training with fully homomorphic encryption (2019). https://eprint.iacr.org/2019/101

11. Carpov, S., Sirdey, R.: Another compression method for homomorphic ciphertexts. In: Proceedings of the 4th ACM International Workshop on Security in Cloud Computing, pp. 44–50. ACM (2016)

12. Chen, H., Han, K.: Homomorphic lower digits removal and improved FHE bootstrapping. In: Nielsen, J.B., Rijmen, V. (eds.) EUROCRYPT 2018. LNCS, vol. 10820, pp. 315–337. Springer, Cham (2018). https://doi.org/10.1007/978-3-319-78381-9_12

13. Cheon, J.H., Kim, J.: A hybrid scheme of public-key encryption and somewhat homomorphic encryption. IEEE Trans. Inf. Forensics Secur. **10**(5), 1052–1063 (2015)

14. Cheon, J.H., Han, K., Kim, A., Kim, M., Song, Y.: Bootstrapping for approximate homomorphic encryption. In: Nielsen, J.B., Rijmen, V. (eds.) EUROCRYPT 2018. LNCS, vol. 10820, pp. 360–384. Springer, Cham (2018). https://doi.org/10.1007/978-3-319-78381-9_14

15. Cheon, J.H., Han, K., Kim, A., Kim, M., Song, Y.: A full RNS variant of approximate homomorphic encryption. In: Cid, C., Jacobson Jr, J. (eds.) SAC 2018. LNCS, vol. 11349. Springer, Cham (2019). https://doi.org/10.1007/978-3-030-10970-7_16

16. Cheon, J.H., Kim, A., Kim, M., Song, Y.: Homomorphic encryption for arithmetic of approximate numbers. In: Takagi, T., Peyrin, T. (eds.) ASIACRYPT 2017. LNCS, vol. 10624, pp. 409–437. Springer, Cham (2017). https://doi.org/10.1007/978-3-319-70694-8_15

17. Chillotti, I., Gama, N., Georgieva, M., Izabachène, M.: TFHE: fast fully homomorphic encryption over the torus. J. Cryptol. **33**(1), 34–91 (2019). https://doi.org/10.1007/s00145-019-09319-x

18. Chillotti, I., Gama, N., Georgieva, M., Izabachène, M.: Faster fully homomorphic encryption: bootstrapping in less than 0.1 s. In: Cheon, J.H., Takagi, T. (eds.) ASIACRYPT 2016. LNCS, vol. 10031, pp. 3–33. Springer, Heidelberg (2016). https://doi.org/10.1007/978-3-662-53887-6_1

19. Coron, J.-S., Naccache, D., Tibouchi, M.: Public key compression and modulus switching for fully homomorphic encryption over the integers. In: Pointcheval, D., Johansson, T. (eds.) EUROCRYPT 2012. LNCS, vol. 7237, pp. 446–464. Springer, Heidelberg (2012). https://doi.org/10.1007/978-3-642-29011-4_27

20. Dathathri, R., et al.: CHET: an optimizing compiler for fully-homomorphic neural-network inferencing. In: Proceedings of the 40th ACM SIGPLAN Conference on Programming Language Design and Implementation, pp. 142–156. ACM (2019)

21. Dobraunig, C., et al.: Rasta: a cipher with low ANDdepth and few ANDs per bit. In: Shacham, H., Boldyreva, A. (eds.) CRYPTO 2018. LNCS, vol. 10991, pp. 662–692. Springer, Cham (2018). https://doi.org/10.1007/978-3-319-96884-1_22

22. Ducas, L., Micciancio, D.: FHEW: bootstrapping homomorphic encryption in less than a second. In: Oswald, E., Fischlin, M. (eds.) EUROCRYPT 2015. LNCS, vol. 9056, pp. 617–640. Springer, Heidelberg (2015). https://doi.org/10.1007/978-3-662-46800-5_24

23. Fan, J., Vercauteren, F.: Somewhat practical fully homomorphic encryption. Cryptology ePrint Archive, Report 2012/144 (2012). https://eprint.iacr.org/2012/144

24. Gentry, C., Halevi, S.: Compressible FHE with applications to PIR. In: Hofheinz, D., Rosen, A. (eds.) TCC 2019. LNCS, vol. 11892, pp. 438–464. Springer, Cham (2019). https://doi.org/10.1007/978-3-030-36033-7_17

25. Gentry, C., Halevi, S., Peikert, C., Smart, N.P.: Field switching in BGV-style homomorphic encryption. J. Comput. Secur. **21**(5), 663–684 (2013)

26. Gentry, C., Halevi, S., Smart, N.P.: Better bootstrapping in fully homomorphic encryption. In: Fischlin, M., Buchmann, J., Manulis, M. (eds.) PKC 2012. LNCS, vol. 7293, pp. 1–16. Springer, Heidelberg (2012). https://doi.org/10.1007/978-3-642-30057-8_1

27. Gentry, C., Halevi, S., Smart, N.P.: Homomorphic evaluation of the AES circuit. In: Safavi-Naini, R., Canetti, R. (eds.) CRYPTO 2012. LNCS, vol. 7417, pp. 850–867. Springer, Heidelberg (2012). https://doi.org/10.1007/978-3-642-32009-5_49

28. Gentry, C., et al.: Fully homomorphic encryption using ideal lattices. STOC **9**, 169–178 (2009)

29. Halevi, S., Polyakov, Y., Shoup, V.: An improved RNS variant of the BFV homomorphic encryption scheme. In: Matsui, M. (ed.) CT-RSA 2019. LNCS, vol. 11405, pp. 83–105. Springer, Cham (2019). https://doi.org/10.1007/978-3-030-12612-4_5

30. Halevi, S., Shoup, V.: Design and implementation of a homomorphic-encryption library. IBM Research (Manuscript) (2013)

31. Halevi, S., Shoup, V.: Algorithms in HElib. In: Garay, J.A., Gennaro, R. (eds.) CRYPTO 2014. LNCS, vol. 8616, pp. 554–571. Springer, Heidelberg (2014). https://doi.org/10.1007/978-3-662-44371-2_31

32. Halevi, S., Shoup, V.: Bootstrapping for HElib. In: Oswald, E., Fischlin, M. (eds.) EUROCRYPT 2015. LNCS, vol. 9056, pp. 641–670. Springer, Heidelberg (2015). https://doi.org/10.1007/978-3-662-46800-5_25

33. Jiang, X., Kim, M., Lauter, K., Song, Y.: Secure outsourced matrix computation and application to neural networks. In: Proceedings of the 2018 ACM SIGSAC Conference on Computer and Communications Security, pp. 1209–1222. ACM (2018)

34. Kim, M., Song, Y., Li, B., Micciancio, D.: Semi-parallel logistic regression for GWAS on encrypted data. BMC Med. Genom. **13**(7), 1–13 (2020)

35. Langlois, A., Stehlé, D.: Worst-case to average-case reductions for module lattices. Des. Codes Crypt. **75**(3), 565–599 (2014). https://doi.org/10.1007/s10623-014-9938-4

36. Lyubashevsky, V., Peikert, C., Regev, O.: On ideal lattices and learning with errors over rings. In: Gilbert, H. (ed.) EUROCRYPT 2010. LNCS, vol. 6110, pp. 1–23. Springer, Heidelberg (2010). https://doi.org/10.1007/978-3-642-13190-5_1

37. Méaux, P., Journault, A., Standaert, F.-X., Carlet, C.: Towards stream ciphers for efficient FHE with low-noise ciphertexts. In: Fischlin, M., Coron, J.-S. (eds.) EUROCRYPT 2016. LNCS, vol. 9665, pp. 311–343. Springer, Heidelberg (2016). https://doi.org/10.1007/978-3-662-49890-3_13

38. Micciancio, D., Peikert, C.: Trapdoors for lattices: simpler, tighter, faster, smaller. In: Pointcheval, D., Johansson, T. (eds.) EUROCRYPT 2012. LNCS, vol. 7237, pp. 700–718. Springer, Heidelberg (2012). https://doi.org/10.1007/978-3-642-29011-4_41

39. Miccianco, D., Sorrell, J.: Ring packing and amortized FHEW bootstrapping. In: 45th International Colloquium on Automata, Languages, and Programming (ICALP 2018). Schloss Dagstuhl-Leibniz-Zentrum fuer Informatik (2018)
40. Naehrig, M., Lauter, K., Vaikuntanathan, V.: Can homomorphic encryption be practical? In: Proceedings of the 3rd ACM Workshop on Cloud Computing Security Workshop, pp. 113–124. ACM (2011)
41. Riazi, M.S., Laine, K., Pelton, B., Dai, W.: Heax: High-performance architecture for computation on homomorphically encrypted data in the cloud. arXiv preprint arXiv:1909.09731 (2019)
42. Microsoft SEAL (release 3.5).: Microsoft Research. Redmond (2020). https://github.com
43. Smart, N.P., Vercauteren, F.: Fully homomorphic SIMD operations. Des. Codes Crypt. **71**(1), 57–81 (2012). https://doi.org/10.1007/s10623-012-9720-4

Author Index

Printed in the United States
by Baker & Taylor Publisher Services